Un-Dead TV

This book is dedicated to my mother, whose strength, courage and humor continue to inspire.

Un-Dead TV

The Ultimate Guide to Vampire Television

SECOND EDITION

Brad Middleton

Foreword by J. Gordon Melton

By Light Unseen Media
Pepperell, Massachusetts

Un-Dead TV
The Ultimate Guide to Vampire Television
Second Edition

Copyright © 2012, 2016 by Brad Middleton. All rights reserved. No part of this publication may be reproduced, stored in a retrieval system or transmitted in any form or by any means, electronic, mechanical, photocopying, recording, or otherwise without the prior written permission of the copyright holder, except for brief quotations in reviews and for academic purposes in accordance with copyright law and principles of Fair Use.

Cover Design by Brad Middleton
Photo Credit: Canadian Broadcasting Corporation (colorized by permission)
Interior design and layout by Vyrdolak, By Light Unseen Media.

Title page photo: Dracula (Norman Welsh) puts the bite on Lucy (Charlotte Blunt) in *Purple Playhouse* - "Dracula" (CBC Still Photo Collection)

Thirsty for more? Visit http://un-dead.tv

Perfect Paperback Edition

ISBN-10: 1-935303-62-7
ISBN-13: 978-1-935303-62-6
LCCN: 2016956181

Published by
By Light Unseen Media
325 Lake View Dr.
Winchendon, Massachusetts 01475

Our Mission:
By Light Unseen Media presents the best of quality fiction and non-fiction on the theme of vampires and vampirism. We offer fictional works with original imagination and style, as well as non-fiction of academic calibre.

For additional information, visit:
http://bylightunseenmedia.com

Printed in the United States of America

0 9 8 7 6 5 4 3 2 1

CONTENTS

Foreword by J. Gordon Melton	7
Introduction	10
About This Book	13
Monsters of the Week: Single Episodes	15
Vampires Among Us: The Series	121
Prominent Bite: Telefilms and Pilots	153
Drawn to Vampires: Animation	189
Myths and Truths: Documentaries and Reality TV	271
Artistic Endeavors: Variety Programming and TV Specials	337
What's in a Name? Non-Traditional Vampires	399
Take a Breather: No Vampires Here!	447
Non-English Programming	473
A Trivial Pursuit	515

Appendices and Index

Appendix 1: Sources Consulted	520
Appendix 2: Country Acronym Legend	523
Appendix 3: Adaptations of Classic Literature and Popular Fiction	524
Appendix 4: Top Rated Productions	526
Appendix 5: Lowest Rated Productions	529
Appendix 6: Yearly Breakdown	532
Appendix 7: Web Series	533
Index of Main Program Titles	534

Photograph and Illustration Credits

Images reproduced in this book are done so in the spirit of publicity, and are not meant to create the appearance of a specially licensed or authorized publication. Efforts have been made to correctly identify copyright holders; any errors will be corrected in a future edition.

The photographs and illustrations in this book were reproduced with permission from the following sources:

BearKatt Productions: 304

Brad Middleton Collection: 15, 24, 29, 30, 50, 54, 56, 62, 63, 68, 69, 70, 71, 76, 82, 84, 110, 116, 117, 120, 124, 126, 127, 136, 137, 141, 146, 147, 149, 152, 154, 156, 157, 159, 161, 162, 166, 167, 168, 172, 174, 175, 176, 180, 181, 186, 188, 189, 191, 209, 217, 218, 230, 269, 270, 282, 298, 307, 311, 327, 332, 336, 338, 341, 344, 349, 351, 355, 358, 364, 372, 376, 379, 383, 385, 392, 398, 399, 423, 430, 440, 447, 458, 462, 473, 514

Canadian Broadcasting Corporation: front cover, title page, 342, 371, 375

David Cremasco: 354, 398

Del Valle Archives: 60, 120, 121, 122, 128, 129, 131, 133, 139, 144, 153, 158, 160, 163, 178, 179, 282, 369, 381

Jibber Jabber Entertainment: 228

Quickfire Media: 271, 315, 316

Vonnie Von Helmolt Film: 337

Acknowledgments

The author also thanks the following individuals and organizations:

Inanna Arthen, Bearkatt Productions (Edmond Buckley); The CBC Library and Archives (Brian Knott, Geoffrey Hopkinson, Michele Melady, Brenda Carroll); Dennis Báthory-Kitsz; Hernan Bouza; Jim Burns; Dan Chambers and David Hodgson; DR Arkiv & Research; Jason Davitt; Documentary.org (Jodi Pais Montgomery, Jon Curry, Tom White); Robert Eighteen-Bisang; Paul Kreppel; Cathy Krusberg; Darío Lavia; José María Marcos and Leandro D'Ambrosio; Janice De La Mare; J. Gordon Melton; The Merril Collection of Science Fiction, Speculation and Fantasy (Lorna Toolis); Elizabeth Miller; Nina Munteanu; Ted Newsom; Christopher Perry; Andy Reaser; Maria Saracen; Steve Schnier; Rick Vanes; David Del Valle; and Vonnie Von Helmolt Film

Foreword

While scholars have, over the last generation, paid significant attention to vampire movies—probing their significance and meaning from a variety of perspectives—the same cannot be said relative to the equally vast presence of vampires on television. Even as Hammer Films was carving out a new and distinctive era for the cinematic vampire, producer/director Dan Curtis was making history with a failing daytime soap opera. His almost flippant introduction of a vampire character not only turned *Dark Shadows* into a daytime media phenomenon, it transformed the many teenagers who rushed home from school to watch it into a huge fan base. They supported the production of numerous books celebrating the series, more than fifty novels utilizing the main characters, and numerous fanzines. Now more than forty years after the show's demise, those same fans continue to gather annually to reminisce about the show, see the stars who brought it to life, and clamor for yet another *Dark Shadows* revival.

Dark Shadows set the stage for the vampire to become a fixture in the nation's living rooms. It provided the inspiration for two *Dark Shadows* films, and led Dan Curtis to produce several made-for-television vampire movies—including the Jack Palance version of Bram Stoker's *Dracula* (1973) and *The Night Stalker* (1972), the latter becoming a pilot show for a new television series. Having come and gone before the rise of the current set of scholars of television, *Dark Shadows* never received the attention its impact suggests it should. But then, neither did any of those that followed it seem worthy of comment.

There is, of course, one exception to the general lack of interest in the television vampire—*Buffy the Vampire Slayer*. In fact, it is the inconvenient truth for vampire scholars that over half of all the scholarly comment on the broad subject of vampires penned through the last century has been directed at *Buffy*, and has been produced in a mere ten years (2003-2012). Interestingly, the attention paid to *Buffy* has not motivated much examination of the vampire in television in general, nor have the many commentators on *Buffy* extended their discussions to include the role played by earlier televised vampires in the development of the *Buffy* series.

Brad Middleton's *Un-Dead TV* addresses the need for a broad overview of the vampire, from the original performance of the live stage production of *Dracula* (1956) starring the legendary John Carradine and the original *Dark Shadows* (1966-1971), to the currently popular prime-time series: *True Blood, Being Human,* and *The Vampire Dairies*. The televised vampire, even more than the cinema vampire, documents the rise of the bloodsucking undead to a key position in popular culture. Over the last half century, screen writers have repeatedly selected the vampire to convey perspectives on a wide spectrum of social issues, from addiction and alienation to sexuality and class warfare.

Television has had a special role in the evolution of the modern vampire. *Dark Shadows*—though not the first vampire television show of note to feature a vampire as a continuing character (remember Grandpa in *The Munsters*)—entered our homes just as two new variant vampire characters were making their appearance. Prior to *Dark Shadows*, the vampire was almost entirely a negative entity, a monster, in whom there dwelt no good, and who possessed little range for development as a character. Few, apart from Dracula, rose to the point of having a name even the most die-hard vampire fan remembered. While some female vampire fans swooned over the bad boy vampires—first, Bela Lugosi and then Christopher Lee—there was little to rally fans to the vampire banner. That situation began to change in 1969 when the comic book introduced the good guy (or good gal) vampire. Vampirella was a survivor from a distant dying planet where blood flowed like water, and once on earth, she appeared as a heroine who melded the comic book super hero with the ancient blood sucker. Having discovered an alternative source for blood that did not require her taking it from human victims, she is transformed into a positive, sexy, and likable character around whom fans could converge and for whom they could cheer as she conquered various foes.

Subsequently, Barnabas Collins, the vampire of *Dark Shadows*, introduced us to the second new vampire type, the conflicted vampire. Barnabas retained enough of his humanity that he understood and agonized over the fact that he had to kill those from whom he took blood in order to stay alive. He continually bemoaned his thirsty condition and pursued any possibility of again becoming human. When not pursuing this quest for his lost humanity, he could participate in a wide variety of alternative activities that allowed him to express the wide range of human emotions.

Long before the movies discovered the potential of the conflicted vampire *(Interview with the Vampire,* 1994) and the good guy vampire *(Underworld,* Blade the Vampire Slayer, *Bloodrayne,* and the *Twilight Saga),* television became the place to nurture the development of both the good guy and the conflicted vampire. Television proved especially hospitable to the heroic vampire, most notably in the person of vampire detective Nick Knight in the *Forever Knight* series. The detective's vocation would prove a popular one for vampires, and Nick Knight would be followed by Henry Fitzroy *(Blood Ties),* Mick St. John *(Moonlight),* and ultimately, of course, Angel from *Buffy the Vampire Slayer.*

The new vampire did not replace the older evil vampire; s/he, if anything, flourished. The new vampire suggested the possibility of a vampire community; the lone vampire could now exist in a world with other vampires—family, lovers, business partners, rivals, friends, and enemies. Far more traditional evil vampires, for example, would appear in *Buffy* (she was, after all, a vampire slayer), than the few good ones that audiences came to know and love—and week after week for seven seasons she dispatched them. Also, many of the vampires proved evil, not just because they were blood suckers, but because they had infiltrated human society and were engaging in a variety of very human evil pursuits.

The good guy vampire would especially flourish in various series aimed at children and youth (most people finding their initial attraction to the vampire as teenagers). Following the introduction of Count von Count to *Sesame Street* during the 1972-73 season, numerous TV series featuring a vampire (and/or youthful vampire hunters), many in animated format, would be produced for Saturday morning and late-weekday afternoon viewing *(Quacula, Count Duckula, Mona the Vampire)*. They would be supplemented by more than a dozen *anime* series introduced from Japan beginning in the 1990s with *Master of Mosquiton '99* and *Vampire Princess Miyu*.

The good guy and conflicted vampires allowed for development and evolution in what had been a fairly limited character in the movies by presenting characters that could love, live with ambiguity, and make moral decisions. At the same time, these vampires also came into peoples' intimate living space, and viewers could allow themselves to develop a deeper attachment to the vampire and quietly nurture that relationship over months, even years. Simultaneously, the good guy vampire would jump from the comic book to romance literature, where it would become the subject of numerous novels in series; no single novel was enough to express the potential of these long-lived characters.

Vampire dramatic series are not, of course, the only contribution of television to the flourishing of the vampire in contemporary pop culture. Even a cursory scanning of the list of television shows begins to uncover the ubiquity of the undead. The pre-existence of a growing television audience, for example, justified the production of numerous made-for-television movies featuring vampires. Countless television shows produced their single vampire episode. The great majority of the more than one hundred vampire documentary films were shot for original viewing on television.

Without television, our awareness of the vampire would be vastly different. The need for some guide through this world carved out by the televised bloodsuckers seems evident. Now we have *Un-Dead TV* as a map that will guide us through it. It will become the foundation volume of future study in the field.

J. Gordon Melton
Waco, Texas
2012

Introduction

Vampires are ubiquitous in our popular culture. From movies to television, in fiction and in art, and even within the hallowed halls of academia, these preternatural creatures of the night are turning up everywhere. But in the not-so-distant past, vampires evoked a sense of extreme terror; they hunted us from the shadows, and were the stuff of nightmares. As these bloodsuckers were being staked in the forests of old, it was Gothic literature that saved them from certain extinction. In his 1897 novel *Dracula,* author Bram Stoker introduced a romantic vampire to the Western world, and our relationship with this once-dreaded revenant has been evolving ever since. As this fear gave way to fascination, the vampire and its nature became a curiosity to be studied, questioned, and understood, which led to an evolution of the myth. The vampire of folklore still exists today, although its modern cousins may turn out to be surprisingly indifferent, if not friendly, while others have become highly sexualized beings. In no other medium has this transformation been so apparent than in television.

By the late 1940s, radio was still the predominant source of entertainment in North American households, although the new medium of television was beginning to take a foothold. Since broadcasters already had an established radio audience, the next logical step was to create television content based on existing radio programming. One of the first televised variety series was *The Texaco Star Theater* on NBC starring comedian Milton Berle, and it was here that the vampire first crossed the threshold into American households. On September 27, 1949, Bela Lugosi, best known for his starring role in *Dracula* (1931), donned the guise of the iconic bloodsucker—heralding an undead presence on television that has ebbed and flowed while steadily increasing over the decades. Both the novel *Dracula* and its undead namesake reappeared on television over the years, beginning with the first televised adaptation of the novel in 1956 starring John Carradine. Bram Stoker's vampire has since been reimagined in countless ways, and although he most often appears in the guise of the Lugosi archetype, his personality, it seems, is ever changing. Dracula truly has become the most ubiquitous vampire in the history of television, followed closely by the iconic creature Vampira, created by the original horror movie host, Maila Nurmi, for *The Vampira Show* (1954). Although her name may not be as well known, her look definitely is, and has clearly influenced most of the female vampires that followed.

In the 1960s, this genre started to be taken more seriously—beginning with sitcoms. Launched in 1964, both *The Addams Family* and *The Munsters* featured ghoulish characters in a lead role. Morticia Addams, who was based on the beatnik character from the *New Yorker* cartoons by Charles Addams, was more of a vamp as opposed to a traditional vampire; as such, all references to *The Addams Family* are found in the section "Take a Breather: No Vampires Here." *The Munsters,* however, had two traditional vampires in the family: Grandpa, a.k.a. Sam Dracula, and his daughter Lily. Despite lasting only two seasons apiece, these shows proved popular enough to spin off several related film and television projects. This decade also gave us the vampire Barnabas Collins, who was introduced to the daytime soap opera *Dark Shadows* as part of a number of supernatural elements added by creator Dan Curtis, in an attempt to prevent the show's cancelation. The changes were an overnight success, and Barnabas became the archetype for the romantic, and often self-loathing, bloodsucker that is so prevalent today. By 1971, *Dark Shadows* ended its run, and the next twenty years saw an intermittent vampire presence on the airwaves; when they did rise from the coffin, it was most often for comedic effect.

By the 1990s, thanks to a number of popular feature films and book series, the networks were once again ready to give vampires a chance—but finding an audience for their stories would prove to be a struggle. Stoker's infamous creation kicked off a new resurgence that began with *Dracula: The Series* in 1990. In this version, the Count was a successful businessman living in the modern world as Alexander Lucard, under the ever-watchful eye of his mortal enemy, Gustav Van Helsing. Dan Curtis returned to Collinwood in 1991, but his updated *Dark Shadows* was canceled due to low ratings after only twelve episodes. Fan favorite *Forever Knight* began as a pilot in 1989, which did not go to series, but after the premise was modified and re-launched in 1992, the show managed to eke out three seasons over four years. By 1996, things were not looking too good for the vampire after another series, *Kindred: The Embraced,* was canceled after only eight episodes. But like a phoenix rising from the ashes, what came next was completely unexpected and would take the world by storm. A show about a teenage vampire slayer finally convinced the Network Brass that supernatural series—especially those featuring vampires—deserved to be front and center in their programming lineup.

Buffy the Vampire Slayer debuted in March 1997, and the series has become so significant that one can classify the periods of undead television as pre-*Buffy* and post-*Buffy*. Crossing social and cultural boundaries, the influence of Joss Whedon's creation has spread outside the confines of the medium, rivaling the impact of Bram Stoker's work on our popular culture. Airing for seven seasons across two networks, *Buffy* led to an equally successful spin-off, *Angel,* as well as a popular comic book run that continued the story after the series ended. Thanks to the rabid success of *Buffy* and *Angel,* more vampires were unearthed, although the first clutch never matched the popularity of their predecessors. Shows like *Blade: The Series* (2006), *Blood Ties* (2007) and *Moonlight* (2007) were each prematurely canceled by the networks before they could firmly establish an audience. It took HBO's *True Blood* (2008) to give the genre the boost it so badly needed, while the teen drama *The Vampire Diaries* (2009)—and its spin-off, *The Originals* (2013)—have since added to this growing wave of popularity, as has Showtime's *Penny Dreadful* (2014). Supporting these traditional bloodsuckers are their cousins from *Sanctuary* (2008) and *Lost Girl* (2010), both of which add to the ever-expanding role that the vampire plays in telling rich, engaging stories.

Once a two-dimensional monster with no voice of its own, the vampire has evolved into something much greater, and television has played a critical role in the creature's enduring hold on the human psyche. It is through their undead voice that storytellers explore the social mores of society, confronting taboos, fears, and prejudices. The image of the vampire is as diverse as the population that it preys upon, and each new generation creates their own interpretation. They have become a reflection of us and our culture, and there is no limit to the ideas that can be explored through these restless creatures of the night. For over sixty-five years, the vampire has spread its influence on the television airwaves, often showing up where you least expect it. This phenomenon demands further study, and I hope that *Un-Dead TV* is a valuable companion to your own journey into this undead world of television history.

About This Book

The content is divided into several categories, based on the nature of the programming, and each is organized alphabetically.

Monsters of the Week: Single Episodes
Individual occurrences of vampire characters in series that do not regularly feature them.

Vampires Among Us: The Series
Series and miniseries that regularly feature vampires.

Prominent Bite: Telefilms and Pilots
Made-for-TV movies, and pilot presentations that are not considered part of a series.

Drawn to Vampires: Animation
Lists all cartoon and anime programming where vampires are found.

Myths and Truths: Documentaries and Reality TV
Factual programming and unscripted television series that feature the undead.

Artistic Endeavors: Variety Programming and TV Specials
Talk shows; sketch comedy; television specials; children's programming.

What's in a Name? Non-Traditional Vampires
Energy drainers, succubi, and other vampire-like creatures (from all categories).

Take a Breather: No Vampires Here!
Catch-all collection of productions thought to feature vampires which do not.

Non-English Programming
The vampire myth is universal; these productions come from several foreign countries.

A Trivial Pursuit
Interesting facts and statistics compiled during the research and review phase.

Appendices
Sources consulted; acronym legend; literary adaptations; best/worst lists; web series.

The Listings

Each entry follows the same basic structure:

Title (includes an episode title, if applicable)
Production Details (broadcast information, cast and crew, etc.)
Synopsis (overview of the production)
Review (if applicable)
Trivia (if applicable, indicated with 📺 icon)

In the production section, Season (S) and Episode (E) numbers are designated as S##E##. If the Director (D) or Writer (W) is not known, then "Anon" is used in lieu of this information; if a credit is shared by many, for the sake of brevity, "Var" is used instead of listing all the names. The Cast (C) list differs based on the nature of the production. For scripted programs, actors are listed, and if a ♀ designation is next to a name, then the person portrayed a vampire. In the case of factual programming, guests and interviewees are listed alongside actors from re-enactments.

If available, the author personally watched and reviewed each entry. Although the synopsis is meant to be spoiler-free, the same cannot be said for the review; it may reveal significant plot details, and possibly give away the ending. Listings that feature a review also include a rating based on the following scale:

🦇🦇🦇🦇	Must-see Un-Dead TV (an excellent production)
🦇🦇🦇	This story has bite (recommended viewing)
🦇🦇	Average fanged fare (easily forgettable)
🦇	Toothless mediocrity (for completists only)
🪵	Horrendous (avoid it like the plague!)

This rating scale is highly subjective, and reflects an overall impression of the production; it is not solely based on the level of vampire content. The author is well versed in vampire fiction, movies, and television shows, and is intimately familiar with screenwriting and television production. Each of these factors has influenced the ratings applied to the listings.

In general, the top-rated entries are entertaining and/or informative, and focus on vampires. However, noteworthy productions may still be recommended even if the vampire content is minimal. Conversely, if an entry is teeming with vampires, but is barely watchable, then it will land on the lower end of the scale. In a few rare cases, the listing is so horrendous that it's been staked! These productions are so awful that they should be avoided altogether, and not viewed by anyone, ever!

Monsters of the Week
Single Episodes

Count Sforza (Vincent Price) takes a liking to Wrangler Jane in *F Troop* (Warner Bros. Television)

Adderly – "Nina Who?"

CBS/Global. Nov 12, 1986 (S01E08). Adventure/Comedy. D: Timothy Bond. W: Carl Binder. C: Winston Rekert, Jonathan Welsh, Dixie Seatle, Ken Pogue, David Calderisi, Jennifer Dale, Nigel Bennett. CAN: English/Color/47m. V.H. Productions Inc./Robert Cooper Productions.

Series follows secret agent V.H. Adderly, who was reassigned to a desk job with the Department of Miscellaneous Affairs—but he ignores his mundane duties to investigate crimes that are overlooked by his superiors. In this episode, Adderly reluctantly "babysits" Nina Olin while her husband, the Ambassador of Beziers, is away on business. Nina is an alcoholic who claims that she's being stalked by a vampire; her husband believes the undead delusion stems from the recent demise of her brother, who bled to death after a car accident. The troubled woman kills herself, but her death doesn't sit well with Adderly—he thinks she was murdered.

This is a garden variety murder-for-inheritance story; the vampire element is minimal, so when Nigel Bennett shows up—in one of his early television roles—one wishes he was there to put the bite on someone (à la Lacroix from *Forever Knight*). Nina was murdered, but we never actually see her, because she's been replaced by her husband's mistress. She's an actress, and her delusional rants incorporate dialogue from her performance in the play *Bride of the Vampire*. The Ambassador is the true vampire here; he preys on Nina, killing her in order to obtain her wealth; upon his death, he's suitably shown with a stream of blood running from his mouth.

Adventure Inc. – "Legacy of a Pirate"

Syndicated. Feb 17, 2003 (S01E14). Action/Adventure. D: Mark Roper. W: Larry Molin. C: Michael Biehn, Karen Cliche, Jesse Nilsson, Ian Duncan ☥, Steven Grives ☥. CAN: English/Color/45m. Fireworks Entertainment/Tribune Entertainment/Valhalla Motion Pictures.

Judson Cross and the team search Bristol Harbor for the wreck of the Black Mantis, a ship believed to have sunk over two hundred years ago in a battle with the pirate Captain John "Blood" Roach. After part of the ship's treasure turns up at auction, Cross traces it back to Krofton Castle, currently occupied by the secretive Baron Pembroke and his son Daniel—both of whom seem to have intimate knowledge of the little-known Captain Blood.

In one of the best entries in this section, this episode features an engaging story with a smart script and some fine British acting. The vampires are a lot of fun to watch; much like humans, they can be either good or bad, and often have conflicting points of view.

Alfred Hitchcock Presents – "The Greatest Monster of Them All"

CBS. Feb 14, 1961 (S06E18). Suspense/Thriller. D: Robert Stevens. W: Robert Bloch. C: William Redfield, Richard Hale ✝, Sam Jaffe, Robert H. Harris, Meri Welles, Charles Carlson, Baruch Lumet, Mike Taylor, Ronnie Sorenson. USA: English/B&W/23m. Shamley Productions.

Film producer Hal Ballew is desperate for a hit, so his writer Fred Logan suggests they make a vampire movie featuring retired actor Ernst von Croft, who was famous in the 1930s for his monster movies. Logan convinces von Croft to come aboard, believing they'll be making a horror picture in the grand tradition of the silver screen—but hack director Morty Lenton has another idea in mind. When von Croft discovers that the film mocks—rather than celebrates—his former screen persona, he exacts revenge befitting to the creature he most often portrayed in the movies. Hosted by Alfred Hitchcock.

A great tale about a once-celebrated horror actor, who ends up appearing in a low-budget B-movie with disastrous results; certainly reminiscent of the waning careers of both Bela Lugosi and John Carradine. Richard Hale is fantastic as the actor who sees his comeback role turned into an object of ridicule, after his voice is intentionally dubbed with something much more comedic. (Although uncredited, the replacement voice sounds very much like a variation of Bugs Bunny as performed by Mel Blanc.) The story reflects on the lost art of serious horror films, once made with integrity but now reduced to cheap creature features riddled with unintentional laughs.

Based on the short story of the same title by Bryce Walton, published in the May 1959 issue of *Ellery Queen's Mystery Magazine* (v. 33 #5, No.186).

Alfred Hitchcock Presents – "Night Creatures"

USA Network. Apr 28, 1989 (Second Series / S04E17). Suspense/Thriller. D: Richard J. Lewis. W: Michael Sloan. C: Brett Cullen, Louise Vallance ✝, Michael Rhoades ✝, Jason Blicker, Ray James. CAN/USA: English/Color/24m. A.H.F. Film Productions Inc./Michael Sloan Productions.

After reporter Holly Sinclair is assigned to cover the record launch of Adam Lust and the Vampires, she ends up in the clutches of the lead singer—who happens to be a real bloodsucker. Hosted by Alfred Hitchcock.

The vampire antagonist is somewhat stereotypical, but it's still an engaging story that's left open-ended, and possibly meant as a backdoor pilot for a spin-off series that never came to be. After Holly is abducted by a mysterious man on horseback (a little silly in this contemporary setting), her boyfriend Coop pledges to hunt down all manner of supernatural beings and psychic phenomena, until he finds the stranger who stole his girl. Teaming up with a friend nicknamed "Freak," a believer who knows all the folklore surrounding such beasts, the episode ends with the two beginning their quest to search for Holly. A similar concept that predates the likes of *The X Files* (1993) and *Supernatural* (2005), which would probably be picked up today thanks to the public's fascination with all things otherworldly.

All Saints – "Lest We Forget"

Channel Seven. Apr 24, 2001 (S04E12). Drama/Medical. D: Scott Hartford Davis. W: Charlie Strachan. C: Georgie Parker, Jeremy Cumpston, Martin Lynes, Judith McGrath, Libby Tanner, Ben Tari, Steven Rooke ☥. AUS: English/Color/46m. 7 Network Australia/Red Heart.

Australian medical drama set in Sydney, which follows the staff of Ward 17 at the fictional All Saints Western General Hospital. The main story in this episode concerns an aging veteran of the Vietnam war, who despite failing health wants to march in his country's national day of remembrance ("Anzac Day," April 25th). One subplot features Gordon Williams, a young man who believes he is a vampire.

The main story arc is rather touching, but the vampire subplot doesn't have much to offer, aside from bringing a little levity to an otherwise somber episode. Gordon hasn't seen the light of day for months; he claims he was bitten by a woman, who sucked his blood and "took his soul." After tests reveal that he's simply suffering from anemia with a vitamin deficiency, the young man is slowly coaxed back into the daylight by Dr. Stevens, who even gets him to agree to a transfusion—despite the fact that Gordon initially thought the process would result in an insatiable craving for blood.

All Together Now – "Bat Out of Hell"

Channel Nine. Sep 24, 1991 (S02E14). Comedy/Family. D: Pino Amenta. W: Anthony Morris. C: Jon English, Rebecca Gibney, Steve Jacobs, Jane Hall, Garry Who, Bruno Lucia, Kerry Armstrong, David Bradshaw ☥. AUS: English/Color/30m. 9 Network Australia.

Series centers on aging rock star Bobby Rivers as he attempts to maintain a music career after discovering he has fifteen-year-old twins, who move in with him after their mother dies in a plane crash. In this episode, Bobby believes that his peculiar new neighbor is a vampire.

Angel – "Corrupt"

WB (Unproduced). 1999 (S01E02). Drama/Fantasy. D: N/A. W: David Fury. C: David Boreanaz ☥, Charisma Carpenter, J. August Richards, Andy Hallett, Glenn Quinn, Elisabeth Röhm. USA: English/Color/60m. Mutant Enemy Productions/20th Century Fox Television/Kuzui Enterprises.

The original script for the second episode of *Angel* was a little too dark—even for this series. Officer Kate Lockley is introduced as an undercover cop posing as a prostitute; she becomes addicted to crack and ends up sleeping with men for money. The episode was put on hold just two days before the start of production, and a new script was ordered. The original story was largely abandoned, but some scenes were reworked into the revised episode, "Lonely Hearts."

A.N.T. Farm – "MutANT Farm"

Disney. Oct 7, 2011 (S01E14). Comedy/Family. D: Adam Weissman. W: Jeny Quine, Dan Signer. C: China Anne McClain, Sierra McCormick, Jake Short ♱, Stefanie Scott, Carlon Jeffery, Zach Steel. USA: English/Color/23m. Disney Enterprises/It's a Laugh Productions/Gravy Boat.

Series follows musical prodigy Chyna Parks, a first year student enrolled in the A.N.T. (Advanced Natural Talents) program at Webster High School in California. In this alternate, Halloween-themed retelling of the pilot episode, Chyna is now a Medusa attending her first day at the M.U.T.A.N.T. program—where she's befriended by a vampire, a zombie, a mummy and a mad scientist.

Standard Disney fare for teens with an underlying lesson about equality—be you monster or human, under the skin, we all look the same. The episode culminates with the performance of a generic, lifeless pop song, which is much more horrific than any monster in this tale.

Are You Afraid of the Dark? – "The Tale of the Nightly Neighbors"

Nickelodeon/YTV. Oct 3, 1992 (S01E08). Family/Suspense. D: Jacques Payette. W: Chloe Brown. C: Raine Pare-Coull, Jason Alisharan, Rachel Blanchard, Suzanna Schebib, Johnny Morina ♱. CAN/USA: English/Color/25m. Family Channel Canada/YTV Canada Inc./CINAR/Nickelodeon.

Series follows a group of teenagers—"The Midnight Society"—who meet at night once a week to tell each other a scary story. In this episode, Betty Ann recalls the tale of Emma and Dayday, siblings who think their new neighbors, the Brauns, are an odd bunch. Originally from the Ukraine, the family dresses only in black, are very private, and have only been seen at night. After several townspeople begin to get sick, the kids believe the Brauns are actually a family of vampires.

A fun tale with a not-so-happy ending, much to the delight of The Midnight Society members. It's a different take on the usual "kids think so-and-so is a vampire" tale; here the older and wiser sister has to convince the younger brother (and horror movie lover) that vampires are real and are living right next door.

📺 The magic dust the kids throw onto the fire was a concoction that included Nestlé Coffee Mate.

Are You Afraid of the Dark? – "The Tale of the Midnight Madness"

Nickelodeon/YTV. Jun 26, 1993 (S02E02). Family/Suspense. D: D.J. MacHale. W: Chloe Brown. C: Jason Alisharan, Raine Pare-Coull, Eddie Robinson, Melanie Wiesenthal, Harry Standjofski, Christopher Heyerdahl ♱. CAN/USA: English/Color/25m. YTV/CINAR/Nickelodeon.

As told by Frank: the Rialto, an old marquee theatre, is set to close due to poor attendance. A mysterious movie director named Dr. Vink claims he can help fill the seats once again—but only if they play his classic silent film *Nosferatu: The Demon Vampire*. It's a great story that includes a faithful homage to Max Schreck's iconic bloodsucker, and fans will take great pride in Vink's take on *Nosferatu;* in his movie, the vampire wins at the end.

🜚 Christopher Heyerdahl (Nosferatu) also played Todd the Wraith in the series *Stargate Atlantis* (2004); the dual roles of John Druitt and Bigfoot in *Sanctuary* (2008); Volturi member Marcus in the *Twilight* films; and the ancient vampire Dieter Braun in Season 5 of *True Blood*.

Are You Afraid of the Dark? - "The Tale of the Night Shift"

Nickelodeon/YTV. Feb 3, 1996 (S05E11). Family/Suspense. D: D.J. MacHale. W: Chloe Brown. C: Joanna Garcia, Ross Hull, Raine Pare-Coull, Emmanuelle Chriqui, Jorge Vargas ♀, Andreas Apergis ♀, Elizabeth Rosen ♀. CAN/USA: English/Color/25m. YTV/CINAR/Nickelodeon.

As told by Sam: A hospital attendant working the night shift notices that her co-workers are beginning to act strange. After one of them turns up dead in the morgue, she discovers the horrible truth behind their change in behavior. This series told vampire stories very well, and this is another wonderful episode that features solid acting with a smart script, and successfully mixes humor and horror.

Are You Afraid of the Dark? - "The Tale of Vampire Town"

Nickelodeon/Family. Apr 24, 1999 (2nd Series / S01E11). Family/Suspense. D: Mark Soulard. W: Alison Lea Bingeman. C: Kareem Blackwell, Elisha Cuthbert, Daniel De Santo, Kyle Downes, Richard Jutras ♀. CAN/USA: English/Color/25m. CINAR/Family Channel/Nickelodeon.

As told by Quinn: Adder, a teen obsessed with the undead, convinces his parents to take him to Wisteria, a town fabled to have once been plagued by vampires. But his over-zealous interest in finding the crypt of the legendary bloodsucker Dreyfus leads some locals to believe that Adder is himself a creature of the night. This isn't as outstanding as previous vampire stories in this series, but it still has a couple of good moments—and features one ugly-looking ancient vampire.

B.J. and the Bear - "A Coffin with a View"

NBC. Mar 10, 1979 (S01E03). Adventure/Drama. D: Ray Austin. W: Michael Sloan. C: Greg Evigan, Pamela Hensley, John Carradine, George Lazenby ♀, Christopher Carroll, Foster Brooks ♀. USA: English/Color/48m. Glen A. Larson Productions/Universal TV.

Star International Pictures hires B.J. to transport two coffins recovered from Dracula's castle in Poenari, which will be used in a promotional stunt to advertise an upcoming vampire movie. Accompanying him is the elderly caretaker of the castle, who warns of dire consequences if the coffins are opened—and B.J. wonders if he should have taken the man more seriously, after a homicide victim is found with bite marks on his neck and his body drained of blood.

I had low hopes for this episode going in, but was pleasantly surprised by just how good it was. It's worth watching provided you skip through what must be the worst theme song in television history. George Lazenby is effective as the mysterious Desmond, and Foster Brooks is hilarious as the drunken actor who stars as the vampire from the film-within-the-TV-show (and his busty female companion is straight out of a Hammer horror movie). I won't give away the ending, but as with most stories, the vampire element is eventually explained away—even though the caretaker isn't convinced, and ultimately, neither is the audience.

📺 John Carradine, who played the caretaker, starred as Dracula on several occasions: in *House of Frankenstein* (1944); *House of Dracula* (1945); the "Dracula" episode of *Matinee Theatre* (1956); *Billy the Kid versus Dracula* (1966); and in *Nocturna: Granddaughter of Dracula* (1979).

The Basil Brush Show – "Taste the Blood of Brushcula"

BBC One. Dec 31, 2003 (2nd Series / S02E09). Comedy/Family. D: Dez McCarthy. W: Dan Tetsell, Danny Robins. C: Michael Windsor, Christopher Pizzey, Georgina Leonidas, Ajay Chabra. UK: English/Color/30m. BBC/Entertainment Rights/Link Entertainment/The Foundation.

Ignoring the warnings of his friends, the mischievous fox Basil Brush eats some old cheese and watches a midnight marathon of horror films just before going to bed. He ends up having a nightmare filled with vampires, Dr. Frankenstein and his assistant Igor.

Baxter – "Vampire Movies"

Family. Oct 10, 2010 (S02E07). Comedy/Family. D: Paul Fox. W: Alex Pugsley. C: Evan Williams, Holly Deveaux, Brittany Bristow, Kyle Mac, Melanie Scrofano, Simon Ahmadi, Addison Holley, Tara Joshi. CAN: English/Color/30m. Shaftesbury Films.

Follows a group of students attending the Northern Star School of the Arts, including slacker Baxter McNab, his best friend Emma Ruby, and his rival Marcus Crombie. In this episode, Baxter avoids writing an essay about vampires; he convinces Ms. Mansfield to let him shoot a video instead. The production is jeopardized after he and Emma argue over which student will play the lead bloodsucker.

Baywatch – "Search & Rescue"

Syndicated. Jan 13, 1997 (S07E10). Action/Adventure. D: Gregory J. Bonann. W: Michael Berk. C: David Hasselhoff, Pamela Lee, Yasmine Bleeth, David Chokachi, Jeremy Jackson, Gena Lee Nolin. USA: English/Color/43m. The Baywatch Company/All American Television.

A huge fire at the pier has the lifeguards and firefighters working side-by-side, and it's such a success that they combine their disciplines to form a new search and rescue unit. Cody, Neely and Rick are offered the chance to become part of this new elite team, but they must give up lifeguarding if they want to take on these new positions.

The opening rescue effort tries to be overly dramatic, but let's face it, no one is ever in any real danger; it's difficult to believe such a premise, since everyone looks so nicely coifed even after intense rescue efforts. A minor story arc involves Mitch, and alludes to his nocturnal activities from the spin-off series *Baywatch Nights,* which at this point had become a full-blown supernatural drama. He's been investigating someone who thinks they're a vampire; he shows up carrying a cross, smelling of garlic, and sporting a bandage on his neck. (The vampire episode from *Baywatch Nights* is unrelated to this particular scene.)

Baywatch Nights – "Night Whispers"

Syndicated. Nov 23, 1996 (S02E09). Action/Drama. D: Reza Badiyi. W: Donald R. Boyle, Carey W. Hayes, Chad Hayes. C: David Hasselhoff, Angie Harmon, Arthur Taxier, Felicity Waterman ☥. USA: English/Color/43m. Baywatch Nights Production Co./All American Television.

This failed spin-off series, where *Baywatch* meets *The X Files,* sees former lifeguard Mitch Buchannon moonlighting as a private investigator alongside gal pal Ryan McBride. In this episode, Ryan discovers the body of a man with a gaping slash across his chest; he died from massive blood loss, but there is very little of it at the scene. Ryan worries for Mitch's safety after the prime suspect, Francesca Bryce, takes an interest in him—because she may be a real vampire.

This is the story of a beautiful four-hundred-year-old vampire who has been searching all this time for the perfect mate, someone who will continually fascinate and amaze her. Oddly enough, this man of her dreams turns out to be Mitch Buchannon, a middle-aged lifeguard who likes to run around all night playing detective. Really? Is the Hoff that much of a catch?

📺 The first season was a traditional drama, but it had dismal ratings. For season two, supernatural elements were introduced, and it became a monster-of-the-week series. This change of focus worked for Dan Curtis when he added Barnabas Collins to *Dark Shadows,* but here the idea fails miserably.

Being Erica – "Erica the Vampire Slayer"

CBC. Mar 25, 2009 (S01E12). Comedy/Drama. D: Holly Dale. W: Aaron Martin, Jana Sinyor. C: Erin Karpluk, Tyron Leitso, Vinessa Antoine, Reagan Pasternak, Morgan Kelly, Michael Riley, Jessica Huras ☥, Jonas Chernick ☥. CAN: English/Color/46m. Temple Street Productions/CBC.

Erica gets kicked out of a management training program, which puts her recent promotion in jeopardy. She needs to challenge her self-perception, so Dr. Tom sends her back to 2001 and into the arms of a former boyfriend, Ivan Frankel. Back then, Erica learned that Frankel participated in a live-action role playing game—as a vampire. When he created a character for her, Erica wasn't

amused; but rather than express how she really felt, she just abandoned the relationship. This time around, she breaks it off with Frankel face to face—but that isn't enough to send her back to her own time. Erica realizes that she must actually attend the L.A.R.P. to resolve this issue.

Despite being able to go back in time to correct past emotional blunders, the trip often doesn't work out as planned; yet Erica always learns something that helps her confront an issue in the present. In this case, she attends the vampire L.A.R.P., but because she's so worried about the perception others have of her, she ruins the night for Frankel. Erica realizes that the only one judging her is herself, so if she can learn to step outside of the box, she may be surprised at just how capable she is at handling conflict. It's an interesting episode with a strong message, and the roleplaying scenes are very entertaining (the story treats both the L.A.R.P., and those who participate in it, with the utmost respect).

Bette – "Halloween"

CBS. Oct 25, 2000 (S01E03). Comedy/Family. D: Andrew D. Weyman. W: Meg DeLoatch. C: Bette Midler, Kevin Dunn, James Dreyfus, Marina Malota, Joanna Gleason, Dolly Parton, John Farley ☥. USA: English/Color/22m. All Girl Productions/Miss M Productions.

After Bette tapes a TV special with Dolly Parton, she dresses up as the Country Music star and drags Rose out trick-or-treating. After the two get in trouble with the L.A.P.D., they flee back to the studio where police mistakenly arrest the real Dolly Parton in Bette's place.

This painfully unfunny self-promotional sitcom barely lasted one season, and based on this episode it's easy to see why. The vampire component is minor; a homeowner is dressed as Dracula while giving out candy. The best part is seeing his two dogs also dressed for the occasion, each wearing an opera cape—perhaps the canines are fans of *Zoltan, Hound of Dracula* (1978).

Beyond Belief: Fact or Fiction – "Morning Sickness" / "The Curse of Hampton Manor" / "Wax Executioner" / "Blood Bank" / "Ring Toss"

SyFy. Jan 21, 2000 (S03E01). Drama/Mystery. D: Skip Schoolnik. W: Bob Wolterstorff, Mike Scott. C: Michele Lamar, Adam Gierasch ☥, Janet Rotblatt, Andrew Hawtrey. USA: English/Color/44m. Maybe Productions/Dick Clark Productions.

This series presented stories based on true events, alongside others of pure fiction; at the end of the episode, it was revealed which was which. In the segment "Blood Bank," a John Doe is admitted to hospital suffering from severe malnutrition and acute anemia. He's given a series of blood plasma transfusions; surprisingly, less than a day later, he fully recovers. That night, two hundred bags of plasma are stolen from the hospital's blood bank, and a nurse discovers dozens of empty blood bags in the patient's bathroom. Presented by Jonathan Frakes with narration by Campbell Lane.

Before the man can be held for questioning, he leaps out of a sixth story window and runs off into the night. Did the John Doe steal the blood to sell it, or was he really a vampire? It's up for the viewer to decide. The suspect is quite creepy, and this segment gets bonus marks because it's based on a true story: it apparently happened in the 1980s, at a hospital on the East Coast of the United States.

Beyond Belief: Fact or Fiction – "Moonstruck Beach" / "Healing Hands" / "Aspen Sunny Side" / "Night Walker" / "Hot Car"

Promotional advertisement for the FOX paranormal series *Beyond Belief: Fact or Fiction* (Dick Clark Productions/TV Guide)

SyFy. Aug 15, 2002 (S04E10). Drama/Mystery. D: Penelope Buitenhuis. W: Bob Wolterstorff, Mike Scott. C: Michael Rogers , Ona Grauer ☥, Gustavo Moreno ☥, Ulla Friis. USA: English/Color/43m. Maybe Productions/Dick Clark Productions.

In "Night Walker," Wade Harris makes a living through identity theft; he hacks into the bank account of an affluent couple, Stokely and Marta Vradma, and steals hundreds of thousands of dollars. Marta is onto his scheme, but surprisingly, she offers to team up with Wade to steal even more from her husband. Presented by Jonathan Frakes with narration by Campbell Lane.

Even though a story about identity theft is rather timely and most certainly could be true, it's clear from the outset that this is a tale of fiction. Marta transfers twenty-five million dollars into Wade's account and spends the night at his place. He wakes up the next day alone, penniless, and with a fresh bite mark on his neck. Although we only see her husband in passing, Marta is quite alluring and could certainly pass for a vampire, but the story is too vague to be certain. The ambiguity is likely intentional, but the story would have benefited from a clearer resolution.

Beyond Reality – "The Passion"

USA Network. Feb 6, 1993 (S02E18). Horror/Sci-Fi. D: Bruce Pittman. W: Marc Scott Zicree. C: Shari Belafonte, Carl Marotte, Leon Pownall ☥, Nikki de Boer ☥, Sam Malkin ☥. CAN/USA: English/Color/24m. Paragon Entertainment Corporation.

Series follows Laura Wingate and J.J. Stillman, two university professors who investigate paranormal happenings outside of the classroom. In this episode, a stranger gives J. J. the journal of his great-grandfather, Jeremiah Baker, a physician who gave up a promising medical career and then fell out of contact with his family. The journal relates a tale from London, 1888: Baker treats Mrs. Winter, who is stricken by a strange blood disease after a man attacks her in the night. A mysterious Caribbean woman believes that the culprit is the same man who killed six prostitutes in the Whitechapel district—and that Mrs. Winter can only be saved *after* she dies.

The majority of the episode takes place in the past, and the three series regulars take on different characters. Shari Belafonte plays Ariel, the Caribbean woman; Carl Marotte plays Jeremiah Baker, the physician; and Nikki de Boer plays Mrs. Winter. Baker and Ariel don't see eye-to-eye on the situation; he wants to cure the vampire, while she wants to kill him. It's an average story with elements of Jack the Ripper, but the plot holes and the actors' inconsistent accents are too distracting.

The Big Easy – "Vamps Like Us"

USA Network. Mar 2, 1997 (S01E20). Crime/Drama. D: Vern Gillum. W: Fred Golan. C: Tony Crane, Susan Walters, Barry Corbin, Fabiana Udenio ⚲, Faber Dewar ⚲, Michael Cahill, Hunt Scarritt ⚲. USA: English/Color/44m. Grosso-Jacobson Productions/ITC Entertainment Gp.

🦇 🦇

Writer Madeline Knox came to New Orleans to research a local vampire cult called The Nightwings; she turned up dead the day after a secret meeting with their leader, Antoine Matthias. The author's body was found drained of blood, with bite marks on the neck, and she was placed upon the tomb of a local occult practitioner who died in 1894. His name was also Antoine Matthias.

A predictable story with a few twists and turns that are not entirely unforeseen. The killer's identity is obvious from the outset, as is the identity of the real man behind the vampire Matthias. The cult members are a group of stereotypes, but they add a bit of color to an otherwise bland story; the direction and editing is so stagnant that even the major chase scene seems as though it's moving in slow motion.

Big Wolf on Campus – "Fangs for the Memories"

YTV/ABC Family. Jul 23, 1999 (S01E15). Action/Comedy. D: Peter Svatek. W: Peter Knight, Christopher Briggs. C: Brandon Quinn, Danny Smith, Rachelle Lefevre, Philip Le Maistre ⚲, Shawn Baichoo ⚲. CAN: English/Color/22m. CinéGroupe/Telescene Film Group Productions.

🦇 🦇 🦇

High school comedy that follows werewolf Tommy Dawkins and his best friend Merton Dingle, a Goth who helps him protect the town of Pleasantville from supernatural baddies. In this episode, to impress Stacey, Tommy donates to a blood drive—but later realizes that his werewolf blood will kill a normal human being. When he and Merton break into the blood bank to steal it back, they meet a group of vampires who are also there to make a withdrawal.

A fun episode with a lot of in-jokes relating to various vampire movies. Case in point: Tommy and Merton argue over who was the better actor in *The Lost Boys* (1987)—Corey Feldman or Corey Haim—which foreshadows the fact that both actors appear in later episodes.

 Rachelle Lefevre (Stacey) later portrayed the vampire Victoria in the feature films *Twilight* (2008) and *The Twilight Saga: New Moon* (2009).

Big Wolf on Campus – "Blaim It on the Haim"

YTV/ABC Family. Jun 10, 2000 (S02E11). Action/Comedy. D: Peter D. Marshall. W: David Wolkove, Sandy Brown. C: Brandon Quinn, Danny Smith, Aimée Castle, Corey Haim ☥. CAN: English/Color/22m. CinéGroupe/Fox Family Channel/Telescene Film Group Productions.

Tommy, Merton and Lori stop a vampire attack, but the bloodsucker is actually actor Corey Haim, who's in town shooting his latest movie. Haim starts spending a lot of time with Lori, and Merton discovers that the actor may in fact be a bona fide neck nibbler.

Another great episode with a lot of inside jokes at the expense of Haim, who shows that he can laugh at himself and his former teen-idol status. The ending sets up Corey Feldman's appearance in season three.

Big Wolf on Campus – "Everybody Fang Chung Tonight"

YTV/ABC Family. Nov 3, 2001 (S03E02). Action/Comedy. D: Daniel Grou. W: Christopher Briggs. C: Brandon Quinn, Danny Smith ☥, Aimée Castle, Erika Rosenbaum ☥, Jennifer Rae Westley ☥. CAN: English/Color/22m. CinéGroupe/Telescene Film Group Productions.

Merton's late-night radio show draws the unwanted attention of Cassandra, a Goth girl who's also a vampire; he falls in love with her despite the fact that she only drinks werewolf blood. Fearing for Tommy's life, Merton tries to hide his friend's true nature.

Another charming undead entry from this series, and definitely recommended for those who like their vampire tales told through a comedic lens. This story arc continues in episodes #19 and #20.

Big Wolf on Campus – "What's the Story, Mourning Corey"

YTV/ABC Family. Apr 20, 2002 (S03E19). Action/Comedy. D: Erik Canuel. W: Christopher Briggs. C: Brandon Quinn, Danny Smith, Aimée Castle, Corey Feldman ☥, Jessica Welch. CAN: English/Color/22m. CinéGroupe/Fox Family Channel/Telescene Film Group Productions.

Corey Feldman is in town to enquire about his best friend Corey Haim, who disappeared after filming a vampire movie two years earlier. He's not surprised when told that Haim was a vampire, and the news of his demise doesn't seem to bother Feldman one bit. This is part one of a two-part story that concludes in the next episode.

Big Wolf on Campus – "Thanks"

YTV/ABC Family. Apr 27, 2002 (S03E20). Action/Comedy. D: Erik Canuel. W: Christopher Briggs, Peter Knight. C: Brandon Quinn, Danny Smith, Aimée Castle, Jessica Welch, Tod Fennell. CAN: English/Color/22m. CinéGroupe/Telescene Film Group Productions.

🦇 🦇 🦇

Although he's equally as smitten with Sloan, Tommy concedes and allows Merton to ask her to the prom. Surprise! She's actually a supernatural bounty hunter, who's been hired by the Werewolf Syndicate to get rid of Tommy and Merton once and for all.

This two-part series finale ties up three story arcs: Cassandra (Merton's former vampire girlfriend), the Werewolf Syndicate, and the actor/vampire Corey Haim. One might also argue that Sloan is a succubus of sorts, for she steals Merton's life by means of a kiss. All are safe by the end, however it turns out that the Resident Advisor at Tommy's new school may be a vampire—a notion that delights Merton immensely. A fitting conclusion to a gem of a TV series.

Bigfoot and Wildboy – "Return of the Vampire"

ABC. Aug 4, 1979 (S02E10). Adventure/Family. D: Leslie H. Martinson. W: Donald R. Boyle. C: Ray Young, Joseph Butcher, Yvonne Regalado, Deborah Ryan ☥, Ken Scott, Mickey Morton. USA: English/Color/25m. Krofft Entertainment.

🦇 🦇 🦇

Series follows the adventures of the legendary Bigfoot and his charge Wildboy, an orphan that the creature raised in the wilds of the Pacific Northwest; the two protect the area from evildoers. In this episode, prospectors unearth a cave filled with gold and treasure, but they accidentally disturb The Countess—a vampire.

This episode is recommended because of its outlandish premise and exceptionally cheesy execution; it's a guilty pleasure that would make Ed Wood proud. The Countess is quite striking, however her prosthetic teeth are so cumbersome that the poor actress has trouble speaking while wearing them. The vampire is not affected by sunlight, but can turn into a bat, which resembles every fake-looking bat that appears in such stories. Bigfoot is essentially a hirsute version of the Six Million Dollar Man; he runs in slow motion, throws around heavy objects, and can jump really high. Wildboy wears clothing made from animal skins, and his short-shorts do not befit a twenty-five-year-old man. Truly a show that must be seen to be believed.

Blue Murder – "Asylum"

Global. Oct 19, 2001 (S02E02). Crime/Drama. D: Tim Southam. W: Michael Melski. C: Maria del Mar, Joel Keller, Jeremy Ratchford, Maurice Dean Wint, Mimi Kuzyk, Geoffrey Pounsett ♀. CAN: English/Color/46m. Blue Murder II Productions Inc./North Bend Film Company.

Canadian drama series that follows a group of police detectives in Toronto. In this episode, Castillo and Sweet investigate the murder of a doctor at a psychiatric hospital, who was strangled and stabbed—and then the killer drank his blood.

Although Renfield's Syndrome (clinical vampirism) is mentioned in passing, none of the doctor's patients are blood drinkers. But one of them is the killer; he feared that if the doctor reassessed him, he'd be considered sane and then sent to a real prison. His partner in crime is a security guard, a disturbed man who believes that his blood is turning to sand—and he drank the doctor's blood because he thought it would cure him.

Burke's Law – "Who Killed Purity Mather?"

ABC. Dec 6, 1963 (S01E11). Crime/Drama. D: Walter Grauman. W: Harlan Ellison. C: Gene Barry, Gary Conway, Regis Toomey, Leon Lontoc, Telly Savalas, Charlie Ruggles, Wally Cox ♀, Janet Blair, Gloria Swanson, Nancy Kovack. USA: English/B&W/52m. Four Star/Barbety.

Burke investigates the murder of Purity Mather, a self-proclaimed witch who, realizing she would be killed, furnished him with a list of possible suspects upon her death. One of them is Count Carlo Szipesti—"the world's only living vampire"—who lives in a hearse and makes special appearances at theatres running horror movie marathons.

A delightful story with smart dialogue, a twist ending, and several comedic moments, most of which are centered around the five quirky individuals suspected of murder. Szipesti is a hoot and not at all imposing; he drinks Bloody Marys for image sake, claims to be descended from a long line of Transylvanian royalty, and makes personal appearances at horror movies because "it's better than collecting unemployment." An all-around great episode from a series with a film noir feel that starred ridiculously attractive actors dressed to the nines.

📺 Swanson was nominated for a Golden Globe award ("Best TV Star - Female") for her performance in this episode.

The Casebook of Sherlock Holmes – "The Last Vampyre"

ITV/PBS. Jan 27, 1993 (S01E08). Crime/Drama. D: Tim Sullivan. W: Jeremy Paul. C: Jeremy Brett, Edward Hardwicke, Keith Barron, Roy Marsden ♀, Maurice Denham, Richard Dempsey ♀, Yolanda Vazquez. UK/USA: English/Color/102m. Granada Television/WGBH Boston.

In this story, loosely based on "The Adventure of the Sussex Vampire" by Sir Arthur Conan Doyle,

Holmes and Watson travel to the hamlet of Lamberly to investigate two mysterious deaths. Locals believe the culprit is John Stockton, a descendent of a once-prominent family in town, who were all killed a century earlier after villagers were convinced they were vampires.

A good all-around Sherlock Homes story, with a few scenes that are straight out of a Hammer horror film. As expected, Holmes has no patience for the supernatural angle; he eventually reasons out that Stockton is a delusional man who believes he's a bloodsucker. Fans of vampire stories will find this better than average, while Conan Doyle purists will balk at the liberties it takes with the original text. Interestingly, one scene shows a character reading an edition of *Varney the Vampire,* which began as a series of "penny dreadfuls" in 1845.

📺 Considered as S06E03/04 of the umbrella series *The Adventures of Sherlock Holmes* (which aired in the United States under the *Mystery!* banner).

Sherlock Holmes (Jeremy Brett) and Dr. Watson (Edward Hardwicke) investigate two mysterious deaths that locals believe were at the hands of a bloodsucker, in "The Last Vampyre" (Granada Television/WGBH Boston)

Castle – "Vampire Weekend"

ABC. Oct 26, 2009 (S02E06). Crime/Drama. D: Karen Gaviola. W: Terri Edda Miller. C: Nathan Fillion, Stana Katic, Susan Sullivan, Molly Quinn, Samantha Shelton ☥, Rob Arbogast ☥. USA: English/Color/42m. Beacon Pictures/Experimental Pictures/ABC Studios.

🦇 🦇 🦇

Suffering from writer's block, crime novelist Richard Castle shadows Detective Kate Beckett for inspiration, and his unique perspective helps solve various cases. In this episode, Castle and Beckett investigate the murder of a man found in a graveyard with a wooden stake driven through his heart. He was working on a graphic novel called *Blood Everlasting,* which surprisingly contains several clues to the identity of his killer—as well as insight into an unsolved murder committed eighteen years earlier.

A great episode where the sanguinists and vampires aren't the criminals that they are initially assumed to be. The main antagonist, Morlock, actually suffers from acute cutaneous porphyria, a condition that the episode addresses fairly accurately (although the effect of sunlight on his skin is more quickly pronounced for dramatic effect).

📺 Nathan Fillion played Caleb in the seventh season of *Buffy the Vampire Slayer;* his co-star, Stana Katic, played the vampire Simone Renoir in the telefilm *The Librarian: The Curse of the Judas Chalice* (2008).

Charmed – "Bite Me"

WB. Apr 18, 2002 (S04E18). Comedy/Drama. D: John Kretchmer. W: Curtis Kheel. C: Alyssa Milano, Holly Marie Combs, Rose McGowan ☥, Julian McMahon, Elizabeth Gracen ☥, Samuel Ball ☥. USA: English/Color/44m. Spelling Television/Northshore Productions Inc.

🦇🦇🦇

Series follows the Halliwell sisters—the "Charmed Ones"—who come from a long line of virtuous, powerful witches. In this episode, after being banished from the Underworld by Cole, an exiled vampire queen seeks to defeat him by biting Paige and turning her into one of the undead.

Not a lot of blood sucking here, but there are some pretty decent human-turns-into-bat effects, and you can't go wrong with a sexy vampire queen played by Elizabeth Gracen! This episode marks the third appearance of the pseudo-vampires known as the Grimlock, demonic humanoids that live underground (and therefore are sensitive to light), who use their power to steal the eyesight from innocent children. This gives them the temporary ability to see the aura that surrounds good-natured people; the Grimlock then drain this positive energy (aura), killing their victims in the process.

In *The Chronicle* episode "The King is Undead," a team of tabloid newspaper reporters goes undercover in search of Elvis, but they end up finding vampires (The Greenblatt-Janollari Studio/Stu Segall Productions)

chromiumblue.com – "The Eternal" / "The Eternal II"

Showtime. Sep 6/13, 2002 (S01E06/07). Adult/Drama. D: Zalman King. W: Elise D'Haene, Greg Hittelman. C: Erica Prior, Summer Altice, Ian Abercrombie, Dominic Keating, Lucas Babin ☥, Matt King ☥. LUX/GER: English/Color/120m. ApolloMedia/Carousel Films.

In this two-part story, Maria falls in love for the first time, but there's a problem: the object of her affection is a vampire named Joe. But things could be worse. Joe is in fact an Eternal—a type of vampire that craves blood, but only takes enough for sustenance and never kills; there is still goodness and mercy deep within his soul. Unfortunately for both of them, his maker—an evil bloodsucker nicknamed The Dutchman—doesn't tolerate his progeny's good nature. He sets a plan in motion to finally turn Joe into a malicious vampire, and uses his new lover Maria as bait.

Aimed directly at adult fans of paranormal romance novels, this erotic tale about a self-loathing vampire is cheesy, poorly-acted and overwrought. Joe escapes the "anguish" of immortality by participating in illegal street races, which inexplicably seems to temporarily dull his pain…and he also plays guitar. If that isn't silly enough, how about flashbacks where The Dutchman tries to look menacing while running around wearing a bicorne hat? If you like watching beautiful people in stories that are all style with no substance, and often unintentionally funny, then this one is for you.

The Chronicle - "The King is Undead"

SyFy. Mar 8, 2002 (S01E20). Comedy/Fantasy. D: Krishna Rao. W: Javier Grillo-Marxuach. C: Chad Willett, Rena Sofer, Reno Wilson, Joe Sagal, Michael Phillip ☥, Curtis Armstrong. USA: English/Color/43m. The Greenblatt-Janollari Studio/Stu Segall Productions.

🦇 🦇 🦇

Tucker and Wes go undercover at "Elvisopolis 3000," in an attempt to track down the real King of Rock 'n' Roll. Meanwhile, Grace goes underground to investigate a vampire sighting within the sewers below. The three cross paths with a man who is the spitting image of Elvis Presley, and he's on a mission to hunt down a nest of vampires masquerading as Elvis impersonators.

Could Elvis still be alive, secretly hunting the undead? Or is it actually his twin brother Jesse, who supposedly died at birth? Perhaps he's just a really good impersonator. We may never know, but this quirky story delivers the laughs while both honoring the King and showcasing the sometimes absurd goings-on at Elvis events. This series, about a tabloid newspaper that reports on real paranormal events, was short-lived; try to catch it in repeats or on DVD, it's well worth your time.

ChuckleVision - "Out for the Count"

CBBC. Feb 16, 2000 (S12E09). Comedy/Family. D: Martin Hughes. W: John Sayle. C: Paul Elliot, Barry Elliot, Hugo Myatt ☥, David Brett ☥. UK: English/Color/15m. BBC.

🦇 🦇

The Chuckle Brothers take a walk-about holiday, and Barry is upset because they chose Transylvania; he believes it's filled with umpires who like to bite people on the neck. His brother Paul explains that he's actually thinking of vampires, which don't exist, although the local tinker they run into believes otherwise—and warns the brothers to avoid Castle Vlad at all costs. They end up staying there anyway; Paul's main concern is supper, while Barry fears that their host is really a vampire—and they're the main course.

This is a harmless kids' program with a stereotypical East European vampire, who turns out to be nothing of the sort—but the same can't be said for his manservant Igor.

Classics Dark and Dangerous – "Mrs. Amworth"

CBC/HTV. 1975 (S01E01). Drama/Suspense. D: Alvin Rakoff. W: Hugh Whitemore, E.F. Benson. C: Glynis Johns ♀, Derek Francis, John Phillips, Pip Miller, Rex Holdsworth. CAN/UK: English/Color/31m. Highgate Associates Ltd./HTV West-Bristol/OECA-Toronto.

Residents in a quaint English village welcome Mrs. Amworth with open arms; she's a charming, outgoing yet slightly eccentric woman who has brought life back into their sleepy little town. After locals are stricken with anemia, some wonder if Amworth is to blame; the same sickness occurred centuries earlier when her distant relative, Elizabeth Chaston, died suddenly in 1644.

Based on the 1922 short story of the same title by E.F. Benson, this is not a tale for those only interested in vampires that bare fangs, hiss at the camera, and spill blood everywhere as they drink—this fiend is more of a vampire/spirit in the classical sense. Johns' performance is remarkable, and her transition from a friendly free spirit to a sinister predator is quite well done (especially considering the short running time). This was the first episode in the CAN/UK co-production *Classics Dark and Dangerous,* a series of six half-hour dramas that starred an international cast of A-list actors. Other tales included "The Silver Blaze" (Sir Arthur Conan Doyle); "The Rocking Horse Winner" (D.H. Lawrence); "The Island" (L.P. Hartley); "The Ugly Little Boy" (Isaac Asimov); and "The Mannikin" (Robert Bloch). "Mrs. Amworth" was combined with "The Island" and "The Mannikin," and released as *Three Dangerous Ladies* (1977); in the 1980s, the remaining episodes were released together as *Three Tales Dark and Dangerous* (which also aired on television).

📺 The air date for this episode is an approximation; it was likely produced in 1975 and would have aired shortly thereafter (in 1978, it was rebroadcast on ITV in the UK). Copies still exist on both 16mm film and VHS, largely because they were distributed into the public school system and libraries.

The Collector – "The Vampire"

Citytv. Jan 31, 2006 (S03E04). Action/Drama. D: Jonathan A. Rosenbaum. W: Catherine Girczyc. C: Chris Kramer, Christine Chatelain, Daniella Evangelista ♀, Kyla Hazelwood ♀, Angela Moore, Richard Side. CAN: English/Color/60m. Lietuvos Kinostudija/No Equal Entertainment.

Morgan Pym is a soul collector who helps those who struck a deal with the Devil; he assists them in redeeming themselves, so they can avoid going to Hell after the bargain has expired. In this episode, Pym has forty-eight hours to aid Ashley Merrin, a girl who made a deal to become a vampire. Pym discovers that Ashley also turned her best friend—but she's an uncontrollable, murderous creature of the night.

The tale started out fine, but it competed with other sub-plots that were too dry and took me right out of the story (one assumes these were part of the overall story arc). Sadly, the vampire plot became so schmaltzy that by the end I was convinced I was watching a Lifetime or Hallmark movie of the week. When Ashley staked her friend, it looked so fake that my first reaction was "Wow. She couldn't bring herself to kill the vampire. Instead, she stabbed a pillow." But no, it was supposed to appear as though she actually did the deed; however, I've pressed push-pins into corkboard with more force than she used ramming the stake through the vampire's chest.

📺 Daniella Evangelista (Ashley Merrin) portrayed the "hanging victim" in the Supernatural vampire episode "Fresh Blood" (2007).

Coming Up Rosie – "Frankenflakes"

CBC. Nov 22, 1976 (S02E11). Comedy/Family. D: Trevor Evans. W: Barbara Evans, Stuart Northey. C: Barrie Baldaro ⚱, John Candy, Dan Hennessey, Catherine O'Hara, Rosemary Radcliffe, John Stocker, Gerald Ainsley. CAN: English/Color/29m. Trevor Evans Productions Ltd./CBC.

Film school graduate Rosie Tucker lands a job as a documentary producer for Zonk Productions, a company that shares a building with several businesses run by a group of oddball characters. In this episode, to try something different, Rosie's boss agrees to shoot a commercial for a new breakfast cereal: sugar frosted Frankenflakes. To cut costs for this monster-themed production, Rosie is forced to use non-professional actors—and her boss ends up playing Dracula.

The performances of John Candy and Catherine O'Hara hint at the comedic talent they later honed on the series *SCTV*. But their scenes are overshadowed by the main story arc, which follows two small-time gangsters who attempt to recover stolen diamonds hidden within a mannequin. The best part is the actual two minute commercial for Frankenflakes, which opens with Igor as he prepares breakfast for Dracula. In a very funny scene, the Count awakens from his coffin at the stroke of midnight, and complains to his vampire teddy bear that he's tired of the same old gruel. Candy and O'Hara then show up dressed as teenage glee club members, and perform a song and dance routine to promote the benefits of the breakfast cereal.

Coronation Street – Ep. #4745

ITV1. Jan 1, 2000 (S41E01). Comedy/Drama. D: David Kester. W: Peter Mills. C: Bruce Jones, Jane Danson, Julie Hesmondhalgh, David Neilson, Barbara Knox, Johnny Briggs, Jacqueline Pirie, Martin Hancock, Thomas Ormson. UK: English/Color/60m. Granada Television.

British soap opera that follows the trials and tribulations of residents in the fictional town of Weatherfield in Greater Manchester county. The focus of this special hour-long episode is a party held in honor of the millennium; residents come dressed as a wide variety of characters, including Dracula.

Coronation Street – Ep. #5618-5622

ITV1. Nov 3-10, 2003 (S44E207-211). Comedy/Drama. D: Tim O'Mara. W: Carmel Morgan, Peter Whalley. C: John Savident, Malcolm Hebden, Anne Kirkbride, Sally Whittaker, William Roache, Chris Gascoyne, Betty Driver, Bill Ward. UK: English/Color/150m. Granada Television.

In this multi-episode story arc, Fred Elliot comes up with a new product, "Dracula Pie," and praises its "full-blooded" nature; he even displays a large cardboard cut-out of the Count outside of his butcher shop. The pies sell like hot cakes, up until Kirk and Les cause a fuss—they claim it gave them food poisoning. To revive flagging sales, Fred gets the local press to cover a promotional event where he hands out free samples, but his plan backfires once Kirk and Les show up to voice their concerns.

Criminal Minds – "The Performer"

CBS/CTV. Nov 11, 2009 (S05E07). Crime/Drama. D: John Badham. W: Holly Harold. C: Joe Mantegna, Paget Brewster, Shemar Moore, Matthew Gray Gubler, Thomas Gibson, Gavin Rossdale ♀. USA: English/Color/42m. The Mark Gordon Company/CBS Television Studios.

The FBI's Behavioral Analysis Unit heads to Los Angeles to investigate the third death in a string of murders, where each victim was strangled and then bled out through two small lesions on the neck. The prime suspect is a Goth musician named Paul Davies—whose persona is a vampire called "Dante"—and the team believes he's now lost within his alter-ego, and has become the real deal off-stage.

A pretty good episode overall; it would have received a higher rating were it not for a few problems with the acting and the script (and it's far too obvious from the get-go who the real killer is).

📺 Gavin Rossdale (Dante) is the former lead singer of Bush; the song he performs at the start of the episode is "Love Will Tear Us Apart" by Joy Division.

Crossing Jordan – "Revealed"

NBC. May 9, 2004 (S03E10). Crime/Drama. D: Allan Arkush. W: Damon Lindelof, Tim Kring. C: Jill Hennessy, Miguel Ferrer, Ravi Kapoor, Kathryn Hahn, Steve Valentine, Jerry O'Connell, Silas Weir Mitchell ♀. USA: English/Color/44m. NBC Studios/Tailwind Productions.

Detective Hoyt investigates the bizarre death of struggling author Samuel Burnham, whose exsanguinated body was found with bite marks on the neck—and locked within his apartment, the door bolted from the inside. An overly-enthusiastic Dr. Townshend genuinely believes that a real vampire may be behind the attack, although Dr. Macy is convinced that there is nothing supernatural going on (and he doesn't want the investigation to turn into an episode of *The X Files*). The prime suspect is the man that Burnham was researching for his latest book: Alastair Dark, a self-proclaimed vampire who seems to play the role all too well.

Engaging story about an unpopular man who reinvents himself to become a respected member of the vampire subculture, a community where he finally fits in. Ultimately the real (yet somewhat mundane) explanation behind the murder is revealed, although the more supernatural version—supplied by the Gothic-loving Dr. Townshend—is much more appealing.

Crown Court – "The Death of Dracula"

ITV1. Mar 28-30, 1973 (S02E37-39). Crime/Drama. D: Mark Cullingham. W: David Fisher. C: Edward Jewesbury, Bernard Gallagher, Charles Keating, John Blythe, John Alkin, David Ashford, Valerie Bell, Luan Peters. UK: English/B&W, Color/90m. Granada Television/Thames.

In this three-part story, renowned illusionist Count Alucard is killed on stage after his most famous trick takes a deadly turn. Fulchester Crown Court must determine if his death was an accident, or premeditated murder instigated by his wife (and stage assistant) Rita Mattson.

As part of the spectacular act that made his reputation, Alucard—dressed up as Dracula—rises from inside a coffin and has two audience members fire silver bullets at him. Although his chest always bleeds, he reveals that there are no wounds to his skin; he then spits out uniquely-marked bullets from within his mouth. He then "attacks" his assistant Rita and bites her on the neck… and so ends the show. However, this time around, his chest is penetrated by the bullets, and the illusionist is killed—but by whom? It's an interesting courtroom drama with some eccentric characters and a sharp script, and is well worth a look.

CSI: Crime Scene Investigation – "Suckers"

CBS. Feb 5, 2004 (S04E13). Crime/Drama. D/W: Danny Cannon. C: William Petersen, Marg Helgenberger, Gary Dourdan, Paul Guilfoyle, James Haven ♀, Joel Bissonnette ♀. CAN/USA: English/Color/44m. Alliance Atlantis/Jerry Bruckheimer Television.

After a teenage Goth girl named Daegana is found dead with all the blood removed from her body, Catherine and Warrick question sanguinist Lazarus Kane. The investigation leads to an odd lab technician, who also seems to have an insatiable taste for the red stuff.

The vampire part of the episode is a nice change from the norm; here the Goth kids and stereotypical blood drinkers are red herrings for the real killer. He's actually quite average but very creepy, and truly seems to think he's a vampire in the classical sense.

CSI: Crime Scene Investigation – "Committed"

CBS. Apr 28, 2005 (S05E21). Crime/Drama. D: Richard J. Lewis. W: Sarah Goldfinger, Uttam Narsu. C: William Petersen, Jorja Fox, Paul Guilfoyle, Wallace Langham, Richard Wharton ♀. CAN/USA: English/Color/40m. Alliance Atlantis/Jerry Bruckheimer Television.

Grissom and Sara investigate the murder of a patient at a mental institution, home to criminally insane and sexually violent prisoners. The man was found in his room bludgeoned to death in a pool of his own blood—and another patient, Kenny Valdez, was drinking it. But the CSI team isn't convinced that Valdez is the one who killed him.

Valdez suffers from Renfield's Syndrome (clinical vampirism), but he wasn't the killer; he just capitalized on the situation to satiate his thirst for blood. After he's cleared of suspicion, there's no longer any vampire component to the story. It's actually a dark tale of incest, with several creepy characters, but the mood is ruined by a couple of ridiculous, implausible scenes.

CSI: Crime Scene Investigation – "Blood Moon"

CBS. Oct 7, 2010 (S11E03). Crime/Drama. D: Brad Tanenbaum. W: Treena Hancock, Melissa R. Byer. C: Laurence Fishburne, Marg Helgenberger, George Eads, Jorja Fox, Max Beesley ♀. USA: English/Color/44m. Jerry Bruckheimer Television/CBS Television Studios.

Michael Wilson is murdered the night before his wedding; in what initially looks like a ritual killing, his body is posed and mutilated. The investigation leads to a local "Coven and Clans" convention, where groups of "vampires" and "werewolves" take their chosen lifestyle very seriously; they believe they are ancient enemies. The CSI team thinks someone has taken the rivalry a little too far, after they discover that Wilson had lived the life of a vampire, and the prime suspect appears to be a werewolf.

A very graphic yet silly story where groups of vampires and werewolves just come off as laughable role players, each an amalgam of cartoonish character traits gleaned from any recent horror movie. The story throws in a red herring with someone suffering from porphyria, where his affliction (in this case, cutaneous) is misused as a plot device, and poorly at that. The conclusion is absolutely ludicrous, and suggestive of an uninspired attempt to cash in on the vampire/werewolf craze.

⚰ This story makes a reference to a previous episode, "Justice is Served" (2001), which also featured a character who suffers from porphyria.

CSI: Miami – "By the Book"

CBS. Oct 30, 2011 (S10E06). Crime/Drama. D: Gina Lamar. W: Melissa Scrivner. C: David Caruso, Emily Procter, Jonathan Togo, Rex Linn, Eva LaRue, Omar Miller, Orlando Jones, Chad Todhunter ♀. USA: English/Color/42m. Jerry Bruckheimer Television/CBS Television Studios.

On Halloween night, an anonymous tip sends the CSI team to an exclusive island mansion owned by popular vampire novelist Marilyn Milner, where they discover the author's housekeeper dead. Her body is found hung upside down and exsanguinated, with two puncture wounds on the neck—a crime that directly mirrors a scene from Milner's latest novel.

Average episode with a story that in many ways points to the *Twilight* series of books, complete with a rabid fan that has pronounced fangs, and even climbs a tree in an attempt to escape from the police. But he's just a red herring, for the real killer is one of Milner's staff who, along with the deceased housekeeper, is one of a group of ghost writers responsible for the majority of her work. Despite a rather dark and chilling pre-credit sequence (and the ghost writer revelation), the story falls a little flat, and the killer's motivation is highly questionable. As with this series in general, the use of advanced (perhaps alien?) technology is laughably distracting.

CSI: NY – "Sanguine Love"

CBS/CTV. Feb 3, 2010 (S06E14). Crime/Drama. D: Norberto Barba. W: Carmine Giovinazzo. C: Gary Sinise, Melina Kanakaredes, Carmine Giovinazzo, Robert Joy, Hill Harper, Carlo Rota ☥. CAN/USA: English/Color/41m. Jerry Bruckheimer Television/CBS Television Studios.

A young woman's body is found in Central Park, her death caused by exsanguination through a small, deep laceration on the side of her neck. After determining the source of an oddly-shaped scar on her wrist, the investigation leads to a local vampire cult headed by the mysterious Joseph Vance.

This painfully predictable story has the CSI: NY team investigating a sanguinist who leads a cult of willing donors, apparently for no other reason than to host pretentious parties with fancy *hors d'oeuvres* and wine...and to sample a little of the real red stuff. Peppered with scenes that are a little too *deus ex machina* to be believed, the story also features the most tame vampire cult ever presented on television. It may be realistic, and for once portray sanguinists as the "good guys," but the story overall is too pedestrian. How's that for being pretentious?

Daring & Grace: Teen Detectives – "The Case of the Voracious Vampire"

CBC. Oct 21, 2000 (S01E03). Family/Mystery. D: John L'Ecuyer. W: Mark Shekter. C: Jeremy Guilbaut, Kristin Booth, Alex Leblanc, Amy Bartlett, R. Steven Bond, Scott A. McRae. CAN: English/Color/30m. Dick & Tracy Entertainment Inc./Microtainment Plus International/CBC.

Teen adventure series where a basketball star teams up with his girlfriend to run his father's detective agency. In this episode, while investigating a series of robberies, Dick and Tracy come across a teen vampire club.

Dark Realm – "Murder One"

Syndicated. May 5, 2001 (S01E10). Horror/Suspense. D: Eric Summer. W: Guy J. Louthan, Whitney Smith. C: William Katt, Frank Grimes, Jane Mar, Wolf Larson, Alison Armitage, John Blakey, Michael Brandon ☥. CAN/FRA/USA: English/Color/60m. Sapphire Films/Warner Brothers.

A lawyer joins a local law firm and discovers that his new co-workers are all vampires. Presented by Eric Roberts.

Darkroom – "The Bogeyman Will Get You" / "Uncle George"

ABC. Dec 4, 1981 (S01E02). Suspense/Thriller. D: John McPherson. W: Robert Bloch. C: James Coburn, Helen Hunt, Gloria DeHaven, Randolph Powell ☥, Quinn Cummings, Arlen Dean Snyder, Gloria DeHaven, R.G. Armstrong. USA: English/Color/60m. Universal TV.

In the segment "The Bogeyman Will Get You," on the way home from the Drive-In, sisters Nancy and DiDi have a run-in (literally) with an odd neighbor, Phil Ames. Nancy becomes attracted to him, but after witnessing some peculiar habits, DiDi is convinced he's a vampire. When her best friend turns up dead, Nancy wonders if her sister may be right. Presented by James Coburn.

Overall a pretty good vampire tale, with a twist ending that leads to a cheerfully unhappy conclusion. A teenage Helen Hunt is excellent here, as is Quinn Cummings as her younger sister. Randolph Powell as Ames brings a certain level of creepiness to the tale; you instantly sense something's wrong with him, even though it might not be what you expect.

Days of Our Lives – Ep. #6119

NBC. Oct 31, 1989 (S24E253). Drama/Romance. D: Anon. W: Leah Laiman, Anne Howard Bailey. C: Matthew Ashford, John de Lancie, Judith Chapman, Charles Shaughnessy, Frank Parker, John Aniston ☥, Genie Francis, Peggy McCay. USA: English/Color/60m. NBC.

For this year's Halloween party, Victor Kiriakis dresses as a Lugosi-inspired Dracula.

Diagnosis Murder – "The Bela Lugosi Blues"

CBS. Jan 6, 1995 (S02E13). Crime/Mystery. D: Lee Philips. W: Michael Gleason. C: Dick Van Dyke, Barry Van Dyke, Victoria Rowell, Scott Baio, Julie Carmen ☥, Tim Dunigan, Phil Morris. USA: English/Color/60m. Dean Hargrove Productions/Fred Silverman Company.

A body is found with massive head and neck trauma, but there is little blood in the wound, and even less at the crime scene. Dr. Sloan suspects nothing out of the ordinary, until a closer examination reveals two puncture wounds near the jugular. While searching the residence of the prime suspect,

Sloan notices no mirrors, and discovers a coffin; he believes the killer has a psychological disorder that has led to vampire delusions. After two other bodies show up with similar wounds, Sloan worries that Dr. Stewart may be the next victim.

Wow. A *real* vampire in a non-supernatural series? This one is a head-scratcher! Not only are the series regulars unfazed by facing what appears to be a classic vampire, the elderly Van Dyke is still agile enough to be thrown across a room—twice—and has no trouble getting up afterward. But that's nothing compared to the fact that they kill a woman who ultimately wasn't even the prime suspect in a murder case! Yikes. Huge suspension of disbelief required for this one.

Dr. Terrible's House of Horrible – "Lesbian Vampire Lovers of Lust"

BBC Two. Nov 12, 2001 (S01E01). Comedy/Horror. D: Matt Lipsey. W: Steve Coogan, Graham Duff, Henry Normal. C: Steve Coogan, Ronni Ancona ♀, Honor Blackman, Sally Bretton, Ben Miller, Basil Moss, Anouska Bolton-Lee ♀. UK: English/Color/30m. Baby Cow Productions.

A six-part anthology series that lampooned horror films of the 1960s and 1970s; each episode was a pastiche of several familiar productions. This story takes place in 1877, where newlyweds Captain Hans Brocken and his wife Carmina are trapped inside the castle of Countess Kronsteen, a beautiful vampiress who wants to take their blood—and their virginity. This sly spoof of the vampire genre is overflowing with sexual innuendo; it's a well-written story that provides a lot of genuine laughs.

Doctor Who – "A Journey Into Terror"

BBC One. Jun 12, 1965 (S02E33). Adventure/Sci-Fi. D: Richard Martin. W: Terry Nation. C: William Hartnell, William Russell, Jacqueline Hill, Maureen O'Brien, John Maxim, Malcolm Rogers ♀. UK: English/B&W/25m. BBC.

This is episode four of the six-part story "The Chase," where the Doctor and his companions are pursued through time and space by the Daleks. They seek refuge in a haunted mansion; it's filled with traps, bats, and other things that go bump in the night. While exploring cobwebbed rooms, the Doctor and Ian run into the Frankenstein Monster, while Barbara and Vicki are surprised by Count Dracula himself.

It's an extremely dated but enjoyable tale from a series where hip, nonchalant spacefarers explored unknown planets with nary a weapon between them. In this chapter, they end up in "Frankenstein's House of Horrors," a scary attraction at a futuristic theme park (c. 1996); the monsters eventually get Medieval on the gang's pursuers. Speaking of which, the Daleks were considered scary at the time, but I just can't get past their toilet-plunger appendages.

Doctor Who – "State of Decay"

BBC One. Nov 22 – Dec 13, 1980 (S18E13-16). Adventure/Sci-Fi. D: Peter Moffatt. W: Terrance Dicks. C: Tom Baker, Lalla Ward, Matthew Waterhouse, Emrys James ☥, William Lindsay ☥, Rachel Davies ☥. UK: English/Color/100m. BBC.

In this four-part story, the TARDIS, traveling through E-Space, lands on a feudal planet where the inhabitants live under the harsh rule of three lords—Aukon, Camilla and Zargo. They bear an uncanny resemblance to officers from the Earth cargo vessel Hydrax, lost one thousand years ago. The Doctor discovers that residents are being systematically taken and drained of blood, which is being used to revive the King of the Great Vampires—who's entombed within the earth below.

A little campy at times, especially with the vampires Camilla and Zargo, although Lord Aukon—played by Shakespearean actor Emrys James—effectively steals every scene; the interactions between him and the Doctor are priceless. It's a great performance that makes up for the fact that we barely get a glimpse of the King of the Great Vampires. This story was originally planned to open Season 15 three years earlier in 1977, but the idea was shelved by the top brass at the BBC. They were concerned that it would compete with their high-profile adaptation of *Dracula* starring Louis Jordan, also produced that year.

📺 The vampires reappear in *Project: Twilight*, an audio drama, as well as in the novels *Goth Opera, Blood Harvest, The Eight Doctors,* and *Vampire Science*.

Doctor Who – "The Curse of Fenric"

BBC One. Oct 25-Nov 15, 1989 (S26E08-11). Adventure/Sci-Fi. D: Nicholas Mallett. W: Ian Briggs. C: Sylvester McCoy, Sophie Aldred, Dinsdale Landen, Alfred Lynch, Nicholas Parsons, Joann Kenny ☥, Joanne Bell ☥. UK: English/Color/100m. BBC.

In this four-part story, the TARDIS takes the Doctor and Ace to England in 1943; they land near a naval base where several soldiers have been killed under mysterious circumstances. The locals think it's an old Viking curse, and believe an evil presence is buried within the crypt underneath the church. The Doctor discovers the ancient evil is called "Fenric," and its minions terrorizing the area—Haemovores—are actually mutated humans from the future, who have evolved into creatures with an insatiable hunger for blood.

A pretty decent story with several layers, but those unfamiliar with the series may find the more character-centric threads less interesting. The futuristic Haemovores are suitably menacing, and the two female vampires are quite effective as undead sirens of the sea.

Doctor Who – "Smith and Jones"

BBC One/CBC. Mar 31, 2007 (2nd Series / S03E01). Adventure/Sci-Fi. D: Charles Palmer. W: Russell T. Davies. C: David Tennant, Freema Agyeman, Anne Reid ♀, Roy Marsden, Adjoa Andoh. CAN/UK: English/Color/45m. BBC/CBC.

Medical student Martha Jones is having a strange day indeed. Her mysterious patient, "The Doctor," has irregular physiology, and the hospital has somehow been transported to the moon. A strange-looking group has taken over the building, and they claim to be an interplanetary police force on the lookout for a fugitive "plasmavore"—an alien disguised as a human and hidden somewhere inside.

Although the main antagonist is the blood-sucking plasmavore, the plot is really just a means to introduce the new Companion, Martha Jones. Still, it's a fun tale with a quirky villain, who uses a bendy straw, inserted into the neck, to suck the blood from her victims.

The Dresden Files – "Bad Blood"

SyFy/Space. Feb 25, 2007 (S01E05). Crime/Drama. D: Rick Rosenthal. W: Jack Bernstein. C: Paul Blackthorne, Terrence Mann, Joanne Kelly ♀, Conrad Coates, Natalie Lisinska ♀, Lyriq Bent ♀. CAN/USA: English/Color/43m. Dresden Files Productions/Saturn Films.

Wizard and private investigator Harry Dresden receives an impromptu visit from Bianca, a former lover who happens to be Chicago's most powerful vampire. Collecting on a debt for helping him five years earlier, Bianca begs Dresden to find out who's behind a recent attempt on her life.

A great episode from an underrated series that was canceled well before its time. Here we have an alluring, sympathetic and believable vampiress who finds herself in the middle of a turf war over a drug called "third eye," specifically engineered for use by the undead.

📺 This version of the vampire Bianca varies significantly from her counterpart in the novels. The literary character is a vicious predator who runs a brothel—and she'd prefer it if Dresden was dead and buried.

The Dresden Files – "Storm Front"

SyFy/Space. Mar 18, 2007 (S01E08). Crime/Drama. D: David Carson. W: Hans Beimler, Robert Hewitt Wolfe. C: Paul Blackthorne, Valerie Cruz, Rebecca McFarland, Raoul Bhaneja, Conrad Coates, Joanne Kelly ♀. CAN/USA: English/Color/43m. Dresden Files Productions/Saturn Films.

A local mobster and his girlfriend are murdered in an occult-like fashion, and the High Council blames Dresden; they think he's using black magic again. As the wizard attempts to clear his name, other murders are committed—and each victim is somehow tied to the nightclub owned by the vampire Bianca. On the run and running out of time, can Dresden find the real killer before he becomes the next victim?

A solid episode with a good mix of humor, horror, magic and character development. Plus, the lovely Bianca vamps out while beating up our hero—yet she's ultimately subdued by magic. Great fun!

📺 This is an edited version of the unaired pilot that was later broadcast as a TV movie in 2008.

The Drew Carey Show – "It's Halloween, Dummy"

ABC. Oct 31, 2001 (S07E07). Comedy/Drama. D: Bob Koherr. W: Mike Teverbaugh, Linda Teverbaugh. C: Drew Carey, Diedrich Bader, Christa Miller, Kathy Kinney, John Carroll Lynch ☥, Ryan Stiles. USA: English/Color/21m. Mohawk Productions/Warner Bros. Television.

Drew is amazed by the new owner of Winfred-Louder, Broderick Newsome, who seems to like (and hate) everything that he does. When Drew is asked to set up a Halloween haunted house for charity, he offers his own home to stage the event. Newsome is very impressed with the turnout, and offers Drew a management position with the company—but things take a turn for the worse after it becomes evident that the man has a very weak heart.

A fun story that garners a lot of laughs, especially in the secondary plot where Lewis seeks out a Russian oral surgeon to take care of a problematic tooth. As for vampires, during the Halloween party, Drew's brother Steve dresses up as Dracula.

Everybody Loves Raymond – "Halloween Candy"

CBS. Oct 26, 1998 (S03E06). Comedy/Family. D: Steve Zuckerman. W: Steve Skrovan. C: Ray Romano, Patricia Heaton, Brad Garrett, Madylin Sweeten, Doris Roberts, Peter Boyle, Vinnie Buffolino ☥. USA: English/Color/23m. Where's Lunch/Home Box Office/Worldwide Pants.

Ray decides not to get a vasectomy and instead brings home a variety pack of colored condoms. Things go awry after Frank mistakes the contraceptives for chocolate coins, and hands them out to the neighborhood kids on Halloween night.

This charming episode has Frank handing out the very last condom to a kid dressed as Dracula, whom Ray chases throughout the neighborhood after realizing what happened. After chasing down fifteen Draculas, he finds the condom—but discovers it's just a candy wrapped in red foil.

📺 Peter Boyle (Frank) is dressed up as Frankenstein's Monster, a character he portrayed in *Young Frankenstein* (1974).

The Evil Touch – "The Fans"

Nine Network. Feb 10, 1974 (S01E19). Horror/Thriller. D: Vic Morrow. W: Ron McLean. C: Vic Morrow ☥, Alfred Sandor, Enid Lorimer, Queenie Ashton, Mike Dorsey, Kevin Howard. AUS: English/Color/27m. Amalgamated Pictures Australasia Productions/Olola Productions.

In the spirit of *The Twilight Zone* and *Night Gallery,* each episode in this weekly anthology series explores a macabre story—from monsters to witchcraft and other supernatural happenings. In this outing, famous horror actor Purvis Greene needs to improve his poor public image, so he makes a personal appearance at the home of two elderly sisters—his biggest fans. But fiction becomes reality when Greene is imprisoned by the women, who actually abhor the depravity he represents on screen—and they've decided to put him on the path of true righteousness. Hosted by Anthony Quayle.

I wasn't convinced by parts of the story (or Vic Morrow's performance), but the two elderly sisters were a hoot, and were the highlight of this episode. The idea was interesting as well: the Pfeiffer sisters, who in 1937 killed a horror actor named "Gulosi," were committed to an insane asylum. The building burnt to the ground in the mid-sixties, and it was believed that all the inmates had died. The women have returned to seek out another soul to save, telling Greene, "there is no morality in your world, where life is valueless, where decency and honesty are dead virtues. You…the depravity you represent! Vampire! Cannibal! Freak Show!" One can only imagine what these ladies would think about today's horror films, and their "torture porn" tendencies.

F Troop – "V is for Vampire"

ABC. Feb 2, 1967 (S02E22). Comedy/War. D: Hollingsworth Morse. W: Austin Kalish, Irma Kalish. C: Forrest Tucker, Larry Storch, Ken Berry, Melody Patterson, Vincent Price ☥. USA: English/Color/30m. Warner Bros. Television.

The pale-skinned, cape-wearing Count Sforza arrives from Transylvania, and wants to buy an old haunted house at the edge of town. Corporal Agarn suspects the stranger is a vampire, and after Wrangler Jane goes missing, the other men of F Troop are equally convinced. It's an average episode that features jokes that show their age, but it's always a pleasure to see the great Vincent Price—especially in the guise of a vampire!

Family Matters – "Dark and Stormy Night"

ABC. Oct 28, 1994 (S06E06). Comedy/Family. D: John Tracy. W: Fred Fox, Jr., Jim Geoghan. C: Reginald VelJohnson ☥, JoMarie Payton Noble, Jaleel White ☥, Rosetta LeNoire ☥, Darius McCrary ☥. USA: English/Color/22m. Bickley-Warren Productions/Miller-Boyett Productions.

After a storm cancels their plans for Halloween trick-or-treating, the family stays in to play "pass the ghost story," and trade off on a tale about a family of nineteenth century vampires. In the story, the Count and Countess von Winslow have an unexpected house guest, Sir Steven the Duke of Urkel, who requires assistance after his carriage breaks down.

The scenes involving the vampire tale do have some funny moments, but at this point in the series, Urkel had become way too annoying. His predictable pratfalls, enhanced by canned laughter, make this episode far less enjoyable than it could have been.

Fantasy Island - "The Lady and the Longhorn" / "Vampire"

ABC. Dec 16, 1978 (S02E13). Comedy/Drama. D: Arnold Laven. W: Dan Ullman. C: Ricardo Montalbán, Hervé Villechaize, Lloyd Bochner, Jack Elam, Eva Gabor, Robert Reed ⚱, Julie Sommars, Erica Yohn. USA: English/Color/49m. Spelling-Goldberg Productions/Columbia Pictures Television.

In "Vampire," famous method actor Leo Drake comes to the island to prepare for his most challenging role yet: Count Dracula. His fantasy is to become a real vampire, but as he disappears into the fanged façade, he loses touch with reality—and locals fear there's a real bloodsucker in their midst.

Upon arrival, Drake and his wife are whisked off to a "sinister" castle on the edge of a village, where—inexplicably—locals still live a feudal existence and are prone to superstition. Descended from a group of Transylvanians that fled their country generations ago, the villagers believe there's an evil presence in the castle. To make matters worse, Drake is the spitting image of the *real* Count Dracula, whose portrait hangs inside the local Inn (although in the picture he looks more like a mustachioed Bert Convy). In record time—he is *method,* after all—Drake disappears into the role, and before long there's a dead girl with a bite mark on her neck, and an angry mob chasing him around town—with torches! Nothing more needs to be said about this train wreck, except that Drake isn't a vampire—but he'd fit right in on the dance floor of Studio 54.

📺 The castle scenes were filmed at Shea's Castle in Antelope Valley, California, built in 1924 by real estate mogul Richard Shea. It's been used as a location for several notable TV series, including *Buffy the Vampire Slayer,* as well as films such as *Blood of Dracula's Castle* (1969).

Fear Itself - "The Sacrifice"

NBC. Jun 5, 2008 (S01E01). Drama/Suspense. D: Breck Eisner. W: Mick Garris. C: Jeffrey Pierce, Jesse Plemons ⚱, Rachel Miner, Mircea Monroe, Stephen Martines, Reamonn Joshee, Bill Baksa ⚱, Walter Phelan ⚱. CAN/USA: English/Color/44m. Fear Itself Productions/Industry Entertainment.

After their car breaks down, four criminals seek refuge in an isolated fort occupied by three alluring sisters, all of whom are living a Colonial existence. Something is amiss with the family, and once the sun goes down, the men are attacked by a creature lurking in the shadows.

Although the premise is a little far-fetched, the story itself is well-told; thankfully, we see very little of the vampire close up, because the makeup effects are laughably bad. Based on the short story "The Lost Herd" by Del Howison, this version takes liberties with the plot, and turns it into a more traditional vampire tale (missing is the original premise and ending, which would have been unsuitable for television). Truth be told, I enjoyed this adaptation way more than the original short story.

📺 This episode was filmed in part at Fort Edmonton Park, Canada's largest living history museum, which includes original and rebuilt structures representing the history of Edmonton from the Fur Trade Era (1795-1859) to the Metropolitan Era (1914-1929).

Fearless Fosdick – "Batula"

NBC. Sep 14, 1952 (S01E13). Adventure/Family. D: Mary Chase. W: Everett Crosby. C: John Griggs, Gilbert Mack, Jean Carson, Frank Sullivan, Silvia Meredith, Donald Sommers. USA: English/B&W/24m. Louis G. Cowan, Inc.

Featuring marionettes by celebrated puppeteer Mary Chase, this short-lived children's show was based on the comic strip-within-a-strip of the same name created by Al Capp, which appeared in his *Li'l Abner* comic. In this episode, the intrepid detective battles a vampire bat that steals toupees whilst hanging upside down. Also known as *Fearless Fosdick Meets Dracula*.

5th Quadrant – "Vampire of the Sun" / "Can You Keep a Secret Society?"

Space. Apr 14, 2002 (S01E13). Comedy/Sci-Fi. D/W: Lee Smart. C: Lee Smart, Jennifer Baxter, Paul Van Wart, Noah Cappe ☥, Michael Rhoades. CAN: English/Color/30m. Garland Freewin Productions/S&S Productions.

In "Vampire of the Sun," the team investigates the horrifying world of modern-day vampires, when they meet up with a strange woman named Nosferata.

Frasier – "Halloween"

NBC. Oct 28, 1997 (S05E03). Comedy/Family. D: Pamela Fryman. W: Suzanne Martin. C: Kelsey Grammer, Jane Leeves, David Hyde Pierce, Peri Gilpin, John Mahoney, Joey Zimmerman ☥. USA: English/Color/22m. Grub Street Productions/Paramount Network Television.

A scatter-brained Roz discloses to Frasier that she's pregnant, although she's still awaiting test results from her doctor. During a literary-themed Halloween party hosted by Niles, hilarity ensues when the rest of the Crane clan mistakenly think that Daphne is the one who's pregnant—and that Frasier is the baby daddy.

Unfortunately, the hilarity didn't quite ensue; with many forced jokes and setups falling flat, this is one of the less amusing episodes from an overall great series. The vampire component is limited to a trick-or-treating child who arrives at the door dressed as Dracula.

Freddy's Nightmares – "Prime Cut"

Syndicated. Jan 21, 1990 (S02E15). Horror/Suspense. D: David Calloway. W: Michael Kirschenbaum. C: Robert Englund, Sandahl Bergman ♀, Tony Dow, Amy Lyndon, Donovan Scott. USA: English/Color/60m. Lorimar Telepictures/New Line Television/Warner Bros. Television.

While on a camping trip, three businessmen are strangely attracted to their guide, Ginger "Tracker" Morgan. After witnessing her aversion to the holy cross and wooden tent stakes—and her apparent fondness for blood—one of the men believes she might be a vampire.

Initially the story was interesting, but then halfway through it was revealed that the vampire thing was only a dream. Actually, a charter plane crash-landed in a remote area, and the three men and their guide have been munching on those who did not survive. Once the vampire aspect is written away, it turns into a bland tale of survival and cannibalism. Granted, the resulting story may be of general interest to horror fans, but for vampire lovers, it's a major letdown.

Freaks and Geeks – "Tricks and Treats"

NBC. Oct 30, 1999 (S01E03). Comedy/Drama. D: Bryan Gordon. W: Paul Feig. C: Linda Cardellini, John Francis Daley, James Franco, Samm Levine, Seth Rogen, Jason Segel, Martin Starr, Becky Ann Baker, Joe Flaherty ♀. CAN/USA: English/Color/45m. Apatow Productions.

On Halloween night, Lindsay ditches her mom in favor of hanging out with her new friends, but ends up in the middle of a vandalism spree. Meanwhile, her younger brother Sam goes trick-or-treating with his pals, but after several unfortunate incidents, he realizes it's time to let go of his childhood.

A charming episode about the pains of growing up and trying to figure out where you fit in, where no one in the Weir family ends up celebrating Halloween exactly in the way they had planned. In a nice nod to the "Count Floyd" character he originated on *SCTV*, Joe Flaherty dresses up as a vampire to help his wife dish out the goodies, but he inadvertently frightens a group of young children who show up at their doorstep. Seems as though after years of failing to provide any real scares on the *SCTV* segment "Monster Chiller Horror Theatre," Count Floyd finally manages to pull it off with great aplomb.

Friday the 13th: The Series – "The Baron's Bride"

Syndicated. Feb 15, 1988 (S01E13). Horror/Suspense. D: Bradford May. W: Larry Gaynor. C: Louise Robey, John D. LeMay, Tom McCamus ♀, Chris Wiggins, Kevin Bundy. CAN: English/B&W, Color/60m. Lexicon Productions/Variety Artists International/Hometown Films.

The team is transported back to nineteenth century London along with newly-turned vampire

Frank Edwards. They cross paths with a young author named Abraham Stoker, to investigate a series of murders committed by Jack the Ripper.

The sub-par acting doesn't dull the charm of the story, which was primarily shot in glorious black and white. It does infer that real vampires inspired Bram Stoker to write his classic novel *Dracula,* which may bother those who dislike seeing real people fictionalized in this manner.

Friday the 13th: The Series – "Bottle of Dreams"

Syndicated. Jul 25, 1988 (S01E26). Horror/Suspense. D: Mac Bradden. W: Roy Sallows. C: Louise Robey, John D. LeMay, Chris Wiggins, Elias Zarou, Tom McCamus ⚲. CAN: English/Color/60m. Lexicon Productions/Variety Artists International/Hometown Films.

In this flashback episode that includes scenes from "The Baron's Bride," Micki and Jack relive their most horrible moments after a strange gas puts them into a trance. It's more like *bottle of nightmares*—this throw-away clip show forces the audience to relive some horrible acting.

Friday the 13th: The Series – "Night Prey"

Syndicated. Nov 13, 1989 (S03E08). Horror/Suspense. D: Armand Mastroianni. W: Peter Mohan. C: Louise Robey, Steven Monarque, Chris Wiggins, Genevieve Langlois ⚲, Michael Burgess ⚲, Eric Murphy ⚲. CAN: English/Color/60m. Lexicon Productions/Variety Artists International.

Vampire hunter Kurt Blackman steals a Medieval crucifix to exact revenge on Evan Van Hellier, the vampire who stole his bride twenty years earlier. But this cursed "Cross of Fire" must first be activated by killing a mortal, using the blade hidden within the handle.

One of the best vampire episodes in this section! Lost love, passion, revenge, traditional vampires—this one has it all. Plus some fine acting from Chris Wiggins, Michael Burgess and Genevieve Langlois.

Friends – "The One Where Chandler Can't Cry"

NBC. Feb 10, 2000 (S06E14). Comedy/Romance. D: Kevin S. Bright. W: Andrew Reich, Ted Cohen. C: Jennifer Aniston, Courteney Cox Arquette, Lisa Kudrow, Matt Le Blanc, Matthew Perry, David Schwimmer, Douglas Looper ⚲. USA: English/Color/24m. Bright-Kauffman-Crane Productions.

Emotions run high as Rachel tries to stop Ross from dating her sister, while Monica freaks out after Chandler admits that he hasn't cried since childhood. But they get distracted by Phoebe's extracurricular activities, after Joey discovers that she's been making adult films.

Convinced that Phoebe is secretly a porn star, the gang rent *Buffay the Vampire Layer*—in the film, Buffay confronts a Dracula-type vampire. They discover it's actually her twin sister Ursula who's been making the films, using Phoebe's name as a pseudonym.

Fries With That? - "Ben Bites"

YTV. Sep 9, 2004 (S01E27). Comedy/Family. D: Carl Goldstein. W: Jackie May, Alan Silberberg. C: Giancarlo Caltabiano ☥, Anne-Marie Baron, Stéfanie Buxton, Morgan Kelly, Jeanne Bowser. CAN: English & French/Color/30m. 9124-1737 Quebec Inc./Tele-Action.

Tess tries her homemade makeup on Ben, who ends up looking like a vampire. But the other staff at Bulky's believe that a bat bite is responsible for his transformation.

General Hospital - Ep. #12727- 12761

ABC. Jan 14 – Mar 4, 2013 (S50E197- 231). Drama/Romance. D: Scott McKinsey. W: Ron Carlivati, Shelly Altman. C: Michael Easton ☥, Lynn Herring, Kelly Monaco, Lisa Lo Cicero, Jane Elliot, Jimmy Deshler, Sean Kanan. USA: English/Color/2040m. American Broadcasting Company.

About a decade after the demise of *General Hospital's* supernatural spin-off *Port Charles,* several of its actors returned to GH, which led to a retcon of the vampire storyline from PC. In this version, vampire slayer Lucy Coe returns to the city, and mistakes police officer John McBain for the bloodsucker Caleb Morley. With a serial killer on the loose, McBain entertains the possibility that his undead doppelgänger may be the culprit; however, it turns out that "Caleb" was once the stage persona of musician Stephen Clay, who went insane after the death of his wife, and now believes he's a real vampire. At the climax of this story arc, Caleb is killed by a silver arrow to the chest, after which it is revealed that he was wearing fake fangs. Was he human, after all? His mystical, glowing ring—the source of his supposed immortality—is stuck on his finger, as if it doesn't want to let go. That is, until a mysterious coroner easily removes it from the corpse, and keeps it for himself. When this character is introduced three months later, he is none other than Caleb/Stephen Clay's estranged older brother, Silas.

Get Smart - "Weekend Vampire"

NBC. Dec 18, 1965 (S01E14). Comedy/Spy. D: Bruce Bilson. W: Gerald Gardner, Dee Caruso. C: Don Adams, Barbara Feldon, Edward Platt, Martin Kosleck ☥, Ford Rainey, Roger Price. USA: English/Color/22m. Talent Associates-Paramount Ltd.

🦇 🦇 🦇

After three agents wind up dead with two suspicious bite marks on their necks, Max and 99 suspect that former CONTROL scientist Dr. Drago—relieved of duty after performing unauthorized experiments—may be responsible. Yet his replacement, Professor Sontag, is also a strange man, and the two wonder if he is in league with the disgruntled doctor. While undercover, Max and 99 trail Sontag to Drago's creepy Gothic castle, where they discover the doctor about to climb into a very large coffin…

An appealing story that rises above the standard trappings of the typical "criminal masquerading as a vampire" plot. The usual wit is abundant here, with side characters often providing some of the most memorable scenes.

Get Smart – "The Wax Max"

NBC. Feb 24, 1968 (S03E20). Comedy/Spy. D/W: James Komack. C: Don Adams, Barbara Feldon, Edward Platt, Richard Devon, Robert Ridgely ☥, Robert Lussier. USA: English/Color/22m. Talent Associates Ltd/Paramount.

While on a day off at an amusement park, Max and 99 inadvertently intercept radioactive material hidden within a Kewpie doll, booty that was intended for a smuggling ring. They are surrounded by KAOS agents headed by the great Waxman, a madman who plans to make Max and 99 a permanent display in his "Chamber of Horrors" wax figure exhibit.

A take-off of *House of Wax* (1953), this is unfortunately not one of the better episodes, although we are treated to a horde of classic movie monsters—including Dracula and the Frankenstein Monster. These two villains aren't given much to do, and although it has a smart ending, the story is essentially just an extended chase scene through an empty amusement park.

📽 The end of the episode takes place within an exhibit based on the final scene from Dickens' *A Tale of Two Cities*. Don Adams channels actor Ronald Colman from the 1935 film adaptation, as he recites the last words spoken by the Sydney Carton character (Dracula even quotes *Hamlet* for good measure).

The Ghost Busters – "The Vampire's Apprentice"

CBS. Nov 8, 1975 (S01E10). Comedy/Family. D: Larry Peerce. W: Marc Richards. C: Forrest Tucker, Larry Storch ☥, Bob Burns, Dena Dietrich ☥, Billy Holms ☥. USA: English/Color/30m. Filmation Associates.

This slapstick series follows a team of detectives—Eddie Spenser, Jake Kong, and Tracy the gorilla—who investigate ghostly happenings. In this episode, the ghosts of Count and Countess Dracula have returned, and they find an unwilling donor in Eddie. It's three against two as Kong and Tracy try to rescue their friend before they too become creatures of the night.

Another successful comedic take on vampires, with Holms and Dietrich turning in great performances as Count Dracula and his much younger bride. This episode also showcases Storch's comedic chops and ear for accents, and Tracy the gorilla—as she mimes her way through some crazy situations—has some of the funniest moments. Aimed at a more youthful audience, the man-in-an-ape suit looks a little cheesy, but it's actually more realistic-looking than the gorilla costume used in *Escape from the Planet of the Apes*.

📺 Storch and Tucker co-starred in *F Troop* (1965), a series that also had a vampire episode.

Ghost Story – "Elegy for a Vampire"

NBC. Dec 1, 1972 (S01E10). Horror/Thriller. D: Don McDougall. W: Mark Weingart, Elizabeth Walter. C: Hal Linden ⚥, Marlyn Mason, Mike Farrell, Arthur O'Connell, Sheila Larken, John Milford. USA: English/Color/47m. William Castle Productions/Screen Gems Television.

🦇🦇

After a student is found dead, her body drained of blood, professor David Wells is the first to volunteer for a nightly civilian patrol—although he secretly worries that he's the killer. As the murders continue, the professor's colleagues believe that a real vampire may be on the loose. Once Wells realizes that he is indeed responsible, he tries to end his life—but the evil growing inside of him has an overpowering need for self-preservation. Presented by Sebastian Cabot as Winston Essex.

In a different take on the standard vampire story, the killer is revealed early on, so it's really the tale of a man as he reluctantly transforms into a vampire, unable to control the evil inside. Wells was secretly the patient

Laura Benton (Marlyn Mason) is unaware that her boyfriend, Professor David Wells (Hal Linden), is descending into darkness in "Elegy for a Vampire" (William Castle Productions/Screen Gems Television)

of the late William Pendergast, a medical scholar studying the link between vampirism and blood diseases; he believed that a chemical imbalance could lead to an unnatural desire for the taste of human blood. Unfortunately, we aren't invested enough in the character of Wells to feel any empathy towards him, and as he succumbs to his evil nature and eventually dies, there's no reason to mourn (and the "surprise" ending isn't exactly a shocker).

📺 A similar premise was the subject of a largely forgotten yet excellent novel by Peter Tonkin, *The Journal of Edwin Underhill* (1981). Narrated by the eponymous anti-hero, it's a series of journal entries detailing his transition from average Joe to evil bloodsucker.

Ghost Whisperer – "Endless Love"

CBS. May 8, 2009 (S04E22). Fantasy/Romance. D: Ian Sander. W: P.K. Simonds. C: Jennifer Love Hewitt, David Conrad, Christoph Sanders, Jamie Kennedy, Camryn Manheim, Alexa Vega, Jake Thomas ☥. USA: English/Color/44m. Sander-Moses Productions/Wintergreen Productions.

Series follows Melinda Gordon, who has the uncanny ability to communicate with spirits, and helps those still earthbound find a way to cross over into the light. In this episode, a troubled teenager is haunted by the ghost of a former classmate, and becomes enchanted by the spirit after it taps into her romantic vampire fantasies. Melinda worries that the prospect of an eternal undying love may sway the girl to take a dramatic step so the two can be together forever.

An overly-dramatic tale that will be of interest to those who enjoy the *Twilight* genre of romantic vampire stories, but most fans will simply roll their eyes at the way the episode panders to the "Emo vamp" crowd.

Gilligan's Island – "Up at Bat"

CBS. Sep 12, 1966 (S03E01). Comedy/Family. D: Jerry Hopper. W: Ron Friedman. C: Bob Denver ☥, Alan Hale Jr., Jim Backus, Natalie Schafer, Tina Louise, Russell Johnson, Dawn Wells. USA: English/Color/24m. Gladasya Productions/United Artists Television.

Gilligan is bitten on the neck by a bat, and is convinced that he'll turn into a vampire. He hides in a cave to protect his friends, and dreams it's 1895. In the dream he's a bloodsucker living in Transylvania; Ginger is his bride and the Howells are his unfortunate house guests. Caretaker Mary Ann has summoned Holmes and Watson—here known as "Sherlock" and "Dr. Watney"—to investigate the strange goings-on in the castle.

Some fun, lightweight entertainment that still offers a number of laughs to this day. The dream sequence is the best part, with Hale donning an authentic British accent and Wells barely recognizable in her role as the ugly hag—and Denver makes a pretty convincing vampire.

Glee – "Theatricality"

FOX. May 25, 2010 (S01E20). Comedy/Drama. D/W: Ryan Murphy. C: Chris Colfer, Lea Michele, Cory Monteith, Matthew Morrison, Jenna Ushkowitz ☥, Idina Menzel, Iqbal Theba. USA: English/Color/44m. Ryan Murphy Productions/20th Century Fox Television.

Shy girl Tina is learning to express herself through the clothes she wears, but her latest Goth look has landed her in the office of Principal Figgins. He's worried that students are experiencing a serious case of "Twilight Fever," and are transforming from normal teenagers into real vampires obsessed with the occult.

Although the Goth/vampire story arc is minor, the related scenes are very funny and make up for what is at times a lackluster episode—but it's worthwhile viewing mainly for the digs it takes at the *Twilight* franchise.

Glory Days – "The Lost Girls"

WB. Feb 13, 2002 (S01E05). Comedy/Drama. D: Randy Zisk. W: Elizabeth Craft, Sarah Fain. C: Eddie Cahill, Poppy Montgomery, Jay R. Ferguson, Emily VanCamp, Sonya Salomaa ⚲. USA: English/Color/60m. Dimension Television/Outerbanks Entertainment.

Sam discovers a body completely drained of blood; Rudy and Mike believe that three young girls, new to town and claiming to be vampires, may actually be the real thing.

Goosebumps – "Vampire Breath"

FOX. Nov 23, 1996 (S02E17). Family/Thriller. D: Ron Oliver. W: R.L. Stine, Rick Drew. C: Zack Lipovsky ⚲, Meredith Henderson ⚲, Earl Pastko ⚲, Krista Dufresne ⚲. CAN: English/Color/30m. Hyperion Pictures/Protocol Entertainment/Scholastic Productions.

🦇 🦇 🦇

Twins Freddy and Cara Renfield dig through the basement in search of hidden birthday presents; instead, they find the entrance to the lair of Count Nightwing, a bloodthirsty six-hundred-and-fifty-year-old vampire.

Freddy and Cara discover that they come from a family of vampires—and that Count Nightwing is their grandfather. On their birthday this year, they'll finally turn into real bloodsuckers; naturally, their gift is a set of bunk-bed coffins. This episode has some of the worst fang props in television history, but it's still overall a fun story.

The Gregory Hines Show – "Eight and a Half Months"

CBS. Oct 31, 1997 (S01E08). Comedy/Family. D: Andrew D. Weyman. W: Sy Dukane, Denise Moss. C: Gregory Hines, Brandon Hammond, Mark Tymchyshyn ⚲, Judith Shelton. USA: English/Color/30m. Darric Productions/Katlin-Bernstein Productions/Montrose Productions.

Series follows widower Ben Stevenson as he balances being a single parent of a twelve-year-old boy, while slowly trying to get back into the dating scene. In this episode, Ben hosts a Halloween party where friends Alex and Angela show up dressed as Count Dracula and Xena, the Warrior Princess.

Grosse Pointe – "Halloween"

WB. Oct 20, 2000 (S01E05). Comedy/Family. D: Jake Kasdan. W: Wendy Engelberg. C: Kohl Sudduth, Lindsay Sloane, Irene Molloy, Al Santos, Bonnie Somerville. USA: English/Color/30m. Artists Television Group/Darren Star Productions.

Short-lived series about the antics, both on and off screen, of five young actors who star in a teen television drama about life at Grosse Pointe High School. In this episode that spoofs *Buffy the Vampire Slayer*, the show-within-a-show films a fantasy sequence where their characters become vampire slayers.

Happy Days – "The Evil Eye"

ABC. Oct 31, 1978 (S06E09). Comedy/Family. D: Jerry Paris. W: Allen Goldstein. C: Ron Howard, Henry Winkler, Marion Ross, Anson Williams ♀, Donny Most, Erin Moran, Al Molinaro, Tom Bosley. USA: English/Color/26m. Henderson Productions/Miller-Milkis Productions.

A superstitious Al Delvecchio becomes convinced that he's been cursed by an old witch. Richie and the gang perform a mock exorcism to make him believe that the hex has been lifted.

For Halloween, Potsie is dressed as Dracula. As the band practices their version of "Monster Mash," Ralph ridicules Potsie's singing style, and says he should sound like Bela Lugosi, not Pat Boone. The episode concludes with a performance of the song, but it doesn't seem right that Dracula is singing words meant to be sung by Doctor Frankenstein.

Happy Days – "Welcome to My Nightmare"

ABC. Feb 3, 1981 (S08E11). Comedy/Family. D: Jerry Paris. W: Mark Rothman. C: Henry Winkler, Marion Ross, Tom Bosley, Richard Gautier ♀. USA: English/Color/24m. Henderson Productions/Miller-Milkis Productions.

After a day of doing favors for his friends, the Fonz is too feverish to donate to a blood drive. He falls asleep while watching "Frankenstein's Doctor" on TV, and dreams that a mad M.D.—who resembles Count Dracula—is trying to drain his coolness to transfer into a clone named "Dougie."

This gets top marks for the dream sequence, which was well-written with some great comedic acting from Henry Winkler. Top honors, though, go to Richard Gautier as the Mad Doctor, in an over-the-top performance that had me in stitches. It's one of the best comedic takes on a vampiric character that you'll find on television.

The Hard Times of RJ Berger – "The Berger Cometh"

MTV. Jun 21, 2010 (S01E03). Comedy/Family. D: Anton Cropper. W: Eric Siegel, Eric Wasserman. C: Paul Iacono, Jareb Dauplaise, Kara Taitz, Amber Lancaster, Jayson Blair, Beth Littleford, Larry Poindexter, Natalija Nogulich. USA: English/Color/30m. MTV/Remote Productions.

So he can be closer to Jenny, RJ auditions for a part in the school's vampire-themed take on *West Side Story*—and he inadvertently lands the lead role.

The Hardy Boys/Nancy Drew Mysteries – "The Hardy Boys and Nancy Drew Meet Dracula"

ABC. Sep 11/18, 1977 (S02E01/02). Family/Mystery. D: Joseph Pevney. W: Glen A. Larson, Michael Sloan. C: Shaun Cassidy, Parker Stevenson, Pamela Sue Martin, John van Dreelen, Lorne Greene ☥, Paul Williams, Bernie Taupin. USA: English/Color/120m. Glen A. Larson Productions/Universal TV.

🦇🦇🦇🦇

While investigating their father's disappearance in Romania, Joe and Frank Hardy (Shaun Cassidy, Parker Stevenson) seek the help of Inspector Stavlin (Lorne Greene) in *The Hardy Boys/Nancy Drew Mysteries* (Glen A. Larson Productions/Universal TV)

In this two-part story, Frank and Joe travel to Paris in search of their father, who went missing while investigating a series of art thefts. The brothers work alongside Nancy Drew and Inspector Stavlin of the Romanian police force, both of whom had been helping their dad. All clues point to a rock festival at Dracula's Castle in Transylvania, headlined by superstar Allison Troy, whom the sleuths believe is tied to the stolen paintings. The investigation takes a supernatural turn after a man is found unconscious with a bite mark on the neck. Has Dracula been awakened by the festivities at his castle?

Having read Hardy Boys books growing up, I'm sure nostalgia played a role in the high rating. The story features Shaun Cassidy's bubblegum pop tunes, Paul Williams performing a song from *Phantom of the Paradise* (1974), and a wonderful turn from Lorne Greene. This Gothic tale has a fun twist ending, and is wrapped up in cheesy 1970s goodness. Add to this some bad acting and even worse bat props—with a cast that includes Elton John's lyricist—and you've got a quirky recipe for an entertaining couple of hours.

📺 Co-writers Michael Sloan and Glen A. Larson have a long history with vampires. Sloan also penned the *B.J. and the Bear* episode "A Coffin with a View," as well as "Night Creatures" from *Alfred Hitchcock Presents*. Larson wrote "McCloud Meets Dracula" from the series *McCloud*, and "Constant Craving" from *NightMan*. Lorne Greene previously starred as Dracula in a 1949 CBC Radio drama adaptation of Bram Stoker's novel.

Harry & Cosh – "Vampire"

Channel 5. Oct 19, 2002 (S04E01). Comedy/Family. D: Daniel Peakcock. W: Anon. C: Harry Capehorn, Coshti Dowden, Gemma Butler, Lucinda Rhodes-Flaherty, Jennifer Guy ☥, Beccy Armory, Frankie Fitzgerald. UK: English/Color/24m. Two Hats Productions/Channel 5.

British children's series that followed two teenagers and their friends and families. In this episode, the gang is hypnotized, and they experience past life regression. In 1783, Harry and Cosh were a duo of highwaymen who preyed upon unsuspecting travelers. They seek refuge in the dilapidated Crowbrook Manor, and end up in the clutches of a vampire known as The Mistress of the Dark—who turns out to be their teacher, Miss Spackman. They come out of the trance believing she's still a bloodsucker—so they strike first before she can take a bite out them.

Although the leads are appealing enough, this episode is dead on arrival. The story jumps back and forth through time, but it's so poorly executed that it becomes far too confusing, and requires too much concentration to follow.

Hercules: The Legendary Journeys – "Darkness Visible"

USA Network. Oct 18, 1999 (S06E04). Action/Adventure. D: Philip Sgriccia. W: Phyllis Strong. C: Kevin Sorbo, Michael Hurst ☥, Jeffrey Meek ☥, Rafe Battiste ☥, Tiffany de Castro ☥. USA/NZL: English/Color/45m. Renaissance Pictures/Studios USA Television.

Hercules and Iolaus travel to Dacia at the behest of their friend Vlad, who needs their help to rid his kingdom of *strigoi*. They discover that Vlad's been busy with a new war tactic—impaling his enemies—and he may be hiding an even darker secret within the cold walls of his castle.

Vlad is a vampire; he's based on Vlad Țepeș, the fifteenth century warlord, which may annoy those who dislike seeing historical figures fictionalized in this manner. Surprisingly, this is a good story, and the actor playing Vlad does a very convincing job in the role. This episode is a good mix of humor and horror, and filled with vampires of the traditional sort; just ignore the huge plot hole regarding Vlad and his father.

Hi Honey, I'm Home! – "Grey Skies"

ABC/nick@nite. Aug 16, 1991 (S01E05). Comedy/Family. D: Doug Rogers. W: Suzanne Collins. C: Charlotte Booker, Stephen Bradbury, Pete Benson, Julie Benz, Eric Kushnick, Al Lewis ☥. USA: English/B&W, Color/30m. ABC/Nickelodeon.

After taking part in the "Sitcom Relocation Program," the Neilson family—stars of the canceled 1950s American television show *Hi Honey, I'm Home!*—continue to live out their lives, unchanged, in modern-day New Jersey. Each episode guest-starred an actor in a role from a classic television show, and this one featured Al Lewis as Grandpa Munster. It was advertised as "Television's first instant rerun," since ABC would debut an episode each Friday, and then nick@night would rebroadcast the same episode two days later.

Highlander – "The Vampire"

Syndicated. Mar 7, 1994 (S02E16). Action/Fantasy. D: Dennis Berry. W: J.P. Couture. C: Adrian Paul, Stan Kirsch, Michel Modo, Jim Byrnes, Jeremy Brudenell ♀, Trevor Peacock, Denis Lill. CAN/FRA: English/Color/49m. Davis-Panzer Productions Inc./Gaumont Télévision/Rysher Entertainment.

🦇 🦇 🦇 🦇

A friend of Duncan's is found dead in a swimming pool, and he suspects foul play after catching a glimpse of an old nemesis—the immortal Nicholas Ward. They first met in France in the 1800s, while Duncan was investigating two suspicious deaths. Locals feared that a vampire was on the loose, since the victims were found with puncture wounds on the neck and bodies completely drained of blood. Ward was the killer, and used the guise of a vampire to cover up the murders—and Duncan fears he's returned to Paris for another killing spree.

This story is largely told in flashback, which works in favor for the tale of a man posing as a vampire, back when such a scare was commonplace in Europe. The art direction and guest stars are top-notch: Jeremy Brudenell effectively plays Ward as a psychotic killer with a sharp wit, and he's surrounded by an excellent supporting cast. This includes Denis Lill as Alan Baines, the vampire hunter who meets an unfortunate end after staking Ward through the heart (which of course does little to impede an immortal). Granted, Ward's *modus operandi* for faking the vampire attacks may be a little far-fetched, but it doesn't detract from an exceptionally enjoyable hour of television.

Nurse Jane Reynolds (Margot Kidder) steals from the wrong patient in *The Hitchhiker* (Quintina Productions Inc/Markowitz-Chesler)

Hill Street Blues – "Film at Eleven"

NBC. Feb 7, 1981 (S01E06). Crime/Drama. D: Georg Stanford Brown. W: Anthony Yerkovich. C: Daniel J. Travanti, Bruce Weitz, Taurean Blacque, Kiel Martin, Tony Plana ♀. USA: English/Color/50m. MTM Enterprises/NBC.

🦇 🦇 🦇

Sgt. Belker books a man suspected of biting a prostitute on the neck: Kevin Dracula, who believes he's a real vampire. After causing a disturbance in the precinct, Dracula is locked up in an isolated cell that officers jokingly call "the vampire lounge"—with tragic results.

A good episode from a series that was known for telling effective dramatic stories with some humor thrown into the mix. The Dracula storyline isn't overly developed, yet it's clear that the man suffers from a psychological disorder; Belker recognizes this fact, and acts accordingly. The scenes with him and Dracula are well written and acted; the ending is sad, shocking, and completely unexpected.

The Hitchhiker – "Nightshift"

HBO. Sep 15, 1985 (S03E01). Horror/Thriller. D: Phillip Noyce. W: April Campbell, Bruce Jones. C: Margot Kidder, Stephen McHattie, Darren McGavin ☥, Dorothy Davies, Enid Saunders, Kenneth Gordon. CAN/FRA/USA: English/Color/26m. Quintina Productions Inc./Markowitz-Chesler.

🦇 🦇 🦇 🦇

Cruel nurse Jane Reynolds commands her patients at the retirement home with an iron fist, treating them with disregard and stealing anything of value that they have. After she pilfers an expensive ring off the comatose body of a new arrival, Reynolds awakens a predator much more evil than she. Presented by Page Fletcher as The Hitchhiker.

This is a well-written and very atmospheric episode, with a couple of genuine scares, and features Darren McGavin as a vampire. Although he has no dialogue, he grunts and groans his way through a believable performance (McGavin, of course, dispatched a couple of the undead in his role as reporter Carl Kolchak in the telefilm *The Night Stalker* and in the series *Kolchak: The Night Stalker*).

📺 Stephen McHattie starred as the love interest of the female vampire in the TV movie *Deadly Love* (1995).

The Hitchhiker – "New Blood"

USA Network. Feb 22, 1991 (S06E20). Horror/Thriller. D: Joël Farges. W: Elizabeth Baxter, Jean-Vincent Fournier. C: Rae Dawn Chong, Didier Sauvegrain ☥, Joanna Pavlis ☥, Jerry Di Giacomo ☥, Geoffrey Carey ☥. CAN/FRA/USA: English/Color/24m. Quintina Productions Inc./Markowitz-Chesler-Rothstein.

🦇 🦇

Leesa White is an avant-garde performer of the macabre, a self-important *artiste* who longs for the day when her talents will be recognized by her peers. She hopes to join the famous performance company, La Troupe du Monde, and lands an impromptu audition—but she's laughed off the stage. The group claims that Leesa only speaks of darkness, but doesn't feel it; so she shows them just how dark she can be. Presented by Page Fletcher as The Hitchhiker.

Art is immortal, and so are the actors from La Troupe du Monde, who are looking for some new blood for their latest production, "Songs of Despair." The real audition comes when Leesa stabs the lead actress, a crime of passion that finally lands her a spot in the cast—where she discovers it's a company of vampires. It's a morality play where the actors could have been any sort of creature, as long as they can return from the dead—so the vampire element just serves the plot, and we end up with nothing more than cookie-cutter bloodsuckers.

Hot in Cleveland – "Everything Goes Better with Vampires"

TV Land. March 28, 2012 (S03E16). Comedy/Family. D: Andy Cadiff. W: Chuck Ranberg, Anne Flett-Giordano. C: Valerie Bertinelli, Jane Leeves, Wendie Malick, Betty White, Rhea Perlman, Georgia Engel, Rick Springfield. USA: English/Color/22m. SamJen Productions/Hazy Mills Productions.

🦇 🦇 🦇

Three fortysomething veterans of the entertainment industry are sidelined in Cleveland after their plane makes an emergency landing en route to Paris—and it's such welcome change from their lives in Hollywood that they decide to remain there. In this episode, Joy lives out a high school fantasy after a chance meeting with Rick Springfield, while Elka believes that her radio adaptation of *Gone with the Wind* will appeal to a younger audience if she adds some vampires.

A charming, modern spin on *The Golden Girls* (1985) that features notable guest stars from popular television series of the past. Although there are no bloodsuckers seen in this episode, they are part of the revamped radio play: Elka and her writing partner read through a scene that features Rhett Butler and Scarlett O'Hara—who are now vampires—drinking "bloody juleps."

📺 Rick Springfield played the vampire detective Nicholas Knight in the TV movie *Nick Knight* (1989).

Hotel Trubble – "Fangs for the Memories"

BBC One. Oct 25, 2010 (S02E06). Comedy/Drama. D: Natalie Bailey. W: Neil Gibbons, Rob Gibbons. C: Dominique Moore, Gary Damer, Sam Phillips, Sheila Bernette, Tanya Franks, Vincent Ibrahim ☥. UK: English/Color/30m. BBC.

Kid's series that follows the hapless trio of Sally, Jamie and Lenny as they attempt to run a hotel. In this episode, a new guest named Dave Racula turns out to be a vampire, and the staff fear for Mrs. Poshington's safety after the man invites her out for a bite.

The Hunger – "A Matter of Style"

Showtime/TMN. Oct 26, 1997 (S01E13). Comedy/Drama. D: John Hamilton. W: Craig Miller, Mark Nelson. C: Chad Lowe ☥, Isabelle Cyr ☥, Janine Theriault, Claudia Besso ☥, Marie-Josée Croze. CAN/UK/USA: English/Color/27m. Telescene Film Group Productions/Scott Free Productions.

🦇 🦇 🦇

Neville Burlington, a socially-awkward young man, is pleased to discover that he's been turned into a vampire, and is all too eager to relish in his new undead form. He discovers that even as a bloodsucker he lacks the prowess to seduce a victim, and time is running out—he needs to feed. It's up to Carmilla—the sexy mentor assigned to aid Neville in his transition—to mold him into the styled, suave vampire that he needs to be. Otherwise, he'll never survive as a creature of the night. Presented by Terence Stamp.

There are a number of entertaining scenes; although Chad Lowe effectively plays the loveable loser, his transition into confident, commanding vampire is not quite as believable. However, it is a nice change to find a story where being "turned" doesn't necessarily mean instantly becoming cool (nor being well-versed in Kung-Fu, for that matter). In this story, the bloodsucker first has to work at his social skills before he can transform into a charming, seductive creature of the night.

Released into the home video market as part of the DVD collection *Hunger: Vampires,* along with the episodes "Fly By Night," "Necros" and "Footsteps."

The Hunger – "Fly-By-Night"

Showtime/TMN. Jan 31, 1998 (S01E15). Drama/Horror. D: Pierre Dalpé. W: Terry Curtis Fox, Gemma Files. C: Giancarlo Esposito ⚥, Kim Feeney, Don Jordan, Gouchy Boy. CAN/UK/USA: English/Color/27m. Telescene Film Group Productions/Scott Free Productions.

Sonia Kopek suffers from shell shock; memories of her time as a soldier during the Gulf War are having a great impact on her present life. After assaulting her psychiatrist, she's placed in a cell next to a man whom she instinctively knows is a vampire. He offers a means to end the suffering, and quell the voices in her head. Presented by Terence Stamp.

Although this gets top marks for a believable, self-serving vampire, the rest of the story is pretty flaccid, even though there's an attempt to spice it up with superfluous soft-core sex scenes. The lead actress—and I use that term loosely—is horribly miscast, and completely unbelievable in the role.

The Hunger – "Nunc Dimittis"

Showtime/TMN. Oct 10, 1999 (S02E05). Drama/Horror. D: Russell Mulcahy. W: Gerald Wexler, Tanith Lee. C: David Warner, Jacob Tierney, Marina Orsini ⚥, Philippe Ross. CAN/UK/USA: English/Color/28m. Telescene Film Group Productions/Scott Free Productions.

Vassu, the dying servant of the vampire Princess Daragan Draculus, has one last task to perform for her: to find his replacement before he takes his final breath. Vassu meets up with a homeless hustler named Snake, a man who usually trades sex for money, but this time around he ends up with much more than he had bargained for. Presented by David Bowie.

In this story, vampires take on a human servant for protection and companionship, and although the human gets the perk of an extended life span, they ultimately die after decades of service. Vassu is a man facing the final days of his existence, and it's quite touching watching the journey as he seeks out another to take his place. This new, younger servant infuses the vampire with renewed vigor—an interesting exploration of the symbiotic relationship between the two. "Nunc Dimittis" is a Christian hymn that uses the words of Simeon from The Gospel According to Luke

(2:29-32), beginning with "Nunc dimittis servum tuum" ("Now lettest thou thy servant depart" or "Now you can dismiss your servant in peace").

📺 Jacob Tierney (Snake) starred as kid vampire hunter Max Townshend in *Dracula: The Series*.

I Love Mummy – "The Mummy Meets Dracula"

YTV/CBBC. Mar 14, 2003 (S01E26). Comedy/Family. D: Gail Harvey. W: William Flaherty, Jackie May. C: Gina Sorell, Mark Caven, Elyes Gabel, Kelly Turner, Neil Crone. CAN/UK: English/Color/24m. Breakthrough Entertainment/Winklemania Productions Ltd.

Follows the adventures of a five-thousand-year-old living mummy, Prince Nuffratuti, and the family that befriends him. In this episode, Nuff, after watching a marathon of Dracula movies, is convinced that a visiting school principal is a vampire.

Reporter Carl Kolchak (Darren McGavin) investigates a series of bizarre exsanguinations in *Kolchak: The Night Stalker* (Francy Productions/Universal TV)

Kids Unlimited – "Kids Undead"

The CW. Nov 17, 2007 (S01E04). Comedy/Family. D: Nick Tabri. W: Nick Tabri, George Leonardopoulos. C: Garland Carter, Nicholas Lobue, Elizabeth Machabeli, Angel Manila, Robert Rench, Sabrina Triunfante, Kenyi Turner ♀. USA: English/Color/27m. Be Productions.

In this take-off of zombie movies, the Kids Unlimited crew produce their first horror film. Former child star Bucky Walters is raised back from the dead by ex-manager Max Mostel, and he exacts revenge on the gang.

This children's series followed the adventures of a self-run kid's talent agency, but suffers from poor production values and a general lack of acting skill. Dracula and other vampires make a brief appearance in the opening segment, which is a commercial for the fictional "Costume Corner" shop.

Kolchak: The Night Stalker – "The Vampire"

ABC. Oct 4, 1974 (S01E04). Horror/Thriller. D: Don Weis. W: David Chase, Bill Stratton. C: Darren McGavin, Simon Oakland, William Daniels, Suzanne Charny ⚲, John Doucette, Jan Murray, Larry Storch. USA: English/Color/52m. Francy Productions/Universal TV.

🦇 🦇 🦇 🦇

A trail of murders has stretched from Las Vegas to Los Angeles. Each victim was exsanguinated, and authorities believe they're dealing with a satanic cult of blood drinkers. Kolchak uncovers the true killer—a bloodthirsty vampire—but since the police don't believe him, he takes matters into his own hands (along with a crucifix and a wooden stake).

This series produced a number of memorable stories, and this is definitely at the top of the list. Kolchak learns that the killer is Catherine Rawlins, a victim of Janos Skorzeny—the vampire in the original *Night Stalker* telefilm. During his investigation, Kolchak, as always, butts heads with the local police force. These scenes add a hint of levity to counterbalance the more thrilling parts of the story, especially those involving Rawlins, a beautiful seductress who becomes a feral vampire when it's time to take down her prey. Kolchak overwhelms Rawlins using a giant flaming cross, and as he puts her to rest with a stake through the heart, the police arrive just in time to catch him in the act. Although he's booked for murder, the charges are eventually dropped; it's determined that she appears to have been dead for over three years.

The L Word – "Lifeline" / "Lone Star"

Showtime. Feb 5/19, 2006 (S03E05/07). Drama/Romance. D: Kimberly Peirce, Frank Pierson. W: Ilene Chaiken, Elizabeth Ziff. C: Leisha Hailey, Erin Daniels, Pam Grier, Alan Cumming, Erica Cerra ⚲. CAN/USA: English/Color/105m. Anonymous Content/Dufferin Gate Productions.

🦇 🦇

In this minor story arc that spans two episodes, Alice tries out a bisexual speed-dating service and meets a vampirologist named Uta Refson, who teaches a course on queer vampire literature at Loyola Marymount University. After she becomes intimately involved with the woman, Alice thinks that Uta may be a real bloodsucker.

It's never quite clear if Alice's new lover—whose name is actually "Nosferatu" spelled backwards—is a vampire in any sense of the word. Before the matter can be resolved, the couple part ways once Uta realizes that Alice is still hooked on a former girlfriend.

L.A. Heat – "Fangs"

TNT. Apr 20, 1999 (S02E01). Action/Crime. D: Richard Pepin. W: Nick Stone. C: Wolf Larson, Steven Williams, Reneé Tenison, Rebecca Chaney ♀, Paul Logan ♀, Tim Haldeman, Christopher Boyer, Jessica Cushman, Debbie James, Kenneth Tigar. USA: English/Color/48m. PM Entertainment Group.

Detectives McDonald and Brooks investigate the murder of a woman whose body was found with a bite mark on the neck and completely drained of blood. The prime suspect is Eric Sommers, who's part of a vampire role-playing club where members drink tomato juice instead of blood—but he seems to have crossed the line between fantasy and reality.

Enjoyable episode from a series shaped in the mold of the *Lethal Weapon* franchise, teeming with beautiful women, improbable shootouts, ridiculous car chases and frequent explosions—it's pure, cheesy fun. The vampire in question, Eric Sommers, was discharged from the army after developing a taste for blood while working for the medical corps; his crime spree is nicknamed "The Bela Lugosi Murders." The focus of the story is the hunt for the vampire killer, and Sommers isn't really given a voice of his own; he's not much more than a bloodsucking boogeyman that occasionally shows up to bare fangs and hiss at the camera.

📺 Paul Logan (Sommers) starred as Dracula in the feature film *Way of the Vampire* (2005).

Land of the Giants – "Comeback"

ABC. Nov 23, 1969 (S02E11). Fantasy/Sci-Fi. D: Harry Harris. W: Richard Shapiro. C: Gary Conway, Don Matheson, Stefan Arngrim, Don Marshall, Deanna Lund, Heather Young, Kurt Kasznar, John Carradine ♀, Jesse White, Fritz Feld, Olan Soulé, James Jeter, Janos Prohaska. USA: English/Color/50m. Irwin Allen Productions/Kent Productions, Inc.

Series followed the crew of the sub-orbital spaceship Spindrift, which during its maiden voyage was inadvertently transported to a giant, Earth-like planet, where everything was twelve times larger than back home—making them appear as though they were the size of toy dolls. In this episode, Egor Crull—a washed-up horror actor—is at the end of his rope, and about to take his own life when he comes across the 'little people' on a freeway overpass. He absconds with the group, hoping to revitalize his long-dead career by using them in a new film. But his plans go awry thanks to a disreputable

Egor Crull (John Carradine) is an out-of-work horror actor attempting to resurrect his dead career in the *Land of the Giants* episode "Comeback" (Irwin Allen Productions/Kent Productions Inc)

B-movie director, who puts the gang in mortal danger at the hands of their King Kong-sized co-star. Egor Crull (John Carradine) portrays a vampire in the film.

Las Vegas – "Hide and Sneak"

NBC. Apr 25, 2005 (S02E21). Crime/Drama. D: Rick Wallace. W: Keith Kaczorek. C: James Caan, Josh Duhamel, James Lesure, Vanessa Marcil, Victor Webster ☥. USA: English/Color/60m. NBC Universal Television/DreamWorks Television/Gary Scott Thompson Productions.

Sam Marquez is intrigued by a high-rolling East European named Estefan, who invades the Montecito with his Gothic vampire entourage in tow.

The vampires here—if they are, in fact, "real" vampires—are not the focus of the main story, so we rarely see them. However, they do act like traditional undead; they sleep (and do other things) in coffins, cover up all mirrors, and never go out during the day. Their leader, Estefan, appears to have the power of levitation. The group is dismissed by the end of the episode, without any further questioning of their nature, or explanation of exactly what they are. I never followed this series, but some of the technology used in this episode seems as far-fetched as what is presented on *CSI: Miami*. But who cares? Based on the eye candy, it's obvious no one watches this show for the believable plot lines.

The Last Precinct – "Never Cross a Vampire"

NBC. May 6, 1986 (S01E05). Comedy/Crime. D: Michael Lange. W: Paul Bernbaum. C: Jonathan Perpich, Ernie Hudson, Wings Hauser, Randi Brooks, Rick Ducommun, Lucy Lee Flippen, Adam West, Richard Lynch ☥, Nat Christian ☥. USA: English/Color/60m. Stephen J. Cannell Productions.

A short-lived TV series that followed a group of misfit law enforcement officers stationed at the notorious 56th Precinct in Los Angeles. In this episode, a tabloid journalist brings unwanted attention to a case involving a thief who has stolen several pints of blood from a local hospital.

📺 Richard Lynch played the vampire Anton Voytek in the TV movie *Vampire* (1979).

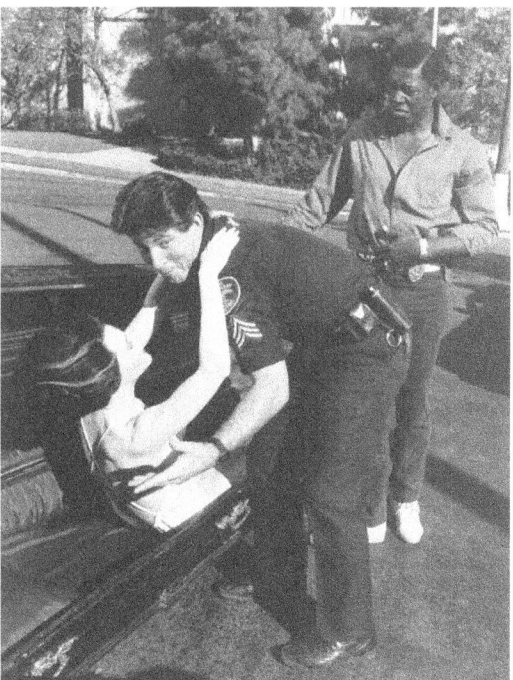

Officers Pascall (Jonathan Perpich) and "Night Train" Lane (Ernie Hudson) rescue one of Dracula's victims in *The Last Precinct* (Stephen J. Cannell Production/NBC-TV)

Law & Order: Criminal Intent – "Collective"

NBC. Jan 30, 2005 (S04E12). Crime/Drama. D: Frank Prinzi. W: René Balcer, Gerry Conway. C: Vincent D'Onofrio, Kathryn Erbe, Jamey Sheridan, Courtney B. Vance, Jamie Harrold, Jordan Gelber, Kim Director, Shannon Burkett, Peter Kim. USA: English/Color/44m. Wolf Films.

The accidental shooting by police of a fanatical toy collector puts detectives on the trail of a female con artist, who poses as a fan at fantasy conventions so she can find men to fleece for their valuable collections. After the woman turns up dead, the investigation leads to members of The Carlotta Francis Society of Manhattan, a group devoted to a deceased author of popular vampire fiction, who go to extremes to better understand the undead characters she wrote about in her novels.

An intriguing and plausible story about a woman who takes advantage of the wrong geek. Although the episode has some good twists and turns, the ending just isn't believable. However, the group from the "vampire club," who live their mundane lives by day and take on roles from the books by night, is very credible; this kind of thing takes place throughout modern society.

Law & Order: Criminal Intent – "Lost Children of the Blood"

USA Network. Jun 8, 2010 (S09E11). Crime/Drama. D: John David Coles. W: Christine Bailey. C: Jeff Goldblum, Saffron Burrows, Mary Elizabeth Mastrantonio, Matt Burns ☥, Clayne Crawford ☥, Dan Butler, Christopher Abbott ☥, Leslie Hendrix. USA: English/Color/42m. Wolf Films.

College student Sara Price turns up dead in her dorm room, completely exsanguinated, the day after an encounter with a mysterious man at a Goth club. The investigation leads to Anton, the charismatic leader of a coven of blood drinkers, but he may just be a pawn in a larger game controlled by another member of the group—a psychotic who believes he's a real vampire. It's a thought-provoking episode that delves into the human psyche and uses modern vampirism as a means to explore the darker side of humanity—very dark and dramatic.

The Legend of Dick and Dom – "Vampire Baby"

CBBC. Mar 20, 2009 (S01E12). Adventure/Family. D: Jeremy Wooding. W: Anon. C: Richard McCourt, Dominic Wood, Terry Jones, Danielle Isaie ☥. UK: English/Color/30m. BBC.

As the two princes continue their search for the antidote needed to cure the plague consuming Fyredor, they end up in Pramsylvania, where they discover a vampire baby named Alan who may hold the key to the next ingredient required for the cure.

Lexx – "Walpurgis Night" / "Vlad"

Space. Aug 24/Sep 7, 2001 (S04E07/08). Comedy/Sci-Fi. D: Colin Bucksey, Christoph Schrewe. W: Tom De Ville, Paul Donovan. C: Brian Downey, Xenia Seeberg, Michael McManus, Peter Guinness, Keith-Lee Castle, John Standing ☥, Minna Aaltonen ☥. CAN/UK: English/Color/92m. Salter Street Productions/Silver Light.

In this two-part story, the Lexx crew continues their exploration of the planet Earth, and end up in Transylvania where Kai is on the hunt for a mysterious castle. The group receives a mixed reaction from residents in a nearby village; they are very superstitious, and believe that Kai is a creature of local legend: a vampire. But they are not the only strangers in town: three Goth girls have also arrived, hoping to meet an alleged bloodsucker named Lord Dracul, who traditionally hosts a great feast at his castle on this night. But Kai learns that there is a creature far more threatening than Dracul, and it's about to be awakened within the cold depths of the castle.

An entertaining story that's very funny at times, with several elements that will be of special interest to fans of Bram Stoker's *Dracula*. In a sense this is almost a re-imagining of the novel; Kai and his group fill in for Harker and company, the three Goth girls are akin to Dracula's Brides, and there's even Van Helsing, who comes from a family of vampire hunters but now runs the local pub. Of course there's Dracul(a)—who isn't what he appears to be—but there's a far more evil vampire-like character called Vlad. That just leaves Renfield, and genre fans will be amused to learn that he's played by Keith-Lee Castle, who starred as the infamous vampire in the UK television series *Young Dracula* (2006). For those unfamiliar with this series, the character of Kai is undead, but he's not a vampire. He's a "Divine Assassin" who relies on a substance called "protoblood" to survive, for it provides the ability to temporarily resurrect the dead. The effects are limited, as is his supply of the liquid, so Kai must often remain in cryogenic suspension to prolong his existence after the effects have worn off. Vlad, on the other hand, is much more akin to a traditional vampire, and she (yes, she!) makes a couple more appearances later on in the series.

📺 "Walpurgis Night" is a translation of "Walpurgisnacht," a traditional spring festival in many parts of Europe that takes place exactly six months prior to Halloween. This day plays an important role in Bram Stoker's short story, "Dracula's Guest" (1914), when on that night, "according to the belief of millions of people, the devil was abroad—when the graves were opened and the dead came forth and walked."

Lexx – "Magic Baby"

Space. Sep 28, 2001 (S04E10). Comedy/Sci-Fi. D: Colin Bucksey. W: Paul Donovan, Lex Gigeroff. C: Brian Downey, Xenia Seeberg, Michael McManus, Alun Lewis, Minna Aaltonen ☥, Jeffrey Hirschfield, Jeremy Peters. CAN/UK: English/Color/43m. Salter Street Productions/Silver Light.

Trapped on *terra firma,* the Lexx crew steals the Space Shuttle and returns to their ship, with the help of a Druid who recognizes them as figures from the divine prophecies of his Order. But their fortunes take a downward spiral after Vlad—the vampiric Divine Assassin—is awakened and released from her cryo-chamber prison.

Average episode that sees the return of Vlad, who causes the crew a great deal of discomfort before she is destroyed by an ancient Druidic staff wielded by Stanley Tweedle. It's worth noting that Vlad only uses her fangs to inject a serum into her victims, which turns them into mindless minions. However, she has a unique proboscis-like appendage that she uses to suck the "protoblood" from Kai. Like all Divine Assassins, she also has a bladed device that shoots out from an apparatus attached to her wrist; in this episode, it's charmingly referred to as "Vlad's impaler."

📺 Vlad returns in Episode 18, "The Game," where she portrays the White Bishops in a chess match between Kai and Prince. She makes one final appearance in Episode 22, "Trip," where she is one of a number of hallucinations that Xev experiences after eating a rare berry.

Lights Out – "Pit of the Dead"

NBC. Jun 11, 1951 (S03E42). Mystery/Thriller. D: William Corrigan. W: Wyllis Cooper. C: Beatrice Kraft, Joseph Buloff, John Dall, Frank Gallop. USA: English/B&W/30m. Admiral Corporation/Erwin, Wasey & Co. Inc./NBC.

In Mexico, two scientists excavating Aztec ruins unexpectedly dig up evil vampires. Hosted by American radio and television personality Frank Gallop.

The Littlest Hobo – "Day for Fright"

CTV. Nov 25, 1982 (S04E12). Adventure/Family. D: Allan Eastman. W: Martin Lager. C: David Calderisi ♀, Jim Henshaw ♀, John-Peter Linton, Peter Jobin, Philip Akin, Ralph Benmergui. CAN: English/Color/24m. Glen-Warren Productions Limited/CTV.

The wandering canine, London, comes across the film set of *Vampire's Revenge,* which is shooting exterior scenes after recently returning from production in Mexico. Things are not quite as they seem; two crew members have smuggled in an antique Spanish cross within a prop coffin—but unbeknownst to them, one of the actors is a Federal Agent in disguise. This lighthearted story has a few funny scenes, most of which involve the over-the-top actor playing the role of the vampire. It's a fine example of wholesome, undead family entertainment.

Lost Tapes – "Vampire"

Animal Planet. Sep 29, 2009 (S02E01). Culture/Drama. D: Anon. W: Anon. C: Rosemary Ellen Guiley, Joe Nickell, Jessica Lynch Alfaro, Craig Stanford, Dallas Tanner, Gavin Perry, Mark Fier, Ivan Djurovic ♀, Jack Harding. USA: English/Color/21m. Go Go Luckey Entertainment.

This pseudo-documentary series erases the line between fact and fiction as it presents tales of horrific encounters with cryptozoids (creatures of folklore and urban legend); each episode mixes scripted scenes with actual news reports, as well as real interview clips with scholars discussing the subject. In this episode, the Redding family moves into a fixer-upper, but it seems there's already something living there: a humanoid creature with a thirst for blood.

Features a creepy, feral vampire, which is about the only positive thing about this production. Due to the shaky camera work, the dramatic segments ("found footage") are barely watchable, while the documentary portions, at times loose with the facts, bring nothing new to the discussion.

Lost Tapes – "Strigoi Vampire"

Animal Planet. Oct 5, 2010 (S03E03). Culture/Drama. D: Anon. W: Anon. C: Rosemary Ellen Guiley, Lee Kats, Dallas Tanner, Jessica Lynch Alfaro, Troy Mittleider, Elizabeth Maxwell, Theresa Deveaux. USA: English/Color/21m. Go Go Luckey Entertainment.

The PaliCo Oil Company has lost all contact with its remote drilling encampment in the New Mexico desert. A private security firm is hired to investigate, and upon arrival, they discover all the workers dead, their bodies drained of blood.

Using rehashed interview clips from the "Vampire" episode (and the same unwatchable camera work), this outing features the Romanian bloodsucker known as a *strigoi,* which has the ability to turn invisible or transform into an animal. In this interpretation, when in human form, they just look like a cookie-cutter vampire with fangs and colored contact lenses. (Why a traditional Romanian vampire is hanging out in the New Mexico desert is anyone's guess.)

The Lost World – "Blood Lust"

Syndicated. Oct 30, 1999 (S01E07). Adventure/Fantasy. D: Richard Franklin. W: James Thorpe. C: Peter McCauley, Rachel Blakely, Will Snow ☥, David Orth, Jennifer O'Dell, Michael Sinelnikoff, Shanyn Asmar ☥. AUS/CAN: English/Color/60m. Coote Hayes Productions/Telescene Film Group Productions.

Loosely based on the novel by Sir Arthur Conan Doyle, this series follows a group attempting to uncover the existence of a prehistoric world hidden within the Amazon jungle. In this episode, while setting up camp, Roxton is attacked by a feverish stranger and bitten on the neck. Later that night, he tries to attack Marguerite, but Challenger fends him off and he escapes into the jungle. As the two track Roxton, they discover several animal corpses with bite marks on the neck and bodies drained of blood. Has their friend been turned into a vampire?

If you're willing to accept the premise of this series, then it should come as no surprise that the team would eventually come across a vampire—who lives in a dilapidated castle in the middle of the jungle! (Really?) The bloodlust is strong among these ones, very true to form; however, they can easily be killed by a shotgun blast, or cured through a hefty dose of the belladonna plant. These concepts ruined this episode for me; I guess I'm just tired of stories where vampires are set up as being incredibly strong and powerful, but then they're subsequently killed off in the third act with little difficulty.

Love, American Style – "Love and the Big Game" / "Love and the Nutsy Girl" / "Love and the Vampire"

ABC. Jan 29, 1971 (S02E18). Comedy/Romance. D: Charles Rondeau. W: Jim Parker, Arnold Margolin. C: Judy Carne, Robert Reed, Tiny Tim ☥. USA: English/Color/30m. Parker-Margolin Productions/Paramount Television/ABC.

🦇 🦇

In "Love and the Vampire," newlyweds Myrna and Wayne spend the night in a creepy old house after their car breaks down during a storm. Although Wayne just finds their host a little peculiar, his wife suspects that he's actually a vampire—and is convinced that her husband has been turned as well.

Tiny Tim dresses up as Dracula to play an eccentric man who's not a vampire, but someone who's just in costume for a midnight horror show at the local movie house. The story is a little silly, although some of the banter between the couple is charming at times, especially once a werewolf is introduced into the mix.

Love, American Style – "Love and the Dream Burglar" / "Love and the Hotel Caper" / "Love and the Single Sister" / "Love and the Monsters"

ABC. Sep 24, 1971 (S03E02). Comedy/Romance. D: Hy Averback. W: Jim Fritzell, Everett Greenbaum. C: James Darren ☥, Maud Adams, George Chandler, Jack Mullaney, Dick Yarmey, Alice Borden. USA: English/Color/30m. Parker-Margolin Productions/Paramount Television/ABC.

Newlyweds spend an unforgettable night at the home of Mr. Foss (Tiny Tim) in the *Love, American Style* segment "Love and the Vampire" (Parker-Margolin Productions/Paramount Television)

🦇 🦇 🦇

In "Love and the Monsters," handsome lothario Roger Barnes stars as Dracula in *Song of the Blood Suckers,* and his friend Brian co-stars as The Mummy. While on a break from filming, they see a statuesque woman in the studio commissary. Brian places a bet with his friend: he believes that because of the vampire makeup, Roger won't stand a chance landing a dinner date with the woman.

The Love Boat - "Ship of Ghouls"

In the episode "Ship of Ghouls," the *Love Boat* crew join in on the Halloween festivities aboard the Pacific Princess (Aaron Spelling Productions/Douglas S. Cramer Company)

ABC. Oct 28, 1978 (S02E07). Comedy/Drama. D: Roger Duchowny. W: Mickey Rose, Jeraldine Saunders. C: Gavin MacLeod, Bernie Kopell, Fred Grandy ⚲, Ted Lange, Lauren Tewes, Vincent Price, Charlie Aiken, Barbara Anderson, Joan Blondell, Gary Collins, Mary Ann Mobley. USA: English/Color/60m. Aaron Spelling Productions/Douglas S. Cramer Company.

Onboard for this episode is The Amazing Alonzo (Vincent Price), an illusionist whose fiancée becomes quite upset after he hides their engagement from his adoring fans. For a costume party, the Pacific Princess crew get in on the fun: Captain Stubing dresses up as Captain Hook, Isaac as Frankenstein's Monster, Doc Bricker as the Wolf Man, Julie as a cat, and Gopher as Dracula (complete with a stereotypical Lugosi façade).

The Love Boat: The Next Wave – "Don't Judge a Book by Its Lover"

UPN. Jan 1, 1999 (S02E09). Comedy/Drama. D: Neal Israel. W: Nicole Avril. C: Robert Urich, Phil Morris, Randy Vasquez, Kyle Howard, Ian Ziering, Patrick Cassidy ⚲, Robin Givens. USA: English/Color/60m. Spelling Entertainment/Worldvision Enterprises.

Follows the adventures of the crew and vacationers aboard the cruise liner Sun Princess. In this episode, a famous author is pursued onboard by a man who claims to be Tristian, the vampire from one of her books.

The Lucy Show – "Lucy and the Monsters"

CBS. Jan 25, 1965 (S03E18). Comedy/Family. D: Jack Donohue. W: Garry Marshall, Jerry Belson, Maury Thompson, Art Thompson. C: Lucille Ball, Vivian Vance, Gale Gordon ⚲, Jimmy Garrett ⚲, Ralph Hart, Shep Sanders ⚲. USA: English/Color/22m. Desilu Productions Inc.

After discovering that their kids went to see a horror double feature, Lucy and Vivian watch the films for themselves—and get scared out of their wits. That night, Lucy has a nightmare where she and Vivian cross paths with the classic movie monsters, including Dracula.

Although the episode initially stretches for laughs, it features some inspired moments once Lucille Ball appears wearing a wreath of garlic around her neck and brandishing a large wooden tent stake. Gale Gordon as the wicked Count Dracula is a pleasure to watch, and the rest of the monsters—including a gorilla named Loretta—were definitely out of the norm for television in 1965.

📺 Three actors are dressed as a Dracula character in this episode: Jimmy Garrett (Lucy's son Jerry), Gale Gordon (in the dream sequence), and Shep Sanders (who shows up at Lucy's door after she awakes from her dream).

Madame's Place – Ep. #1.--

Syndicated. 1982 (S01E--). Comedy/Satire. D: Paul Miller. W: Anon. C: Wayland Flowers, Susan Tolsky, Johnny Haymer, Judy Landers, Bill Kirchenbauer ☥, Carl Balantine. USA: English/Color/30m. Brad Lachman Productions/Madame Inc./Paramount.

Series centers around the exploits of Madame (voiced by puppeteer Wayland Flowers), an aging film star who has a knack for witty repartee that's often peppered with double entendre, and who currently hosts her own talk show. In this episode, after Madame has an encounter with the vampire Baron von Leer, she pays a visit to Dr. Steiner—who transforms her into the Bride of Frankenstein.

McCloud – "McCloud Meets Dracula"

NBC. Apr 17, 1977 (S07E06). Crime/Drama. D: Bruce Kessler. W: Glen A. Larson. C: Dennis Weaver, J.D. Cannon, Terry Carter, John Carradine ☥, Diana Muldaur, Michael Sacks, Ken Lynch, Ken Scott. USA: English/Color/71m. Glen Larson Productions/Universal TV.

🦇🦇

Someone is killing people and drinking their blood, and McCloud believes that the perpetrator is a vampire fanatic with deep psychological problems. He turns to retired horror film actor Loren Belasco—a known Dracula expert—to help build a profile of the killer. But the investigation soon focuses on Belasco himself, after McCloud realizes that the actor is living out his life in the guise of Dracula,

Retired film actor Loren Belasco (John Carradine) is unable to let go of his most famous role from the silver screen in "McCloud Meets Dracula" (Glen Larson Productions/Universal TV)

his most famous role from the silver screen.

Although we only get a glimpse of the killer, it's pretty clear from the outset that it's Belasco, especially considering that the audience sees more of his vampire antics than McCloud does. His home, which is lit by candlelight and has no mirrors, is maintained by a creepy manservant. Belasco sleeps in a coffin and only rises upon sunset—but is he a real blood-drinking vampire, or simply a senile actor reliving his glory days through the role that made him famous? This is left up to interpretation, with no clear resolution to the story—we last see Belasco jumping off of a bridge, but his body is never recovered from the river below. What if the Dracula character wasn't just a role in a movie, but a convenient façade perfectly suited to the undead?

📺 This episode uses footage of Carradine when he starred as Dracula in the films *House of Frankenstein* (1944) and *House of Dracula* (1945).

McHale's Navy – "The Vampire of Taratupa"

ABC. May 4, 1965 (S03E33). Comedy/War. D: Hollingsworth Morse. W: Myles Wilder, William Raynor. C: Ernest Borgnine, Joe Flynn, Tim Conway ☥, Ann Elder, Bob Hastings. USA: English/B&W/25m. Sto-Rev Co.

Captain Binghamton transfers Parker to hazardous duty, but reconsiders after he learns that they both share a rare blood type. Parker is forced to stay out of harm's way; stuck by Binghamton's side, he asks McHale to help him escape the clutches of their commanding officer.

It's a silly premise, but there are a few laughs thanks to Conway's portrayal of Dracula, a guise he uses as a means to scare Binghamton from wanting his blood.

Ensign Charles Parker (Tim Conway) pretends he's Dracula to escape the clutches of Captain Binghamton (Joe Flynn) in *McHale's Navy* (Sto-Rev Co.)

Masters of Horror – "The V Word"

Showtime. Nov 10, 2006 (S02E03). Horror/Suspense. D: Ernest Dickerson. W: Mick Garris. C: Michael Ironside ☥, Branden Nadon, Arjay Smith, Jodelle Ferland, Lynda Boyd, Keith Humphrey. CAN/USA: English/Color/60m. Starz Productions/Nice Guy Productions/Industry Entertainment.

Two videogame-loving teens break into the Collinswood funeral home, hoping to see the body of a recently deceased classmate; instead, they're stalked by their former teacher. The first half of the story is quite suspenseful, but surprisingly, it becomes lackluster once the vampire stuff really kicks in.

📺 The name of the funeral home is an obvious nod to the *Dark Shadows* TV series, which followed the goings-on of the Collins clan in their Collinwood mansion.

Mentors – "Nothing to Fear"

Family. Mar 17, 2003 (S03E09). Family/History. D: Rick Stevenson. W: Mark Leiren-Young, Scot Morison. C: Stevie Mitchell, Samantha Krutzfeldt, Brian Martell, Jane Sowerby, Nick Mancuso ☥, Kett Turton. CAN: English/Color/30m. Minds Eye Entertainment/Anaïd Productions.

Series follows two siblings who use a powerful computer to temporarily summon historical figures to help them solve problems. In this episode, Simon uses the VisiCron to summon the real Dracula, Vlad Țepeș, to scare the wits out of a Goth kid who bullied him. Once he learns that Vlad is out for blood, Simon realizes that vengeance is not the answer.

The Middleman – "The Vampiric Puppet Lamentation"

ABC Family. Aug 18, 2008 (S01E10). Comedy/Sci-Fi. D: Sandy Smolan. W: Andy Reaser. C: Matt Keeslar, Natalie Morales, Brit Morgan, Mary Pat Gleason, Drew Tyler Bell, Jake Smollett, Steve Valentine, Gideon Emery ☥, Sadie Stratton ☥. USA: English/Color/44m. ABC Family.

🦇🦇🦇

Centuries ago, Vlad the Impaler, the king of all vampires, was murdered alongside his wife, the Vampire Queen. Their blood spilled onto their two favorite puppets—exact replicas of the couple—damning their souls into the dolls for all eternity. After Vlad's puppet is inadvertently brought back to life, the Middleman must stop it before it finds its better half. If the couple is reunited, they will regain human form—and champion an undead army that will plunge the Earth into an eternal night of blood.

Generally any story that turns Vlad the Impaler into a real vampire makes me groan, however this one was a hoot, not in small part due to the fantastic puppet created in Vlad's image. There are also several nods to the *Dracula* novel ("John Seward Home for the Criminally Insane" and "Holmwood Drive"), as well as other hints of vampire pop culture (*Buffy, Blade,* Hammer films, and the *Tomb of Dracula* comic book series).

📺 One character states that she is familiar with "three of the major Canadian syndicated vampire detective shows." Two obvious answers are *Forever Knight* (1992) and *Blood Ties* (1997), but what of the third? I posed this question to writer Andy Reaser, but have been sworn to secrecy regarding the answer. Let's just say he wants to keep you guessing!

Midsomer Murders – "Death and the Divas"

ITV. Jan 2, 2013 (S15E04). Crime/Drama. D: Nick Laughland. W: Rachel Cuperman, Sally Griffiths. C: Neil Dudgeon, Jason Hughes, Fiona Dolman, Tamzin Malleson, Sinéad Cusack, Harriet Walter, Henry Goodman, Pearce Quigley, Alice Sykes, Joseph Beattie, David Bark-Jones, John Carson ♀, Georgina Beedle ♀. UK: English/Color/90m. Bentley Productions Ltd.

Long-running British crime series that follows various murder investigations in the idyllic (but deadly) fictional county of Midsomer. In this episode, author Eve Lomax, who was writing a book about local horror actress Stella Harris, appears to have been murdered by a vampire, much like a character from one of Harris's films. This coincides with the return of the actress's estranged sister Diana Davenport, a much more successful movie star. As the body count rises, each victim is also killed in a manner from one of Harris's films. This leads Detective Chief Inspector John Barnaby to wonder, could life be imitating art? And are the murders related to Harris and Davenport's forty year-old sibling rivalry?

DCI Barnaby's wife, Sarah, is played by Fiona Dolman, who co-starred as Mike's skeptical ex-, Frances, in the 1998 BBC miniseries, *Ultraviolet*.

The Monkees – "Monstrous Monkee Mash"

NBC. Jan 22, 1968 (S02E18). Comedy/Music. D: James Frawley. W: Neil Burstyn, David Panich. C: David Jones ♀, Micky Dolenz, Michael Nesmith, Peter Tork, Ron Masak ♀, Arlene Martel, David Pearl. USA: English/Color/25m. Screen Gems Television/Raybert Productions.

Davy falls for a mysterious girl named Lorelei, who is secretly in cahoots with her uncle, a vampire who wants to turn the musician into Dracula reborn (even though he's a bit too short). Soon the Monkees are on the run from the other classic movie monsters, and they discover that the vampire has a nefarious plan for all of them. It's a fun episode with some hilarious moments, and guest star Ron Masak steals the show with his over-the-top vampire antics—it's pure lighthearted lunacy.

Mr. Majeika – "Fangs for the Memory"

ITV1. Jan 10, 1990 (S03E02). Comedy/Family. D: Michael Kerrigan. W: Jenny McDade. C: Stanley Baxter, Claire Sawyer, Simeon Pearl, Roland MacLeod, Fidelis Morgan, Richard Murdoch, Sanjiv Madan, Philip Herbert ♀. UK: English/Color/25m. Television South (TVS).

Vegetarian vampire Billy Bloodcup shows up in Britland, but he seems to have confused Empire Day with Vampire Day.

Monsters – "The Vampire Hunter"

Syndicated. Nov 12, 1988 (S01E04). Horror/Suspense. D: Michael Gornick. W: Edithe Swensen. C: Robert Lansing, Jack Koenig, Page Hannah, John Bolger ☥, Sylvia Short. USA: English/Color/30m. Laurel EFX Inc./Tribune Broadcasting Company/Worldvision Enterprises Inc.

Victorian-era vampire hunter Ernest Chariot has retired, but fate intervenes when a young woman seeks his help, fearing her brother has been turned into a vampire. He refuses to assist, but is drawn into a game of revenge after his young protégé Jack takes the case.

Another good story from the *Monsters* series, set in a believable Victorian setting, with an excellent performance from Lansing as the pompous, somewhat jaded vampire hunter. The undead antagonist provides some soap opera-level acting, but still holds his own even though the lower half of his face is covered by a mask (which hides the injury given to him by Chariot). True to form, Chariot shows no mercy; when he stakes the vampire, the scene feels very real—Van Helsing would be proud.

Monsters – "The Legacy"

Syndicated. Dec 3, 1988 (S01E07). Horror/Suspense. D: Jeff Wolf. W: John Sutherland, Robert Bloch. C: David Brisbin, Lara Harris, Mary Ann Gibson, Kevin Jeffries ☥. USA: English/Color/22m. Laurel EFX Inc./Tribune Broadcasting Company/Worldvision Enterprises Inc.

Character actor Fulton Pierce was renowned for completely disappearing into the monster roles he created, and no one since has been able to reproduce his makeup techniques. To better understand the man and his methods, his biographer rents the private Hollywood retreat once owned by the actor. After the writer finds Pierce's old makeup kit, he discovers the nefarious source behind the actor's amazing transformations.

Pierce was so good at his craft because he literally *became* each role; he transformed into a number of monsters that were trapped within the mirror of his makeup kit. One fiend in particular—an evil vampire—exerted some control over Pierce, and directed each transformation. Late in his career, the actor took on the guise of the vampire, but paid the ultimate price for becoming such a malevolent monster; the vampire controls the biographer in the same manner. This story is ostensibly a tribute to Lon Chaney, the legendary character actor who had a great influence on early Hollywood filmmaking. Not only does the series of transformations follow the same chronology as the roles Chaney himself performed, the monsters even stay true to character in how they react to the woman they love.

📺 The characters featured are Quasimodo from *The Hunchback of Notre Dame* (1923), Erik from *The Phantom of the Opera* (1925), and Edward Burke from *London After Midnight* (1927)—a man who technically wasn't an evil vampire, but a police inspector in disguise.

Monsters – "Pool Sharks"

Syndicated. Dec 17, 1988 (S01E09). Horror/Suspense. D/W: Alan Kingsberg. C: Tom Mason, Irving Metzman, Rebecca Downs , Page Johnson. USA: English/Color/22m. Laurel EFX Inc./Tribune Broadcasting Company/Worldvision Enterprises Inc.

Gabe is a hustler who takes on a beautiful and mysterious woman named Natasha, who happens to be a vampire—and is also very adept at playing pool. But she's not the only one out for blood; Gabe has been tracking her ever since his brother was murdered, after Natasha beat him in a similar high-stakes game of pool months earlier.

A so-so story that is a little cheesy at times, and becomes somewhat convoluted once it attempts to explain why this vampire "pool shark" uses the game to draw in her victims. At least we're presented with a traditional, seductive bloodsucker, who is affected by the standard trappings such as crosses and stakes.

Monsters – "Shave and a Haircut, Two Bites"

Syndicated. Nov 18, 1990 (S03E08). Horror/Suspense. D: John Strysik. W: Dan Simmons. C: Wil Wheaton, Matt LeBlanc, John O'Leary, Al Mancini. USA: English/Color/22m. Laurel EFX Inc./Tribune Broadcasting Company/Worldvision Enterprises Inc.

Every small town has a barber shop, its trademark pole swirling red and white, as if it were blood continually dripping and spilling. At least that's how Kevin sees it, for he believes that the local establishment is actually a front for a vampire guild that stretches back centuries—and that proprietors Innis and D'Onofrio are looking for victims more than customers.

So many aspects of this tale ring true; most barber shops remain open despite a limited clientele, and offer prices that seem decades out of date. Also, the elderly men running the shop never seem to age—and what's the story behind the iconic pole displayed outside? In this story, the proprietors aren't vampires, but they do take care of one, and get an extended lifespan in return. The only major letdown is the revelation that the real vampire is actually a human-sized leech, which looks a little ridiculous as it drinks blood through a giant straw. Apparently this is its natural form, which it has reverted to after centuries of hiding from the outside world. If this is what happens to all vampires, then I doubt there will be too many members of Team Edward in about five hundred years.

During Medieval times, barbers performed other duties aside from haircuts, including surgery and dental work, and often used leeches for bloodletting. The red and white stripes represented bloody bandages wrapped around a pole, hung out to dry after washing.

Monsters – "The Waiting Game"

Syndicated. Dec 9, 1990 (S03E10). Horror/Suspense. D: Bruno Spandello. W: John Fox. C: Doug McKeon ☥, Stephen Burleigh, Carrington Garland ☥, Leo Garcia ☥. USA: English/Color/22m. Laurel EFX Inc./Tribune Broadcasting Company/Worldvision Enterprises Inc.

🦇 🦇 🦇 🦇

For Lieutenant Tyler and Captain Levitt, it's just another day at the office until they're given a surprise order to launch a nuclear arsenal; days later, a nuclear winter envelopes the Earth. Safe within a military bunker, Tyler and Levitt believe they're the only ones left alive—so what could be making the scratching noise outside the building?

As the officers lose their grip on sanity, Tyler exits the safety of the bunker to find the cause of the noise—which turns out to be vampires (who seem to thrive in such conditions). Captain Levitt remains within the shelter, and the door can't be unlocked without his security code. But the creatures outside are a persistent lot, and they only have to try about one hundred thousand permutations before they find the correct code—and time is on their side. This suspenseful episode is heavy on dialogue but light on action, blood and gore—yet the payoff for learning so much about the characters is that you care about what happens to them by the end. This is a prime example of a memorable vampire tale that doesn't rely on large set pieces or in-your-face horror; it's just a strong story that's told very well.

Mr. Meaty - "Nosferateens" / "I Love Lizzy"

Parker and Josh, teen fast-food workers-turned vampires, cozy up to a crew member between takes on *Mr. Meaty* (Nickelodeon Productions/Author Photo)

CBC/Nickelodeon. Oct 27, 2006 (S01E06). Comedy/Family. D/W: Jamie Shannon. C: Jason Hopley ☥, Jamie Shannon ☥, Todd Doldersum, Marty Stelnick, Troy Baker. CAN/USA: English/Color/22m. Nickelodeon Productions/The Canadian Broadcasting Corporation.

This kids series follows teens Parker and Josh, who work at a fast food restaurant at Scaunchboro Mall. In "Nosferateens," the boys discover a vampire hiding in the freezer. As a means to alleviate the crushing boredom inherent with working at Mr. Meaty, they force the creature to turn them into one of the bloodsucking undead.

Murder, She Wrote – "The Perfect Foil"

CBS. Apr 13, 1986 (S02E21). Drama/Mystery. D: Walter Grauman. W: Robert E. Swanson. C: Angela Lansbury, Barbara Babcock, Peter Bonerz, Cesare Danova, George DiCenzo, Robert Forster, Wendy Oates ⚲. USA: English/Color/48m. Corymore Productions/Universal TV.

Jessica Fletcher travels to New Orleans to check up on a distant cousin, and discovers that he's been charged in the murder of a local thug. The story takes place during Mardi Gras, and one participant appears in costume as "Madame Dracula" (she dons an elaborate mask with white skin, red lips, and pronounced fangs).

Murder, She Wrote – "The Legacy of Borbey House"

CBS. Oct 3, 1993 (S10E03). Drama/Mystery. D: Walter Grauman. W: Danna Doyle, Debbie Smith. C: Angela Lansbury, Ron Masak, Richard Gilliland, William Windom, David Birney ⚲, Roy Dotrice, Christopher Neame. USA: English/Color/46m. Corymore Productions/Universal TV.

Occult specialist Dr. Howard Sorenson is in Cabot Cove researching the legendary Borbey family, who were supposedly a group of vampires that lived there in the mid-1800s. When it's discovered that the grave of William Borbey stands empty, and a mysterious man has recently purchased his old Victorian mansion, some locals wonder if a vampire has returned from the dead.

I'm sure fans of the show enjoyed this one, but for those more interested in a vampire tale, it's pretty middle-of-the-road; it's really only a sub-plot to help drive the overall murder-mystery story. Like many of these single-episode vampire outings, there is a twist ending that has been used before, but here it doesn't have quite the same impact.

📺 Roy Dotrice, a vampire hunter of sorts in this tale, portrayed a bloodsucker in the *Tales from the Darkside* episode "My Ghostwriter: The Vampire" (1987). Christopher Neame appeared in two Hammer vampire films, *Lust for a Vampire* (1971) and *Dracula A.D. 1972* (1972), in which he starred as vampire wannabe Johnny Alucard.

Murdoch Mysteries – "Bloodlust"

Alibi/Citytv. Apr 26, 2011 (S04E11). Crime/Drama. D: Gail Harvey. W: Paul Aitken, Graham Clegg, Phil Bedard, Larry Lalonde. C: Yannick Bisson, Hélène Joy, Thomas Craig, Jonny Harris, Jonathan Watton, Ephraim Ellis, Leah Pinsent. CAN: English/Color/46m. Shaftesbury Films.

Follows the exploits of William Murdoch, a Victorian-era police detective working in Toronto, who employs the latest techniques in forensic science to solve crimes. In this episode, a young schoolgirl has drowned, but the crime is sensationalized after it's revealed that she also suffered major blood loss—and has two strange marks on her neck. Due to the recent publication of Bram Stoker's Dracula, locals believe that her death was at the hands of a vampire.

This episode starts out well, and plays on the sensationalism surrounding the publication of Stoker's novel, which brought a romantic vampire into the Western world. The perpetrator is actually a hemophiliac who's capitalizing on the popularity of the book to lure young women; he drains a small amount of their blood, which his doctor uses in experiments to treat his condition. The series takes place in the late 1890s, so it's questionable whether so many residents would already have a copy of the novel (the US edition of *Dracula* wasn't published until 1899). This is forgivable, but the story is completely ruined when one character insists that the perpetrator is Vlad Țepeș! A "noted vampire!" Are you kidding me? There's absolutely no way that anyone in the Western world would have known about Vlad back then. Granted, this is fiction, and artistic liberties are expected, but for those who know the real connection (or lack thereof) between Vlad and vampires, this revelation is sure to drive them batty.

My Parents are Aliens – "Joshferatu"

ITV1. Nov 15, 2004 (S06E04). Family/Sci-Fi. D: Tom Poole. W: Brian Lynch. C: Tony Gardner ☥, Carla Mendonça, Alex Kew ☥, Charlotte Francis, Danielle McCormack, Olisa Odele, Dan O'Brien. UK: English/Color/30m. Granada Kids/Yorkshire Television.

Follows the lives of three orphans adopted by Brian and Sophie Johnson, two aliens from the planet Valux left stranded after crashing their spaceship. In this episode, on Halloween night, Brian morphs into a vampire—and seeks out Mr. Whiteside as his first victim.

Nash Bridges – "Superstition"

CBS. Feb 12, 1999 (S04E14). Action/Drama. D: Jim Charleston. W: Reed Steiner, Jed Seidel. C: Don Johnson, Cheech Marin, Yasmine Bleeth, Jenny McShane, Renee Smith ☥, Matt O'Toole ☥. USA: English/Color/44m. Rysher Entertainment Inc./The Don Johnson Company/Carlton Cuse Productions.

A man is found murdered with a ceremonial knife piercing his heart and bite marks on his neck. The investigation leads Nash to a group of modern-day vampires, who believe that the blood of musician Finn Rivers will give them eternal youth, beauty and immortality.

A generic story about a whacked-out cult teeming with vampire posers. Their hangout, called the "Blood Club," is the most tame-looking Goth club ever depicted on television. Naturally, the knives used by cult members are replicas of that once owned by Vlad the Impaler ("that Dracula guy"), I guess because the writers assumed that a little name-dropping would give the story more authenticity. They were wrong.

NCIS: New Orleans – "Master of Horror"

CBS. Oct 28, 2014 (S01E06). Crime/Drama. D: Terrence O'Hara. W: Scott D. Shapiro. C: Scott Bakula, Lucas Black, Zoe McLellan, Rob Kerkovich, CCH Pounder, Paige Turco, Rod Rowland, Eyal Podell, Adam Rose, Aubrey Deeker, Cyd Strittmatter, Steven Weber, Brooke Hurring. USA: English/Color/42m. Wings Productions/When Pigs Fly Productions.

Series follows a team of investigators, based in New Orleans, who are assigned to crimes involving members of the United States Navy and Marine Corps. In this episode, which takes place during Halloween, a Judge Advocate General of the Navy is found dead in a cemetery, dressed in Victorian garb with two small puncture wounds on her neck. This is a spin-off series of the long-running *NCIS*.

Ned's Declassified School Survival Guide – "Halloween" / "Vampires, Werewolves, Ghosts and Zombies"

Nickelodeon. Oct 29, 2006 (S03E03). Comedy/Family. D: Savage Steve Holland. W: Scott Fellows, Lazar Saric. C: Devon Werkheiser ♀, Lindsey Shaw, Daniel Curtis Lee, Daran Norris, John Bliss. USA: English/Color/25m. Jack Mackie Pictures/ApolloProMovie GmbH/Filmproduktion KG.

In the segment "Vampires, Werewolves, Ghosts and Zombies," the kids become their Halloween costumes. As Ned studies for a Vampire Aptitude Test (V.A.T.), a Frankenstein Monster chases Cookie (now a werewolf) throughout the school. Meanwhile, Moze attempts to bring a student to the other side so she can have another ghost pal to hang out with, and a zombified Gordy tries to catch a vampire weasel that is terrorizing the hallways.

Good fun all around, geared towards kids but adults will get a kick out of this one too. I particularly liked the nod to *Caddyshack* (1980), the film which saw groundskeeper Carl hunting down a gopher that was terrorizing an upscale golf course. Each kid has fun with their otherworldly characters, and in particular, there are some great moments as Ned studies for his V.A.T.'s.

NightMan – "Constant Craving"

Syndicated. Jan 18, 1998 (S01E12). Action/Adventure. D: Bud Bashore. W: Janet Curtis, Stephen A. Miller, Glen A. Larson. C: Matt McColm, Earl Holliman, Michael Woods, Lysette Anthony ♀, François Guétary ♀. CAN/USA: English/Color/44m. Nightman Productions Inc./Glen Larson Entertainment Network Inc.

After a freak accident, jazz musician Johnny Domino gained the ability to detect evil; as NightMan, he uses this new skill to fight crime in San Francisco. In this episode, Countess Erica Bolen is on the hunt for new blood. Specifically, she requires certain DNA sequences to alter her blood chemistry, which should cure her vampirism. Domino's father holds the final key sequence within his veins; can NightMan intervene before he becomes an unwilling donor?

Although the premise is interesting, the way it's developed and resolved is riddled with so many plot holes that it doesn't hold up, no matter how much you suspend your disbelief. When the story isn't great, it draws too much attention to the poor special effects and laugh-inducing flying sequences. I've been told that the "Night Man" comic book series (*Malibu,* 1993-95) was an excellent read, however it did not translate well to the small screen.

Über-producer Glen A. Larson has created many entertaining series over the past thirty years, some of which included a vampire-themed episode.

NightMan – "Book of the Dead"

Syndicated. Oct 26, 1998 (S02E04). Action/Adventure. D: George Mendeluk. W: D.G. Larson. C: Matt McColm, Jayne Heitmeyer, Derwin Jordan, Claudette Mink, Mark Lindsay Chapman, Rebecca Reichert ♀. CAN/USA: English/Color/44m. Nightman Productions Ltd./Glen Larson Entertainment Network.

A scientist digs up the grave of a long-dead magician, who was buried with a book that contains an ancient Sumerian spell to raise the dead—which he uses to bring back his wife. But her resurrection comes with a price: she's now a bloodthirsty vampire. Domino must stop the reunited couple before they can perform yet another ritual, which will bring forth the Lord of the Dead and his horde of zombie minions, who will arise to sweep the Earth and devour the living.

If the synopsis alone isn't enough to steer you away from this mess, then perhaps a more direct warning will: it's awful. The plot is ridiculous and hard to follow, the roles painfully acted, and the special effects, as always, look just terrible (don't get me started on the *papier mâché* zombies). As for the bloodsucker, is seems the only reason why the wife was resurrected as a vampire is because, well, vampires are popular. In the opening scene, the scientist is warned about stealing from the grave: "He who takes this book from me takes with it the curse of eternity." Well, he who watches this episode takes with it the curse of stupidity.

Night Court – "Death Takes a Halloween"

NBC. Oct 26, 1990 (S08E05). Comedy/Family. D: Jim Drake. W: Harry Anderson. C: Harry Anderson, John Larroquette, Markie Post, Charles Robinson, Richard Moll, Stephen Root, Douglas MacHugh ♀. USA: English/Color/22m. Starry Night Productions/Warner Bros. Television.

On Halloween, a man claims to be the Spirit of Death, and is put in the lockup for the night. Harry wonders if he was telling the truth, because now that Death is behind bars, no one seems to be dying. There's minimal vampire content here; Dracula shows up in the Courthouse cafeteria, and borrows a bottle of ketchup from Christine—not quite the red stuff he usually seeks, but this is wholesome family entertainment after all.

Night Gallery – "The Boy Who Predicted Earthquakes" / "Miss Lovecraft Sent Me" / "The Hand of Borgus Weems" / "Phantom of What Opera?"

NBC. Sep 15, 1971 (S02E01). Suspense/Thriller. D: Gene Kearney. W: Jack Laird. C: Joseph Campanella ⚲, Sue Lyon. USA: English/Color/30m. Universal Studios Television.

In the vignette "Miss Lovecraft Sent Me," Betsy worries about her latest babysitting gig after she notices that the man of the house is quite pale, doesn't cast a reflection, and has an eclectic taste in reading material. Her suspicions mount after the man goes to check in on his son, who he claims is "difficult with strangers"—and she hears the sound of chains and growling noises coming from the bedroom.

Not a bad story, but as with many of the *Night Gallery* vignettes, it ends poorly. Although it's not fully explained, the vampire's wife is probably a werewolf, and their son is some sort of hybrid beast. (These are the kind of details that I apparently obsess about.)

Night Gallery – "A Question of Fear" / "The Devil Is Not Mocked"

NBC. Oct 27, 1971 (S02E06). Suspense/Thriller. D: Gene Kearney. W: Gene Kearney, Manly Wade Wellman. C: Helmut Dantine, Francis Lederer ⚲, Hank Brandt, Martin Kosleck, Gino Gottarelli, Mark de Vries. USA: English/Color/30m. Universal Studios Television.

In "The Devil Is Not Mocked," a man recounts a heroic tale from World War II, when a Nazi General and his SS officers were on the trail of an underground resistance movement. They followed the group to a large castle in Transylvania, where they were met by a friendly Count who invited them in for food and drink. Although the General believed that the host was actually the leader of the resistance forces, all they found was a warm welcome and a dozen Slavik servants—until the clock struck midnight. Hosted by Rod Serling.

Based on the 1943 short story of the same title by Manly Wade Wellman, this is an excellent supernatural tale about Dracula and his small army of werewolves. They've sworn to protect their country from the encroaching Nazi threat—and literally have the soldiers for dinner.

📺 Francis Lederer starred as Dracula in the feature film *The Return of Dracula* (1958).

Night Gallery – "The Diary" / "A Matter of Semantics" / "Big Surprise" / "Professor Peabody's Last Lecture"

NBC. Nov 10, 1971 (S02E08). Suspense/Thriller. D: Jack Laird, Jeannot Szwarc. W: Gene Kearney, Richard Matheson. C: Cesar Romero ⚲, E.J. Peaker, Monie Ellis, John Carradine ⚲, Vincent Van Patten, Marc Vahanian. USA: English/Color/30m. Universal Studios Television.

In the vignette "A Matter of Semantics," out-of-towner Count Dracula visits a local blood bank, unaware that it's a place to make donations—not ask for a loan. In the segment "Big Surprise,"

the elderly Mr. Hawkins offers three local boys a big surprise, but they first have to dig it up from beneath a large oak tree. Hosted by Rod Serling.

The vignette is one of the better ones from this season, with Romero hamming it up as Count Dracula on holiday, who wants to withdraw a few pints. Yet "Big Surprise" is the standout, with Carradine giving an effective and creepy performance—but is he a vampire? It's never quite made clear; even though he's unearthed as the sun sets, sunlight doesn't seem to affect him, and he has no classic undead features.

Night Gallery – "House: With Ghost" / "A Midnight Visit to the Neighborhood Blood Bank" / "Dr. Stringfellow's Rejuvenator" / "Hell's Bells"

NBC. Nov 17, 1971 (S02E09). Suspense/Thriller. D: William Hale. W: Jack Laird. C: Victor Buono ♀, Journey Laird. USA: English/Color/30m. Universal Studios Television.

Count Dracula (Cesar Romero) visits a blood bank in the *Night Gallery* vignette "A Matter of Semantics" (Universal Studios Television)

In the vignette "A Midnight Visit to the Neighborhood Blood Bank," a vampire flies in to the bedroom of a potential victim to make a withdrawal, yet he's stopped at the last minute after she tells him she's already made a donation. Hosted by Rod Serling.

Another example of just how hard it is to pull off a successful story within a two-minute time constraint; everything relies on the punch line, which in this case isn't all that funny: it turns out that the woman already "gave at the office."

📺 This exact same joke was told at the start of a *Barris & Company* episode broadcast on November 9, 1968.

Night Gallery – "Green Fingers" / "The Funeral" / "The Tune in Dan's Café"

NBC. Jan 5, 1972 (S02E15). Suspense/Thriller. D: John Meredyth Lucas. W: Richard Matheson. C: Joe Flynn, Werner Klemperer ♀, Harvey Jason, Charles Macaulay ♀, Jack Laird, Laara Lacey, Leonidas D. Ossetynski ♀, Diana Hale ♀. USA: English/Color/30m. Universal Studios Television.

In "The Funeral," the affluent Ludwig Asper visits Morton Silkline's Cut Rate Catafalque to arrange for a memorial service, and the cost is of no concern. Asper reveals that he's a vampire who's planning his *second* funeral—and this time around he wants to go out in style. Hosted by Rod Serling.

A light-hearted story with several funny moments leading up to the hilarious antics of Asper's fiendish friends after they arrive at his memorial service. Klemperer is great as a meticulous vampire trying to plan the perfect funeral, which is ultimately ruined by the creatures he invites; it seems as though monsters just can't put aside their differences, even during such an important occasion.

Night Gallery – "You Can Come Up Now, Mrs. Millikan" / "Smile, Please"

NBC. Nov 12, 1972 (S03E07). Suspense/Thriller. D/W: Jack Laird. C: César Danova ☥, Lindsay Wagner. USA: English/Color/30m. Universal Studios Television.

In the vignette "Smile, Please," a gentleman accompanies a young woman to a dilapidated castle, where she hopes to take the first-ever photograph of a real vampire. The man assures her that the undead are quite harmless when they're asleep, but much to the dismay of the photographer, the coffin is empty. Yet the man claims that there is indeed a vampire nearby. Hosted by Rod Serling.

A predictable story that falls flat, as do many of the other vignettes in this series. Thankfully it's over quickly so we don't have to spend too much time listening to Wagner's horrible attempt at a British accent.

Night Gallery – "Death on a Barge"

NBC. Mar 4, 1973 (S03E12). Suspense/Thriller. D: Leonard Nimoy. W: Halsted Welles, Everil Worrell. C: Lesley Ann Warren ☥, Lou Antonio, Brooke Bundy, Robert Pratt. USA: English/Color/30m. Universal Studios Television.

A dockside worker is attracted to a mysterious woman named Hyacinth, whom he only sees at night and is apparently trapped on an anchored barge due to her fear of crossing running water. Although she refuses to let him come aboard, the woman longs to be with him, and he too wants that day to come—if only to confirm his suspicion that she's a vampire. Hosted by Rod Serling.

Although I like the premise—we don't often see a sympathetic vampire—I just couldn't buy into this one. Maybe because it was overdramatic, or because the acting was so bad. The father seemed to be doing everything in his power to protect his undead daughter, which is why the ending made no sense at all—he sides with the prey and not the predator. You'd think he wouldn't care so much that she has a snack now and again—after all, a girl's got to eat!

Night Gallery – "Hatred Unto Death" / "How to Cure the Common Vampire"

Two vampire hunters have second thoughts in the *Night Gallery* vignette "How to Cure the Common Vampire" (Universal Studios Television)

NBC. May 27, 1973 (S03E15). Suspense/Thriller. D/W: Jack Laird. C: Richard Deacon, Johnny Brown. USA: English/Color/30m. Universal Studios Television.

In the vignette "How to Cure the Common Vampire," a group of men approach a coffin with weapons in hand. As one of them places a stake over the vampire's chest, he questions the deed about to be done. Hosted by Rod Serling.

Where's a rim shot when you need it? This tale has one hesitant hunter asking another, "are you sure?" to which he replies, "well, it couldn't hurt." It feels like a hastily-sketched single-panel cartoon that tries to be funny but fails miserably in the execution.

Ninja Turtles: The Next Mutation – "Unchain My Heart"

FOX Kids/TV Asahi. Feb 20 – Mar 13, 1998 (S01E22-25). Adventure/Family. D: Robert Lee. W: Dan Clark, Michael Mayhew. C: Jarred Blancard, Mitchell Lee Yuen, Richard Yee, Gabe Khouth, Nicole Parker, Kira Clavell ♀, Justin Soon ♀, Lauren Attadia ♀. JPN/USA: English/Color/88m. Saban Entertainment/Toei Company.

While Bonesteel hunts the Turtles throughout New York, in China, undead minions awaken their mistress—the two-thousand-year-old vampire Vam-Mi. Time is of the essence; she must find her heart to complete her reanimation, and it just happens to be in the possession of Venus de Milo.

Allotting four episodes to one story doesn't always make it better—and such is the case for this tale. It becomes far too repetitive, and easily could have been told in fewer episodes. The most annoying aspect of the production is its over-use of sound effects—bells, whistles, animal noises, and everything in between.

Nip/Tuck – "Giselle Blaylock & Legend Chandler"

Syndicated. Mar 3, 2009 (S05E22). Drama/Medical. D: Lyn Greene. W: Lyn Greene, Richard Levine. C: Dylan Walsh, Julian McMahon, John Hensley, Roma Maffia, Wendy Glenn ♀, Graham Shiels ♀. USA: English/Color/43m. Hands Down Entertainment/The Shephard-Robin Company/Ryan Murphy Productions.

Sanguinists Legend and Giselle are trying to curb their taste for each other's blood, and require plastic surgery to repair the damage caused by their activities. But patching up their skin may not be enough of an incentive to halt the bloodlust that they share for each other.

It's tough to gauge this one, since it's only a sub-plot used to drive the overall story arc for this series. Yet within the short time they're given, the sanguinists paint a clear picture of what it means to be a blood drinker in modern society, and the issues that result from such a habit. The theme of the vampire also ties in well to a person's search for eternal youth through plastic surgery, as well as Christian's personal search for longevity (he was diagnosed with terminal cancer).

📺 Graham Shiels (Legend Chandler) portrayed the vampire Liam on HBO's *True Blood* (2008). Giselle Blaylock is the namesake of Miriam Blaylock, the ancient vampire in *The Hunger* (1983).

The Odyssey – "Night Life"

CBC. Oct 24, 1994 (S03E04). Family/Sci-Fi. D: Stacey Curtis. W: Leila Basen. C: Illya Woloshynm, Tony Sampson, Ashley Rogers, Andrea Nemeth, Ryan Reynolds, Laura Harris ☥, Xantha Radley ☥, Nicole Penny ☥. CAN: English/Color/24m. Water Street Pictures Ltd./CBC.

🦇🦇

Much to Jay's dismay, a trio of "in" girls take an interest in Donna, and believe she has what it takes to be a member of their clique. Meanwhile, in the fantasy world, Alpha is drawn toward a group of vampires that believe she would be a worthwhile addition to their ranks.

The series follows the adventures of Jay Ziegler, a boy who falls into a coma and ends up existing within two different realities. In the real world, his family and friends attempt to bring Jay out of the coma; but within his subconscious, Jay lives in a place where there are no adults, and his friends exist as alternate personalities. *The Odyssey* has been hailed by many as one of the better sci-fi shows geared towards kids, and although the vampire storyline may seem a little bland to adults, it's definitely suitable for the target audience.

One Foot in the Grave – "Tales of Terror"

BBC One. Oct 23, 2000 (S06E02). Comedy/Drama. D: Christine Gernon. W: David Renwick. C: Richard Wilson ☥, Annette Crosbie, Owen Brenman, Doreen Mantle, Leila Hoffman, John Rutland. UK: English/Color/33m. BBC.

🦇🦇🦇

Victor is asked to don the fangs for Mr. Swainey's latest production, *Nosferatu the Vampire,* after the actor previously picked for the starring role decided he had issues with the blood-drinking aspect of the character. After a medical test finds blood in Victor's digestive system, many wonder if he's taken the role a little too seriously.

We never get to see the actual stage production, however the situations surrounding it are pretty funny, and it's entertaining to watch cantankerous couple Victor and Margaret interact—imagine Archie Bunker if he had an equally acerbic wife.

Parks and Recreation – "Time Capsule"

NBC. Feb 3, 2011 (S03E03). Comedy/Satire. D/W: Michael Schur. C: Amy Poehler, Rashida Jones, Aziz Ansari, Nick Offerman, Aubrey Plaza, Chris Pratt, Adam Scott, Rob Lowe, Jim O'Heir, Retta, Will Forte. USA: English/Color/22m. Deedle-Dee Productions.

City bureaucrat Leslie Knope plans to bury a time capsule that will contain items representing the life and times of present-day Pawnee, Indiana. She denies one man's request to include Stephenie Meyer's *Twilight* books, and is unprepared for the lengths to which he'll go to ensure his demands are met.

A decent episode that vilifies *Twihards* all the while celebrating the impact the books have had on all walks of life. Like it or not, the *Twilight* series has had a major cultural impact on the tween generation, for better or for worse.

The Phil Silvers Show – "Bilko's Vampire"

CBS. Oct 1, 1958 (S04E02). Comedy/War. D: Aaron Ruben. W: Arnie Rosen, Coleman Jacoby. C: Phil Silvers, Joe E. Ross ☥, Harvey Lembeck, Maurice Gosfield, Beatrice Pons. USA: English/B&W/25m. CBS.

Originally titled *You'll Never Get Rich*, this series features Master Sergeant Ernest Bilko, who spends much of his time trying to make extra money through various get-rich-quick schemes. In this episode, Ritzik forgoes the nightly poker game to watch *Shriek Theater* on TV. This upsets Bilko, who tries to scare Ritzik back into the game by telling him that this increasing obsession with vampires will turn him into one.

Bilko's plan backfires, so he looks for some other way to glean money from Ritzik—and learns that a production company wants an unknown actor to star in a new series of *Dracula* films. Ritzik, who now believes he's a real vampire, is perfect for the role—and as his agent, Bilko stands to make quite a bit of cash. It's a very funny episode with a great performance from Joe E. Ross as Ritzik, whose increasing obsession with vampires is a hoot to watch (he appears dressed in a full Dracula outfit).

📺 *Shriek Theater* alludes to *Shock Theater*, a package of 52 horror films from Universal Studios that were released into television syndication in 1957. All the classics from the silver screen were available for broadcast, including *Dracula*, *The Wolf Man*, *Frankenstein* and *The Mummy*.

Podge & Rodge: A Scare at Bedtime – "The Vampire Leprechaun"

RTÉ Two. Mar 19, 1997 (S01E14). Adult/Comedy. D: Damian Farrell. W: Mick O'Hara, Ciarán Morrison. C: Mick O'Hara, Ciarán Morrison. UK: English/Color/6m. Double Z Enterprises.

Rodge boasts about the beautiful girl he just met, but Podge has a dire warning for his brother. The woman is actually the zombie bride of Séamus Shenanigans, the vampire leprechaun, who craves the blood of young bachelors—especially those with low moral standards. Podge claims that Rodge is now doomed to a life of "undeadness," but he has a sure-fire way to get his brother out of the predicament.

You can't go wrong with lewd puppets recounting illicit tales filled with sexual innuendo! The brothers live in an abandoned insane asylum; Podge is clever and devious, while Rodge is dumber and has looser morals. The story of the vampire leprechaun is quite funny, as is the wicked banter between the two of them.

📺 The puppets also hosted a Halloween special over the course of three nights, which featured movies such as *Dracula* and *Interview with the Vampire*.

Police Academy: The Series – "Lend Me Your Neck"

Syndicated. Apr 21, 1998 (S01E25). Comedy/Crime. D: Anon. W: Anon. C: Matt Borlenghi, Rod Crawford, Toby Proctor, Jeremiah Birkett, Heather Campbell, Christine Gonzales, Joe Flaherty, Michael Winslow. USA: English/Color/30m. Goodman-Rosen Productions/Paul Maslansky Productions.

Annie gains the unwanted romantic attentions of Cesare, a troubled man who recently escaped from a local mental hospital—and believes he's a vampire.

Poltergeist: The Legacy – "Darkness Falls" / "Light of Day"

Showtime. Jan 23/30, 1998 (S03E01/02). Horror/Sci-Fi. D: Michael Robison. W: Michael Sadowski. C: Derek de Lint, Robbi Chong, Martin Cummins, Helen Shaver, Anthony Palermo, Sarah Strange. USA: English/Color/120m. PMP Legacy Productions/Trilogy Entertainment Group.

In this two-part story, Alex encounters an old friend in New Orleans, who's changed since college—she's now a vampire. After the woman bites Alex, her transformation into the undead begins, but the process will only be completed after she succeeds in killing the object of her bloodlust: Nick.

Poltergeist: The Legacy – "The Darkside"

Showtime. Aug 21, 1998 (S03E22). Horror/Sci-Fi. D: Michael Robison. W: Grant Rosenberg. C: Derek de Lint, Robbi Chong, Martin Cummins, Helen Shaver, Anthony Palermo, Sarah Strange. USA: English/Color/60m. PMP Legacy Productions/Trilogy Entertainment Group.

In this clip show, a bloodsucker from the Darkside points out past failures of the Legacy organization, in an attempt to turn Alex against it. Features clips from the vampire-themed episodes "Darkness Falls" and "Light of Day."

Private Practice – "Love Bites"

ABC. Feb 11, 2010 (S03E14). Drama/Medical. D: Matthew Penn. W: Dana Baratta. C: Kate Walsh, Tim Daly, Audra McDonald, Paul Adelstein, Taye Diggs, Kaitlyn Dever, Colin Ford ☥. USA: English/Color/43m. ShondaLand/The Mark Gordon Company/ABC Studios.

Dr. Freedman treats Paige, a feverish and pale young girl who has a bite mark on her neck; she claims that her eternal love and soul mate Seth did the deed. But the young man confesses that he's just posing as a two-thousand-year-old bloodsucker, because so many girls are into that "romantic vampire crap."

Finally we have a story that addresses the annoying trend of cuddly, loveable vampires, such as those found in the *Twilight* universe. It actually does a good job of exploring the reality of preteen girls who become too enthralled with vampires of this ilk, and the unfortunate result of such an obsession.

Providence – "Things That Go Bump in the Night"

NBC. Nov 1, 2002 (S05E05). Drama/Medical. D: Tony Wharmby. W: Jennifer Cecil. C: Melina Kanakaredes, Seth Peterson, Mike Farrell, George Newbern, Denis Arndt, Alex D. Linz, Matt Champagne, Paul Eiding ☥. USA: English/Color/60m. NBC Studios.

It's Halloween night and Sydney is confronted by all manner of costumed creatures at the hospital, including a distraught man who claims to be a vampire.

PSI Factor: Chronicles of the Paranormal – "Valentine"

Syndicated. Feb 14, 1999 (S03E14). Drama/Sci-Fi. D: Ross Clyde. W: Sheila Prescott-Vessey. C: Matt Frewer, Nancy Anne Sakovich, Barclay Hope, Colin Fox, Nigel Bennett, Peter MacNeill, Winston Rekert ☥, C. J. Fidler ☥. CAN: English/Color/46m. Alliance Atlantis/Eyemark Entertainment.

The OSIR team investigates the brutal murder of a man whose corpse was found completely drained of blood—but he won't be the last. As the body count rises, they discover that each victim was hooked on heroin, and suspicion falls on Marc Hagan, a man with a checkered past. He possesses an old human skull, complete with retractable fangs—the remains of a local man thought to be a vampire, and killed over a century ago. Hosted by Dan Aykroyd.

In a Valentine's Day story that moves about as fast as coagulated blood, a vampire junkie runs amok, feeding her need for both blood and heroin—which she got hooked on before she died. I guess being lonely on this particular day will lead someone to do questionable things, but I don't think I've ever seen a story where a character investigating a series of murders gets romantically involved with *both* prime suspects. Professional ethics be damned!

The character "Marc Hagan" is most likely in homage to Mark Rein-Hagen, creator of the role-playing game *Vampire: The Masquerade*.

Psych – "This Episode Sucks"

USA Network. Oct 26, 2011 (S06E03). Comedy/Crime. D: James Roday. W: Todd Harthan, James Roday. C: James Roday ⚘, Dulé Hill ⚘, Timothy Omundson, Maggie Lawson, Kirsten Nelson, Kristy Swanson, Corey Feldman ⚘, Tom Lenk. USA: English/Color/43m. GEP Productions/Tagline Pictures.

After a body is found drained of blood, with two bite marks on the wrists and neck, Shawn and Gus take an overzealous approach to their investigation—believing the perpetrator is a bona fide bloodsucker. Meanwhile, Detective Lassiter is in a conflict of interest after discovering that the prime suspect might be the pale and mysterious woman he recently met at a bar.

A fun episode that features many references to genre films, and includes actors who have starred in related movies and television series. Highlights include the two amateur sleuths dressed up as Lestat and Blacula; Gus is constantly mistaken for Count Chocula, because according to Shawn, no one remembers *Blacula* except for them and Quentin Tarantino. Kristy Swanson—the original Buffy the Vampire Slayer—is great as the enigmatic love interest of detective Lassiter, while both Tom Lenk (Andrew from the *Buffy* TV series) and Corey Feldman (from the *Lost Boys* movies) shine in their brief cameos. Definitely recommended viewing!

Quantum Leap – "Blood Moon"

NBC. Feb 9, 1993 (S05E15). Adventure/Drama. D: Alan J. Levi. W: Tommy Thompson. C: Scott Bakula ⚘, Dean Stockwell, Shae D'Lyn, Ian Buchanan ⚘, Deborah Maria Moore ⚘, Rod Loomis. USA: English/Color/47m. Belisarius Productions/Universal TV.

Series follows physicist Dr. Sam Beckett, who after a failed time travel experiment ends up jumping back and forth through the decades, "leaping" into the body of another and temporarily taking over their life. Before he can move on—with the hope that the next "leap" will take him back home—he must change history for the better. He remains connected to his own time through a military observer named Al Calavicci, who appears as a hologram to assist Sam with his objective. In this episode, it's March 10, 1975, and Sam "leaps" into Nigel Corrington—and awakes inside a coffin. His wife, the Lady Alexandra, eagerly anticipates the upcoming "Blood Moon" ritual, a sacrifice where the undead honor Count Bathory.

Sam is there to prevent Alexandra's murder, and believes the vampire shtick is just a way for Corrington—a highly-paid and eccentric artist—to prop up the cost of his work. Yet both Al, and the guests at the ritual, believe Corrington really is a centuries-old vampire. It's a well-written comedic episode, especially in the scenes that highlight Al's superstitious nature towards vampires. The premise is loosely based on the legend of Elizabeth Báthory, who in this story was a man, and "one of the first vampires in recorded history."

R.L. Stine's The Haunting Hour - *"Grampires"*

The Hub. Oct 13, 2012 (S03E01/02). Family/Suspense. D: Neill Fearnley. W: Erik Patterson, Jessica Scott. C: Christopher Lloyd ⚥, Mitchell Kummen, Chanelle Peloso, Mary Black, Patti Allan, Ken Camroux, Rebecca Toolan, Brenda McDonald, Gina Stockdale. CAN/USA: English/Color/46m. Front Street Pictures/Haunting Hour Productions.

In this 2-part season premiere, Cristen and her brother Mike learn something unexpected about their Grandfather during a visit to his retirement community, Sunset Estates. It seems residents only come out at night—and they'd love to have the kids over for dinner!

The Ray Bradbury Theater – *"The Man Upstairs"*

USA Network/Global. Mar 5, 1988 (S03E05). Horror/Sci-Fi. D: Alain Bonnot. W: Ray Bradbury. C: Adam Negley, Féodor Atkine ⚥, Micheline Presle, Henri Poirier, Kate Hardie. CAN/FRA: English/Color/25m. Atlantis Films/Granada Television International/ Wilcox Productions Inc.

Douglas is suspicious of the new hotel lodger, Mr. Koberman; he sleeps during the day, has an aversion to silver and sunlight, and has arrived in Paris at a time when young women are mysteriously vanishing. After a girl is found dead, white as snow and drained of blood, Douglas suspects that Koberman is a vampire.

A strange story with an ambiguous ending that begs the question, who's terrifying whom? Douglas, on one hand, knows of Koberman's aversion to silver and sunlight, yet he goes out of his way to pester him with both. Is Koberman actually a vampire, or just someone who, in his travels, discovered a means to extend his life? Douglas ultimately kills Koberman by slicing him open while he sleeps; he removes some sort of endosymbiotic organism, and then fills Koberman's body cavity with silver coins. Since the man is never shown to be more than just a peculiar person with odd health issues—who happens to be forty going on one hundred and twenty-five—I vote for Douglas as the real monster in this tale.

Read All About It! – "An Evil Smile"

TVO. Oct 30, 1983 (S02E08). Education/Literature. D: Jeremy Pollock. W: Clive Endersby. C: David Craig Collard, Lydia Zajc, Michael Dwyer, Edwina Follows, A. Frank Ruffo ⚲, Robert Windsor. CAN: English/Color/15m. TV Ontario.

This educational series taught kids about history, reading and writing. In this episode, teenagers Lynne and Alex are trying to find the Book Destroyer, who's attempting to erase all villains from classic literature; in the process, the stories are inadvertently eradicated forever. They discover the home of Count Dracula, who offers to assist them in their quest. The teens are impressed by Dracula's cooperation, that is, until sunset—when the vampire has a change of heart.

Dracula, despite his harmless façade—he even belts out a catchy tune about good storytelling—stays true to his nature. He traps the kids and tries to put the bite on them, but the Book Destroyer intervenes; the poor Count is erased from existence before he can do the deed.

Reaper – "I Want My Baby Back"

The CW. Mar 31, 2009 (S02E05). Comedy/Drama. D: John Fortenberry. W: Thomas Schnauz. C: Bret Harrison, Tyler Labine, Rick Gonzalez, Missy Peregrym, Ray Wise, Heather Doerksen ⚲, Ken Marino. CAN/USA: English/Color/42m. The Mark Gordon Company/Fazekas & Butters.

After Sam captures the escaped soul of Tracy Reid, a self-proclaimed vampire, it turns out she had an IBOH—an intentional birth out of hell—and produced a daughter. Faced with this unexpected turn of events, Sam must find a way to protect Reid's baby before the Devil forces him to claim the infant's soul.

An excellent episode from an equally great (but short lived) supernatural series. Although the vampire arc shares screen time with several other sub-plots, it still results in an entertaining story that includes a nod to *Buffy the Vampire Slayer* (1997).

Relic Hunter – "Possessed"

Syndicated. May 8, 2000 (S01E20). Action/Adventure. D: Jean-Pierre Prévost. W: Rob Gilmer. C: Tia Carrere, Christien Anholt, Lindy Booth, Zeta Graff ⚲, Jonathan Firth, Jane March. CAN/FRA/GER/USA: English/Color/43m. Fireworks Entertainment/Gaumont Télévision/M6 Métropole Télévision.

Sydney and Nigel travel to Brussels at the behest of Eric Dalt, an author who believes his girlfriend is part of an ancient Lamae cult, and is slowly killing him. Complications arise when Nigel falls under the spell of a cult member, which leaves Sydney on her own to find the sacred sundial of Zeus—the only object that can save the two men.

The story is a little over the top, but nothing out of the ordinary for this series. The cult members are somewhat trite, but their leader—an ancient bloodsucker named Emmanuelle—is a seductive beauty. As is the case with most TV vampire villains, she's killed way too easily.

Relic Hunter – "Vampire's Kiss"

Syndicated. Oct 29, 2001 (S03E07). Action/Adventure. D: Ian Toynton. W: M.A. Lovretta. C: Tia Carrere, Christien Anholt, Tanja Reichert, Adrian Paul ⚲, Lawrence Bayne. CAN/FRA/GER/USA: English/Color/60m. Fireworks Entertainment/Gaumont Télévision/M6 Métropole Télévision.

Gothic romance novelist Lucas Blackmer asks Sydney to help recover a legendary chalice that once belonged to Vlad Țepeș—an object said to infuse its bearer with vampiric powers. But Nigel and Karen suspect the author may be a bloodsucker himself, after they discover that he wears contact lenses, uses SPF-50 sunblock, and his residence "looks like the Halloween aisle at Wal-Mart."

One of the better vampire episodes, with a well-plotted "is he or isn't he a vampire" story, featuring some funny scenes with Nigel and Karen as they try to figure out if the author really is a vampire. Of course the tale gets no props for once again tying Vlad Țepeș to his fictional counterpart, but even this fiasco isn't enough to deter from one's enjoyment.

Renegade – "Blood Hunt"

USA Network. Mar 7, 1997 (S05E18). Action/Adventure. D: Bruce Kessler. W: Richard Gilbert Hill. C: Lorenzo Lamas, Branscombe Richmond, Stephen J. Cannell, Virginya Keehne, Madison Mason, Scott N. Stevens, Ash Adams, Allison Dunbar. USA: English/Color/42m. Renegade TV Enterprises.

Framed for a murder he didn't commit, Reno Raines goes on the run while he attempts to clear his name, and teams up with a bounty hunter to help those in need. In this episode, Raines comes to the aid of a runaway, who claims she's being pursued by a vampire.

Road to Avonlea – "After the Honeymoon"

CBC. Mar 15, 1992 (S03E10). Drama/Family. D: Don McBrearty. W: Janet MacLean. C: Sarah Polley, R.H. Thomson, Jackie Burroughs, Kate Nelligan ⚲, Zachary Bennett ⚲. CAN/USA: English/Color/46m. Rose Cottage Productions Inc./Sullivan Films Inc./CBC.

Jasper's new "vampire spectrum" experiments have garnered the attention of Sydney Carver, a quirky scientist who travels to Avonlea to observe his bat studies first-hand. Sara and Felix are convinced that the woman is a vampire, and that she plans to turn Jasper into a creature of the night.

A good story with a quirky guest character and a fun subplot involving the kids as they become hunters, believing that vampires have invaded their town. The only issue I have with this story is the fact that Felix mentions Vlad the Impaler, certainly an anachronism, since this fifteenth century prince of Wallachia would have been unknown to Western society in the early 1900s.

📺 When Sara is surprised by Felix—who's dressed as a vampire and wearing an opera cape and fake fangs—she's reading aloud from Chapter 2 of the novel *Dracula* by Bram Stoker.

Round the Twist – "Quivering Heap"

ABC (AUS). Jun 12, 1993 (S02E11). Comedy/Family. D: Esben Storm. W: Paul Jennings, Esben Storm. C: Ben Thomas ☥, Jeffrey Walker ☥, Joelene Crnogorac, Richard Moir, Jasper Bagg ☥, John Frawley, Richard Young ☥. AUS: English/Color/20m. Australian Children's Television Foundation.

Pete's lead role in the school's production of Dracula has Gribbs up in arms, especially since the character gets to bite Fiona on the neck—so he keeps Pete from attending opening night and takes over the part. But the tables are turned after Pete meets a ghost who needs to give someone a really good scare, and the school play offers the perfect opportunity for the apparition to get his wish—and for Gribbs to get a taste of his own medicine. It's an amusing story for kids where the bully gets what's coming, although Pete's smug attitude towards getting the role results in much less sympathy for him once he loses it to Gribbs.

Sabrina, the Teenage Witch – "Really Big Season Opener"

ABC. Oct 5, 2001 (S06E01). Comedy/Family. D: Andrew Tsao. W: Jon Vandergriff. C: Melissa Joan Hart, Caroline Rhea, Beth Broderick, Nick Bakay, Trevor Lissauer, Elisa Donovan, Soleil Moon Frye, Sisqó ☥, Winston Story ☥. USA: English/Color/22m. Warner Bros. Television.

Sabrina and Miles are having a hard time casting the lead role for their new student horror film, so they place an ad "desperately seeking a vampire," hoping to land an experienced actor between jobs. The man who responds, Vladimir Kortensky, shows up already in character, and he seems to play the part all too well.

The audition scenes for the vampire are the highlight of this episode, as are Vladimir's interactions with the other actors. But the story digresses as Sabrina channels Buffy to battle the undead, squaring off in ridiculous fight scenes inspired by *The Matrix*—a likely parody that falls flat. The episode culminates in a horrible musical number, with cheerleaders dancing around a coffin while they lip synch to an instantly-forgettable pop song.

St. Elsewhere – "Loss of Power"

NBC. Dec 11, 1985 (S04E10). Drama/Medical. D: Mark Tinker. W: Tom Fontana, John Masius, Bruce Paltrow. C: Ed Flanders, William Daniels, Norman Lloyd, Ed Begley Jr., Stephen Furst, Mark Harmon, Howie Mandel, David Morse. USA: English/Color/47m. MTM Productions.

Medical drama series that takes place at St. Eligius, a fictional teaching hospital in Boston. In this episode, while the other doctors deal with various problems during a city-wide blackout, Axelrod and Morrison help a man who believes he's a vampire.

Scrubs – "My Missed Perception" / "My Cabbage" / "My Fallen Idol" / "My Urologist"

NBC. Jan 17/Feb 28/May 2/May 16, 2006 (S05E06/12/21/23). Comedy/Drama. D: Bill Lawrence, John Inwood. W: Kevin Biegel, Ryan Levin. C: Zach Braff ♀, Sarah Chalke, Donald Faison ♀, Neil Flynn, Ken Jenkins, John C. McGinley, Judy Reyes. USA: English/Color/88m. Doozer/Touchstone Television.

🦇 🦇 🦇

Over the course of Season 5, J.D. hints at a screenplay he's been working on—*Dr. Acula*—which follows the misadventures of a bloodthirsty vampire whose name, of course, alludes to *Dracula*. There are a handful of fantasy sequences with J.D. as the titular vampire, and the final segment—and certainly the best—is a scene between J.D. and Turk, who deems his role as a pimp is borderline racist, and ends up forcing J.D. to let him be the vampire.

The Secret Adventures of Jules Verne – "Rockets of the Dead"

Syndicated. Jul 2, 2000 (S01E03). Action/Adventure. D: Pierre de Lespinois. W: Brian Finch. C: Francesca Hunt, Chris Demetral, Michael Praed, Patrick Duffy ♀, Michel Courtemanche. CAN/UK: English/Color/42m. Filmline International/Talisman Crest.

🦇 🦇 🦇

Rebecca Fogg goes undercover to attract the attention of Angelo Rimini, the Duke of Carpathia, who is the prime suspect in the recent murder of a British diplomat. After Rimini returns to his castle with Rebecca in tow, she discovers he's a vampire—but they fall in love. Rimini's undead army is about to attack every capital in Europe, which will spread vampirism throughout the continent—and in this new world, he'll reign as King with Rebecca at his side.

In this mythology, vampires cannot turn into bats—and therefore cannot travel very quickly—so Rimini steals a formula for a powerful explosive. It fuels the rockets that take his undead army to the skies; this results in a thousand opera-caped vampires—with jet packs strapped to their backs—flying towards every major European center. Yes, it's as silly as it sounds, but it's really just a device to drive the plot; the real story is the romance between the vampire Rimini and Agent Fogg. I really enjoyed this one, and I don't usually gravitate towards mushy vampire romances. It's quite well-written, and the strong acting makes up for a few campy bloodsucker moments. Think of it as a steampunk romance, with a lead vampire portrayed in the same vein as Frank Langella's performance in *Dracula* (1979).

Secret Diary of a Call Girl – Ep. #4.7

ITV2. Mar 15, 2011 (S04E07). Drama/Romance. D: Samuel Donovan. W: Dan Sefton. C: Billie Piper, Paul Nicholls, Iddo Goldberg, Lily James, Karl Dobby, Alex Lowe ♀. UK: English/Color/30m. Silver Apples Media/Tiger Aspect Productions.

Follows the adventures of Hannah Baxter, who lives a secret life as a high-class call girl named "Belle." In this episode, she takes part in a vampire role play with a new client, but things get complicated after the man dies in bed.

Shades of Darkness – "Feet Foremost"

BBC One. Jun 10, 1983 (S01E03). Horror/Suspense. D: Gordon Flemyng. W: Alan Plater, L.P. Hartley. C: Jeremy Kemp, Joanna Van Gyseghem, Heather Chasen, Peter Machin, Carol Royle. UK: English/Color/60m. Granada Television.

Real estate tycoon Charles Ampleforth buys Low Threshold Hall, a remote manor abandoned one hundred and fifty years ago over the belief that it was haunted by the ghost of Lady Elinor, a sixteen-year-old newlywed who was murdered by her husband. Local legend claims she killed the previous occupants one by one, by possessing them and then infecting their bodies with a deadly disease. Ampleforth jokes that considering the price he paid for the estate, there *should* be a decent ghost inside—but there may be truth to the tale after one of his guests becomes infected by a strange illness. This episode was rebroadcast in 1984 on PBS in the United States (under the *Mystery!* banner), and is a remake of the story first presented in the UK series *Mystery and Imagination* (1968).

The term "feet foremost" means "feet first," and superstition dictates that this is how a corpse should be carried out of a home—so it won't find its way back. In some folklore, if a child is born feet foremost, it will become a vampire.

She-Wolf of London – "Habeas Corpses"

Syndicated. Mar 13, 1991 (S01E16). Comedy/Crime. D: Chuck Bowman. W: William Rabkin, Lee Goldberg. C: Kate Hodge, Neil Dickson, Dan Gilvezan, Barry Van Dyke ☥, Marta DuBois ☥, Sandra Kerns ☥, David Sage ☥. USA: English/Color/47m. Finnegan-Pinchuk/MTE.

Originally called *Love & Curses,* this series follows American student Randi Wallace, who was studying overseas in London when she was attacked by a werewolf. Her mentor, Professor Ian Matheson, now helps her search for a cure. In this episode, a man claims that his ex-wife and her lawyers are draining him dry—then he keels over dead from exsanguination. Ian and Randi go undercover to infiltrate the law firm, which appears to be run by vampires.

An example of one of those cheesy, image-conscious series that aired during this period, with bad hair and even worse fashion sense. Still, this one has a few good one-liners, and a story about lawyers as vampires *does* seem like a natural fit.

Sledge Hammer! – "Last of the Red Hot Vampires"

ABC. Nov 19, 1987 (S02E09). Comedy/Family. D: Bill Bixby. W: Alan Spencer. C: David Rasche, Anne-Marie Martin, Harrison Page, Bernie Kopell ☥, Deborah Wakeham, Bud Cort ☥, Greta Blackburn. USA: English/Color/25m. Alan Spencer Productions/New World Television.

Elderly horror actor Vincent Lagarski dies shortly after being fired from the set of his latest film, *Touch of the Vampire.* After the film's director and lead actress turn up dead, their bodies drained of blood, many believe that Lagarski has returned from the grave.

Another great episode from this gem of a series from the mid-1980s, with a wonderful guest-starring performance from Bernie Kopell, who does a fitting tribute to Bela Lugosi. This story has a lot to say about aging movie stars and their legacy on-screen—not to mention that it emphasizes that movie producers are the worst vampires of them all.

📺 This episode is dedicated to "Mr. Blasko," as in Béla Blaskó, better known as Bela Lugosi.

Sliders – "Stoker"

FOX. May 9, 1997 (S03E24). Adventure/Sci-Fi. D: Jerry O'Connell. W: Josef Anderson. C: Jerry O'Connell, Sabrina Lloyd, Cleavant Derricks, Kari Wuhrer, Ryan Alosio ☥, Duff McKagan ☥, Danny Masterson, Tommy Chong. USA: English/Color/45m. St. Clare Entertainment/Universal TV.

Series follows a group of interstellar travelers who use a special device to "slide" from one parallel dimension to another via wormholes; each world they visit is different than the Earth they know. In this episode, Wade falls for Morgan, the lead singer of "Stoker"—a rock band implicated in the disappearance of several women. Her friends fear for her safety, and rightly so: the musicians are all vampires.

On this world, *Dracula* was never written by Bram Stoker, but he still has influence on the story itself; many character names were lifted from the novel, and the band is named after the author. The acting is the weakest part of this production, and some scenes are B-movie bad; the vampire extras are the worst of the lot, and even this diehard fan rallied for their demise.

Smallville – "Thirst"

WB. Oct 27, 2005 (S05E05). Adventure/Fantasy. D: Paul Shapiro. W: Steven S. DeKnight. C: Tom Welling, Kristin Kreuk ☥, Michael Rosenbaum, Allison Mack, Brooke Nevin ☥, James Marsters. USA: English/Color/42m. Tollin Robbins Productions/Smallville Films.

Lana pledges to the Tri Psi Sorority at Metropolis University, unaware that it's a sisterhood of bloodthirsty vampires—and she joins their ranks. As Clark looks for a means to cure Lana of her affliction, the investigation leads to LuthorCorp and the mysterious "Project 1138."

When we learn that the sorority is headed by "Buffy Sanders," it's pretty clear that the episode isn't going to take itself too seriously. Unfortunately it's filled with stereotypes, from the vapid vampires to the vacuous sorority girls, and when it fails to be funny, we're reminded that "dying is easy, but comedy is hard." For example, when Milton Fine tells Clark that "there are no such thing as vampires," we're expected to find this amusing, since Fine is played by James Marsters, who of course starred as Spike in *Buffy the Vampire Slayer* (1997). The writer previously worked on both

Buffy and *Angel,* but the type of humor that worked so well in those series fails miserably here.

So Weird – "Vampire"

Disney. May 20, 2000 (S02E22). Family/Mystery. D: Patrick Williams. W: Jay Bryant. C: Cara DeLizia, Patrick Levis, Mackenzie Phillips, David Paetkau ☥, Kett Turton ☥, Melissa Barker-Sauer ☥, Nicole McKay ☥. USA: English/Color/24m. Sugar Entertainment/Fair Dinkum Productions/Disney.

Series follows siblings Fiona and Jack, who tour across the country with their rock star mom. In this episode, Jack has been invited to the headquarters of OSSN, a nationwide online study group that plans to induct him as a full member. Fi discovers that the organization is actually based in Romania, and is a front for a network of modern-day vampires that want to expand their ranks.

These vampires are sinister, but there is one good guy (of course) who's fighting his inner bloodsucker; he helps the family escape the clutches of the OSSN. I like the idea of vampires using the Internet to seek out the best and brightest to expand their numbers, although two prominent members are pretty dim-witted and don't quite fit the profile—so there's a bit of a mixed message here. Regretfully, during an opening vignette, Fi claims the original vampire was Vlad Țepeș—but then states that he didn't actually drink blood, have fangs, or sleep in a coffin. Huh?

📺 The program includes a still of Bela Lugosi as Dracula from the 1931 film—with fangs digitally added to the picture! Ridiculous! Lugosi never wore them when he portrayed Dracula. It was Christopher Lee and the 1958 Hammer production *Horror of Dracula* that first gave the Count his fangs on film (discounting, of course, *Nosferatu, Eine Symphonie des Garuens*).

Starsky & Hutch – "The Vampire"

ABC. Oct 30, 1976 (S02E07). Crime/Drama. D: Bob Kelljan. W: Michael Grais, Mark Victor. C: David Soul, Paul Michael Glaser, Antonio Fargas, John Saxon ☥, Phil Leeds, G.W. Bailey, Suzanne Somers. USA: English/Color/50m. Spelling-Goldberg Productions.

Series follows Starsky and Hutch, two police detectives in fictional Bay City, California. In this episode, victims in a series of bizarre murders are strangled and then drained of blood through two marks on the neck. Starsky is convinced they're dealing with a bona fide vampire.

When you have two characters playing off of one another—where one believes in vampires and the other does not—you're guaranteed some very funny scenes. Such is the case in *Quantum Leap's* "Blood Moon," and the same is true for this story. Starsky's growing obsession with the undead is a joy to watch, as is Hutch's dismissal of his partner's antics. The "vampire" in this tale, René Nadasy, has been killing women to collect their blood, perhaps to use in a sacrifice to resurrect his dead wife (it's never fully explained). Unfortunately, this character is very confusing. He certainly acts like a bloodsucker when he's attacking his victims: he bares fangs, wears a cape, and has a seemingly heightened agility. But when he's his "normal" self, he's reserved, fangless, and walks with a limp. Is he a real vampire, or just a psychotic devil worshiper, distraught over losing his wife and looking for any means to bring her back? It's never made clear, and the episode ends with too many unanswered questions—but it's still an enjoyable journey.

📺 The name "René Nadasy" may allude to Count Ferenc Nádasdy, the husband of Elizabeth Báthory—the sixteenth century Hungarian "blood countess" considered to be the most prolific female serial killer in history.

Struck by Lightning - "The Movie"

CBS. Oct 3, 1979 (S01E03). Comedy/Family. D: Joe Zwicke. W: Michael Russnow. C: Jeffrey Kramer, Jack Elam, Jeff Cotler, Millie Slavin, Bill Erwin, Richard Stahl, Jonathan Goldsmith ☥, Keene Curtis. USA: English/Color/30m. Fellows-Keegan Company/Paramount Television.

The series follows a high school science teacher named Ted Stein, who inherits his grandfather's Inn, an eighteenth century lodge that had fallen into disrepair. Ted learns that he's the great-great-grandson of the infamous Doctor Frankenstein, and the creepy caretaker who resides at the Inn—who goes by the name of Frank—is actually the monster that his ancestor created over two hundred and thirty years ago. In this episode, the Inn is being used as a set for a horror film, and Frank thinks that the Dracula character in the movie is the real deal.

Superboy - "Young Dracula" / "Run, Dracula, Run"

Syndicated. Oct 28, 1989/Feb 3, 1990 (S02E04/16). Adventure/Sci-Fi. D: David Nutter, Richard J. Lewis. W: Ilya Salkind, Cary Bates. C: Gerard Christopher, Stacy Haiduk, Ilan Mitchell-Smith, Kevin Bernhardt ☥, Lloyd Bochner ☥. USA: English/Color/44m. Alexander & Ilya Salkind/Cantharus Productions N.V.

In this two-part story, Dr. Byron Shelley is a vampire on the run, hiding out from his father—Count Dracula—who has sent a more powerful bloodsucker to bring his son back home. The doctor is a good man who believes that vampirism is a disease and ultimately curable, and to this end, he's created a serum that controls some aspects of his affliction. But Shelley reverts to his old vampire self after his medicine is stolen, and preys upon Lana and Superboy.

The first episode has a couple of fun moments, but it's plagued by poor acting and oddball storytelling, issues that were prevalent throughout this series. Sadly, the vampire sent to retrieve Shelley is as stereotypical as you can get, and his fight scenes are unintentionally laugh-inducing. The second installment is a vast improvement, but unfortunately the audience never gets to see Dracula—certainly a missed opportunity—yet the resolution to the story is still a satisfactory one. (On a positive note, Shelley is never cured of his affliction.)

📺 David Nutter directed some of the more popular episodes of *The X Files*, including "2Shy," a story about a fat-sucking vampire.

Supernatural (UK) – "Dorabella"

BBC One. Aug 6, 1977 (S01E08). Horror/Suspense. D: Simon Langton. W: Robert Muller. C: Jeremy Clyde, David Robb ☥, Ania Marson ☥, John Justin ☥, Esmond Knight, Jonathan Hyde. UK: English/Color/52m. BBC.

This anthology series featured stories of vampires, werewolves, ghosts and other beings; supernatural tales told by prospective members trying to gain entry into the secret society called "The Club of the Damned." In this episode, a man recounts the tale of an adventure with a friend, where the two traveled across Europe in search of the unusual and the forbidden. On one fateful evening they met a beguiling young woman named Dorabella, who enticed them to travel North to her family's remote estate—but terror and death followed in their wake.

Although there is very little blood and no fangs to be found, this episode is still very engaging. The vampires are of the traditional sort, who use the façade of romance to capture their prey. One noteworthy scene has a bard named Amadeus reciting the last five stanzas of "We Are Seven" by William Wordsworth, first published in 1798. This haunting poem works quite well in the context of a vampire tale.

Supernatural – "Dead Man's Blood"

The CW. Apr 20, 2006 (S01E20). Horror/Thriller. D: Tony Wharmby. W: Cathryn Humphris, John Shiban. C: Jared Padalecki, Jensen Ackles, Jeffrey Dean Morgan, Warren Christie ☥, Anne Openshaw ☥. USA: English/Color/43m. Kripke Enterprises/Wonderland Sound and Vision.

As Sam and Dean look into the suspicious death of a Hunter named Daniel Elkins, their father unexpectedly shows up to join the investigation. Elkins had in his possession an antique Colt handgun, which legend says has the ability to kill any supernatural being—but it's now in the possession of the vampires that killed him. The three must face down the nest of bloodsuckers to retrieve the mystical gun, which John needs to kill the demon that murdered his wife.

A jam-packed episode that introduces the vampire lore for the series, as well as the importance of the Colt handgun; it even finds time to delve deeper into the complex relationship between John Winchester and his two sons. The vampires are truly evil, yet the writers give them a sympathetic edge, an idea that is further explored in the episode "Bloodlust."

📺 Elements of this story were incorporated into "Saikai: Reunion," the fourteenth episode from the Japanese OVA anime series *Supernatural: The Animation*.

Supernatural – "Bloodlust"

The CW. Oct 12, 2006 (S02E03). Horror/Thriller. D: Robert Singer. W: Sera Gamble. C: Jared Padalecki, Jensen Ackles, Sterling K. Brown, Amber Benson ☥, Samantha Ferris, Ty Olsson ☥, Derek McIver. USA: English/Color/43m. Kripke Enterprises/Wonderland Sound and Vision.

Sam and Dean head to Red Lodge, Montana, to investigate a rash of cattle mutilations and two suspicious murders. They initially believe that a satanic cult may be behind the killings, but after examining one of the victims, they realize that vampires are to blame. They team up with a Hunter named Gordon Walker, but working alongside him is not at all what they expected; Walker may be as much a danger to them as he is to the creatures he's after.

An interesting episode where the vampires aren't necessarily the most evil characters in the story. Amber Benson, who played Tara in the *Buffy the Vampire Slayer* TV series, disappears into the role of vampire matriarch Lenore. To torture the undead, Walker uses the blood of a dead man; it effectively acts like an acid, and burns the vampire's skin—and causes a great deal of pain in the process. This lore was first introduced in the Season 1 episode "Dead Man's Blood."

This story was loosely adapted as "Yajuu no Chi: Savage Blood," the fifth episode from the Japanese OVA *anime* series *Supernatural: The Animation*.

Supernatural – "Fresh Blood"

The CW. Nov 15, 2007 (S03E07). Horror/Thriller. D: Kim Manners. W: Sera Gamble. C: Jared Padalecki, Jensen Ackles, Lauren Cohan, Sterling K. Brown ✞, Michael Massee, Matthew Humphreys ✞, Mercedes McNab ✞. USA: English/Color/41m. Kripke Enterprises/Wonderland Sound and Vision.

A bloodsucker has been dealing a new drug at a local club—vampire blood—and he's already turned at least one woman into one of his kind. But she doesn't understand what she's become, and the bodies are piling up as she tries to satiate her unrestricted lust for blood. As the Winchester brothers hunt down this reckless vampire and the one who created her, rogue Hunter Gordon Walker is out of jail and out for some blood of his own. He wants to kill Sam, because he thinks the man is the anti-Christ.

In this intense and often gruesome episode, the creators continue to weave their own take on vampire mythology, with yet another example of an evil but sympathetic bloodsucker. The man believes he's a dying breed, and is only creating more like him because Hunters have killed off his entire "family." The story also drives home the point that being bitten by a vampire won't turn you into one—their blood must be taken in directly, akin to a viral infection, after which the human slowly takes on the aspects of the vampire. (An important plot device used here, as well as in a later episode from the sixth season.) This episode is a highlight of Season 3, and one of the best episodes of the entire series run.

Mercedes McNab is the second alumnus of the *Buffy the Vampire Slayer* series to appear on *Supernatural* as a vampire; the first was Amber Benson (Tara from *Buffy*). McNab, who played the effervescent blonde vampire Harmony in *Buffy* (and in the spin-off series, *Angel*) fares well in a dramatic turn, as a woman who made a wrong choice and paid the ultimate price for her mistake.

Supernatural – "Monster Movie"

The CW. Oct 16, 2008 (S04E05). Horror/Thriller. D: Robert Singer. W: Ben Edlund. C: Jared Padalecki, Jensen Ackles, Todd Stashwick ☥, Melinda Sward, Holly E. Dignard, Michael Eklund, Gary Chalk. USA: English/B&W/43m. Kripke Enterprises/Wonderland Sound and Vision.

Sam and Dean travel to Pennsylvania to investigate a vampire attack, which turns into an honest to goodness monster hunt after a second victim appears to have been killed by a werewolf. They discover that the creatures are not acting as expected, and the eyewitness accounts describe the monsters as if they were straight out of a horror movie. They're actually dealing with a shape shifter that's a fan of the classic monsters of the silver screen, and the brothers become unwilling participants in the creature's own version of a monster movie.

Series that deal with dramatic, life-and-death situations sometimes take a break to offer up a more light-hearted, non-canon episode that is not to be taken seriously—such is the case with this story. In homage to the classic Universal horror films, this episode is shot in glorious black and white, a modern story told through the lens of these iconic movies. The shape shifter character is a sympathetic one; he spends most of the time in the guise of a vampire, and his story plays out as a mix of *Frankenstein* and *Dracula*. This humorous tale is in the same vein as *The X Files* episode "Bad Blood" (1998), both of which are prime examples of stand-alone episodes that still hold up after repeated viewings.

📺 The Season 6 episode "Clap Your Hands If You Believe" (2010) dealt with suspected alien abductions, and took a similar tongue-in-cheek approach in homage to the TV series *The X Files*.

Supernatural – "Free To Be You and Me"

The CW. Sep 24, 2009 (S05E03). Horror/Thriller. D: J. Miller Tobin. W: Jeremy Carver. C: Jared Padalecki, Jensen Ackles, Misha Collins, Adrianne Palicki, Jim Beaver, Mark Pellegrino, Demore Barnes, Ed Welch ☥. USA: English/Color/42m. Kripke Enterprises/Wonderland Sound and Vision.

The Winchester brothers go their separate ways; Sam gives up hunting in an attempt to escape his destiny, while Dean continues his search for the archangel Raphael. There's minor bloodsucker content here: an opening montage shows Dean investigating a case of exsanguination. Later, as he's about to destroy the vampire, Dean quips, "Eat it, Twilight!"

📺 During Seasons 4 and 5, Sam becomes addicted to demon blood, which affects the evil inside of him and boosts his psychokinetic powers; he often uses these enhanced abilities to exorcise demons from their human hosts.

Supernatural - "Live Free or Twihard"

The CW. Oct 22, 2010 (S06E05). Horror/Thriller. D: Rod Hardy. W: Brett Matthews. C: Jared Padalecki, Jensen Ackles ♀, Cindy Sampson, Mitch Pileggi, Nicholas Elia, Joseph D. Reitman ♀, Elise Gatien ♀. USA: English/Color/42m. Kripke Enterprises/Wonderland Sound and Vision.

After seven teenage girls go missing in as many days, Sam and Dean believe they're dealing with a nest of vampires that are luring naïve young women—by impersonating the romantic bloodsucker so common in popular culture. Dean becomes infected and discovers the group's master plan: they're actively increasing their ranks to build up an army, and to make matters worse, they're no longer afraid of Hunters.

Another great vampire episode that starts with a humorous dig at the *Twilight* franchise, but becomes much darker once Dean is infected. He learns a horrible truth about Sam, which plays into the main story arc of the season. Included are some brief glimpses of the Alpha vampire—the oldest and first of its kind—which will feature prominently in a later episode.

Supernatural - "Family Matters"

The CW. Nov 5, 2010 (S06E07). Horror/Thriller. D: Guy Bee. W: Andrew Dabb, Daniel Loflin. C: Jared Padalecki, Jensen Ackles, Misha Collins, Mitch Pileggi, Corin Nemec, Jessica Heafey, Rick Worthy ♀. USA: English/Color/42m. Kripke Enterprises/Wonderland Sound and Vision.

After learning that Samuel Campbell and his group have discovered the location of the Alpha vampire, Sam and Dean tag along to kill the bloodsucker—but the hunt goes horribly wrong. Sam confesses to Dean that their grandfather has actually been capturing—not killing—the Alpha monsters, in order to interrogate them for some unknown reason.

This would have been an outstanding episode were it not for the overwrought family drama and laughable dialogue, which at times seems straight out of a B-grade horror film. Although the Alpha vampire is a badass and gets some major screen time, surprisingly—despite being a centuries-old bloodsucker—he still can't stave off the effects of "Dead Man's Blood." As for the reason behind Samuel Campbell's deception, it turns out he's working for a major demon character, in a story arc that will play out over the next couple of episodes.

📺 The Alpha vampire makes one final, brief cameo in the excellent episode "Caged Heat," where it's assumed that he's been killed by the angel Castiel—along with all the other creatures captured by Samuel Campbell.

Supernatural - "Alex Annie Alexis Ann"

The CW. Apr 22, 2014 (S09E19). Horror/Thriller. D: Stefan Pleszczynski. W: Robert Berens. C: Jared Padalecki, Jensen Ackles, Kim Rhodes, Katherine Ramdeen, Ashley Crow ♀, Reilly Dolman, Greyston Holt, Jarrett Knowles ♀, Liam Sproule ♀, Bill Marchant, Alexis Kellum-Creer. USA: English/Color/42m. Kripke Enterprises/Wonderland Sound and Vision.

Sheriff Jody Mills summons Sam and Dean to Sioux Falls after a teenager brought to her police station was attacked by a vampire in the holding cell—and the young girl knew the assailant. Turns out she is on the run from a nest of vampires, who had been holding her captive for almost eight years, and she had been repeatedly used to lure in unsuspecting victims for her adoptive undead family to feed on. Unwilling to reveal the location of the nest, as if she were suffering from some sort of vampiric Stockholm syndrome, the girl is taken by the Sheriff into hiding while Sam and Dean search for the bloodsuckers. But the Winchesters are unable to find the vampires, because they're well on their way to tracking down the girl and taking back what's theirs.

Supernatural – "Bloodlines"

The CW. Apr 29, 2014 (S09E20). Horror/Thriller. D: Robert Singer. W: Andrew Dabb. C: Jared Padalecki, Jensen Ackles, Lucien Laviscount, Nathaniel Buzolic, Sean Faris, Melissa Roxburgh, Danielle Savre, Stephen Martines, Bryce Johnson, Erinn Westbrook, Michael Rogers, Larry Hoe. USA: English/Color/42m. Kripke Enterprises/Wonderland Sound and Vision.

Ennis Roth planned a night to remember with his girlfriend, and was about to propose marriage when they were attacked—and she died in his arms. His claim that the assailant was some sort of monster was enough to gain the attention of the Winchester brothers, who soon discover that Chicago is secretly being run by five monster families, including werewolves, shapeshifters, and the djinn. Bent on revenge, Ennis vows to find the thing responsible for killing his girlfriend, which forces Sam and Dean to reveal who they really are, and what the young man is truly going to be facing.

Vampires play a background role in this tale of rival monster families vying for control of Chicago. This episode had been planned as a backdoor pilot for a *Supernatural* spin-off series, but was so poorly received that the idea died with this one-off story, and it's easy to see why. The overall premise involving the warring families is far too derivative of *Kindred: The Embraced*, substituting vampire clans with monster families. And the major story arc involving forbidden love between a werewolf and a shapeshifter hints at an otherworldly *West Side Story* (not to mention *Twilight*). Clearly they were aiming for something that would capture the interest of *The Vampire Diaries* fans, but the young adult angle did not mesh well with the brutal, often horrific universe in which *Supernatural* is set. Producers tried a handful of such pilots, none of which really caught on. My vote is to give Sheriffs Jody Mills and Donna Hanscum their own spin-off! These are two of the strongest, and most interesting, female characters that have been written into the show over the past few seasons—and are more than capable of carrying their own series.

Supernatural – "Hibbing 911"

The CW. Dec 2, 2014 (S10E08). Horror/Thriller. D: Tim Andrew. W: Jenny Klein, Phil Sgriccia. C: Jared Padalecki, Jensen Ackles, Kim Rhodes, Briana Buckmaster, Morgan Taylor Campbell ⚢, Fred Ewanuick ⚢, Aren Buchholz, Ellie Harvie, Michael Karl Richards, Andy Nez, Cody Wells ⚢, Matthew Mylrea ⚢. USA: English/Color/42m. Kripke Enterprises/Wonderland Sound and Vision.

Sheriff Jody Mills reluctantly attends a retreat for police officers, where she meets Sheriff Donna

Hanscum, unaware that they have mutual friends: the Winchester brothers. Sam and Dean are quickly summoned after a body is discovered with the throat torn out, and the culprit is a vampire—who also happens to be one of the officers among the group. But they soon realize that this bloodsucker may not be the true killer, but rather someone from his past who is looking to reconnect after he severed ties with them decades earlier.

Supernatural – "Brother's Keeper"

The CW. May 20, 2015 (S10E23). Horror/Thriller. D: Phil Sgriccia. W: Jeremy Carver. C: Jared Padalecki, Jensen Ackles, Misha Collins, Mark A. Sheppard, Ruth Connell, Julian Richings, Robert Moloney, Roger Haskett, Fiona Hogan, Emilija Baranac, Darren Mann, Jeffrey C.R. Wallace, Lucas David Morgan ☥. USA: English/Color/42m. Kripke Enterprises/Wonderland Sound and Vision.

In this finale episode of the tenth season, Sam continues searching for a cure for Dean's destructive behavior, while his brother takes on a case with a fellow Hunter named Rudy. And the affect that the Mark of Cain is having on Dean comes to a head after Rudy is captured while investigating a vampire nest—and Dean attacks the bloodsuckers head-on, completely focused on the kill, with no concern for those in peril.

Supernatural – "Baby"

The CW. Oct 28, 2015 (S11E04). Horror/Thriller. D: Thomas J. Wright. W: Robbie Thompson. C: Jared Padalecki, Jensen Ackles, Misha Collins, Teach Grant ☥, Sarah-Jane Redmond, Matt Cohen, Danyella Angel, Catherine Jack, Megan Kaptein. USA: English/Color/42m. Kripke Enterprises/Wonderland Sound and Vision.

Sam and Dean come across a creature they've never seen before, which seems to feed on both human hearts and blood. At first believing it's some sort of werewolf-vampire hybrid, they soon learn it's actually a cross between a vampire and a ghoul—and it's very, very, hard to kill! To make matters worse, these creatures can completely pass for human, which makes them all the more difficult to hunt—and the monster they're after is someone they'd never suspect.

Supernatural – "Don't You Forget About Me"

The CW. Feb 3, 2016 (S11E12). Horror/Thriller. D: Stefan Pleszczynski. W: Nancy Won. C: Jared Padalecki, Jensen Ackles, Kim Rhodes, Kathryn Love Newton, Katherine Ramdeen, Ben Cotton ☥, Jedidiah Goodacre ☥, Ty Wood, Angela Palmer, Preston Vanderslice, Veena Sood, Merren McMahon. USA: English/Color/42m. Kripke Enterprises/Wonderland Sound and Vision.

Claire Novak, the daughter of the man that the angel Castiel has been using as a human vessel, has been living with Sheriff Jody Mills along with Alex Jones, the young woman who was rescued two years ago from a nest of vampires. Sam and Dean visit the trio after Claire starts causing mischief, believing that recent deaths in town were at the hands of monsters—and it seems that a vampire from Alex's past has come calling, bent on revenge.

The Super Mario Bros. Super Show! – "Bats in the Basement" / "Mario and the Beanstalk"

Syndicated. Sep 13, 1989 (S01E08). Adventure/Family. D: Dan Riba. W: George Atkins. C: Lou Albano, Danny Wells, Jim Ward ☥, Jeannie Elias, Harvey Atkin, John Stocker. USA: English/Color/22m. Binder Entertainment/DiC Entertainment/Nintendo of America Inc.

In the live-action segment "Bats in the Basement," the brothers host a foreign exchange student from Transylvania, Count Zoltan Dracula. Although they think he's a little odd—he arrived in a coffin, for instance—they just figure that everyone has their own peculiarities. After he racks up bills for withdrawals from the blood bank, eye wash for his red eyes, and dental floss for his big teeth, the brothers realize they're dealing with a vampire.

This segment has a number of fun moments, especially when the brothers look for ways to resolve their predicament. As they read through the book "How to Get Rid of a Vampire," the Count tells them flat out: "Just ask me to leave!"

📺 Jim Ward dons fangs once again in Episode 32, where he plays a vampire in the segment "Vampire Until Ready." Although he looks identical in both episodes, it's only here that he's referred to as Dracula.

The Super Mario Bros. Super Show! – "Vampire Until Ready" / "20,000 Koopas Under the Sea"

Syndicated. Oct 17, 1989 (S01E32). Adventure/Family. D: Dan Riba. W: David Bennett Carren, J. Larry Carroll. C: Lou Albano, Danny Wells, Jim Ward ☥, Jeannie Elias, Harvey Atkin, John Stocker. USA: English/Color/22m. Binder Entertainment/DiC Entertainment/Nintendo of America Inc.

In the live-action segment "Vampire Until Ready," Mario and Luigi hire an exterminator to get rid of a pesky bat. But the man is very odd; he wears a long, flowing cape, and speaks with a foreign accent. The brothers soon believe that the bat and the exterminator are one and the same—a vampire.

Harmless but enjoyable story for kids, where the Dracula-like vampire comes up with a scheme to meet new people: he infiltrates a house in bat form, with the hope that the occupants will call his exterminating service. He then arrives to save the day, and tries to make new friends while he's there.

Swamp Thing – "Powers of Darkness"

USA Network. Jul 17, 1992 (S03E02). Drama/Sci-Fi. D: Chuck Bowman. W: W. Reed Moran. C: Scott Garrison, Dick Durock, Jeremy Licht ☥, Bobbi Evors, Larry Manetti, Marc Macaulay, Donna Rosae ☥. USA: English/Color/24m. BBK Productions/Batfilm Productions Inc./DiC Enterprises Inc./MTE Inc.

Series follows Dr. Alec Holland, who was transformed into a swamp creature after his lab in the Louisiana bayou was sabotaged; he now fights injustice with the help of his confidante, a local named Will Kipp. In this episode, a troubled teen named Dorian believes he's a vampire, but Will thinks it's just a façade that the kid uses to escape the reality of his tormented life at home. After his mother's alcoholic boyfriend is overly abusive, Dorian threatens to kill him—and when the man is found dead the next day, the teen is the prime suspect in his murder.

In this melodramatic episode teeming with stereotypes, the Swamp Thing isn't given much to do, so he just hangs out in the boggy forest to offer up vague advice. The story is inconsistent; there are several deliberate scenes that indicate Dorian is a real vampire, and the teen is shown in full undead mode—complete with pale skin, a bald head, and a pair of fangs. To add to the confusion, a dream-like sequence shows the boyfriend killing the vampire that supposedly turned Dorian. Yet these scenes are completely ignored in the last act, when it's revealed that his mother accidentally killed her boyfriend. Are these scenes simply the demented fantasies of a teen with deep psychological problems? It's never made clear, which leads to a puzzling episode that doesn't know what kind of story it's trying to tell.

T-Bag and the Rings of Olympus – "Vampires"

ITV1. Feb 4, 1991 (S07E05). Adventure/Family. D: Glyn Edwards. W: Grant Cathro, Lee Pressman. C: Georgina Hale ♀, John Hasler, Natalie Wood, Gavin Richards ♀, Denise Coffey. UK: English/Color/30m. Thames Television.

In this series, Tabatha Bag searches across time and space for The Rings of Olympus, which form a powerful necklace once worn by the Goddess Athena. Pollyzena, who is Athena's handmaiden, attempts to find the rings first. In this episode, Polly travels to Transylvania, where she meets a vampire named Count Igor von Fledermaus. He promises to give her one of the rings—if she'll come back to his castle for a quick bite.

T-Bag and the Wonders in Letterland – "Debbie in the Land of V"

ITV1. Apr 16, 1985 (S01E07). Adventure/Family. D: Leon Thau. W: Grant Cathro, Lee Pressman. C: Elizabeth Estensen, John Hasler, Jennie Stallwood, Jim Norton ♀, John Thirtle. UK: English/Color/30m. Thames Television.

In this first incarnation of the series, Debbie is on a quest to find a group of golden letters. In this episode, she arrives in the Land of V—where she meets a friendly vampire named Vic.

Tales from the Crypt – "The Secret"

HBO. Jul 31, 1990 (S02E18). Horror/Thriller. D: Michael Riva. W: Doug Ronning. C: Larry Drake, Grace Zabriskie ♀, Mike Simmrin, Georgann Johnson, Stella Hall, William Frankfather ♀, John Kassir. USA: English/Color/25m. Home Box Office.

A strange couple adopts a young orphan named Theodore, who finds his new parents quite eccentric. They pamper him to no end; he feasts on succulent meals with delicious desserts, and has every toy he ever wanted. Since his parents are out every night and are never around during the day, Theodore is left in the company of their manservant Tobias—who questions his role in the deadly plan that his masters have in store for the boy.

An average vampire tale with a couple of kooky bloodsuckers, who are sweetening up the boy's blood in order to make him all the more delicious when it's time to feed. Their servant Tobias is in on the plan; he's been promised immortality if he goes along with the sacrifice, but he ultimately tries to save the boy from the clutches of the couple. Although Tobias fails to protect him, Theodore is actually a werewolf—and he learns that vampire blood is quite tasty.

 "Gaines Orphanage," where Theodore initially lives, is named after the publisher of EC comics: William Maxwell Gaines. This tale is based on the story of the same title by Carl Wessler, from *The Haunt of Fear* #24 (EC, Mar-Apr 1954).

Tales from the Crypt – "The Reluctant Vampire"

HBO. Jul 10, 1991 (S03E07). Horror/Thriller. D: Elliot Silverstein. W: Terry Black. C: Malcolm McDowell ♀, Sandra Dickinson, George Wendt, Michael Berryman, Paul Gleason, John Kassir. USA: English/Color/28m. Home Box Office.

Donald Longtooth is a vampire with the best job in town—he works as a security guard at a blood bank. He's free to drink from its stores each night so long as he adjusts the records, otherwise someone will notice that pints have gone missing. One evening the record book can't be found, so Longtooth hits the streets to restock the blood bank—and gains the unwanted attention of the notorious vampire hunter Rupert Van Helsing.

Longtooth is a sensitive bloodsucker who's all talk and no bite; smitten with his co-worker Sally, the vampire has a tough time hiding his true nature from her. Cutbacks put their jobs in jeopardy, so Longtooth goes on a killing spree to exponentially increase the blood supply at the clinic—and he wipes the city clean of criminals in the process. It's a charming episode with many humorous moments, and even the Crypt Keeper gets in on the fun: he introduces the episode dressed as Dracula.

 Based on the story of the same title by Al Feldstein from *The Vault of Horror* #20 (EC, Aug-Sep 1951).

Tales from the Crypt – "Werewolf Concerto"

HBO. Sep 9, 1992 (S04E13). Horror/Thriller. D: Steve Perry. W: Scott Nimerfro. C: Timothy Dalton, Dennis Farina, Walter Gotell, Charles Fleischer, Reginald VelJohnson, Lela Rochon, Beverly D'Angelo ♀, Wolfgang Puck, John Kassir. USA: English/Color/23m. Home Box Office.

Vacationers stranded at a mountainside resort are being stalked by a werewolf. One of the guests is a hunter that specializes in exterminating such beasts, but they need to remain anonymous to effectively do the job. As the identity of the mysterious hunter is exposed, it's revealed that more than one guest is hiding a dark secret.

Red herrings abound in this enjoyable story, where the werewolf isn't the only monster hiding behind a façade. This episode succeeds largely due to the performances of Timothy Dalton and Beverly D'Angelo, who play off of one another with great aplomb.

📺 Based on the story of the same title by Johnny Craig from *The Vault of Horror* #16 (EC, Dec 1950-Jan 1951).

Tales from the Crypt – "Cold War"

HBO. May 31, 1996 (S07E06). Horror/Thriller. D: Andy Morahan. W: Scott Nimerfro. C: Ewan McGregor, Jane Horrocks, Colin Salmon ☥, John Salthouse, Willie Ross, John Kassir. USA: English/Color/22m. Home Box Office.

Ford and Cammy are two reckless thieves who end up in a lover's spat after a convenience store robbery goes horribly wrong. Cammy seeks refuge in the arms of another man, but a one night stand reveals far more about him than she could have ever imagined.

An amusing tale of conflict, where two ghouls and a vampire argue over which species is the most superior of the undead. Bloodsuckers are widely known to take issue with their werewolf cousins, but it seems they also despise their zombie brethren.

📺 Based on the story of the same title by Jack Kamen in *Tales from the Crypt* #43 (EC, Aug-Sep 1954).

Tales from the Darkside – "Strange Love"

Syndicated. May 11, 1986 (S02E21). Horror/Thriller. D: Ted Gershuny. W: Edithe Swensen. C: Harsh Nayyar ☥, Marcia Cross ☥, Patrick Kilpatrick ☥. USA: English/Color/22m. Laurel Entertainment Inc./Jaygee Productions/Tribune Entertainment.

Dr. Philip Carrol makes a house call at the behest of Edmund Alcott, whose wife Marie has hurt her leg after a fall—and he discovers the two are vampires. Alcott imprisons the doctor, who must remain until Marie recovers; she becomes enamored by their reluctant house guest, and looks for a way to free both of them from the evil grip of her husband.

The antagonist is one of the most annoying vampires you'll ever find on television, so it is a happy ending when he gets what's coming to him. The saving grace is Marie, played by a young Marcia Cross; the actress makes for quite a seductive vampiress, and she fits right in with a story that takes place in 1935.

Tales from the Darkside – "The Circus"

Syndicated. Sep 28, 1986 (S03E01). Horror/Thriller. D: Michael Gornick. W: George A. Romero, Sydney J. Bounds. C: William Hickey, Kevin O'Connor, Ed French ⚲, Jacques Sandulescu. USA: English/Color/22m. Laurel Entertainment Inc./Jaygee Productions/Tribune Entertainment.

Bragg is a cynical, alcoholic newspaper reporter who specializes in debunking charlatans. His next target is "Dr. Nis's Exhibition of Wonder," a traveling supernatural circus that features a number of strange creatures. He's convinced that the spectacles are nothing but a sham, that is, until he sees the first attraction: a demonic vampire that appears to actually kill a baby lamb and drink its blood. Narrated by Paul Sparer.

A creepy story thanks to the presence of actor William Hickey as the eerie Ringmaster, which counterbalances the unremarkable performance by the actor playing the reporter. The monsters are quite ghoulish, especially the vampire—who is mistakenly referred to as a "succubus" even though he is clearly male (and should have been called an "incubus").

Tales from the Darkside – "My Ghostwriter: The Vampire"

Syndicated. Feb 1, 1987 (S03E14). Horror/Thriller. D: Frank De Palma. W: Peter O'Keefe. C: Jeff Conaway, Roy Dotrice ⚲, Jillie Mack, Chi Chi Navarro. USA: English/Color/21m. Laurel Entertainment Inc./Jaygee Productions/Tribune Entertainment.

Peter is a struggling horror author who's run out of ideas, until one fateful night when Count Draco enters his life. In exchange for sanctuary, the bloodsucker offers to tell him nine hundred years of vampire stories—tales that will fill a dozen books. After the first volume is published to great acclaim, Peter makes the grave mistake of prematurely ending the partnership. Narrated by Paul Sparer.

There's a good mix of comedy and horror in this morality tale, where the conniving author pays dearly for his dishonor. Roy Dotrice is effective as the menacing vampire, and carries a gravitas befitting to one so ancient.

📺 Based on a story of the same title by Scott Edelman from *The Unexpected* #197 (DC Comics, Apr 1980).

Tales of the Unexpected – "The Nomads"

NBC. Feb 23, 1977 (S01E04). Horror/Thriller. D: Allen Reisner. W: Earl W. Wallace, Anthony Wilson. C: David Birney, Lynne Marta, Eugene Roche, David Huddleston, Katherine Justice, Read Morgan, Alvah Stanley. USA: English/Color/60m. Quinn Martin Productions.

Not to be confused with the long-running UK series of the same name, this single-season show was also known as *Quinn Martin's Tales of the Unexpected*. In this episode, Vietnam veteran Paul

Rogers has a history of hallucinating, which is why he's unable to convince anyone that he's seen a UFO. Things get worse after he discovers the ship is transporting a race of "space vampires," who plan on taking over the Earth. Presented by William Conrad.

📺 This story is a remake of "Beachhead" from the series *The Invaders* (1967).

Third Watch – "Kingpin Rising" / "How Do You Spell Belief?" / "End of Tour"

NBC. Feb 25 – Apr 29, 2005 (S06E17/20/21). Crime/Drama. D: Nelson McCormick. W: Charles Murray. C: Coby Bell, Nia Long, Molly Price, Anthony Ruivivar, Skipp Sudduth, Tia Texada, Jason Wiles, Luke Robertson ☥. USA: English/Color/180m. Warner Bros. Television/ John Wells Productions.

In a minor story arc that spans three episodes, Detective Yokas investigates the case of a missing teen. She traces the disappearance to a vampire cult headed by a young man named Dante—and he seeks revenge against her for meddling in his affairs.

A Vietnam vet (David Birney) investigates a UFO sighting despite the hesitation of his girlfriend (Lynne Marta) in the *Tales of the Unexpected* episode "The Nomads" (Quinn Martin Productions)

Thriller – "God Grante That She Lye Stille"

NBC. Oct 23, 1961 (S02E05). Horror/Thriller. D: Herschel Daugherty. W: Robert Hardy Andrews. C: Ronald Howard, Henry Daniell, Sarah Marshall ☥, Victor Buono, Madeleine Holmes, Avis Scott. USA: English/ B&W/60m. Hubbell Robinson Productions Inc.

In 1661, Elspeth Clewer was found guilty of the abominable crime of witchcraft and vampirism, accused of slaughtering beasts, birds and humans to drink their blood. She placed a curse upon her family, and was burned at the stake—but the evil force that consumed Elspeth did not die along with her. Three hundred years later, that same evil targets Lady Margaret Clewer, who has returned to her ancestral home to celebrate her twenty-first birthday. Hosted by Boris Karloff.

Thriller – "Masquerade"

NBC. Oct 30, 1961 (S02E06). Horror/Thriller. D: Herschel Daugherty. W: Donald S. Sanford, Henry Kuttner. C: Elizabeth Montgomery ☥, Tom Poston ☥, John Carradine, Jack Lambert, Dorothy Neumann. USA: English/B&W/51m. Hubbell Robinson Productions Inc.

Caught in a raging storm, Charlie Denham and his wife Ros get sidelined from their honeymoon, and seek refuge in a creepy guest house run by a family of hillbillies. Although his wife worries about their situation—she thinks their hosts are murderers—Charlie relishes in the macabre nature of it all. Legend has it that vampires hunt in the area, masquerading as regular people, and as the couple explores the house, they get the feeling that they're not meant to leave alive. Hosted by Boris Karloff.

A smart, tongue-in-cheek story about a couple of vampires who have adapted to the times, living under the guise of normal human beings—no thick accents or long flowing capes here. In an amusing twist, the newlyweds often point out all the macabre storytelling clichés that they face in the story, as if entirely expected. There are several red herrings dropped along the way as to who could be masquerading as human, and the ending is wholly satisfying and a fitting conclusion to the tale.

📺 The building used as the exterior for the guest house is the infamous "Bates Motel" from the classic Alfred Hitchcock film *Psycho* (1960).

Thrills – "Club Plasma"

Cinemax. Jul 6, 2001 (S01E06). Adult/Fantasy. D: Lucas Riley. W: Alon Kaplan. C: Lauren Hays, Antoinette Abbott, Duke Champagne ☥, Catalina Larranaga ☥, Charles D. Cherrier, Raquel Ann Moore ☥, Logan Degan ☥, Susan Hale ☥. USA: English/Color/27m. Advanced Media Entertainment.

Studly tabloid reporter Rob Constantine teams up with his sultry co-worker Felicia Reynolds to investigate a self-proclaimed vampire named Portia Valera, who owns a new underground hotspot called Club Plasma. As they dig deeper to get to the meat of the story, Felicia becomes mesmerized by a masked man with a special gift, while Rob learns that there's a high price to pay for uncovering the naked truth.

About as good a story as one expects from soft-core pornography; the flaccid script and wooden acting results in mostly laughable scenes—and the sex isn't all that exciting either. Well, at least there are vampires!

Trapper John, M.D. – "Dark Side of the Loon"

CBS. Dec 16, 1984 (S06E09). Drama/Medical. D: Gregory Harrison. W: John Whelpley. C: Pernell Roberts, Gregory Harrison, Charles Siebert, Timothy Busfield, Marc McClure ☥. USA: English/Color/45m. 20th Century Fox Television.

🦇🦇🦇

On the night of a full moon, J.T. begins a house-sitting gig at a stately abode, which was put up for sale after the recent death of the owner. He's surprised by a pale occupant named Luthor, the owner's grandson, who claims to be a vampire—and hasn't eaten for days.

It's not often that porphyria, the "vampire disease," is written into a prime-time television series. But here we have an interesting story of a man who was brought up to believe that he was a real vampire, because the affliction that was genetically passed down to him was misunderstood (he was even fed blood on a regular basis). This is an entertaining psychological vampire story, which deftly examines the real effects of porphyria—and includes a nod to *Interview with the Vampire*, surely one of the earliest mentions in scripted television of Anne Rice's groundbreaking novel.

The Twilight Zone – "Monsters!" / "A Small Talent for War" / "A Matter of Minutes"

CBS. Jan 24, 1986 (S01E15). Suspense/Thriller. D: B.W.L. Norton. W: Robert Crais. C: Ralph Bellamy ☥, Oliver Robins, Kathleen Lloyd, Bruce Solomon, Lewis Dauber. CAN/UK/USA: English/Color/60m. Atlantis Films Limited/London Film Productions/MGM Television.

🦇🦇🦇

In the segment "Monsters!" a horror-loving kid, Toby Michaels, befriends his new neighbor, Emile Bendictson—an elderly man who claims to be a vampire and has come back home to die.

Engaging story about a kind, grandfatherly vampire who shows Toby some of the magic that he's seen over the years—despite knowing that the boy is part of the group that will end his life. It's a unique take on our perception of evil, and the monsters that lurk inside us all.

The Twilight Zone – "Need To Know" / "Red Snow"

CBS. Mar 21, 1986 (S01E21). Suspense/Thriller. D: Jeannot Szwarc. W: Michael Cassutt. C: George Dzundza ☥, Barry Miller ☥, Vladimir Skomarovsky, Victoria Tennant ☥, Rod Colbin, Andrew Divoff. CAN/UK/USA: English/Color/60m. Atlantis Films Limited/Persistence of Vision/MGM Television.

🦇🦇🦇

In "Red Snow," Colonel Ulyanov of the Russian KGB is sent to a gulag north of Vorkuta, in the Arctic Circle, to investigate the deaths of two Communist Party officials. He meets a woman who hasn't aged in fifty years, and discovers that those exiled to this harsh, frigid land—where there's no sun between October and April—include a group of undead *vorvolaka*.

Highly entertaining story thanks to a wonderful performance by Dzundza as an aging, idealistic KGB agent, who's trapped within a corrupt system that he once believed he could change. He discovers that the exiled residents have a symbiotic relationship with their undead neighbors; the humans protect the vampires during the daylight periods of the summer, while the relationship is reversed throughout the sunless stretches of winter. Ulyanov expects to be killed after learning their secret, just like the officials before him; instead, he's offered a gift that will give him the power to fight the crooked system he wants so desperately to fix. It's a smart episode that integrates real folklore with actual historical events, and makes for a compelling tale.

Unhappily Ever After – "Ryan, Vampire Slayer"

WB. Oct 26, 1997 (S04E07). Comedy/Family. D: Andrew Susskind. W: J. Stewart Burns. C: Geoff Pierson, Stephanie Hodge, Kevin Connolly, Nikki Cox, Justin Berfield, Bobcat Goldthwait, Bridget Flanery. USA: English/Color/22m. Touchstone Television/Buena Vista Television.

As a way to avoid dating Ryan, cheerleader Bunny Muffowitz jokingly admits that she's a vampire slayer, and her activities keep her far too busy. After she gets hurt and no longer has an excuse, Bunny manages to sidestep his advances by convincing him that he's been chosen as her replacement.

In an obvious take on the cult show *Buffy the Vampire Slayer,* this episode is more about making fun of the undead than slaying them (the only appearance of a vampire is a Dracula dummy that Ryan uses for practice). Still, it's quite a funny story, and has a priceless running joke about the existence of vampires: "Of course they are real! How else do you explain Yoko Ono and Priscilla Presley living off the dead?"

Urban Gothic – "Vampirology"

Channel 5/Bravo. May 24, 2000 (S01E02). Horror/Sci-Fi. D: Colin Bucksey. W: Tom de Ville. C: Keith-Lee Castle ☥, Julienne Davis, Emily Hamilton, Charles De'Ath, Danny Edwards. UK: English/Color/24m. Golden Square/BlackJack.

Rex, a vampire living in London, allows a documentary film crew to follow him for one night in and around Soho. As he hangs out with his friends and searches for his evening meal, we get a glimpse into the playboy lifestyle of this modern-day bloodsucker. He becomes less charming as his hunger grows, and soon reveals the wolf inside the sheep's clothing. Scream queen Ingrid Pitt has a cameo.

Initially I wasn't all that impressed with this one; it's a typical "interview with a vampire" scenario, where the subject goes through the common misconceptions surrounding bloodsuckers. But the character of Rex grew on me, and once the human prey is killed—mercilessly in a dark alley—I was struck by the authenticity of the scene; Rex is brutal, savage, and only shows a moment of regret. Yet is he a real vampire, a murderous sociopath, or something else entirely? It's left up for the viewer to decide.

📺 Keith-Lee Castle starred as Count Dracula in the family-oriented UK series *Young Dracula* (2006).

Virtual Murder – "A Dream of Dracula"

BBC One. Aug 21, 1992 (S01E05). Crime/Mystery. D: Philip Draycott. W: Bennett Sims. C: Nicholas Clay ⚰, Kim Thomson ⚰, Stephen Yardley, Alan David, Julian Clary, Ronald Fraser, Jill Gascoine, Alfred Marks ⚰. UK: English/Color/49m. BBC/Pebble Mill.

🦇🦇🦇

Follows psychology professor Dr. John Cornelius and his partner Samantha Valentine, as they investigate a series of bizarre cases. In this episode, a vampire victimizes several locals, but Cornelius believes that the perpetrator is simply in the grip of an obsession, consumed by every aspect of the Dracula myth. He fears the attacks will eventually lead to murder, and finds unexpected help from a man who calls himself Van Helsing.

Discounting the cheesy music and flashy editing tricks, this episode is quite interesting, with a few inspired moments and quirky characters. It's unclear if the attacker—who believes he's really Dracula—is simply a man obsessed, or actually someone who's become a real vampire by adopting the habits of the legendary Count (he's an elderly man who drinks small amounts of blood, and has surprising strength and agility for his age). What of the man who calls himself Van Helsing? He studies bats and blood, and knows quite a bit about vampire hunting—is he also mired in a deep obsession, or is there something more to him as well?

The Watcher – "The Human Condition" / "The Blood of Our Children" / "Rita" / "The Comic"

UPN. Mar 14, 1995 (S01E08). Drama/Mystery. D: Tucker Gates. W: Dan Peterson. C: Sir Mix-A-Lot, Bobbie Phillips, Ely Pouget, Paula Barbieri ⚰, Randi Ingerman, Dana Barron. USA: English/Color/60m. Christopher Crowe Productions/Paramount Television.

Set in Las Vegas, this anthology series features stories introduced by The Watcher, a mysterious man who uses surveillance monitors inside his hotel room to spy on the lives of others. In the segment "The Blood of Our Children," an alcoholic woman enlists the help of a vampire as she searches for her runaway daughter.

Weird Science – "Gary & Wyatt's Bloodsucking Adventure"

USA Network. Jun 1, 1996 (S04E19). Comedy/Sci-Fi. D: Les Landau. W: Kari Lizer, Alan Cross, Tom Spezialy. C: Michael Manasseri ⚰, John Mallory Asher ⚰, Vanessa Angel ⚰, Krista Allen ⚰, Mark Lindsay Chapman ⚰. USA: English/Color/22m. St. Clare Entertainment/Universal Television.

🦇🦇🦇

Based on the 1985 movie of the same title, this series follows the misadventures of Gary and

Wyatt, two teens who create their dream woman on a computer—and she has the power to temporarily grant their wishes. In this episode, Lisa turns her makers into vampires so they can be cool enough—"like Tom Cruise and Brad Pitt"—to gain entrance into Club Lust. But since she's turned off by the blood-drinking aspect, Lisa makes them crave Yoo-Hoo (a chocolate-flavored beverage) instead of blood.

This was far more amusing than expected, and surprisingly, it contains some mature language and adult situations. It's a typical boy-falls-for-girl-who-is-a-vampire story, but it's nicely fleshed out—and features stereotypical vampires and amusing secondary characters.

What I Like About You – "Halloween"

WB. Oct 28, 2005 (S04E06). Comedy/Drama. D: Shelley Jensen. W: Amy Engelberg, Wendy Engelberg. C: Amanda Bynes, Wesley Jonathan, Leslie Grossman, Allison Munn, Jennie Garth, Jason Priestley ☥, Dan Cortese ☥. USA: English/Color/22m. Weller-Grossman Productions/Tollin-Robbins Productions.

While away for the weekend in Vermont, Holly decides she's ready to spend the night with Vince. Meanwhile, back home in New York, Valerie worries that her relationship with Charlie is moving way too fast. Despite the title, this episode has very little to do with Halloween, and although two characters dress up as vampires, only one has any fun with it.

Wild Kat – "Blood Sisters"

Channel Ten. Mar 23, 2001 (S01E08). Adventure/Family. D: Steve Peddie. W: Ron Elliott. C: Pia Prendiville, Daniel Daperis, Paris Abbott, Luke Pegler, Nicolette Findlay, Karin Hampton. AUS: English/Color/30m. Carlton International/ATV Family Entertainment AG/Barron Entertainment Ltd.

Series follows Katrina, a teen who's able to mind-meld with a female tiger named Garang, which imprints the cat's emotions onto her, and gives her extraordinary abilities. In this episode, after testing samples of their blood, Dr. Raushark discovers that both Kat and Garang have a rare gene that may explain the psychic link they share. But Kat's friend Jasmin is suspicious of Raushark, and believes she's really a vampire.

Wings – "The Gift of Life"

NBC. Oct 30, 1996 (S08E06). Comedy/Family. D: Leonard R. Garner, Jr. W: Michael Sardo. C: Tim Daly, Steven Weber, Crystal Bernard ☥, David Schramm, Rebecca Schull, Tony Shalhoub, Amy Yasbeck. USA: English/Color/22m. Grub Street Productions/Paramount Television.

Series followed two brothers who run an independent airline out of a regional airport in Nantucket, Massachusetts. In this episode, as the gang prepares for a Halloween festival, a medical courier on a priority-one delivery inadvertently leaves behind a cooler that contains a very important donation. It's an amusing episode with minimal vampire content: Helen Chappel is dressed up as a sexy, bouffant-haired vampiress.

Women: Stories of Passion – "The Little Vampire"

Showtime. Aug 23, 1997 (S02E07). Adult/Romance. D/W: Mary Woronov. C: Elisa M. Rothstein, Shannah Laumeister ☥, Steven Langa, Horacio Anthony ☥. USA: English/Color/30m. Showtime Networks.

Series features erotic stories of love, passion, and sexual fantasy. In this episode, a woman claims to have once been a vampire, but was saved after falling in love.

The Wonderful World of Disney – "The Mystery in Dracula's Castle"

NBC. Jan 7/14, 1973 (S19E11/12). Family/Mystery. D: Robert Totten. W: Sue Milburn. C: Johnny Whitaker, Scott C. Kolden ☥, Mariette Hartley, Clu Gulager, John Fiedler, Mills Watson. USA: English/Color/91m. Walt Disney Productions.

In this two-part story, Alfie Booth wants to make a vampire film, and it takes some convincing to get his reluctant little brother Leonard to star as Dracula (he'd rather play Sherlock Holmes). When they use a local lighthouse to film part of the movie, the kids come across two men who, unknown to them, are behind the recent robbery of a very expensive necklace.

The castle may be a lighthouse and Dracula may be a ten-year-old kid, but for an old Disney episode, this one is better than average. It's a fun story that isn't too cheesy or sugar-coated, and stars many familiar faces of the day; it even has a cute dog that gets into all sorts of mischief.

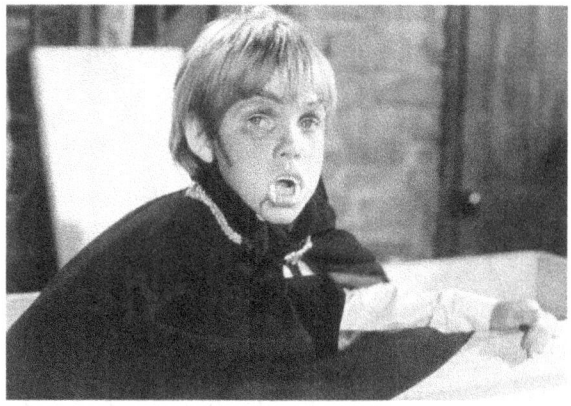

Leonard Booth (Scott C. Kolden) stars as Dracula in a home movie from *The Wonderful World of Disney* - "The Mystery in Dracula's Castle" (Walt Disney Productions)

The X Files – "3"

FOX. Nov 4, 1994 (S02E07). Mystery/Sci-Fi. D: David Nutter. W: Chris Ruppenthal, Glen Morgan, James Wong. C: David Duchovny, Gillian Anderson, Justina Vail ☥, Perrey Reeves ☥, Frank Military ☥, Gustavo Moreno ☥. USA: English/Color/46m. Ten Thirteen Productions/20th Century Fox Television.

With Scully still missing, Mulder heads to Los Angeles to investigate a bizarre case that involves a trio of serial killers who have already claimed six victims—and they seem to be real blood drinkers. As he is drawn into the world of vampire fetishism, Mulder falls for a woman who may be linked to the murderers.

This episode got a bad rap from fervent fans when it first aired, but to this day, it still holds up quite well as a serious vampire story (it's a worthy companion to the very humorous "Bad Blood" episode from Season 5). Perrey Reeves is excellent as a sanguinist on the run, hounded by an "unholy trinity" of vampires that has been following her across the country—they want to make her one of their own. The final minutes of the episode are quite thrilling; however, additional lore is hastily added to serve the story, which is a little too convenient. It remains a strong close to one of the better episodes from this season.

The X Files – "Bad Blood"

FOX. Feb 22, 1998 (S05E12). Mystery/Sci-Fi. D: Cliff Bole. W: Vince Gilligan. C: David Duchovny, Gillian Anderson, Mitch Pileggi, Luke Wilson ☥, Patrick Renna ☥, Forbes Angus, Brent Butt. USA: English/Color/46m. Ten Thirteen Productions/20th Century Fox Television.

While investigating a rash of exsanguinations in rural Texas, Mulder kills a teenage boy whom he mistakes for a real vampire—and faces a $446 million lawsuit from the victim's family. As Mulder and Scully try to get their stories straight before a meeting with Skinner, it's a case of he said/she said as they each give their own take on events.

Promotional advertisement for *The X Files* episode "Bad Blood" on FOX (Ten Thirteen Productions/20th Century Fox Television/TV Guide)

This hilarious episode gives insight into how Mulder and Scully see themselves and each other, as they recount their experiences working on a recent case. In one of the finest self-contained episodes of the series, this tale of trailer-trash vampires is a winner all around. It receives top marks for its humor, and for the return of real bloodsuckers—which were last seen in the decidedly more serious episode "3" from Season 2.

Xena: Warrior Princess – "Girls Just Wanna Have Fun"

Syndicated. Oct 21, 1996 (S02E04). Action/Adventure. D: T.J. Scott. W: Adam Armus, Nora Kay Foster. C: Lucy Lawless, Renée O'Connor, Ted Raimi, Matthew Chamberlain, Kym Kristalie ⚥. USA: English/Color/43m. MCA Television/Renaissance Pictures/Studios USA Television.

While investigating the disappearance of several young women, Xena and Gabrielle find the den of the god Bacchus, whose followers are bloodthirsty vampires known as "Bacchae." This mess of a story is a mishmash of several vampire legends, and is plagued by hyperkinetic editing and nausea-inducing camera work. Yet most fans of the show will be distracted by the fact that Xena and Gabrielle do a little neck nibbling in this episode.

📺 Vampires are also referenced in the Season 4 episode "The Play's the Thing," when a character speaks of seeing the play *Buffus the Bacchae Slayer*—clearly an allusion to the TV series *Buffy the Vampire Slayer* (1997).

You Wish – "Halloween"

ABC. Oct 31, 1997 (S01E06). Family/Fantasy. D: Jeff McCracken. W: Steve Pepoon. C: John Ales, Harley Jane Kozak, Jerry Van Dyke, Alex McKenna, Nathan Lawrence, Sylvain Cecile, Andrew Masset ⚥, Larry Cedar. USA: English/Color/30m. Touchstone Television.

Series follows the Apple family after they inadvertently release a friendly, two-thousand-year-old genie imprisoned within a rug. In this episode, after the genie grants a wish for real Halloween costumes, he accidentally brings to life the decorations of Dracula and the Mummy.

Young Hercules – "The Lure of the Lyre"

FOX. Oct 30, 1998 (S01E19). Adventure/Fantasy. D: Chris Graves. W: Michael Reaves. C: Ryan Gosling, Dean O'Gorman, Chris Conrad, Kevin Smith, Jodie Rimmer ⚥, Angela Marie Dotchin, Morgan Fairhead ⚥. USA: English/Color/21m. Renaissance Pictures/MCA Television.

Hercules and friends are drawn into the realm of Bacchus, where fun is the priority and the party never ends. But after Lilith gets bitten, she changes into a vampire-like creature—and Hercules realizes that something is amiss within the den of the god of good times.

There's a lot of hissing and posing with these vampires, but not much bite. The story will be familiar to fans of *Xena: Warrior Princess* (see "Girls Just Wanna Have Fun"), and this episode is just as silly. it includes a scene where the followers of Bacchus dance as if at a modern-day rave—complete with a pulsating soundtrack. Although not called vampires by name, these "Bacchae" have prominent fangs, and create others through a bite on the neck; they also fear the sunlight, and can transform into wolves.

The Young Indiana Jones Chronicles – "Transylvania, January 1918"

ABC. Aug 21, 1993 (S02E20). Action/Adventure. D: Dick Maas. W: Jonathan Hensleigh. C: Sean Patrick Flanery, Keith Szarabajka, Bob Peck ☥, Simone Bendix, Paul Kynman, Sam Kelly, George Hall. USA: English/Color/60m. Paramount Pictures/Lucasfilm LTD/Amblin Entertainment.

Follows the adventures of Indiana Jones in his youth, before he became a professor and wielded his trademark whip. In this episode, Indy joins a group of special agents investigating General Targo, a Romanian who raided a German P.O.W. camp to liberate the captured soldiers—only to hold them hostage himself. Things take a supernatural turn after the team confronts the man, who appears to be a vampire—and thinks he's a modern-day Vlad Țepeș.

At the time of broadcast, several countries considered this episode too violent for television, so it was pulled from some markets (it does have its gory moments). As Indy travels from Venice to Transylvania, chatting up the mission and meeting his team members, it takes up so much story that it almost feels like you're watching the journey in real time. There's a great payoff once they reach the castle, but unfortunately everything goes downhill from there. By the time they finally meet Targo—who looks like a cross between a Musketeer and Nosferatu—there's only fifteen minutes left to tell his story. Too bad, since from here on in, the tale begins to redeem itself. There are too many unanswered questions: is he the real Vlad the Impaler, a sociopath who thinks he is, or a reincarnation of the man? How did he become a vampire? Most importantly, how can such a powerful undead being be so easily dispatched by a no-whip-wielding whippersnapper?

📺 The DVD release includes the inspired documentary *Dracula: Fact and Fiction* (2007) as part of the special features.

The Young Ones – "Nasty"

BBC Two. May 29, 1984 (S02E03). Comedy/Music. D: Geoff Posner. W: Ben Elton, Rik Mayall, Lise Mayer. C: Adrian Edmondson, Rik Mayall, Nigel Planer, Christopher Ryan, Alexei Sayle ☥, Terry Jones, Mark Arden, Helen Atkinson Wood. UK: English/Color/35m. BBC.

Series follows the misadventures of four undergrad students attending Scumbag College, who live together in squalor. In this horror-themed episode, the flat mates try to hook up their very first VCR, so they can watch some "video nasties." A large package arrives from the Transvaal in South Africa—and it contains a vampire. Features a song by the Gothic punk band The Damned.

This surreal sitcom often stretched beyond the traditional boundaries of the medium, frequently breaking the fourth wall and making humorous, *non sequitur* plot turns. The vampire's first appearance leads to some unintentional (or possibly deliberate) funny moments, as the actor struggles to speak through a set of cheap plastic fangs—which are nowhere to be found in later scenes. The overall story is quite difficult to summarize, but it's definitely must-see Un-Dead TV!

📺 The term "video nasty" refers to low-budget horror films that were released into the home video market in the early 1980s.

Promotional advertisement for Alan Ball's hit series *True Blood* (Home Box Office)

Promotional advertisement for the FOX TV movie *Blood Ties* (Richard and Esther Shapiro Entertainment Inc./TV Guide)

Vampires Among Us
The Series

Richard Straker (James Mason) and his vampire partner Kurt Barlow (Reggie Nalder) prey on the local populace in *Salem's Lot* (Warner Bros. Television)

American Horror Story: Hotel

FX. Oct 7, 2015 - Jan 13, 2016 (S05E01-12). Horror/Suspense. D: Ryan Murphy, Bradley Buecker. W: Ryan Murphy, Brad Falchuk. C: Kathy Bates, Sarah Paulson, Evan Peters, Lady Gaga ☥, Wes Bentley, Finn Wittrock ☥, Matt Bomer ☥, Chloë Sevigny ☥, Denis O'Hare, Cheyenne Jackson, Angela Bassett. USA: English/Color/720m. Brad Falchuk Teley-Vision/Ryan Murphy Productions.

Season five of this horror anthology series takes place at Los Angeles's Hotel Cortez, which was built almost a century earlier and is haunted by the ghost of a serial killer, among other nefarious beings. One such creature is The Countess, a glamorous bloodsucker who was born in 1904, and then borne into darkness by Rudolph Valentino, who had acquired vampirism from director F.W. Murnau (who himself contracted the virus while working on *Nosferatu, eine Symphonie des Grauens*). These vampires are known as The Afflicted, each of whom has been granted eternal life, among other benefits, so long as they feast on human blood. Elizabeth, as The Countess is also known, has sired several others, including a brood of vampire children who also live at the hotel.

Angel

WB. Oct 5, 1999 – May 19, 2004 (110 Episodes). Drama/Fantasy. D: James A. Contner, Joss Whedon. W: Joss Whedon, David Greenwalt. C: David Boreanaz ☥, Alexis Denisof, Charisma Carpenter, J. August Richards, Andy Hallett, Amy Acker, Stephanie Romanov, Vincent Kartheiser, James Marsters ☥. USA: English/Color/6600m. Mutant Enemy Productions/20th Century Fox Television/Kuzui Enterprises.

🦇 🦇 🦇 🦇

Angel, the vampire with a soul, teams up with Doyle, a half-demon who receives painful premonitions of future events from The Powers That Be. Together with fledgling actress Cordelia Chase, the three form Angel Investigations, and use Doyle's "visions" as a guide in their quest to "help the helpless" of Los Angeles. Wolfram & Hart, an evil, interdimensional law firm, believes that Angel will play a major role in their plan for an upcoming apocalypse. Spin-off of the *Buffy the Vampire Slayer* TV series.

Angel is a character-driven series best viewed in chronological order; otherwise, some events in both the overall and individual story arcs may have less impact. It's darker and grittier than its

Angel (David Boreanaz) helps the helpless of Los Angeles in *Angel* (Mutant Enemy Productions/20th Century Fox Television)

precursor, and is a shining example of television drama at its best—supernatural or otherwise. It's all about redemption, fighting for what you believe in, and if necessary, sacrificing your life for a cause. The series had many high points, and even though it struggled at times with the story, it definitely concluded with a bang. The ending stayed true to the theme of the show; it pulled no punches, and was both a heartbreaking and satisfying conclusion to the series.

📺 IDW published a canonical continuation of the series in comic book form, beginning in 2007. Entitled *Angel: After the Fall,* the series was initially plotted by the show's creator, Joss Whedon. He based these storylines on ideas that would have been told in Season 6 of *Angel,* had the series not been canceled.

Bad Blood

ITV1. Apr 18 – May 2, 1999 (3 Episode Miniseries). Horror/Suspense. D: Tim Fywell. W: Tony Marchant. C: Alex Jennings ☥, Lia Williams, Steven Mackintosh, Taro J. Sherabayani, Trevor Martin, Emilia Fox, Serban Celea, Ileana Iordache. UK: English/Color/180m. Carlton Television.

In a story loosely based on *Dracula,* Father Irving helps infertile couple Joe and Nina Harker adopt Valentin, a young boy from Romania. As the child settles into his new environment, Nina sees a change in her husband's demeanor—he becomes increasingly hostile and alienated. Desperate for answers, Nina turns to Father Irving for assistance, and the priest discovers the horrible truth behind Joe's erratic behavior.

Big Bad Beetleborgs/Beetleborgs Metallix

FOX. Sep 7, 1996 – Mar 2, 1998 (88 Episodes). Family/Sci-Fi. D: Var. W: Var. C: Wesley Barker, Herbie Baez, Shannon Chandler, Brittany Konarzewski, Billy Forester, Joe Hackett ☥, David Fletcher, Frank Adelia. USA: English/Color/2640m. Saban Entertainment.

Series follows The Beetleborgs, a group of cyborg warriors who defend their city against the evil Magnavores. Features a cast of supporting characters that include the vampire Count Fangula, as well as other fiends based on classic movie monsters.

Being Human (UK)

BBC Three. Jan 25, 2009 – March 10, 2013 (36 Episodes). Drama/Fantasy. D: Philip John, Colin Teague. W: Toby Whithouse, Jamie Mathieson. C: Aidan Turner ☥, Russell Tovey, Lenora Crichlow, Sinead Keenan, Michael Socha, Damien Molony ☥, Annabel Scholey, Jason Watkins ☥, Kate Bracken. UK: English/Color/2160m. Touchpaper Television.

🦇🦇🦇

Three twentysomethings share a flat in contemporary Bristol, each hiding a dark secret: Mitchell is a vampire who's sworn off human blood, George is an intelligent man cursed with lycanthropy, and Annie is the ghost of a woman who died in the flat under mysterious circumstances.

A unique mix of horror, humor, and pathos in a modern-day setting, and one of the most notable series since *Buffy the Vampire Slayer*. By the third season it seemed as though the creative spark was lost, but it ended strong with the departure of a major cast member. The fourth season proved to be an entirely new beast altogether; it was a transitional story arc, and led to a completely new cast taking over for Season 5. It's a rare example of a series that has managed to successfully reboot itself after replacing all the original characters, yet still remained true to the heart and soul of the story.

Being Human (CAN)

SyFy/Space. Jan 17, 2011 – Apr 7, 2014 (52 Episodes). Drama/Fantasy. D: Paolo Barzman, Stefan Pleszczynski. W: Jeremy Carver, Anna Fricke. C: Sam Witwer ☥, Sam Huntington, Meaghan Rath, Mark Pellegrino ☥, Vincent Leclerc ☥, Kristen Hager, Gianpaolo Venuta, Connor Price. CAN: English/Color/2288m. Muse Entertainment Enterprises.

Three twentysomethings share an apartment in modern-day Boston, each hiding a dark secret: Aidan is a vampire who's sworn off human blood, Josh is an intelligent man cursed with lycanthropy, and Sally is the ghost of a woman who died in the apartment under mysterious circumstances.

This reimagining of the UK series features the same basic premise and characters, although some story arcs are different, as are various plot points. Unfortunately it's a little lifeless, seemingly dumbed down from its predecessor, and often heads into soap opera territory. It's too flashy for its own good, and relies on an overstuffed soundtrack to cover up weak storylines (which often pale in comparison to the original).

Blade: The Series

Spike TV. Jun 28 – Sep 13, 2006 (12 Episodes). Action/Fantasy. D: Peter O'Fallon, Michael Robison. W: David S. Goyer, Geoff Johns. C: Kirk Jones ☥, Jill Wagner ☥, Neil Jackson ☥, Jessica Gower ☥, Nelson Lee, Larry Poindexter. USA: English/Color/720m. Phantom Four/Marvel Entertainment.

Krista Starr, a former soldier, searches for answers in the mysterious death of her twin brother Zack; she learns that he was a "familiar"—the servant of a vampire. His killer is part of "The House of Chthon," a vampire organization that wants to rule mankind. She teams up with Blade, the half human/half vampire warrior, to stop them. Although the

Blade (Kirk Jones) teams up with a former soldier whose brother was a vampire slave in *Blade: The Series* (Phantom Four/Marvel Entertainment)

pilot aired as "Blade: House of Chthon," it's not distinct from the series itself, and is chronologically considered to be the first episode (an extended version was released on DVD).

Blood Ties

Lifetime. Mar 11 – Dec 7, 2007 (22 Episodes). Drama/Romance. D: Allan Kroeker, James Dunnison. W: Peter Mohan, Mark Leiren-Young. C: Christina Cox, Dylan Neal, Kyle Schmid ☥, Gina Holden, Nimet Kanji, Françoise Yip, Keith Dallas. CAN: English/Color/1320m. Insight Film Studios.

Private eye Vicki Nelson investigates a strange case in Toronto, and has a fateful run-in with the vampire Henry Fitzroy. They team up to solve a number of crimes with a supernatural bent, along with the help of Vicki's Goth-loving assistant Coreen, and her reluctant ex-partner Mike Celluci.

Based on the Blood Books by Tanya Huff, this is an excellent series that never received proper support from the network, and was canceled after a single season—despite its rabid fan base. The unique cast of characters includes Henry Fitzroy, the illegitimate son of Henry VIII, and Vicki Nelson, a strong-willed woman who reluctantly left the police force after being diagnosed with *retinitis pigmentosa* (a genetic eye condition that can lead to blindness).

When released on DVD, the show was divided up into two "seasons" of twelve and ten episodes respectively (even though, technically, only one season was produced).

Buffy the Vampire Slayer

WB/UPN. Mar 10, 1997 – May 19, 2003 (144 Episodes). Action/Fantasy. D: Joss Whedon, James A. Contner. W: Joss Whedon, Marti Noxon. C: Sarah Michelle Gellar, Alyson Hannigan ☥, Nicholas Brendon ☥, Anthony Stewart Head, James Marsters ☥, Charisma Carpenter, Kristine Sutherland, Michelle Trachtenberg, David Boreanaz ☥. USA: English/Color/8640m. Mutant Enemy Productions/20th Century Fox Television/Kuzui Enterprises.

Buffy Summers relocates to Sunnydale after she was expelled from a high school in Los Angeles, the result of an "unfortunate incident" that led to the destruction of the school gymnasium. Chosen by fate to be The Slayer—a warrior with heightened abilities who battles supernatural evil—Buffy tries to defy destiny and just be a normal teenager. But her hope of a fresh start is dashed after she learns that Sunnydale is located atop a portal to Hell—and the city quickly becomes the center of evil activity. Guided by her mentor, Rupert Giles, Buffy confronts a bevy of supernatural creatures, with the help of computer geek Willow and loveable loser Xander.

A ground-breaking show that proved the allure of vampires was significant enough to sustain an ongoing series. Although the undead were the catalyst, the stories told were not limited to these creatures alone; this allowed the writers to explore numerous modern-day issues facing society.

Overall, the storytelling was exceptional; however, having set such a high standard of excellence, a number of episodes didn't quite make the cut—especially in the later seasons. There's no denying the impact that *Buffy* continues to have on our popular culture, and it's doubtful there would be as many vampires on television today if it wasn't for this series.

📺 In 2007, *Buffy* was revived in comic books, and the series was so successful that creator Joss Whedon did the same for his other canceled series, *Angel*.

In an alternate *Buffy* universe, Willow (Alyson Hannigan) and Xander (Nicholas Brendon) are vampires (Mutant Enemy Productions/20th Century Fox Television)

Sarah Michelle Gellar is Buffy Summers, chosen by fate to battle evil on *Buffy the Vampire Slayer* (Mutant Enemy Productions/20th Century Fox Television)

Cliffhangers!

NBC. Feb 27 – May 1, 1979 (10 Episodes). Drama/Romance. D: Jeffrey Hayden, Sutton Roley. W: Craig Buck, Myla Lichtman. C: Michael Nouri ⚥, Carol Baxter ⚥, Stephen Johnson, Bever-Leigh Banfield ⚥, Louise Sorel ⚥, Antoinette Stella ⚥. USA: English/B&W, Color/200m. Universal TV.

🦇🦇🦇

Features three distinct storylines, split into chapters much like old movie serials, and each episode ends on a cliffhanger. In the segment "The Curse of Dracula," in present-day San Francisco, the Count lives under the assumed identity of a college professor. He secretly longs for Mary Gibbons, the daughter of a woman he once loved—but she's trying to destroy him with the help of Kurt von Helsing (the grandson of the renowned vampire hunter). Narrated by Brad Crandall.

Michael Nouri's performance as Dracula is sympathetic and endearing, but Louise Sorel (as Amanda

Gibbons) is the standout. Gibbons was turned by Dracula years ago, but to protect her daughter Mary, she is faced with destroying the man she still loves. Two different TV movies were compiled from "The Curse of Dracula" storyline: *The World of Dracula* combined episodes one through seven, while *The Loves of Dracula* included episodes seven through ten. Another version, *Dracula '79,* supposedly included the first four episodes; this may have aired during the initial series run as a means to recap the story (it's possible that a third film, *The Curse of Dracula,* compiled all ten episodes). The most expensive production at the time, *Cliffhangers!* also featured "Stop Susan Williams" (a photographer tries to solve her brother's murder) and "Secret Empire" (a sheriff in 1880 discovers an alien civilization hidden underground).

Promotional artwork of Michael Nouri as Count Dracula from the NBC series *Cliffhangers!* (Universal TV/K. McVey)

Dark Shadows (1966)

ABC. Jun 27, 1966 – Apr 2, 1971 (1225 Episodes). Drama/Romance. D: Lela Swift, Dan Curtis. W: Dan Curtis, Art Wallace. C: Jonathan Frid ☥, Alexandra Isles, Joan Bennett, Grayson Hall, Louis Edmonds, Nancy Barrett, David Selby, Kathryn Leigh Scott, Lara Parker, David Henesy. USA: English/B&W, Color/36750m. Dan Curtis Productions Inc.

Victoria Winters arrives at the Collinwood mansion to serve as governess to David Collins, the youngest of the extended family living in the manor home. She discovers strange goings-on within its walls; events take a darker turn upon the arrival of Barnabas Collins, a distant cousin visiting from England.

Daytime soap opera *Dark Shadows* always had a Gothic feel, but it took a distinctly supernatural turn when ghosts were added six months into the production. The show's popularity skyrocketed with the introduction of Barnabas Collins, a centuries-old vampire, and this character became the model for all the self-doubting, romantic vampires to come. This newfound success led to the addition of even more otherworldly elements, including time travel, werewolves, zombies and witches. The cast created a memorable group of characters, with many actors portraying different roles when the storyline switched time periods. The series lasted for five years, spawned a number of tie-in novels and comics, and was remade on television in 1991. In 2012, a feature film adaptation from Tim Burton starred Johnny Depp as Barnabas Collins.

📺 Some of Robert Cobert's original music from *Dark Shadows* was used in the paranormal soap opera *Passions* (1999). Tabitha Lenox, an immortal witch in the latter series, claimed she was once courted by Barnabas Collins before his engagement to Josette du Pres.

Jonathan Frid bares fangs in his iconic role as the vampire Barnabas Collins on the Gothic soap opera *Dark Shadows* (Dan Curtis Productions Inc.)

Barnabas Collins (Ben Cross) tries to cure the vampire within after falling in love on *Dark Shadows* (Dan Curtis Productions Inc./MGM Television)

Dark Shadows (1991)

NBC. Jan 13 – Mar 22, 1991 (12 Episodes). Drama/Romance. D: Dan Curtis, Armand Mastroianni. W: Dan Curtis, Hall Powell. C: Ben Cross ♀, Barbara Blackburn, Jim Fyfe, Joanna Going ♀, Joseph Gordon-Levitt, Veronica Lauren, Ely Pouget, Barbara Steele, Roy Thinnes. USA: English/Color/598m. Dan Curtis Television Productions Inc./MGM Television.

🦇 🦇 🦇

Victoria Winters travels to the remote Collinwood mansion to work as a private tutor, and falls in love with Barnabas Collins, a distant cousin of her employers. Barnabas is actually a centuries-old vampire, who believes that Victoria is the reincarnation of his long-dead fiancée. He desperately wants to build a life with her, but is unable to control his bloodlust—so he forms an uneasy alliance with Dr. Julia Hoffman, who believes that she can cure his affliction by altering his blood chemistry.

This short-lived primetime revival of the original series began as a two-part miniseries, and then continued on as a mid-season replacement. It was canceled after one season, even though it quickly established an audience and garnered excellent ratings. The majority of the roles were well cast, and Ben Cross was a compelling Barnabas—a vampire barely able to contain the evil within. Dramatic, bloody, and campy at times, the series retained the same Gothic elements that made the original such a hit. It's worthwhile viewing that still holds up today, even though it ends on a cliffhanger with no resolution to the story.

📺 Comic book company *Innovation Publishing* planned to produce several four-issue miniseries based on this revival. Two were published in their entirety, but only the first issue of the third was printed before the company went out of business. They also produced adaptations of the Anne Rice novels *Interview with the Vampire, The Vampire Lestat,* and *Queen of the Damned.*

Dr. Julia Hoffman (Barbara Steele) believes she can cure Barnabas Collins (Ben Cross) of his vampirism in the remake of *Dark Shadows* (Dan Curtis Productions Inc)

Death Valley

MTV. Aug 29 – Nov 21, 2011 (12 Episodes). Fantasy/Satire. D: Eric Appel. W: Curtis Gwinn, Eric Weinberg. C: Tania Raymonde, Vene L. Arcoraci, Toby Meuli, Charlie Sanders, Bryan Callen, Texas Battle, Bryce Johnson, Vince Lozano ♀. USA: English/Color/360m. Liquid Theory.

A dark comedy/mockumentary series in the same vein as COPS, where an Undead Task Force faces off against a bevy of supernatural creatures running amok in the San Fernando Valley.

Demons

ITV1. Jan 3 – Feb 7, 2009 (6 Episodes). Drama/Fantasy. D: Tom Harper, Matthew Evans. W: Peter Tabern, Lucy Watkins. C: Christian Cooke, Zoe Tapper ♀, Philip Glenister, Holliday Grainger, Richard Wilson, Saskia Wickham. UK: English/Color/360m. Shine.

Teenager Luke Rutherford learns that he is the last descendant of a long line of demon slayers. He reluctantly teams up with mentor Rupert Galvin and the mysterious Mina Harker, to protect London from the dark forces of evil. Originally titled *The Last Van Helsing,* this tepid series borrows shamelessly from the *Buffy* franchise—minus the good storytelling, witty dialogue and talented actors.

Dracula

NBC/Sky. Oct 25, 2013 – Jan 24, 2014 (10 Episodes). Drama/Romance. D: Andy Goddard, Brian Kelly. W: Cole Haddon, Daniel Knauf. C: Jonathan Rhys Meyers ♀, Jessica De Gouw, Thomas Kretschmann, Victoria Smurfit, Oliver Jackson-Cohen, Nonso Anozie, Katie McGrath ♀, Ben Miles, Robert Bathurst, Miklós Bányai, Alastair Mackenzie, Phil McKee, Joseph Kowalski. UK/USA: English/Color/430m. Flame Ventures/Universal Television.

Fifteen years after being unearthed in Romania, Dracula resurfaces in England under the guise of Alexander Grayson, an American entrepreneur who wants to bring wireless electricity to Victorian society. His real goal, however, is to destroy the Order of the Dragon—a secret, nefarious group that was responsible for killing his wife back when he was human (and known as Vlad Țepeș, the Romanian warlord). As Dracula sets his plan in motion, things become complicated after he discovers that Mina Murray, a London socialite, may in fact be the reincarnation of his long-dead wife.

Much of this may sound familiar, because this pastiche of a story really doesn't offer anything new to *Dracula* lore—and is so far removed from Bram Stoker's novel that, except for some familiar faces and places, there's little to connect it to the original story. This series isn't meant for die-hard **Dracula** fans; it's for those in the vampire romance camp, who swoon over the eye candy that is Jonathan Rhys Meyers (let's face it, the character from Bram Stoker's novel, and the historical Vlad Țepeș, weren't exactly sex symbols sporting six-packs). Another glaring fault is that there's little horror to be found; Dracula is a dull schemer, who spends fifteen years developing an elaborate plan to introduce wireless electricity, just so he can supplant mankind's dependency on oil (the profits of which feed the activities of the Order of the Dragon). The Dracula I knew would have simply created a horde of vampire minions, and then commanded them to tear apart every single member of the group. As more take up their cause, they are struck down in kind. This Dracula, unfortunately, is patient to a fault. Although the series achieved good ratings, it wouldn't prove to grow long in the tooth; it was cancelled after a single season.

Dracula
[Il bacio di Dracula / Dracula's Curse]

Rai Uno. May 29/31, 2002 (2 Episode Miniseries). Drama/Horror. D: Roger Young. W: Roger Young, Eric Lerner. C: Patrick Bergin ♀, Giancarlo Giannini, Hardy Krüger Jr., Stefania Rocca, Muriel Baumeister ♀, Kai Wiesinger, Alessia Merz ♀. GER/ITA: English/Color/173m. RAI Radiotelevisione Italiana/Barnholtz Entertainment.

Lawyer Jonathan Harker is hired to purchase the Carfax Estate on behalf of Count Vladislav Tepes. He's actually an ancient vampire, who wants to use Harker and his friends as undead envoys in his quest to conquer the New World.

This contemporary—and often faithful—adaptation interweaves a morality tale about worldly success and making the right choices in life. Unfortunately it's plagued by uneven acting, and the pan-European cast speaks in accented (and often dubbed) English—which may be distracting to some audiences. The actors portraying Dracula and Professor Valenzi (the Van Helsing character) are well-suited in their roles, but the standout performer is Brett Forrest as "Béla Roenfield." Even though he has little screen time, the gaunt actor is mesmerizing as Dracula's crazed, insect-eating harbinger. Scholars debate over the novel's homoerotic overtones—if any—in the relationship between Dracula and Harker; this adaptation is not so subtle. In one scene, after Dracula stops his brides from attacking, Harker lies in bed, shocked and shirtless. Dracula then floats over Harker, straddles him on the bed, and whispers, "Oh yes I have loved…and I can love, can't I Jonathan? My love will give you freedom—freedom of choice…But you must come to me. You must love me. You must want me. You *must* love me!" Later, Dracula tells Lucy, "Every man can be yours… and then mine."

📺 Features a mish-mash of vampire lore: Dracula can morph into mist, a wolf, a bat, or even a mischief of rats; he's repelled by religious icons, is extremely wounded by holy water, and casts no reflection—but is unharmed by sunlight.

Dracula: The Series

Max (Jacob Tierney) and Christopher (Joe Roncetti) confront their nemesis Alexander Lucard (Geordie Johnson) in *Dracula: The Series* (RHI Entertainment/ Homescreen Entertainment)

Syndicated. Sep 29, 1990 – May 11, 1991 (21 Episodes). Adventure/Family. D: Allan Eastman, René Bonnière. W: Glenn Davis. C: Geordie Johnson ♀, Jacob Tierney, Joe Roncetti, Mia Kirshner ♀, Bernard Behrens, Geraint Wyn Davies ♀. USA: English/Color/630m. RHI Entertainment/ Homescreen Entertainment.

Dracula may have been a pain in the neck to the local villagers in Transylvania, but now that he's relocated to a major European center, he's become an international threat. Living under the guise of Alexander Lucard, the legendary bloodsucker is now a successful businessman, and with his corporate connections, he's in a position to take over the world's financial institutions. His activities are being closely monitored by Gustav Helsing, who's trying to find some way to expose Dracula for what he really is. Things take a complicated turn upon the arrival of Max and Christopher, Helsing's nephews from America.

An entertaining series for all ages, although adults will find some of the storylines and acting a little too camp. The devilish Alucard is a hoot, as is his "bromance" with his cackling offspring Klaus. The magnificent locations in Luxembourg, where the series was shot, add a stunning look to the show. Despite being canceled, the series ended on a cliffhanger: Gustav disappears into a mystical portal, chasing Alucard and Klaus; he leaves all his vampire-hunting notes to Max, who is set to return to the States with the rest of his family.

📺 Mia Kirshner (Sophie) starred in *The Vampire Diaries* and *30 Days of Night: Dark Days,* while Jacob Tierney (Max) starred in the episode "Nunc Dimittis" from the TV series The Hunger. Geraint Wyn Davies portrayed Nicholas Knight in *Forever Knight;* here he plays Klaus Helsing—and personal redemption is the last thing on this vampire's mind!

Forever Knight

CBS/USA Network. May 5, 1992 – May 18, 1996 (70 Episodes). Crime/Drama. D: Allan Kroeker. W: James D. Parriott, Barney Cohen. C: Geraint Wyn Davies ☥, John Kapelos ☥, Catherine Disher, Nigel Bennett ☥, Gary Farmer, Natsuko Ohama, Deborah Duchene ☥, Ben Bass ☥. CAN/GER: English/Color/4200m. Paragon Entertainment/Glen Warren Productions.

Nick Knight is an eight-hundred-year-old vampire who's atoning for his past misdeeds, although his maker, Lucien Lacroix, is offended by this desire for redemption. Knight works as a homicide detective in Toronto, and his one human confidant—Dr. Natalie Lambert—is using modern science to find a way for him to become mortal once again.

This ground-breaking series was the first of the "vampire cop" sub-genre, and paved the way for such shows as *Angel, Blood Ties* and *Moonlight*—but it was continually threatened by cancelation. The second season aired eighteen months after the first, and a third wouldn't have been produced were it not for the efforts of the ardent fan base—yet this final season suffered from major cast changes and inconsistent storytelling. The finale episode received mixed reviews from fans, despite an ambiguous ending that left the door open for continuing the series in some other form. In 1997, three novels based on the series were published by Boulevard Books.

📺 In the Season 2 episode "Stranger Than Fiction," Nick's human partner Schanke appears in a dream sequence dressed as a Dracula-type vampire.

From Dusk Till Dawn

El Ray. Mar 11, 2014 – 2016 (30 Episodes). Action/Horror. D: Robert Rodriguez, Dwight H. Little. W: Robert Rodriguez, Robert Kurtzman. C: D.J. Cotrona, Zane Holtz ☥, Eiza Gonzalez ☥, Jesse Garcia, Madison Davenport, Brandon Soo Hoo ☥, Wilmer Valderrama ☥, Robert Patrick, Jake Busey, Don Johnson, Samantha Esteban, Jamie Tisdale. USA: English/Color/1035m. Sugarcane Entertainment/Rodriguez International Pictures.

Seth and Richie Gecko are on the lam after a bank heist went horribly wrong. As they flee towards Mexico, Seth notices that his brother is becoming increasingly unstable—and he keeps adding to the body count, which isn't helping their cause one bit. Richie claims to be having visions of a woman who "needs to be set free," and he believes all questions will be answered once they reach the Titty Twister, a biker bar just over the border that turns out to be harboring all sorts of

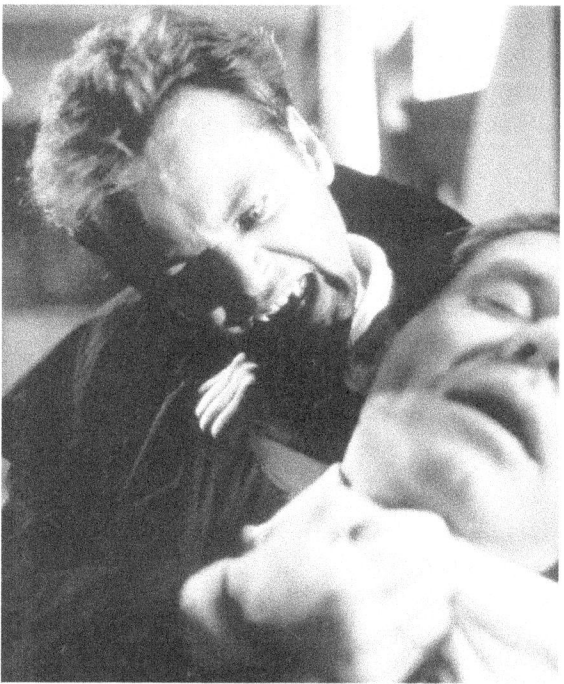

Nick Knight (Geraint Wyn Davies) is an 800-year old vampire atoning for his past misdeeds in *Forever Knight* (Paragon Entertainment/Glen Warren Productions)

Detective Nicholas Knight (Geraint Wyn Davies) uses his vampiric powers for good on *Forever Knight* (Paragon Entertainment/Glen Warren Productions)

monsters.

Based on the cult horror film *From Dusk Till Dawn* (1996), which starred George Clooney and Quentin Tarantino (who also wrote the screenplay), the first season retells the same story that was presented in the movie. What's markedly different is that the supernatural element is introduced from the get-go; this is a far cry from the film, which at first blush was a crime/drama that inexplicably took a hard-left turn into horror/comedy. The Gecko brothers are still the driving force behind the story, and are not your everyday anti-heroes; one is a sociopath, while the other is a psychopath. Much like in the film, they're villains through-and-through, yet in the adaptation, Richie has changed somewhat. In the movie, he was a sadist, rapist, and all-around creepy guy. He's equally as unstable in the series, but his sex-offending nature has been toned down, and his amorous hallucinations in the film have been replaced by supernatural ones (which tie into the larger story). Although the monsters here demonstrate traditional vampire traits, including subsisting on human blood, Rodriguez doesn't consider them as such; they're Mesoamerican in origin, dating back to an ancient sun-and-snake worshiping cult that had a penchant for human sacrifice. As the series progresses, he plans to expand on this mythology, which was first hinted at in the last scene of the 1996 film. Santánico Pandemonium, the vampire queen who in the movie was a one-dimensional monster, is given much more of voice in the series. She's still the hitherto antagonist in season one, but will become the heroine of the story in season two, as she faces enemies that are much more powerful than she. These changes, as well as the addition of new characters—and having a multi-episode platform to explore them at greater depth—results in a major improvement over the original film.

 Don Johnson's character, Texas Ranger Earl McGraw, also appeared in the original film, as well as in *Kill Bill* (2003/4), *Death Proof* (2007), and *Planet Terror* (2007).

The Gates

ABC. Jun 20 – Sep 19, 2010 (13 Episodes). Drama/Romance. D: Terry McDonough. W: Richard Hatem, Grant Scharbo. C: Rhona Mitra ☥, Luke Mably ☥, Frank Grillo, Marisol Nichols, Skyler Samuels, Travis Caldwell, Paul Blackthorne ☥. USA: English/Color/780m. Fox Television Studios/Summerland Entertainment.

Nick Monohan relocates his family to The Gates, an exclusive neighborhood where he's been hired as the new chief of police. All is not well within this strange, gated community: his first assignment is to solve the murder of the man he just replaced.

This supernatural soap opera followed residents of an exclusive community that housed a bevy of creatures, including vampires, werewolves, witches, and even a succubus. The main plot focused on a vampire couple and their human daughter, while the secondary story was a *Twilight*-infused melodrama that followed the lives of the teens in the neighborhood. Although the show was poorly promoted by the network, it developed a solid fan base, but the summer schedule—and low ratings—led to its demise.

Greg the Bunny (1st Series)

FOX. Mar 27 – Aug 11, 2002 (13 Episodes). Comedy/Satire. D: Jim Ellis. W: Dave Jeser, Matt Silverstein. C: Eugene Levy, Seth Green, Bob Gunton, Sarah Silverman, Dina Waters, Drew Massey ☥. USA: English/Color/390m. Steven Levitan Productions/20th Century Fox Television.

Greg the Bunny is just one of the many "Fabricated Americans" who live and work alongside the human population. The father of Greg's roommate is the director of the low-budget kids' puppet show "Sweetknuckle Junction," so he uses that connection to get an office job at the television station—but inadvertently lands a starring role on the TV show.

Entertaining series that parodies *Sesame Street* (1969) with a hint of *Meet the Feebles* (1990). The eclectic mix of characters include the vampire puppet Count Freddie Blah, and Junction Jack—a "racist" human actor with a deep hatred towards puppets (he calls them "socks," which they consider to be the most offensive racial slur). Some of the best bits are when they slag that "other muppet show" on PBS, and make derogatory references to its cast of characters.

Greg the Bunny (2nd Series)

IFC. Aug 19, 2005 – Dec 16, 2006 (20 Episodes). Culture/Satire. D/W: Sean Baker, Spencer Chinoy, Dan Milano. C: Dan Milano ☥, Sean Baker, Spencer Chinoy. USA: English/Color/240m. Monkeys With Checkbooks/Independent Film Channel.

In this reimagined series, Greg the Bunny is a struggling entertainer who befriends his idol, Count Blah—a foul-mouthed vampire and former television horror movie host (he's often mistaken for Count von Count from *Sesame Street*, which annoys him to no end). Most episodes parody films and television series, and the opening credit sequence is in homage to *The A-Team*.

Hemlock Grove

Netflix. Apr 19, 2013 – Oct 23, 2015 (33 Episodes). Mystery/Horror. D: David Straiton, Deran Sarafian. W: Brian McGreevy, Lee Shipman. C: Famke Janssen ☥, Bill Skarsgård ☥, Landon Liboiron, Joel de la Fuente, Kaniehtiio Horn, Dougray Scott, Madeleine Martin, Michael Andreae. USA: English/Color/1485m. Gaumont International Television/Mad Hatter Entertainment.

This Netflix series, based on Brian McGreevy's book of the same name, explores the strange goings-on at a fictional town in Pennsylvania following the brutal murder of a teenage girl. Residents include Peter Rumancek, who is a werewolf, and Roman Godfrey, who is half *Upir* (a blood-drinking vampire from European folklore).

House of Frankenstein

NBC. Nov 2/3, 1997 (2 Episode Miniseries). Action/Horror. D: Peter Werner. W: J.B. White. C: Adrian Pasdar, Greg Wise ☥, Teri Polo, CCH Pounder, Miguel Sandoval, Jorja Fox ☥, Richard Libertini, Karen Austin, J.A. Preston. USA: English/Color/168m. Big Productions Inc./Michael R. Joyce Productions.

🦇 🦇 🦇

Detective Vernon Coyle surveys the scene of another grisly murder, possibly the work of a serial killer. Meanwhile, Crispin Grimes, a wealthy night club owner, sends a crew to the Arctic Circle to search for the Frankenstein Monster—a creature that he believes is very real and buried somewhere in the ice flows. As Coyle investigates another attack, the trail leads to Grimes and his associates, and the detective realizes he's dealing with a very dangerous group. The case takes a strange turn upon the arrival of Dr. Shauna Kendall, an anthropologist who believes the murders were committed by a vampire.

A thoroughly enjoyable miniseries that features the three classic horror movie monsters, in a modern story that begins as a police drama, and then transitions into a full-fledged creature feature. The vampire isn't Dracula, but a centuries-old bloodsucker who appears human until he shows his true nature, which is gargoyle-like. He commands dozens of his kind, all of whom appear as traditional undead, and has authority over werewolves. Only the third terror, Frankenstein's Monster, is the real deal, and closely resembles the creature from Mary Shelley's

In *House of Frankenstein,* a Master Vampire (Greg Wise) terrorizes Los Angeles, and Frankenstein's Monster (Peter Crombie) is unearthed (Big Productions Inc/ Michael R. Joyce Productions)

Grace Dawkins (Teri Polo) and Crispin Grimes (Greg Wise) each have a dark secret in the 2-part miniseries *House of Frankenstein* (Big Productions Inc/Michael R. Joyce Productions)

novel. Considering how the story ends, it seems as though the intention was to make a sequel, or perhaps turn it into a series—neither of which ever came to pass.

Kindred: The Embraced

FOX. Apr 2 – May 8, 1996 (8 Episodes). Drama/Romance. D: Peter Medak. W: John Leekley, P.K. Simonds. C: Mark Frankel ☥, C. Thomas Howell, Kelly Rutherford, Stacy Haiduk ☥, Patrick Bauchau ☥. USA: English/Color/368m. John Leekley Productions/Spelling Television.

Detective Frank Kohanek desperately wants to arrest local businessman Julian Luna, whom he believes is a powerful mob boss controlling a large cartel in San Francisco. Kohanek is drawn into a strange new world after he discovers that Luna is actually a vampire, who rules over several disparate clans of the undead. The two form an uneasy alliance, and work together to solve cases involving wayward vampires.

The series was based on the role-playing game *Vampire: The Masquerade,* but it only used the basic premise—where several vampire clans secretly rule the government and other influential organizations—and then created a more traditional story that focused on Luna and Kohanek. Ardent fans of the source believed the series didn't delve enough into the politics between the clans, and much of what they loved about the game was lost in translation. The first episode was horribly written, confusing, and melodramatic; subsequent episodes were more inspired, and Luna turned out to be a fascinating character (while Kohanek remained a mess of clichés). There's no clear indication as to why the series was canceled; just months after the final episode aired, Mark Frankel (Julian Luna) was killed in a motorcycle accident.

Julian Luna (Mark Frankel) keeps the peace among several disparate clans of vampires in *Kindred: The Embraced* (John Leekley Productions/Spelling Television)

The Lair

here!. Aug 1, 2007 – Nov 27, 2009 (28 Episodes). Adult/Drama. D/W: Fred Olen Ray. C: David Moretti, Colton Ford, Dylan Vox ☥, Peter Stickles ☥, Brian Nolan, Johnny Hazzard, Grant Landry, Bobby Rice. USA: English/Color/840m. here! TV.

Small town journalist Thom Etherton investigates a series of bizarre murders, and discovers that a private gay club, known as The Lair, is run by vampires. His activities put his life in danger, but lucky for him, head bloodsucker Damien believes he's the reincarnation of a long dead lover.

The Little Vampire

ITV/CBC/NDR. Dec 31, 1986 – Mar 22, 1987 (13 Episodes). Adventure/Family. D: René Bonnière. W: Richard Nielsen. C: Christopher Stanton, Joel Dacks ☥, Michael Gough, Gert Fröbe, Susan Hogan, Michael Hogan. CAN/GER/UK: English/Color/325m. Norflicks Productions Ltd./Allarcom Limited.

An anti-social kid, Anton Besker, befriends a boy named Rüdiger, whom he discovers is a vampire—and is being hunted by a local police officer. Based on the books *Little Vampire* (1982) and *The Little Vampire Moves In* (1982) by Angela Sommer-Bodenburg.

The Lost Boys

The CW. 2017. Drama/Romance. D: Anon. W: Rob Thomas. C: Anon. USA: English/Color/--m. Gulfstream TV/Warner Bros Television.

Joel Schumacher's cult 1987 vampire film is being adapted for television, and will tell a story spanning several decades—only the main vampire characters will remain constant as the years go by. It's being eyed as the successor to *The Vampire Diaries,* with a planned 7-season story arc that will span seventy years, with each season covering about a decade. The first season kicks off in San Francisco, 1967, during the Summer of Love.

Midnight, Texas

NBC. 2016-2017 (-- Episodes). Drama/Fantasy. D: Niels Arden Oplev. W: Monica Owusu-Breen. C: François Arnaud, Dylan Bruce, Joanne Camp, Peter Mensah ☥, Parisa Fitz-Henley, John-Paul Howard, Arielle Kebbel, Bob Jesser, Jason Lewis, Shannon Lorance, Lora Martinez-Cunningham, Kyle Pierson, Sarah Ramos. USA: English/Color/--m. Universal Television/David Janollari Entertainment.

Based on Charlaine Harris's book trilogy of the same name, this series takes place at a small town in Texas where no one is quite what they seem. From witches to psychics, and vampires to werewolves, humans and supernatural creatures joined forces to form this tightknit community to protect themselves from outsiders who would do them harm. In the pilot, traveling psychic Manfred Bernardo heeds the advice of his deceased Grandmother and puts down roots in Midnight, unaware of just how special his neighbors really are. NBC execs, happy with the final product, have slated *Midnight, Texas* for their 2016/2017 schedule.

Monster Squad

NBC. Sep 11 – Dec 4, 1976 (13 Episodes). Adventure/Family. D: Herman Hoffman, James Sheldon. W: Charles Isaacs. C: Fred Grandy, Mike Lane, Henry Polic II ☥, Buck Kartalian, Edward Andrews. USA: English/Color/390m. D'Angelo-Bullock-Allen Productions.

Walter is a criminology student who works as a night watchman at a wax museum, and spends his time tinkering with an invention he calls a "crime computer." The machine inadvertently reanimates the wax statues of Dracula, Frankenstein, and the Wolf Man. Wishing to atone for their past misdeeds, with Walter's help, the three become supernatural crime fighters.

Moonlight

CBS/CTV. Sep 28, 2007 – May 16, 2008 (16 Episodes). Drama/Romance. D: Fred Toye. W: Trevor Munson, Ron Koslow. C: Alex O'Loughlin ☥, Sophia Myles, Jason Dohring ☥, Brian J. White, Tami Roman, Shannyn Sossamon ☥. USA: English/Color/960m. Silver Pictures Television/Warner Bros. Television.

In the 1950s, Mick St. John had the surprise of his life: on his wedding night, his new wife Coraline turned him into a vampire, and he's been struggling with this undead existence ever since. He now works as a private investigator in Los Angeles, and develops feelings for reporter Beth Turner, whom he saved as a child from the clutches of his wife.

Moonlight Desire

(Unproduced.) 1992. D/W: Alexander Galant.

Writer/director Alexander Galant researched Bram Stoker's own handwritten notes as he was developing this series, and he intended to present a darker version of the Count—because at the time, vampires had become too romantic. Set in the present day, pirates intercept artifacts recovered from the Titanic, and one of the crates holds Dracula—who's been trapped underwater for eighty years. The Count escapes; he discovers the descendants of those who wronged him are now scattered across the globe, unaware of their connection to the hunters in Stoker's novel (they believe it's a work of fiction). One of the descendants is a homicide detective named Van Helsing, and her partner is Detective Cotford—a name Galant discovered in Bram Stoker's notes. The series would have featured other literary and historical figures, including Elizabeth Báthory, Carmilla, Lord Ruthven, and Count Saint-Germain. Some of these elements resurfaced in the novel *Dracula the Un-dead* (2009), written by Dacre Stoker and Ian Holt; Alexander Galant was the historical researcher for this book.

The Munsters

CBS. Sep 24, 1964 – May 12, 1966 (70 Episodes). Comedy/Family. D: Lawrence Dobkin, David Alexander. W: Joe Connelly, Bob Mosher. C: Fred Gwynne, Yvonne De Carlo ♀, Al Lewis ♀, Beverley Owen, Pat Priest, Butch Patrick, Paul Lynde. USA: English/B&W/2100m. Kayro-Vue Productions.

🦇 🦇 🦇

A family of friendly monsters have a series of misadventures, never quite understanding why people react so strangely to them. Features the vampires Lily and Grandpa (who is later revealed to be Count Dracula).

A family of friendly monsters, whose patriarch is Count Dracula, see themselves as typical working-class suburbanites in *The Munsters* (Kayro-Vue Productions)

The Munsters Today

Syndicated. Oct 9, 1988 – May 24, 1991 (72 Episodes). Comedy/Family. D: Peter Isacksen, Russ Petranto. W: Noah Taft, Bryan Joseph. C: John Schuck, Lee Meriwether ☥, Howard Morton ☥, Jason Marsden, Hilary Van Dyke. USA: English/Color/2160m. The Arthur Company/MCA Television.

After one of Grandpa's experiments goes horribly wrong, The Munster family ends up in suspended animation for twenty-two years. They wake up in 1988, and have a great deal of difficulty adjusting to this image-conscious, technology-driven, self-help society.

This revamp may offend fans of the original series, especially by the second season, when it barely resembled the premise of its predecessor. The story was turned into a generic, vapid and horribly-written sitcom, populated with terrible jokes and canned laughter.

📺 Prior to airing the first episode, TBS broadcast *The Best of the Munsters,* a retrospective of the original series that reunited Al Lewis, Butch Patrick and Pat Priest.

My Babysitter's a Vampire: The Series

TeleToon/Disney. Feb 28, 2011 – Dec 6, 2012 (26 Episodes). Comedy/Family. D: Bruce McDonald. W: Tim Burns, Alice Prodanou. C: Matthew Knight, Vanessa Morgan ☥, Atticus Mitchell, Cameron Kennedy ☥, Kate Todd ☥, Ella Jonas Fargliner. CAN: English/Color/572m. Fresh TV.

Based on the telefilm/pilot of the same name, this series follows the further adventures of Ethan Morgan (a "seer" who can glimpse into the future), his best friend Benny (a spell caster), and his babysitter Sarah (a fledgling vampire).

The Originals

The CW. Oct 3, 2013 - 2017 (79 Episodes). Drama/Horror. D: Chris Grismer, Jeffrey G. Hunt. W: L.J. Smith, Michael Narducci. C: Joseph Morgan ☥, Daniel Gillies ☥, Phoebe Tonkin ☥, Charles Michael Davis ☥, Leah Pipes, Danielle Campbell, Claire Holt ☥, Daniella Pineda, Eka Darville, Steven Krueger, Todd Stashwick, Sebastian Roché ☥. USA: English/Color/3555m. My So-Called Company/Alloy Entertainment.

The first vampires in all of history, The Original Family, return to New Orleans, a city they helped build three centuries ago. But these undead siblings—Klaus, Elijah, and Rebekah—find a city at war; Klaus's progeny, Marcel, leads a vampire army against an increasingly-desperate coven of witches. Klaus isn't impressed by what's become of *his* city, so he decides to reclaim it for his own, and schemes to once again become the king of New Orleans. As he plays the witches against the vampires, his attention shifts to protecting the werewolf who is carrying his baby; a miracle child that is just like him—a hybrid, part werewolf and part vampire.

A spin-off of *The Vampire Diaries, The Originals* is geared towards an older audience, and focuses on the family drama between vampire siblings; although they share a bloodline, they couldn't be any more different. There's also greater attention given to the other supernatural beings who inhabit New Orleans, with less focus overall on romantic entanglements; *The Originals* is to *The Vampire Diaries* as *Angel* was to *Buffy the Vampire Slayer*. In its fledgling season, *The Originals* quickly established itself as a compelling supernatural drama in its own right, with a well thought-out universe. It's a worthwhile alternative for those looking for something more than what is offered by *The Vampire Diaries*, which is a teen-oriented series that revolves around an ever-dramatic love triangle.

📺 This series began as a backdoor pilot that aired as Episode 20 from Season 4 of *The Vampire Diaries*. The premiere episode of *The Originals* was a retelling of that same story, except rather than focus on Klaus, there were additional scenes featuring his siblings Elijah and Rebekah.

Penny Dreadful

Showtime/Sky. May 11, 2014 - Jun 19, 2016 (27 Episodes). Drama/Horror. D: J.A. Bayona, Coky Giedroyc. W: John Logan. C: Reeve Carney, Timothy Dalton, Eva Green, Rory Kinnear, Billie Piper, Danny Sapani, Harry Treadaway, Josh Harnett, Olivia Llewellyn ☥, Robert Nairne ☥, David Warner. CAN/UK/USA: English/Color/1620m. Desert Wolf Productions/Showtime Networks, Inc.

🦇 🦇 🦇 🦇

In pursuit of finding his daughter Mina, who fell under a dark influence and has since disappeared, Sir Malcolm Murray enlists the assistance of a brilliant, young doctor, as well as an American gunslinger. Vanessa Ives, Mina's best friend, feels responsible for her disappearance, so she often puts herself in harm's way as the group chases leads among the dank depths of London—where they uncover wicked, supernatural forces. And as more is revealed about each member of the group, it seems as though they're each dealing with demons of their own.

The story takes place in Victorian England, and features characters from classic Gothic literature including *Frankenstein* (1818), *The Picture of Dorian Gray* (1890), and *Dracula*

Promotional poster for the third and final season of John Logan's smash hit *Penny Dreadful* (Showtime)

(1897). In fact, is the latter novel that this series draws on the most, using a few of Bram Stoker's characters, as well as utilizing vampires as the main antagonist. As the first season progresses, Vanessa Ives becomes the most compelling original character; it's through her that the theme of the series, "there is some *thing* within us all," is most evident. Although there are some familiar faces and places, this is an original story, featuring a core group of reimagined characters who are on a quest to save a young woman's soul—and the journey thus far has proven to be a dark, horrific, and completely engaging one. This is must-see Un-Dead TV!

The title of the series is taken from a cheap, sensational form of 19th-century British fiction collectively known as "penny dreadfuls." These typically featured lurid stories that spanned several weeks, with each issue costing a penny. One of the better-known examples is *Varney the Vampire; or, the Feast of Blood,* which began as a series of penny dreadfuls before being collectively published as a novel in 1847.

Port Charles

ABC. Jun 2, 1997 – Oct 3, 2003 (1633 Episodes). Drama/Romance. D: Jill Ackles, Anthony Morina. W: Carole Real, Kelly Brown, Judy Farrell. C: David Holcomb, Jay Pickett, Lisa Lord, Michael Easton ☥, Ian Buchanan ☥, Lynn Herring, Thorsten Kaye ☥, Rebecca Staab ☥. USA: English/Color/48990m. ABC.

This spin-off of *General Hospital* initially focused on the lives of a handful of doctors in residence, and for the first couple of years was a traditional daytime soap opera. As if taking a cue from *Dark Shadows,* the storylines evolved to include Gothic elements; eventually vampires, angels and werewolves were introduced. Much as with Spanish *telenovelas,* each story arc spanned thirteen weeks, two per season, and had a distinct beginning, middle and end.

Power Rangers Mystic Force

ABC Family/Toon Disney. Feb 20 – Nov 13, 2006 (32 Episodes). Action/Fantasy. D: Mark Beesley. W: John Tellegen, Bruce Kalish. C: Firass Dirani, Angie Diaz ☥, Richard Brancatisano, Melanie Vallejo, Donogh Rees ☥. USA: English/Color/960m. Ranger Productions Ltd./BVS Entertainment Inc.

To battle a resurgence of evil forces, a powerful sorceress calls upon five teens, each destined to become legendary warriors known as The Power Rangers. One of the main villains in this series is Necrolai, the Dark Mistress of the Underworld and Queen of the Vampires. During the two-part story "Stranger Within," one of the Power Rangers is turned into the undead.

Preacher

AMC. May 22, 2016 – 2017 (23 Episodes). Drama/Fantasy. D: Evan Goldberg, Seth Rogen. W: Steve Dillon, Garth Ennis. C: Dominic Cooper, Joseph Gilgun ☥, Ruth Negga, Ian Colletti, Graham McTavish, Lucy Griffiths, W. Earl Brown, Derek Wilson, Tom Brooke, Anatol Yusef, Jackie Earle Haley, Ricky Mabe. USA: English/Color/1380m. AMC Studios/DC Entertainment.

Preacher Jesse Custer returns to his hometown of Annville, Texas, to reclaim his faith and lead his father's church, All Saints Congregational. But his blessed verses take on new meaning after a renegade soul, the offspring of a demon and an angel, merges with his own—and he gains the ability to control people with simply a word. Custer soon befriends Cassidy, a hedonistic, Irish vampire who's on the run from unusual government agents. *Preacher* is based on the Garth Ennis/Steve Dillon comic book series of the same name.

Real Vampire Housewives

(In Development). 2012. Comedy/Drama. D/W: Andre Jetmir. C: Metta World Peace.

Los Angeles Lakers forward Metta World Peace plays a vampire elder in the pilot for a proposed series about a group of mischievous women who are all married to vampires. While their husbands sleep during the day, the housewives get into all sorts of wicked trouble. In the pilot episode, a recently-engaged couple seeks the blessing of the Clan's Elder to wed. Although the pilot was set to shoot in September, 2012, in Encino, California, there has been no further information released about this production.

Sanctuary

SyFy. Oct 3, 2008 – Dec 30, 2011 (59 Episodes). Drama/Sci-Fi. D: Martin Wood. W: Damian Kindler, Sam Egan. C: Amanda Tapping, Robin Dunne, Ryan Robbins, Emilie Ullerup, Christopher Heyerdahl, Agam Darshi, Jonathon Young ⚥. CAN/USA: English/Color/3540m. Stage 3 Media/Sanctuary Productions.

In Victorian England, a group participated in experiments that used ancient vampire blood to test the boundaries of science and nature—with remarkable results. Dr. Helen Magnus received an extended lifespan, while her lover John Druitt gained the ability to teleport through time and space. James Watson attained a markedly higher intellect, while Nikola Tesla was turned into a vampire—and gained the power over electricity. The fifth member of the group, Nigel Griffin, attained the ability to turn invisible. Magnus now operates the "Sanctuary," a refuge for otherworldly creatures, and with the help of psychologist Will Zimmerman, she searches out these "abnormals" to protect, treat and study them. But a shadow organization known as The Cabal has a different attitude, and believes the creatures are a real threat to the survival of the human race—and should be destroyed.

The first season was hit and miss; the monster of the week stories were average, and often borrowed ideas from other Sci-Fi/Fantasy series. The main story arc that dealt with the five scientists and The Cabal was quite engaging, and made up for the lackluster episodes. The second season was a disappointment; it focused on character development and procedural crime investigation, and introduced split screens and fancy editing (overused eye candy that quickly became an annoyance). The most noteworthy aspect of the show was the character Nikola Tesla, deftly played by actor Jonathon Young. Witty, self-absorbed, and with charisma to spare, Tesla remains one of the most memorable vampire characters on television.

📺 *Sanctuary* used green screen technology combined with computer-based virtual sets, and began as a series of webisodes before it was picked up as a traditional television series.

Ben Mears (David Soul) battles master vampire Kurt Barlow (Reggie Nalder) in *Salem's Lot* (Warner Bros. Television)

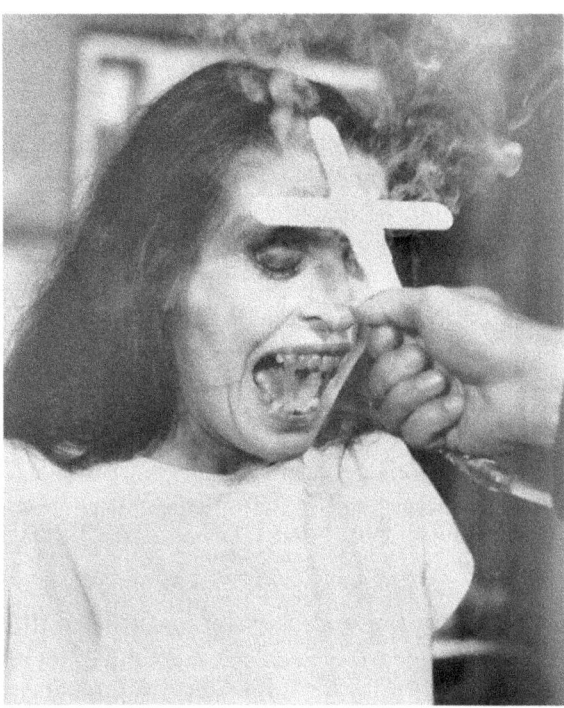

Newly-turned vampire Marjorie Glick (Clarissa Kaye) is seared by a holy cross in *Salem's Lot* (Warner Bros. Television)

Salem's Lot (1979)

CBS. Nov 17/24, 1979 (2 Episode Miniseries). Horror/Suspense. D: Tobe Hooper. W: Paul Monash. C: David Soul, James Mason, Lance Kerwin, Bonnie Bedelia ☥, Lew Ayres, Julie Cobb, Elisha Cook, George Dzundza, Ed Flanders, Reggie Nalder ☥, Brad Savage ☥. USA: English/Color/184m. Warner Bros. Television.

🦇 🦇 🦇

Author Ben Mears returns to his hometown to study the Marsten House, a stately home that he believes is inherently evil—a malevolent force that draws wicked men towards it. The house was recently purchased by Richard Straker, an eccentric antiques dealer who eagerly awaits the arrival of his partner, Kurt Barlow. After a local boy goes missing, Mears discovers that a great evil has awakened in the town—and it's living inside the walls of the Marsten House.

One of the better adaptations of Stephen King's work, produced at a time when TV movies weren't all just family-friendly fare. Although some liberties were taken with the story (especially with the character Kurt Barlow), this production still holds up to this day. It's a chilling tale of an evil force that spreads throughout a small town in Maine, and features one of the scariest-looking vampires ever seen on television.

In foreign markets, the miniseries was edited down to two hours and released theatrically, and the initial North American home video release was based on this version. Several scenes were re-edited or excised altogether, the most notable being the prologue and epilogue, which take place in Ximico, Guatemala. The complete version has since been restored and released on DVD.

Salem's Lot

NBC (Unproduced). 1979.

NBC had planned to spin-off the original story—a two-part miniseries on CBS—into a new original series that followed Ben Mears and Mark Petrie across the country, in their ongoing struggle against the vampires. Despite having renowned author Robert Bloch attached to the project, it never saw the light of day.

'Salem's Lot (2004)

TNT. Jun 20/21, 2004 (2 Episode Miniseries). Drama/Suspense. D: Mikael Salomon. W: Peter Filardi. C: Rob Lowe, Andre Braugher, Donald Sutherland, Samantha Mathis ✝, Rutger Hauer ✝, James Cromwell. USA: English & French/Color/182m. The Wolper Organization/Warner Bros. Television.

Author Ben Mears returns to his hometown of Jerusalem's Lot to research a new book about the Marsten House, a lofty estate with a horrific past. When Mears was nine years old, on a dare, he broke into the home and witnessed a murder-suicide, an event that has haunted him ever since. Mears discovers that the house was recently purchased by an eccentric antiques dealer named Richard Straker—and the arrival of his business partner coincides with a rash of tragic events.

This adaptation is quite different from the 1979 version, and in some ways more closely resembles the original novel by Stephen King. It's an interesting story about the nature of evil and those who are drawn towards it, and demonstrates how quickly a picture-perfect town can crumble under calamitous influences. Unfortunately parts of the story are weak, from the acting to the direction and writing, and some scenes are just downright laughable. The saving grace is actor Donald Sutherland, who is a delight to watch as the kooky, psychotic Richard Straker—the most interesting character of the "Lot."

Scully

Channel 4. May 14 – Jun 25, 1984 (7 Episode Miniseries). Drama/Fantasy. D: Les Chatfield. W: Alan Bleasdale. C: Andrew Schofield, Ray Kingsley, Mark McGann, Richard Burke, David Mallinson, Joe Briath, Tony Haygarth ♀. UK: English/Color/190m. Granada Television.

Delinquent teenager Francis Scully wants to be a professional soccer player, and hopes to one day join the Liverpool Football Club. The trouble is, his active imagination interferes with the reality around him, and he often sees visions of star athlete Kenny Dalglish. The caretaker at Scully's school is nicknamed Count Dracula, because he's a major pain in the neck—and he appears as a real vampire in some of Scully's fantasy scenarios.

Shadow Chasers – "Blood and Magnolias"

ABC (Unaired). 1986 (S01E12). Comedy/Mystery. D: Chuck Bowman. W: Mary Ann Kasica, Michael Scheff. C: Dennis Dugan, Trevor Eve, Nina Foch, Mary-Margaret Humes, Cameron Mitchell ♀, Frank Ashmore, Warren Munson, Frank Farmer. USA: English/Color/60m. Warner Bros. Television

This short-lived series followed a journalist and an anthropologist who teamed up to solve cases involving the paranormal—usually butting heads along the way (only nine of thirteen episodes went to air before it was canceled). In this episode, the team travels to North Carolina to investigate a vampire attack. They uncover a local legend about the lost colony of Roanoke, which vanished in the late sixteenth century; it's believed a vampire eradicated the entire population, but the creature was eventually killed and then buried in the area. As the investigation continues, the team meets an eccentric millionaire named Edwin Greaves—and he may actually be the infamous Roanoke Vampire.

A journalist and an anthropologist (Dennis Dugan, Trevor Eve) investigate paranormal cases in *Shadow Chasers* (Warner Bros. Television)

Shadowhunters: The Mortal Instruments

Freeform. Jan 12, 2016 – 2017 (23 Episodes). Fantasy/Romance. D: J. Miles Dale, Mairzee Almas. W: Ed Decter, Y. Shireen Razack. C: Katherine McNamara, Dominic Sherwood, Alberto Rosende ♀, Emeraude Toubia, Harry Shum Jr., Matthew Daddario, Isaiah Mustafa, Jon Cor, Alan Van Sprang, Maxim Roy, Paulino Nunes, Kaitlyn Leeb ♀. USA: English/Color/966m. Constantin Film/Don Carmody Television.

The series is based on *The Mortal Instruments* fantasy novels by Cassandra Clare, the first book of which was adapted to film as *The Mortal Instruments: City of Bones* (2013). The story centers on

Clary Fray, whose world changes overnight upon her 18th birthday, when she learns that she was born with angelic blood and destined to be a "Shadowhunter"—those who protect humans from demons, werewolves, vampires, and other nefarious creatures of the night.

Slayer School

(Unproduced.) 2003.

This concept never really developed beyond the pitch stage, when producers tossed around ideas for a replacement series as *Buffy* neared its end. The show would have followed a group of potential Slayers and feature other characters from *Buffy,* but the idea didn't sit well with Whedon—so it wasn't developed any further.

Smoke and Shadows

(Unproduced.) 2010.

In 2010, an idea was shopped around for a new vampire TV series based on the "Smoke" trilogy of books by Canadian fantasy author Tanya Huff—which features the return of Henry Fitzroy, the four-hundred-and-seventy-four-year-old vampire from her *Blood Ties* novels. The series follows Fitzroy to Vancouver, Canada, where production is beginning on a new TV show based on one of his graphic novels; he ends up investigating a series of paranormal happenings in the city. Initially entitled *Smoke & Mirrors,* the production was previously in development by Kaleidoscope Entertainment and The Fremantle Corporation.

The Strain

FX. Jul 13, 2014 - Oct 30, 2016 (36 Episodes). Drama/Horror. D: Guillermo del Toro, David Semel. W: Regina Corrado, Justin Britt-Gibson. C: Corey Stoll, David Bradley, Mia Maestro, Kevin Durand, Jonathan Hyde, Richard Sammel ☥, Sean Astin, Jack Kesy, Natalie Brown, Miguel Gomez, Ben Hyland, Robin Atkin Downes ☥. USA: English/Color/1584m. Double Dare You/ Carlton Cuse Productions.

🦇 🦇 🦇

This life-size statue of The Master (Robin Atkin Downes), from *The Strain,* caused a number of scares while on display at a pop culture convention (Author Photo)

Dr. Ephraim Goodweather and his team from the CDC investigate Regis Air Flight 753, which mysteriously went dark upon landing at JFK airport in New York City. All souls on board were lost, save for four survivors, none of whom remember anything beyond landing on the tarmac. An elderly man named Abraham Setrakian seems to have inside information about what happened aboard the plane, and he claims that it's tied to an ancient evil that dates back centuries. Although Goodweather dismisses the man's wild accusations, he fears they may be facing a catastrophic pathological event after all 206 corpses from Flight 753 disappear from the city morgue—and the surviving passengers start to show signs of infection from an unknown virus.

If nothing else, this series will be remembered as one that took its time to tell a story. Nothing of great consequence happens in the first couple of episodes, although there are a handful of chilling scenes that help keep the viewer interested. But even once the virus takes a hold of the city, leading to more mayhem, there still seems to be a lot of unnecessary scenes—and the writing seems padded at times. This seriously affects the pacing, and prevents this series from truly becoming must-see Un-Dead TV. Still, the story includes some interesting, if subtle, nods to traditional vampire folklore—and the creatures themselves are definitely not the kind that teenage girls will swoon over! (Which is definitely a plus in my book.)

📺 In 2006, Guillermo del Toro pitched the idea for *The Strain* to FOX television, but disagreed with the execs on how to tell the story. Rather than adapt it as a feature film, he teamed up with writer Chuck Hogan to pen a three-book series, which were published yearly beginning in 2009. That same year, *Variety* reported that the trilogy would be adapted into a three-season television series, but it wasn't until 2012 that cable channel FX—a division of FOX—requested a pilot, and then ordered a full series in November, 2013.

Summer in Transylvania

Nickelodeon (UK). Oct 25, 2010 – Jun 15, 2011 (20 Episodes). Comedy/Family. D: Simon Hynd. W: Andy Watts. C: Amy Wren, Charlie Evans ☥, Kane Ricca, Daniel Black, Sophie Stuckey, Richard Lumsden, Phillipa Peak, Andrew Harrison ☥. UK: English/Color/600m. The Foundation.

Summer Farley enrolls at Stoker High in Transylvania, and discovers that her classmates are all monsters—literally. The halls are teeming with teenage horrors, including zombies, werewolves, vampires and mummies.

True Blood

HBO. Sep 7, 2008 – Aug 24, 2014 (80 Episodes). Horror/Romance. D: Michael Lehmann, Scott Winant. W: Alan Ball, Charlaine Harris, Brian Buckner. C: Anna Paquin, Stephen Moyer ☥, Ryan Kwanten, Rutina Wesley ☥, Sam Trammell, Chris Bauer, Nelsan Ellis, Deborah Ann Woll ☥, Carrie Preston, Alexander Skarsgård ☥, Kristin Bauer van Straten ☥, Jim Parrack. USA: English/Color/4800m. Home Box Office.

🦇 🦇 🦇

The Japanese have developed a synthetic product known as Tru Blood, and vampires couldn't be happier. They've come out of the coffin and are freely living among the human population, but this uneasy co-existence is tenuous at best. Sookie Stackhouse is a barmaid who has a secret of her own—she can read minds—and her life changes forever upon the arrival of the vampire Bill Compton, who has returned home in search of his family roots.

After a synthetic blood product has eliminated their need to feed on humans from the shadows, many vampires now live out in the open in *True Blood* (Home Box Office)

This series is best described as going in like a lion, and out like a lamb. *True Blood* lost its focus about halfway through its seven-season run, and never fully recovered—and should have been staked a couple of seasons earlier than it was. Still, it was a ground-breaking series, and should be fondly remembered for its dark, sexy storytelling, which was often splattered with horrifically-bloody scenes, as well as its viral marketing campaigns and innumerable merchandising lines. What should be forgotten are its array of undeveloped and often dropped subplots, Sookie's bevy of supernatural suitors, and the finale episode that was pretty much panned by every fan who stuck with the series right up until the bitter end.

Ultraviolet

Channel 4. Sep 15 – Oct 20, 1998 (6 Episodes). Drama/Horror. D/W: Joe Ahearne. C: Jack Davenport, Susannah Harker, Idris Elba, Philip Quast, Stephen Moyer ♀, Fiona Dolman, Colette Brown, Corin Redgrave ♀. UK: English/Color/360m. World Productions Inc.

Detective Michael Colefield investigates the disappearance of his best friend Jack, and discovers that he's been turned into a vampire. Colefield reluctantly joins a paramilitary organization with ties to the Vatican, and learns that their mission is threefold: track vampires, discover their agenda, and eliminate them if necessary.

 Stephen Moyer starred in the HBO hit *True Blood,* while Corin Redgrave starred in the "Dracula" episode of *Mystery and Imagination* (1968).

The Vampire Diaries

The CW. Sep 10, 2009 - May 2017 (171 Episodes). Drama/Romance. D: Chris Grismer, Marcos Siega. W: Kevin Williamson, Julie Plec. C: Nina Dobrev ♀, Paul Wesley ♀, Ian Somerhalder ♀, Steven R. McQueen, Candice Accola ♀, Kat Graham, Zach Roerig, Michael Trevino. USA: English/Color/7695m. Alloy Entertainment/ Bonanza Productions.

In search of a normal life, Stefan Salvatore—a good-hearted vampire—returns home to Mystic Falls, where he masquerades as a teenager and enrolls in high school. He falls for fellow student

Elena Gilbert, a shy girl who reminds him of a past love. Stefan's quest for peace is shattered upon the arrival of his older brother Damon, a dangerous man who excels at being a vampire—and wants to make Stefan's life a living hell.

This series centres around a love triangle between Elena, Stefan, and Damon, and is therefore meant for those who prefer stories that are smothered in vampire romance. Unfortunately, it relies too much on the doppelgänger trope as a plot device, but the target audience likely doesn't care, because they're too distracted by all the eye candy. On a more positive note, this series introduced The Original Family—three vampire siblings, the first of their kind, who would end up with a spin-off series of their own: *The Originals* (2013).

Ian Somerhalder auditioned for the role of Jason Stackhouse on *True Blood*, but that's not where the connections between the two series ends. Both shows use the same fake blood, and also share editors.

Vampire High

YTV. Sep 15, 2001 – May 4, 2002 (26 Episodes). Drama/Family. D: Jim Kaufman. W: Mark Shekter, Laura Kosterski. C: David McIlwraith, Jeff Roop ☥, Meghan Ory, Karen Cliche ☥, Paul Hopkins ☥, Ilona Elkin ☥. CAN: English/Color/780m. Microtainment/Les Productions La Fête Inc.

Mansbridge Academy is a remote boarding school home to two groups of students: in the daytime, the wealthy and privileged wander the halls, while overnight, a group of vampires take part in a secret experiment meant to make them more civilized. Guided by Dr. Reginald Murdoch, the students try to curb their predatory nature as they cope with everything else that a normal teenager has to face.

Vampires: Brighter in Darkness

SKY. Jan 7 – Mar 2011 (8 Episodes). Drama/Romance. D/W: Jason Davitt. C: Tim Benge, Kyle Chester, Dan Briggs, Rhys Howells ☥, Rebecca Eastwood, Abigail Law-Briggs ☥, Dorival Mota, James MacCorkindale. UK: English/Color/240m. Witchward Productions.

After ending a disastrous relationship, a young gay man falls for a mysterious stranger named Lucas Delmore—who turns out to be an ancient vampire.

Van Helsing

SyFy. Sep 23, 2016 – 2017 (13 Episodes). Action/Sci-Fi. D: Michael Nankin, Simon Barry. W: Simon Barry, Jonathan Walker. C: Kelly Overton, Jonathan Scarfe, Christopher Heyerdahl, Rukiya Bernard ☥, David Cubitt, Vincent Gale ☥, Hilary Jardine, Trezzo Mahoro, Aleks Paunovic ☥, Alison Wandzura, Laura Mennell ☥, Paul Johansson ☥. USA: English/Color/780m. Nomadic Pictures.

This futuristic story follows Vanessa Helsing, a single mom who was killed by a vampire—or was she? A few years later, she awakens into a post-apocalyptic world overrun by the undead. She learns that she's immune to the vampire's bite, and her peculiar blood composition gives her the ability to transform the creatures back into their former humans selves!

Vlad Dracula

Starz (In Development). 2012. Action/Drama. W: J. Michael Straczynski, Roy Lee.

Created by J. Michael Straczynski *(Babylon 5)* and Roy Lee *(The Ring)*, this series will intertwine the life and times of the historical Vlad Țepeș with Bram Stoker's fictional vampire. Announced in 2012, the story follows Vlad's life as a fifteenth century warlord, as he struggles to hold on to his humanity while he slowly becomes a vampire. The first season will take place during the 1400s, while the second will take place in the present day.

Wizards of Waverly Place

Disney. Oct 12, 2007 – Aug 27, 2010 (77 Episodes). Family/Sci-Fi. D: Victor Gonzalez. W: Todd J. Greenwald, Perry M. Rein. C: Selena Gomez, Jake T. Austin, David Henrie, Maria Canals-Barrera, David DeLuise, Bridgit Mendler ♀. USA: English/Color/2310m. It's a Laugh Productions.

The Russo children—Alex, Justin and Max—are typical kids except for one major difference: they're all wizards in training. Their sibling rivalry runs deeper than most, because once they turn eighteen, only one of them gets to keep their magical abilities. The second season features the Van Heusens, a family of friendly vampires who open a competing sandwich shop.

Young Dracula

CBBC. Sep 21, 2006 – Mar 13, 2014 (66 Episodes). Comedy/Family. D: Joss Agnew. W: Danny Robins, Dan Tetsell. C: Gerran Howell ♀, Clare Thomas ♀, Keith-Lee Castle ♀, Simon Ludders, Andy Bradshaw, Craig Roberts, Lucy Borja, Ben McGregor. UK: English/Color/1650m. BBC Wales.

After his wife leaves him for a werewolf, Count Dracula relocates with his children to a small town in Britain. To his dismay, his kids actually want to befriend the townspeople—rather than eat them—and since they have not yet attained their full vampiric nature, they can still freely walk among the humans. With the help of their bumbling servant Renfield and a talking, stuffed wolf named Zoltan, the family adjusts to their strange new lives abroad.

This exceptional comedy series is filled with unique and interesting characters. The most enjoyable is Count Dracula, a fish out of water, who still attempts to be the embodiment of evil despite being distracted by the modern trappings of his new surroundings. He's old fashioned and doesn't believe that women make good vampires—which is why instead of his daughter, he chose her younger brother to be his successor. Such intense family drama has never been so much fun! Highly recommended.

Craig Roberts played the vampire Adam in the UK series *Being Human* and its spin-off web series, *Becoming Human*.

Zombies vs. Vampires

NBC (Unproduced). 2010. W: Austin Winsberg. Wonderland Productions/Warner Bros. Television.

In the summer of 2010, NBC bought a spec script for a comedy series described as a "buddy cop procedural," where the two main characters are a human and a vampire (who hides his true nature). They investigate "zombie crimes" in a world where these brain munchers are integrated into society—since they can be controlled through medication.

Spied on the streets of Toronto, Canada, was this sign for crew members working on Guillermo del Toro's *The Strain*. This begs the question, who was in holding? And were they on the menu? (Author Photo)

Lost Girl stars Zoie Palmer (Dr. Lauren Lewis) and Anna Silk (Bo Dennis) meet fans at a pop culture convention (Author Photo)

Lost Girl stars Kris Holden-Ried (Dyson Thornwood) and Ksenia Solo (Kenzi Malikov) meet fans at a pop culture convention (Author Photo)

PROMINENT BITE
TELEFILMS AND PILOTS

Dracula (Louis Jourdan) offers his blood to Mina (Judi Bowker) in a scene from *Count Dracula* (British Broadcasting Corporation)

13 Thirteenth Avenue

CBS. Aug 15, 1983. Comedy/Family. D: John Bowab. W: Lenny Ripps, Steve Zacharias. C: A.C. Weary, Ilene Graff, Ernie Sabella, Paul Kreppel ♀, Robert Harper, Wil Wheaton, Clive Revill, Elizabeth Savage, Stanley Brock. USA: English/Color/30m. Paramount Pictures.

In this pilot episode for an unsold series, psychiatrist Dr. Carey looks after several otherworldly beings that live in an apartment building on 13 Thirteenth Avenue in New York City. Residents include a vampire lawyer, a werewolf accountant, and a witch who's a model—and the superintendent is a troll. They fear their secrets will be exposed upon the arrival of the new, "normal" tenants: a recently-widowed Assistant District Attorney and his young son. The vampire lawyer is a traditional bloodsucker; he dislikes sunlight and avoids garlic.

In *13 Thirteenth Avenue,* a psychiatrist (Clive Revill) discovers that several of his neighbors are supernatural beings, including Roland Keats (Paul Kreppel), who's a vampire (Paramount Pictures)

Angel - Pilot

WB (Pilot). 1998. Drama/Fantasy. D: Anon. W: Joss Whedon, David Greenwalt. C: David Boreanaz ♀, Charisma Carpenter, Glenn Quinn, Sarah Michelle Gellar, Julie Benz, Eliza Dushku, Juliet Landau. USA: English/Color/6m. Mutant Enemy Productions.

Angel, the vampire with a soul, recaps the story of his life—from his days as mortal in Ireland, to the main events in the *Buffy* series. This unaired presentation pilot uses footage from *Buffy* and adds new scenes featuring Angel, Cordelia and Doyle—to illustrate the premise of "helping the helpless" in Los Angeles.

Angel / Spike / Willow / Faith

WB (Unproduced). 2004-2006.

When *Angel* was canceled in 2004, it was reported that the WB network was interested in a television movie based on the show. However, David Boreanaz said that he'd only return if it was released theatrically—but the WB declined. That same year, James Marsters—who played Spike on both *Buffy* and *Angel*—said that a movie based on his character was a possibility, and he'd participate as long as it was made within five years (otherwise he'd have aged too much to play an immortal character). In 2005, Joss Whedon asked Tim Minear *(Angel, Firefly, Dollhouse)* to write and direct a Spike movie, and by early 2006 the WB was open to discussing the project. But later that year, Whedon said that funding was an issue, and Amy Acker—who would have co-starred with Marsters—said the project was officially dead. She also revealed that three telefilms had been proposed, each a separate story that would have focused on Spike, Willow, and Faith.

Asylum Night

HorrorChannel. Dec 19, 2004. Comedy/Horror. D: Brad Watson. W: Brad Watson, Darren Mills. C: Adrienne Carlyle ⚱, David Horton, Michelle Esclapez ⚱, Elliot Hill, Nicolas Levene ⚱, Robert Cargill, Lucy Casson ⚱, Lauren Bigby, James MacLeod. UK: English/Color/120m. Revolt Films.

Investigative reporter Ellen Cole goes undercover at a local mental institution that's rumored to be involved in questionable practices. She's deeply concerned about her brother, who's one of the patients there, and discovers a number of inmates are missing. The staff are using them as part of a nefarious experiment that also involves a nest of vampires held captive within the dank basement of the facility.

Low budget indie horror that's high on blood, gore and other bodily fluids, but the coagulated script doesn't offer anything new to the genre—and the film overstays its welcome long before the end credits begin to roll.

Being Human

BBC Three. Feb 18, 2008. Drama/Fantasy. D: Declan O'Dwyer. W: Toby Whithouse. C: Guy Flanagan ⚱, Russell Tovey, Andrea Riseborough, Claire Foy, Adrian Lester ⚱, Dylan Brown, Dominique McElligott. UK: English/Color/60m. Touchpaper Television.

In modern-day Bristol, three supernatural twentysomethings share a flat while they attempt to lead normal lives despite their otherworldly nature: Mitchell is a vampire, George a werewolf, and Annie is a ghost. This is the pilot for what would become the hit UK series, and aside from actor Russell Tovey, all other characters were re-cast.

Bloodsuckers

SyFy. Jul 30, 2005. Horror/Sci-Fi. D/W: Matthew Hastings. C: Joe Lando ⚱, Dominic Zamprogna, Natassia Malthe ⚱, Leanne Adachi, Aaron Pearl, A.J. Cook, Michael Deluise, Michael Ironside ⚱. CAN: English/Color/100m. Vega Productions Inc./Kandu Entertainment/Sci-Fi Pictures.

The human race has spread throughout the universe, and discovered other intelligent life, most of it vampiric. To prevent these creatures from attacking the Earth, vampire sanitation crews—dubbed V-SANs—explore the depths of space to seek out and kill whatever undead species they find. After responding to an emergency call from a remote mining colony under attack, a V-SAN team barely escapes with their lives. The vampires responsible are in league with a human faction known as the Cosmosis, a group dedicated to halting mankind's expansion into outer space; they also believe that vampires have every right to co-exist. It's a race against time as the wayward V-SAN team struggles to track down the Cosmosis ship, before her crew can jeopardize more lives in pursuit of their peculiar vision of utopia.

Released on DVD as *Vampire Wars: Battle for the Universe,* this is a better than average SyFy production (which isn't saying much)—although the concept of vampires in space is a little silly. Michael Ironside shows up intermittently to chew the scenery as the bad-ass vampire Muco, and really only exists to serve the plot; he's killed off by the third act. The special effects are pretty good across the board, but the same can't be said for most of the acting, nor the "action" scenes. Natassia Malthe is suitably sexy as the vampire Quintana, the daughter of two vampirized humans, a role which perhaps inspired director Uwe Boll to cast her as Rayne in the two completely unnecessary sequels to his feature film *BloodRayne* (2005).

Blood Ties

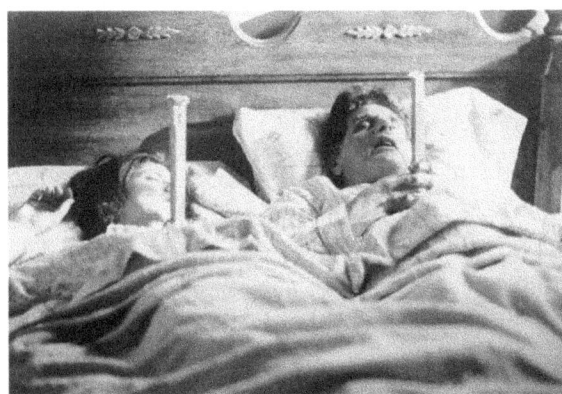

A teenager learns of his unique ancestry after his parents (Anne Marie Gillis, Michael Bellomo) are brutally murdered in *Blood Ties* (Richard and Esther Shapiro Entertainment Inc./Barb Lakin)

FOX. May 27, 1991. Drama/Romance. D: Jim McBride. W: Richard Shapiro. C: Harley Venton ☥, Patrick Bauchau ☥, Kim Johnston-Ulrich, Michelle Johnson ☥, Salvator Xuereb ☥, Jason London ☥, Bo Hopkins. USA: English/Color/91m. Richard and Esther Shapiro Entertainment Inc.

🦇 🦇 🦇

Teenager Cody Puckett discovers that crossbow-wielding intruders have brutally attacked his parents; they were impaled with wooden stakes, had their mouths filled with dirt, and were set on fire. Blamed for their deaths, he flees to a group of distant relatives in California, where he learns that he's one of many "Carpathian-Americans" living in the United States—a group that refuses to use the term "vampire" to describe themselves (because it's derogatory). The clan is divided; while some members try to integrate into the human population, others believe they shouldn't mix with what they consider a lesser species. As Cody tries to figure out exactly where he fits in, the Carpathians are faced with a new enemy in town: the Southern Coalition Against Vampires, which includes the same group of zealous hunters who killed his parents.

The Carpathians are descendants of Adam's first wife Lilith, the result of her liaison with a creature known as Mobius; they're not immortal nor are they bothered by sunlight, but they are stronger than humans, and heal more quickly. Much of the conflict is between the "assimilationists"—those who feel they should be up front about what they are—and the traditional bloodsuckers, who believe that the two species should never mix. The vampires are the heroes in this tale of family loyalty, race relations, and good versus evil, and the story features a healthy dose of humor, sex and drama. It was rumored that based on the success of the *Dark Shadows* revival in early 1991, producers Richard and Esther Shapiro (of *Dynasty* fame) were able to sell FOX on this story. With a strong cast and interesting premise, *Blood Ties* would have translated easily into a series—but unfortunately it never made it past the pilot stage. It has since been released into the home video market as a standalone movie.

📺 Patrick Bauchau played the vampire Archon Raine in the short-lived series *Kindred: The Embraced* (1996).

Buffy the Vampire Slayer – Pilot

(Unaired.) May 1996. Action/Fantasy. D/W: Joss Whedon. C: Sarah Michelle Gellar, Nicholas Brendon, Riff Regan, Charisma Carpenter, Anthony Stewart Head, Mercedes McNab, Julie Benz ☥. USA: English/Color/26m. 20th Century Fox Television/Mutant Enemy.

🦇 🦇 🦇

Buffy Summers relocates to Sunnydale, hoping to leave destiny and slaying far behind her. But she's forced to battle the undead once again, after a man is killed by a vampire. Her new Watcher, Rupert Giles, is an Englishman who serves as the librarian at her school.

Although some of the acting and direction is weak, this unaired pilot is still very well-written with some sharp dialogue and funny moments. The familiar cast of characters are all here, and the story acts as a blueprint for what the series would become. This is technically a "presentation" production, used to sell the series to networks, and was never meant to be broadcast on television. It was leaked onto the Internet, much to the chagrin of Joss Whedon. The story was expanded and reshot as "Welcome to the Hellmouth" (1997), the first episode of the series.

The Scoobies battle supernatural forces of evil that are a constant threat to their beloved town of Sunnydale in *Buffy the Vampire Slayer* (Mutant Enemy Productions/20th Century Fox Television)

Cast a Deadly Spell

HBO. Sep 7, 1991. Drama/Fantasy. D: Martin Campbell. W: Joseph Dougherty. C: Fred Ward, David Warner, Julianne Moore, Clancy Brown, Alexandra Powers. USA: English/Color/96m. HBO Pictures/Pacific Western.

🦇 🦇 🦇

This story takes place in an alternate 1940s universe, where monsters are real and magic is practiced by everyone—except for Detective H. Philip Lovecraft. He's hired by a wealthy man to recover the Necronomicon, a mystical tome stolen by a former employee. The mystical and magical are simply a part of everyday life, as are monsters and other fanciful creatures. Bloodsuckers play a negligible role; in one scene, a police detective complains about the vampires in West Hollywood, and one of them bares her fangs behind the bars of a jail cell.

Count Dracula

Dracula (Louis Jourdan) haunts the Whitby cemetery in the 1977 BBC adaptation *Count Dracula* (British Broadcasting Corporation)

BBC Two. Dec 22, 1977. Drama/Horror. D: Philip Saville. W: Gerald Savory. C: Louis Jourdan ☥, Frank Finlay, Susan Penhaligon ☥, Judi Bowker, Mark Burns, Jack Shepherd, Bosco Hogan, Richard Barnes, Susie Hickford ☥, Belinda Meuldijk ☥, Sue Vanner ☥. UK: English/Color/151m. BBC.

🦇 🦇 🦇

In this faithful adaptation of Bram Stoker's novel, Jonathan Harker travels to Transylvania to assist Count Dracula, who wants to emigrate to England. Imprisoned in the castle, Harker discovers his sinister host is actually a bloodthirsty vampire.

Aside from a veiled reference to Vlad Țepeș, this adaptation follows the novel quite closely—except for the conclusion, which ends in typical staking fashion. The primary focus is Lucy, who's now Mina's sister, and she only has two suitors this time around. Quincey Morris and Arthur Holmwood have merged to become Quincey P. Holmwood, a Texan who works for the Embassy in London—and has the worst American accent you could ever imagine. Louis Jourdan's Dracula exudes charm, arrogance and menace. His low-key performance is a welcome change from the norm, as is that of Jack Shepherd as Renfield, a man deeply disturbed by the dark influence of the vampire; he's not the over-the-top lunatic that is usually seen on screen. This is a fine production and one of the top adaptations, with some stunning locations that include Whitby. It also features some dated video effects that were cutting edge in the 1970s, but appear awkward to modern audiences.

📺 In the United States, this was rebroadcast in March 1978 on PBS under the "Great Performances" banner. In some regions it aired as a complete program in one evening, while in other markets it was split into two or three parts, airing as a miniseries over days and even weeks. Subsequent airings in the UK were also split into three parts.

The Curse of Dracula

NBC. 1979. Drama/Romance. D: Jeffrey Hayden, Sutton Roley, Kenneth Johnson. W: Craig Buck, Myla Lichtman, Renee & Harry Longstreet. C: Michael Nouri ♀, Carol Baxter ♀, Stephen Johnson, Bever-Leigh Banfield ♀, Louise Sorel ♀. USA: English/Color/120m. Universal TV.

In modern-day San Francisco, the infamous Count Dracula now lives and works under the assumed identity of a college professor, teaching East European History at Southbay College. Although he has a few students under his spell, he secretly longs for Mary Gibbons, the daughter of a woman he once loved. His plans, however, are constantly interrupted by Kurt von Helsing, the grandson of the legendary vampire hunter. This telefilm supposedly combines all ten chapters of the segment "The Curse of Dracula" from the series *Cliffhangers!*, edited together as a standalone movie.

Dark Shadows (2004)

(Unaired.) May 2004. Drama/Fantasy. D: P.J. Hogan. W: Mark Verheiden. C: Alec Newman ♀, Marley Shelton, Matt Czuchry, Ivana Milicevic, Blair Brown, Martin Donovan, Jessica Chastain, Kelly Hu, Jason Shaw. USA: English/Color/40m. Dan Curtis Productions/Warner Bros. Television.

In the *Cliffhangers* segment "The Curse of Dracula," the Count (Michael Nouri) secretly longs for Mary Gibbons (Carol Baxter), the daughter of a woman he once loved (Universal TV)

On Halloween night, Victoria Winters arrives at the majestic estate known as Collinwood mansion. Later that evening, caretaker Willie Loomis unexpectedly lets loose the vampire Barnabas Collins, who had been trapped for centuries within the family crypt.

This re-imagined pilot featured an all-new cast in a contemporary setting. It was originally going to be directed by Rob Bowman *(The X Files),* who had previously helmed some episodes from the 1991 revival series. Instead he chose to direct a feature film, and was replaced by P.J. Hogan—who was unfamiliar with the franchise (this was allegedly one of the reasons why the production did not "gel" in the way that WB executives had hoped). The series was never picked up and the pilot was never broadcast; however, it has been screened at several Dark Shadows Festivals.

Daughter of Darkness

CBS. Jan 26, 1990. Horror/Thriller. D: Stuart Gordon. W: Robert Reynolds ♀, Dezsö Garas, Jack Coleman, Erika Bodnár ♀, Kati Rák ♀, Ági Margittai. USA: English/Color/88m. King Phoenix Entertainment Inc./Accent Entertainment Corporation.

Katherine Thatcher travels to Bucharest in search of a father that she never knew. She discovers the pendant she wears—his only gift to her—is actually the family crest of Prince Constantin Ciprian, a man who local legend says disappeared over two hundred years ago after becoming a vampire. Katherine is captured by a group that believes she is of unique birth—the daughter of a vampire—and they plan to use her as a vessel to breed a race of human immortals, which will be able rule the land by night *and* day.

Prince Constantin (Anthony Perkins) protects his daughter from a group of vampires in *Daughter of Darkness* (King Phoenix Entertainment Inc./Accent Entertainment Corp.)

This film is very authentic-looking; shot in Hungary, local actors were used for all but the lead roles, and the production does a good job of recreating the state of Romania towards the end of Ceaușescu's rule (it would have been nearly impossible to actually film in Bucharest at the time). Unfortunately, made-for-television vampire movies tend to be toned down with the blood and gore elements, and this is no exception. The vampires aren't terrifying enough, and the relationships that Katherine has along the way—with an undead gigolo and a straight-laced diplomat—completely lack believability. Perkins effectively disappears into the role of the alpha bloodsucker, but his performance is not enough to elevate this production beyond a low-budget, B-movie feel.

 These vampires have no fangs; instead, they feed using a proboscis, which extends from within their tongue after it splits open. This is reminiscent of a similar method of feeding used by the vampire Dr. Weyland in the modern classic *The Vampire Tapestry* (1980) by Suzy McKee Charnas.

Deadly Love

Lifetime. Oct 9, 1995. Drama/Romance. D: Jorge Montesi. W: Rob Gilmer, Sherry Gottlieb. C: Susan Dey ♀, Stephen McHattie, Eric Peterson, Julie Khaner. CAN: English/Color/92m. Power Pictures/Alexander Enright and Associates/Victor Television.

Lonely vampire Rebecca Barnes is a successful photographer by day and stalker of evil men by night, who becomes intimately involved with Sean O'Connor, a detective investigating a series of bizarre murders. As Barnes struggles with revealing her true nature to the man she loves, O'Connor is torn by the suspicion that she may be the killer who's stalking the city.

Based on the novel *Love Bite* by Sherry Gottlieb, this is essentially a romantic drama with fangs (but no blood or gore). As is not often the case, the vampire protagonist is a woman, and Susan Dey is quite stunning in the role. It's a strong story with some fine acting, and those who enjoy the romantic side of vampirism will appreciate this one.

📺 Stephen McHattie played another star-crossed lover in the vampire-themed episode "Nightshift" from *The Hitchhiker* (1985).

Rebecca Barnes (Susan Dey) has a taste for evil men in the TV movie *Deadly Love* (Power Pictures/Alexander Enright and Associates)

Dead of Night

ABC (Unproduced). 1975/77. Horror/Suspense. D: Dan Curtis. W: Richard Matheson.

Two pilots were produced for a proposed anthology series; neither went beyond the telefilm stage, despite being created by the horror dream team of Dan Curtis and Richard Matheson. The first, *Trilogy of Terror* (1975), featured a succubus story, while the second, *Dead of Night* (1977), included a period piece about a vampire attack. Curtis was part of a similar venture for an unsold pilot called *Dead of Night: A Darkness at Blaisedon*. In that story, two supernatural investigators check out strange goings-on at a house believed to be haunted. Produced by a team closely associated with *Dark Shadows*, this pilot has the same look and feel; it was broadcast in 1969, but not commissioned into a full series.

Dead of Night

NBC. Mar 29, 1977. Fantasy/Horror. D: Dan Curtis. W: Richard Matheson, Jack Finney. C: Ed Begley Jr., E.J. André, Patrick MacNee, Anjanette Comer, Elisha Cook, Horst Buchholz ♀, Joan Hackett. USA: English/Color/73m. Dan Curtis Productions Inc./Metromedia Producers Corporation.

🦇🦇🦇

Legendary producer/director Dan Curtis teamed up with renowned author Richard Matheson for this anthology of three tales: "Second Chance," "No Such Thing as a Vampire," and "Bobby."

The second story takes place in Solta, Romania in 1896, where a distraught professor seeks the help of his superstitious butler to protect his wife, who's being preyed upon by a vampire. But even as the men defend the woman by all means possible, the attacks continue, which leads them to believe that the vampire may be hiding somewhere within the estate.

Although "Bobby" is hands-down the best story, "No Such Thing as a Vampire" still gets honorable mention for its strong acting and the smart twist ending. However, the scant twenty-one-minute running time doesn't leave much room for an elaborate story or extensive character development. This trilogy was the second pilot for a proposed anthology series to be called *Dead of Night;* the first attempt was the 1975 TV movie *Trilogy of Terror.*

📺 "No Such Thing as a Vampire" was originally published in the October 1959 issue of Playboy magazine. Richard Matheson first adapted the story for television in 1968, for the UK anthology series *Late Night Horror*—no known archive for this version exists, and it is considered a lost production.

Dracula (1973)

CBS. Feb 8, 1974. Drama/Horror. D: Dan Curtis. W: Richard Matheson, Bram Stoker. C: Jack Palance ⚰, Simon Ward, Nigel Davenport, Pamela Brown, Fiona Lewis ⚰, Penelope Horner, Murray Brown ⚰. USA: English/Color/99m. Dan Curtis Productions Inc.

🦇🦇

Mrs. Westenra (Pamela Brown) unknowingly hosts a bloodthirsty vampire who believes that her daughter Lucy is his reincarnated bride in *Dracula* (Dan Curtis Productions Inc)

Solicitor Jonathan Harker travels to Transylvania at the behest of Count Dracula, who wants to relocate to England and purchase some property there. Harker discovers that Dracula is not quite human, and after the Count leaves for England, he's imprisoned within the walls of the dilapidated castle. Dracula sets his sights on Lucy Westenra, a woman whom he believes is the reincarnation of his long-dead wife. Vampire hunter Van Helsing, and Lucy's fiancé Arthur Holmwood, try to stop the Count before he can turn her into his undead bride.

This adaptation diverges from the novel quite a bit, especially with the characters of Jonathan Harker and Lucy Westenra; she's now Dracula's love interest, and the main reason why he relocates to England. Borrowing elements from *Dark Shadows,* this version introduces new aspects to the Dracula tale, including the reincarnation of a lost loved one. It's also most likely the first film to reimagine Dracula as Vlad Țepeș, the fifteenth century Wallachian prince—yet it is never explained how he became a vampire. Palance plays the Count as more animal than human, which works most of the time, but overall the story falls short from the lofty expectations of such a

In *Dracula*, solicitor Jonathan Harker (Murray Brown) gets more than he bargained for while on a business trip to Transylvania (Dan Curtis Productions Inc)

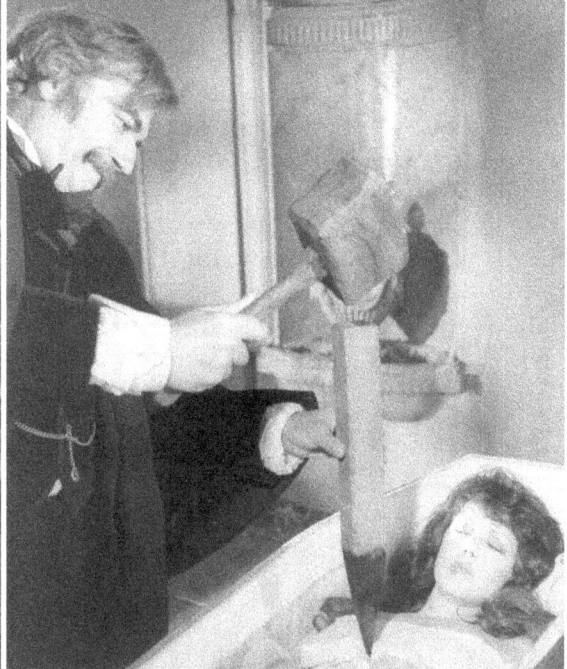

Van Helsing (Nigel Davenport) dispatches the vampiress Lucy Westenra (Fiona Lewis) in the 1973 TV movie *Dracula* (Dan Curtis Productions Inc)

horror dream-team as Curtis and Matheson. Eagle-eyed fans will notice that when Mina's body is discovered, the scene almost matches frame-by-frame a similar sequence in *House of Dark Shadows*, when Carolyn's body is found; this sequence is reproduced for a third time in the 1991 revival of *Dark Shadows*, when Daphne's body is discovered!

 This production was originally slated to air on October 12, 1973 but was pre-empted by a live television address by President Richard Nixon. He announced that Gerald Ford was nominated to replace Spiro Agnew as Vice President.

Dracula (2006)

BBC One. Dec 28, 2006. Horror/Romance. D: Bill Eagles. W: Stewart Harcourt. C: Marc Warren ☥, Tom Burke, Stephanie Leonidas, Sophia Myles ☥, Rafe Spall, Dan Stevens, Donald Sumpter, David Suchet. UK: English/Color/90m. Granada Television/BBC Wales.

🦇

Arthur Holmwood is a desperate man. Recently engaged, he just learned that he contracted syphilis at birth; his parents both died from the horrible disease, and he's beginning to show signs of infection. A cure may be found with a Transylvanian nobleman named Count Dracula, who some believe possesses extraordinary occult powers. Holmwood arranges for Dracula to come to England, but the foreigner turns out to be a vile creature bent on spreading evil across the land.

In this atmospheric telefilm, loosely based on Bram Stoker's novel, Holmwood finances Dracula's trip, purchases real estate for him, and secures his residency—all in a bid to gain a cure for his illness. Jonathan Harker still travels abroad to facilitate the move, but Dracula kills him once the arrangements are finalized. Van Helsing, who is ostensibly Renfield in this story, was initially sent to Transylvania as an envoy for a secret occult society. This "Brotherhood of the Undead" worships Dracula, and they use Holmwood as a pawn in their scheme to get the vampire onto British soil. Dracula is pure evil, with no redeeming qualities or inherent charm; he's a run-of-the-mill bloodsucker that shares little with the character from the novel. This production differs so much from the source that it can barely be considered an adaptation; it's more of a generic vampire tale that just happens to include some familiar places and faces from *Dracula*.

In the United States, it was first broadcast on PBS stations on February 11, 2007. Actress Sophia Myles (Lucy Westenra) starred as Beth Turner in the short-lived vampire series *Moonlight* (2007).

The Dresden Files

SyFy/Space. Jan 5, 2008. Crime/Drama. D: David Carson. W: Hans Beimler, Robert Hewitt Wolfe. C: Paul Blackthorne, Valerie Cruz, Rebecca McFarland, Raoul Bhaneja, Conrad Coates, Joanne Kelly ⚥, Terrence Mann. CAN/USA: English/Color/85m. BOC Inc./Saturn Films.

After a local mobster and his girlfriend are murdered in an occult-like fashion, the High Council blames wizard Harry Dresden; they believe he has fallen off the wagon, and is using black magic once again. As Dresden attempts to clear his name, other murders are committed, and each victim is tied to a nightclub owned by the vampire Bianca. On the run and running out of time, can Dresden find the real killer before he too becomes a victim?

This unaired pilot was actually produced *after* the series was green lit, and already airing on television. It's a solid production with a good mix of humor, horror, magic and character development. The stunning vampiress Bianca makes an appearance, and dukes it out with our hero before being subdued by magic. This is a great stand-alone movie that can be enjoyed by fans, and even those not familiar with the series.

This production is considered out of continuity with the series, since there was no way to make it fit without specific, costly reshoots.

Drink, Slay, Love

Lifetime. 2017. Comedy/Drama. D: Vanessa Parise. W: Eirene Donohue. C: Cierra Ramirez ⚥, Zach Peladeau, McKaley Miller, Angelique Rivera, Gregg Sulkin, Sarah Desjardins, Jasmine Sky Sarin. USA: English/Color/90m. Sepia Films/Just Singer Entertainment.

Based on author Sarah Beth Durst's YA novel of the same name, this TV movie is being adapted with the assistance of actress Bella Thorne for Lifetime. The story follows Pearl, a sixteen-year-old vampire who, after a bizarre altercation, is able to walk in sunlight. This draws the attention of New England's Vampire King, who wants to use her special gift for his own nefarious purposes. Unfortunately for Pearl, the accident also gave her a conscience, and she no longer wants to treat humans as simply walking blood bags.

Emmanuelle, the Private Collection: Emmanuelle vs. Dracula

Cinemax. Oct 1, 2004. Adult/Horror. D: KLS. W: Rafael Glenn. C: Natasja Vermeer, Beverly Lynne ⚲, Kelsey ⚲, Mollie Green ⚲, Valerie Baber ⚲, Ernesto Perdomo ⚲, Marcus Deanda ⚲. USA: English/Color/87m. Oranton Ltd./Riouw Beleggingen B.V./Click Productions Inc.

After a mysterious stranger interrupts their bachelorette party, Emmanuelle and friends are overpowered by his dark influence. One by one they are turned into creatures of the night, until only Emmanuelle is left untouched—figuratively *and* literally. Now it's up to the internationally-renowned Mistress of Pleasure to battle the King of the Undead as only she can, in an erotic showdown where her very soul is on the line.

No one expects adult movies to have much of a script or feature classically-trained actors, yet this is by far one of the worst soft-core films out there—and even the vampire component can't save it. The undead antagonist is a greasy-looking incubus, who claims that through the power of his gaze he can give women the most pleasurable experience imaginable. After each bachelorette falls under his spell—which is a surprise, considering he simply stares blankly at them and speaks as if reading from a book on theoretical physics—he turns them into vampires through a penetrating combination of sex and a bite on the neck. Each woman in turn becomes a sexual predator, and dons so much makeup that they look as though they belong in *The Rocky Horror Picture Show.* But wait! There's a twist to this tale, for this man is just a minion of the real vampire king, who arrives late to this bacchanalian orgy. Emmanuelle shows Dracula what real pleasure is—but still stakes him in the not-so-thrilling climax.

Faith the Vampire Slayer

(Unproduced.) 2003.

Writer/director Tim Minear *(Angel, Firefly, Dollhouse)* pitched an idea for a *Buffy* spin-off that would feature a globetrotting Faith who's trying to find her place in the world, à la *Kung Fu* (1972). The project was dropped after Eliza Dushku decided to do something different—she starred in the series *Tru Calling* (2003) for two seasons.

The Fixer

(Unaired.) Action/Comedy. D: Anon. W: Jon F. Merz. C: Brandon Stumpf, Devon Diep, Steve Triebes, Andria Blackman, Jules Hindman, Nigel Gore, Eric R. Eastman. USA: English/Color/420m. New Ronin Entertainment.

The story follows a jaded man who was chosen at birth to help protect the balance between humans and a secret race of vampires. Based on the *Lawson Vampire* books by Jon F. Merz, the series is set in New England and is currently in pre-production.

Fred 2: Night of the Living Fred

Nickelodeon. Oct 22, 2011. Comedy/Family. D: John Fortenberry. W: David A. Goodman. C: Lucas Cruikshank ☥, Jake Weary ☥, Siobhan Fallon Hogan, Stephanie Courtney, Carlos Knight ☥, Seth Morris ☥, Daniella Monet, Ariel Winter. USA: English/Color/83m. The Collective/Varsity Pictures.

In this ghoulish sequel to *Fred: The Movie* (2010), Fred has some misgivings about his new music teacher, Mr. Devlin—a pale man who wears black, avoids direct sunlight, and prefers steak that is very, very bloody. Fred believes that Devlin is a vampire, and tries to expose him after he shows interest in his mother.

There's no denying the talent of star Lucas Cruikshank, but it's hard to fathom that anyone would purposely watch a movie that features his creation, Fred Figglehorn—an annoying, hyperactive teen with an overactive imagination. For much of the film, Fred talks directly to the camera, which is interspersed with scenes that help drive the plot along. There are a few inspired moments, but this production is definitely only watchable by the target audience—whoever that may be.

Louis B. Latimer (Paul Lynde) attends a film festival dressed as Dracula in *Gidget Gets Married* (Screen Gems Television/ABC)

Gidget Gets Married

ABC. Jan 4, 1972. Comedy/Drama. D: E.W. Swackhamer. W: John McGreevey, Frederick Kohner. C: Monie Ellis, Michael Burns, Don Ameche, Paul Lynde ☥, Joan Bennett, Elinor Donahue, Macdonald Carey. USA: English/Color/73m. Screen Gems Television/ABC.

Gidget's recent marriage is tested after she discovers that her husband's company likes to meddle in the private lives of its employees. Paul Lynde reprises his role as Louis B. Latimer, a former child actor who manages the Greenwich Village apartment complex where Gidget once lived. He appears in one scene made up as a Lugosi-inspired Dracula, having just returned from a film festival where the patrons dressed up as their favorite actors.

📺 E.W. Swackhamer also directed the 1979 telefilm *Vampire* for ABC.

Gothica

ABC (Unaired). 2013. Drama/Fantasy. D: Anand Tucker. W: Matt Lopez. C: Melissa George, Tom Ellis, Janet Montgomery, Seth Gabel, Raza Jaffrey, Tracie Thoms, Emma Booth, Christopher Egan, Tom Degnan, Laysla De Oliveira, Lori Graham, Howard Rosenstein ☥, Mélodie Simard, Matthew Kabwe. USA: English/Color/60m. ABC Studios/The Mark Gordon Company.

The pilot for this modern-day Gothic soap opera incorporated legendary characters from classic works of fiction, from the likes of Stoker's *Dracula*, Wilde's *The Picture of Dorian Gray*, and Shelley's *Frankenstein*. However, ABC passed on greenlighting a series, and the pilot never aired on television. It was rumored that execs didn't feel as though the mix of these literary characters worked—something that writer John Logan managed to get right for his series *Penny Dreadful*, which was in production around the same time as *Gothica*.

The Halloween That Almost Wasn't

ABC. Oct 28, 1979. Comedy/Family. D: Bruce Bilson. W: Coleman Jacoby. C: Judd Hirsch ☥, Mariette Hartley, Henry Gibson, Jack Riley, John Schuck, Robert Fitch, Josip Elic, Andrew Duncan, Jamie Ross, Maggie Peters Ross. USA: English/Color/24m. Concepts Unlimited/New Horizons.

🦇🦇🦇🦇

Dracula is annoyed that his monster friends have become too mild-mannered, so he delivers an ultimatum: either go back to being scary, or be replaced at Halloween. Winnie the Witch is fed up with being feared, so she threatens to quit altogether if the Count doesn't abide by her own list of demands. If he refuses, she won't do her traditional ride over the moon, and since Halloween can't begin without it, for the first time in two thousand years, the festive event is in jeopardy.

Released on VHS as *The Night Dracula Saved the World*, this production was nominated for four Emmy Awards, and won one for makeup. It features a smart script, a priceless ending, and great performances from Judd Hirsch, Mariette Hartley and Henry Gibson. Even the minor characters—the Mummy, especially—have a

Dracula (Judd Hirsch) is all smiles as he tries to convince his monster friends that they need to be scary again in *The Halloween That Almost Wasn't* (Concepts Unlimited/New Horizons)

few shining moments of their own. Frankenstein's Monster is played by John Schuck, who a decade later would be reassembled to play Herman Munster in the TV series *The Munsters Today* (1988).

📺 This was filmed at Lyndhurst castle in Tarrytown, New York, where both *House of Dark Shadows* (1970) and *Night of Dark Shadows* (1971) were shot.

Here Come the Munsters

FOX. Oct 31, 1995. Comedy/Family. D: Robert Ginty. W: Bill Prady, Jim Fisher, Jim Staahl. C: Edward Herrmann, Veronica Hamel ♀, Robert Morse ♀, Christine Taylor, Mathew Botuchis, Troy Evans, Mary Woronov. USA: English/Color/89m. Bodega Bay Productions/St. Clare Entertainment.

🦇 🦇 🦇

Promotional photo for the FOX pilot
Here Come the Munsters
(St. Clare Entertainment/Steve Schapiro)

While fleeing from an angry mob in Transylvania, Lily comes across a scorched letter from Marilyn, Herman's niece, who lives in California with her parents Elsa and Norman Hyde. Realizing this is an opportune time for a change of scenery, the Munsters head Stateside for a visit. Marilyn is very glad to see them, because her father has gone missing, and her mother is in a coma. They discover that Norman was the victim of his own experiments; he's been transformed into Brent Jekyll, a congressional candidate with a singular message: it's time for the United States to deport of all of its immigrants.

This satire of middle-class America, with a strong (yet often subtle) message about immigration, starts out well but unfortunately falters towards the end. Elsa, Herman's sister, is a "Bride of Frankenstein" type of monster, and it's clear that if a series had been commissioned, she and her husband would be minor characters at best. One scene features a cameo appearance by the surviving cast from the original TV series (Yvonne De Carlo, Al Lewis, Butch Patrick and Pat Priest). It's great to see the old gang together again, but the scene comes off as too contrived. As far as the new cast, Veronica Hamel is quite charming as Lily—she even gets to bite someone on the neck!—while Robert Morse as Grandpa Dracula effectively fills the shoes of Al Lewis. But it's Edward Herrmann who steals the show with his take on Herman Munster; although he adds a few of his own touches, it's definitely in homage to Fred Gwynne's characterization. This pilot successfully updates the classic 1960s sitcom while maintaining the same premise, and captures the heart and humor of the original—it's a far better attempt than the abysmal 1988 series *The Munsters Today*.

📺 The opening sequence includes footage of the mob scene from *Frankenstein* (1931), and while on the airplane trip to America, the Munsters watch *Bride of Frankenstein* (1935).

I, Desire

ABC. Nov 15, 1982. Romance/Suspense. D: John Llewellyn Moxey. W: Robert Foster. C: David Naughton, Dorian Harewood, Brad Dourif ⚥, Barbara Stock ⚥, Marilyn Jones. USA: English/Color/95m. Columbia Pictures Television/Green-Epstein Productions.

David Balsiger, a coroner's aide, is obsessed with a killer who is stalking the streets of Los Angeles. Each victim was completely drained of blood, and David believes that a real vampire may be responsible. As the body count rises and his obsession consumes him, David has a fateful run-in with an excommunicated priest—who believes that he can stop the vampire's killing spree.

Also known as *Desire, the Vampire,* this is an enjoyable telefilm even though one correctly guesses the identity of the vampire about ten minutes into the story. It's an engaging tale about a man's increasing obsession with stalking a killer, after the bubble of innocence is shattered and he realizes that vampires truly exist. It's a bit slow-going until Brad Dourif gets some major screen time; from then on in, it's a quick run to the finish line. The most unfortunate aspect is the inclusion of animal sound effects whenever the vampire is stalking her prey, which leads to some unintentionally hilarious scenes.

📺 John Llewellyn Moxey also directed the telefilm *The Night Stalker* (1972).

Laurell K. Hamilton's Anita Blake: Vampire Hunter

IFC (Unproduced). 2009. After Dark Films/Lionsgate.

In what was to be their first original telefilm, IFC green lit this production in early 2009, adapted by Glen Morgan *(The X Files, Millennium, Final Destination);* principle photography was supposed to start that summer, with an air date sometime in 2010. However, in late 2009, Laurell K. Hamilton revealed that the telefilm was no longer happening—the IFC deal was dead. Although there's been no official word as to why the production was canceled, perhaps Hamilton provided a hint when she wrote in her blog, "I would rather have no television show than a bad one."

The League of Extraordinary Gentlemen

FOX (Unaired). 2013. Action/Adventure. W: Michael Green. USA: English/Color/60m.

Little is known about the television pilot that FOX commissioned for the Alan Moore/Kevin

O'Neill property in 2013, which execs described as a drama where Victorian-era characters team up to fight a common enemy. In the original graphic novel, the central character, Wilhelmina "Mina" Murray, achieved immortality after bathing in a mystical pool in Africa. She was also an immortal in the 2003 feature film adaptation, however, that was because the character was reimagined as a vampire. It is unknown if Michael Green, who penned the pilot script, also made Mina one of the undead.

Let the Right One In

TNT. 2017. Horror/Thriller. D: Anon. W: Jeff Davis. C: Anon. USA: English/Color/60m. Tomorrow Studios/Studio T.

Based on the best-selling novel by John Ajvide Lindqvist, this pilot follows the story of a young boy in small-town Vermont, who's being tormented by bullies and finds solace in a new friendship with a young girl. Her arrival coincides with a string of unusual murders; as it turns out, she's vampire. The property was twice adapted on film, as *Let the Right One In* (2008) and *Let Me In* (2010), and was previously in development at A&E for possible broadcast on Showtime.

The Librarian: The Curse of the Judas Chalice

TNT. Dec 7, 2008. Action/Adventure. D: Jonathan Frakes. W: Marco Schnabel. C: Noah Wyle, Stana Katic ☥, Bruce Davison ☥, Dikran Tulaine, Bob Newhart, Jane Curtin. USA: English/Color/91m. Electric Entertainment.

🦇 🦇 🦇

While on vacation in New Orleans, Flynn Carsen falls for a mysterious lounge singer named Simone Renoir, a woman he dreamed of when he first arrived in the city. She's there to protect the Judas Chalice, a powerful artifact that a group of Russians want to use to raise a notorious vampire back from the dead.

Good lighthearted entertainment in the same vein as *Raiders of the Lost Ark,* with a nice mix of comedy and suspense that's wrapped within a pulp serial sensibility. Story-wise, this one is grounded in history more so than other such tales, although it still takes some liberties. It's refreshing to see a hero who's a bookworm and who "talks in paragraphs," as well as a heroine who holds her own, and isn't just a damsel in distress.

London After Midnight

TCM. Nov 1, 2002. Drama/Suspense. D: Rick Schmidlin, Tod Browning. W: Tod Browning, Waldemar Young, Joseph Farnham. C: Lon Chaney ☥, Andy MacLennan, Marceline Day, Polly Moran, Conrad Nagel, Edna Tichenor ☥. USA: English/B&W/47m. Metro-Goldwyn-Mayer/Turner Classic Movies.

🦇 🦇 🦇

Five years after socialite Roger Balfour took his own life, a strange couple rents out his estate that up until now had sat abandoned. His daughter Lucille believes that the new tenants are vampires, so the Inspector who originally investigated her father's death returns to reopen the case. Hosted by Robert Osborne.

In 1965, a fire in MGM's Vault #7 resulted in the loss of several early silent films, including Tod Browning's *London After Midnight* (1927); this was the last known surviving print of the film. It's been reconstructed here using hundreds of still photographs taken during production, using the original continuity script as a guide (and includes reproductions of the original interstitial titles). For the first time, modern audiences get a deeper glimpse into the fantastic makeup achievement of Lon Chaney, which is beautifully illustrated in the black and white photography presented here.

Tod Browning loosely remade the film as *Mark of the Vampire* in 1935.

The Loves of Dracula

NBC. 1979. Drama/Romance. D: Jeffrey Hayden, Sutton Roley, Kenneth Johnson. W: Craig Buck, Myla Lichtman, Renee & Harry Longstreet. C: Michael Nouri ♀, Carol Baxter ♀, Stephen Johnson, Bever-Leigh Banfield ♀, Louise Sorel ♀. USA: English/Color/120m. Universal TV.

In modern-day San Francisco, the infamous Count Dracula lives under the assumed identity of a college professor. He teaches East European History at Southbay College, and although he has a few students under his spell, he secretly longs for Mary Gibbons, the daughter of a woman he once loved. His plans, however, are constantly interrupted by Kurt von Helsing, the grandson of the legendary vampire hunter. This telefilm is actually episodes seven through ten of "The Curse of Dracula" storyline from the series *Cliffhangers!*, edited together as a standalone movie.

The Midnight Hour

ABC. Nov 1, 1985. Comedy/Horror. D: Jack Bender. W: Bill Bleich. C: Lee Montgomery ♀, Shari Belafonte-Harper ♀, LeVar Burton ♀, Peter DeLuise, Dedee Pfeiffer ♀, Jonna Lee, Jonelle Allen ♀, Kevin McCarthy, Cindy Morgan ♀, Dick Van Patten ♀. USA: English/Color/95m. ABC.

To add authenticity to a Halloween party, a group of high school friends sneak into a museum to steal some historical artifacts. They break the seal on an old scroll and read the passage within; this awakens a centuries-old vampire-witch, as well as a horde of demons buried in the local graveyard. As the dark influence blankets the town, two teenagers must find the scroll and re-seal it before midnight—otherwise the awakened terrors will be a permanent addition to this serene New England town.

This exceptional Halloween tale has achieved cult status, and rightly so; it's a perfect mix of comedy, horror, and all-around great storytelling. Ignoring the fact that the lead actors are all too old to be playing teenagers, *The Midnight Hour* is a strong telefilm that should please any fan of the genre. With an amazing soundtrack enhanced by the voice of Wolfman Jack (who knew that The Smiths' "How Soon Is Now?" would work so well in a vampire attack scene?), this remains an exceptional TV movie that warrants repeated viewing.

📺 In what is certainly in homage to Michael Jackson's *Thriller* video, at one point the partygoers break into a catchy, fully choreographed undead dance!

Mockingbird Lane

NBC. October 26, 2012. Comedy/Fantasy. D: Bryan Singer. W: Bryan Fuller, Norm Liebmann, Ed Haas. C: Jerry O'Connell, Portia de Rossi ☥, Charity Wakefield, Mason Cook, Eddie Izzard ☥, Cheyenne Jackson, Beth Grant. USA: English/Color/40m. Living Dead Guy/ Bad Hat Harry Productions.

Herman and Lily Munster unexpectedly have to relocate their family, after their son causes a disturbance when his werewolf tendencies surface as he hits puberty. They find the perfect new home: 1313 Mockingbird Lane, a decrepit abode with a horrific past—which their neighbors have coined "the hobo murder house." As the couple adjusts to their new suburban surroundings, they look for the best way to delicately tell their son that he's not quite human. And it doesn't help that Grandpa Munster, a.k.a. Dracula, relishes in the fact that his grandson is a true chip off the old block— and wants to show him what it really means to be a Munster (and a monster).

Initially planned as a reboot of *The Munsters* classic television series, which would delve deeper into the origins of the famous family, this was instead presented as a television special and never went beyond the pilot stage. It was a rocky road just to get to that point; Bryan Fuller first delivered a pilot script in 2010, which was

Melissa Cavender (Shari Belafonte-Harper) calls forth a centuries-old vampire, which heralds a tide of dark influence that overwhelms a serene New England town in *The Midnight Hour* (ABC-TV)

A group of high school friends undergo a transformation after they mistakenly awaken an ancient evil in the ABC television movie *The Midnight Hour* (ABC-TV)

rejected by NBC, but approved a year later after revisions made it "edgier and darker." All the familiar faces from the original series are here, updated to contemporary times, but that's where the similarities end. The light humor of the original has been replaced by darker fare, and the Munsters themselves, at times, seem more like the Addams family. In the original series, they superficially resembled the Universal Monsters, but were never really threatening; here they're more human-looking, but are more closely in tune with their monstrous tendencies. Some may argue that, by today's standards, sticking with the original premise would have been absurd, yet it still worked quite well in the television movie *Here Come the Munsters* (1995). All in, *Mockingbird Lane* wasn't that much of a disappointment, and could have come into its own had it been given a chance to develop. If nothing else, it should be remembered as being far more enjoyable than all three seasons of the moronic *Munsters Today* (1988-91).

In 2013, NBC exec Bob Greenblatt claimed that they didn't go ahead with a series because they weren't able to successfully balance the supernatural (and other oddball elements) with the central family drama. He added that they're not against bringing back *The Munsters* again in the future, in some other incarnation.

Mom's Got a Date with a Vampire

Disney. Oct 13, 2000. Family/Fantasy. D: Stephen Boyum. W: Robert Keats, Lindsay Naythons. C: Caroline Rhea, Charles Shaughnessy ⚰, Matthew O'Leary, Robert Carradine, Laura Vandervoort, Karl Pruner ⚰. CAN/USA: English/Color/83m. Upstart Productions/Walt Disney Pictures.

Adam Hansen and his sister Chelsea are grounded for the weekend, so in order to sneak out of the house on Friday night, they conspire to get a date for their mom. Everything goes as planned, that is until their younger brother Taylor discovers that the charming man they set her up with is actually an evil vampire. With the help of a mysterious stranger named Van Helsing, the kids hatch a plan to stop the bloodsucker before he can make their mom his undead bride.

Definitely made for kids, this is a predictable tale that drops a few references to *Dracula*. It's a little heavy-handed with its message about staying true to oneself, the importance of family, and the power of true love. Not really what most look for in a vampire story, but to each his own.

Mother, May I Sleep with Danger?

Lifetime. Jun 18, 2016. Romance/Thriller. D: Melanie Aitkenhead. W: Amber Coney, James Franco. C: Emily Meade ⚰, Leila George, Emma Rigby ⚰, Amber Coney, Tori Spelling, Ivan Sergei, Nick Eversman, Christie Lynn Smith, Ashli Haynes, Taylor Laughlin, Mirela Burke, Christopher Allen, Zoë Bleu ⚰, Gabrielle Haugh ⚰, James Franco. USA: English/Color/86m. Rabbit Bandini Productions/Sony Pictures Television.

College student Leah Lewisohn falls in love with Pearl, a Goth-girl who just happens to be a "Nightwalker"—who appears human by day, but can transform into a vampire at night (and her victims of choice are abusive men, unlike others of her kind who are far less discriminating). This is a remake of the 1996 television movie of the same name, which starred Tori Spelling as a college athlete, struggling with personal demons, who falls in love with an abusive man who turns out to be a murderer. James Franco reimagined the overwrought story as a lesbian vampire tale, which also features Spelling—although this time around, she plays Leah's mother.

Mr. and Mrs. Dracula

ABC. Sep 5, 1980. Comedy/Family. D: Doug Rogers. W: Robert Klane. C: Dick Shawn ⚥, Carol Lawrence ⚥, Barry Gordon, Anthony Battaglia ⚥, Gail Mayron ⚥, Rick Aviles, Johnny Haymer, Paula Prentiss ⚥. USA: English/Color/30m. Marble Arch Productions/ABC Circle Films.

After angry villagers force him out of his castle in Transylvania, Vladimir Dracula relocates his family to the Bronx, New York. As the clan adjusts to their new homeland, Vlad plans a six-hundred-and-eighteenth wedding anniversary celebration for his wife Sonia.

This pilot also featured Dracula's grandfather Gregor, an ancient vampire who's stuck in bat form because he's forgotten how to change back into a human being. After the pilot aired in 1980, it was revamped and reshot, with Paula Prentiss taking over the role of Sonia from Carol Lawrence. Broadcast in early 1981, this version still didn't catch on, so it was not picked up as a series.

Vladimir Dracula and his wife Sonia (Dick Shawn, Carol Lawrence) relocate to the Bronx in *Mr. and Mrs. Dracula* (Marble Arch Productions/ABC Circle Films)

Munster, Go Home!

(Unaired.) 1966. Comedy/Family. D: Earl Bellamy. W: George Tibbles, Joe Connelly, Bob Mosher. C: Fred Gwynne, Yvonne De Carlo ⚥, Al Lewis ⚥, Butch Patrick, Debbie Watson, Hermione Gingold, Terry-Thomas, John Carradine, Robert Pine. USA: English/Color/96m. Universal Pictures.

Herman inherits the land and title of Lord of Munster Hall in Shroudshire, England. When the family relocates to Britain, they receive a less than enthusiastic welcome from their distant cousins.

The story picks up from where the original series left off, and was meant to be a pilot for a new series that followed the Munsters and their new lives in England. However, no network was interested in airing it, and understandably so; it's a terrible production with transparent jokes and zero laughs. Instead, it was released theatrically in the summer of 1966. The only actor who didn't reprise their role was Pat Priest; at age thirty, she was considered "too old" by producers to play the part.

The Munsters' Revenge

NBC. Feb 27, 1981. Comedy/Family. D: Don Weis. W: Arthur Alsberg, Don Nelson. C: Fred Gwynne, Al Lewis ☥, Yvonne De Carlo ☥, K.C. Martel, Jo McDonnell, Bob Hastings, Peter Fox, Herbert Voland, Colby Chester, Sid Caesar. USA: English/Color/97m. Universal TV.

A demented doctor uses robotic statues from a wax museum to commit crime sprees throughout the city. But this is merely a prelude to the main event: on Halloween night, he plans to steal precious jewels from the tomb of a mummy king. Unfortunately for Herman and Grandpa, two of the robots look exactly like them, and they are charged with theft. On the run from the authorities, the Munsters must clear their names and stop the doctor's evil scheme before the police can capture them.

In yet another attempt to bring the Munster family back to television, this story ostensibly takes place in present-day (1981), but the characters of Marilyn and Eddie are recast with younger actors. This isn't a major distraction, because the telefilm focuses on Herman and Grandpa, and gives little screen time to the rest of the family. Fred Gwynne, who was reportedly paid a lot of money to return, makes the best of a bad situation. There's a new quirky relative, the Phantom of the Opera; he's an attention hog who loves to sing, especially in the upper registers, and can shatter glass with the sound of his voice. At first this character is a lot of fun, but he quickly wears out his welcome as his glass-breaking shtick is repeated time and time again. With no redeeming qualities, very few laughs, and a lot of filler, this production fails on all fronts.

A clan of friendly monsters don't quite look like the other suburbanites in the CBS series *The Munsters* (Kayro-Vue Productions)

Promotional advertisement for the NBC TV movie *The Munsters' Revenge* (Universal TV/TV Guide)

The Munsters' Scary Little Christmas

FOX. Dec 17, 1996. Comedy/Family. D: Ian Emes. W: Ed Ferrara, Kevin Murphy. C: Sam McMurray, Ann Magnuson ♀, Bug Hall, Sandy Baron ♀, Mary Woronov, Ed Gale, Arturo Gil, Mark Mitchell. USA: English/Color/90m. Michael R. Joyce Productions/St. Clare Entertainment.

Christmas has always been Eddie's favorite holiday, but this year he's depressed over missing out on an authentic Transylvanian festivity. His family bands together to lift his spirits, but Grandpa—as he often does—messes up an experiment: instead of making it snow, he accidentally transports Santa Claus into the Munster home. Although Eddie is glad to see the jolly red elf, Christmas may be in jeopardy unless they can figure out a way to get Santa back home.

The beloved Munster clan is resurrected once again in this family-friendly story, updated to modern times, which sticks to the premise of the original series. For the most part, the actors do a good job of paying homage to the original, yet the role of Grandpa is horribly miscast. There are a few inspired moments; these include the macabre installations that decorate the Munster home, and Herman's Christmas gift for Eddie: a Marquis de Sade Dungeon Action Play Set. Unfortunately these scenes are not enough to save a story that's too derivative and exceptionally sappy. Unlike rum and eggnog, the Munsters and Christmas just don't go well together.

Promotional advertisement for the FOX TV movie *The Munsters' Scary Little Christmas* (St. Clare Entertainment/TV Guide)

The Munsters Today – "Still the Munsters After All These Years"

(Unaired.) 1988. Comedy/Family. D: John M. Robins. W: Lloyd J. Schwartz. C: John Schuck, Lee Meriwether ♀, Howard Morton ♀, Jason Marsden, Mary-Ellen Dunbar, Dave Madden, Richard Horvitz. USA: English/B&W, Color/15m. The Arthur Company/MCA Television.

Grandpa persuades his family to try out his latest invention—a custom-designed sleeping chamber in the shape of a coffin. The machine malfunctions; instead of being set for thirty minutes of rest, the duration switches to "forever." Twenty-two years later, the family is inadvertently reawakened by a land developer, who thinks the house is abandoned; he wants to tear it down to build a parking lot. Initially the Munsters believe it's still 1966, but then realize the extent of their "nap"—and their back taxes are so high that they may have to sell their beloved home in order to pay the bills.

This unaired presentation pilot revamps the iconic 1960s television show, and opens with a new cast in a black and white flashback, detailing Grandpa's experiment gone awry. Fast-forward twenty-two years later, and the Munsters face the first of many predicaments as they adjust to the strange new world of 1988. The production is awful, laced with dumb jokes and an abundance of canned laughter, yet it was still deemed good enough to be turned into a series.

Must Be Santa

CBC/Starz. Dec 12, 1999. Family/Drama. D: Brad Turner. W: Douglas Bowie. C: Arnold Pinnock, Deanna Milligan, Dabney Coleman, Keenan Macwilliam, Peter Millard, Brian Miranda, Steven McCarthy, Gerard Parkes, Jordy Benattar, Joe Flaherty ⚧. CAN: English/Color/120m. CBC.

It's time for Santa to retire. The jolly elf's replacement, Floyd Court, is trying to re-establish ties with his estranged daughter. He reluctantly takes on the role, but misuses the new powers granted to him. What does this Christmas story have to do with the undead, you ask? Surprisingly, Joe Flaherty has a cameo appearance in the guise of "Count Floyd," the vampire horror movie host character that he originated on *SCTV*.

My Babysitter's a Vampire

TeleToon. Oct 9, 2010. Comedy/Family. D: Bruce McDonald. W: Tom McGillis, Jennifer Pertsch, Tim Burns. C: Matthew Knight, Vanessa Morgan ⚧, Atticus Mitchell, Cameron Kennedy ⚧, Kate Todd ⚧, Joe Dinicol ⚧, Ella Jonas Fargliner. CAN: English/Color/90m. Fresh TV.

Ethan Morgan's overprotective parents hire a babysitter for the night, because they don't trust him enough to take care of his little sister. Upset by the situation, his attitude changes once the cute babysitter arrives—until he discovers she's a vampire.

A harmless telefilm geared towards the "Emo vamp" crowd, even though it makes fun of them; it also celebrates geeks while taking a jab at them too. The story becomes too convoluted with the introduction of a prophecy and other supernatural elements, common themes nowadays that here seem like a trite retread. The most interesting aspect is the film-within-a-film, *Dusk III: Unbitten*, which is a direct satire of the *Twilight* franchise. There's also a reference to the popular series *The Vampire Diaries*, which in this story is referred to as *The Bloodsucker Diaries*.

📺 This pilot was commissioned into a television series, which ran for two seasons.

My Fair Munster

CBS. 1964. Comedy/Family. D: Norman Abbott. W: Norm Liebmann, Ed Haas. C: Joan Marshall ☥, Beverly Owen, Happy Derman, Al Lewis ☥, Fred Gwynne. USA: English/Color/14m. Kayro-Vue Productions.

As their date comes to a close, Marilyn invites Jack to meet her family, but he's a little hesitant after seeing their creepy-looking house. After being introduced to her uncle Herman, Jack makes a beeline for his car—because Marilyn is a normal woman who lives with a family of monsters. The Munsters, however, believe that *Marilyn* is the ugly duckling of the clan—so Grandpa concocts a love potion that will make her irresistible, forever ending her unlucky streak with men.

This short color pilot was used to sell the series to CBS, and although it was never broadcast, some footage was later used in Episode 2 (and has since been released on DVD). In this production, Lily is known as "Phoebe" and is played by a different actress, who takes on more of a Vampira-like look and persona. The other major difference is with Eddie, who is much more of a feral werewolf (and is also played by a different actor).

The NBC Wednesday Mystery Movie: The Snoop Sisters: A Black Day for Bluebeard

NBC. March 19, 1974. Crime/Mystery. D: David Friedkin. W: Tony Barrett, Robert Foster, Jackson Gillis. C: Helen Hayes, Mildred Natwick, Lou Antonio, Bert Convy, Vincent Price ☥, Tammy Grimes, Roddy McDowall. USA: English/Color/75m. Talent Associates/Norton Simon Inc./Universal TV.

Part of a series of four telefilms that followed the adventures of Ernesta and Gwendolin Snoop, two elderly sisters who write mystery novels and use their talents to solve real-life crimes. In this story, has-been horror actor Michael Bastion hopes his career will be reinvigorated after a horror film festival is held in his honor. On the night of the premiere, his wealthy wife is murdered, and the cash-strapped actor is the prime suspect—because she left him a sizeable inheritance in her will.

Hollywood legends Helen Hayes and Mildred Natwick are a joy to watch as the Snoop Sisters,

Michael Bastion (Vincent Price) is suspected of murdering his wife in *The Snoop Sisters: A Black Day for Bluebeard* (Talent Associates/Universal TV)

but it's the great Vincent Price who steals the show with his charming performance as Bastion—a vain, aging actor who has a penchant for the melodramatic. Long since typecast as a horror villain, Bastion arrives at the film festival dressed as a vampire, and makes a grand entrance from within a coffin delivered via hearse. Rounding out the exceptional cast is Roddy McDowall as Lionel Standish, the cousin of the deceased.

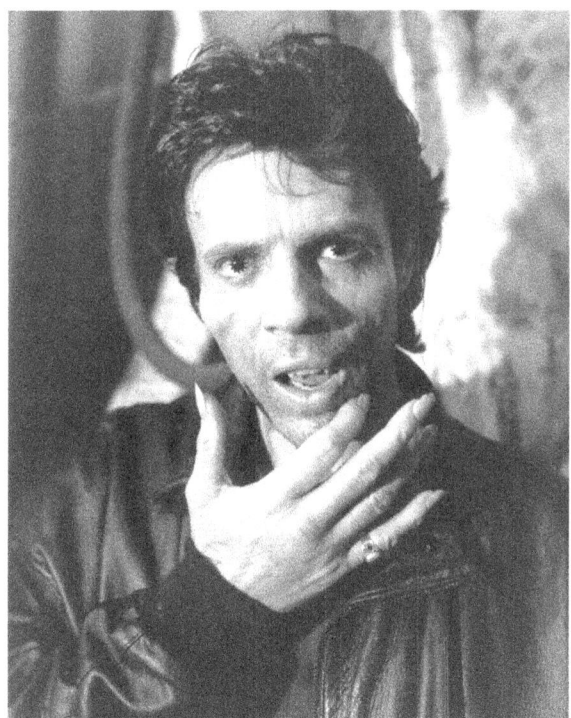

Los Angeles police detective Nicholas Knight (Rick Springfield) is a vampire looking for a cure in *Nick Knight* (Barry Weitz Films Inc./New World Television)

Michael Nader is Lacroix, the vampire who turned Nicholas Knight in the TV movie *Nick Knight* (Barry Weitz Films Inc/New World Television)

Nick Knight

CBS. Aug 20, 1989. Crime/Drama. D: Farhad Mann. W: James D. Parriott, Barney Cohen. C: Rick Springfield ☥, John Kapelos, Robert Harper, Laura Johnson, Michael Nader ☥. USA: English/Color/92m. Barry Weitz Films Inc./Robirdie Pictures Inc./New World Television.

An investigation into a series of bizarre murders leads Detective Nick Knight to a stolen jade goblet. Knight is a vampire, and this artifact may be the key in curing his affliction. Lacroix, the vampire who turned Knight, is after the goblet as well—but he wants to destroy it.

My expectations were low for this telefilm, because the premise changed significantly before it resurfaced three years later as the series *Forever Knight*. (In this version, Knight is four centuries younger, has a different origin story, works in Los Angeles, and his human confidant is male.) But I was pleasantly surprised, especially with Springfield's earnest performance; Knight's struggle with his vampiric nature is more believable than the way it was portrayed by Geraint Wyn Davies in the television series. Much like the bloodsuckers in *Buffy* and *Angel,* when Knight is in full vampire mode, his face transforms into something more demonic. This was against the norm at the time; most romanticized vampires simply grew fangs and had a change in eye color.

📺 This story was remade as the first two episodes of the series ("Dark Knight"). John Kapelos (Detective Donald Schanke) was the only actor to appear in both versions.

Nightlife

USA Network. Aug 23, 1989. Comedy/Drama. D: Daniel Taplitz. W: Daniel Taplitz, Anne Beatts. C: Ben Cross ☥, Maryam d'Abo ☥, Keith Szarabajka ☥, Jesse Corti, Camille Saviola, Glenn Shadix ☥. USA: English/Color/90m. Cine Enterprises Mexico/MCA Television Entertainment.

🦇🦇🦇

A century ago, the vampire Angelique buried herself underground to escape Vlad, her controlling, evil lover. She's accidentally unearthed outside a monastery in present-day Mexico City, and put under the care of Dr. Zuckerman. He's a hematologist, and believes that her vampirism can be treated by science. Unfortunately for Angelique, Vlad is still undead, and now that she's resurfaced, he can easily track her down.

A lighthearted romantic comedy that has a sharp script with some very funny scenes, and showcases the stunning beauty of Mexico City by night. Not quite on par with one of the best undead rom-coms, *Love at First Bite* (1979), but it's still one of the better vampire TV movies.

📺 Ben Cross (Vlad) also bared fangs as Barnabas Collins in the short-lived *Dark Shadows* remake from 1991.

Promotional advertisement for the USA Network TV movie *Nightlife* (MCA Television Entertainment/TV Guide)

The Night Stalker

ABC. Jan 11, 1972. Horror/Thriller. D: John Llewellyn Moxey. W: Richard Matheson, Jeff Rice. C: Darren McGavin, Carol Lynley, Simon Oakland, Ralph Meeker, Claude Akins, Charles McGraw, Kent Smith, Barry Atwater ♀. USA: English/Color/77m. Dan Curtis Productions/ABC.

🦇🦇🦇🦇🦇

Reporter Carl Kolchak's abrasive personality has gotten him fired from all the major newspapers, so he's been reduced to working for a small publication in Las Vegas. On the lookout for any story that might bring him national attention—and a better job back in New York City—Kolchak covers any crime, any time. While investigating a series of unusual murders, he learns that each victim died from shock induced by massive blood loss—yet there is never any blood found at the scene. As the evidence points to a real, flesh-and-blood vampire killer, Kolchak realizes he's got a Pulitzer Prize-winning story on his hands—but his publisher and the local police force don't believe a word of it.

Carl Kolchak's (Darren McGavin) latest investigation unearths a real bloodthirsty vampire (Barry Atwater) in *The Night Stalker* (Dan Curtis Productions Inc)

The antagonist isn't just another faceless creature of the night; he's been given a full back story, which adds authenticity to the tale. His name is Janos Skorzeny, a traditional vampire that fears the cross, is weakened by sunlight, and sleeps in a coffin lined with earth from his homeland. Publicly, he's a rich Romanian who travels the world under false identities, and wherever he goes, death and destruction follow. Initially the police don't believe he's the real killer, because he's over seventy years old, but Kolchak knows the truth—and it takes some convincing to get the law on his side. Yet he's charged with first-degree murder after he stakes Skorzeny, and the police only release him after he reluctantly agrees to suppress the story—and leave Las Vegas forever. The working title for this production was *The Kolchak Tapes*, which producer Dan Curtis reused for his 1973 TV movie *The Norliss Tapes*.

📺 The spin-off series, *Kolchak: The Night Stalker* (1974), included a vampire episode that featured one of Skorzeny's victims as the antagonist.

Ripper

BBC (Unproduced). 2001.

This spin-off of *Buffy the Vampire Slayer* was first proposed by Joss Whedon in 2001, and was to follow Rupert Giles and his exploits in England after leaving Sunnydale for good (he was nicknamed "Ripper" in his youth). Whedon said the miniseries would be made in the tradition of classic British ghost stories, and it was reported that he wrote a two-hour pilot (and several other *Buffy* scribes penned outlines for other episodes). As Whedon became involved in other projects, *Ripper* was put on hold, yet it still evolved; by 2007 he reported that a ninety-minute telefilm was close to being commissioned by the BBC (and Anthony Head was still attached). By 2009 the project was still in limbo, and the main stalling point was rights issues with the Rupert Giles character; everyone involved wants to see this project happen, but they can't do a thing until this matter is cleared up.

Roger Corman's The Phantom Eye

AMC. Oct 30, 1999. Comedy/Drama. D: Gwyneth Gibby. W: Benjamin Carr. C: Roger Corman, Sarah Aldrich, David Sean Robinson, Jonathan Haze, Jude Farese, Lisa Boyle ☥, Linda Porter, François Giroday ☥, Frank Gorshin. USA: English/Color/63m. Concorde-New Horizons.

🦇 🦇 🦇

Two interns are sent to the AMC Horror Film Library to assist Dr. Gorman, who's trying to locate a missing movie called "The Phantom Eye," which is scheduled to air at midnight. They split up to quicken their search, but each door they try leads into a different classic horror movie; now trapped, they're forced to play out a role within each film. Gorman is actually testing their cinematic knowledge, and in order to survive, the interns must figure out the resolution to the movie—or they will be trapped inside it forever.

A fun little production that will appeal to aficionados of older horror movies. There's a lot of humor to be found as the interns weave their way through several B-movie situations, and they often bring in an audience's perspective as they attempt to figure out a resolution. The ending to the tale is both fitting and classic, and won't be spoiled here.

📺 This production was originally split up into several chapters that were broadcast separately over the course of a month, as part of AMC's *Monsterfest* horror movie marathon.

Roxy Hunter and the Horrific Halloween

The N. Oct 26, 2008. Adventure/Family. D: Eleanor Lindo. W: James Kee, Robin Dunne. C: Aria Wallace, Robin Brûlé, Demetrius Joyette, Yannick Bisson, Connor Price ☥, Juan Chioran, Devon Bostick. USA: English/Color/120m. Dolphin Entertainment/Winding Road Entertainment/Creative Capers Entertainment.

Roxy is about to experience her first Halloween in Serenity Falls, but the irrepressible nine-year-old expects it'll be pretty boring—until she discovers that her classmate from Transylvania is a real vampire. Robin Dunne co-wrote several of these *Roxy Hunter* telefilms, but he's best known to genre fans as the actor who portrayed Dr. Will Zimmerman in the TV series *Sanctuary*.

Shadow Zone – "The Undead Express"

Showtime. Oct 27, 1996. Drama/Family. D: Stephen Williams. W: Roy Sallows. C: Ron Silver ☥, Chauncey Leopardi, Natanya Ross, Tony T. Johnson, Sherry Miller, Ron Lea, Ron White ☥, Frank Moore ☥, Wes Craven. USA: English/Color/98m. Hallmark Entertainment/Lynch Entertainment.

While waiting for the subway, teenager Zach meets Valentine, a vampire who has been trapped for decades underneath the streets of New York City. He invites Zach onto the "Undead Express," a subway train used by vampires to ride along the old and largely forgotten rail lines separated from the modern system. Valentine has a proposal: in exchange for showing Zach the abandoned parts of the subway line, which will help a great deal with a school project, the teen must lead him up to the surface—which he can only access through the help of an innocent person.

Aimed at pre-teens, this low-budget and bloodless tale moves at a snail's pace, and feels like an after-school special with vampires—most of whom do very little until they meet their horrible demise in the surprisingly graphic finale. The predictable plot is populated with stereotypical characters, and the vampires are just plain boring—all fangs and no bite (Valentine is so lethargic that he often struggles to get any words out). The target audience will find this entertaining yet forgettable, and anyone over the age of thirteen should probably avoid it altogether.

📺 The story is based on the book *The Undead Express* from the series *Shadow Zone*, a collection of thirteen children's horror novels written by different authors but published under the same pen name of J. R. Black. One other book in this series, *My Teacher Ate My Homework*, was broadcast a year later under the *Shadow Zone* banner.

Sherlock Holmes: The Case of the Whitechapel Vampire

Hallmark Channel/CTV. Oct 27, 2002. Crime/Drama. D/W: Rodney Gibbons. C: Matt Frewer, Kenneth Welsh, Shawn Lawrence, Neville Edwards, Michel Perron, Tom Rack ☥. CAN: English/Color/89m. Hallmark Entertainment/MUSE Entertainment Enterprises Inc.

Brother Marstoke summons Sherlock Holmes to investigate the murder of a fellow monk, and believes that a South American demon is responsible. Known as "Desmoto," the creature often appears as a giant bat, and Marstoke is convinced that it followed them back to England after their recent mission in Guyana.

A lackluster tale that is peppered with dialogue that seems too modern (or perhaps just too out of place) within a Sherlock Holmes story, and there's not much action to boot. It seems a stretch at ninety minutes, with too many red herrings and a couple of implausible scenes; frankly, the story isn't engrossing, mysterious or suspenseful enough to hold interest for that long. Matt Frewer as Holmes looks the part, and Kenneth Welsh is a genuine Watson, but most of the other roles are hit and miss; they run the full gamut of acting prowess and believable British accents. If that's not enough to keep you away—it turns out there are no real vampires!

📺 This was the last entry in a series of four Sherlock Holmes TV movies produced in Canada; unlike the previous outings, this one is a pastiche of sorts, and not based on any specific work by Sir Arthur Conan Doyle (it bears no resemblance to his short story "The Adventure of the Sussex Vampire").

Slayer

SyFy. Jul 8, 2006. Horror/Thriller. D/W: Kevin VanHook. C: Casper Van Dien, Tony Plana ♀, Kevin Grevioux ♀, Jennifer O'Dell, Alexis Cruz, Joyce Giraud ♀, Ray Park ♀, Danny Trejo, Lynda Carter. USA: English/Color/88m. IDT Entertainment Inc./SyFy Channel.

It's been six months since Captain Hawk and his elite commandos were viciously ambushed in the rainforests of South America, and the survivors believe they were attacked by vampires. Hawk returns to the area to look for a company of missing soldiers, but this time around the assignment is much more personal: his ex-wife is also there, and she's completely unaware of the supernatural creatures that hunt for human blood under the dense canopy of the rainforest.

Original programming produced by The SyFy Channel is usually hit and miss, and *Slayer* is a prime example of a movie to avoid. It's obvious that this cliché-ridden, no-budget yarn was produced as quickly as humanly possible; it often seems like the actors are reading their lines for the first time. Casper Van Dien gives his standard B-movie performance, while Kevin Grevioux proves that he should just stick to screenwriting. Seeing Lynda Carter in an army uniform only makes one long for the comparatively high-brow premise that was her *Wonder Woman* series. Stuntman-turned-actor Ray Park, who plays vampire twins, is the best thing about this movie; he even tops the requisite über-vamp, who is centuries old yet remarkably easy to kill.

Transylvania

NBC (Unproduced). 2004.

While Stephen Sommers was directing the film *Van Helsing* (2004), he came up with an idea for a spin-off television series set in the same world as the movie, but which would feature different characters (and use the sets created for the film). The response to the pilot script was very enthusiastic, and NBC tapped David Fury *(Buffy the Vampire Slayer, Angel, Lost)* to help develop the series. The story followed a young cowboy from Texas who relocates to Transylvania to become the local sheriff, and he ends up battling supernatural creatures. The project was ultimately dropped by NBC, with no official reason given.

Transylvania

The CW. 2016. Drama/Thriller. D: Jason Ensler. W: Hugh Sterbakov. C: Max Ryan, Sofia Pernas, Laura Brent, Luke Allen-Gale, Evan Stern, Tom Reed, Jake Fairbrother, Constantine Meglis, Anthony Gerbrandt, JaNae Armogan. USA: English/Color/90m. Midnight Radio/CBS Studios.

This period drama, set in the 1880s, follows Victoria Harker, an adventurous woman who travels to Transylvania in search of her missing father, who had journeyed there from New York City in pursuit of an infamous creature of the night. Teaming up with Godrey Lestrade, formerly of Scotland Yard, the two cross paths with a young Dr. Frankenstein, as well as a horde of supernatural

Twilight

CBS (Unaired). 2007. Crime/Romance. C: Alex O'Loughlin ☥, Shannon Lucio, Rade Serbedzija ☥, Amber Valetta ☥, James Black, Benjamin Benitez ☥. USA: English/Color/28m. Silver Pictures Television/Warner Bros. Television.

Commissioned by CBS, this presentation pilot resulted in the TV series *Moonlight,* which was retitled to avoid confusion with the book and film franchise of the same name. The story takes place in New York City, and features Alex O'Loughlin as the vampire Mick St. John—but all other roles are played by different actors. This production actually works better than most of the episodes from the series; in this version, vampires avoid sunlight—a standard that was abandoned when the story was revamped and relocated to Los Angeles.

Ultraviolet

FOX. Apr 2000. Drama/Romance. D: Mark Piznarski. W: Chip Johannessen, Howard Gordon. C: Eric Thal, Spence Decker ☥, Joanna Going, Mädchen Amick, Idris Elba, Carlo Rota, Lindy Booth ☥, Joel S. Keller. USA: English/Color/41m. 20th Century Fox Television/TCFTV Canpro II Inc.

Officer Viggo Bartoli resurfaces from a three-year undercover assignment just in time for his bachelor party. But he disappears on the morning of his wedding, and takes all the evidence he gathered while undercover. His partner, John Cahill, investigates the disappearance, and uncovers a secret medical facility run by a hematologist who's in league with a Federal agent. The two are part of a shadow organization entrenched in a war with vampires—and they're also very interested in Bartoli's whereabouts.

Considering the pedigree behind this project—Howard Gordon *(Buffy the Vampire Slayer, Angel)* and Chip Johannessen *(Millennium, Moonlight)*—it's a surprise that it turned out so bad; it's more romantic drama than supernatural thriller, so perhaps these two weren't the best choice. The vampires are very sympathetic and appear to be a docile minority—so the whole "war" aspect doesn't make sense. It's a little too reminiscent of *Kindred: The Embraced,* and feels like a supernatural soap opera aimed at those more interested in the power of love rather than the power of evil. Had it been pitched today, the project may well have been commissioned into a series, considering the rabid popularity of the "glampire" archetype. The story is based on the six-part UK series of the same name, but it bears no similarity; the pilot was set to premiere in the winter of 2001, but it was deemed such a failure that it was never broadcast.

Untitled Kevin Williamson Project

(Unproduced.) 2010.

Thanks to the success of *The Vampire Diaries,* the CW asked Kevin Williamson to develop a companion series—a one-hour drama about a group of paranormal investigators. Characters from *The Vampire Diaries* probably wouldn't cross over into this new series, however it would still deal with the supernatural. A pilot was tentatively planned for the 2011/12 season, but there's been no further news about the project. It was possibly put aside in order for Williamson to concentrate on *The Secret Circle,* a teen drama about a high school that's teeming with witches.

Vampire

ABC. Oct 7, 1979. Drama/Suspense. D: E.W. Swackhamer. W: Steven Bochco, Michael Kozoll. C: Jason Miller, Richard Lynch ✝, E.G. Marshall, Kathryn Harrold ✝, Barrie Youngfellow, Michael Tucker, Jonelle Allen, Jessica Walter. USA: English/Color/90m. MTM Enterprises.

Anton Voytek (Richard Lynch) exacts revenge on those who wronged him in the ABC TV movie *Vampire* (MTM Enterprises)

The lives of architects John and Leslie Rawlins are forever changed upon the arrival of European businessman Anton Voytek. He's searching for priceless family heirlooms, and believes the valuables are buried underneath a new development project spearheaded by the couple.

In this story, much like in *Dracula,* the identity of the vampire isn't hidden from the audience for very long. Voytek initially appears to be a friend, a suave businessman who only wants to recover what belongs to him. But the valuables are well-documented items, stolen over the centuries, so Voytek is arrested for conspiracy to commit grand theft. His trust betrayed, Voytek shows his true colors, and exacts revenge against all of those involved. It's a tragic tale of lives ruined by a vengeful vampire, and most of the horror is left up to the audience's imagination. Compelling and suspenseful, this character-driven telefilm features a great performance by Richard Lynch as a classical vampire—a cross between Dracula and Lestat.

📺 Meant to be a backdoor pilot, the story is left open-ended with Voytek on the run. Since no series was commissioned, the tale ends here.

The Van Helsing Chronicles

NBC. 1997. Suspense/Thriller. D: Geoffrey Sax. W: Javier Grillo-Marxuach, Brian Henson. C: Dan Gauthier, Teri Polo, Paul Hipp, Sophie Ward. USA: English/Color/30m. Jim Henson Productions/NBC Studios.

In the fall of 1997, NBC desperately needed to fill the void left by a brand new series that was canceled after only two episodes. The network announced a revamped Saturday lineup immersed in the paranormal, and resurrected an abandoned pilot that was produced earlier that year. Called *The Van Helsing Chronicles* (retitled *Legacy*), the story follows the descendants of Van Helsing and Jonathan Harker as they battle a horde of supernatural creatures. It was reported at the time that the concept was being reworked, and a new pilot would be commissioned—but nothing ever came of it (even though NBC ordered six episodes up front).

Wolvesbayne

SyFy. Oct 12, 2009. Fantasy/Horror. D: Griff Furst. W: Leigh Scott. C: Mark Dacascos ☥, Jeremy London, Christy Romano, Rhett Giles, Stephanie Honore ☥, Taylor Roppolo ☥, Yancy Butler ☥. USA: English/Color/93m. Bullet Films/Active Entertainment/Nu Image.

A self-absorbed real estate developer becomes cursed with lycanthropy, and reluctantly seeks the help of a fellow werewolf who's learned to keep her affliction under control. They team up with an elite group of vampire hunters, who are trying to stop a plan to resurrect an ancient, powerful creature of the night.

For a movie billed as a werewolf story, the lycanthrope arc just introduces a tale about warring vampire clans, one of which wants to take over humanity by resurrecting an ancient bloodsucker. This is too bad, because the opening half of the movie—which focuses on the man dealing with his werewolf affliction—is much more interesting than what follows. Once the vampire plot takes over (featuring characters and ideas that have been rehashed *ad infinitum*), the film derails, and it becomes a mess of clichés. Fans of vampire stories will find nothing new here, and those expecting some major werewolf action will be sorely disappointed.

📺 This is a sequel to the direct-to-DVD movie *Dracula's Curse* (2006).

The World of Dracula

NBC. 1979. Drama/Romance. D: Jeffrey Hayden, Sutton Roley, Kenneth Johnson. W: Craig Buck, Myla Lichtman, Renee & Harry Longstreet. C: Michael Nouri ☥, Carol Baxter ☥, Stephen Johnson, Bever-Leigh Banfield ☥, Louise Sorel ☥. USA: English/Color/95m. Universal TV.

In modern-day San Francisco, the infamous Count Dracula lives under the assumed identity of a college professor. He teaches East European History at Southbay College, and although he has a few students under his spell, he secretly longs for Mary Gibbons, the daughter of a woman he once loved. His plans, however, are constantly interrupted by Kurt von Helsing, the grandson of the legendary vampire hunter.

This telefilm is actually the first seven chapters of "The Curse of Dracula" storyline from the series *Cliffhangers!*, edited together as a standalone movie. Produced haphazardly, it retains several flashbacks that were originally meant to be viewed week-by-week as a story recap. This makes for an odd viewing experience; one must re-watch scenes that were witnessed less than twenty minutes earlier, and the story concludes halfway through the seventh chapter of the series—so the ending makes little sense.

Promotional advertisement for the ABC TV movie
The Midnight Hour (ABC/TV Guide)

Drawn to Vampires
Animation

Quacula, the vampire duck, is Theodore Bear's unwanted house guest in the "Quacula" segment from *The New Adventures of Mighty Mouse and Heckle and Jeckle* (Filmation Associates)

Aaahh!!! Real Monsters – "The Switching Hour"

Nickelodeon. Oct 29, 1994 (S01E01). Comedy/Family. D: Jim Duffy. W: Marcy Gray Rubin, David Adam Silverman. C: Charlie Adler, Christine Cavanaugh, David Eccles, Gregg Berger, Steven L. Harman, Andrew Leeds. USA: English/Color/23m. Klasky-Csupo Inc./Nickelodeon.

Despite being told to remain indoors on Halloween night, monsters Ickis, Krumm and Oblina venture out to scare some humans. Amazed that they can receive free treats by simply going door-to-door, the monsters forego their original plan, and focus on gathering candy. But things take a turn for the worse when Ickis is switched for Nicky, a boy who's dressed up in a costume that looks just like him. This series about young monsters in training doesn't feature classic movie creatures, however this episode does have a couple of scenes with kids dressed up as vampires.

Abbott & Costello – "A Goose Misuse" / "Invader Raider" / "Monster Muddled" / "Monsterkeet"

Syndicated. Dec 9, 1967 (S01E14). Comedy/Fantasy. D: Joseph Barbera, William Hanna. W: Neal Barbera, Jack Mendelsohn. C: Bud Abbott, Stan Irwin, Don Messick, John Stephenson, Hal Smith, Mel Blanc, Janet Waldo ♀. USA: English/Color/30m. Hanna-Barbera Productions Inc.

In the segment "Monster Muddled," police officers Abbott and Costello respond to a disturbance of the peace call at 806 Weirdo Place. Inside, Costello finds an out-of-control masquerade party where everyone is dressed up as monsters—but it turns out the revelers aren't wearing costumes.

Harmless cartoon that features all the major creatures and creeps, including a green-skinned, red-haired female vampire. She transforms into a large bat, but Costello flees the festivities before she can put the bite on him.

The ABC Saturday Superstar Movie – "Mad, Mad, Mad Monsters"

ABC. Sep 23, 1972 (S01E03). Comedy/Family. D: Arthur Rankin Jr., Jules Bass. W: William J. Keenan, Lou Silverstone. C: Allen Swift ♀, Bradley Bolke, Rhoda Mann, Bob McFadden. USA: English/Color/44m. Rankin-Bass Productions/Videocraft International Inc.

Henry von Frankenstein has created a bride for his monster, and the couple will wed on Friday the 13th at the Transylvania Astoria Hotel. But the wedding guests become a little too enthralled with the bride, so Frankenstein's assistant Igor hides her away in the mountains—where she's captured by the evil creature Modzoola.

A disappointing outing from the team that delivered a number of classic holiday programs for kids during the 1960s and 1970s. The fault lies with the story and not the animation; it's visually stunning, and successfully brings all the classic movie monsters to life, including Count Dracula (who has a vampire son named Boobula).

📺 Ostensibly a sequel to the 1967 Rankin/Bass animated theatrical film *Mad Monster Party*.

The ABC Saturday Superstar Movie – "Daffy Duck and Porky Pig Meet the Groovie Goolies"

ABC. Dec 16, 1972 (S01E15). Comedy/Family. D: Hal Sutherland. W: Chuck Menville, Len Janson. C: Mel Blanc ☥, Larry Storch ☥, Howard Morris, Joanne Louise, John Erwin, Larry D. Mann ☥, Dallas McKennon. USA: English/Color/44m. Filmation Associates/Warner Bros. Animation.

Drac confronts the Phantom of the Flickers in "Daffy Duck and Porky Pig Meet the Groovie Goolies" (Filmation Associates/Warner Bros. Animation)

Daffy Duck's new production of *King Arthur and His Knights of the Round Table* has been sabotaged by a mysterious stranger, the Phantom of the Flickers, who vows to destroy every cartoon that Daffy and his friends have ever made. Upset by the news, Frankie—Daffy's biggest fan—heads to Hollywood along with the other Groovie Goolies, to stop the criminal before he can cause any more damage.

This classic mash-up features Filmation's musical monsters alongside several Looney Tunes characters. About a third of the movie is a cartoon-within-a-cartoon (the *King Arthur* film); the Goolies take on roles in Daffy's production, until he mistakenly believes they're in cahoots with the Phantom. The monsters then must stop the saboteur on their own, and just when they have him in their grasp, the Phantom escapes into "mad mirror land"—the real world—where he morphs to his human counterpart (as do Frankie, Drac and Wolfie). Upon capture, the Phantom reveals he's actually Drac's long-lost uncle, Claude Chaney, a master of disguise and former silent film star. Since Chaney can only be seen as black and white, color films like Daffy's have ruined his career. After making amends, Daffy hires Chaney as the new monster in his movie, and thanks to his many disguises, this "ghoul of a thousand faces" lands the comeback role of his career. It's a rare classic cartoon that even features a scene where Daffy Duck appears as a vampire!

📺 The character Claude Chaney is probably based on two actors: Claude Raines, who played the title role in *The Phantom of the Opera* (1943); and Lon Chaney, who was nicknamed "The Man of a Thousand Faces," and was best known for his groundbreaking makeup techniques in early cinema. He also starred as the Phantom in a 1925 adaptation of the Gaston Leroux novel.

The ABC Saturday Superstar Movie – "The Mini-Munsters"

ABC. Oct 27, 1973 (S02E03). Comedy/Family. D: Anon. W: Anon. C: Richard Long, Cynthia Adler ♀, Al Lewis ♀, Henry Gibson, Bobby Diamond, Ron Feinberg. USA: English/Color/60m. Fred Calvert Productions/Universal TV.

Eddie wants to play in a band, but he has to find some way to prevent all the loud noise from annoying his parents. So Grandpa builds a new invention: a car that runs on music instead of gasoline. Al Lewis was the only star of the original live-action series to reprise his role in this production, which was a pilot for an unproduced spin-off series. A thirty minute version was broadcast in the 1980s.

ABC Weekend Specials – "Bunnicula: The Vampire Rabbit"

ABC. Jan 9, 1982 (S05E03). Adventure/Family. D: Don Sheppard, Gordon Kent. W: Mark Evanier. C: Jack Carter, Howard Morris, Alan Dinehart, Josh Milrad, Pat Peterson, Janet Waldo, Alan Young. USA: English/Color/23m. Ruby-Spears Enterprises.

🦇🦇🦇🦇

Toby and Pete Monroe find a shoebox hidden within some tall weeds, and inside they discover a cute bunny rabbit fast asleep. Aside from a bit of dirt, the box also contains a note (in Romanian) that reads, "Take good care of my baby." The Monroe family takes in the stray rabbit; after a few days, they discover that some vegetables have turned completely white, as if every drop of juice was drained. As the phenomenon spreads throughout the neighborhood, worried locals fear it has something to do with the recent accidents at the WorldCo food processing plant. Narrated by Jack Carter (as Harold the dog).

A charming story that has all the great elements of a vampire movie, but toned down for the enjoyment of children; there's even a mob of angry locals, who in this case are wearing housecoats and slippers. Much like in *Dracula*, rather than seeing the vampire in action, the majority of the story focuses on others reacting to his nocturnal activities. Bunnicula is harmless, only showing his true nature at night; in vampire form, he has elongated fangs and red glowing eyes, and can fly using membranes under his arms (akin to the wings of a bat). He also has a psychokinetic ability, which he uses to trap the real menace that threatens WorldCo. Many of the characters in the story are familiar with the novel *Dracula*, and Chester the cat is a vampire expert; he even consults the book after realizing what Bunnicula really is. Harold eventually convinces Chester that Bunnicula is just a normal rabbit; the vampire saves the day without revealing his true identity. Highly recommended for kids of all ages.

📖 Based on *Bunnicula: A Rabbit-Tale of Mystery* by Deborah Howe and James Howe, this adaptation gives several vampiric powers to the rabbit, none of which appear in the book.

The Adventures of Jimmy Neutron: Boy Genius – "Nightmare in Retroville"

Nickelodeon. Oct 29, 2003 (S02E05). Adventure/Comedy. D: Mike Gasaway. W: Steven Banks. C: Debi Derryberry, Rob Paulsen ⚲, Jeffrey Garcia, Mark DeCarlo, Frank Welker, Carolyn Lawrence ⚲. USA: English/Color/24m. DNA Productions Inc./O Entertainment/NickToon Productions.

🦇 🦇 🦇 🦇

Jimmy uses his new invention, the Monster Maker, to turn his friends into realistic-looking creatures for Halloween. Unfortunately, Carl morphs into the real Dracula, while Sheen transforms into an actual werewolf. Jimmy has to find a way to turn them back to normal, before an angry mob gets hold of them.

A hilarious story that references several horror movies and TV series; one character even dresses up as "Muffy the vampire annihilator." It's a veritable celebration of classic movie monsters, and should be viewed by anyone with a pulse—and even those without!

Adventure Time with Finn & Jake

Cartoon Network. Mar 11, 2010 – 2017 (238 Episodes). Adventure/Comedy. D: Larry Leichliter. W: Adam Muto, Bert Youn, Sean Jimenez. C: Jeremy Shada, John DiMaggio, Olivia Olson ⚲, Hynden Walch, Tom Kenny, Pendleton Ward. USA: English/Color/2618m. Frederator Studios.

Follows a boy named Finn and his best friend Jake the dog, in a series of adventures in the Land of Ooo. One recurring character is Marceline the Vampire Queen, who drinks "shades of red" instead of blood; she's still affected by sunlight, and can turn into a giant bat. Despite having an evil vampire for a father, Marceline becomes good friends with Finn and Jake.

📺 The season seven mini-series "Stakes" was an 8-episode story arc that saw Finn & Jake join forces with Marceline to battle ghosts from her past.

The All-New Popeye Hour – "The Ski's The Limit" / "To Boo or Not To Boo" / "The Terrifyink Transylvanian Treasure Trek" / "Fantastic Gymnastics"

CBS. Sep 16, 1978 (S01E02). Adventure/Family. D: Var. W: Var. C: Jack Mercer, Marilyn Schreffler, Daws Butler, Allan Melvin. USA: English/Color/60m. King Features Syndicate/Hanna-Barbera Productions Inc.

In the segment "The Terrifyink Transylvanian Treasure Trek," Count Dracula asks Popeye and Olive Oyl to recover his lost treasure, but Bluto overhears the plan, and tries to get to the booty before they can. The three meet up at Dracula's castle, where they confront the Frankenstein Monster, but the greatest surprise of all comes when they discover exactly what the treasure is.

The All-New Scooby and Scrappy-Doo Show – "Wizards and Warlocks" / "Who's Minding the Monster?"

ABC. Sep 24, 1983 (S01E03). Adventure/Family. D: Anon. W: Richard Merwin, Robert Goldblatt. C: Casey Kasem, Don Messick, Heather North. USA: English/Color/23m. Hanna-Barbera Productions Inc.

In the segment "Who's Minding the Monster?" the gang heads to Transylvania to see if there's any truth behind the rumor that Frankenstein is terrorizing the local populace. They pose as babysitters in order to infiltrate Frankenstein's castle.

In this silly episode, Frankenstein is the Dracula family's babysitter, but they lost his controller unit, and he wandered off the castle grounds. The couple finds him, but they need to restore energy to his brain—so they capture Shaggy and Scooby to use as unwilling donors. The monsters are very tame; one cringe-worthy scene sees Dracula and his wife strolling along a canal pushing a baby carriage. What's really strange is that their baby is actually a werewolf—one wonders if Dracula has any inclination that he probably isn't the father.

📺 Technically this series had a vampire in every episode. In the opening credits, Shaggy, Scooby and Scrappy-Doo come face to face with a bloodsucker while on the run from a horde of monsters. This segment was rebroadcast on September 21, 1985 (S01E03) as part of the rerun series *Scooby's Mystery Funhouse*.

The Amazing Adrenalini Brothers! – "Fangs of Horror"

ITV. Jan 14, 2006 (S01E03). Adventure/Family. D: Dan Chambers, Claire Underwood. W: Nick Ostler. C: Dan Chambers ⚥, Sartaj Garewal, Mark Huckerby, Nick Ostler, Manny Lipman, Olly Smith. CAN/UK: English/Color/10m. Pesky/Studio B Productions/Bejuba! Entertainment.

Hailing from Réndøosîa, the Adrenalini brothers—Adi, Enk and Xan—travel the world to perform death-defying stunts. In this episode, the showmen crash-land in Transylvania, just steps from an old castle inhabited by someone named "Dracula"—and he's terrorizing the locals. Mayhem ensues after the brothers discover that the man is the spitting image of Xan. There are no real vampires in this story, but there is, however, a colony of giant bats that have large fangs.

📺 In Canada, this was broadcast on YTV as part of the premiere episode in March 2007, and was combined with the cartoons "Saddles of Insanity" and "Guitars of Destiny."

The Amazing Screw-On Head – Pilot

SyFy. Jul 27, 2006. Adventure/Fantasy. D: Chris Prynoski. W: Bryan Fuller, Mike Mignola. C: Paul Giamatti, David Hyde Pierce, Patton Oswalt, Mindy Serling, Corey Burton, Molly Shannon ⚥. USA: English/Color/22m. Kickstart Productions/Living Dead Guy Productions/The Sci-Fi Channel.

It's 1862, and an ancient parchment known as the Kalakistan Fragment is taken from The Museum of

Dangerous Books and Papers, along with the scholar who was attempting to decipher it. President Abraham Lincoln asks his top secret agent, Screw-On Head, to investigate the matter. Emperor Zombie is the culprit; he's looking for a way to unlock the secrets of the ancient document, so he can obtain the power of a demi-god.

Adapted from a one-shot comic book by Mike Mignola, this steampunk adventure mixes humor and Lovecraftian horror, and is animated in a style that suits the story perfectly. SyFy aired the pilot in the summer of 2006, and set up a special website to get feedback so they could determine whether or not to commission a full series. The survey has since closed, but no results were ever published—and there's been no word from SyFy as to the status of the series.

The Amazing Spider-Man and The Incredible Hulk – "The Transylvania Connection"

NBC. Sep 24, 1983 (S03E02). Adventure/Family. D: Donald L. Jurwich. W: Jack Mendelsohn. C: Dan Gilvezan, Frank Welker, Kathy Garver, Stanley Jones ⚥, Hans Conried, Jerry Dexter, June Foray, John Stephenson. USA: English/Color/24m. Marvel Productions Ltd./Mihan Inc.

After Firestar is hypnotized by a stranger at the E.S.U. Spring Dance, Spidey and Iceman discover she's under the control of Count Dracula—and he wants her for his undead bride. The two superheroes pursue the vampire to his castle in Transylvania, where they're confronted by the Wolf-Thing and the Frankenstein Monster—creatures intent on keeping the two at bay until Dracula can perform his unholy wedding. Narrated by Stan Lee.

In this charming yet cheesy story, Dracula is all fangs and no bite, and uses hypnosis to control both Firestar and his two monster minions. He is affected by sunlight and can turn into a bat, and causes the superheroes some degree of discomfort before succumbing to them in the end. But apparently only Dracula's "vampiric nature" is destroyed; he reverts back to human, and is completely unaware of what has transpired. (It should be noted that Dracula has a private jet that can transform into the shape of a giant bat! How cool is that?)

📺 This episode was retitled "The Bride of Dracula!" when it aired in reruns. The series ran under three different umbrella titles: *Spider-Man and His Amazing Friends* for season one, *The Incredible Hulk and the Amazing Spider-Man* for season two, and *The Amazing Spider-Man and The Incredible Hulk* for season three.

American Dragon: Jake Long – "Bite Father, Bite Son"

Disney. Jun 17, 2007 (S02E27). Action/Family. D: Nick Filippi. W: Chris Bowman. C: Dante Basco, John DiMaggio, Tress MacNeille ⚥, Matt Nolan, Jeff Bennett, Charlie Finn, Phil Morris, Dee Bradley Baker. USA: English/Color/23m. Walt Disney Television Animation.

Jake Long can transform into a dragon, which makes his blood type very special indeed. A group of vampires come to town in search of their next meal, and as it turns out, these strigoi can only be sustained by such rare (and delicious) blood.

Animaniacs – "Draculee, Draculaa" / "Phranken-Runt"

FOX. Oct 29, 1993 (S01E29). Comedy/Family. D: Michael Gerard, Byron Vaughns. W: John P. McCann. C: Rob Paulsen, Jess Harnell, Tress MacNeille, Dan Castellaneta ⚥. USA: English/Color/30m. Amblin Entertainment/Warner Bros. Television Animation.

In the segment "Draculee, Draculaa," the Warner siblings are en route to Pennsylvania when they inadvertently end up in Transylvania. They stay overnight at Dracula's castle, and the vampire is all too willing to accommodate them—that is, until they start to drive him batty.

An enjoyable cartoon that is reminiscent of the Bugs Bunny short *Transylvania 6-5000*. Dan Castellaneta, best known for his vocal work on *The Simpsons*, is a suitably menacing Dracula, and the character design is one of the better interpretations of the infamous vampire.

Archie's Weird Mysteries – "Scarlet Night" / "I Was a Teenage Vampire" / "Halloween of Horror"

PAX. Feb 9-11, 2000 (S01E31-33). Family/Mystery. D: Louis Gassin. W: Brian Swenlin. C: Andy Rannells ⚥, Chris Lundquist ⚥, Danielle Young ⚥, Camille Schmidt ⚥, Paul Sosso ⚥, Michele Phillips ⚥. USA: English/Color/66m. Les Studios Tex/DiC Productions, L.P.

In this three-part story, Veronica is suspicious of a new girl in town, Scarlet Van Helsing, who has a keen interest in Archie and the subject he's writing about: vampires. As if that wasn't bad enough, a stranger tells her that she's The Chosen One, and is destined to battle Medlock, an ancient vampire that wants to plunge the world into eternal darkness. Unfazed by all of this, Veronica is more concerned with how these events might ruin her upcoming Halloween party.

Vampires are introduced into the Archie universe in this fun multi-episode story arc, influenced by *Buffy the Vampire Slayer*. The tale builds on the traditional mythology of vampires; these bloodsuckers are more folkloric than romantic, but regretfully, they succumb too easily to the heroes by the end.

📺 These three episodes were combined as the feature-length cartoon *Archie and the Riverdale Vampires*.

Aqua Teen Hunger Force – "Bus of the Undead"

Cartoon Network. Sep 30, 2001 (S01E03). Comedy/Satire. D: Jay Edwards. W: Matt Maiellaro, Dave Willis. C: Dana Snyder, Carey Means, Dave Willis, C. Martin Croker, H. Jon Benjamin, Don Kennedy ⚥, Mary Kraft. USA: English/Color/12m. Radical Axis/Williams Street.

Late one night, Shake is watching a vampire movie when he hears a disturbance outside. He's convinced it's Count Dracula, and that a vehicle parked on the street is an "undead bus" that wants drain his blood. To convince him that Dracula is dead and not actually parked outside their home, Frylock takes Shake on a trip to Memphis to visit the vampire's grave.

A very funny episode that features live-action clips from the fake movie *Assisted Living Dracula*, where the vampire is shown in his later years under the care of a nurse. Highlights include a roadside sign for the Memphis attraction Dracula's Grave and Gift Shop, which features The Count in the guise of Elvis, playing guitar and surrounded by bats.

Aqua Teen Hunger Force – "Little Brittle"

Cartoon Network. Sep 5, 2004 (S03E06). Comedy/Satire. D: Ned Hastings. W: Matt Maiellaro, Dave Willis. C: Dana Snyder, Carey Means, Dave Willis, Andy Merrill, Mike Schatz, Chris Ward ☥, Matt Maiellaro ☥. USA: English/Color/12m. Radical Axis/Williams Street.

🦇 🦇 🦇

The group has another run-in with MC Pee Pants, but this time he's been reincarnated as an elderly rapper who calls himself "Little Brittle." Near death and hoping to extend his life, the musician finds a way to get turned into a vampire—but it doesn't work out exactly as planned. It's another enjoyable episode from this series, and features a senile rapper whose lyrics reflect his advanced age and its effect on his daily routine.

Attack of the Killer Tomatoes – "Spatula, Prinze of Dorkness"

FOX. Nov 24, 1990 (S01E10). Comedy/Family. D: Karen Peterson. W: Richard Mueller. C: John Astin, Chris Guzek, Kath Souci, Neil Ross, Thom Bray, Maurice La Mare ☥. USA: English/Color/23m. Akom Productions Ltd./Four Square Productions Inc./Marvel Productions Ltd.

🦇 🦇 🦇 🦇

Zoltan imbibes a bottle of vampire serum and transforms into Spatula, an undead tomato whose kiss can turn anyone into a ketchup vampire. As the evil menace spreads throughout San Zucchini, Doctor Gangreen rebrands the town "Doc Gangreen's Vampire Village." It's all part of his nefarious plan to use a horde of vampire tomatoes to attack the unsuspecting crowds that will flock to this new tourism mecca.

This well-crafted and surprisingly inventive story is hijacked in the opening moments by Count Dracula himself, who often breaks the fourth wall as he hosts this Halloween-themed tale. To spice up the story, he deliberately sends the serum to Gangreen, who refuses to use it—and tells Dracula that he should stop interfering with events and just stick to narrating the cartoon. This self-aware story even has one character noting that the violence has been toned down because it's a cartoon for kids, which is why there's no biting or blood. This humorous and imaginative tale spoofs vampire movies, censorship, capitalism, and many points in between, and is highly recommended viewing.

📺 One scene features characters watching *Wack-O Spooko Chiller Theater*, hosted by Wigvira, Mistress of the Dank. This is an allusion to the horror movie hostess Elvira, Mistress of the Dark.

Baby Looney Tunes – "Log Cabin Fever" / "A Mid-Autumn Night's Scream"

Cartoon Network. Apr 11, 2005 (S02E06). Adventure/Family. D: Ron Myrick. W: Tim Cahill, Julie McNally Cahill. C: Ian James Corlett, Brian Drummond ☥, June Foray, Janyse Jaud, Terry Klassen, Britt McKillip, Sam Vincent. CAN/USA: English/Color/30m. Warner Bros. Animation.

In "A Mid-Autumn Night's Scream," Floyd dresses up as Dracula and takes the kids out trick-or-treating for Halloween. Daffy ends up with no candy whatsoever, so he debates whether he should make the long, scary trek up to Hilltop Manor. Rumor has it that if you can make it to the front door—while avoiding the giant spiders, quicksand, and trees that grab little children along the way—you'll be rewarded with as much candy as you can carry.

A fun little cartoon for toddlers, but probably annoying to anyone else. Some of the costumes worn are based on other cartoon characters: Bugs Bunny is dressed as Yosemite Sam, Daffy as Duck Dodgers, and Granny takes on the guise of Witch Hazel. An award is presented for the most realistic costume, and the winners are three aliens who resemble Marvin the Martian's "Instant Martians."

The Baskervilles

TeleToon/CITV/FR2/ABC (AUS). 1998–2000 (26 Episodes). Comedy/Family. D: Nick Martinelli. W: Alastair Swinnerton, Tony Barnes. C: Suzy Aitchison, Rob Brydon, Rachel Preece, Gary Martin. CAN/UK: English/Color/780m. CINAR/Gaumont-Alphanim/France 2.

The Baskerville family is on holiday at the new tourist attraction Underworld: The Theme Park, where people pay good money to have a bad time. It's actually a Gothic, suburban landscape where everything is opposite than in the real world; trapped inside, they have no choice but to live there. Their neighbors include several monstrous families: The Draculas (vampires), The Lucifers (demons), and The Frankensteins (reanimated people).

Batman: The Brave and the Bold – "Shadow of the Bat!"

Cartoon Network. Apr 22, 2011 (S03E03). Action/Adventure. D: Michael Goguen. W: J. M. DeMatteis. C: Diedrich Bader ☥, Dee Bradley Baker, John DiMaggio ☥, Tom Everett Scott ☥, Will Friedle ☥, Nika Futterman ☥, Grey DeLisle ☥, Nicholas Guest, Jennifer Hale ☥, Jeremy Shada. USA: English/Color/22m. Warner Bros. Television.

Holy vampires, Batman! While assisting The Demon in hunting down the bloodsucker Dala, the Caped Crusader is bitten by her—and becomes a vampire. Despite his best efforts, he fails to stave the hunger for blood, feeding on both Alfred and the Black Mask. Still not satiated, Batman attacks the Justice League International, creating a horde of superhero bloodsuckers—which The Demon then incinerates using the power of the sun. Turns out that Batman was only hallucinating; he was indeed bitten by Dala, but never actually became a vampire.

The Beatles – "Baby's in Black" / "Misery"

ABC. Oct 23, 1965 (S01E05). Comedy/Family. D: Graham C. Sharpe, John Dunn. W: Bruce Howard, Heywood Kling. C: Lance Percival, Paul Frees. AUS/CAN/UK/USA: English/Color/19m. King Features Production/Canawest Studios/TVC London.

In "Baby's in Black," the Fab Four mistakenly end up in Transylvania, because Ringo misunderstood the travel agent; he thought they booked a trip to Pennsylvania. The group seeks refuge in a creepy castle, where a mad scientist kidnaps Paul to use as a husband for his latest creation—a woman who is half human and half bat. In the segment "Misery," the band visits a wax museum to view the figures made in their image, and they're terrorized by a reanimated statue of Dracula.

This episode is quite enjoyable, even though it's poorly animated, and the voices sound nothing like the musicians themselves. To the tune of "Misery," Count Dracula chases The Beatles throughout the wax museum; it's a quirky segment equally matched by the intermission between the cartoons, which is a sing-along to "I'll Get You."

Beavis and Butt-Head – "Werewolves of Highland" / "Crying"

MTV. Oct 27, 2011 (S08E01). Comedy/Satire. D: Tony Kluck, Roy Smith. W: John Altschuler, Dave Krinsky. C: Mike Judge, Toby Huss, Lori Nasso, Sam Johnson, Monica Keena, Thomas Middleditch. USA: English/Color/22m. 3 Arts Entertainment/Judgmental Films/MTV.

In "Werewolves of Highland," Beavis and Butt-Head want to become creatures of the night, because girls are going crazy over the men from *Twilight*. Since the bite from any undead creature will do, they solicit the help of a homeless man—whom they mistake for a werewolf.

The dysfunctional duo return to MTV after fourteen years, in an episode that skewers the *Twilight* franchise, and deftly points out some of its more vapid characteristics. After being bitten, Beavis and Butt-Head end up in the hospital, suffering Gangrene, Gonorrhea, Staph, MRSA, and Hepatitis A, B & C. Welcome back, guys!

Boo to You Too! Winnie the Pooh

CBS. Oct 25, 1996. Adventure/Family. D: Rob LaDuca. W: Carter Crocker, A.A. Milne. C: Peter Cullen, Jim Cummings ⚥, John Fiedler, Michael Gough, Ken Sansom. USA: English/Color/21m. Walt Disney Television Animation.

As Pooh and the gang prepare for Halloween, everyone is excited aside from Piglet, who's too afraid to participate. But he must face his fears head-on after he discovers that a scary monster is roaming the Hundred Acre Wood, and it's heading towards his friends. Narrated by John Rhys-Davies.

Tigger sings the song "I Wanna Scare Myself" as he tries on several costumes, one of which is a vampire outfit—and he's briefly seen with jet-black hair, pronounced canines, and wearing a long flowing cape.

Brand Spanking New! Doug – "Doug's Bloody Buddy"

ABC. Oct 26, 1996 (S01E08). Adventure/Family. D: Jim Jinkins, Jack Spillum. W: Joe Fallon. C: Connie Shulman, Doug Preis, Alice Playten, Chris Phillips, Fred Newman, Thomas McHugh, Becca Lish, Greg Lee. USA: English/Color/30m. Jumbo Pictures Inc./Walt Disney Television Animation.

Doug and Roger investigate a rumor that Skeeter is really a vampire, and they wonder if it might be true after they see him hanging out with bats.

Brandy & Mr. Whiskers – "The Curse of the Vampire Bat" / "The Monkey's Paw"

Disney. Oct 29, 2004 (S01E11). Adventure/Family. D: Timothy Björklund. W: Brian Swenlin. C: Kaley Cuoco, Charlie Adler, Alanna Ubach, Tom Kenny, Sherri Shepherd, Jennifer Hale. USA: English/Color/30m. Walt Disney Television Animation.

Follows the adventures of Brandy the dog and Whiskers the rabbit, who become stranded in the Amazon rainforest. In "The Curse of the Vampire Bat," their new neighbor Vlad claims that he's just a harmless fruit bat—but he hates garlic and avoids mirrors and sunlight! Whiskers tries to prove to Brandy that Vlad is actually a vampire.

Vlad is indeed a harmless vampire bat (with a Hungarian accent). He explains that he's really just like a big mosquito. He only takes a little bit of blood, but everyone freaks out when they hear the word "vampire"—so he pretends to be a fruit bat because of the intolerance of others.

Buffy the Vampire Slayer: The Animated Series – Pilot

FOX. 2004. Action/Fantasy. D: Anon. W: Joss Whedon, Jeph Loeb. C: Giselle Loren, Alyson Hannigan, Anthony Stewart Head, Nicholas Brendon. USA: English/Color/4m. Mutant Enemy/20th Century Fox Television.

Giles desperately tries to warn the gang about a sect of vampires that are planning an apocalypse, but all Buffy, Xander and Willow can think about is an upcoming party. Just when he's finally getting through to them, a hideous dragon crashes into the library, and takes Buffy away into the night.

In 2001, development began on an animated *Buffy* series to be voiced by most of the original cast members (which, continuity-wise, would start in the middle of Season 1 of the TV show). It was green lit by FOX in 2002, and set to air within their Fox Kids programming block later that year;

but it ended up in limbo, after the network discontinued airing daytime children's programming. In 2004, this unaired presentation pilot was commissioned by FOX, and shopped around to other networks in an attempt to sell the series; none were interested, so it remains unproduced.

 This project is referenced in issue #20 of the *Buffy the Vampire Slayer Season Eight* comic series, in a story where Buffy awakes in an animated world of the past—and finds herself in the middle of events from Season 1.

The Bugs Bunny/Road Runner Hour – Ep. #1.20

CBS. Jan 25, 1969 (S01E20). Comedy/Family. D: Chuck Jones, Maurice Noble. W: John Dunn. C: Mel Blanc, Ben Frommer ☥, Julie Bennett. USA: English/Color/60m. Warner Bros. Animation.

Features the cartoon short "Transylvania 6-5000," where Bugs Bunny takes a wrong turn and ends up in Pittsburgh, Transylvania. He stays overnight at Count Bloodcount's castle, which he thinks is a motel. Unable to sleep, Bugs reads through a book of magic, and he learns a few tricks that prevent him from becoming the vampire's next meal.

Originally released theatrically on November 30, 1963, this classic cartoon's most memorable moments involve Bugs utilizing the magic words *abra-cadabra* and *hocus-pocus* (and various incarnations of each). This transforms Count Bloodcount in and out of bat form at the most inopportune times; by the end of the cartoon, the poor vampire is a little worse for wear.

Promotional advertisement for the CBS animated program *Bugs Bunny's Howl-Oween Special* (Warner Bros. Television/TV Guide)

 This was rebroadcast as part of ABC's *The Bugs Bunny & Tweety Show* on several occasions, including: January 17, 1987 (S01E18); October 1, 1988 (S03E04); February 11, 1989 (S03E23); October 22, 1994 (S09E07); and November 11, 1995 (S10E10).

Bugs Bunny's Howl-Oween Special

CBS. Oct 26, 1978. Comedy/Family. D: Friz Freleng, Chuck Jones, Abe Levitow, Robert McKimson, Maurice Noble. W: John Dunn, Warren Foster, Michael Maltese, Tedd Pierce. C: Mel Blanc, June Foray. USA: English/Color/25m. Warner Bros. Television.

On Halloween night, Witch Hazel's wacky spells target several Looney Tunes characters, including Bugs Bunny, Daffy Duck, Porky Pig,

Sylvester the Cat, and Speedy Gonzales. During a final showdown with Bugs, she drinks a potion that transforms her into Count Bloodcount.

This production uses the framing story from the 1966 cartoon *A-Haunting We Will Go,* and mixes in clips from eight other classic Warner Brothers shorts—all tied together with new scenes used to segue between each. In original form, the cartoons are enjoyable to watch, but here they've been hacked to pieces in a failed attempt to make an overall cohesive story—and the new scenes in no way match the quality or look of the original animation.

Includes scenes from the theatrical shorts *Scaredy Cat* (1948), *Bewitched Bunny* (1954), *Claws For Alarm* (1954), *Hyde and Hare* (1955), *Broom-Stick Bunny* (1956), *A Witch's Tangled Hare* (1959), *Hyde and Go Tweet* (1960) and *Transylvania 6-5000* (1963).

Captain N: The Game Master – "Return to Castlevania"

NBC. Sep 28, 1991 (S03E03). Family/Fantasy. D: John Grusd, Kit Hudson. W: Matt Uitz. C: Matt Hill, Andrew Kavadas, Long John Baldry. USA: English/Color/30m. DiC Entertainment/Nintendo of America Inc.

Follows the adventures of Kevin Keene, a teenager transported to "Videoland" on a mission to defeat the evil Mother Brain. In this episode, on the creepy world of Castlevania, Kevin teams up with Simon Belmont to battle the Poltergeist King—who turns out to be Count Dracula in disguise.

Amusing story that suffers from the inclusion of Dracula's son Alucard, who is depicted as a skateboarding surfer-dude with a rebellious attitude. This episode includes elements from the NES video game *Castlevania III: Dracula's Curse* (1990).

Casper and the Angels – "Fatula" / "T.V. or Not T.V."

NBC. Nov 3, 1979 (S01E07). Adventure/Family. D: George Gordon, Ray Patterson. W: Bob Ogle, Patsy Cameron. C: Julie McWhirter, Diana McCannon, Laurel Page, John Stephenson, Dick Beals, Rick Dees, Frank Welker. USA: English/Color/30m. Hanna-Barbera Studios Inc.

In the segment "Fatula," Minnie and Maxie are surprised to learn that Count Fatula has been released from Space Prison on good behavior. Now free as a bat, he even claims to have turned a new leaf, and wants bygones to be bygones. Casper discovers that Fatula secretly wants to take revenge against his friends.

Uninspired cartoon that features a plump vampire who has difficulty maintaining flight when he transforms into a bat (because he's so overweight). There are several fat jokes and bite jokes that won't garner any laughs—aside from the ones provided by the overbearing laugh track, of course.

CatDog – "CatDogula"

Nickelodeon. Nov 6, 1999 (S02E19). Comedy/Family. D: Rob Porter. W: Steven Banks. C: Jim Cummings ☥, Tom Kenny ☥, Carlos Alazraqui ☥, Billy West ☥, Maria Bamford ☥, John Kassir ☥. USA: English/Color/24m. Peter Hannan Productions/Nickelodeon.

Chronicles the adventures of conjoined animals Cat, the schemer, and Dog, the dreamer. In this episode, as Cat and Dog prepare for Halloween, they see a scary news report about dead, bloodless cattle coming back to life. A horde of Peruvian vampire ticks is responsible, and as a wave of evil blankets the town, Dog succumbs to the bite of the undead. Cat must find a way to reverse the effects before the stroke of midnight, otherwise, Dog will remain a vampire forever. It's a mildly-entertaining story influenced by the legend of el chupacabras, and features a swarm of insects with strong accents led by chief vampire Nosferacho—who provides most of the humor.

Centurions – "Night on Terror Mountain"

Syndicated. Nov 4, 1986 (S01E37). Family/Sci-Fi. D: Anon. W: Mel Gilden. C: Pat Fraley, Neilson Ross, Vince Edwards, Ron Feinberg, Edmund Gilbert, Diane Pershing, Jennifer Darling. USA: English/Color/21m. Ruby-Spears Productions/Nippon Sunrise.

This early North American *anime*-style series features an elite team of warriors with special armor, which allows them to fuse with powerful weaponry. In this episode, the Centurions stop an attack on an air traffic control station in Transylvania. The culprits, Doc Terror and Hacker, flee to a nearby castle. Inside they discover the coffin of Count Dracula, and the three evildoers team up to destroy the Centurions once and for all.

Oh Dracula, will you ever learn? This entertaining episode sees the Count once again bent on world domination, and true to form, he even turns on his co-conspirators. Unfortunately, Dracula succumbs to sunlight at the hands of those do-gooder Centurions.

Challenge of the Super Friends – "Attack of the Vampire"

ABC. Oct 14, 1978 (S01E06). Adventure/Family. D: Ray Patterson, Carl Urbano. W: Jeffrey Scott. C: Danny Dark ☥, Olan Soulé, Casey Kasem, Shannon Farnon, Bill Callaway, Mike Bell ☥, Louise Williams ☥. USA: English/Color/23m. Hanna-Barbera Productions Inc.

High atop the Transylvanian Alps, the world's most infamous vampire rises once again. Dracula wants to turn the Earth's population into his undead legion, and as his vampire horde takes over Austria, even Superman and the Wonder Twins fall under his evil influence. As Aquaman and Wonder Woman try to stop the undead tide from spreading across Europe, Batman and Robin are left to face Dracula on their own.

This excellent adventure features one of the more inspired takes on Dracula: he's pure evil, speaks with a raspy voice, and produces a haunting moan as he struggles to breathe. At first he uses some magic dust to transform unsuspecting airline passengers into vampires; they in turn spread the disease by emitting red lasers from their eyes. The story includes some truly campy moments, such as when Superman uses Batman's "Bat Makeup" to pass himself off as a vampire. The story effectively mixes the Dracula legend with comic book superheroes, and even includes some pretty scary-looking undead.

📺 This "laser method" for making new vampires was also used by Jeffrey Scott in the episodes he wrote for *Spider-Woman* ("Dracula's Revenge," 1979) and *SuperFriends* ("Voodoo Vampire," 1980).

Class of the Titans – "Sybaris Fountain"

TeleToon. May 10, 2006 (S01E24). Adventure/Family. D: Brad Goodchild. W: Brad Birch. C: Kelly Sheridan, Ted Cole, Meghan Black, Doron Bell, Ty Olsson ☥, Laura Sadiq ☥. CAN: English/Color/22m. Studio B Productions/Top Draw Animation/Nelvana Limited.

Descended from the original Greek gods, a group of seven teenage heroes train at Olympus High as they prepare for an eventual battle with the time god Cronus. In this episode, the Titans travel to a remote village to investigate a missing statue, which was part of an old fountain in the town square. Locals believe it's a sign that a great evil has returned; in ancient times, the area was attacked by Queen Sybaris—the first vampire—and the statue had marked the spot where she was defeated. They insist that the missing statue means that Sybaris has been resurrected.

In Greek mythology, Sybaris was a female dragon, and she is depicted here as a cross between a winged snake and a gargoyle, with humanoid features; not your typical vampire by any means. She also takes on some aspects of Lamia, who in the same lore was an ancient Queen of Libya who was turned into a child-eating demon. It's an average but enjoyable story that successfully mixes Greek mythology with a contemporary interpretation of vampire folklore.

The Cleveland Show – "Beer Walk!"

FOX. Dec 5, 2010 (S02E09). Comedy/Satire. D: Jim Shellhorn. W: Aaron Lee. C: Mike Henry, Sanaa Lathan, Kevin Michael Richardson, Reagan Gomez-Preston, Jason Sudeikis, Seth MacFarlane. USA: English/Color/22m. Fuzzy Door Productions/Persons Unknown Productions.

This *Family Guy* spinoff features the Griffins' neighbor, Cleveland Brown, who now lives with his new family in Stoolbend, Virginia. In this episode, to prove to his wife that he's as equally altruistic as her, Cleveland recruits his friends to get drunk for charity. Donna is injured during one of Cleveland's inebriated stunts, so he's forced to take over the housecleaning duties until she recovers.

A rather pointless outing peppered with stale jokes. In one scene, while Donna is recuperating, she asks Cleveland to return some DVDs to the video store. She thought she had rented *True Blood*, but it just seems to be scenes from "some gay guy's nightmare." This cuts to a shot of a shirtless Bill Compton and Eric Northman (vampires from *True Blood*), who scratch and hiss at each other while mugging to the camera.

The Cleveland Show – "A Nightmare on Grace Street"

FOX. Oct 30, 2011 (S03E03). Comedy/Satire. D: Phil Allora. W: Jonathan Green, Gabe Miller. C: Mike Henry, Sanaa Lathan, Kevin Michael Richardson, Reagan Gomez, Jason Sudeikis, Glenn Howerton ⚲. USA: English/Color/22m. Fuzzy Door Productions/Persons Unknown Productions.

Donna forces Rallo and Cleveland to spend Halloween night in a spooky old house, because the two of them are always trying to prove which one is the toughest. Meanwhile, Roberta believes she's in a love triangle with Caleb the werewolf and Edwin the vampire, but the delusional girl doesn't realize that the men only have eyes for each other.

Teeming with lowbrow humor, the episode opens with a distasteful joke that involves the corpse of Vincent Price, and goes downhill from there. It almost rises above mediocrity with a few digs at the *Twilight* franchise, but by now, even these jokes are getting a little stale.

Clifford the Big Red Dog – "Come Back, Mac" / "Boo!"

PBS. Sep 18, 2000 (S01E11). Adventure/Family. D: John Over. W: Lois Becker, Anne-Marie Perrotta. C: John Ritter, Grey DeLisle, Cam Clarke, Gary LeRoi Gray, Kath Soucie, Cree Summer, Kel Mitchell, Tony Plana ⚲. USA: English/Color/30m. Scholastic Entertainment Inc.

In "Boo!" Pedro—dressed as Count Dracula—hosts an outdoor screening of a ghost movie. Most of the kids get a little scared, aside from Jetta, who claims that nothing frightens her. Yet she loses her resolve after she sees a really big ghost wandering around Birdwell Island.

A charming cartoon for kids where they learn that it's normal to be scared, and it's okay to tell others when you feel this way. Interestingly, the name "Dracula" is never mentioned. The character in the costume speaks with a Hungarian accent, wears the typical vampire garments and *accoutrements,* and sports very pronounced fangs—and everyone naturally knows who he's supposed to be. It just goes to show how ubiquitous the Bela Lugosi/Dracula archetype is in our popular culture.

Codename: Kids Next Door – "Operation C.A.K.E.D.-T.H.R.E.E." / "Operation L.O.C.K.D.O.W.N."

Cartoon Network. Aug 6, 2004 (S03E08). Adventure/Family. D: Tom Warburton. W: Tom Warburton, Mo Willems. C: Dee Bradley Baker ⚱, Ben Diskin ⚱, Jennifer Hale, Daran Norris ⚱, Cree Summer, Lauren Tom ⚱. USA: English/Color/30m. Curious Pictures/Rough Draft Studios Inc.

In "Operation L.O.C.K.D.O.W.N.," Number One is en route to the tree house when he purposely activates code L-62, which puts the entire facility into lockdown—and he arrives unconscious. The kids discover that there's an intruder among them: Count Spankulot, a spank-happy vampire. Trapped until sunrise, Number Five must find a way to take control of the situation before it gets out of hand.

An amusing tale where each kid is turned into a vampire after being spanked. They revert back to their normal selves after a healthy dose of sunlight, a process that painfully rips the vampire nature from their very bones.

📺 Count Spankulot returned to wreak havoc in the 2005 platform game *Operation: V.I.D.E.O.G.A.M.E.*

The Comic Strip

Syndicated. Sep 7 – Dec 4, 1987 (65 Episodes). Comedy/Family. D: Anon. W: Julian P. Gardner, Peter Lawrence. C: Bob McFadden, Earl Hammond, Peter Newman, Larry Kenney, Maggie Jakobson, Jim Meskimen, Carmen de Lavallade. USA: English/Color/1950m. Rankin-Bass Productions Inc.

Episodic adventures from four distinct shows: "Mini-Monsters," "The Street Frogs," "Karate Kat" and "Tigersharks." In "Mini-Monsters," two rambunctious siblings are sent to Camp Mini-Mon for the summer, but their parents are unaware that it's actually a camp attended by kids of famous movie monsters—including Dracula's son, Dracky. It's a harmless show for kids with extremely dated dialogue. Some of the "Mini-Monsters" segments were compiled into a thirty-minute home video release titled *The Mini-Monsters: Adventures at Camp Mini-Mon*.

The Completely Mental Misadventures of Ed Grimley

NBC. Sep 10 – Dec 3, 1988 (13 Episodes). Comedy/Family. D: Bob Goe. W: Martin Short, Wayne Kaatz. C: Martin Short, Joe Flaherty ⚱, Catherine O'Hara, Andrea Martin, Jonathan Winters. USA: English/Color/390m. Hanna-Barbera Productions Inc./Wang Film Productions Company.

Hyperkinetic Ed Grimley lives next door to his unrequited love interest, Ms. Malone, a woman for whom he'd do anything—provided it doesn't interrupt the opportunity to watch his favorite TV show, *Count Floyd's Scary Stories*.

This show-within-a-show is a live action segment where Joe Flaherty reprises the role of the vampire character "Count Floyd" that he originated on *SCTV*. He steps out of a coffin to greet a small audience of disinterested children, and then introduces one of his "chiller monster stories." At the last minute he learns that the tale isn't available, so it's substituted with something that is much less frightening.

Count Duckula

ITV1. Sep 6, 1988 – Feb 16, 1993 (65 Episodes). Comedy/Family. D: Chris Randall. W: Jimmy Hibbert, Peter Richard Reeves, John Broadhead. C: David Jason ⚲, Jack May, Brian Trueman, Jimmy Hibbert, Ruby Wax. UK: English/Color/1950m. Cosgrove Hall Productions/Thames.

🦇🦇🦇

For many centuries, Transylvania was the home to a dreadful dynasty of vampire ducks, but the tradition has been broken due to the improper resurrection of Count Duckula. Instead of blood, ketchup was used in the spell that brought him back from the dead—and he's returned as a vegetarian. Narrated by Barry Clayton.

This *Danger Mouse* spin-off follows the misadventures of Count Duckula, brought back to life by his macabre servant Igor; his dimwitted housemaid, Nanny, was the one who mixed up the ingredients in the resurrection spell. The three of them often travel outside of Transylvania thanks to Castle Duckula, which can teleport anywhere across the globe—but it always returns by dawn. Despite being a harmless vegetarian, Duckula is still pursued by the bumbling vampire hunter, Dr. Von Goosewing.

Cow and Chicken – "Chickens Don't Fly" / "P.E." / "I Am Vampire"

Cartoon Network. Sep 9, 1998 (S03E07). Adventure/Comedy. D: David Feiss. W: Maxwell Atoms. C: Michael Dorn ⚲, Charlie Adler ⚲, Mark Hamill, Tom Kenny, David Feiss. USA: English/Color/30m. Hanna-Barbera Productions Inc.

In the segment "I Am Vampire," two harmless bloodsuckers, Weasel and Baboon, are targeted by an infamous vampire hunter—even though they only drink canned blood.

Cyberchase – "Castleblanca"

PBS. Jan 22, 2002 (S01E02). Adventure/Family. D: Larry Jacobs. W: Dan Elish. C: Christopher Lloyd, Gilbert Gottfried, Bianca DeGroat, Novie Edwards, Jacqueline Pillon ⚲, Annick Obonsawin. CAN/USA: English/Color/27m. thirteen WNET New York/Educational Broadcasting Corporation.

🦇🦇🦇

The Hacker captures Dr. Marbles and takes him to the world of Castleblanca, the Transylvania of Cyberspace, and plans to transfer the man's brain power into his new robot monster, Gigabyte.

When the gang arrives in Castleblanca to search for the cyberscientist, they discover a world populated with all sorts of monsters. They must use logic and critical thinking to reason out exactly where The Hacker has hidden their friend.

This Halloween-themed episode teaches kids about creating surveys, gathering data, and mapping the results. Dracula even makes an appearance after the kids mistakenly head to the wrong castle, because they didn't collect information in the best way possible (which led to an improper conclusion based on a poor data set).

D-TV – "Monster Hits"

NBC. Oct 30, 1987. Family/Music. D: Andrew Solt. W: Phillip Savenick, Andrew Solt, Susan F. Walker. C: Jeffrey Jones, Wayne Allwine, Tony Anselmo, Bill Farmer, June Foray, Maurice LaMare. USA: English/Color/48m. Walt Disney Productions/Andrew Solt Productions.

Hosted by the Magic Mirror, this Halloween-themed TV special features a dozen contemporary pop songs set to video montages edited from classic Disney cartoons.

In the mid-1980s, the Disney Channel aired a series of pop music videos, but instead of broadcasting the official video for the song, they created new visuals that were edited from classic cartoons. Initially used to fill small pockets of air time, these videos were later pieced together in a series of television specials that aired on NBC. "Monster Hits" included the spooky standard "Monster Mash" by Bobby "Boris" Pickett, and featured a clip from *Mickey's Gala Premier* (1933). This was an animated short about a film premiere attended by many celebrities, including Dracula, the Frankenstein Monster and Mr. Hyde. It's by far the best video of the lot, and it's surprising just how well the classic cartoons meshed with contemporary pop music.

📺 Other songs in this special include: "Thriller" (Michael Jackson); "Ghostbusters" (Ray Parker Jr.); "Bad Moon Rising" (Creedence Clearwater Revival); "Somebody's Watching Me" (Rockwell); "Evil Woman" (ELO); "Superstition" (Stevie Wonder); "You Better Run" (Pat Benatar); "That Old Black Magic" (Spike Jones); "Dreamtime" (Daryl Hall); and "Sweet Dreams" (The Eurythmics).

Danger Mouse

ITV1/Channel 4. Sep 28, 1981 – Mar 19, 1992 (89 Episodes). Comedy/Family. D: Brian Cosgrove. W: Brian Trueman. C: David Jason ♀, Terry Scott, Edward Kelsey, Brian Trueman, Jimmy Hibbert. UK: English/Color/2670m. Cosgrove-Hall Productions/Thames Television.

Secret agent Danger Mouse and his faithful sidekick Ernest Penfold swap one-liners as they risk life and limb while on assignment. Over the course of the series they occasionally faced Count Duckula, a showbiz-obsessed vampire waterfowl that craved the spotlight and wanted his own TV show.

Wry British humor runs rampant throughout this self-aware series, clearly influenced by Monty Python, Sherlock Holmes and James Bond. Count Duckula is a hoot; he sounds like a cross between Donald Duck and Porky the Pig, is green in color, and dresses in traditional Dracula attire; he can also transform into a bat—a cricket bat, that is. He made three appearances over the course of this series: in "The Four Tasks of Danger Mouse," "The Return of Count Duckula," and "Duckula Meets Frankenstoat." The first two outings were extended stories that ran over the course of five episodes each. Count Duckula was finally granted his wish in 1988, when he starred in his own eponymous spin-off series.

📺 These episodes also featured "vampoids," which were cricket bats infused with Count Duckula's personality. He also had three Dracula-like backup singers.

Count Duckula first appeared in *Danger Mouse* before getting his own eponymous spin-off series (Cosgrove Hall Productions/Thames)

DarkStalkers

UPN. Sep 30 – Dec 30, 1995 (13 Episodes). Action/Adventure. D: Var. W: Var. C: Cree Summer, Bill Switzer, Gary Chalk, Michael Donovan ☥, Ian James Corlett, Kathleen Barr ☥, Tony Jay. USA: English/Color/390m. DiC Entertainment.

Based on the Capcom arcade game, this series follows Harry, a descendent of the wizard Merlin, who teams up with a cat woman named Felicia to battle an army of supernatural creatures known as the DarkStalkers. Features Demitri, the Lord of the Vampires, as well as a succubus named Morrigan.

Darkwing Duck – "Night of the Living Spud"

Syndicated. Sep 11, 1991 (S01E05). Comedy/Family. D: Anon. W: Steve Roberts, Duane Capizzi. C: Jim Cummings, Christine Cavanaugh, Terence McGovern, Tino Insana, Dana Hill, Susan Tolsky, Frank Welker ☥. USA: English/Color/22m. Walt Disney Television Animation.

Darkwing Duck relates a spooky story about the time he faced a vampire potato, the result of an experiment gone horribly awry. A villainous plant, Bushroot, decided to grow a wife of his own, but he added potato starch instead of posy blossom into the mix. This resulted in a monstrous, vampiric potato that terrorized the city, and each of her victims was turned into a couch potato. This is a very different kind of vampire story, but despite the creative premise, it suffers from lame jokes that only kids will find amusing.

Dear Dracula

Cartoon Network. Oct 16, 2012. Comedy/Family. D: Chad Van De Keere. W: Brad Birch. C: Ray Liotta ⚲, Nathan Gamble ⚲, Emilio Estevez, Marion Ross, Ariel Winter, Matthew Lillard, Yuri Lowenthal, Tara Strong. USA: English/Color/42m. Kickstart Productions.

Much like how kids write to Santa Claus at Christmastime, Sam—a young horror buff and vampire fanatic—writes to Dracula at Halloween, asking for the hottest new toy: a Count Dracula action figure! But instead of sending the doll, Dracula decides to pay Sam a visit, with his assistant Myro in tow. Airing as part of Cartoon Network's "Spooky Specials" for Halloween, *Dear Dracula* was adapted from the children's graphic novel of the same name by Joshua Williamson and Vicente Navarrete, which was published in 2008 by Image Comics/Shadowline.

Defenders of the Earth – "Dracula's Potion"

Syndicated. Nov 4, 1986 (S01E42). Adventure/Family. D: Will Meugniot. W: Chris Bunch, Allan Cole. C: Lou Richards, Buster Jones, Peter Renaday, Loren Lester, Peter Mark Richman, Sarah Partridge, William Callaway. USA: English/Color/22m. Marvel Productions Ltd.

🦇 🦇 🦇

Set in the year 2015, this series features a team of superheroes that include the Phantom, Mandrake the Magician, and Flash Gordon. In this episode, the Defenders head to Transylvania at the behest of Doctor Helsing, who's concerned about the well-being of his associate Jonathan Harker. The man traveled there over three months ago to work on an archeological excavation, but he hasn't been heard from since. Their investigation takes them to the castle of a mysterious nobleman, Count Vlad, whose charming façade may be hiding something much more sinister.

This episode is a bare-bones, futuristic adaptation of Bram Stoker's *Dracula*, and several key scenes are reminiscent of the novel. For example, when the Defenders first arrive in Transylvania, they're met by a horse-drawn carriage; inscribed on the back of the vehicle is the phrase "Den die todten rieten shinel" (sic), which one of the team translates as "The dead travel fast." Count Vlad looks and sounds like a typical Dracula; he has the ability to mesmerize women, and can control a pack of wolves. The episode title refers to a magic potion that the Count tricks the team into drinking, which transforms each of them into the animal most representative of their personality.

Dennis the Menace – "Vampire Scare" / "Give Me Liberty or Give Me Dennis" / "Wilson for Mayor"

Syndicated. Nov 21, 1986 (S01E45). Adventure/Family. D: Michael Maliani. W: Var. C: Brennan Thicke, Jeannie Elias, Brian George, Phil Hartman, Marilyn Lightstone, Sharon Noble, Riva Spier, Louise Valance. USA: English/Color/30m. DiC Enterprises/General Mills.

In the segment "Vampire Scare," Dennis and his friends see a strange man heading inside a creepy house, and he looks exactly like the vampire from the scary movie they just watched. The kids sneak inside to see if he's the real deal, but the man has disappeared into thin air; all they find is an empty coffin.

The vampire in question is really just a magician, and the weird objects in his home are simply props he uses in his act—or so he claims. He never explains to the kids why he looks and sounds just like Dracula. (Perhaps the vampire, bored after centuries of killing and whatnot, decided to pick up a new hobby?)

Drak Pack

CBS. Sep 6, 1980 – Sep 12, 1982 (16 Episodes). Adventure/Family. D: Chris Cuddington. W: Doug Booth. C: Bill Callaway, Hans Conried, Jerry Dexter ⚥, Chuck McCann, Julie McWhirter ⚥, Alan Oppenheimer ⚥. USA: English/Color/352m. Hanna-Barbera Productions Inc./Southern Star.

To atone for the past misdeeds of their monstrous forefathers, Drac Jr., Howler and Frankie fight crime and battle evildoers. Under the leadership of Count Dracula, the three teenagers often cross paths with O.G.R.E., a band of criminals headed by their arch nemesis, Dr. Dred.

This entertaining series introduces the archetypal movie monsters to a younger audience, and celebrates the classics of the silver screen through the characters and situations it presents. Part of the charm is its tongue-in-cheek humor, à la *Get Smart*, and there are several running jokes throughout the series. The teenagers invoke their monster powers through a "Drak-whack," a high-five motion that initiates a transformation in each of them. Howler becomes a werewolf with a powerful lung capacity, while Frankie morphs into a Karloff-inspired monster and gains tremendous strength. Drac is the vampire of the group, and can transform into many different entities—including smoke, a bat, and even a seagull; he can also levitate and use his cape to fly. Drac sounds like a teenage Maxwell Smart, and has an uncanny resemblance to Tim Curry as Dr. Frank-N-Furter, complete with pale white skin, eyeliner and lipstick. Truly an inspired series that still holds up to this day, and worthwhile viewing for both kids and adults.

📺 One of Dr. Dred's underlings, Vampira, certainly bears passing resemblance to her famous namesake created by Maila Nurmi. She's a "vamp" in the classic *femme fatale* sense, yet still has transformative abilities; she can morph into a snake, a spider, and other insects, as well as a horse, a sea monster, and even a pterodactyl.

Duck Dodgers – "I'm Going to Get You, Fat Sucka" / "Detained Duck"

Cartoon Network. Sep 20, 2003 (S01E05). Adventure/Sci-Fi. D: Spike Brandt. W: Spike Brandt, Tony Cervone. C: Joe Alaskey, Bob Bergen, Jeff Bennett ☥, Edward Asner, Dee Bradley Baker, Michael Dorn, Grey DeLisle ☥. USA: English/Color/22m. Cartoon Network/Warner Bros. Television Animation.

In the segment "I'm Going to Get You, Fat Sucka," Dodgers and the Cadet land on what they believe is a derelict space station. Inside they find a sole occupant, Count Muerte, who's more than eager to welcome them in. Dodgers—who's used to being the center of attention—is surprised when Muerte completely ignores him; the stranger seems far more interested in his portly subordinate.

This hilarious cartoon is essentially a comedic retelling of Bram Stoker's immortal tale, with Dodgers as Renfield, the Cadet as Harker, and Muerte as a fat-sucking Dracula; even the three vampire brides make an appearance. Count Muerte is reminiscent of the famous Warner Brothers/Looney Tunes vampire Count Bloodcount, although he's more Nosferatu in appearance.

Duck Dodgers – "Till Doom Do Us Part"

Cartoon Network. Mar 11, 2005 (S03E01). Adventure/Sci-Fi. D: Spike Brandt. W: Tony Cervone. C: Joe Alaskey, Bob Bergen, Jeff Bennett ☥, Dick Beals, John Di Maggio, Jim Cummings, Grey DeLisle, Tia Carrere. USA: English/Color/22m. Cartoon Network/Warner Bros. Television Animation.

In a story that spoofs *SuperFriends* (1973), a disgruntled robot assembles a team of the thirteen most sinister villains from the farthest reaches of the galaxy, in an effort to destroy their common enemy: Duck Dodgers. But the nefarious group, "The Legion of Duck Doom," has difficulty agreeing on a single course of action. None of this even registers with Dodgers, since his focus—such as it is—is on the upcoming wedding between Marvin the Martian and Queen Tyr'ahnee; he's been asked to be the Best Man at the ceremony.

Another entertaining episode that features the return of Count Muerte, despite the fact that he was apparently destroyed after his last encounter with Dodgers and the Cadet (you can't keep a good vampire down!). This would have received top marks had the story included more of the fat-sucking vampire, but he's underused in this tale.

DuckTales – "Ducky Horror Picture Show"

Syndicated. Dec 31, 1987 (S01E64). Adventure/Family. D: Terence Harrison. W: Richard Merwin. C: Peter Cullen, Jim Cummings, Dick Gautier, Joan Gerber, Chuck McCann, Alan Oppenheimer, Neil Ross. USA: English/Color/23m. Walt Disney Television Animation.

Always on the lookout for more money, Scrooge McDuck transforms his mansion into a hotel to accommodate fifty conventioneers, unaware that it's a gathering of real monsters. After the creatures run amok, Scrooge is to blame—because everyone thinks that it's just a publicity stunt for the monster movie marathon at his Scroogerama Dome.

The fiends include Quackenstein, the Wolf Duck, and Count Drakeula—who only bites apples, because they keep his teeth nice and shiny. This vampire duck is patterned after Bela Lugosi, with jet-black hair, a red-lined opera cape, and a thick Hungarian accent.

 The sorceress Magica De Spell, one of the main antagonists of this series, was inspired in part by Morticia from *The Addams Family* comic strip by Charles Addams.

Ed, Edd n' Eddy – "Ed, Edd n' Eddy's Boo Haw Haw"

Cartoon Network. Oct 28, 2005. Family/Comedy. D: Danny Antonucci. W: Danny Antonucci, Jono Howard. C: Matt Hill, Samuel Vincent, Tony Sampson, Janyse Jaud ♀, David Paul Grove, Kathleen Barr, Keenan Christenson, Erin Fitzgerald. USA: English/Color/25m. a.k.a. Cartoon Inc.

The gang heads out for Halloween armed with a crudely-drawn map in search of "Spook-E-Ville"—a neighborhood where residents give out bucket loads of candy. En route they run into all sorts of trouble, thanks to Ed's obsession with horror films; he's watched so many movies lately that he believes the costumed kids they encounter are real monsters.

This Halloween special is really only for those who don't mind a cartoon that's coarsely drawn, with characters that spend most of their time yelling. One of the kids they encounter is dressed up as a vampire, who through Ed's distorted vision morphs into a monstrous bloodsucker.

Family Guy – "Former Life of Brian"

FOX. Apr 27, 2008 (S06E11). Comedy/Satire. D: Pete Michels. W: Steve Callaghan. C: Seth MacFarlane ♀, Alex Borstein, Seth Green, Mila Kunis, Mike Henry, Patrick Warburton, Chace Crawford. USA: English/Color/22m. 20th Century Fox Television/Fuzzy Door Productions.

Brian seeks out his long-lost soul mate, Tracy Flannigan, and learns he's the father of her child—who turns out to be a foul-mouthed, angry teenager. The Griffins take him in, and Brian sees it as an opportunity to make everything right with the boy.

Average episode with the standard mix of jokes that are either spot-on funny, completely off the wall, or borderline offensive. After Brian takes up magic to impress women, Stewie suggests that his stage outfit should include Peter's cape from last year's Halloween costume. This leads to a flashback where Peter is dressed as Count Crotchula, the "bulging vampire"—a well-endowed Dracula who makes a point of drawing attention to his considerable assets.

Family Guy – "Halloween on Spooner Street"

FOX. Nov 7, 2010 (S09E04). Comedy/Satire. D: Jerry Langford. W: Andrew Goldberg. C: Seth MacFarlane ♀, Alex Borstein, Seth Green, Mila Kunis, Mike Henry, Johnny Brennan, James Burkholder, Chris Cox. USA: English/Color/22m. 20th Century Fox Television/Fuzzy Door Productions.

Peter, Joe and Quagmire participate in their annual Halloween prank competition, while Brian teaches Stewie all about the fine art of trick-or-treating. Meanwhile, Meg attends her first high school Halloween party, and hopes that her sexy (and anonymous) cat costume will help her score with a boy.

Stewie, who has no concept of Halloween, believes that the costumed kids running around the neighborhood are real undead creatures attacking the town (note: one of them is dressed as Dracula). After Brian explains what Halloween is all about, Stewie dresses up in a duck costume, with one small addition: he's been bitten by a vampire, so he's actually a "modern vampire duck" that "hangs out with Anna Paquin and drives around in a black Mercedes." Stewie and Brian then have a slight disagreement over the series True Blood.

Family Guy – "Lottery Fever"

FOX. Sep 25, 2011 (S10E01). Comedy/Satire. D: Greg Colton. W: Andrew Goldberg. C: Seth MacFarlane, Alex Borstein, Seth Green, Mila Kunis, Mike Henry, Patrick Warburton, Adam West. USA: English/Color/22m. 20th Century Fox Television/Fuzzy Door Productions.

His family isn't impressed when Peter remortgages the house to buy thousands of lottery tickets—but they have a change of heart after he wins the jackpot.

Abysmal episode that includes a scene where Peter pays Joe to watch the entire first season of *True Blood,* for no other reason than to pick out the scenes with female nudity. Peter rants about the dreary nature of the shows created Alan Ball, and has a conversation with Anna Paquin, who's seen with vampire Bill asleep in her arms. It's a painfully unfunny episode, and one of many recent outings that clearly illustrate that *Family Guy* should be put to rest.

Fanboy and Chum Chum – "Fangboy" / "Monster in the Mist"

Nickelodeon. Nov 21, 2009 (S01E05). Adventure/Family. D: Jim Schumann. W: Scott Kreamer. C: David Hornsby ♀, Nika Futterman, Jamie Kennedy, Jeff Bennett ♀, Wyatt Cenac. USA: English/Color/30m. Frederator Incorporated/Nickelodeon Animation Studios.

In the segment "Fangboy," Fanboy discovers two small bite marks on his neck, and thinks he's been turned into a vampire. He'd like to turn his best pal Chum Chum into a bloodsucker as well—but he doesn't have a neck. They visit a neck specialist, Dr. Acula, to see if anything can be done.

The Flintstones Meet Rockula and Frankenstone

ABC. Oct 30, 1980. Comedy/Family. D: Ray Patterson. W: Willie Gilbert. C: Henry Corden ☥, Mel Blanc, Jean Vander Pyl, Gay Autterson, John Stephenson ☥, Ted Cassidy, Lennie Weinrib ☥. USA: English/Color/48m. Hanna-Barbera Productions Inc.

The Flintstones and the Rubbles win a trip to Rockula's Castle in Rocksylvania, where they attend an opening-night masquerade ball. The noise from the party awakens the vampire Count Rockula and his creation The Frankenstone Monster. Asleep for five hundred years, Rockula believes that Wilma is the spitting image of his long lost bride—and he wants to claim her for his own.

Made for kids, this cartoon doesn't have much to offer to the adult viewer. The laugh track begins to annoy after about ten minutes, and the standard monster chase scene goes on for way too long. However, the monster characters themselves are designed well, and Fred Flintstone even dresses up as a vampire—so it's not all bad. But Rockula's plan involves making Wilma a widow, which is a little dark for a children's story.

📺 Frankenstone was voiced by Ted Cassidy, who played Lurch on the original *Addams Family* television show.

The Fonz and the Happy Days Gang – "The Vampire Strikes Back"

ABC. Dec 20, 1980 (S01E07). Adventure/Family. D: George Gordon, Carl Urbano, Rudy Zamora. W: Tom Swale, Duane Poole. C: Henry Winkler, Ron Howard, Donny Most, Frank Welker, Didi Conn. USA: English/Color/22m. Hanna-Barbera Productions Inc./Paramount Television.

In this series, a futuristic alien named Cupcake takes the *Happy Days* gang on a trip through time, but they have a great deal of difficulty making it back to 1957 Milwaukee. In this episode, they fall off course and end up in Transylvania, where they meet a stranger, Count Wolfgang von Wolfenstein, who offers to put them up for the night. Richie and Ralph have doubts about the man, so they look for lodging in the local village—where they learn that the Count is really a vampire. Naturally, the evil bloodsucker has an equally evil plan: he wants to take Cupcake for his bride, so they can rule over a world of darkness as husband and wife.

The vampire character is exceptionally cool-looking; he's a Dracula type, with red eyes, pointy ears and pronounced fangs. Unfortunately, the story doesn't rise above the ludicrous premise of the series.

Freaky Stories – "The Vampire"

YTV. 1997 (S01E--). Adventure/Family. D/W: Steve Schnier. C: James Rankin, Dan Redican. CAN: English/Color/5m. Decode Entertainment Inc./Sound Ventures Productions Ltd./Funbag Animation.

A series of animated shorts that featured kid-friendly urban myths and legends; each tale was bookended by the phrase "This is a true story, and it happened to a friend of a friend of mine." In this episode, a boy suspects his neighbor is a vampire, who secretly serves wine laced with human blood to patrons at an upscale restaurant.

Futurama – "I Dated a Robot"

FOX. May 13, 2001 (S03E15). Comedy/Sci-Fi. D: James Purdum. W: Eric Kaplan. C: Billy West, Katey Sagal, John Di Maggio, Tress MacNeille, Lauren Tom, Phil LaMarr, Maurice LaMarche ♀, Lucy Liu. USA: English/Color/22m. The Curiosity Company/20th Century Fox Television.

Fry admits that he had always wanted to date a celebrity, so the Planet Express crew pays a visit to Nappster, a company that makes humanoid robot copies of any superstar; he chooses Lucy Liu. The gang discovers that Nappster is actually a group of cybercriminals, who kidnap the preserved heads of dead celebrities so they can make illegal copies of their image.

An amusing episode that's a thinly-veiled take on the controversy surrounding Napster, the pioneering peer-to-peer file sharing service once used by millions to obtain digital music files for free. The story actually works quite well even if you aren't aware of the history behind it, and Lucy Liu is a hoot as she mocks the world of celebrity and her films. One in particular, the fake movie *Charlie's Angels III: The Legend of Charlie's Gold,* features two things that Fry loves: vampires and explosions. In the film, the Angels surround a ticking coffin that opens up to reveal Count Dracula—who then explodes.

Other episodes featured minor vampire references, including: "The Series Has Landed" (breakfast cereals of the future include Archduke Chocula); "Love's Labors Lost in Space" (a vampire squid); "Fear of a Bot Planet" (a movie poster for *Buff-Bot: The Human Slayer);* and "Lrrreconcilable Ndndifferences" (a tap-dancing Dracula in the opening scene).

Galaxy Goof-Ups – "Vampire Of Space"

NBC. Nov 18, 1978 (S01E11). Adventure/Sci-Fi. D: Ray Patterson, Carl Urbano. W: Haskell Barkin, Chuck Couch, Mark Fink. C: Mel Blanc ♀, Daws Butler, Joe Besser, John Stephenson ♀. USA: English/Color/23m. Hanna-Barbera Productions Inc.

Count Vampula wants to rule the universe, and the only one standing in his way is Captain Snerdly, the commander of the Galaxy Goof Ups. Despite being warned of the vampire's plan, Snerdly is captured. Can the rest of the gang find a way to rescue their captain, before Vampula and his zombie army take over the galaxy?

A funny yet dated tale of vampires in space, where the heroes still have time to stop by the local discothèque before completing their mission. Count Vampula is the basic Dracula archetype, but he hates being a vampire: awake all night, there's never anything good on TV, and he only has zombies for company; morphing into a bat isn't fun at all, and hanging upside down makes him dizzy. Truly, Count Vampula is one of the most internally-conflicted vampires to ever appear on television.

Garfield and Friends – "Count Lasagna" / "U.S. Acres: Mystery Guest" / "Rodent Rampage"

CBS. Oct 20, 1990 (S03E11). Comedy/Family. D: Jeff Hall, Tom Ray. W: Mark Evanier, Sharman DiVono. C: Lorenzo Music ☥, Thom Huge ☥, Howie Morris, Gregg Berger, Frank Welker, Jack Riley. USA: English/B&W, Color/24m. Film Roman/United Feature Syndicate Inc.

In the segment "Count Lasagna," Jon has a new idea for a comic book: the adventures of Dracula's pet, a lazy vampire cat that terrorizes delivery men from local pizzerias, spaghetti take-outs, and sidewalk macaroni vendors. Unable to get any Italian food, villagers form an angry mob to hunt down the feline. It's an enjoyable, tongue-in-cheek story presented in glorious black and white, and features Jon as Count Dracula and Garfield as Count Lasagna.

Garfield in Disguise

CBS. Oct 30, 1985. Family/Music. D: Phil Roman. W: Jim Davis. C: Lorenzo Music ☥, Thom Huge, Gregg Berger, Lindsay Workman, Desirée Goyette. USA: English/Color/26m. Film Roman/United Media Productions.

Garfield and Odie go trick-or-treating, and end up stuck on an island where they seek shelter in an old house with a secret past. The owner claims that a century ago, a ruthless band of pirates buried their ill-gotten gains under the house, and their ghosts have returned on this very night to reclaim the lost treasure.

Released into the home video market as *Garfield's Halloween Adventure*. As he decides what to wear for Halloween, Garfield tries on a vampire costume and sings, "I could be a scary vampire, and turn myself into a bat!

Promotional advertisement for a rebroadcast of the CBS animated special originally titled *Garfield in Disguise* (United Features Syndicate Inc./TV Guide)

FLAP! FLAP!" This is unfortunately the only vampire reference in the story. It should be noted that this scene, as well as the elderly owner of the house and the pirate ghosts, may be a little too scary for younger audiences.

📺 This special won the 1986 Emmy Award for Outstanding Animated Program.

Ghostbusters – "Shades of Dracula"

Syndicated. Oct 27, 1986 (S01E36). Adventure/Family. D: Bill Nunes. W: Fred Ladd, Bob Forward. C: Pat Fraley, Peter Cullen, Alan Oppenheimer, Susan Blu, Linda Gary, Erik Gunden, Erika Scheimer, Lou Scheimer. USA: English/Color/24m. Filmation Associates/Tribune Broadcasting Co.

Unrelated to the film franchise, this is a sequel to the live-action TV series *The Ghost Busters* (1975), and follows the misadventures of a team of paranormal detectives: Eddie Spenser, Jake Kong, and Tracy the gorilla. In this episode, Count Dracula has returned to Transylvania after one hundred years to reclaim his kingdom. While the team looks for a way to defeat the vampire, intrepid reporter Jessica Wray gets caught up in the story—literally—after she falls under the Count's spell.

Dracula is quite kooky, and is designed using the standards of the day. He wears a black cape with red lining, has exaggerated features with yellow eyes, and has jet-black hair with a widow's peak. He can transform into a bat, or dissolve into mist, and is affected by garlic and sunlight. As with other Filmation cartoons, this story has a positive message for kids—all about the power of friendship.

Count Dracula returns to reclaim his kingdom in *Ghostbusters* - "Shades of Dracula" (Filmation Associates/Tribune Broadcasting Co.)

Ghostbusters – "The Girl Who Cried Vampire"

Syndicated. Nov 14, 1986 (S01E50). Adventure/Family. D: Bill Reed. W: Steven J. Fisher. C: Pat Fraley, Peter Cullen, Alan Oppenheimer, Susan Blu, Linda Gary, Erik Gunden, Erika Scheimer, Lou Scheimer. USA: English/Color/23m. Filmation Associates/Tribune Broadcasting Co.

Time-traveler and fellow ghostbuster Futura takes the gang to the year 2186, to install ghost alarms on Moon Base Alpha. A new food source will be harvested there that could potentially eliminate hunger, but Prime Evil isn't impressed; he sends two vampires into the future to destroy the crop by any means necessary. When they arrive on the base, a girl spies the vampires before they have a chance to don their human disguises. She tries to warn everyone about them, but no one will believe her—because she has a reputation for playing pranks and crying wolf.

The two vampires in this story are Victor and Vampira, identical in design (with minor variations) to Count Dracula and Bella La Ghostly from the Filmation series *Groovie Goolies* (1971). Also from Transylvania, the couple call themselves "The Draculs" when disguised as human, and are about as evil as they can be in a cartoon for youngsters.

📺 When Victor transforms into a bat, it's the exact same animation used for Drac in the Groovie Goolies series.

Gravedale High

NBC. Sep 8, 1990 – Sep 7, 1991 (13 Episodes). Comedy/Family. D: Robert Alvarez. W: Ernie Contreras. C: Rick Moranis, Barry Gordon, Shari Belafonte, Jackie Earle Haley, Maurice LaMare, Ricki Lake, Roger Rose ☥, Frank Welker. USA: English/Color/390m. Hanna-Barbera Productions Inc.

Meek high school teacher Max Schneider instructs a group of teenage monsters, all of whom are based on the classic movie horrors. Students include the vampire Vinnie Stoker, a zombie named Blanche, Frankentyke, and Reggie Moonshroud—who's a werewolf.

The Great Bear Scare

Syndicated. Oct 1983. Adventure/Family. D: Hal Mason. W: John Barrett. C: Tom Smothers, Louis Nye ☥, Hans Conried, Sue Raney, Hal Smith, Lucille Bliss. USA: English/Color/24m. DimenMark International Inc.

Journalist Patti Bear reports that a group of fiends from the unexplored Monster Mountain is about to descend on the city of Bearbank. The Bureau of Bear Affairs sends one resident, Ted E. Bear, to investigate. Led by Count Dracula, the monsters are planning an invasion, and their ultimate goal is to take over the world.

Mediocre adventure for kids that features a menacing Count Dracula and his horde of invading monsters. Their quest fails because the citizens of Bearbank realize that, in reality, the monsters aren't scary at all; it was the fear of the unknown that made everyone so afraid. This is the underlying message for the audience, but it's buried within a convoluted explanation that most kids won't even understand.

The Grim Adventures of Billy & Mandy – "Billy Idiot" / "Home of the Ancients"

Cartoon Network. Jun 30, 2005 (S04E13). Comedy/Family. D: Robert Alvarez. W: Nina Bargiel, C.H. Greenblatt. C: Grey DeLisle, Greg Eagles, Richard Horvitz, Vanessa Marshall, Jane Carr, Chris Cox, Jennifer Darling, Phil LaMarr ☥. USA: English/Color/23m. Cartoon Network Studios.

Series follows Billy and Mandy, two kids who end up with the Grim Reaper as a best friend after he loses a bet. In the segment "Billy Idiot," the famous ballet instructor Mrs. Pollywinkle accepts Billy into her Dance Academy; she's really a dark witch who feeds off of the souls and talent of her students. In "Home of the Ancients," Grim plays a destructive game of bowling, and uses the Moon for a ball. Found guilty of gross misuse of power, he's sentenced to fifty hours of community service at the local retirement complex; it's home to several of his childhood idols, including Dracula, the Wolf Man, and the Bride of Frankenstein.

The first segment is largely forgettable except for the vampire-like headmistress, who drains her students of their talent so she can remain the greatest dancer of all time. The second cartoon is equally as banal, but it features the series debut of Dracula—and Phil LaMarr's take on the vampire is very funny (and seems to be inspired by Fred Sanford from *Sanford and Son*).

The Grim Adventures of Billy & Mandy – "Billy and Mandy Save Christmas"

Cartoon Network. Dec 11, 2005 (S05E07). Comedy/Family. D: Russell Calabrese. W: Maxwell Atoms, Nina Bargiel, Jeremy Bargiel. C: Richard Horvitz, Grey DeLisle, Greg Eagles, Malcolm McDowell ☥, Carol Kane ☥, Gilbert Gottfried. USA: English/Color/37m. Cartoon Network Studios.

After a disastrous encounter with a fake shopping mall Santa, Grim takes Billy and Mandy to the North Pole to prove that the jolly old elf really exists. But Santa is now a vampire, and the only way to save him is to kill the head bloodsucker: Baron von Ghoulish.

A Christmas special that features the undead seems like the best of both worlds, but the story never quite clicks. The vampire element is very entertaining; Baron von Ghoulish is a fastidious, anal-retentive neat freak, and his scenes are the best of the bunch. Unfortunately, he's overshadowed by the scenes featuring Billy, which are often too annoying to stomach.

The Grim Adventures of Billy & Mandy – "Dumb-Dumbs & Dragons" / "Fear and Loathing in Endsville"

Cartoon Network. May 12, 2006 (S06E09). Comedy/Family. D: Shaun Cashman. W: C.H. Greenblatt. C: Grey DeLisle, Greg Eagles, Richard Horvitz, Vanessa Marshall, Louis Anderson, Diedrich Bader, Jane Carr, Phil LaMarr ☥. USA: English/Color/23m. Cartoon Network Studios.

In "Fear and Loathing in Endsville," Grim pays a visit to Dracula at the retirement home, but his gift of peanut butter and blood cookies doesn't go over so well (Dracula hates peanut butter). The vampire invites him out for the early bird special at Fanny's Diner, but the two get lost and end up wandering the desert.

When Dracula makes an appearance in *Billy & Mandy*, he always elevates the quality of the story, and this one garners a few laughs thanks to him. Yet one of the funniest scenes involves Grim, when he meets up with a Tusken Raider (from the *Star Wars* universe) that just happens to have a sandcrawler that he can use to get home.

📺 Dracula makes one more appearance this season, in the episode "Goodbling and the Hip-Hop-Opotamus." Irwin's Grandmama schools Principal Goodvibes in the fine art of "Yo Mama" jokes, and when she says "Yo mama is so ugly that Dracula wouldn't drink her blood!" the vampire chimes in, "Dracula wouldn't touch her with Wolf Man's teeth!"

The Grim Adventures of Billy & Mandy – "Dracula de Bergerac"

Cartoon Network. Feb 14, 2007. Comedy/Family. D: Anon. W: Anon. C: Grey DeLisle, Vanessa Marshall, Phil LaMarr ☥. USA: English/Color/3m. Castle Creek Productions/Cartoon Network.

After witnessing Irwin's pitiful attempt to woo Mandy, Dracula offers to teach him the secret art of picking up girls—for a price. In this take on the classic story *Cyrano de Bergerac,* Dracula tells Irwin to repeat everything he says. Irwin takes him literally, and echoes Dracula's words verbatim; the situation rapidly derails and results in a very funny scene.

The Grim Adventures of Billy & Mandy – "Nergal's Pizza" / "Hey, Water You Doing?"

Cartoon Network. Mar 9, 2007 (S07E04). Comedy/Family. D: Gordon Kent. W: Mike Diederich. C: Grey DeLisle, Greg Eagles, Richard Horvitz, Vanessa Marshall, Debi Derryberry, Martin Jarvis, Amber Hood, Phil LaMarr ☥. USA: English/Color/23m. Cartoon Network Studios.

In "Nergal's Pizza," Nergal claims to have the tastiest pizza in town, so Grim opens up his own restaurant to prove that he can do better. As the competition heats up, both of them add supernatural ingredients to their recipes—but the mystical pizza has an adverse effect on their customers.

As he awaits a pizza delivery, Dracula watches an old horror movie on television, and yells at the screen, "Frankenstein can't act, he just grunt!" Later, as Nergal's son faces the daunting task of delivering thousands of pizzas, he reads a tabloid headline about the infamous "Bat Boy"—and then shape-shifts into dozens of bats.

The Grim Adventures of Billy & Mandy – "Billy & Mandy's Big Boogey Adventure"

Cartoon Network. Feb 14, 2007 (S07E07). Comedy/Family. D: Shaun Cashman. W: Maxwell Atoms, Nina Bargiel, Jeremy Bargiel. C: Greg Eagles, Richard Horvitz, Grey DeLisle, Vanessa Marshall, Fred Willard, Phil LaMarr ☥. USA: English/Color/82m. Cartoon Network Studios.

After Grim loses yet another soul, the Underworld finds him guilty of misusing his power—

again. Stripped of his title, rank and abilities, he's exiled to the River Styx along with Billy and Mandy. The Boogey Man takes over Grim's role as the Angel of Death, but modern kids no longer fear him; so he plans to steal Horrors Hand, an object that will make him the most frightening thing in the universe. This animated feature will only be of interest to die-hard fans, because the more juvenile aspects of the series—such as excessive flatulence and bodily fluids—are in overabundance here. Dracula is one of the jurors who decides Grim's fate.

The Grim Adventures of Billy & Mandy - "Dracula Must Die!" / "Short Tall Tales"

Cartoon Network. Sep 21, 2007 (S07E09). Comedy/Family. D: Juli Hashiguchi, Eddy Houchins. W: C.H. Greenblatt. C: Greg Eagles, Richard Horvitz, Grey DeLisle, Vanessa Marshall, Phil LaMarr ♀, Dorian Harewood. USA: English/Color/23m. Cartoon Network Studios.

In "Dracula Must Die!" the vampire's past has finally caught up with him. His mortal enemy, Lionel Van Helsing, wants to end Dracula's life once and for all—but Grim intervenes to save his childhood idol. This homage to the 1970s includes a flashback to when Dracula and Van Helsing were best friends, until the vampire stole the heart of the woman he loved. In the final showdown, Van Helsing spares Dracula's life, but leaves him to a more horrific fate: domestication (the vampire is forced to reconnect with his long lost family).

The Grim and Courage Hour - "The Uninvited" / "Death of the Party"

Cartoon Network. Oct 26, 2006 (S01E05/06). Comedy/Family. D: Anon. W: Maxwell Atoms. C: Greg Eagles, Grey DeLisle, Jane Carr, Phil LaMarr ♀, Richard Horvitz, Jennifer Hale, Vanessa Marshall. USA: English/Color/6m. Castle Creek Productions/Cartoon Network.

This short-lived programming block re-aired cartoons from *The Grim Adventures of Billy & Mandy* and *Courage the Cowardly Dog*—but one umbrella segment, "Billy's Birthday Shorties," featured new stories. In "The Uninvited," Dracula goes out of his way to prove why he should be invited to Billy's birthday party, while in "Death of the Party," Dracula tries to sneak out early because the festivities are really boring. These shorts were introduced by a life-sized Dracula puppet, voiced by Phil LaMarr, which sat on a throne surrounded by witches, vampires, and other creatures of the night.

Groovie Goolies

CBS. Sep 12, 1971 – Sep 3, 1972 (16 Episodes). Family/Music. D: Hal Sutherland. W: Jack Mendelsohn, Jim Mulligan, Bob Ogle. C: John Erwin, Larry D. Mann, Larry Storch ♀, Dallas McKennon, Howard Morris, Jane Webb ♀. USA: English/Color/480m. Filmation Associates.

A groovy group of friendly fiends lives at Horrible Hall, a boarding house for monsters, where they spend their days telling jokes and playing music. The house band features organist Drac (a vampire), guitarist Wolfie (a werewolf), and percussionist Frankie (a reanimated corpse). Other residents include the vampire twins Ratzo and Batzo, and the switchboard operator Bella La Ghostly.

A *Laugh-In* inspired kid's series that featured a kooky cast of ghoulish characters in several recurring segments. These included Bella La Ghostly, who dished out advice à la Dear Abby; "Weird Window Time," where the entire group participated in a series of rapid-fire jokes; and "Ask-It Casket," where residents posed questions to a coffin with a disembodied voice. Each episode included two bubblegum pop songs; one was performed by the house band, while the second featured guest musicians (including The Mummies and The Puppies, The Bare Bones Band, Rollin' Headstones, and Spirits of '76).

📺 The series was rebroadcast on ABC from October 25, 1975 - September 5, 1976, and upon syndication in 1978, was retitled *The Groovie Goolies and Friends;* this version included additional cartoons from unrelated series. The original working title was *The Kookie Spookies.*

Growing Up Creepie

Discovery Kids. Sep 9, 2006 – Jun 27, 2008 (26 Episodes). Adventure/Family. D: Guy Vasilovich. W: Carin Greenberg Baker, Anthony Gaud. C: Athena Karkanis, Dwayne Hill ⚲, Julie Lemieux, Richard Yearwood, Stevie Vallance. USA: English/Color/780m. Mike Young Productions.

Creepie is an orphan who was abandoned on the doorstep of Dweezwold Mansion; taken in by a family of insects living inside, she was raised as one of their own. Three of her relatives are juice-drinking vegan mosquitoes that have sworn off blood, including her adoptive father Vinnie, who has some vampire characteristics.

Hanna-Barbera Superstars 10 – "Scooby-Doo and the Ghoul School"

Syndicated. 1988 (S01E06). Adventure/Family. D: Charles A. Nichols. W: Glenn Leopold. C: Rene Auberjonois, Susan Blu ⚲, Hamilton Camp, Jeff B. Cohen, Glynis Johns, Casey Kasem, Zale Kessler ⚲, Ruta Lee. USA: English/Color/93m. Hanna-Barbera Productions Inc.

Scooby and Scrappy-Doo join Shaggy in his new job as a gym teacher at a private school for girls. To their surprise, the students are actually ghouls—the daughters of famous movie monsters. They overcome their fear to help the girls prepare for an upcoming volleyball tournament against their rivals from a nearby military academy.

The Mystery Machine and the rest of the Scooby gang are missing from this feature-length adventure, as is most of the humor and quirky storytelling from the original series. The previous Scooby incarnations had monsters that were just humans in disguise, yet these young ghouls are the real deal (but not yet scary like their parents). They include Sibella, Count Dracula's daughter; Elsa Frankensteen; Phantasma the ghost; Winnie the werewolf; and Tanis the mummy. The story concludes at a school dance, where Scrappy-Doo raps about recent events, while a horde of monsters dance around him. Yes, it's as awful as it sounds.

📺 The umbrella series was a set of ten animated feature-length cartoons produced for television syndication, which showcased Hanna-Barbera's most popular characters in new, extended adventures.

Hanna-Barbera Superstars 10 – "Scooby-Doo and the Reluctant Werewolf"

Syndicated. 1988 (S01E10). Adventure/Family. D: Ray Patterson. W: Jim Ryan. C: Don Messick, Casey Kasem, Hamilton Camp ☥, Jim Cummings, Joan Gerber, Ed Gilbert, Brian Mitchell, Pat Musick ☥, B.J. Ward. USA: English/Color/92m. Hanna-Barbera Productions Inc.

Dracula summons his fiendish friends to compete in the annual Transylvania Grand Prix, but this year the event is in jeopardy: the Wolf Man has retired, and the race can't go on without one of his kind participating. But every five hundred years, a new werewolf is born—and the next one in line is Shaggy Rogers.

Most of the *Mystery Inc.* crew is nowhere to be found, since the focus is on Scooby-Doo and Shaggy—who has an "adoring but liberated" girlfriend, Googie. The gang is kidnapped and taken to Transylvania; Dracula promises to cure Shaggy of his affliction if he takes part in the derby. The best bits are the scenes that feature Dracula with his bumbling assistant Wolfgang, and his hunchbacked henchmen Brunch (an aristocratic Brit) and Crunch (an unintelligible mush-mouth). There's one other vampire in this story: Vannapira, the Count's bubbly assistant, whose look is based on the iconic Vampira character (though she's nowhere near as macabre). The premise is ludicrous, but it's a very entertaining story; the only negative aspect is the road race itself, which seems to drag on forever.

📺 The creature competitors and their vehicles are: Frankenstein and Repulsa (Freaky Flunken-Wagon), Swamp Thing (Slime Speedster), The Witch Sisters (Cauldron Coupé), Mr. Bonejangles (Bone Barber), The Mummy (Mummy Mobile), Dr. Jackal and Mr. Snyde (Split Personality Special), and the Dragonfly (Dragon Dragster).

Heathcliff and Dingbat

ABC. Oct 4 – Dec 27, 1980 (26 Episodes). Comedy/Family. D: Charles A. Nichols. W: Var. C: Frank Welker ☥, Don Messick, June Foray, Mel Blanc, Henry Corden, Janet Waldo, Clare Peck, Marilyn Schreffler. USA: English/Color/780m. Ruby-Spears Productions Inc.

This series combined two distinct shows: "Heathcliff," which followed the adventures of a mischievous cat, and "Dingbat and the Creeps," which followed three employment-seeking friends—Dingbat, a vampire dog; Spare Rib, a portly skeleton; and Nobody, a pumpkin.

In a sendup of *The Three Stooges,* the three ghouls call themselves *Odd Jobs Incorporated,* and live inside a belfry attached to a three-wheeled chopper motorcycle (similar in concept to the "Creepy Coupe" driven by Big Gruesome and Little Gruesome in the 1968 series *Wacky Races*). Each five to seven minute segment follows the same basic premise: the gang finds a job, has great difficulty in their new occupation, and is out of work by the end. Dingbat is a standard cartoon dog, aside from his fangs and cape, and can transform into a miniaturized, bat-like version of himself. In one episode, he's described as a "one of a kind vampire bat dog" *(vampira dogus scaredy catus)* that's deathly afraid of garlic toast and loves chocolate milk bones.

Hellboy Animated – "Blood and Iron"

Cartoon Network. Mar 17, 2007. Action/Adventure. D: Victor Cook. W: Mike Mignola. C: Ron Perlman, Selma Blair, John Hurt, Doug Jones, Peri Gilpin, Kath Soucie ♀, Grant Albrecht, Jim Cummings. USA: English/Color/76m. Starz Media/Revolution Studios/Film Roman.

The team investigates a report of hauntings at Hampton House, and discovers the spirits of over six hundred women who were tortured and murdered by Erzsebet Ondrushko, the Hungarian "Blood Countess." Obsessed with her own vanity, Erzsebet killed the women to bathe in their blood; for her crimes, she lost her soul, and was turned into a vampire. She was destroyed in 1939, but after the team finds a body completely drained of blood, they fear that Erzsebet has been resurrected.

A mixed bag of a story with some great scenes interspersed with periods of extreme dullness. The flashback sequences are the most interesting, but if one isn't familiar with the characters, then these scenes may be confusing. The ghost-hunting setup and post-vampire conclusion drag the story down, which sucks the life out of the tale and prevents it from being recommended viewing. Erzsebet Ondrushko is modeled after Erzsébet Báthory, the sixteenth century Hungarian noblewoman who was accused of torturing and killing hundreds of girls.

📺 Loosely based on the five issue miniseries *Hellboy: Wake the Devil* (Dark Horse Comics, June - October 1996).

Hello Kitty's Furry Tale Theater – "Catula" / "Paws of the Round Table"

CBS. Nov 14, 1987 (S01E09). Adventure/Family. D: Michael Maliani. W: Jack Hanrahan, Phil Harnage. C: Tara Charendoff, Sean Roberge, Mairon Bennett, Elizabeth Hanna, Cree Summer ♀, Denise Pidgeon. JPN/USA: English/Color/30m. MGM/UA Television/DiC Enterprises.

Each episode featured two stories adapted from film, television and books, rewritten for kids and acted out by Hello Kitty and friends. In "Catula," the gang travels to Catsylvania at the behest of Grandma Kitty, who worries that a milk-guzzling vampire will suck the town dry of its supply. They spend the night at a creepy castle, which is the home of Countess Catula—a peculiar feline who doesn't cast a reflection.

If you're looking to introduce your children to classic literature at a young age, then this cartoon is a good start—it's loosely based on Bram Stoker's *Dracula*. This charming adaptation has a tame ending: the locals defeat the vampire by using the flashes on their cameras.

Hey Arnold! – "Sid the Vampire Slayer" / "Big Sis"

Nickelodeon. Mar 18, 2000 (S05E03). Adventure/Family. D: Christine Kolosov. W: Michelle Lamoreaux. C: Spencer Klein, Sam Gifaldi, Christopher Walberg ⚥, Ashley Buccille, Nika Futterman, Maurice LaMare ⚥. USA: English/B&W, Color/24m. NickToon Productions.

In the segment "Sid the Vampire Slayer," Sid is a little spooked after watching a vampire movie, so when Stinky jokes that he's one of the undead, Sid believes him. Arnold is skeptical, until he notices that Stinky has some peculiar nighttime habits.

A charming episode that includes a film-within-a-film, inspired by the Hammer horror movies, which stars a vampire based on Dracula. Stinky's strange nocturnal habits include wearing a cape and sleeping in a coffin; these are explained away as normal activities. But at the end of the story, he's seen chatting with his pet vampire bat—and sporting a set of real fangs. It's a fun ambiguous ending that kids will love.

Hotel Transylvania

Disney Channel. 2017. Comedy/Family. D: Anon. W: Anon. C: Anon. USA: English/Color/--m. Sony Pictures Animation/Nelvana.

Based on the film franchise of the same name, this series follows Dracula's daughter, Mavis, and her friends as they navigate through the trials and tribulations of their teenage years. The series is set at her father's hotel, which is a remote resort where monsters are free to take their families on vacation.

House of Mouse – "Gone Goofy"

ABC. Mar 3, 2001 (S01E07). Comedy/Family. D: Tony Craig, Roberts Gannaway. W: Michael Fontanelli, Henry Gilroy. C: Wayne Allwine, Tony Anselmo, Bill Farmer ⚥, Tress MacNeille, Russi Taylor. USA: English/Color/30m. Walt Disney Television Animation.

Includes the cartoon "Donald's Goofy World," where Donald's world is turned upside down after he's knocked unconscious. When he wakes up, he notices that Goofy is everywhere: each story in the local newspaper, the *Goofy Gazette*, features only him, and the same goes for television—including the new show, *Goofy the Vampire Slayer*.

This funny episode includes a segment with Goofy as a vampire, even though he's technically a vampire *slayer* (Angel is an undead vampire slayer, so why not Goofy?). It's still worthwhile viewing despite the minimal vampire content.

Inspector Gadget – "The Haunted Castle"

Syndicated. Oct 29, 1983 (S01E08). Adventure/Family. D: Var. W: Var. C: Don Adams, Cree Summer Francks, Maurice LaMare, Dan Hennessey, Don Francks ☥, Frank Welker. USA: English/Color/23m. DiC Enterprises/Nelvana.

Gadget and company are in Transylvania for a law enforcement convention, unaware that Dr. Claw is hiding out within the decrepit walls of the nearby Castle Dracula. They meet a man who has fangs and wears an opera cape; Penny believes he is Count Dracula himself, but Gadget dismisses it as simply a show for the tourists.

The mysterious man is actually a M.A.D. Agent disguised as Dracula, yet he isn't the only classic movie monster in this story; other Agents masquerade as the Frankenstein Monster and the Wolf Man.

Invader ZIM – "Halloween Spectacular of Spooky Doom"

Nickelodeon. Oct 26, 2001 (S01E12). Adventure/Comedy. D: Steve Ressel. W: Jhonen Vasquez, Rob Hummel. C: Richard Horvitz, Rosearik Rikki Simons, Andy Berman, Melissa Fahn, Lucille Bliss, Mo Collins, Phil LaMarr ☥. USA: English/Color/24m. NickToon Productions.

Follows ZIM, an alien bent on world domination, and his arch-nemesis Dib, a paranoid kid who knows what ZIM is (but his classmates just think he's crazy). In this episode, Ms. Bitters complains that Halloween is just a commercial enterprise that turns kids into candy-starved zombies. ZIM takes her words at face value, and prepares to defend himself against these undead candy munchers. Meanwhile, Dib experiences some nightmarish visions, and he plunges into a frightening, alternate universe—and drags ZIM in along with him.

A bizarre series with a strange premise and an oddball cast of characters, one of which has the annoying habit of yelling every bit of dialogue. As for the vampiric content, one of their classmates is dressed up as Dracula for Halloween.

James Bond Jr. – "The Inhuman Race"

Syndicated. Oct 15, 1991 (S01E22). Action/Adventure. D: Bill Hutten, Tony Love. W: Jeffrey Scott. C: Jeff Bennett ☥, Corey Burton, Julian Holloway, Mona Marshall, Brian Mitchell, Jan Rabson, Susan Silo. USA: English/Color/22m. MWS Inc./MGM/Camelot Entertainment Sales.

James and his friends are in Germany for an international scholastic competition when they're approached by a woman desperate for help. She wants them to investigate a disturbance at a local diamond mine, where workers fear for their lives after being attacked by supernatural creatures.

The attackers—a werewolf and a vampire—are just the disguised henchmen of Dr. Derange, sent to the facility to scare away the workers. Derange wants the diamond mine all to himself, and plans to use his own crew of android mutants to clear it out. There's just one thing missing from the prototype android: the spark of human life. Sound familiar? This story has the classic gruesome threesome: a vampire, a werewolf, and a Frankenstein Monster (the android). The vampire costume is rather atypical; it resembles a bat-like winged humanoid with pronounced fangs. Unfortunately the smart premise doesn't live up to the rest of the story.

The Jetsons – "Haunted Halloween"

ABC. Oct 31, 1985 (S02E26). Comedy/Sci-Fi. D: Anon. W: Mark Young. C: George O'Hanlon ⚥, Penny Singleton ⚥, Daws Butler, Janet Waldo, Don Messick, Jean Vander Pyl, Mel Blanc, Frank Welker. USA: English/Color/22m. Hanna-Barbera Productions Inc.

In preparation for Mr. Spacey's Halloween party, George practices his magic act, while Elroy and Orbity shop for new costumes at Mr. Scarem's Costume Shop and Waxite Museum. The proprietor takes great interest in Orbity, and believes the weird little creature will be a worthwhile addition to his permanent collection of oddities.

This revamped series, produced twenty years after the first, suffers from the addition of a cute yet annoying sidekick—an alien called "Orbity"—that spends most of the time bouncing around the room and murmuring half English/half nonsensical gibberish. At the start of the episode, George tells a creepy Halloween tale, and Orbity gets quite scared. That night, the alien has a dream where George and Jane are vampires, Elroy is a mummy, and Judy is a witch.

Jibber Jabber – "Night of the Vampire" / "No Such Thing As Ghosts"

YTV. Sep 2, 2008 (S01E10). Adventure/Family. D: David Bowes, Dennise Fordham. W: Roger Fredericks, Bronwen Kyffin. C: Ashleigh Ball, Kathleen Barr, Dorla Bell, Bill Mondy, Chantal Strand ⚥, David Bowes. CAN: English/Color/30m. Northwest Imaging & FX/Jibber Jabber Toons Ltd.

Series follows two seven-year-old fraternal twin brothers who share the same imaginative point of view, and get wrapped up in a world of adventure. In "Night of the Vampire," the evil vampiress Count Jessula plans to turn the

Count Jessula wants to turn the entire household into bloodsuckers in *Jibber Jabber* - "Night of the Vampire" (Jibber Jabber Entertainment, Inc.)

entire household into bloodsuckers, and only Sir Duke of Jib and Jabbury stands in her way.

Johnny Bravo – "Going Batty" / "Berry the Butler" / "Red Faced in the White House"

Cartoon Network. Dec 1, 1997 (S01E11). Comedy/Satire. D: Rumen Petkov. W: Steve Marmel. C: Jeff Bennett, Alison La Placa ⚲, Marvin Kaplan ⚲, Dee Bradley Baker, Dan Castelleneta. USA: English/Color/30m. Rough Draft Studios/Hanna-Barbera Productions Inc.

A silly series that features a lead character that's a cross between Arnold Schwarzenegger and Elvis, a narcissistic man who isn't the smartest one in the room (and therein lies the humor). In the segment "Going Batty," vampire couple Lois and Woody split up after two thousand years of undead life together. Lois hunts for a new man with whom she can spend an eternity; she sets her sights on Johnny Bravo, but her ex-boyfriend vows to do whatever it takes to reclaim his eternal damsel of the dark.

The undead odd couple are a hoot; he's a diminutive Woody Allen type, while she's a sultry, statuesque green-haired beauty. Johnny finally clues in that his date is actually a vampire, and the last few moments of the cartoon are completely off the wall and very, very funny.

Kim Possible – "October 31st"

Disney. Oct 11, 2002 (S01E14). Action/Comedy. D: Chris Bailey. W: Mark Palmer. C: Christy Carlson Romano, Will Friedle, Nancy Cartwright, Tahj Mowry, Gary Cole ⚲, John Di Maggio, Shaun Fleming. USA: English/Color/22m. Walt Disney Television Animation/ABC.

Kim liberates the top secret "Centurion Project" from the clutches of Dr. Drakken and Duff Killigan, but the small device gets stuck on her wrist. While she juggles her plans for Halloween night, Kim tells a few little white lies—which triggers the device to expand and encase her completely within a set of futuristic body armor.

A charming episode with some good laughs, mostly at the expense of Duff Killigan, the irate Scottish mercenary and self-proclaimed "World's Deadliest Golfer." Kim's father dresses up as Dracula when he volunteers at the "Scare for Care House of Horror."

Little Dracula

FOX Kids. Sep 3 – Oct 31, 1991 (6 Episodes). Adventure/Family. D: Joe Pearson. W: Anon. C: Edan Gross ⚲, Joe Flaherty ⚲, Kath Soucie ⚲, Jonathan Winters, Neil Ross, Brian Cummings, Joey Camen, Melvyn Hayes. USA: English/Color/180m. Kalato Studios/Walker Hahn Productions.

Based on the books by Martin Waddell and Joseph Wright, this series tells the story of a little vampire who idolizes his father, Dracula. Along with his best friend Werebunny, the cast includes a group of oddball characters from Transylvania. In October 1999, the FOX Family channel briefly resurrected the series, and broadcast several episodes that were part of the original English production run of thirteen (which were previously unaired).

In France, a full twenty-six episodes were produced under the title Draculito mon saigneur, and broadcast from 1991-93. In 1992, *Harvey Comics* published a three-issue miniseries.

A young vampire idolizes his infamous father in *Little Dracula,* based on the books by Martin Waddell and Joseph Wright (Kalato Studios/Walker Hahn Productions)

Lucy, the Daughter of the Devil – "The Special Fathers vs. The Vampire Altar Boys"

Cartoon Network. Oct 21, 2007 (S01E08). Adult/Comedy. D: Loren Bouchard. W: Loren Bouchard, Holly Schlesinger. C: H. Jon Benjamin, Melissa Bardin Galsky, Jon Glaser, Eugene Mirman, Todd Barry ⚲. USA: English/Color/12m. Lauren Bouchard/Williams Street.

Series follows Lucy, a young woman forced to fulfill her destiny as the Antichrist despite her objections; a religious group, The Special Clergy, vow to protect the world from her. In this episode, the Archbishop sidelines the holy team from their main mission to investigate an all-out vampire assault against the Church: undead altar boys and choir boys are preying on priests. Inexperienced in the art of slaying bloodsuckers, the Special Sister manages to hold her own, but her overzealous nature also proves fatal to a few humans along the way.

A fun and creepy black comedy that features a band of evil altar boys who resemble old Playmobil toy figures; except, of course, these guys are homicidal undead with a penchant for blood drinking. It takes a worthwhile jab at the usual tropes of vampire movies, including the ever-present scene where it's explained what can and cannot kill a bloodsucker.

Mad Jack the Pirate – "The Horror Of Draclia"

FOX Family. Oct 31, 1998 (S01E06). Adventure/Comedy. D: Jeff DeGrandis. W: Bill Kopp. C: Charlie Adler, Jocelyn Blue, Cam Clark, Rob Daniels, Sandy Fox, Brad Garrett, Sherman Howard, Bill Kopp, Billy West ⚲. USA: English/Color/22m. Saban Entertainment.

Jack discovers a map to Count Draclia's hidden treasure inside a box of breakfast cereal. Despite Snuk's objections, they set sail to Vulgaria to search for the booty. Snuk believes that the Count is a bloodthirsty vampire—as do all the residents of Vulgaria—but Jack wants to sneak into the castle and grab the treasure anyway.

Draclia was expecting them; he planted the map in the breakfast cereal, so he could trap Jack and use him as a never-ending blood supply. The vampire—which resembles a green-skinned Nosferatu—is the best part of the episode, but unfortunately he alone cannot save the story from being extremely lifeless.

Magic School Bus – "Going Batty"

PBS. Sep 30, 1995 (S02E04). Adventure/Family. D: Charles E. Bastien. W: Ronnie Krauss. C: Lily Tomlin, Malcolm-Jamal Warner, Tyne Daly, Dana Elcar, Elliot Gould, Eartha Kitt, Edward James Olmos, Stuart Stone ♀. CAN/USA: English/Color/26m. Nelvana/Scholastic Productions Inc.

Ralphie fails to convince his classmates that Ms. Frizzle is a vampire, even though she showed up at school acting very strange and wearing a cape. The kids have a change of heart after she takes their parents to a creepy castle for a nighttime field trip—where they witness "Count Frizula" turning them into creatures of the night.

An educational tale that explores the habits and misconceptions of bats, in the guise of a fun vampire story. The kids even transform into the furry fliers themselves, and get first-hand experience using echolocation.

Martin Mystery – "Journey into Terrorland"

YTV. Feb 13, 2006 (S03E20). Action/Adventure. D: Stéphane Berry, Gregory Panaccione. W: Rhonda Smiley. C: Samuel Vincent, Dale Wilson ♀, Kelly Sheridan, Teryl Rothery. CAN/FRA: English/Color/22m. Marathon Animation/Image Entertainment Corporation Inc.

On Martin's one-year anniversary with the Agency, his co-workers take him to the grand opening of Terrorland, a horror-themed amusement park based on real places (with genuine artifacts). After Billy is captured by a vampire, Martin discovers that one of the attractions is a little too authentic.

In this entertaining story, an evil Egyptian spirit transforms all the fake amusement park horrors into the real thing, and most of the characters are turned into movie monsters. Billy the Martian becomes a vampire, which results in a creature that looks very much like "Little Dracula" from the animated series of the same name—except he's much more menacing, and sports the traditional look that includes jet-black hair with a widow's peak.

Mary Shelley's Frankenhole

Cartoon Network. Jun 27, 2010 – Mar 25, 2012 (20 Episodes). Adult/Comedy. D: David Tuber. W: Dino Stamatopoulos. C: Jeff B. Davis, Scott Adsit, Britta Phillips, Chris Shearer ☥, Jay Johnson. USA: English/Color/300m. Fragical Productions/ShadowMachine Films/Williams Street.

A stop-motion series that follows the exploits of an immortal Dr. Victor Frankenstein, who has created a number of wormholes ("Frankenholes") that link his home to the past, present and future; he's visited by historical figures and celebrities looking for help. All the major horrors are represented, including Dracula, who is constantly putting the moves on Victor's wife Elizabeth.

An atmospheric series that is painfully unfunny, unless you prefer adult-oriented stories that are racist, sexist, and politically incorrect—all in the name of "black comedy." Unlike *South Park* or *Robot Chicken,* this series isn't satire, nor is it smart; it's just gutter humor that serves no purpose other than to offend. Too bad, because the stop-motion animation is quite excellent, and would be highly recommended were it not for the terrible writing.

Mighty Max – "Fly by Night"

Syndicated. Oct 19, 1994 (S02E18). Action/Adventure. D: Gordon Bressack, Jules Dennis. W: Matthias Weber. C: Rob Paulsen, Tony Jay, Richard Moll, JoBeth Williams ☥, B. J. Ward, Clive Revill, Hamilton Camp. USA: English/Color/21m. Bluebird Canal/Bohbot Entertainment.

A vampire is attacking the citizens of London, but the culprit isn't Dracula. Max and company have a run in with the beast, but it isn't affected by the usual undead trappings. As the trail leads to Transylvania, they discover it's a very different kind of bloodsucker.

This atmospheric cartoon comes with a message: don't always rely on established knowledge and facts; question what's come before, and use your intuition to solve problems. The vampire in this story is linked to the fly and not to the bat; in human form, it can take to the air using fly-like wings, and has a large proboscis that it uses to feed (it can also transform into a human-sized fly). At the end of the episode, the audience learns a bit about the common house fly; you can't go wrong with a vampire story that is both educational and entertaining.

Mighty Mighty Monsters in Halloween Havoc

Teletoon. Oct 28, 2013. Comedy/Family. D: Adam Wood. W: Ben Burden Smith, Gil Rimmer, Scott Oleszkowicz. C: Reece Thompson, Donavon Stinson ☥, Vincent Tong, Travis Turner, Doug Abrahams, Kendra Anderson, Doron Bell, Brett Dier, Jeff Gladstone, John Stewart. CAN: English/Color/44m. Bron Studios.

Before they became known as Dracula, the Wolf Man, and Frankenstein's Monster, Vlad, Gunnar and Frankie were the best of friends who liked to play practical jokes on their schoolmates at Monster Academy. But after being expelled and sent to a Human Immersion program at an ordinary suburban middle school, they come face-to-face with the greatest horror of all: tween culture! Based on the graphic novel created by Sean Patrick O'Reilly.

Mighty Mighty Monsters in New Fears Eve

Teletoon. Dec 31, 2013. Comedy/Family. D: Adam Wood. W: Ben Burden Smith, Gil Rimmer, Scott Oleszkowicz. C: Reece Thompson, Donavon Stinson ☥, Vincent Tong, Travis Turner, Doug Abrahams, Kendra Anderson, Diana Kaarina, Jimi Cuell, Brett Dier. CAN: English/Color/44m. Bron Studios.

The monster friends are bribed by Dr. Scherbatova to appear on his television show, and if it gets huge ratings, they'll get to return to Monster Academy for good! But the infighting soon begins, and as tempers flare as they each try to grab the spotlight, Vlad, Frankie and Gunnar have to put aside their own personal aspirations to work together in order to make the show a resounding success. Based on the graphic novel created by Sean Patrick O'Reilly.

Mighty Mighty Monsters in Pranks for the Memories

Teletoon. June, 2015. Comedy/Family. D: Adam Wood, Jimi Cuell. W: Shane Simmons, Adam Wood. C: Donavon Stinson ☥, Vincent Tong, Travis Turner, Doug Abrahams, Doron Bell, Diana Kaarina, Jimi Cuell. CAN: English/Color/44m. Bron Studios.

Set to return to Monster Academy in the fall, Vlad wants to leave their human classmates an unforgettable prank to remember them by, even though his monster friends Frankie and Gunnar want nothing to do with it. But it turns out that someone else is planning even more mischief, which leads to damaging the school and the possibility of facing the most horrific thing imaginable: summer school! Based on the graphic novel created by Sean Patrick O'Reilly.

Milton the Monster Show – "Fly Meets the Monsters" / "Crumb-Bumming" / "V for Vampire"

ABC. Dec 28, 1965 (S01E16). Comedy/Family. D: Hal Seeger. W: Heywood Kling, Jack Mercer, Kin Platt. C: Bob McFadden, Larry Best ☥, Dayton Allen. USA: English/Color/30m. Hal Seeger Productions/ABC Films/Siren Entertainment.

🦇 🦇 🦇

Milton, a dimwitted Frankenstein Monster, was created by mad scientist Professor Weirdo, who lives in a creepy castle along with his assistant Count Kook and the monsters Heebie (a ghoul/zombie) and Jeebie (a werewolf/cyclops). In the segment "V for Vampire," for several nights, a vampire has entered Professor Weirdo's bedroom, scaring him half to death. After the intruder bypasses several traps set for him, the Professor believes that he's actually a housemate in disguise.

Lighthearted kid's entertainment in the same vein as *The Munsters* and *The Addams Family*. The vampire is really Count Kook in a bat costume; he's trying to scare the Professor out of the room, so he can have it for himself—because it has the best view of the nearby cemetery.

The Modifyers

Nickelodeon (Unproduced). 2007. D: Collette Sunderman. W: Lynne Naylor, Amy Wolfram, Chris Reccardi. C: Mae Whitman, Jeff Bennett, Paul Rugg ♀. USA: English/Color/12m. Nicktoons.

This failed pilot for an animated series follows Agent Xero, a master of disguise, and her modular sidekick Mole; they're part of a secret mystery-cracking team known as The Modifyers. In this story, under the guise of Lacey Shadows, Agent Xero attempts to thwart the plans of the rodent villain named Rat, who's stolen "The All Seeing Eye." Rat hopes the loot will impress his boss, Baron Vein, who's a kooky, Nosferatu-like vampire that hates sunshine and Country Music. This enjoyable, Steampunk-infused take on 1960s British spy films has a lot going for it—but apparently both the Cartoon Network and Nickelodeon passed on turning it into a series.

Mona the Vampire

YTV/CBC. Sep 13, 1999 – 2003 (65 Episodes). Family/Mystery. D: Louis Piche. W: Jason Bogdaneris. C: Emma Taylor-Isherwood ♀, Justin Bradley, Carrie Finlay, Marcel Jeannin, Carole Jeghers, Tia Caroleo. CAN/FRA: English & French/Color/1950m. Cinar/New Films International/Canal J.

Ten-year-old Mona has an extremely active imagination, and believes that her town is filled with monsters. In the guise of her alter-ego (a vampire), she solves ghoulish mysteries with the help of her two best friends, Lily and Charley.

Monster Auditions – "Sam"

SBS. Apr 18, 2009 (S01E03). Comedy/Family. D: Suren Perera. W: Stu Connolly. C: Libby Bramble ♀. AUS: English/Color/1m. Sticky Pictures Pty Ltd/Screen Australia.

A short animated monologue from Sam, a vampire who has a crush on her star co-worker and employee of the month, Dennis.

Monster Force

Syndicated. Sep 18 – Dec 11, 1994 (13 Episodes). Action/Family. D: Chris Schouten. W: Marv Wolfman, Paul Edick. C: Philip Akin, Lawrence Bayne, Robert Bockstael ♀, Paul Haddad, David Hewlett, Carolly Larson. USA: English/Color/390m. Universal Cartoon Studios/Lacewood Productions.

In the distant future, a group of teenagers equipped with high-tech weaponry defend the populace against nefarious beings, including Count Dracula, the Mummy, and the Wolf Man. These teen heroes have some monstrous abilities of their own; Luke Talbot is stricken with lycanthropy, which he can control at will unless there's a full moon, while Shelley Frank is a psychic who can communicate telepathically with various creatures. Her family is connected to Frankenstein, a benevolent monster that often aids the group in battle.

The quality of the episodes fluctuates, but the overall story arc is pretty interesting, and it's great seeing all the classic Universal movie monsters together in one series (although they aren't carbon-copies of their silver screen counterparts). Bloodsuckers abound thanks to the group's arch-nemesis, Count Dracula, who has a servant named Renfield and three female cohorts (akin to his brides from Bram Stoker's novel). Bent on destroying the Monster Force, Dracula often attempts to trick Luke Talbot into killing another human being—an act that will make him a true monster and bring him over to the dark side.

Monster High

Nickelodeon. Oct 30, 2011 – 2017. Comedy/Family. D: Audu Paden. W: Anne D. Bernstein, Lauren Rose. C: Kate Higgins, Salli Saffioti, Debi Derryberry ☥, Laura Bailey, Yuri Lowenthal, Audu Paden. USA: English/Color/919m. WILDBRAIN/DHX Media.

Mattel's *Monster High* dolls, which feature the kids of the classic Universal Monsters, has become a cash-cow media empire with various animated properties saturating television and the Internet. The core group of *ghoul-friends* are Frankie Stein, Clawdeen Wolf, and Draculaura, while several other characters—including Cleo de Nile, Holt Hyde, and Deuce Gorgon—were part of the initial line of toys. First introduced in 2010, each new release of these dolls produces a related animated special, created specifically to promote the new product. The first, *New Ghoul @ School* (2010), debuted on the Monster High YouTube channel on Halloween. This was followed a year later by *Fright On!* (2011), the first of such specials to air on television. Since then, there have been numerous TV specials to date, anywhere from two to four per year that range from forty-six to seventy-one minutes in length. A fifteenth production, *Electrified,* is set to premiere on TV in the spring of 2017.

Monster Mash

WB. Oct 31, 1999. Comedy/Family. D: Guido Manuli. W: Guido Manuli, Judy Rothman Rofé. C: French Tickner ☥, David Sobolov, Scott McNeil, Janyse Jaud, Patricia Drake, Tabitha St. Germain, Jim Byrnes, Phil Hayes, Dave Ward. ITA/USA: English/Color/64m. DiC Enterprises/ RAI Radiotelevisione Italiana.

The classic movie monsters used to be scary, but ever since the novelty song "Monster Mash," no one has taken them seriously. Such horrors as Dracula, The Wolfman, and Frankenstein's Monster were once the bringers of nightmares, but now they're just "fun" entertainers appearing on such variety shows as Foolish Monster Tricks. These original fiends, however, are given one more chance to prove that they can still be scary—otherwise, modern slashers such as Freddy and Jason will take over their territory for good!

¡Mucha Lucha!: Gigante – "Blue Demon"

WB. Feb 26, 2005 (S03E17). Adventure/Family. D: Ken Kessel. W: Anon. C: Carlos Alazraqui, Kimberly Brooks, Tasia Valenza, Candi Milo, Scott McNeil, Michael Donovan, Jason Marsden ☥. USA: English/Color/30m. Warner Bros. Animation.

In this episode, alternately titled "The Magnificent 3," the team joins forces with the famous wrestler Blue Demon Jr. to fend off a group of marauding vampires.

The New Adventures of Captain Planet – "Going Bats, Man"

TBS. Mar 5, 1994 (S04E16). Adventure/Education. D: Robert Alvarez. W: Nick Boxer. C: David Coburn ☥, LeVar Burton, Joey Dedio, Janice Kawaye, Scott Menville, Kath Soucie, Margot Kidder. USA: English/Color/24m. Hanna-Barbera Cartoons Inc./TBS Productions Inc.

Environmentally-themed cartoon that features a multi-racial team of five youths, who are given special powers to defend the Earth against disaster; when the task is too overwhelming, they combine their strengths to summon Captain Planet. In this episode, locals in New Mexico want to destroy a colony of bats; they believe the creatures are responsible for a rash of attacks on the populace. The Planeteers band together with a biologist to find the real source of the disturbance, and it has something to do with a horror movie that's being filmed in the area.

There's some bloody content to be found, even though the main story concerns the preservation of a generic bat species, and not *Desmodus rotundus* (the common vampire bat). The episode includes a scene from the horror film that features a dark-haired vampiress, while Suchi (an annoying monkey character) dresses up in the guise of a vampire bat—and has fangs dripping with blood. At the end of the cartoon, there's a "Planeteer Alert" where Captain Planet appears as a Dracula-type bloodsucker. He enters the bedroom of an unsuspecting maiden, but he's not all that scary; would you be afraid of a vampire wearing a white unitard, who sports a green-colored mullet?

The New Adventures of Mighty Mouse and Heckle and Jeckle

CBS. Sep 8, 1979 – Sep 4, 1982 (32 Episodes). Adventure/Family. D: Ed Friedman, Lou Kachivas. W: Ted Pedersen, Ron Card, Bill Danch. C: Frank Welker ☥, Alan Oppenheimer ☥, Diane Pershing, Norm Prescott. USA: English/Color/960m. Filmation Associates.

Features the cartoon *Quacula,* which follows the misadventures of a vampire duck who lives in the basement of a house owned by Theodore Bear (who constantly tries to rid himself of the vampire pest). Quacula has two pronounced fangs, jet-black hair, and wears a blue jacket with a red-lined black cape; he sleeps in a white coffin in the shape of a large duck's egg. This series also features a vampire in the *Mighty Mouse* episode "Catula," where Pearl Pureheart travels to Transylvania and rents a room in the creepy castle of Count Catula (Oilcan Harry).

📺 Sixteen *Quacula* shorts were produced, and this vampire duck pre-dates the first appearance of the better-known Count Duckula from *Danger Mouse* (1981). In reruns, the series was retitled *The New Adventures of Heckle & Jeckle and Quacula*.

The New Scooby-Doo Mysteries – "Scooby's Peep-Hole Pandemonium" / "The Hand of Horror"

ABC. Sep 15, 1984 (S02E02). Adventure/Comedy. D: Oscar Dufau, Rudy Zamora. W: Cynthia Friedlob, John Semper. C: Don Messick, Casey Kasem, Heather North, Maria Frumkin, Frank Welker, Rene Auberjonois. USA: English/Color/30m. Hanna-Barbera Productions Inc.

In "Scooby's Peep-Hole Pandemonium," a tabloid magazine hires the gang to get the inside scoop on the famous horror movie queen Norma Deathman, who hasn't been seen in public since retiring from the craft in 1933.

The annoying laugh track from the previous Scooby series is gone, but it's been replaced by the equally-annoying character Scrappy-Doo. Yet it's not all bad; the story features a bevy of monsters, including: a Mummy (the maid); the Frankenstein Monster (the butler "Franklin Stein"); a werewolf (a pet); and Norma Deathman—who's actually a three-hundred-year-old vampire.

The New Scooby-Doo Mysteries – "A Halloween Hassle at Dracula's Castle"

ABC. Oct 27, 1984 (S02E08). Adventure/Comedy. D: Oscar Dufau, Rudy Zamora. W: Paul Dini. C: Don Messick, Casey Kasem, Heather North, Maria Frumkin, Frank Welker. USA: English/Color/30m. Hanna-Barbera Productions Inc.

The gang attends a Halloween party at Dracula's Castle, where the hosts are vampires and the guests are all classic movie monsters. But the creatures have renounced their evil ways and are in dire straits; the ghost of Van Helsing is terrorizing them, and they want the Scooby gang to get rid of the apparition.

Despite the nauseating opening theme (with monsters dancing in unison), this episode is better than average, and has an interesting twist: the Scooby gang aligns with a group of monsters to combat an even worse fiend. The ghost is just a man in disguise, however, but everyone else is the real deal—and the monsters return to their evil ways by the end of the story. Happy ending!

📺 As with *The All-New Scooby and Scrappy-Doo Show*, this series features a vampire in the opening credit sequence.

The New Shmoo – "The Return of Dracula"

NBC. Feb 16, 1988 (S01E02). Comedy/Mystery. D: Ray Patterson. W: Gene Ayers, Doug Booth. C: Bill Idelson, Delores Cantú-Primo, Chuck McCann, Frank Welker, Daws Butler, Don Messick, John Stephenson, Janet Waldo. USA: English/Color/22m. Hanna-Barbera Productions Inc.

Mickey, Nita and Billy Joe are three young reporters who work for Mighty Mysteries Comics; they investigate supernatural happenings with the help of their lovable pal Shmoo, a creature that has the ability to transform into anything it chooses. In this episode, the group travels to Transylvania to investigate a report of missing locals near the vicinity of Dracula's Castle.

An average outing from this *Scooby-Doo* knockoff that features some creepy vampire characters, who turn out to be just humans in disguise. A troupe of theater actors was using the castle to rehearse their new *Dracula* play, when they discovered a vast treasure hidden within the depths below. These struggling thespians had no money (naturally), so greed got the best of the them; they captured some locals to use as slave labor to remove the booty, while the vampire ruse kept everyone else away from the castle. The moral of the story? Greed is bad and money changes people. One day you're a starving artist suffering for your craft, and the next you're a cruel thief who will stop at nothing—including slavery—to steal vast riches from right under the noses of the poor.

Octonauts – "The Vampire Squid"

CBeebies. Dec 8, 2010 (S01E28). Adventure/Family. D: Darragh O'Connell. W: Stephanie Simpson. C: Ross Breen, Teresa Gallagher, Simon Greenall, Paul Panting, Rob Rackstraw, Keith Wickham, Jo Wyatt. UK: English/Color/11m. Brown Bag Films/Chorion.

Based on the children's books by Vicki Wong and Michael C. Murphy, this series follows the adventures of a group of undersea explorers. In this episode, Peso prepares for a training exercise in the Midnight Zone, and Kwazii warns him about the vampire squid—a fanged creature with large, glowing eyes, which wears a cape covered in spikes, and lives in a haunted castle in the deepest, darkest part of the region. As Peso completes the exercise, he encounters a creature in distress, one that he's never seen before—could it be the infamous undersea dweller that Kwazii warned him about?

Peso meets the vampire squid, but discovers that rumor and misunderstanding has led to tall tales about the shy cephalopod. This great little story for tots features the cutest and most disarming vampire you'll ever find on television. Although he doesn't resemble the Dracula-like creature he's purported to be, the squid still sounds very much like Bela Lugosi. Awesome!

Oh Yeah! Cartoons – "ChalkZone: Snap Out of Water" / "Earth to Obie" / "Mina and The Count: The Ghoul's Tribunal"

Nickelodeon. Dec 19, 1998 (S02E04). Comedy/Family. D/W: Rob Renzetti. C: Jeff Bennett, Tara Charendoff, Mark Hamill ♀. USA: English/Color/30m. Frederator Studios/NickToon Productions.

In "The Ghoul's Tribunal," a group of monsters learn about the flourishing friendship between The Count and Mina. The vampire is put on trial for having a healthy, loving relationship with a human child—which is criminal behavior in their eyes. Hosted by Kenan Thompson.

Amusing short that features other horrors from the silver screen, including the Mummy, the Frankenstein Monster (and his bride), and the Creature from the Black Lagoon; even a werewolf shows up by the end of the story.

📺 This series was similar in concept to *What a Cartoon Show* (1995), and "Mina and The Count" is the only cartoon to appear in both.

Oh Yeah! Cartoons – "ChalkZone: Secret Passages" / "Kid From S.C.H.O.O.L." / "Mina and The Count: The Vampire Who Came to Dinner"

Nickelodeon. Dec 26, 1998 (S02E05). Comedy/Family. D: Rob Renzetti. W: Rob Renzetti, Alex Kirwan. C: Jeff Bennett, Tara Charendoff, Mark Hamill ♀, Michael Bell. USA: English/Color/30m. Frederator Studios/NickToon Productions.

🦇🦇🦇🦇

In "The Vampire Who Came to Dinner," Mina invites The Count to her house for supper; he's unaware that she has an older sister Lucy—who's of legal age for biting. As the vampire fights temptation, the situation worsens when Mina presents the special dish she made for him: garlic soufflé. Hosted by Kenan Thompson.

A great little story that sees Mina and Lucy fighting for the attention of The Count. Before she met him, Lucy disregarded Mina's friend as a "creepy violin teacher"—but upon being introduced, The Count becomes a "European nobleman" in her eyes.

Oh Yeah! Cartoons – "ChalkZone: ChalkDad" / "A Dog & His Boy" / "Mina and The Count: Playing a Hunch"

Nickelodeon. Jan 9, 1999 (S02E07). Comedy/Family. D: Rob Renzetti. W: Andy Bialk, Zac Moncrief. C: Jeff Bennett, Tara Charendoff, Mark Hamill ♀. USA: English/Color/30m. Frederator Studios/NickToon Productions.

In "Playing a Hunch," The Count tries to get his assistant Igor out of the castle; Mina is on her way for a visit, and he disapproves of their friendship. But the vampire's scheme backfires; Mina arrives before Igor can leave, so it becomes a game of hide and seek as he desperately tries to ensure that the two don't meet. Hosted by Kenan Thompson.

This sub-par entry has only a few funny moments, and pales in comparison to previous episodes. The main problem lies with Igor, who seems very out of character when compared to his earlier appearances.

Oh Yeah! Cartoons – "ChalkZone: Chalk Rain" / "The Dan Danger Show" / "Mina and The Count: My Best Friend"

Nickelodeon. May 8, 1999 (S02E09). Comedy/Family. D: Rob Renzetti. W: Paul Rudish, Dan Krall. C: Jeff Bennett, Tara Charendoff, Mark Hamill ☥, Robbie Rist, Mari Weiss. USA: English/Color/30m. Frederator Studios/NickToon Productions.

🦇 🦇 🦇

In the segment "My Best Friend," Mina presents a report to her class that details her friendship with the blue-skinned vampire. Her classmates ridicule her, and Mina gains the unwanted attention of Nick, the schoolyard bully. Hosted by Kenan Thompson.

The segment starts off well yet flounders in the middle, but redeems itself with a great payoff at the end. The Count comes up with a devious plan to help Mina get back at Nick—there's nothing more precious than a story about a little girl who's trained to look and act like a vampire.

Oh Yeah! Cartoons – "Jelly's Day: Aunt Broth's Makeover" / "Terry and Chris" / "Mina and The Count: FrankenFrog"

Nickelodeon. Aug 14, 1999 (S02E13). Comedy/Family. D: Rob Renzetti. W: Alex Kirwan, Rob Renzetti. C: Jeff Bennett, Tara Charendoff, Mark Hamill ☥, Robbie Rist, Mari Weiss. USA: English/Color/30m. Frederator Studios/NickToon Productions.

🦇 🦇

In "FrankenFrog," on a particularly glorious night for defying the laws of nature, The Count repairs Mina's favorite doll—he "restores its life" à la Doctor Frankenstein. The next day, Mina's class dissects a frog, but the experiment doesn't go very well—so she attempts to "repair" the amphibian in the same way that The Count fixed her doll. Mina succeeds, and the frog comes back to life—but it goes on a rampage, terrorizes the school, and creates all sorts of monstrous mayhem. Hosted by Kenan Thompson.

This is the last cartoon to feature these two best friends; unfortunately, this average story is missing the charm that made the early shorts so wonderful. The best part is The Count's reaction to Mina's creation; despite all the resulting havoc, the vampire seems quite proud of what she accomplished.

Olliver's Adventures – "Raisin Hell" / "What a Pain in the Neck" / "Wolfman Zack"

TeleToon. Nov 16, 2002 (S01E11). Adventure/Family. D: Ron Doucet. W: Edward Kay, Michael Best. C: Joanne Miller, Glenn Lefchak, Lex Gigeroff, Jeremy Webb, Tara Doyle. CAN: English/Color/30m. Collideascope Digital Productions Inc./Ollies III Productions.

Follows an imaginative boy who turns every day events into grand adventures. In the segment "What a Pain in the Neck," Olliver and family eat at a fancy restaurant, and their waiter bears a striking resemblance to Dracula.

Pac-Man – "Pacula" / "Trick-or-Chomp"

ABC. Oct 16, 1982 (S01E04). Adventure/Family. D: Anon. W: Jeffrey Scott. C: Marty Ingels, Barbara Minkus, Neil Ross ☥, Chuck McCann ☥, Susan Silo ☥, Barry Gordon ☥, Allan Lurie. USA: English/Color/30m. Hanna-Barbera Productions Inc.

In "Pacula," Mezmaron replaces his five ghost-monster cronies with a new creation, Count Pacula. The vampire descends onto Pac-Land, and threatens to chomp the daylights out of the locals unless Pac-Man reveals the secret location of the hidden power pellet forest.

This series is based on the iconic video game *Pac-Man,* where a yellow orb travels through a maze and eats dots while being chased by ghosts. You can't expect much from such thin source material, yet this particular story is quite amusing. The gaming and vampire worlds collide to produce a strange hybrid that features Dracula in the form of Pac-Man, as well as five vampiric ghost monsters.

Pac-Man and the Ghostly Adventures – "A Berry Scary Night"

Disney XD/Tokyo MX. Oct 12, 2013 (S01E22). Adventure/Family. D: Motohito Nasu. W: Sean Catherine Derek, Glenn Leopold. C: Erin Mathews, Sam Vincent Andrea Libman, Ashleigh Ball, Ian James Corlett, Brian Drummond, Lee Tockar ☥, Matt Hill. CAN/JPN/USA: English/Color/26m. 41 Entertainment/Arad Productions Inc.

Series follows Pac-Man and his ghost-fighting friends as they protect Pac-World from nefarious spirits and monsters that escape into their realm from the Nether-World (which is controlled by Lord Betrayus). This story takes place on Halloween, which is a special one, because there's a double blue moon on Pac-World. This rare, celestial event gives Count Pacula the power boost needed to sink his fangs into Pac-Man and drink the yellow right out of him—until he's just a colorless husk! The Count looks and sounds like Lugosi's Dracula, has mesmerizing ability, and when transformed into a bat, he can shoot lasers from his eyes.

Pac-Man and the Ghostly Adventures – "Pac's Scary Halloween"

Disney XD/Tokyo MX. Oct 24, 2016 (S03E10/11). Adventure/Family. D: Makoto Sato, Kensuke Suzuki. W: Sean Catherine Derek, Ken Pontac. C: Erin Mathews, Sam Vincent Andrea Libman, Ashleigh Ball, Ian James Corlett, Brian Drummond, Lee Tockar ⚥, Matt Hill. CAN/JPN/USA: English/Color/45m. 41 Entertainment/Arad Productions Inc.

In this 2-part story, Pac and his pals are invited to an all-you-can-eat Halloween dinner at Dr. Pacenstein's Transylpacia Castle, unaware that it's a trap! Pacenstein is in cahoots with Lord Betrayus, but instead of building a Pac-destroying mega monster as promised, he transplants his brain into Pac-Man! But the wrench in his plan is Count Pacula, the doctor's neighbor, who's tired of Pacenstein's wretched, never-ending experiments, which are disrupting the neighborhood. So he joins forces with Pac and his friends, believing that an enemy of his enemy is a friend, after all.

Phineas and Ferb – "That's the Spirit" / " The Curse of Candace"

Disney. Oct 7, 2011 (S03E13). Adventure/Family. D: Robert F. Hughes, Jay Lender. W: Martin Olson, J.G. Orrantia. C: Vincent Martella, Ashley Tisdale ⚥, Thomas Brodie-Sangster, Caroline Rhea, Richard O'Brien. USA: English/Color/22m. Walt Disney Television Animation.

Series follows the inventive step-brothers Phineas and Ferb, their controlling older sister Candace, and their pet platypus Perry—a secret agent assigned to circumvent the nefarious plans of the evil scientist Dr. Doofenshmirtz. In "The Curse of Candace," after watching a horror movie, Candace is attacked by a bat at the theater. She believes that she's been turned into a vampire, because she no longer has a reflection, can lift heavy objects, and can levitate.

This cartoon opens strong with a scene from *Early Evening,* a teen vampire film that skewers the Twilight franchise. As Candace is drawn into her imagined world of darkness, her plight is showcased in an inspired music segment, where the outcast, undead teen tries to deal with her brightly-lit suburban surroundings.

📺 The opening movie features the voices of Michael J. Fox (as the werewolf Michael), Stephen Moyer (as the vampire Jared) and Anna Paquin (as the human Kristen).

The Pink Panther and Friends – "Pink Plasma" / "The Ant from Uncle" / "The Pink Tail Fly"

NBC. Aug 8, 1975 (S01E03). Adventure/Family. D: Art Leonardi. W: John W. Dunn. C: Art Leonardi. USA: English/Color/30m. Mirisch-Geoffrey-DePatie Freleng Productions.

In "Pink Plasma," the Pink Panther is in Transylvania, where he stays overnight in a castle—

unaware that it's the home of a vampire. After sidestepping some life-threatening situations, Pink ends up in the basement and discovers a coffin; fittingly, he buries it and has an impromptu memorial for the deceased. But once the sun sets, the vampire inside the coffin digs his way out—and he isn't very happy. This amusing short is a little repetitive, but features a fun Dracula-type vampire who can never seem to get the drop on the Pink Panther.

The Pink Panther Show – "Pink Panic" / "Transylvania Mania" / "An Ounce of Pink"

NBC. Oct 11, 1969 (S01E08). Adventure/Family. D: Gerry Chiniquy. W: John W. Dunn, Tony Benedict, Don Jurwich. C: Pat Harrington, Jr. USA: English/Color/30m. Mirisch-Geoffrey-DePatie Freleng Productions.

In the segment "Transylvania Mania," Clouseau travels to Transylvania to investigate a scientist who's making monsters without a license. The Inspector arrives just in time, because the man needs a fresh brain for his latest experiment.

A terribly bland cartoon that has a vampire villain for no other reason than to have a villain who's a vampire; this bloodless Dracula spends most of his time chasing Clouseau around the castle. Originally a theatrical short produced in 1968, the running joke towards the end is a direct rip-off from the Bugs Bunny cartoon *Transylvania 6-5000* (1963)—and doesn't work nearly as well in this recycled form.

The Plastic Man Comedy/Adventure Show – "Wham Bam, Beware of the Clam" / "The Day the Ocean Disappeared" / "There is Nothing Worse Than a Stony Curse" / "Anthead" / "Never Retire with Mr. & Mrs. Van Pire" / "The Mysterious Robot Critic Caper"

ABC. Sep 29, 1979 (S01E02). Comedy/Family. D: Rudy Larriva, Manny Perez, Charles A. Nichols. W: Var. C: Peter Cullen, Frank Welker, John Stephenson ☥, Marlene Aragon, Keith Barbour, Daws Butler. USA: English/Color/120m. Ruby-Spears Productions.

In the *Mighty Man and Yukk* segment "Never Retire with Mr. & Mrs. Van Pire," the crime fighting duo travels to Paradise Island, to investigate reports of wealthy vacationers gone missing.

Turns out that a vampire couple is preying on their affluent guests; they steal their fortunes, and then turn them into bats. It's a silly episode where no one realizes what the Van Pires really are, even though they look and sound exactly like stereotypical vampires: they have pale faces, fangs, and wear opera capes—the entire package. This is a kid's cartoon, so the Van Pires have little bite; they're using their guests for money, not blood.

The Real Ghostbusters – "No One Comes to Lupusville"

ABC. Oct 5, 1987 (S02E16). Family/Fantasy. D: Masakazu Higuchi. W: J. Michael Straczynski. C: Arsenio Hall, Maurice La Mare ⚢, Lorenzo Music, Laura Summer, Frank Welker. USA: English/Color/23m. Columbia Pictures Television/DiC Enterprises.

This series follows the adventures of a group of paranormal investigators, and is based on the 1984 film *Ghostbusters*. In this episode, a mysterious man hires the team to rid his town of vampires, and they end up in the middle of a monster turf war.

This tale of warring vampire factions is mostly enjoyable, except for a handful of groan-worthy jokes. The Ghostbusters find an unlikely ally in the original residents of the town—a group of werewolves. The story answers this age-old question: what happens if a werewolf bites a vampire, or vice-versa? Answer: probably the coolest group of monsters around, that's what!

The Real Ghostbusters – "Transylvanian Homesick Blues"

ABC. Dec 11, 1987 (S02E65). Family/Fantasy. D: Richard Raynis, Masakazu Higuchi. W: Michael Reaves. C: Dave Coulier, Arsenio Hall, Maurice La Mare, Kath Soucie, Frank Welker. USA: English/Color/23m. Columbia Pictures Television/DiC Enterprises.

The Ghostbusters travel to Boldavia at the behest of Count Vostak, an aristocrat who's being haunted by some ghostly vampire bats. But as the attacks expand into the nearby village, the locals believe that Vostak is responsible—and the team must find the real culprit before an angry mob can seek revenge.

This average story features a good-guy vampire, the last of his line, who's being hunted down by the last descendent of the infamous Van Helsing. The story includes the notion that Bram Stoker based his immortal tale on the feud between two families—a group of vampires, and those who hunt them.

The Ri¢hie Ri¢h/Scooby-Doo Show – "A Close Encounter with a Strange Kind" / "The Robotnappers" / "A Fit Night Out for Bats" / "Piggy Bank Prank" / "The Chinese Food Factory" / "Muscle Beach"

ABC. Nov 8, 1980 (S01E01). Adventure/Family. D: Anon. W: Anon. C: Sparky Marcus, Nancy Cartwright, Stanley Jones, Joan Gerber, Casey Kasem, Don Messick. USA: English/Color/60m. Hanna-Barbera Productions Inc.

Fred, Daphne and Velma are missing from this series, and the stories featured broad comedic situations instead of focusing on solving a mystery. In "A Fit Night Out for Bats," the Mystery Machine gets a flat tire, so the Scooby gang seeks shelter in a creepy house on a nearby hill. Inside they find Mr. Sylvester, a peculiar man who is more than happy to have them in for dinner.

Sylvester claims that it's the cook's night off, so the gang has to make their own meals; but when they can't find any food, they realize that their host is a vampire. It's a silly story that hints of *Dracula* and *The Fearless Vampire Killers,* but Sylvester isn't very menacing—and he has the quirky habit of breaking the fourth wall to speak to the audience.

The Ri¢hie Ri¢h/Scooby-Doo Show – "Hardhat Scooby" / "Money Talks" / "Hothouse Scooby" / "Mischief Movie" / "Pigskin Scooby" / "An Ordinary Day"

ABC. Oct 24, 1981 (S02E06). Adventure/Family. D: Anon. W: Mark Jones, Bob Ogle. C: Sparky Marcus, Nancy Cartwright, Stanley Jones, Joan Gerber, Casey Kasem, Don Messick. USA: English/Color/60m. Hanna-Barbera Productions Inc.

In "Hardhat Scooby," the gang works overnight at a construction site, and fear that the creepy foreman will have their necks if they don't get the structure finished by dawn. In "Hothouse Scooby," they eke out a living as gardeners, and come face to face with a horde of cannibalistic plants.

This episode features two examples of vampires played for humor, who break the fourth wall when they chat to the audience about the nefarious plans they have in store for the Scooby gang. In "Hardhat Scooby," the building under construction is called "The Vampire State Building"—an allusion to the Empire State Building in New York City.

Both of these vampire-themed episodes were rebroadcast as part of *The All-New Scooby and Scrappy-Doo Show* (1983) and *Scooby's Mystery Funhouse* (1985).

Ripley's Believe It or Not! – "The Vampire Kit"

FOX Family. Aug 4, 1999 (S01E05). Adventure/Family. D: François Brisson. W: Michael O'Mahony. C: Teddy Lee Dillon, Rick Jones ⚥, Jennifer Morehouse, Bob Brewster, Carlo Essagian, Neil Kroetsch. CAN/FRA: English/Color/24m. Cinar Animation Inc./Alphanim.

In Poenari, a young woman is found with two bite marks on her neck, the apparent victim of a vampire. This attack coincides with the return of a descendent of Vlad Dracula, who has taken up residence in his ancestral home nearby. Michael Ripley and friends investigate the matter, and although they aren't sure if a real bloodsucker is involved, they bring along his uncle's "Vampire Killing Kit"—just in case.

An amusing episode that is surprisingly accurate regarding both the fifteenth century warlord Vlad Dracula, and the Vampire Killing Kit (which is an actual item in the Ripley archives). The story isn't exactly correct regarding Vlad's lineage, but he is mentioned as being "a national hero, not a vampire." Still, faux bloodsuckers abound, thanks to a despicable tycoon from Texas. He's orchestrated the vampire scare in order to frighten away the locals, so he can buy up the land at a cheap rate and gain access to the rich oil reserves that flow underneath. The true riddle of the tale is Jarvis, the butler at Dracula's castle; he claims to have been working there "forever," and casts no reflection in mirrors, nor can he be recorded on videotape. Was he a real vampire after all? Believe it or not!

📺 Each episode features a green-skinned Dracula-type vampire in the opening title sequence.

Robot Chicken – "Nutcracker Sweet"

Cartoon Network. Feb 27, 2005 (S01E02). Adult/Comedy. D: Doug Goldstein. W: Doug Goldstein, Tom Root. C: Seth Green, Dan Milano, Michael Benyaer, Mike Henry, Kurtwood Smith, Sarah Michelle Gellar. USA: English/Color/12m. Shadowmachine Films/Stoopid Monkey/Williams Street.

This sub-par episode features a vignette where several people, including Dracula, have their testicles crushed to the tune of Tchaikovsky's *The Nutcracker Suite*. Also includes a short segment where a homeless man sells baby vampires on a street corner (and has three juvenile bloodsuckers in a box next to him).

Robot Chicken – "Plastic Buffet"

Cartoon Network. Mar 13, 2005 (S01E04). Adult/Comedy. D: Tom Root. W: Doug Goldstein, Tom Root. C: Seth Green, Sarah Michele Gellar, Mark Hamill, Mike Henry, Dan Milano, Ryan Seacrest. USA: English/Color/11m. Shadowmachine Films/Stoopid Monkey/Williams Street.

Features a segment where Sarah Michele Gellar explains how Season 8 of *Buffy the Vampire Slayer* would have started, had it not been canceled. It's a typical *Robot Chicken* story of mayhem and mash-up—a cross between the *Chucky* films, pop culture (the Cabbage Patch Kid dolls), and the iconic *Buffy* series.

Gellar's synopsis: With the police hot on his trail, a killer doll lays low until he can find a way to reverse a gypsy curse and get his human body back. He takes refuge in a farmer's field, but inadvertently disturbs a group of zombified dolls trapped within a lettuce patch; they escape from their wretched confines by consuming the killer's soul, and attack the populace. Only one woman can stop these undead, unholy creatures from destroying the world: Buffy.

Robot Chicken – "Celebrity Rocket"

Cartoon Network. Apr 23, 2006 (S02E04). Adult/Comedy. D: Tom Root. W: Doug Goldstein, Tom Root. C: Seth Green, Abe Benrubi, Ginnifer Goodwin, Jamie Kaler, Breckin Meyer, Chad Morgan. USA: English/Color/12m. Shadowmachine Films/Stoopid Monkey/Williams Street.

A man escapes from the clutches of a vampire and speeds off in his car. A check of the rear-view mirror reveals no one behind him, so the man thinks he's safe—but he's forgotten that vampires don't cast a reflection.

A silly vignette where the oblivious man—unable to see the vampire—drives back and forth over the poor undead creature several times. The best segment, however, is a *Highlander* parody that stars Lindsay Lohan and several other former child actresses.

Robot Chicken – "Dragon Nuts"

Cartoon Network. Apr 30, 2006 (S02E05). Adult/Comedy. D: Doug Goldstein. W: Doug Goldstein, Tom Root. C: Seth Green, Abe Benrubi, Bruce Campbell, Macaulay Culkin, Peter Gallager. USA: English/Color/12m. Shadowmachine Films/Stoopid Monkey/Williams Street.

Opens with a short vignette that features two Dracula-type vampires discussing office politics at the "blood" cooler. Minimal vampire content, but the episode features a number of very funny segments, the best of which is "The NeverEnding Party," a takeoff of *The NeverEnding Story* (1984).

Robot Chicken – "Tubba-Bubba's Now Hubba-Hubba"

Cartoon Network. Apr 1, 2008 (S03E15). Adult/Comedy. D: Chris McKay. W: Seth Green, Mike Fasolo. C: Seth Green, Mocean Melvin ☥, Breckin Meyer, Dan Milano, Kevin Shinick, Mindy Sterling. USA: English/Color/12m. Shadowmachine Films/Stoopid Monkey/Williams Street.

Counter Terrorist Unit agent Count Dracula tracks down a bomb set to detonate onboard an airplane. Although the vampire is effective at hunting down the terrorists, once the bloodlust takes over, he doesn't discriminate between who's good and who's evil. This hilarious *24* spoof starts off slowly—after all, Dracula sleeps during the day—but picks up once the sun goes down and the Count gets to work. The payoff at the end is priceless!

Robot Chicken – "Maurice Was Caught"

Cartoon Network. Aug 2, 2009 (S04E12). Adult/Comedy. D: Chris McKay. W: Mike Fasolo, Seth Green. C: Seth Green ♀, Jean-Claude Van Damme ♀, Hugh Davidson, Soleil Moon Frye, Adrianne Palicki. USA: English/Color/12m. Shadowmachine Films/Stoopid Monkey/Williams Street.

In a spoof of the *Castlevania* video game, Simon Belmont battles Count Dracula and his werewolf servants; they don't take the whip-wielding hero seriously, until they learn just how effective such a weapon can be. In another segment, where *Wall Street* meets *Sesame Street,* Count von Count has a cameo in a scene where Kermit introduces a group of children to his cousin, Gordon the gecko.

The *Castlevania* segment is the funnier of the two; the monsters are shocked by Belmont's actions, and call him a sadist for using a whip as a weapon. The best non-vampire segment is *Frankly My Dear, I Don't Give a Van Damme.* It's a remake of *Gone with the Wind,* and features action movie stars Jean-Claude Van Damme as Rhett Butler, and Cynthia Rothrock as Scarlett O'Hara.

Roger Ramjet – "Dr. Evilkisser" / "The Sheik" / "Bat Guy" / "The Shaft"

Syndicated. Sep 11, 1965 (S01E01). Adventure/Family. D: Fred Crippen. W: Gene Moss, Jim Thurman. C: Bob Arbogast, Dick Beals, Joanie Gerber, Dave Ketchum, Gene Moss, Gary Owens. USA: English/Color/30m. Pantomime Pictures Inc./Snyder-Koren Productions Inc.

In "Bat Guy," Roger and the American Eagle squadron wing their way towards Pennsylvania. They make a navigation error and end up in Transylvania, where the evil Count Bat Guy absconds with Doodle.

Roger saves the day (yet again) by taking one of his special "proton energy pills," which gives him the strength of twenty atom bombs for twenty seconds. He goes on a vicious rampage, and destroys the Count, his castle, and his servant Sheldon (a Frankenstein Monster). The vampire is of the Nosferatu archetype, even though he speaks in broken English with a Hungarian accent. He has a bald head, a pallid complexion, and long fingernails—but no fangs.

Roswell Conspiracies: Aliens, Myths and Legends

Syndicated. Aug 27, 1999 – Jun 3, 2000 (40 Episodes). Action/Adventure. D: Bradley Charles Rader. W: Bob Forward. C: Scott McNeil, Eli Gabay, L. Harvey Gold, Saffron Henderson, Janyse Jaud ♀, Dale Wilson ♀. USA: English/Color/840m. BKN Entertainment Inc./Jirech Productions.

The famous Roswell UFO incident was a hoax, a staged event to detract from the real truth: aliens have been living among us for centuries. Human encounters with the various alien species resulted in the folklore about vampires, werewolves, and other creatures. In the present day, bounty hunter Nick Logan teams up with rogue alien Sh'lainn Blaze; they form an uneasy coalition with The

Alliance, a group dedicated to capturing wayward aliens in order to keep their existence hidden from humanity.

This series is great entertainment for kids, with complex storylines and well-defined characters, aspects that make it equally enjoyable for adults (especially for fans of *The X Files*). The three primary alien species—vampires, werewolves and banshees—mask themselves as human until they reveal their true nature. The vampires are snake-like, yet still feature traditional characteristics; they're technology-driven corporate tycoons, with organized families (akin to the Mob) that are collectively known as the Dark Empire. Some of the more charming moments involve the "Fugitive Collection and Transport" team, members of The Alliance that cover up alien mishaps in public, by feeding misinformation to witnesses and the media. As with any series, the quality of the episodes fluctuates, but the overall story arc is well-plotted and very engaging, and ends with a satisfying conclusion that is uplifting yet tinged with pathos.

📺 In a nod to *Kolchak: The Night Stalker*, a nosey reporter featured in the series is named Carl McGavin, based on actor Darren McGavin and his character Carl Kolchak.

Rugrats – "Curse of the Werewuff"

Nickelodeon. Oct 28, 2002 (S08E26). Adventure/Family. D: Joseph Scott. W: Peter Egan. C: E. G. Daily ☥, Christine Cavanaugh, Kath Soucie, Cheryl Chase, Dionne Quan, Debbie Reynolds, Joe Alaskey, Jack Riley ☥. USA: English/B&W, Color/24m. Klasky-Csupo Inc./Nickelodeon.

The babies are dressed up as scary monsters for Halloween, and Angelica jokes that they'll soon transform into the real thing. She guarantees that she can turn them back to normal later—but only if they give her all their candy.

In this amusing Halloween episode, the babies have mixed feelings about their costumes; Tommy likes being a vampire, and the twins love being bats, yet Chuckie is terrified of permanently becoming a "werewuff." The best moments are with Stu, the adult who still loves Halloween and goes to extremes to celebrate it.

Sabrina the Teenage Witch

CBS. Sep 12, 1970 – Sep 4, 1971 (16 Episodes). Family/Music. D: Hal Sutherland. W: Jack Mendelsohn, Jim Mulligan, Bob Ogle. C: Larry Storch ☥, Howard Morris, Jane Webb ☥, Larry D. Mann, Dallas McKennon, John Erwin. USA: English/Color/480m. Filmation Associates.

Alternately titled *Sabrina and the Groovie Goolies,* this series featured Sabrina, a good-natured teenage witch, and her cousins Drac, Wolfie and Frankie—a group of monsters who reside at Horrible Hall. The group was introduced in the episode "The Bear Facts," while Horrible Hall was first seen in "Child Care." A spin-off of *The Archie Comedy Hour* (1969), this series led to another spin-off, the *Groovie Goolies* (1971), which focused specifically on Sabrina's cousins.

Scary Godmother Halloween Spooktakular

YTV. Oct 31, 2003. Adventure/Family. D: Ezekiel Norton. W: Heath Corson, Jill Thompson. C: Garry Chalk, Noel Callahan, Alex Dodok, Brittney Irvine, Brit McKillup, Danny McKinnon, Scott McNeil ☥, Adam Pospisil ☥. CAN: English/Color/47m. Mainframe Entertainment Inc./YTV.

Jimmy reluctantly takes his younger cousin Hannah out trick-or-treating. His friends want to ditch her, so Jimmy convinces Hannah to leave some candy in the basement of a spooky house, which he claims will protect them from monsters. They lock her inside, and she's so frightened that it draws the attention of a friendly witch—who offers to help Hannah teach the older kids a lesson.

This is a fantastic Halloween special that both kids and adults will enjoy, with a family-friendly message and a number of funny characters. Hannah's "Scary Godmother" (the witch) has several ghoulish friends: a flamboyant skeleton, an aristocratic werewolf, a family of vampires, and a large, multi-eyed monster. The strong story and excellent characterizations make up for the dated CGI, which looks somewhat archaic by today's standards.

The Scooby and Scrappy-Doo Puppy Hour – "The Comic Book Caper" / "The Misfortune Teller" / "Vild Vest Vampire" / "The Puppy and the Reluctant Bull"

ABC. Nov 6, 1982 (S01E07). Adventure/Family. D: Charles A. Nichols. W: Gary Greenfield. C: Casey Kasem, Don Messick, Frank Welker, Michael Bell, Billy Jacoby, Peter Cullen, Nancy McKeon. USA: English/Color/60m. Hanna-Barbera Productions Inc./Ruby-Spears Enterprises.

In the segment "Vild Vest Vampire," Scrappy and Yabba-Doo accidentally unearth a coffin, and out steps the undead outlaw Count Zarko. Can they stop the vampire before he turns the townsfolk into mindless zombies?

This adventure features Scooby's brother Yabba-Doo, a white Great Dane that's more courageous than his sibling, and has a better command of the English language (he's a step up from their annoying cousin, Scooby-Dum). Count Zarko, the vampire cowboy, is quite ridiculous—both he and the story don't have much bite.

The Scooby-Doo/Dynomutt Hour – "The Headless Horseman of Halloween" / "The Harbor Robber"

ABC. Oct 9, 1976 (S01E05). Adventure/Family. D: Charles A. Nichols. W: Dick Conway. C: Casey Kasem ☥, Don Messick, Frank Welker, Pat Stevens, Heather North, Daws Butler, Janet Waldo. USA: English/Color/60m. Hanna-Barbera Productions Inc.

In "The Headless Horseman of Halloween," the gang attends a costume party at the Crane Manor in Sleepy Hollow, and learns that their host is a direct descendant of the Ichabod Crane. To their horror, the infamous Headless Horseman appears on the estate grounds looking for a cursed necklace. Can the amateur sleuths figure out the truth behind the appearance of the ghastly apparition, before he attacks the residents and takes one of their heads for his own?

Zoiks! This average episode is marred by the overuse of a laugh track and the inclusion of a new character, Scooby-Dum, Scooby's annoying country-bumpkin cousin. The highlight is Shaggy, who attends the party dressed as a bloodsucker and eats even more than usual, because, "like, being a vampire really gives you an appetite."

Scooby's All-Star Laff-A-Lympics – "Vampire Bats and Scaredy Cats" / "Acapulco and England" / "Beastwoman, Part Two" / "The Mixed Up Mystery of Deadman's Reef"

ABC. Sep 17, 1977 (S01E02). Adventure/Family. D: Charles A. Nichols. W: Norman Maurer. C: Casey Kasem, Don Messick, Frank Welker, Pat Stevens, Heather North, Daws Butler. USA: English/Color/120m. Hanna-Barbera Productions Inc.

In "Vampire Bats and Scaredy Cats," Lisa Van Hoff invites the Scooby gang to her eighteenth birthday party. They discover that her grandfather is a vampire, and he's returned to mark this special occasion by turning Lisa into one of the undead.

This is one of the better Scooby vampire stories; unfortunately, it features an overbearing laugh track (as usual), and the irritating side-kick, Scooby-Dum. The vampire is suitably evil, but he's not quite what he appears to be—which those do-gooders from *Mystery Inc.* manage to figure out by the end of the story.

Scooby's All-Stars – "A Creepy Tangle in the Bermuda Triangle" / "South America and Transylvania" / "Cavey's Crazy Car Caper"

ABC. Sep 23, 1978 (S02E03). Adventure/Family. D: Charles A. Nichols. W: Neal Barbera, Tom Dagenais. C: Julie Bennett, Mel Blanc, Daws Butler, Scatman Crothers, Casey Kasem, Don Messick, John Stephenson, Frank Welker. USA: English/Color/90m. Hanna-Barbera Productions Inc.

In the *Laff-A-Lympics* segment "South America and Transylvania," three teams compete in a scavenger hunt. In Transylvania, they must find three things: a vampire bat; the Mad Monster's autograph (Frankenstein's Monster); and a strip of wrappings from a mummy. The race to the finish will not be an easy one, for werewolves and other creatures of the night flourish in this dark, creepy land. The "Really Rottens" team, Mr. and Mrs. Creeply, search the eerie castle of a local Count, who villagers believe is a real vampire. Meanwhile, team "Scooby Doobies" confront a colony of bats, one of which transforms into a Dracula-like vampire.

Interestingly, Mr. and Mrs. Creeply were based on Weirdly and Creepella Gruesome, who first made an appearance in *The Flintstones* episode "The Gruesomes" (1964). The Gruesomes were themselves reminiscent of Boris and Goonda Evil Scientist, characters that first appeared in the *Snooper and Blabber* episode "Big Diaper Caper" (1959). The Scientists were in turn inspired by Charles Addams' famous (but nameless) macabre couple from his cartoons in *The New Yorker* magazine—who were given the names Gomez and Morticia upon the creation of the television series.

Scooby-Doo and Scrappy-Doo – "I Left My Neck in San Francisco"

ABC. Nov 24, 1979 (S01E10). Adventure/Family. D: Ray Patterson. W: Willie Gilbert. C: Casey Kasem, Don Messick, Heather North, Frank Welker, Lennie Weinrib, Joan Gerber ☥. USA: English/Color/20m. Hanna-Barbera Productions Inc.

The Scooby gang tours Alcatraz prison and comes face to face with a local legend, the Lady Vampire of the Bay. Shaggy jokes that she's really Daphne in disguise, because neither of them are seen in the same place at the same time. But after he notices that Daphne no longer casts a reflection, Shaggy believes that his friend has been turned into a vampire.

One of the better episodes in this series thanks to the minimal presence of that annoying pup, Scrappy-Doo. Naturally, Fred and Velma reason out who the real vampire is; it's Lefty Callaghan, a thief that has returned to Alcatraz in order to claim the jewels that he hid away before going to prison. Vampire fans will appreciate the glimpse of a Dracula statue when the gang passes by the San Francisco wax museum.

Scooby Doo, Where Are You! – "A Gaggle of Galloping Ghosts"

CBS. Nov 22, 1969 (S01E11). Adventure/Family. D: William Hanna, Joseph Barbera. W: Joe Ruby, Ken Spears. C: Casey Kasem, Don Messick, Frank Welker, Stefanianna Christopherson, Nicole Jaffe, John Stephenson ☥, June Foray. USA: English/Color/22m. Hanna-Barbera Productions Inc.

While en route to Franken Castle (imported stone-by-stone from Transylvania), the gang has their fortunes read by a gypsy. She warns them of certain doom if they continue on to their destination, but they ignore the superstitious seer. Inside the castle they come face to face with three fiendish monsters—a vampire, a werewolf, and a reanimated corpse.

In homage to the classic Universal Studios monsters, the Scooby gang faces three characters based on Dracula, the Wolf Man, and Frankenstein's Monster. These fiends are actually just one (rather talented) thief in disguise; he's trying to keep visitors away, so he can find the hidden treasure inside Franken Castle. The premise is silly, the conclusion even more so, but it's still a classic cartoon that has stood the test of time. Most notably, it features the first time that the culprit utters the iconic line, "Might have gotten away with it too, if it wasn't for these blasted kids and that dog!"

📺 Adapted as "The Ghosts of Grimstone Castle" in issue #10 of the comic book series *Scooby Doo, Where Are You?* (Gold Key, February 1972).

The Simpsons – "Treehouse of Horror IV"

FOX. Oct 28, 1993 (S05E05). Comedy/Satire. D: David Silverman. W: Conan O'Brien, Bill Oakley. C: Dan Castellaneta ☥, Julie Kavner ☥, Nancy Cartwright ☥, Yeardley Smith, Hank Azaria ☥, Harry Shearer ☥. USA: English/Color/22m. Gracie Films/20th Century Fox Television.

🦇 🦇 🦇 🦇

In the segment "Bart Simpson's Dracula," Mr. Burns invites the Simpsons to a midnight repast at his country estate in Pennsylvania. Later that night, the family discovers that Bart has been turned into one of the undead—and the only way to save him is to kill the head vampire: Montgomery Burns.

An enjoyable Halloween episode in homage to Rod Serling's *Night Gallery,* where each tale is introduced by Bart while standing in front of a painting. This segment spoofs Francis Ford Coppola's *Dracula* (1992), and includes references to *Nosferatu, eine Symphonie des Grauens* (1922), *The Addams Family* (1964), *Salem's Lot* (1979), and *The Lost Boys* (1987).

The Simpsons – "Sideshow Bob Roberts"

FOX. Oct 9, 1994 (S06E05). Comedy/Satire. D: Mark Kirkland. W: Bill Oakley. C: Dan Castellaneta ☥, Julie Kavner, Nancy Cartwright, Yeardley Smith, Hank Azaria, Harry Shearer, Kelsey Grammer, Phil Hartman. USA: English/Color/23m. Gracie Films/20th Century Fox Television.

🦇 🦇 🦇

After a right-wing radio talk show host gets Sideshow Bob released from prison, the circus sidekick runs as a Republican in the mayoral election—and wins. As for vampires, Sideshow Bob's campaign is backed by the Republican Party of Springfield, and Dracula is a member.

The Simpsons – "Treehouse of Horror V"

FOX. Oct 30, 1994 (S06E06). Comedy/Satire. D: Jim Reardon. W: Greg Daniels, Dan McGrath. C: Dan Castellaneta, Julie Kavner, Nancy Cartwright, Yeardley Smith, Hank Azaria, Harry Shearer, James Earl Jones, Marcia Wallace. USA: English/Color/23m. Gracie Films/20th Century Fox Television.

🦇 🦇

In the segment "The Shinning," Mr. Burns hires the Simpsons to take care of his wilderness estate during the wintertime, but the lack of beer and cable television drives Homer insane. Marge locks him away inside the walk-in pantry, but he's released by Moe (the ghost bartender) and a horde of ghouls—including Dracula.

The Simpsons – "Home Sweet Home-Diddily-Dum-Doodily"

FOX. Oct 1, 1995 (S07E03). Comedy/Satire. D: Susie Dietter. W: Jon Vitti. C: Dan Castellaneta, Julie Kavner, Nancy Cartwright ☥, Yeardley Smith, Hank Azaria, Harry Shearer, Marcia Wallace, Pamela Hayden. USA: English/Color/22m. Gracie Films/20th Century Fox Television.

The Child Welfare Board deems Marge and Homer unfit parents, so their kids are put in the care of the Flanders family. It's a better-than-average episode with minimal vampire content: Marge scolds Bart for wearing a set of vampire teeth, and she tells him, "It's class photo day, no Dracula fangs!"

The Simpsons – "The Old Man and the Lisa"

FOX. Apr 20, 1997 (S08E21). Comedy/Satire. D: Mark Kirkland. W: John Swartzwelder. C: Dan Castellaneta, Julie Kavner, Nancy Cartwright, Yeardley Smith, Hank Azaria, Harry Shearer, Bret Hart. USA: English/Color/21m. Gracie Films/20th Century Fox Television.

Mr. Burns loses his entire fortune; with Lisa's help, he rebuilds his empire by constructing a recycling plant. There are a couple of vampire references; the fake movie *Colonel Dracula Joins the Navy* airs on television, and a confused Mr. Burns goes grocery shopping for the first time—and notices that the vampire on a box of Count Chocula cereal looks like him.

The Simpsons – "Treehouse of Horror IX"

FOX. Oct 25, 1998 (S10E04). Comedy/Satire. D: Steven Dean Moore. W: Donick Cary, Larry Doyle. C: Dan Castellaneta ☥, Julie Kavner, Nancy Cartwright, Yeardley Smith, Hank Azaria, Harry Shearer, Robert Englund. USA: English/Color/23m. Gracie Films/20th Century Fox Television.

In the segment "The Terror of Tiny Toon," Krusty appears dressed as Dracula as he introduces an *Itchy & Scratchy* special. In "Starship Poopers," the Simpsons watch *How Dracula Got His Groove Back* on television. It's one of the better Simpsons Halloween episodes, even though vampires are only mentioned in passing.

The Simpsons – "The Old Man and The 'C' Student"

FOX. Apr 25, 1999 (S10E20). Comedy/Satire. D: Mark Kirkland. W: Julie Thacker. C: Dan Castellaneta, Julie Kavner, Nancy Cartwright, Yeardley Smith, Hank Azaria, Harry Shearer, Jack La Lanne, Pamela Hayden. USA: English/Color/22m. Gracie Films/20th Century Fox Television.

Springfield will host the next Olympic games; to honor the event, residents participate in a contest to design a mascot—which Kent Brockman hopes will be as memorable as the "Atlanta Whatsit" and the "Montréal Vampire." It's another funny episode with just a passing reference to bloodsuckers; before you get your hopes up, the mascot for the 1976 Summer Olympics in Montréal was actually a beaver named Amik—not a vampire.

The Simpsons – "Brawl in the Family"

FOX. Jan 6, 2002 (S13E07). Comedy/Satire. D: Matthew Nastuk. W: Joel H. Cohen. C: Dan Castellaneta ☥, Julie Kavner, Nancy Cartwright, Yeardley Smith, Hank Azaria, Harry Shearer, Jane Kaczmarek, Delroy Lindo, Pamela Hayden. USA: English/Color/22m. Gracie Films/20th Century Fox Television.

A social worker helps the Simpsons work through their issues, but the situation worsens upon the arrival of Amber and Ginger—the women Homer and Ned married while on a drunken stint in Las Vegas. As for vampires, this episode features a scene at the Springfield Republican Party headquarters—and Dracula is a member of the nefarious group.

The Simpsons – "All's Fair in Oven War"

FOX. Nov 1, 2004 (S16E02). Comedy/Satire. D: Mark Kirkland. W: Matt Selman. C: Dan Castellaneta, Julie Kavner, Nancy Cartwright, Yeardley Smith, Hank Azaria, Harry Shearer, James Caan, Thomas Pynchon. USA: English/Color/22m. Gracie Films/20th Century Fox Television.

Marge realizes that her kitchen needs a serious makeover, so Homer builds her a new one. Thrilled with the result, she enters the "Oven Fresh Bakeoff" contest. The episode features a brief scene from the fake movie *Blacula Meets Black Dracula,* where two funky vampires stop The Man from turning a discothèque into a hockey rink. It's a fun little spoof of the vampire/exploitation films of the 1970s.

The Simpsons – "The Girl Who Slept Too Little"

FOX. Sep 18, 2005 (S17E02). Comedy/Satire. D: Raymond S. Persi. W: John Frink. C: Dan Castellaneta, Julie Kavner, Nancy Cartwright, Yeardley Smith, Hank Azaria, Harry Shearer, Dan Rather, Jon Stewart. USA: English/Color/22m. Gracie Films/20th Century Fox Television.

Homer stops the construction of a new Stamp Museum in the neighborhood, but his plan backfires: to make room for the Museum elsewhere, the Springfield Cemetery is relocated right next door to him. As Maggie watches *Sesame Street* on TV, Marge confesses that she's spooked by Count von Count; she yells at the television screen, and tells the fanged muppet to go back to his own country.

The Simpsons – "Treehouse of Horror XVI"

FOX. Nov 6, 2005 (S17E04). Comedy/Satire. D: David Silverman. W: Marc Wilmore. C: Dan Castellaneta, Julie Kavner, Nancy Cartwright, Yeardley Smith, Hank Azaria, Harry Shearer ☥, Terry Bradshaw, Dennis Rodman, Tress MacNeille. USA: English/Color/22m. Gracie Films/20th Century Fox Television.

In the segment "I've Grown a Costume on Your Face," a woman wins the Springfield Halloween contest for her witch costume, but her prize is revoked after the Mayor discovers she's *really* a witch. To seek revenge, she turns each resident into a real version of the costume that they're wearing. As for vampires, Mayor Quimby thinks Dr. Hibbert is dressed as Blacula, but he's actually just plain old Dracula; after the witch's spell is cast, Hibbert turns into a real vampire.

The Simpsons – "You Kent Always Say What You Want"

FOX. May 20, 2007 (S18E22). Comedy/Satire. D: Matthew Nastuk. W: Tim Long. C: Dan Castellaneta ☥, Julie Kavner, Nancy Cartwright, Yeardley Smith, Hank Azaria, Harry Shearer, Chris "Ludacris" Bridges. USA: English/Color/22m. Gracie Films/20th Century Fox Television.

After Kent Brockman curses on air, an FCC investigation leads to his dismissal from the network. He joins forces with Lisa to broadcast his own show over the Internet, but his left-leaning, anti-corporate message doesn't sit well with the Springfield Republican Party.

The story of Brockman's filthy *faux pas* is a timely one, and deftly satirizes the FCC, censorship, and even the Fox Network. As the members of the Republican Party discuss how to deal with the Brockman threat, Dracula offers to "Dracula-bite him," a plan that draws an exasperated response from the others in the group. This leads to a funny scene between the Count and Rainier Wolfcastle, who chastises the poor vampire for his terrible ideas.

The Simpsons – "E Pluribus Wiggum"

FOX. Jan 6, 2008 (S19E10). Comedy/Satire. D: Michael Polcino. W: Michael Price. C: Dan Castellaneta ☥, Julie Kavner, Nancy Cartwright, Yeardley Smith, Hank Azaria, Harry Shearer, Dan Rather, Jon Stewart. USA: English/Color/22m. Gracie Films/20th Century Fox Television.

Mayor Quimby declares that the Springfield Presidential Primary will take place earlier than usual. The town becomes the center of the political universe, and draws the nationwide attention of politicians, pundits, spin-doctors and the media. Residents tire of the increasingly superficial process, so they vote for the most ridiculous candidate they can think of: Ralph Wiggum.

Dracula appears in a scene at the Republican Party headquarters, where the group debates whether or not to offer Ralph Wiggum the GOP nomination. It's a smart parody of the modern political process, but it can be a little brainy at times.

The Simpsons – "Treehouse of Horror XX"

FOX. Oct 18, 2009 (S21E04). Comedy/Satire. D: Mike B. Anderson. W: Daniel Chun. C: Dan Castellaneta ⚲, Julie Kavner, Nancy Cartwright, Yeardley Smith, Hank Azaria, Harry Shearer, Pamela Hayden ⚲. USA: English/B&W, Color/22m. Gracie Films/20th Century Fox Television.

In the pre-title sequence, a group of classic monsters from the silver screen—Dracula, the Wolf Man, the Mummy, and Frankenstein's Monster—hit the streets of Springfield on Halloween night, when they can walk freely and undetected. They end up at a party hosted by Marge and Homer, where they become quite friendly with the locals—until their wives show up. It's an average episode with an opening sequence that trumps the quality of the three main stories.

The Simpsons – "Treehouse of Horror XXI"

FOX. Nov 7, 2010 (S22E04). Comedy/Satire. D: Bob Anderson. W: Joel H. Cohen. C: Dan Castellaneta ⚲, Julie Kavner, Nancy Cartwright, Yeardley Smith, Hank Azaria, Harry Shearer ⚲, Hugh Laurie, Daniel Radcliffe ⚲. USA: English/Color/22m. Gracie Films/20th Century Fox Television.

In the segment "Tweenlight," Lisa falls for the new boy in town—Edmund, a vampire whose father is Dracula. After the teens run away together, Homer and Dracula team up to find the lovebirds before Lisa can be turned into one of the undead.

This is a spot-on parody of the *Twilight* franchise and is highly recommended. Homer's idea of how to combat the vampire family is priceless; Milhouse, who ostensibly plays the role of Jacob from the films, morphs into a canine much less frightening than a wolf. As they search for the young couple, Dracula takes Homer on a ride through the neighborhood of "Dracula-La-Land," where he sees a variety of vampires, including: Dracula *(Bram Stoker's Dracula)*; Count Orlok *(Nosferatu, eine Symphonie des Grauens)*; Blacula *(Blacula)*; Selene *(Underworld)*; Grandpa *(The Munsters)*; Count Chocula (from the breakfast cereal); and Count von Count *(Sesame Street)*—who's drinking from the neck of Big Bird.

Snorks

NBC. Sep 15, 1984 – May 13, 1989 (65 Episodes). Adventure/Family. D: Ray Patterson. W: Berny Wolf. C: Michael Bell, B.J. Ward, Nancy Cartwright, Barry Gordon, Brian Cummings, Frank Welker ⚲. USA: English/Color/1950m. Sepp S.A./Hanna-Barbera Productions Inc.

Series follows a community of colorful, underwater dwellers living in Snorkland. One of the villains is The Great Snork Nork, a Dracula-inspired, gravel-voiced character that executes his nefarious plans with the help of his two vampire-like minions (which resemble miniature versions of him).

South Park – "The Ungroundable"

Comedy Central. Nov 19, 2008 (S12E14). Adult/Satire. D/W: Trey Parker. C: Trey Parker, Matt Stone ☥, Nico Agnone, Jessie Jo Thomas. USA: English/Color/22m. Braniff/Comedy Partners.

Butters discovers that vampires roam the school hallways, but no one believes him; as more students are turned, he reluctantly joins the group. This rampant increase of straight-A preppy students posing as vampires has the Goth kids up in arms—they dislike the fact that no one can tell the difference between them and the undead wannabes.

This story takes a jab at the *Twilight* posers while saluting the endearing nature of the Goth crowd—even though it also makes fun of them in the process. Butters' induction into the South Park Vampire Society is quite involved: he shops at Hot Topic for dark clothing and vampire *accoutrements,* dies his hair black, and completes the transition with a gulp of vampire blood—which is actually Clamato juice.

Space Ghost and Dino Boy – "The Iceman" / "The Vampire Men" / "The Time Machine"

CBS. Dec 3, 1966 (S01E13). Adventure/Family. D: Joseph Barbera, William Hanna. W: Lew Marshall, Paul Sommer, Bill Perez, Walter Black, Bill Hamilton. C: John David Carson, Mike Road, Don Messick. USA: English/Color/30m. Hanna-Barbera Productions Inc.

The *Dino Boy in the Lost Valley* segment featured a young boy named Todd who gets stranded on an island that is stuck in prehistoric times; he's befriended by Ugh, a caveman who calls him "Dino Boy." In "The Vampire Men," bat-like humanoids capture Dino Boy after he crashes while hang gliding. These "vampire men" are quite ominous, with large fangs, green skin and big yellow eyes—probably as close to a "real" vampire as you'll find in a kid's cartoon from the mid-1960s.

Spawn – "Hunter's Moon"

HBO. May 26, 1999 (S03E04). Fantasy/Horror. D: Anon. W: Rebekah Bradford, John Leekley. C: Keith David, Richard Dysart, Dominique Jennings, James Keane, Michael McShane, Jennifer Jason Leigh ☥. USA: English/Color/24m. Ko-Ko Entertainment/Todd McFarlane Entertainment.

Spawn is blamed for killing some thugs, but Jade the Bounty Hunter discovers that the one responsible is actually a vampire named Lilly—she made a pact with the Masters, and if she destroys Spawn, she will be redeemed. This doesn't sit well with Jade, who wants to kill Spawn on her own. It's an overwrought story that takes itself too seriously, and is mostly forgettable except for a truly evil vampire voiced by Jennifer Jason Leigh.

Spider-Man – "Neogenic Nightmare: The Morbius Saga"

FOX. Oct 28, 1995 – Feb 10, 1996 (S02E06-10). Action/Adventure. D: Bob Richardson. W: John Semper, Brynne Stephens. C: Christopher Daniel Barnes, Susan Beaubian, Nick Jameson ♀, J.D. Hall ♀. USA: English/Color/100m. Marvel Enterprises/New World Entertainment Films/Genesis Entertainment.

Michael Morbius experiments with mutated blood from Spider-Man, but the test goes awry and he transforms into a plasma-sucking vampire. Spider-Man teams up with Blade to stop Morbius, before he can use the Neogenic Recombinator to transform others into creatures just like him.

The overall story arc for Season 2 is dubbed "Neogenic Nightmare," and is based on the "Six Arms Saga" story that spanned issues #100-102 of the comic *Amazing Spider-Man* (1971). This particular five-part arc features Morbius and Blade, but due to censorship restrictions in place by FOX, Morbius was not allowed to drain blood from his victims; instead, he uses suction cups on his hands to drain their plasma (but never kills them in the process). Morbius super-mutates into a giant man/bat creature that superficially resembles the character "Man-Bat" from DC Comics. It's still a good story even though it is poorly animated, although both Blade and Morbius pale in comparison to how they were presented in the comics.

The method Morbius uses for feeding is reminiscent of the *Star Trek* episode "The Man Trap" (1966), which featured a creature that used suction cups on its hands to drain the salt from its victims.

Spider-Man – "Partners in Danger: The Awakening" / "Partners in Danger: The Vampire Queen"

FOX. May 10/17, 1997 (S04E06/07). Action/Adventure. D: Bob Richardson. W: Sean Catherine Derek, Meg McLaughlin. C: Christopher Daniel Barnes, Liz Georges, Nick Jameson ♀, J.D. Hall ♀, Nichelle Nichols ♀. USA: English/Color/60m. Marvel Enterprises/New World Entertainment Films/Genesis Entertainment.

Deborah Whitman tracks down Michael Morbius, who's now highly-mutated, unresponsive, and in a state of hibernation. She transports him back to ESU and continues to work on a cure for his condition. Spider-Man discovers another vampire in town, but for some reason, Blade does not want it destroyed.

These episodes are chapters 6 and 7 of the eleven-part "Partners in Danger" saga. The story is a little too melodramatic, and not as interesting as the five-part arc that features Morbius. The tale concludes in "Secret Wars: The Gauntlet of the Red Skull," where Blade, Morbius and the Black Cat search for the Vampire Queen.

Spider-Man – "Secret Wars: The Gauntlet of the Red Skull"

FOX. Nov 14, 1997 (S05E10). Action/Adventure. D: Bob Richardson. W: Virginia Roth. C: Christopher Daniel Barnes, Robert Hays, Nick Jameson ♀, J.D. Hall ♀, Nichelle Nichols ♀. USA: English/Color/22m. Marvel Enterprises/New World Entertainment Films/Genesis Entertainment.

This episode is chapter 2 of the three-part "Secret Wars" saga. The Black Cat teleports to an alien world, to fight alongside Spider-Man as he battles the Red Skull. Back on Earth, Blade and Morbius team up to take on the Vampire Queen and her undead army.

The majority of the episode takes place off-world, so we don't see too much vampire action. Unfortunately, the alien story isn't very interesting; many scenes just show the Marvel superheroes secretly longing for the Black Cat, who has a penchant for falling off of tall structures (only to be rescued at the last moment from certain death). By the time the episode cuts back to the vampire story, all the evil bloodsuckers have left the building.

📺 This story is based on the twelve-issue comic book series *Marvel Super-Heroes Secret* Wars (Marvel Comics, May 1984 - Apr 1985).

Spider-Woman – "Dracula's Revenge"

ABC. Nov 24, 1979 (S01E10). Action/Adventure. D: Bob Richardson. W: Jeffrey Scott. C: Joan Van Ark ♀, Bruce Miller, Bryan Scott, Vic Perrin. USA: English/Color/22m. DePatie-Freleng Enterprises/Marvel Comics Animation.

In Eastern Grumania, Count Dracula teams up with the Wolf Man and Frankenstein's Monster to inflict pain and suffering on the populace. Can Spider-Woman stop the gruesome threesome before they turn everyone into creatures of the night?

Actual blood-drinking was out of the question for a Saturday morning cartoon at the time. Therefore, in this bizarre story, Dracula makes other vampires by emitting lasers from his hands. Not to be outdone, the Wolf Man creates other werewolves by shooting lasers from his eyes, while the Frankenstein Monster makes his progeny through lasers emitted from the electrodes on his neck. Poor Spider-Woman gets caught in the crossfire, and transforms into something almost indescribable: a were-vamp human arachnid that resembles a furry, fanged super heroine (who occasionally emits guttural cat sounds). Van Helsing is also thrown into the mix; he tempts fate by hosting a dinner party at Dracula's castle, a building in which his family has squatted since defeating the Count five hundred years earlier (talk about adding insult to injury).

📺 Prolific cartoon writer Jeffrey Scott also scripted the equally laser-infused episodes "Attack of the Vampire" from *Challenge of the Super Friends* (1978) and "Voodoo Vampire" from *SuperFriends* (1980).

SpongeBob SquarePants – "Scaredy Pants" / "I Was a Teenage Gary"

Nickelodeon. Oct 28, 1999 (S01E13). Comedy/Family. D: Paul Tibbitt. W: Paul Tibbitt, Peter Burns. C: Tom Kenny, Bill Fagerbakke, Clancy Brown, Rodger Bumpass, Lori Alan, Mary Jo Catlett. USA: English/Color/30m. United Plankton Pictures/Nicktoons Productions.

In "Scaredy Pants," to frighten the locals, SpongeBob dresses up as the ghost of The Flying Dutchman—but his costume is so pathetic that the *real* ghost crashes a Halloween party at the Krusty Krab. This episode garners a few laughs, but the vampires are limited to one guest at the party who's dressed as a bloodsucker.

SpongeBob SquarePants – "Graveyard Shift" / "Krusty Love"

Nickelodeon. Sep 6, 2002 (S03E13). Comedy/Family. D: Sean Dempsey. W: Doug Lawrence, Jay Lender, Dan Povenmire. C: Tom Kenny, Bill Fagerbakke, Dee Bradley Baker, Ralph Giordano, Max Schreck ☥. USA: English/Color/30m. United Plankton Pictures/Nicktoons Productions.

In "Graveyard Shift," SpongeBob works overnight at the Krusty Krab. Squidward scares him with the tale of a former fry cook who accidentally cut off his own hand—and now stalks the night as the "Hash-Slinging Slasher." It's an entertaining episode that features a *non sequitur* scene where Nosferatu (Count Orlok from *Nosferatu, eine Symphonie des Grauens*) fools SpongeBob and Squidward into thinking that the Hash-Slinging Slasher has entered the Krusty Krab.

SuperFriends – "The Voodoo Vampire" / "Invasion of the Gleeks" / "Mxyzptlk Strikes Again"

Syndicated. Oct 11, 1980 (S01E05). Action/Adventure. D: Ray Patterson. W: Jeffrey Scott. C: Danny Dark ☥, Olan Soulé ☥, Casey Kasem ☥, Shannon Farnon, Bill Callaway ☥, Buster Jones. USA: English/Color/30m. Hanna-Barbera Productions Inc.

In "The Voodoo Vampire," Vampirus rises from the lifeless swamps of darkest Africa, and attacks a group of archaeologists. When Batman and Robin intervene, both heroes transform into vampires. As Vampirus and her evil horde race towards the Hall of Justice, can Black Lightning warn the other SuperFriends before they too are turned into her undead slaves?

Trouble alert! It doesn't get much sillier than this: Vampirus creates new progeny by shooting them with lasers emitted from her fangs. Apparently vampires and lasers were deemed a good mix, as similar laser-wielding foes appeared in both *Challenge of the Super Friends* ("Attack of the Vampire," 1978) and *Spider-Woman* ("Dracula's Revenge," 1979).

📺 When the vampires transform into bats, the sound effect used is very similar to what was heard when Steve Austin used his bionics in *The Six Million Dollar Man* (1974).

The Super Hero Squad Show – "This Man-Thing, This Monster!" (Six Against Infinity, Part 3)

Cartoon Network (Unaired). (S02E17). Comedy/Family. D: Patty Shinagawa. W: John Rozum. C: David Boat ☥, Nina Dobrev ☥, Tom Kenny, Rob Paulsen. USA: English/Color/23m. Film Roman/Marvel Animation.

Based on the Hasbro "Super Hero Squad" line of toys, this series is a comedic take on characters from the Marvel universe, with light-hearted adventures aimed at kids. In this episode, after the Dark Surfer scatters the heroes through time, space, and reality, Iron Man lands on a strange world that resembles nineteenth century Transylvania. There are no superheroes, but there is a handful of friendly monsters—including a werewolf named Jack Russell, who teams up with Iron Man to rescue his girlfriend Ellen from the clutches of Dracula.

Purists rejected this series because of its humor and childlike nature, but the target audience will enjoy it—and adult fans of Marvel Comics will really appreciate this episode. The story features Dracula (from *Tomb of Dracula*), Werewolf/Jack Russell (from *Werewolf by Night*), Man-Thing (from *The Man-Thing*), and a number of mummies based on N'Kantu (from *The Living Mummy*). Here the infamous vampire doesn't drink blood, but he drains the life-force from his victims. He combines it with energy produced at his home—a dilapidated windmill called "Windmill Dracula"—to create soulless mummies. Dracula is defeated, but not before Ellen is turned into a vampire; she teams up with Jack (the werewolf) and Man-Thing (the friendly swamp creature) to form the "Supernatural Hero Squad."

📺 Each episode has a title card designed in homage to classic comic book covers; this one is based on *Tomb of Dracula* #1 (Marvel, April 1972).

SWAT Kats: The Radical Squadron – "The Curse Of Kataluna"

Syndicated (Unaired). 1993. Action/Family. W: Glenn Leopold. Hanna-Barbera Productions Inc./Mook Company Ltd.

Commander Feral falls under the spell of a mysterious feline named Kataluna, unaware she's a succubus that wants to drain his life-force. It's believed this episode was at some stage of production when the series was canceled; the premise was re-used for the episode "Eclipse" in *The Real Adventures of Jonny Quest* (writer Glenn Leopold worked on both series).

The Sylvester & Tweety Mysteries – "Is Paris Stinking?" / "Fangs for the Memories"

Kids' WB! Sep 20, 1997 (S03E02). Adventure/Family. D: Anon. W: Anon. C: Joe Alaskey, June Foray, Frank Welker. USA: English/Color/30m. Warner Bros. Television Animation.

In "Fangs for the Memories," Sylvester, Tweety and Grandma end up in a spooky castle, which turns out to be the home of the infamous Count Bloodcount.

Tales from the Cryptkeeper – "The Sleeping Beauty"

ABC. Oct 23, 1993 (S01E06). Family/Horror. D: Laura Shepherd. W: Edithe Swenson, David Finley. C: John Kassir, Stephen Ouimette ♀, John Stocker, Karen Bernstein ♀. USA: English/Color/24m. Nelvana.

Chuck, a narcissistic prince, hopes that a simple kiss will break the evil spell that has kept a wealthy, beautiful princess asleep for over a century. His fraternal brother Melvin, an intelligent but meekly runt of a man, guides Chuck through the dark, impenetrable forest that stands between him and his goal. They survive the journey that has claimed so many would-be heroes before them, but discover that something even more horrific lurks within the castle walls.

This charming story reimagines the well-known fairy tale, with Sleeping Beauty as a vampire; the vain prince pays the ultimate price for his preoccupation with her exorbitant wealth. The real hero is Melvin, who narrowly escapes death on several occasions; he finds the actual (human) beauty asleep elsewhere within the castle—and awakens her with a kiss.

📺 Based on "The Sleeping Beauty!" published in the comic book *Tales from the Crypt* #39 (EC, December 1953/January 1954).

Tales from the Cryptkeeper – "Fare Tonight"

ABC. Nov 13, 1993 (S01E09). Family/Horror. D: Laura Shepherd. W: David Finley. C: John Kassir, Valentina Cardinalli, Marsha Moreau, Robert Bockstael ♀, David Hemblen. USA: English/Color/24m. Nelvana.

Best friends Camille and Mildred are horror aficionados obsessed with vampires, so naturally they're delighted when they hear reports of a possible bloodsucker roaming the area. Armed with a homemade "vampire detector," the girls track down a mysterious man who seems to be stalking their good friend Eugene—or is it the other way around?

An enjoyable cartoon for kids, where the preteen hunters destroy the undead threat thanks to their extensive knowledge of vampire lore. There is also a reference to *Dracula*: the girls track the vampire to an abandoned warehouse that is located on Stoker Street.

📺 Loosely based on "Fare Tonight, Followed by Increasing Clottyness..." published in *Tales from the Crypt* #36 (EC, June/July 1953).

Tales from the Cryptkeeper – "Transylvania Express"

ABC. Dec 10, 1994 (S02E13). Family/Horror. D: Laura Shepherd. W: Peter Sauder. C: John Kassir, Damon D'Oliviara, Colin Fox, Jayne Eastwood, Elizabeth Hanna, Rob Stefaniuk, John Stocker, Stuart Stone. USA: English/Color/24m. Nelvana.

Two surfer dudes, Ben and Mike, search for the perfect wave—but end up in Austria instead of Australia. Ignoring the warnings of locals, the wayward travelers take a midnight train through the Transylvanian countryside—and discover several coffins on board. It's a painfully unfunny story with only one saving grace: the band of nasty-looking undead, led by a master vampire who resembles a green-skinned Nosferatu.

Tales of the Wizard of Oz – "The Count"

Syndicated. 1961 (S01E25). Adventure/Family. D: Harry Kerwin. W: Arthur Rankin Jr. C: Carl Banas, Corinne Conley, James Doohan, Peggi Loder, Larry D. Mann, Bernard Cowan, Alfie Scopp. USA: English/Color/5m. Rankin-Bass Productions/Crawley Films/Videocraft International.

This quirky series of 200 animated shorts features stories based on characters from L. Frank Baum's *The Wonderful Wizard of Oz*. In this episode, the Count tells the Wicked Witch that he's leaving the world for good, never to return. She creates her own vampire in his image; the only thing missing from her new beau is a brain—so she captures Dandy Lion to use his.

A very amusing short that features a red-headed vampire, who broadcasts himself into Wicked's crystal ball with the introduction "Live, from ghost to ghost, we bring you the Count!" The Wicked Witch successfully creates her own bloodsucker, but encounters a problem when she transfers Dandy's brain: the two switch personalities, which turns Dandy into a vampire, and the Count into a coward.

Thundarr the Barbarian – "Stalker from the Stars"

ABC. Dec 6, 1980 (S01E10). Adventure/Family. D: Rudy Larriva. W: Buzz Dixon, Mark Evanier. C: Bob Ridgely, Nellie Bellflower, Henry Corden, Stacey Keach Sr., Keye Luke, Joan Van Ark, Shep Menkin. USA: English/Color/21m. Ruby-Spears Productions.

In the distant future, Thundarr the Barbarian battles the forces of evil in a post-apocalyptic Earth, with the help of sorceress Princess Ariel and Ookla the Mok. In this episode, an alien vampire hunts down villagers living in an old amusement park buried within a frozen wasteland.

This vampire is a large, red, lizard-like creature; it has four arms, snail-like eyes, and pronounced fangs. It shoots webbing out of its claws, which it uses to cocoon its victims, and emits destructive lasers from its eyes. The creature is compared to a Dracula statue found in the amusement park, so one can assume it survives on human blood. But it never feeds on anyone; it only captures and preserves the villagers for the return trip back to its home world.

Tiny Toon Adventures – "Stuff That Goes Bump in the Night"

FOX. Sep 25, 1990 (S01E08). Adventure/Family. D: Art Leonardi. W: Richard Mueller, Pat Allee, Ben Hurst. C: Charlie Adler ⚥, Tress MacNeille, Cree Summer, Don Messick, Frank Welker. USA: English/Color/22m. Amblin Entertainment/Warner Bros. Television Animation.

In the segment "Fang You Very Much," Elmyra's latest adoption from the ACME Pet of the Month Club is a cute little bat that is actually Count Bloodcount in disguise. But the vampire soon realizes that *he's* the one who has landed in the evil clutches of another. In "Easy Biter," a mosquito searches for its next bloody meal within the veins of Hamilton J. Pig.

Elmyra puts the poor Count through a number of painful situations; he hasn't seen this much hostility since he faced Bugs Bunny in *Transylvania 6-5000* (1963). Vampires play a major role in this entire episode—it's nice to see so much screen time devoted to these creatures of the night.

Tiny Toon Adventures – "Night Ghoulery"

FOX. May 28, 1995. Comedy/Family. D: Peter Hastings, Paul Dini. W: Michael Gerard, Rusty Mills. C: Joe Alaskey ⚥, Tress MacNeille ⚥, John Kassir ⚥, Don Messick, Cree Summer, Maurice LaMarche. USA: English/Color/45m. Amblin Entertainment/Warner Bros. Television Animation.

This animated special spoofs Rod Serling's *Night Gallery* as it presents tales that parody popular horror stories and movies. None of the segments feature the undead, but three characters (Buster Bunny, Babs Bunny, and Plucky Duck) appear as vampires in the opening sequence.

Ugly Americans – "So You Want to Be a Vampire?"

Comedy Central/Comedy Network. Apr 21, 2010 (S01E06). Comedy/Fantasy. D: Devin Clark. W: Aaron Blitzstein. C: Matt Oberg, Natasha Leggero, Kurt Metzger, Randy Pearlstein, Larry Murphy. CAN/USA: English/Color/22m. Tookie Wilson Productions/Cuppa Coffee Studios.

New York has an influx of otherworldly immigrants; these aliens, demons, zombies, and other creatures of the night try to assimilate into human society. In this episode, a cordial vampire is convicted of illegally trying to bite and convert his girlfriend. Social worker Mark guides the couple through the steps required for a legal conversion, but he's forced to dig up dirt on the vampire—who once claimed to be hiding a deep dark secret.

In this series, vampires occasionally appear in the background, but this episode places them front and center. This entertaining story spoofs Edward and Bella's relationship from the *Twilight* movies, and takes a well-deserved jab at the brooding vampire and his doe-eyed human girlfriend. Other movie vampires make an appearance, including: Katrina *(Vamp);* Count Orlok *(Nosferatu, eine Symphonie des Grauens);* and David *(The Lost Boys).*

Underfist – "Halloween Bash"

Cartoon Network. Oct 12, 2008 (S01E01). Comedy/Family. D: Shaun Cashman. W: Maxwell Atoms. C: Richard Horvitz, Grey DeLisle, Greg Eagles, Vanessa Marshall ♀, Diedrich Bader, Armin Shimerman, Phil LaMarr ♀. USA: English/Color/62m. Cartoon Network Studios.

On Halloween, Grim and the gang go their separate ways after a disappointing night of trick-or-treating. On his way home, Irwin inadvertently opens up a portal to the Underworld, which unleashes a horde of candy monsters bent on destroying the human race. With the world in chaos, Irwin—along with Hoss Delgado, General Skarr, Jeff the Spider and Fred Fredburger—ventures into the Underworld to put an end to the source of these candy horrors.

As part of Team Underfist—mankind's last defense against the terrors of the Underworld—Irwin finally unleashes the power within, thanks to the vampire/mummy blood that courses through his veins. The story starts out strong with an appearance by Dracula, but it never rises above the great opening few minutes. Too juvenile for adults and too violent for kids, it's hard to see where this one fits in.

A spin-off of *The Grim Adventures of Billy & Mandy*, this TV special was intended as a pilot for a new series, yet none was commissioned. Several sequels are listed in the end credits, including *Underfist Against the Astro-Vampires*.

The Venture Bros.

Cartoon Network. Feb 16, 2003 – Mar 20, 2016 (71 Episodes). Action/Sci-Fi. D: Christopher McCulloch, Jon Schnepp. W: Christopher McCulloch, Doc Hammer. C: Christopher McCulloch, Michael Sinterniklaas, James Urbaniak, Patrick Warburton, Paul Boocock, Charles Parnell ♀. USA: English/Color/2130m. Astro Base Go!/Cartoon Network.

This long-running animated series features re-imagined characters gleaned from all avenues of popular culture—from comics to kids television shows—and follows the antics of Dr. Rusty Venture, his fraternal twin sons Hank and Dean, and Brock Samson, his testosterone-charged body guard. The cavalcade of characters includes a vampire slayer who appeared in ten episodes, beginning with "Fallen Arches" in season two. Jefferson Twilight is a "Blackula Hunter," who collects fangs as trophies that he wears on a necklace. Although his origin story is similar to Marvel's vampire hunter Blade, Jefferson is not one of the undead—however he does resemble Prince Mamuwalde (William Marshall) from *Blacula* (1972). Jefferson Twilight last appeared in the season six special "All This and Gargantua-2" (2016).

Wacky Races

CBS. Sep 14, 1968 – Jan 4, 1969 (17 Episodes). Adventure/Comedy. D: William Hanna, Joseph Barbera. W: Larz Bourne. C: Daws Butler, Don Messick ♀, John Stephenson, Janet Waldo, Dave Willock, Paul Winchell. USA: English/Color/510m. Heatter-Quigley Inc./Hanna-Barbera Productions Inc.

A series of adventurous road rallies that featured eleven vehicles occupied by a large cast of quirky characters. Each group raced for the ultimate prize: the title of "World's Wackiest Racer." Narrated by Dave Willock.

This fun series featured some great moments between The Narrator and the antagonist of the show, Dick Dastardly (accompanied by his snickering dog Muttley). One vehicle, the Creepy Coupe, was driven by Big Gruesome and Little Gruesome; the smaller monster was a short, purple-skinned vampire. Each episode included two different races, and for the record, the Gruesome Twosome won only three of the thirty-four rallies. In 2006, the concept was updated to modern times in the unaired pilot *Wacky Races Forever,* but no new series was commissioned. More recently, life-size working replicas of each vehicle (complete with drivers in costume) have appeared in the UK's *Festival of Speed,* which is held annually on the grounds of the Goodwood Estate in Chichester, West Sussex.

📺 In the late 1980s, a new TV movie was proposed, "Around the World with the Wacky Racers," which would have been part of the *Hanna-Barbera Superstars 10* series. The idea was scrapped, but the concept was incorporated into "Scooby-Doo and the Reluctant Werewolf."

Wacky Races Forever

Cartoon Network (Unaired). 2006. Comedy/Family. D: Spike Brandt, Tony Cervone. W: Mark Banker. USA: English/Color/6m. 6 Point Harness/Warner Bros. Animation.

🦇🦇

This contemporary reboot of the classic Hanna-Barbera cartoon series shared the same basic premise, but the participants were the sons and daughters of characters from the original series (except for the evil Dick Dastardly and his sidekick Muttley the dog). The races were organized by Peter Perfect and his designer Viceroy, who was secretly in league with Dastardly in a bid to take over Perfect's company. Team Gruesome Twosome featured two vampires; one was a bald-headed, Nosferatu-type male, while the second was a stylish female sporting an orange streak through her hair. Although it doesn't retain the charm of the original series, the update stands on its own—but the Cartoon Network passed on it.

What a Cartoon Show – "Mina and The Count: Interlude with a Vampire"

Cartoon Network. Nov 5, 1995 (S01E17). Comedy/Family. D/W: Rob Renzetti. C: Michael Bell, Mark Hamill ⚥, Jeff Bennett, Ashley Johnson. USA: English/Color/8m. Hanna-Barbera Cartoons Inc./Cartoon Network.

🦇🦇🦇

Due to a mix-up by his assistant Igor, the Count enters the home of seven-year-old Mina Harper instead of seventeen-year-old Nina Parker. Mina wakes up, and she won't let the vampire leave until he plays a few dozen games with her. This is a charming introduction to these characters, who returned three years later as part of the Nickelodeon series Oh Yeah! Cartoons (1998).

What's New, Scooby-Doo? – "The Vampire Strikes Back"

Kids' WB. Oct 18, 2003 (S02E05). Adventure/Family. D: Tom Mazzocco. W: Jordana Arkin. C: Casey Kasem, Frank Welker, Grey DeLisle, Mindy Cohn, Jennifer Hale, James Arnold Taylor ♀, Brian Tochi. USA: English/Color/23m. Warner Bros. Animation.

The gang travels to Transylvania to watch The Hex Girls film their new music video, but things aren't going so well. Someone is sabotaging the production, and the band is close to breaking up. To make matters worse, it appears as though a vampire is behind all this misfortune.

Twin brothers Steve and Stu Fortescu pose as vampires to ruin the fortunes of Owen DeCassle, a businessman who purchased their ancestral home—and has rented it out for the video shoot. In a nod to *Dracula,* DeCassle's man servant is named Wretchfield; he doesn't seem to eat bugs, but he certainly likes to have them as pets.

The Wild Thornberrys – "Blood Sisters"

Nickelodeon. Oct 27, 1998 (S01E12). Adventure/Family. D: Peter Avanzino, Carol Millican. W: Tom J. Stern. C: Lacey Chabert, Jodi Carlisle, Tim Curry, Flea, Danielle Harris ♀, Tom Kane, John Kassir ♀. USA: English/Color/24m. Klasky-Csupo Inc./Nickelodeon.

Deep within the Andes Mountains of Peru, the Thornberrys visit the world's foremost expert on vampire bats, Dr. Spinoza. The family discovers he's been spending a little too much time with his test subjects; Spinoza dresses like Dracula, and believes that the bite from a vampire bat will turn its victim into a tormented undead soul.

This enjoyable story features one of the kookiest vampire characters on television. Spinoza is not who he claims to be; a delusional local—who recently bought a satellite dish and has since become hooked on American horror films—is posing as him.

Witch's Night Out

NBC. Oct 27, 1978. Family/Fantasy. D: John Leach. W: John Leach, Jean Rankin. C: Gilda Radner, Bob Church, John Leach, Naomi Leach, Tony Molesworth, Catherine O'Hara, Fiona Reid ♀, Gerry Salsberg. CAN: English/Color/26m. Leach-Rankin Productions Ltd./CBC.

On Halloween night, residents of a small town host a party in an old abandoned house, but the building isn't actually empty; it's the home of a washed up witch, who regains her sense of mischievous adventure once the patrons arrive. She transforms the *hors d'oeuvres* into spiders, and the candy apples into newts; she even grants the wishes of some neighborhood kids, who desperately want to be real monsters. The townsfolk initially fear the witch, but they come to realize that Halloween can be a special night for everyone—because it's the one day of the year when they can be whomever, or whatever, they wish.

This forgotten animated special is definitely a product of its time, and features multi-hued characters drawn over lushly-painted backgrounds. Gilda Radner is a hoot as "The Godmother," a misunderstood witch inspired by Norma Desmond from *Sunset Boulevard*. Although this is a story for children, it's infused with humor that adults will appreciate—including the scene where a character called "Nicely" is transformed into a sexy vampiress. Clad only in a bikini, she looks as though she belongs in a Hammer horror film.

This production was rebroadcast on the Disney Channel in the 1980s-1990s, and was released on VHS in 1995. A prequel of sorts, *The Gift of Winter* (1974), featured some of the same characters and voice actors.

Promotional advertisement for the NBC animated special *Witch's Night Out*
(Leach-Rankin Productions Ltd./TV Guide)

Yogi's Treasure Hunt – "Countdown Drac"

Syndicated. Sep 16, 1985 (S01E03). Adventure/Family. D: Ray Patterson. W: Alex Lovy, Chuck Couch. C: Daws Butler, Dick Erdman, Dick Gautier, Arlene Golonka, Bob Holt, Stacy Keach Sr., Gail Matthius, Don Messick. USA: English/Color/18m. Hanna-Barbera Studios Inc.

This series follows the crew of the SS Jelly Roger, a globetrotting, treasure-hunting group that includes Yogi Bear, Boo Boo, and several other Hanna-Barbera cartoon characters. In this episode, musician Count-Down Drac tries to make it in America, but his hit single in Europe, "Transylvania Swing," fails to crack the charts in the United States. Yogi and the gang travel to Transylvania to retrieve the vampire's treasure, which he believes is necessary to attain success in America.

Count-Down Drac plays guitar and looks like a cross between Dracula and Elvis Presley. His "treasure" is actually his former band mates, whom he abandoned when he moved to the United States to pursue a solo career. The three musicians—a vampiress (clarinet), mad scientist (trumpet) and the Frankenstein Monster (saxophone)—don't really add much to "Transylvania Swing." It's a horrible tune that neither Elvis nor Dracula would be caught dead singing.

Zombie Hotel

BBC Two/France 3. 2006 (26 Episodes). Adventure/Family. D: Luc Vinciguerra. W: Peter Saisselin, Catherine Cuenca. C: Aileen Mythen, Hilary Kavanagh, Roger Gregg, Susan Slott, Rod Goodall, Paul Tylack, Danna Davis. FRA/IRL/LUX/UK: English, French/Color/676m. Alphanim/TeleGaël/Canal J.

Fungus and Maggot are twin zombies whose parents run a local hotel, which houses an odd assortment of employees—including a chef who's a vampire. The series begins with the siblings trying to pass for human as they enroll in a local school; they're befriended by a boy named Sam, who knows what they are but is willing to keep it a secret.

📺 John Stocker voiced the vampire chef in the English version of the series.

Horror aficionado Tal Zimerman travels the globe to investigate why people love to be scared in the documentary *Why Horror?* (Don Ferguson Productions/Gary Pullin)

Myths and Truths
Documentaries and Reality TV

Revealed - "Mysteries of the Vampire Skeletons" explores three superstitious burials from a twelfth century mass grave (Quickfire Media)

10 Vampires We Love

E!. Nov 16, 2009. Culture/Media. D: Anon. W: Anon. C: Anne Rice, Julie Plec, Tricia Wood, Kevin Williamson, Molly Goodson, Ben Lyons, Katherine Ramsland, Steve Biodrowski, Lotti Pharriss Knowles, Theresa Bane. USA: English/Color/24m. E! Entertainment Networks.

Since Bela Lugosi's iconic turn as Dracula, vampires have transformed into something much more mainstream—becoming sexier and less sinister. These creatures now reign supreme in popular culture, but what has led to this current resurgence in popularity? Numerous voices weigh in on why vampires are in vogue, as *E!* counts down their top ten favorite bloodsuckers. Narrated by Sylvia Villagran.

If you prefer a program filled with screaming pre-teens that isn't too concerned with factual accuracy, then this one is for you. As the top ten glamorous vampires ("glampires") are counted down, dozens of rehashed interview clips are used to demonstrate how these undead creatures have become "much younger and a lot hotter." This essentially boils down to actors relishing in the superficial beauty of one another; there are no bald headed, hairy-palmed revenants with halitosis found in this lot. A handful of new interviews attempt to speak to this current cultural phenomenon, but they're short and used sparingly, lest they draw any attention away from all the eye candy.

For the record, here are the top ten vampires: #10: Damon Salvatore (Ian Somerhalder / *The Vampire Diaries*); #9: Alice Cullen (Ashley Greene / *The Twilight Saga*); #8: Angel (David Boreanaz / *Buffy the Vampire Slayer* and *Angel*); #7: Bill Compton (Stephen Moyer / *True Blood*); #6: Satanico Pandemonium (Salma Hayek / *From Dusk Till Dawn*); #5: Dracula (Gerard Butler / *Dracula 2000*); #4: Blade (Wesley Snipes / *Blade* trilogy); #3: Selene (Kate Beckinsale / *Underworld*); #2: Eric Northman (Alexander Skarsgård / *True Blood*) and #1: Edward Cullen (Robert Pattinson / *The Twilight Saga*).

20/20 – "Summer of the Vampire"

ABC. Aug 26, 2005 (S26E50). Culture/History. D: George Paul, Eric Siegel. W: Richard Gerdau. C: Elizabeth Vargas, Nicolae Paduraru, Elizabeth Miller, Michael Barsanti, David J. Skal, Elizabeth Kostova, Katherine Ramsland. USA: English/Color/60m. ABC News.

Is Dracula just a sinister vampire legend, or something much more, perhaps a metaphor for our deepest fears about life and death? With the success of the new bestseller *The Historian,* a tale that weaves the lives of the historical Vlad Țepeș with the fictional Count Dracula, vampires are once again a hot topic of discussion. But who was this fifteenth century Wallachian warlord, and just how much influence did he have on the immortal Count from Bram Stoker's classic novel? Elizabeth Vargas hunts for the truth behind the most enduring creature of all time.

Interesting news documentary that gets all the facts straight but doesn't necessarily break any new ground. Several well-known scholars are interviewed regarding the real and historical Dracula, and author Elizabeth Kostova makes her first trip to Transylvania. This adventure in a land that she's written about but never experienced firsthand—just like Bram Stoker—would have been an interesting focal point, but unfortunately little of this venture is included in the program.

20/20 – "Howie Mandel" / "Real-Life Vampires" / "Serial Surrogacy"

ABC. Nov 27, 2009 (S29E48). Culture/History. D: Anon. W: Anon. C: John Quinones. USA: English/Color/60m. ABC News.

In the segment "Real-Life Vampires," correspondent John Quinones explores modern day sanguinists, and the surprising etiquette surrounding their blood exchanges.

100 Greatest – "Scary Moments"

Channel 4. Oct 25/26, 2003. Culture/Horror. D: Mark Murray, Helen Spencer. W: Les Keen. C: John Carpenter, David Skal, Robert Englund, Rick Baker, Kim Newman, Alice Cooper, John Landis, Joss Whedon, Christopher Lee. UK: English/Color/205m. Channel Four Television Corporation/Tyne Tees Television.

🦇 🦇 🦇

Presented by comedian Jimmy Carr, this lengthy special counts down the one hundred scariest moments in the history of film and television, as voted by viewers of Channel 4 in the UK. Along with movies and television shows, entries include music videos, public service announcements, and commercials.

Fans of the genre will already recognize most of these scariest moments, although there are some inclusions that non-UK residents will be unfamiliar with. Unfortunately, the program suffers from poorly-written jokes delivered in a bland manner by the host, and features too many clips from lesser-known film critics and performers. Even if you disagree with the choices made, it's still an interesting overview of the horror genre, but due to the sheer number of productions listed, it's only a slim introduction to each of them. Vampires didn't make the top ten, but they were responsible for a handful of scariest moments: #90 - *Dracula* (1931), #38 - *Nosferatu, eine Symphonie des Grauens* (1922), #36 - *Dracula, Prince of Darkness* (1966), and #24 - *The League of Gentlemen Christmas Special* (2000).

100 Years of Horror – "Bela Lugosi"

SyFy. 1995. History/Horror. D/W: Ted Newsom. C: Bela Lugosi Jr., Caroll Borland, Hugh Hefner, Mark Gilman Jr., Ralph Bellamy, John Carradine, Robert Wise, Sara Karloff. USA: English/Color/23m. Passport International Productions Inc.

🦇 🦇 🦇

Christopher Lee has portrayed Dracula more often than any other actor, but it's the face and voice of Bela Lugosi that is inexorably linked to the infamous Count. This episode takes a look at the fluctuating career and personal life of Lugosi post-*Dracula,* and his on-screen rivalries with Boris Karloff and Lon Chaney Jr. Hosted by Christopher Lee.

Lugosi's starring role in *Dracula* (1931) was both a blessing and a curse. His peers have nothing but praise for him, yet one can't help but feel sorry for the man. Lugosi was integral in bringing horror to movie theaters and television screens, and he deserved more positive recognition during his lifetime. In his later years, when asked if his ties to the vampire will ever end, Lugosi replied, "No, Dracula never ends." In 1956, he was hired to host a *Shock Theater* program on television, but he died one week after the contracts were signed. He was buried in one of his *Dracula* stage play costumes at the request of his fourth wife, Lillian Arch, and their son.

 Lugosi once suggested a Technicolor remake of *Dracula,* but no studios were interested; in 1958, Hammer Film Productions ignited the career of Christopher Lee with their color adaptation.

100 Years of Horror – "Blood-Drinking Beings"

SyFy. 1995. History/Horror. D/W: Ted Newsom. C: D.P. Smith, Brinke Stevens, Roy Ward Baker, Jimmy Sangster, Ferdy Mayne, Robert Cornthwaite, Charlton Heston, Roger Corman, Dick Miller, Caroline Munro. USA: English/Color/23m. Passport International Productions Inc.

Dracula may be a household name, but dozens of other vampires have entertained us over the years. This program examines the breadth and diversity of the vampire on screen, as well as the real bloodsuckers that live in the world around us. Hosted by Christopher Lee.

One of the least interesting episodes in this series, despite the number of vampire films highlighted; the use of trailers, instead of actual film clips, makes for a lesser quality production. There are also some dubious entries, namely *Planet of the Vampires* (1965) and *The Omega Man* (1971)—neither of which had any vampiric element. A 1996 video release, *100 Years of Horror – The Count and Company,* probably combined this production with the episode "Dracula and His Disciples."

The series had a first-run in the UK on the fledgling Sci-Fi (SyFy) channel, while a few episodes were broadcast in the United States on TLC.

100 Years of Horror – "Dracula and His Disciples"

TLC. Oct 1996. History/Horror. D/W: Ted Newsom. C: Bela Lugosi Jr., Caroll Borland, Fred Olen Ray, Nina Foch, John Carradine, Francis Lederer, Peter Cushing, Jimmy Sangster, Veronica Carlson, Freddie Francis. USA: English/Color/24m. Passport International Productions Inc.

This episode celebrates the various film adaptations based on Bram Stoker's infamous Count, from the 1931 Universal production to the Hammer revivals of the 1950s and onward. It explores the evolution of the Dracula adaptation, where erotic subtext led to overt sexuality, and also notes the various Broadway productions. Hosted by Christopher Lee.

As with other episodes in this series, the most interesting parts are the rare archival interviews with actors and the other creative people behind the classic films. Highlights include Lugosi's infamous 1931 interview with Dorothy West, some outtakes from *Abbott and Costello Meet Frankenstein* (1948), and a few sound bites from Peter Cushing recorded later in his life.

100 Years of Horror – "Frankenstein and Friends"

TLC. Oct 1996. History/Horror. D/W: Ted Newsom. C: Ira Lawson, Boris Karloff, David J. Skal, Hugh Hefner, Sarah Karloff, Ralph Bellamy, Jack Hill, Bela Lugosi Jr., Glenn Strange, Don Medford. USA: English/Color/23m. Passport International Productions Inc.

This episode examines the history of Mary Shelley's creation as explored through the major film adaptations, starting with Edison's 1910 version (which was once thought to be lost). Includes archival interviews with the actors who brought the Frankenstein Monster to life, and highlights the other creatures that often co-starred alongside him—including Dracula and the Wolf Man. Hosted by Christopher Lee.

There are not a lot of bloodsuckers in this episode, but the inclusion of some rare archival footage still makes for an interesting half hour. There's an eclectic mix of new interviews, including one with *Playboy* magazine founder Hugh Hefner—an odd choice indeed.

The 700 Club – "Haiti" / "Michele Bachmann" / "Anne Rice"

Syndicated. Jan 14, 2010 (S38E--). News/Faith. D: Anon. W: Anon. C: Pat Robertson, Terry Meeuwsen, Bill Horan, Lee Webb, Scott Ross, John Jessup. USA: English/Color/60m. Christian Broadcasting Network.

In this episode, correspondent Scott Ross visits Anne Rice, who discusses her journey from writing best-selling vampire books to her latest focus: stories about Angels and God.

This is a revealing look into the life of the now-evangelical Anne Rice, yet it still feels a little strange seeing her extol such virtues; if she has truly found peace through regaining her faith, then fans should be happy for her. The rest of the program is a lesson in blind faith and extreme right-wing religious views, and won't be of much interest to vampire fanatics.

The introduction to Rice's segment erroneously states that her best-selling *Vampire Chronicles* was a trilogy; there are actually ten books in the series.

ABC News Nightline – Ep. #32.07

ABC. Apr 5, 2011 (S32E07). Culture/News. D: Anon. W: Anon. C: Cynthia McFadden, Jeremy Hubbard, Andre Berger, Lynn Piper, Shelly McCarthy. USA: English/Color/30m. ABC.

In the segment "Vampire Beauty," correspondent Jeremy Hubbard investigates one of the latest fads in cosmetic surgery: the "vampire facelift." This new technique lasts for up to eighteen months and costs from $800 to $1200 per treatment, twice as long and half the price of other similar procedures. The process involves extracting the patient's own blood; the plasma-rich proteins are separated out, and re-injected into wrinkles and cheeks to stimulate natural collagen growth (which apparently masks the effects of aging).

This is more of an infomercial for the treatment itself rather than a critical look at the bigger picture of false beauty and the fear of aging. The report follows two women as they get the vampire facelift procedure; they have already had the standard run of plastic surgeries, and this is yet another fad that sucks them in as they pursue a never-ending quest to maintain their youth. The segment uses clips from *True Blood* and *Twilight,* and mentions the Blood Energy Potion, an energy drink that's marketed in a blood bag.

AFI's 100 Years: 100 Heroes & Villains

CBS. Jun 3, 2003. History/Horror. D: Gary Smith. W: Bob Gazzale. C: Kathy Bates, Anthony Hopkins, Hayden Christensen, Glenn Close, Wes Craven, Geena Davis, Kirk Douglas, Robert Englund. USA: English/Color/60m. AFI/The Gary Smith Company/SFM Entertainment.

The American Film Institute counts down the top fifty film heroes and villains of all time; Count Dracula, from Tod Browning's *Dracula* (1931), is #33 on the list of villains. This is the sixth in a series of twelve specials that honor the top movies produced in the United States over the last century. Hosted by Arnold Schwarzenegger.

America Undercover – "Vampire Murders"

HBO. Aug 19, 1999 (S--E--). Crime/Drama. D: Eames Yates. W: Eames Yates, John Parsons Peditto. C: Rod Ferrell, Dana Cooper, Sondra Gibson, April Doeden, Jaden Murphy, Rod Odom. USA: English/Color/60m. American Undercover/Home Box Office.

Tells the story of a group of teenagers from Kentucky, who were part of a vampire clan led by Rod Ferrell; in 1996, he brutally murdered the parents of one of the members.

Ancient Aliens - "Aliens and the Undead"

History. Oct 26, 2011 (S03E14). History/Sci-Fi. D: Melissa Tittl. W: Andy Papadopoulos. C: David J. Skal, Tok Thompson, Bob Curran, Max Brooks, Doc Barham, Jonathan Young, Giorgio Tsoukalos, George Noory. USA: English/Color/45m. Prometheus Entertainment/A&E Television Networks.

For centuries, mankind has told tales of encounters with strange, soulless creatures—zombies, vampires, and humans trapped between heaven and hell. Are these incidents simply myths, or could 'ancient astronauts' be the source of such strange occurrences of life beyond death? Narrated by Robert Clotworthy.

Ancient Mysteries – "Origin of the Vampire"

A&E. Jan 14, 1994 (S01E04). Folklore/History. D: J. Charles Sterin, Lars Ullberg. W: Lars Ullberg. C: Anne Rice, Michael Bell, Raymond McNally, Matthew Bunson, Paul Barber, Badescu Cezar, Ruth Kelly, Henry Strozier. USA: English/Color/48m. The Voyagers Group/Hearst Entertainment.

From the ghastly undead of antiquity to their contemporary romantic counterparts, this documentary examines the origin and evolution of vampires over the past three hundred years. Historical accounts of suspected vampirism are interspersed with the works of Montague Summers and Dom Augustin Calmet. The production includes interviews with scholars and writers familiar with the genre. Narrated by Leonard Nimoy (Stanley Anderson for the video release).

This interesting look at vampire myths from Romania to Rhode Island includes a present-day account from the village of Arafu, where superstitious locals believed a suicide victim would return from the dead as a vampire. The production also discusses the vampire's transition to film, and includes artwork, illustrations, and a few cheesy reenactments. Unfortunately it claims that Bram Stoker's immortal vampire was based on Vlad Țepeș, the extent of which has since been disputed by scholars; most now believe that Stoker knew only the name and very little of the man.

America's Next Top Model – "America's Next Top Vampire"

The CW. Mar 31, 2010 (S14E04). Drama/Reality. D: Allison Chase. W: Anon. C: Tyra Banks, Nigel Barker, J. Alexander, André Leon Talley, Jay Manuel ☥, Dania Ramirez, Krista White ☥, Raina Hein ☥. USA: English/Color/60m. 10 by 10 Entertainment/Bankable Productions.

The amateur models perform in a commercial that is broadcast live on a large outdoor monitor at Times Square. They later pose as fledgling vampires, in a photo shoot that involves a bathtub and whole a lot of fake blood.

Jumping on the bloodsucker bandwagon, the women pose as newly-turned vampires, and literally become blind as a bat when white-out lenses are placed over their eyes (which elicits even more faux drama than usual). Host Jay Manuel gets in on the game; his vampire guise actually looks good, whereas the models just resemble vapid, underfed caricatures from bloody bad B-movies.

American Vampires

Channel 4. Jun 26, 2001. Culture/Media. D/W: Mark Soldinger. C: Vincent, Sinner, Ghost, Mikel, Sue, Michael, Raven, Spigot Girl, Sarah, Scott. UK: English/B&W, Color/52m. XYTV Productions.

From the major centers of New York and Los Angeles to the sleepy suburbs of Cincinnati, vampires thrive throughout the United States. Beyond the role players, who are in it just for fun, "lifestylers" participate in a much more serious manner; in an age where blood-borne diseases are commonplace, they face great risk from their blood-drinking activities. Narrated by Mark Soldinger.

The host travels across the country to meet real sanguinists, and witnesses their blood exchanges and related activities; it's an unflinching look at modern vampirism without flash or flare. Viewers take a dark journey into the subculture, and witness activities that many will find quite unnerving. Most participants are in it for pleasure; some genuinely crave blood, while others offer themselves as donors. There are also extreme cases, such a blood performance artist who blurs the line between entertainment and self-mutilation. It's a compelling glimpse into the lives of real vampires that has never been seen until now.

📺 Occult and metaphysical author Michelle Belanger is part of a group that gathers in Cincinnati; she leads an energy circle where participants imbibe some blood-laced mead.

The Anatomy of Horror

UPN. Aug 22, 1995. History/Film. D: John Fuller. W: Anon. C: George A. Romero, Clive Barker, Tobe Hooper, Wes Craven, Quentin Tarantino, Robert Rodriguez, Gary J. Tunnicliffe, Doug Bradley, Leo Braudy, Robert Kurtzman. USA: English/B&W, Color/60m. Miramax Films.

Traces the evolution of horror, from early examples of cave paintings and the Bible, to movies from the silent era through the present day. Features clips from *Nosferatu, eine Symphonie des Grauens* (1922), as well as a section that highlights KNB EFX Group, a company that produced special effects for the film *From Dusk Till Dawn* (1996). Hosted by Jeff Yagher.

Anna in Wonderland – "Vampires"

BBC Three. Sep 30, 2003 (S01E07). Culture/Reality. D: Anon. W: Anon. C: Lucius, Jason, Mogsy, Tara Daynes. UK: English/Color/60m. XYTV Productions.

In her search for self-proclaimed vampires living in Britain, the host travels to Wellingborough and meets Jason, a thirty-two-year-old man who's part of the "National Vampire Association"—and he contacts teenagers to encourage their "vampirism." In one scene, Jason cuts his arm with a razor blade, and directs a sixteen-year-old to suck his blood. Other interviewees include Lucius, a young woman who sleeps in a coffin and had her eye teeth filed down to points. Presented by Anna Nolan.

📺 When this episode was rebroadcast in Ireland, an official complaint was launched under the Broadcasting Act specific to the blood-drinking scene. The complainant believed that Jason's alleged behavior was criminal, abusive, and hinted of pedophilia—but it was determined that the show did not breach any broadcasting standards.

Arrest & Trial – "Vampire Cult Killers"

Syndicated. Nov 2, 2000 (S01E38). Crime/Drama. D: Rob Port, Eddie Barbini. W: Anon. C: Jennifer Pfalzgraff, Jamie Lauren. USA: English/Color/30m. Wolf Films/MoPo Entertainment.

Features the story of teenager Heather Wendorf, whose longtime friend Rod Ferrell murdered her parents in 1996, so she could run away from home. Ferrell once led a group called the "Vampire Clan," and believed he was a five-hundred-year-old vampire named "Vassago." Hosted by Brian Dennehy (Rob Butler for the UK broadcast).

Auction Kings – "Vampire Hunting Kit" / "Meteorite"

Discovery. Oct 26, 2010 (S01E01). History/Lifestyle. D/W: Amanda Crane. C: Paul Brown, Cindy Shook, Jon Hammond, Delfino Ramos, Bob Brown. USA: English/Color/22m. Authentic Entertainment Inc.

In the segment "Vampire Hunting Kit," up for bid is an authentic, mid-1800s era travel kit that contains over thirty items thought to protect one from vampires…or even kill them if necessary. The items include: knives crafted from silver; an old Bible; a silver crucifix; a serrated knife (for beheading); vials of holy water; silver nitrate; a rosary; and a crossbow with silver tipped arrows (instead of the standard pistol found in most kits).

The owner hopes to sell it for $7500; a bidding war ensues, and the winning offer is for $12,000. It's an interesting segment, especially for those who have never seen one of these kits up close; it's a unique item from our superstitious past, and the show features some great shots of the contents. The episode also includes clips from the film *Nosferatu, eine Symphonie des Grauens* (1922).

Backstory – "Buffy the Vampire Slayer"

AMC. May 20, 2002 (S03E03). History/Film. D: Stacey Dowdy Travis. W: Anon. C: Fran Rubel Kuzui, Howard Rosenman, Donald Sutherland, Luke Perry, Sarah Michelle Gellar, David Boreanaz. USA: English/Color/60m. Prometheus Entertainment/Foxstar Productions/Fox Television Studios/AMC.

A behind-the-scenes look at the 1992 film starring Kristy Swanson, which explores how this lackluster movie paved the way for the television series that became a pop culture phenomenon.

Behind the Fame – "The Munsters" / "Addams Family"

TLC. Oct 31, 2002. Culture/History. D: Robert Corsini. W: Robert Corsini, Geoffrey Mark Fidelman. C: Al Lewis, Pat Priest, Lisa Loring, Felix Silla. USA: English/B&W, Color/60m. Starcast.

Released on video as *Inside Television's Greatest – Addams Family & The Munsters,* this Halloween special takes an affectionate look at these two classic sitcoms, both of which launched in 1964. The actors share anecdotes about their respective shows, and discuss how their careers changed after cancelation.

Being Human Unearthed

BBC Three. Mar 28, 2009. Culture/Media. D: Colin Teague. W: Toby Whithouse. C: Colin Teague, Matthew Bouch, Rob Pursey, Toby Whithouse, Lenora Crichlow, Russell Tovey, Rob Mayor, Aidan Turner, Annabel Scholey. UK: English/Color/57m. Touchpaper Television/BBC.

From behind the scenes and beyond the grave, this promotional documentary takes a look at the genesis of the smash UK hit *Being Human*. It explores the major characters and storylines, and hints at what to expect from the second season. Narrated by Alex Price.

Fans will enjoy this inside look at the popular TV series about three otherworldly housemates who try to lead normal human lives. Creator Toby Whithouse compares the pilot to the series, and cast members discuss the characters they play, and what's in store for them.

Beyond - "Vampires"

Space. Jan 20, 2007 (S04E05). Folklore/History. D/W: Steven Rumbalow. C: Jeremy Parnes, David Temrick, Richard Tilson, Jan Drummond, Anton Brejak. CAN: English/B&W, Color/25m. Renegade Motion Pictures.

Canadian paranormal documentary series that explored myths and truths about the occult, psychics, hauntings, and a bevy of supernatural creatures—all tied together in loosely-themed seasons. This episode explores folklore and vampires, and how they are connected to numerous otherworldly predators. Presented by Alannah Myles.

I cannot speak for the rest of this series, but if this episode indicates anything, it's that producers did a poor job of pre-screening their interview subjects. Case in point: the "vampire expert" who talks at length about "Wake 'em Stake 'em Stephen," a notorious serial killer who murdered almost 1,000 vampire lifestylers and role-players in the early 1800s. How odd is it that, after dozens of such documentaries have been produced over the years, this is the first time that this obviously noteworthy killer has been mentioned? Granted, this aficionado—who seems to actually be a writer and satirist—may have been embellishing the story of Burl "Wake 'em and Stake 'em" Purry, the tough-as-nails slayer of the undead from Texas who had racked up an equal number of vampire kills—which were celebrated in the pages of *Weekly World News* (Vol. 21 No. 8, Nov. 16, 1999).

Biography – "Dracula"

A&E. Oct 26, 1995. Culture/Literature. D: Daniel Wiles. W: Melvyn Bragg. C: Leonard Wolf, Christopher Frayling, Tina Rath, Daniel Farson, Elaine Showalter, Stephen Jones, Christopher Lee, Carole Bohanan, Stephen Kaplan, Seán Manchester. USA: English/Color/47m. A&E Networks.

From the shores of Whitby to the Hollywood Hills, this documentary explores the origins of Bram Stoker's immortal creation, and speculates on how much the author incorporated his own life into the novel—and how his writing was influenced by personal relationships and the anxieties of Victorian England. Broadcast as part of "Biography: Tricks and Treats Week" on A&E, and hosted by Jack Perkins.

It's unfortunate that by the end of his life, Bram Stoker believed he was a failure; if he'd only known what impact his creation would have on the world. This documentary discusses the author and the genesis of his novel, and explores the erotic subtext and the link between blood and sex. It also covers the continuing hold that both Dracula and other vampires have on our collective psyche, and examines the legacy on film, from Murnau to Coppola.

📺 This is a repackaged edit of a British documentary presented in *The South Bank Show* episode "Dracula" (1993).

Biography – "Bela Lugosi: Hollywood's Dark Prince"

A&E. Oct 27, 1995. Culture/Literature. D: Kevin Burns. W: David J. Skal. C: Bela Lugosi, Jr., Ray Walson, Martin Landau, Ronald V. Borst, Forrest J Ackerman, Robert Wise, Dick Scheffield. USA: English/B&W, Color/45m. Van Ness Films Inc./Twentieth Television Inc.

🦇 🦇 🦇 🦇

Considered a renowned theatre actor in his native land, Bela Lugosi had always dreamed of becoming an actor, and through sheer perseverance he landed his first role at the age of twenty. After achieving everything he could on the Hungarian stage, he emigrated to the United States in 1921. In 1927, at age forty-four, he landed the title role in the Broadway production of *Dracula*. Lugosi wasn't the first choice for the film adaptation, but he fought hard to land the role. His iconic performance made him famous, but it was a detriment to his career; he was unable to shake his association with the infamous vampire. Narrated by Richard Kiley.

Broadcast during "Tricks and Treats" week on A&E, this excellent documentary traces the life of actor Bela Lugosi, from his humble childhood in Hungary to his pre-*Dracula* fame in the United States, and his roller-coaster career after the release of the classic 1931 Universal movie. In his later years, Lugosi fought a very public battle with drug addiction, which he eventually won; yet his hope for a comeback ended with his death at age seventy-three.

📺 Repackaged as part of Image Entertainment's "Heroes of Horror" two-disc DVD set, which also includes expanded *Biography* episodes of Boris Karloff, Lon Chaney Jr., Peter Lorre and Vincent Price.

Biography – "Fred Gwynne: More Than a Munster"

A&E. Oct 19, 1999. Culture/History. D: Lawrence Williams. W: Jerry Decker. C: Al Lewis, Madyn Gwynne, Foxy Gwynne, Deb Gwynne, Beverley Owen, Butch Patrick, Ralph Macchio. USA: English/B&W, Color/60m. A&E Networks.

The life and career of Fred Gwynne is profiled in this episode of *Biography,* which includes clips from *The Munsters* (1964) and *Munster, Go Home!* (1966). Presented by Harry Smith.

Fred Gwynne takes a break from filming *The Munsters* and tries his hand at operating a camera (Kayro-Vue Productions)

Yvonne De Carlo is Lily Munster, the daughter of Count Dracula, in the CBS series *The Munsters* (Kayro-Vue Productions)

Biography – "Yvonne De Carlo: Gilded Lily"

A&E. Jul 18, 2000. Culture/History. D: Lawrence Williams. W: Gidion Phillips. C: James Parish, Robert Stack, Al Lewis, Joyce Arthur, Pat Priest, Bari Morgan Miller. USA: English/B&W, Color/45m. A&E Networks.

Profiles the life of actress Yvonne De Carlo, who had a flourishing film career in the 1940s and 1950s, but by the 1960s, her career was in a decline. She auditioned for the role of Lily Munster—and the rest is television history. Presented by Peter Graves.

Biography – "Anne Rice: Vampires, Witches and Bestsellers"

A&E. Oct 24, 2000 (S14E104). Culture/Literature. D/W: Sandra Zweig. C: Pat Harberson, Alice Borchardt, Anne Rice, Stan Rice, Ginny Hiebert, Margaret Rice, Michael Riley, Karen O'Brien, Victoria Wilson, Tina Jordan, Ross Tafaro. USA: English/Color/45m. ABC News Productions.

This episode profiles author Anne Rice; it traces her childhood in New Orleans to her life in San Francisco, and the genesis of *Interview with the Vampire,* her groundbreaking first novel. Numerous interviews detail Rice's personal tragedies, her passion for writing, and her rise to fame. Hosted by Jack Perkins with narration by Deborah Amos.

Anne Rice was born into a city of contradictions, so it is no surprise that her strict Catholic upbringing in New Orleans was abandoned for a free-spirited life in San Francisco. Always an avid writer, her literary career took a back seat to that of her husband, the poet Stan Rice, up until the loss of their daughter to leukemia in 1972. As she worked through her grief, Anne wrote *Interview with the Vampire,* but the manuscript was universally rejected by publishers in 1974. She persisted, and a year later it was picked up by Knopf; the rest, as they say, is history. The documentary includes a wide range of interviews with key people in Anne's life, yet it feels somewhat clinical—all facts and no emotion. A superior production, *Bookmark* - "The Vampire's Life" (BBC 1993), should be sought out by those looking for a more personal glimpse into the author's life.

Biography – "Al Lewis: Forever Grandpa"

A&E. Nov 30, 2000. Culture/History. D: Anon. W: Colin Powers. C: Al Lewis, Butch Patrick, Pat Priest, David Lewis, Henry Meister, Craig Seeman, Karen Ingenthron, Charlotte Rae, Ted Lewis. USA: English/B&W, Color/45m. Foxstar Productions/A&E Networks.

Profiles Al Lewis, the actor best known for his role as Grandpa Dracula on *The Munsters*. Features interviews with his friends, family, and peers. Presented by Harry Smith.

Biography – "Buffy the Vampire Slayer"

A&E. May 14, 2003 (S17E41). Culture/History. D: Jack Walworth. W: Carolyn Townsend. C: Joss Whedon, Gail Berman, Sarah Michelle Gellar, Anthony Stewart Head, David Boreanaz, Alyson Hannigan, James Marsters, Nicholas Brendon. USA: English/Color/60m. Prometheus Entertainment.

Takes a look at the hit TV series inspired by the 1992 film, which led to a spin-off featuring Angel, the vampire with a soul.

Biography – "The Munsters: America's First Family of Fright"

A&E. Jul 8, 2003. Culture/History. D: Rick Hull. W: Jerry Decker. C: Donald Glut, Norman Abbott, Al Lewis, Yvonne De Carlo, Butch Patrick, Pat Priest, Edward Herrmann, Karl Silvera, Beverley Owen, George Barris. USA: English/B&W, Color/50m. A&E Networks.

Explores the history of the classic sitcom and the numerous attempts at revival. Features interviews with the original cast, who reflect on the popularity of the show and its lasting legacy.

Biography – "Bram Stoker"

A&E. Dec 11, 2004 (S18E--). Culture/Literature. D: Anon. W: Anon. C: Eartha Kitt, Michael Barsanti, Anthony Bianchi, Eva La Rue, Tom Hewitt, Vincent Pastore, Elizabeth Miller. USA: English/Color/60m. Prometheus Entertainment.

Profiles author Bram Stoker, best known for his 1897 novel *Dracula*. Narrated by Neil Ross.

Bloodlines – The Dracula Family Tree

History Channel. Nov 11, 2003. Culture/History. D: David Paradine. W: Trevor Poots. C: Radu Florescu, Razvan Teodorescu, Cristiana Zavoianu, Matei Cazacu, Myron Yorra, Stephen Keefe, Silvia Chitimia, John Florescu. USA: English/B&W, Color/47m. A&E Television Networks.

The Florescu family is forever tied to Vlad Țepeș, through a marriage centuries ago between his half-brother, Vlad the Monk, and their ancestor, Maria Florescu. Vlad the Monk, backed by the

Florescu family, attempted to overthrow his half-brother; they failed, and the two families became bitter enemies. The bloodlines of both Vlad Țepeș and Vlad the Monk died out long ago, but the descendants of Maria's brother, Vintilla Florescu, live on to this day—but have they been cursed to a lifetime of misfortune? Narrated by Jeff Harding.

Also known as *Bloodlines: Dracula's Family Tree,* this documentary follows historian Radu Florescu and his son John, as they travel to Romania to explore the history of both families. Florescu's relatives have been touched by eerie misfortune over the years; this is a fascinating look into the history of the family, and how their possible ties to Vlad Țepeș has resulted in a "supernatural" curse that has affected several generations. It's also a first-hand glimpse into the life and research of Radu Florescu, who along with Raymond McNally discovered the link between Vlad Țepeș and Bram Stoker's Count Dracula, which they first published in the book *In Search of Dracula: A True History of Dracula and Vampire Legends* (1972).

Bloodsucking Cinema

Starz. Oct 26, 2007. Film/History. D/W: Barry Gray. C: Uwe Boll, Cheech Marin, John Carpenter, Everett Burrell, Corey Haim, Harry Jay Knowles, Kristanna Loken, David S. Goyer, John Landis, Leonard Maltin, Gregory Nicotero. USA: English/Color/56m. Insight Film Studios/Vamp Productions.

Explores the origins and birth of the vampire, and its evolution into Hollywood as one of the silver screen's most enduring characters.

Bookmark – "The Vampire's Life"

BBC One. Oct 20, 1993. Culture/Literature. D/W: Anand Tucker. C: Anne Rice, Stan Rice, Bill Murphy, Alice Borchardt, Karen O'Brien, Gertrude Helwig, Michael Riley, Chris Rice. UK: English/Color/46m. Oxford Television Company/BBC Lionheart Television/Lifetime Television.

Anne Rice became a household name after the publication of *Interview with the Vampire,* her groundbreaking first novel that was inspired by real events in her personal life. This documentary takes a look at Rice before she became a writer, as told by the author, her family, and her friends. Narrated by Neville Watchurst.

Anne Rice's writing is heavily influenced by her upbringing in New Orleans; she was raised in a deeply religious family that still held a strong belief in the supernatural. Through various interview clips we get a glimpse into her formative years, from the Garden District in New Orleans to the Haight-Ashbury neighborhood of San Francisco. Heartbreaking at times, this is a compelling and deeply personal look into the events that influenced her first book—including the death of her daughter Michelle, who was the inspiration behind the vampire child Claudia.

Released on video as *Anne Rice – Birth of the Vampire.* In 1994 it was bestowed with a BAFTA (British Film & TV Academy) award for best arts documentary.

Books into Film – "Anne Rice"

Bravo. 2006 (S01E14). Film/Literature. D: Chris Krieger. W: Lori Jansen, Jenny Steele, Carey Roberts, Michael Tobin. C: Anne Rice, Elizabeth Miller. CAN: English/Color/25m. Pyramid Productions Inc./Chum Television.

Series examines the journey of classic and contemporary literature from the page to the screen. This episode features the adapted novels of Anne Rice, and showcases the films *Interview with the Vampire* (1994), *Queen of the Damned* (2002), and *Exit to Eden* (1994). Hosted by Judy Gabriel.

Cheaply made, this episode is comprised almost entirely of old, rehashed press junket clips, most of poor quality, and really suffers by not including interviews from the creators behind these films. Anne Rice gives her own take on these adaptations; only *Interview with the Vampire* was endorsed by her, and she provides some frank statements about the other box office disasters. Yet the program just becomes a forum for Rice to vent about these terrible films; her words may be justified, but there's no one to counterbalance her opinion. She hopes to be more involved in the creative process for any future adaptions, the next of which may be based on her first Christian novel, *Christ the Lord: Out of Egypt*.

Cake Boss – "Coffins, Costumes and a Cake on a Gurney"

TLC. Oct 31, 2011 (S04E32). Culture/Reality. D: Anon. W: Anon. C: Buddy Valastro, Mauro Castano, Danny Dragone, Joey Faugno, Frankie Amato Jr., Ralph Attanasia, Lisa Valastro, Mary Sciarrone. USA: English/Color/21m. High Noon Entertainment/Discovery Communications.

Reality series that follows Buddy Valastro and *la Famiglia* at Carlo's Bakery in Hoboken, New Jersey. In this episode, as Halloween approaches, Buddy often gets a few odd requests—and this year is no exception. One client needs a life-sized coffin, complete with a resting corpse inside, and the body has to bleed when bitten.

This special cake is requested by Betty, a self-proclaimed vampire who needs it for an official induction ceremony. It's clear from the outset that Buddy and his crew don't take her too seriously, yet they do put in a serious effort to fulfill her request. Betty is obviously a role player, and her attempt to be taken seriously is hampered upon the arrival of her vampire pals; they hiss and bare fangs to the camera, which looks quite odd in the middle of a bakery. The cake is delivered to a cemetery at night; unfortunately, Betty's induction ceremony looks completely staged, as if the television production team had a hand in the presentation of the event. Nevertheless, the coffin cake looks amazing!

Cities of the Underworld – "Dracula's Underground"

History. Jul 9, 2007 (S01E11). History/Mystery. D: Anne Etheridge. W: Sean Dash. C: Don Wildman, Vadim Bondar, Gabrielle Constantin, Petra Diaconescu, Monica Findlay, Dona Matache. USA: English/Color/45m. Authentic Entertainment Inc./Thirty Four Productions.

Host Don Wildman visits the locations linked to Vlad "The Impaler" Țepeș, and heads underground to explore hidden caves, hideouts, tombs and tunnels. He separates fact from fiction, and discusses the infamous fifteenth century prince and his lasting legacy to the region.

An entertaining yet melodramatic look at Vlad Țepeș, which accurately presents the real history of the man, and the locations associated with his life. Interesting locales include a massive salt mine, and an extensive network of subterranean caves that run throughout Romania.

The Conspiracy Show

VisionTV. 2011 (S01E13). Folklore/History. D: Jalal Merhi. W: Richard Syrett, Ron Craig. C: Seán Manchester, Rosemary Ellen Guiley, Joe Nickell, Neil Arnold. CAN: English/Color/22m. Film One/TFC.

It is often the case that, behind a myth, there is a sliver of truth—so what of the vampire? Could there really have been a creature such as this, which fed on human blood? This episode explores vampire facts versus fiction, and the infamous Highgate Vampire case of the 1970s. Hosted by Richard Syrett.

Creepy Canada – "Belle Island Hag" / "Empress Theatre" / "Wilno Vampire" / "The Olde Angel Inn" / "Magnetic Hill" / "Mather-Walls House"

OLN. Dec 9, 2003 (S02E07). Folklore/History. D: William P. Burke, Larry Santos. W: Matthew Hood. C: Hendry Crane, Gerard Gibbs, Samantha Ling, Cathy Brady, Tim Davidson. CAN: English/B&W, Color/47m. Eyebeam Media/Creepy Canada Inc.

Paranormal documentary series covering historical supernatural happenings across Canada, which expanded in the third season to include other spooky locales in the United States. The segment "Wilno Vampire" explores the lore tied to this rural Ontario village, founded by Kashubian (Polish) immigrants in 1858. Yet the tale itself—about a turn of the century newlywed who committed suicide and returned as a vampire to feed on her loved ones—seems to be a fictional account based on the (now much-disputed) findings first reported by folklorist Jan Perkowski in the pages of his infamous study, "Vampires, Dwarves, and Witches Among the Ontario Kashubs" (1972). *Creepy Canada* was hosted by Terry Boyle, with narration by David Pritchard. When rebroadcast in the United States, the series was rebranded as *Hauntings and Horrors*. The "Wilno Vampire" segment was incorporated into the DVD compilation *Alien Creatures From Beyond: Monsters, Ghosts and Vampires,* repackaged and retooled in the vein of contemporary paranormal investigation series.

Deadliest Warrior – "Vampires vs. Zombies"

Spike. Sep 14, 2011 (S03E10). History/War. D: David Dale Dryden, David Hogan. W: Anon. C: Richard Machowicz, Geoff Desmoulin, Armand Dorian, Steve Niles, Scott Bowen, Max Brooks, Robert Daly, Matt Mogk. USA: English/Color/43m. 44 Blue Productions/Morningstar Entertainment.

This supernatural-themed episode tries to answer an age-old question: which creatures are the deadliest undead warriors, blood-drinking vampires, or brain-eating zombies? Under the advice of a panel of horror experts, the crew devises a set of characteristics and capabilities for each group—and then sets them loose in an undead showdown for the ages. Narrated by Drew Skye.

For the first time, the excessive blood, gore and violence presented in *Deadliest Warrior* has a legitimate purpose. Let's face it; the next major apocalypse will probably result in this exact scenario, so why not figure out which monster will win? To level the playing field, the vampires are outnumbered sixty-three to one, yet even this massive zombie horde fails to stop the fanged and furious.

📺 One vampire "expert" perpetuates the myth that Bram Stoker's immortal creation was based on the warlord Vlad Țepeș. Don't believe a word of it!

Deadly Women – "Obsession"

Discovery Channel. Feb 8, 2005 (S01E01). Crime/History. D/W: Christopher Thorburn. C: Dennis Báthory-Kitsz, Candice DeLong, Janis Amatuzio, Michael Kelleher, Kalila Smith, Gregg Olsen, Georgina Anderson ♀. USA: English/Color/44m. Beyond Productions.

Elizabeth Báthory is profiled along with three other female serial killers, each of whom had an obsession that drove them to murder. Their lofty positions in society allowed for their crimes to be kept under wraps; that is, until it was far too late for their victims. Narrated by Marsha Crenshaw.

Often melodramatic, this episode sheds some light onto a group of female mass murderers, most of whom are outside of the public radar. The real draw is Elizabeth Báthory, the most infamous of the lot, and the story of Dennis Báthory-Kitsz is an interesting one. He believes that he is related to the Blood Countess, and his journey takes him from the United States to Slovakia. On behalf of his family line, he apologizes for her crimes, and officially reconciles with the descendants of her victims. In a setting most appropriate, the group shares a meal at the Pizzeria Báthory in Čachtice.

📺 Dennis Báthory-Kitsz is an Elizabeth Báthory aficionado; his opera about her life, Erzsébet, premiered in Vermont in 2011.

Disappeared – "Dancing Into Darkness"

Discovery Channel. Jan 16, 2012 (S04E12). Crime/Mystery. D: Anon. W: Anon. C: Melissa Hines, Jill Morley, Floyd Merchant, James Ridgeway, Glenn Kenny, John Rhein, Steve Rogers. USA: English/Color/44m. Peacock Productions/Discovery Communications.

Former *Village Voice* reporter Susan Walsh was thirty-six years old when she vanished from Nutley, New Jersey on July 16, 1996; now a cold case, her friends and family still wonder what happened. Did she leave on her own accord, or was she abducted? Could it have something to do with her investigations into a vampire cult, or the Russian Mob? Narrated by Christopher Walker.

The disappearance of Susan Walsh last received national attention on *Unsolved Mysteries* in 1997, and there have been no new leads since then. Her cold case file was reopened in 2005; all the evidence was re-examined, yet nothing substantial was found. Although this production once again brings attention to her case, it presents nothing new, and essentially rehashes everything from the 1997 report. There's little mention of Walsh's research into the vampire subculture; however, it's revealed that her investigation was triggered by a report that claimed a cult of vampires was stealing blood from New York City hospitals (something the 1997 production neglected to mention).

Dracula: Fact and Fiction

HIC. Nov 29, 2007. Culture/History. D/W: Adam Sternberg. C: Roger Corman, Elizabeth Miller, J. Gordon Melton, Radu Florescu, Margaret Carter, Joe De Francesco. USA: English/B&W, Color/25m. Lucasfilm Ltd./JAK Films Inc.

The vampire of folklore kept to the shadows. It was a myth that was created to help explain the unexplainable, but that all ended once Bram Stoker introduced a romanticized version to the Western world. Narrated by John Parsons.

Since the publication of *Dracula* in 1897, vampires have become integrated into popular culture worldwide. In this program, scholars discuss the historical Dracula, Vlad Țepeș, and his influence on Bram Stoker's infamous creation. This short documentary skillfully separates fact from fiction, and does an excellent job of clearing up the most common misconceptions that continue to plague other productions.

Included on the *Young Indian Jones* DVD set (Volume 3, Disc 2) as part of the special features for "Masks of Evil" ("Chapter 17, Istanbul/Transylvania 1918").

Dracula: The True Story

Syndicated. 1997. Folklore/History. D/W: Matthias Kessler. C: Dan Berindei, Raymond McNally, Brianna Caradja, Christian Reiter, Herbert Hönigsmann, Paul Daian, Roman Polanski, Steve Barton. GER: English & German/Color/44m. Langbein & Skalnik TV.

A century has passed since the initial publication of Bram Stoker's *Dracula,* and the book's popularity has resulted in a thriving, undead tourism industry in Romania. From the Dracula Hotel at Borgo Pass, to Dracula's sexy playmates at a vampire-themed club, bloodsuckers are a hot commodity; they've even infected the country's national hero, Vlad Țepeș, whose face adorns countless kitschy souvenirs.

This excellent documentary focuses on the real Dracula, Vlad Țepeș, and his legendary exploits against the Turks—as well as his own people. His life and times are illustrated through clips from several films, including: *Nosferatu, eine Symphonie des Grauens* (1922); *Vlad Țepeș* (1979); and *Bram Stoker's Dracula* (1992). Experts also discuss the real medical conditions that could have inspired local vampire folklore.

Dracula's Bram Stoker

RTE1. Mar 4, 2003. Literature/History. D/W: Sinead O'Brien. C: Christopher Lee, Neil Jordan, Donald Sinden, Roy Foster, Owen Killian, Caitríona Ní Mhurchú, Patrick Sutton, David Norris. IRL: English/Color/52m. Ferndale Films/NRK-TV International.

Takes a look at the complex life of Bram Stoker, one of Ireland's most elusive authors, and the events that may have influenced his masterpiece, *Dracula.* Narrated by John Hurt.

Encounters: The Hidden Truth – "New England Vampires"

FOX. Mar 19, 1995 (S02E--). Culture/News. D: John Jopson. W: Anon. C: Michael Bell. USA: English/Color/60m.

This magazine-style series explores subjects outside of traditional science, such as hauntings, the supernatural, aliens, and other unexplained phenomena. This episode includes a purported tale of vampires in New England. Hosted by John Marshall.

Explorer – "Vampire Forensics"

NGC. Feb 23, 2010 (S24E12). Folklore/Mystery. D: Gareth Harvey. W: Gareth Harvey, Max Salomon. C: Matteo Borrini, Eric Nuzum, Michael Bell, Bill Rodriguez. USA: English/Color/46m. National Geographic Society/National Geographic Television.

A team excavates a sixteenth century mass grave in Venice, and discovers a skull with a brick inserted between the jaws. Was this part of an ancient, macabre ritual meant to kill a vampire?

Forensic anthropologist Matteo Borrini attempts to put a face to this "Vampire of Venice," who may be tied to the hysteria surrounding the Black Plague of 1575. Narrated by Peter Coyote.

This beautiful-looking documentary tells the year-long tale of Matteo Borrini's investigation into this five-hundred-year-old mystery: was the victim really a vampire, or just another Venetian who fell to the Black Plague? Unfortunately, this search for the truth won't be of much interest to anyone outside of those who enjoy science or anthropology. The find itself was a sensation in 2006, but this behind-the-scenes look at the quest for answers is bloody boring; it would have benefited from more interviews and less narration. Borrini discovers that the mysterious corpse was definitely not a vampire; it was a female, sixty to seventy years of age, and aside from living much longer than most women in Venice during that period, there's nothing else remarkable about her. What of the brick inserted into her mouth? Chalk this one up to superstitions of the past; locals believed that the cause of the epidemic was a "shroud eater," a creature that fed on buried corpses and then rose from the earth to infect the living—so the brick was inserted to prevent her from eating. For a far more engaging take on a similar subject, check out the episode "Mysteries of the Vampire Skeletons" from the long-running UK series *Revealed*.

Faces of Evil

TNT. April 6, 2000. History/Occult. D: Phil Tuckett. W: Phil Tuckett. C: Andrew Delbanco, Peter Cooper, John Douglas, Poppy Z. Brite, Mark Edmundson, Marilyn Manson, Molefi Kete Asante, Peter Levenda, John Carpenter, Emanuel Milingo, Laurel Geller. USA: English/Color/70m. Bristlecone Films/Turner Network Television.

This documentary is an investigation into the devil and the nature of evil, exploring both historical accounts, and fictional examples found in literature, film, and music. The wide range of perspectives include musician Marilyn Manson (*Antichrist Superstar*), author Poppy Z. Brite (*Lost Souls*), and filmmaker John Carpenter (*Vampires*). Narrated by Malcolm McDowell.

Fang vs. Fiction: The Real Underworld of Vampires and Werewolves

AMC. Sep 17, 2003. Film/Folklore. D/W: David Grabias. C: J. Gordon Melton, Daniel Cohen, Brad Steiger, Katherine Ramsland, Nicolae Paduraru, Gypsy Zanval, David Farrant, Kalila Smith, Freddie Salazar, Linda Godfrey, Crudelia. USA: English/Color/48m. Artifact Studios.

Experts explore the dark side of history, and separate fact from fiction as they deconstruct the legends of vampires and werewolves—creatures that have been reported in practically every culture on the planet. This promotional documentary for the film *Underworld* (2003) also features a number of clips from classic monster movies. Narrated by Tatiana Yassukovich.

This entry should be avoided by everyone, with the hope that it will eventually disappear and be lost to history. Buried within this factually inaccurate sham of a production are elements of a real documentary, and I'm sure that the experts interviewed believed that they were taking part in one. The line between fact and fiction is completely erased; movie mythology that the narrator describes from *Underworld* is fully entwined with the words of experts as they discuss historical folklore and real science. This makes it appear as though everyone is talking about the same thing, as if the scholars actually support the theory of an eternal struggle between werewolves and vampires (taking place in the shadows, over centuries). Then there are the interviews with "real" vampires and werewolves, who only come off as glorified role players, and lend no credence to the actual subcultures that they supposedly represent. This production should technically be listed under variety programming, because it's not a documentary in any sense of the word. Avoid this mind-numbing mess at all costs!

📺 Originally meant to air as part of AMC's *Monsterfest* 2003 on Halloween weekend, the documentary was instead broadcast earlier, in order to promote the theatrical release of *Underworld*.

Flesh and Blood: The Hammer Heritage of Horror

BBC One. Aug 6/14, 1994 (2 Episodes). History/Film. D/W: Ted Newsom. C: Roy Ward Baker, James Bernard, Martine Beswicke, Veronica Carlson, Michael Carreras, Hazel Court, Joe Dante. UK/USA: English/B&W, Color/100m. Heidelberg Films/BBC.

🦇 🦇 🦇 🦇

Hammer Film Productions has made films from all genres, which have played in practically every country in the world, but it's their iconic images of horror and terror for which they're best remembered. This documentary explores the history of the studio with a focus on the *Dracula* and *Frankenstein* franchises, and the string of sequels that each film produced. Features new and archival interviews with many of the key players, including writers, directors and actors, who reflect on the importance of one of the world's most influential film studios. Narrated by Peter Cushing and Christopher Lee.

An excellent program geared towards anyone interested in the history of Hammer Film Productions, or horror filmmaking in general. It's a very detailed look at the films that the studio produced, and includes some great interviews with many people who have since passed away. Produced in 1994, this documentary often asks if Hammer Film Productions will ever return, because by that point, the company had been on hiatus for almost a decade. Indeed, the studio has returned from the grave, but it wasn't until 2008 with their production of the web-based series *Beyond the Rave*.

📺 This was Peter Cushing's last project and final collaboration with longtime friend Christopher Lee. Cushing passed away in August 1994, three months after recording the narration.

FRONTLINE/World – "Cambodia, Pol Pot's Shadow" / "Romania, My Old Haunts" / "India, Hole in the Wall"

PBS. Oct 31, 2002 (S01E02). Education/History. D: Marian Marzynski. W: Andrei Codrescu. C: Andrei Codrescu, Mircea Dinescu, Nicolae Marinescu, Vadim Tudor, Maria Campina. USA: English, Romanian/Color/60m. WGBH Boston.

In "Romania, My Old Haunts," journalist Andrei Codrescu returns to his homeland thirteen years after the downfall of dictator Nicolae Ceaușescu; he finds a post-Communist nation immersed in capitalism, yet still struggling with the freedom that it brings. He explores how the historical ruler Vlad Țepeș has been reimagined through Western eyes as Count Dracula, a vampire who has returned from the dead to promote Romanian tourism.

In this excellent short documentary, former poet Andrei Codrescu witnesses first-hand the changing face of Romania. From the emerging hip-hop scene to young women learning English (and exotic dancing), this program is a fascinating and often disparaging look at how locals are adjusting to their new found freedoms—with some faring better than others. From Club Dracula, Dracula's Castle, and the Dracula Travel Agency, see how liberty has led to a new breed of monster that's terrorizing the Romanian landscape.

Ghost & Vampire Legends of Rhode Island

PBS. Oct 26, 2002. History/Folklore. D: Scott Saracen. W: Maria Patsias. C: Michael Bell, Charles Turek Robinson, Christopher Rondina, Eleyne Austen Sharp, Harle Tinney, Virginia Smith. USA: English/Color/60m. 3rd Story Productions.

From ghosts, to spirits and vampires, the Ocean State has a colorful supernatural past. From one of the most infamous vampires in America to the Princess Augusta Ghost Ship and the elusive specters of Benefit Street, the folklore of Rhode Island runs deep with the undead. Experts uncover the chilling facts behind the local legends of Mercy Brown, Nellie Vaughn and Sarah Tillinghast, and explore the haunted histories of Belcourt Castle and the Inn at Shadow Lawn.

Ghost Hunters International – "Dracula's Castle"

SyFy. Aug 20, 2008 (S01E14). History/Fantasy. D: Dave Hobbes. W: Anon. C: Robb Demarest, Andy Andrews, Barry Fitzgerald, Brandy Green, Dustin Pari, David Baxter, Irene Bede. USA: English/B&W, Color/44m. Alan David Management/Pilgrim Films and Television Inc.

The GHI team travels to Romania to investigate the supernatural goings-on at Poenari Castle, which is north of the city of Curtea de Argeș. Nicknamed "Dracula's Castle," this was a fortress constructed in the fifteenth century by warlord Vlad Țepeș, who expanded existing ruins that were built two hundred years earlier. Purported to be one of the most haunted places on Earth, the team stays overnight in the castle to find any proof that can back up this claim.

In a series that at times feels like *Bill and Ted's Excellent Paranormal Adventure,* a group of twentysomethings travel the world to explore the supernatural hot spots, and utilize a "scientific" approach in their investigations. This equates to non-scientists using techno-gadgets to measure things that humans can't normally see or hear, over a time period of such a limited scope that no real conclusions can ever be made. The result is a sequence of melodramatic segments where the team sees or hears something that the audience does not; this is often revealed to be nothing at all, or simply an odd occurrence they deem "supernatural" just because it can't be explained. Poor old Vlad Țepeș isn't held in high regard; the team constantly mispronounces his name, and they only focus on his atrocities, even though he's considered a national hero to Romanians. The spirits were often asked to present themselves, but nothing ever came to pass; this is understandable, because the team was speaking English. Had they spoken Romanian, the ghosts would have understood what the heck they wanted.

In an earlier episode, the GHI team investigated the historic Citadel Rasnov; they briefly touched on Vlad Țepeș, and his favorite form of torture—impalement.

Great Books – "Dracula"

TLC. Oct 30, 1999. Culture/History. D/W: Trish Mitchell. C: David J. Skal, Elizabeth Miller, James V. Hart, Nina Auerbach, Leonard Wolf, Barbara Belford, Donald Sutherland. USA: English/Color/50m. The Cronkite Ward Company/Discovery Communications Inc.

This overview of the classic novel is illustrated with clips from the films *Nosferatu, eine Symphonie des Grauens* (1922), *Count Dracula* (1977) and *Bram Stoker's Dracula* (1992), as well as Victorian-era drawings and other visual media. Scholars put the story in context with the time in which it was written, and speculate how Stoker's personal life played a role in creating the tale. Interviews with modern-day vampires, who haunt nightclubs instead of cemeteries, illustrate the novel's impact on modern popular culture. Narrated by Donald Sutherland.

This is an excellent introduction to the novel, one of the better attempts to dissect the story to examine the subtext lurking below the surface. Its impact on the Goth subculture is illustrated through interviews with modern sanguinists; they tend to come off as cliquey and pretentious, and most likely don't reflect the attitude of the community as a whole.

This documentary clearly states a fact that has been lost in most film adaptations: Dracula was *not* staked by Van Helsing, or anyone else for that matter. Jonathan Harker sliced open his throat, as Quincey Morris plunged a knife into his heart.

Halloween Wars – "Zombies vs. Vampires"

Food Network. Oct 16, 2011 (S01E03). Culture/Reality. D: Anon. W: Anon. C: Shinmin Li, Miles Teves, Rob Zombie. USA: English/Color/43m. Television Food Network G.P.

In this scrumptiously horrific reality series, five teams attempt to win over the judges with exotic, spooky desserts; the winners will bring home a cool $50,000. In this episode, the three remaining teams must depict an ultimate (and tasty!) battle between vampires and zombies. Hosted by Justin Willman.

Now that producers are officially running out of ideas for reality series, we're starting to see cheaply-made shows like this one, with judges you've never heard of (except for, perhaps, each week's celebrity guest). Each team is comprised of a pumpkin carving expert, a candy craftsman, and a cake artist. These confectionery connoisseurs are indeed skilled artists, but considering their overwrought demeanor (and the faux drama added through editing), you'd think they were struggling to find a cure for cancer. The series would be forgettable were it not for some of the more macabre creations, and this episode features an amazing shadowbox presentation of a Marie Antoinette-era vampire facing off against a decaying zombie.

Hammer: The Studio That Dripped Blood!

BBC Two. Jun 26, 1987. History/Film. D/W: Nick Jones, David Thompson. C: Martin Scorsese, Peter Cushing, Christopher Lee, Anthony Hinds, Michael Carreras, Jimmy Sangster, Aida Young, David Pirie, Don Sharp, James Bernard, James Carreras, Ingrid Pitt. UK: English/B&W, Color/50m. BBC.

In honor of the thirtieth anniversary of *The Curse of Frankenstein* (1957), this documentary explores the history of Hammer Film Productions, and includes cast and crew interviews with those who made some of the studio's most memorable movies. Features clips from the films *Horror of Dracula* (1958), *Dracula Prince of Darkness* (1966), and *The Vampire Lovers* (1970). Narrated by Charles Gray.

Hammer was encouraged to produce more horror films with the success of *The Quatermass Xperiment* (1955). With *The Curse of Frankenstein,* they resurrected the celebrated movie monster—and the rest is history. This excellent documentary gives insight into the inner workings of Hammer Film Productions, its knack for stretching a budget, and its ability to transform Bray Studios—originally a small but stately country home—into whatever the script demanded.

To cut costs, Hammer filmed four movies back to back that shared many of the same sets and cast members: *Rasputin the Mad Monk; The Reptile; Dracula Prince of Darkness;* and *The Plague of the Zombies.*

HBO First Look – "Blood Lines: Dracula – The Man, The Myth, The Movies"

HBO. 1992 (S01E--). Film/History. D: Jeff Werner. W: Kincaid Jones. C: Francis Ford Coppola, Gary Oldman, Donald A. Reed, James V. Hart, Anthony Hopkins, Keanu Reeves, Norine Dresser, Winona Ryder, Michael Ballhaus. USA: English/Color/30m. Columbia Pictures.

To promote upcoming movies, this series offers a behind-the-scenes look at feature film production. In this episode, the cast and crew of *Bram Stoker's Dracula* (1992) discuss the movie, their roles, and the enduring legend of the Count. Alternately titled "Making *Bram Stoker's Dracula*" and "Bloodlines: Making Coppola's *Dracula*."

This interesting chronology begins inside Sony Studios, where Francis Ford Coppola attends an early pre-production meeting. It then takes an unfiltered look at the movie making process, and features candid interviews with the creative minds behind the production. With a focus on actor meetings, preparations, and early rehearsals, many will be turned off by the lack of glamor; but those interested in filmmaking will really enjoy this journey.

Rebroadcast in the UK (BBC, January 30 1993), this documentary was also included in the 1999 DVD release for the feature film.

Heartstoppers: Horror at the Movies

Syndicated. Oct 31, 1992. History/Horror. D: Steve Purcell. W: Mitchell Barry. C: John Landis, Wes Craven, Rick Baker, Samuel Z. Arkoff, Charles Band, Tom Woodruff, George Romero, Forrest J Ackerman, Cassandra Peterson. USA: English/B&W, Color/93m. Riverstreet Productions.

This look at the history of horror movies shines a spotlight onto the creative teams behind many of Hollywood's most well-known productions, including the classic Universal monster movies. Noteworthy segments feature the work of special effects master Rick Baker, the contributions of Forrest J Ackerman, the gimmicks of William Castle, and the B-movie productions of Samuel Z. Arkoff. Hosted by George Hamilton.

This beautiful mess of a documentary retains some nostalgic value, and George Hamilton does his best with the poorly-scripted host segments. There is a lot of interesting content, including an interview with Forrest J Ackerman at his Ackermansion, but there's way too much filler. Despite the many faults, this production gets high marks for showcasing the brilliant (and often peculiar) creative minds that work behind the scenes to bring these horrors to life. Several vampire films are featured, including: *Nosferatu, eine Symphonie des Grauens* (1922); *Dracula* (1931); *The Vampire Bat* (1933); *Horror of Dracula* (1958); *Love at First Bite* (1979); *Transylvania Twist* (1989); *Innocent Blood* (1992); *Bram Stoker's Dracula* (1992); and *Buffy the Vampire Slayer* (1992).

Hidden – "World's Bloodiest Dungeons"

Travel Channel. Oct 31, 2001 (S01E04). Culture/History. D: Anon. W: Anon. C: Dennis Báthory-Kitsz. UK: English/Color/60m. London Weekend Television.

Part of "Haunted Travels Week," this episode features a trip to Čachtice Castle in Slovakia, once home to the infamous serial killer Elizabeth Báthory.

Hideous Crime – "Vampire Killers"

Channel 5. May 6, 2003 (S01E01). Crime/Culture. D: Adam Murch. W: Penny Chimes. C: Tessa Mayes, Gavin Baddeley. UK: English/Color/60m. Sky News.

This documentary miniseries explores murderous crimes in Great Britain and Germany, and the focus of this episode is "vampire" offenses. The first segment concerns troubled Welsh teenager Matthew Hardman; he stabbed an elderly woman to death, removed her heart, and drank her blood. The second segment tells the story of Daniel and Manuela Ruda, a mentally unstable couple that role-played as vampires; they killed a friend and drank his blood. Were these killings simply the result of disturbed individuals, or can a subculture be held responsible for negatively influencing young minds?

A History of Horror with Mark Gatiss

BBC Four. Oct 11/18/25, 2010 (3 Episodes). Culture/Film. D: John Das, Rachel Jardine. W: Mark Gatiss. C: Carla Laemmle, Sara Karloff, Gloria Stuart, John Carpenter, Jimmy Sangster, Barbara Steele, Roger Corman, Barbara Shelley, Roy Ward Baker, George A. Romero, Tobe Hooper. UK: English/B&W, Color/180m. BBC.

🦇 🦇 🦇

Mark Gatiss—actor, screenwriter, and lover of all things macabre—explores the three greatest eras in horror filmmaking. The first episode, "Frankenstein Goes to Hollywood," begins with the silent film era and *The Phantom of the Opera* (1925), and traces the careers of horror pioneers Lon Chaney, Boris Karloff and Bela Lugosi. In part two, "Home Counties Horror," Gatiss travels to the birthplace of Gothic tradition and the films of Hammer Film Productions, which created a groundbreaking mix of gore, wit and sexuality. The final episode, "The American Scream," finds Gatiss back in the United States, where he explores the third great era that began with *Psycho* (1960) and ended with *Halloween* (1978).

Presented in the same manner as Christopher Frayling and his exploration of Dracula in *Nightmare: The Birth of Horror* (1996), Gatiss travels the globe to reveal his list of the standout horror movies made from 1925 through 1978. He fully admits that this is a biased account of the history of horror films, yet the personal nature of the journey makes up for the fact that it doesn't thoroughly cover the subject. The highlights include: a look at Lon Chaney's actual makeup kit; one of the vampire bat props used in *Dracula* (1931); and a charming short tribute to Hammer mainstay Peter Cushing. It's a love letter to classic horror filmmaking; with the genre now reduced to "torture porn" and over the top gore, this series is a wonderful look back to when these types of films were actually respectable.

Hollywood and The Stars - "Monsters We've Known and Loved"

NBC. Jan 13, 1964 (S01E--). Comedy/History. D: Jack Haley, Jr. W: Draper Lewis, Jack Haley, Jr., Al Ramrus. C: Joseph Cotten. USA: English/B&W/25m. United Artists Television/Wolper Productions.

Early television documentary series about Tinseltown, its movies, and its star talent. This episode takes a look back at some of the nightmare creatures that have invaded Hollywood—including vampires, ghouls, and werewolves! Beginning with horrors of the silent era, narrator Joseph Cotten takes us on an affectionate (and often humorous) tour that also covers the Universal monsters, mad doctors, atomic-age creatures, and things from other worlds. Includes film clips showcasing the many faces of Lon Chaney and Boris Karloff, as well as John Barrymore, Bela Lugosi, Vincent Price, and Peter Lorre.

A wonderful, tongue-in-cheek overview of classic silver screen terrors, which features a compilation of great clips for the monster lover in all of us. This short-lived documentary series included episodes covering comedians, gangster films, the Oscars, and swashbuckler pictures—as well as others that focused on stars like Humphrey Bogart, Rita Hayworth, Al Jolson, and Bing Crosby.

Hollywood Chronicles – "The Nightmare Factory"

Discovery Channel. Oct 30, 1989 (S01E09). Culture/Film. D: James Forsher. W: Laurie Jacobson. C: Forrest J Ackerman, Samuel Z. Arkoff, Roger Corman. USA: English/B&W, Color/23m. James Forsher Productions Inc./Facets Entertainment Group.

An ambitious series that covers ninety years of Tinseltown history over twenty-six episodes. This outing offers a short overview of the history of Hollywood horror films, from the early 1900s through the present day. Features clips from silent movies and early talkies, as well as a segment about Bela Lugosi and *Dracula* (which includes newsreel footage of the actor). Hosted by Jackie Cooper.

From within the walls of Hollywood's legendary Magic Castle, the host narrates this brief yet authoritative look at the evolution of creature features. Modern-day terrors are given some mention, but the primary focus is early horror and supernatural films through the drive-in classics of the 1950s and 1960s. Features several actors who brought these creatures to life, including Lon Chaney, Boris Karloff, Claude Rains, Peter Lorre and John Carradine. Special mention is given to Bela Lugosi; his iconic performance as Dracula ignited his film career, yet it was ultimately a curse that affected both his professional and personal life. It's an interesting look at early Hollywood, and is a fitting introduction to the genre; those looking for more should check out the excellent AMC documentary *Monster Mania* (1997).

The Horror of It All

PBS. Feb 23, 1983. Culture/Film. D/W: Gene Feldman. C: Rouben Mamoulian, Roger Corman, John Carradine, Robert Bloch, Curtis Harrington, Gloria Stuart, Herman Cohen, Dana Andrews, Martine Beswicke, David Del Valle. USA: English/B&W, Color/59m. Wombat Productions Inc.

🦇 🦇 🦇 🦇

We've become well versed in the language of horror, thanks to folklore, books, comics, and most importantly, motion pictures. This program documents the history of horror movies, from the early silent productions through the recent spate of splatter films. Features interviews with writers, actors and directors who helped bring these tales to life, and includes clips from *Nosferatu, eine Symphonie des Grauens* (1922), *Dracula* (1931) and *Horror of Dracula* (1958). Narrated by José Ferrer.

Released into the home video market as *The Hollywood Collection: The Horror of It All,* this fantastic documentary should be required viewing for all Film Lit classes. It features a number of interviews with those intimately familiar with the genre, who offer up their own take on horror filmmaking—and reveal charming anecdotes along the way. Many relay a sense of disillusionment towards the current state of horror films, which have become explicit, violent and bloody. They hope the genre reverts back to a time when these movies were filled with wonder, fantasy and terror. I couldn't agree more!

Hot Type – "Queen of Vampire Lit: Anne Rice in New Orleans"

Newsworld. Oct 29, 2000 (S04E04). Culture/Literature. D: Anon. W: Evan Solomon. C: Anne Rice. CAN: English/Color/18m. CBC.

🦇 🦇 🦇

With the publication of *Merrick,* the seventh book in Anne Rice's "Vampire Chronicles" series, host Evan Solomon travels to New Orleans to chat with the author about vampires, sexuality and pornography—as well as her recent reconciliation with the Catholic Church. Features clips from movies based on her books, including *Interview with the Vampire* (1994) and *Exit to Eden* (1994).

Anne Rice, and her Vampire Chronicles, have been a hot topic of discussion since *Interview with the Vampire* was first published in 1976 (Author Photo)

The pre-interview segment explores the author's life, from her early days in New Orleans and her marriage to Stan Rice, to the death of her daughter Michelle in 1972. The focus then shifts to her career as a successful author; the interview begins with a discussion of *Merrick,* yet it quickly shifts focus to the character of Lestat, as Rice reflects on vampires, immortality, and the nature of evil. The conversation concludes with a discussion of her pornographic work, most notably the *Beauty* series, and how she has returned to Catholicism after over forty years as an atheist.

Hot Type – "Anne Rice: Christ the Lord"

Newsworld. Sep 1, 2005 (S09E08). Culture/Literature. D: Anon. W: Evan Solomon. C: Anne Rice. CAN: English/Color/23m. CBC.

🦇 🦇 🦇

Host Evan Solomon chats with Anne Rice about her new novel, *Christ the Lord: Out of Egypt,* which depicts the life of Jesus Christ as a boy—and is a major departure from her best-selling "Vampire Chronicles" series. The author left the Catholic Church at the age of eighteen and became an atheist, and she discusses her path back to Christianity. Features clips from the films *Jesus Christ Superstar* (1973), *Exit to Eden* (1994) and *Interview with the Vampire* (1994).

Anne Rice laid her vampires to rest with the publication of *Blood Canticle* in 2003. She has since become an evangelist of sorts, and will only use her talents to promote the life and teachings of Jesus Christ. She describes how she slowly regained her faith and rediscovered the Catholic Church, despite her opposition to its stance on certain social issues (including abortion, gay rights and birth control). It's another intimate and engaging conversation between Rice and Solomon, and is an excellent companion piece to their previous *tête-à-tête* from 2000.

📺 Anne Rice publicly renounced the Catholic Church in 2010, stating she could no longer justify being part of a group that is "hostile, disputatious and deservedly infamous." She still retains her faith, and has only abandoned organized religion.

How'd They Do That? – Ep. #4.--

CBS. 1997 (S04E--). Culture/Horror. D: Morris Abraham, Patrick Taulère. W: Bill Paolantonio, Earl Durham, Eric Schotz, Tom Seligson. C: Robert Kurtzman. CAN/USA: English/Color/60m. LMNO Productions/Telepicture Productions/Warner Bros. Television.

Co-hosts Pat O'Brien and Wendy Walsh present topics that range from the silly to the serious: medicine, technology, filmmaking, natural wonders, unusual professions…you name it. This episode highlights KNB Effects Group, a company that created special effects for the film *From Dusk Till Dawn* (1996). The SFX crew demonstrates how several effects were created, including bloodlettings, a dismemberment, and the staking of a vampire.

In Search of... - "Dracula"

NBC. Jun 8, 1977 (S01E16). Culture/History. D: H.G. Stark. W: Jeremy Brink. C: Nikolai Paduraru. USA: English/Color/24m. Alan Landsburg Productions.

Vlad Țepeș and his homeland are forever linked to the most renowned monster of Gothic literature: Count Dracula. Are tales of Vlad's fiendish exploits mere fiction, or are they based in reality? This episode investigates the legend of Dracula through the life of Vlad the Impaler, the fifteenth century prince of Wallachia. Hosted by Leonard Nimoy.

Excellent documentary that delves into the real Vlad Dracula, and takes a balanced look at the atrocities associated with his reign. The host explores the man versus the myth, without the superficial hype that pollutes modern documentaries about the subject. What can be better than a factually-accurate program narrated by Mr. Spock? Features clips from *Nosferatu, eine Symphonie des Grauens* (1922) and stills from various Hammer horror films.

In Search of... - "In Search of Dracula with Jonathan Ross"

ITV. Oct 26, 1996. Culture/History. D: Luke Jeans. W: Mark Tinkler. C: Christopher Lee, Stephanie Beacham, Richard E. Grant, Grace Jones, Jack Palance, Ingrid Pitt, James Herbert, Ken Russell, Bela Lugosi, Jr., Alexandra Caradja, Frank Wheeler, Daniel Farson. UK: English/Color/52m. London Weekend Television.

To mark the one hundredth anniversary of the publication of *Dracula*—which has since been translated into dozens of languages, and adapted into hundreds of movies—host Jonathan Ross takes a satirical look at Bram Stoker's infamous creation. He explores the history of the novel, the inherent eroticism (which was exploited in the movies), and the folklore that influenced the author.

Despite the glaring factual errors, this program is a worthwhile look into the allure of Dracula, and includes some charming interviews with the actors and filmmakers who brought this undead character to life. Features a wide variety of clips from horror films, with a focus on those from Hammer Film Productions.

📺 Michael Ripper has a cameo in one host segment; he appeared in more Hammer films than any other actor, and often portrayed a working-class character.

In Search of History - "The Real Dracula"

History Channel. 1998. Culture/History. D: Anon. W: Charlie Ryan. C: Radu Florescu, Raymond McNally, David J. Skal, J. Gordon Melton. USA: English/Color/47m. FilmRoos Inc./A&E Television Networks.

Venture into the life of the historical Dracula, Vlad Țepeș, the fifteenth century Wallachian warlord. He ruled from a mountain fortress with an iron fist, and had a penchant for impaling his enemies—and often his own countrymen. A hero to some and a horror to others, discover the link between the man and the immortal vampire created by Bram Stoker. Narrated by David Ackroyd.

Incredible Stories – "The Vampire Hunters"

ITV1. Oct 10, 2003 (S01E01). Culture/History. D: Tim Hopewell. W: Anon. C: Anon. UK: English/Color/30m. Granada Television.

A documentary miniseries that examines popular myths and legends. This episode traverses Spain, Transylvania and New England, in search of any scientific truth behind the vampire myths.

The Independent Lens - "Wonder Women! The Untold Story of American Superheroines"

PBS. Apr 15, 2013 (S14E12). Culture/History. D: Kristy Guevara-Flanagan. W: Kristy Guevara-Flanagan , Kelcey Edwards. C: Gloria Steinem, Lynda Carter, Lindsay Wagner, Andy Mangels, Trina Robbins, Jen Stuller, Katie Pineda, Carmela Lane, Kathleen Hanna. USA: English/Color/80m. Vaquera Productions.

This documentary explores the genesis of the fictional comic book heroine Wonder Woman, and her lasting legacy on popular culture. Questioning the inherent contradictions found with such characters, filmmakers presents other superheroines (both real and fictional) who have become positive role models for girls—including Buffy Summers, vampire slayer.

Insomniac with Dave Attell – "Nashville"

Comedy Central. Dec 26, 2002 (S03E04). Comedy/Reality. D: Anon. W: Anon. C: Dave Attell. USA: English/Color/30m. Comedy Central.

American stand-up comedian Dave Attell explores the nightlife in Nashville, Tennessee. He visits an adult bookstore, hangs out with some vampires, and delivers milk in the wee hours of the morning.

Is It Real? – "Vampires"

NGC. Oct 23, 2006 (S02E10). History/Mystery. D/W: Vicky Matthews. C: Don Henrie, Kevyn Settle, Michael Bell, Nicholas Bellantoni, Elizabeth Miller, Moody Mustafa, Seán Manchester, Nicholae Paduraru. USA: English/Color/46m. National Geographic Television and Film.

🦇🦇🦇

This episode explores ancient legends and contemporary culture, to better understand the myths, reality and folklore surrounding vampires. From historical bloodsuckers to modern blood drinkers, various cases of vampirism are deconstructed through the lens of forensic science. Narrated by Ian Gregory.

An interesting documentary that presents facts without too much flare, aside from some re-enactments that include a Dracula character. The program examines Vlad Țepeș, historical tales of vampires in New England, and a 2004 incident in Romania. A hematologist tests modern-day vampire Don Henrie, to see if there is any medical basis for why he craves human blood. Even though he resembles an overly-enthusiastic role player, Henrie comes across as a very well-informed and stable individual—a refreshing change from the posers who tend to be interviewed for these types of productions.

The Jerry Springer Show – Ep. #16.95

Syndicated. Jul 13, 2007 (S16E95). Culture/Reality. D: Anon. W: Anon. C: Jerry Springer. USA: English/Color/60m. NBC Universal Television/Universal TV.

In the segment "Jerry and the Vampire," a young man named Zack travels to the studio within a coffin. He claims to have grown fangs four years earlier, after his vampire girlfriend took a bite out of him.

The Journal – Ep. #1253

CBC. Jan 9, 1987 (S05E--). Arts/Culture. D: Anon. W: Anon. C: Daniel Richler, Richard Ouzounian, Anne Rice. CAN: English/Color/40m. CBC.

This episode explores the story of Count Dracula, which has become an inspiration to countless writers and filmmakers. From a play produced at the Neptune Theatre in Halifax, to recent films such as The Hunger, vampires are now commonplace in popular culture. Includes a clip from Anne Rice, who discusses her recent book, *The Vampire Lestat*. Hosted by Daniel Richler.

Kentucky Teenage Vampires

Channel 5. Nov 4, 1998. Crime/Reality. D: Mark James. W: Anon. C: Rod Ferrell. UK: English/Color/50m. United Productions.

Documents the story of Rod Ferrell, and features an interview with him from death row. He was once the leader of a "vampire cult," and responsible for the brutal murder of his ex-girlfriend's parents in 1996. Includes reaction from residents of Murray, Kentucky, where Ferrell and the group had lived.

Killer Trials: Judgment Day – "The Lesbian Vampire Killers"

ID. Feb 3, 2012 (S01E02). Crime/Culture. D/W: Kim Hogg. C: Stephen Kerin, Pat Glancy, Adrian Gundelach. USA: English/Color/22m. WMR Productions/IMG Entertainment.

True crime series that explores sensational murder cases from across the globe. This episode features the story of Tracey Wigginton, who in 1989 killed Edward Baldock outside a rowing club on the banks of the Brisbane River in Australia. Her three co-accused each claimed the same defense: they were under the "evil spell" of Wigginton, who had vampiric tendencies, and planned the murder so she could drink the man's blood. Narrated by Erik Dellums.

This episode provides a brief overview of the case, and features archival television footage as well as new interviews with those who brought the killer to justice. Wigginton was caught because her ATM card was found in Baldock's shoe; she pled guilty and was given no trial. Of her three co-accused, one was acquitted, while the other two served time and have since been released. After nearly twenty-three years in jail, Tracey Wigginton was granted parole in early 2012—despite the concerns of the original crown prosecutor and some of Tracey's relatives, who all believe she's still a dangerous individual.

Lugosi: The Forgotten King

PBS. Jul 12, 1986. Culture/Film. D: Mark S. Gilman Jr., Dave Stuckey. W: Mark S. Gilman Jr., Dave Stuckey, Forrest J Ackerman. C: Ralph Bellamy, Carroll Borland, John Carradine, Alex Gordon. USA: English/B&W, Color/60m. Operator 13 Productions.

A portrait of horror film star Bela Lugosi, best known for his iconic role in Tod Browning's *Dracula* (1931). Includes clips from this film, as well as *Mark of the Vampire* (1935), *The Return of the Vampire* (1944), *Abbott and Costello Meet Frankenstein* (1948) and *Plan 9 from Outer Space* (1959). Also features a clip from the actor's appearance on the television show *You Asked For It* (1953). Presented by Forrest J Ackerman.

Lost Worlds: The Real Dracula

History. Sep 4, 2006 (S01E10). History/Military. D/W: Shaun Trevisick. C: Mei Trow, Tessa Dunlop, Aryeh Nusbacher, Ed McCann, Nicolae Paduraru, David Baxter, Bogdan Popovici. UK: English/Color/44m. Atlantic Productions.

🦇🦇🦇🦇

Focusing on the *real* Dracula, this documentary examines Vlad Țepeș and his legendary actions on and off the battlefield (and his lasting legacy in modern-day Romania). Experts utilize computer animation to recreate buildings and other fortifications associated with Vlad's reign, many of which still exist in some form to this day—each a symbol of the indelible mark that he left on his country. Narrated by David Robb (UK version) and Corey Johnson (US version).

This fascinating documentary presents facts, not fantasy, and takes a look at Vlad in the context of being a man very much of his times; a brutal yet successful leader who brought order to an unruly land. One of the most unique aspects is the focus on Vlad's legacy, through the recreation of structures built during his time in power, and how these battlements factored into his military campaigns. Highly recommended.

MSNBC Investigates – "Dark Heart, Iron Hand: The Vampire Killers"

MSNBC. Apr 3, 2001 (S01E--). Crime/Culture. D: Anon. W: Anon. C: Brad King, Aphrodite Jones, Al Gussler, Heather Wendorf, Harry Krop, Dana Cooper, Matt Goodman, Candace Hawthorne, Elizabeth McHahon, Charity Keesee, Scott Anderson. USA: English/Color/43m. MSNBC.

🦇 🦇 🦇

In the mid-1990s, outcasts in a small Kentucky town fell under the influence of Rod Ferrell, a teenager who believed that he was a real vampire named "Vassago." Ferrell's ultimate goal was to cross over from man to god, in a ritual that would involve taking a human life. Hosted by John Seigenthaler.

Documents the events that led to the murders of Naomi and Richard Wendorf, whose daughter Heather was Ferrell's ex-girlfriend; she was part of his "vampire cult," and wanted to run away from home. It's clear that Ferrell was an unstable, alienated teen, who immersed himself in dark fantasies; his mother was also into vampirism, and believed that they were both immortal. Except for Wendorf, each member of the group was convicted of a crime associated with the killings, and most of them get a chance to tell their side of the story. The standout interview is with Heather Wendorf, who was legally cleared of any wrongdoing. It is presented in such a way that viewers can judge for themselves as to whether or not the jury made the correct decision in her case.

MSNBC Investigates – "Interview with a Vampire"

MSNBC. Mar 6, 2011 (S11E--). Crime/Culture. D: Andy Webb. W: Edmond Buckley. C: Rod Ferrell, April Lindsey, Sondra Gibson, Jaden Murphy, Heather Wendorf, Jeremy Hueber, Jeff Taylor, Jake Caudill, Candace Hawthorne, Gina Maria Ferrell. UK: English/Color/45m. BearKatt Productions.

🦇 🦇 🦇 🦇

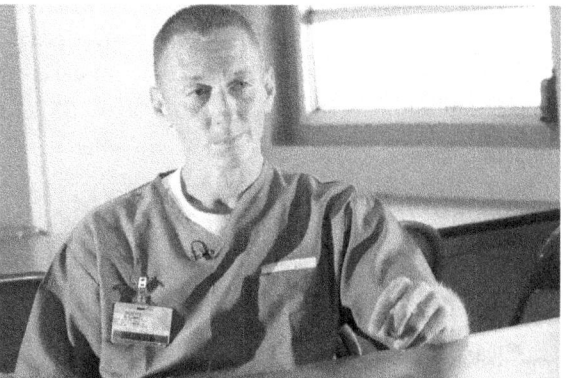

Rod Ferrell reflects on his crimes from inside Florida State Prison on *MSNBC Investigates* - "Interview with a Vampire" (BearKatt Productions/MSNBC)

Fifteen years after he killed his ex-girlfriend's parents, Rod Ferrell, the former leader of a teenage "vampire cult," discusses the brutal double murder he committed in 1996. In an interview from within Florida State Prison, Ferrell reflects on his crimes, his life behind bars, and his dubious status as a sinister celebrity. Includes new interviews with former acquaintances that help illustrate how Ferrell went from a mistreated child to an alienated teen, when reality lost out to dark fantasy and a killer named "Vassago" was born.

Rod Ferrell cites his mother as the root cause for all his troubles; she introduced him to the vampire subculture when he was still a boy. A former friend asserts that Ferrell was repeatedly fed on by the sanguinists in his mother's group, and he claims to have witnessed a human sacrifice. Perhaps these tales are meant to soften how one looks at his heinous crimes, yet it's clear that he did not have a normal childhood. Ferrell now claims that the murders had nothing to do with the occult, or any particular group, and insists that he was just a confused teenager. He's now a changed man on a path to redemption, and married a former nurse in 2010. His mother, with whom Ferrell is no longer in contact, claims that she was a vampire lifestyler and not an advocate; this is in stark contrast to statements she made during her son's trial, when she asserted that they were both "immortal." What of Heather Wendorf, the daughter of the deceased couple, and the only member not convicted of any crime? She declined to be interviewed for this documentary, and only appears in archival footage; she's now married and has a child of her own. It's an intriguing but sad story, the details of which seem to change over time, and it's doubtful we've heard the last from any of those involved. This is an excellent companion piece to the equally first-rate MSNBC documentary from a decade earlier, "Dark Heart, Iron Hand: The Vampire Killers" (2001).

Mad Mad House

SyFy/Space. Mar 4 - Apr 29, 2004 (10 Episodes). Culture/Reality. D: Brian Smith. W: Anon. C: Fiona Horne, Art Aguirre, Iya Ta'Shia Asanti, Don Henrie, David "Avocado" Wolfe, Jamie Ethridge. USA: English/Color/435m. A. Smith & Co. Productions/USA Cable Entertainment.

Ten average people share a house with a group that embraces alternative lifestyles: a vampire, a witch, a modern primitive, a voodoo priestess, and a naturist. Each contestant is judged on their ability to perform different challenges relating to the "alts'" beliefs and practices, and are voted out of the competition if they don't respond suitably to the tests.

A disclaimer states that "the challenges presented to the residents of the house are not necessarily reflective of the actual practices of any particular religion or belief." This makes sense, considering the trials appear to be over-dramatic, made for television nonsense.

Magnificent Obsessions – "Sand Castles" / "Dracula"

Life Network. Nov 5, 2002 (S01E05). Culture/Reality. D: Shereen Jerret, Noah Erenberg. W: Stephen Lawson, Erika MacPherson, Noah Erenberg. C: Marjon Katerberg, Angelique Werner, Johan Roggeman, Elizabeth Miller, Adam Such. CAN: English/Color/22m. Summit Films.

In "Dracula," from the shores of Newfoundland to the streets of Romania, Elizabeth Miller spreads her undying passion for Bram Stoker's immortal tale. But this mild-mannered university professor doesn't just lecture about the novel—she lives it, and travels the globe to present scholarly papers on all things Dracula. For her efforts, she has been honored with the title "Baroness of the Transylvanian Society of Dracula" (a historical-cultural organization based in Bucharest), and is considered a leading expert on the subject.

If you can ignore the distracting camera angles and overt editing tricks that plague this production, you'll discover an entertaining look at the renowned *Dracula* scholar. From her eclectic collection of vampire paraphernalia, to her love of vampire movies and expert knowledge on the subject, Miller infectiously proves that some obsessions can truly be magnificent.

Martina Cole's Lady Killers – "Elizabeth Bathory"

ITV3. Nov 17, 2008 (S01E06). Crime/History. D: Sean Crotty. W: Anon. C: Ingrid Pitt, Karen Krizanovich, Dennis Báthory-Kitsz, Susanna Fiore, Wesley Nike. UK: English/Color/60m. Free @ Last TV.

Six notorious female serial killers are profiled by British crime author Martina Cole; she investigates why women kill, and why it's a surprise to all of us when they do. This episode examines the case of the sixteenth century Hungarian aristocrat Countess Elizabeth Báthory, who was accused of killing upwards of six hundred young women.

MonsterFest 2000: The Classics Come Alive

AMC. Oct 27, 2000. History/Film. D: Anon. W: Anon. C: Whoopie Goldberg, Linda Blair. USA: English/B&W, Color/60m. American Movie Classics.

Co-hosts Whoopie Goldberg and Linda Blair introduce clips from classic films from the 1930s through the 1960s. This anchored a six-day run of monster movies on AMC that included *Dracula* (1931), *Drácula* (Spanish version,1931), *Dracula's Daughter* (1936), *Son of Dracula* (1943), *Return of the Vampire* (1944), *House of Frankenstein* (1944), *House of Dracula* (1945), *Brides of Dracula* (1960) and *Dracula, Prince of Darkness* (1966).

MonsterQuest – "Vampires in America"

History. Aug 6, 2008 (S02E10). History/Mystery. D: Anon. W: Joanna Chejade-Bloom, Joe Danisi. C: Nicholas Bellantoni, Michael Bell, Konstantinos, Katherine Ramsland, Lawrence Ossias, Joy Poulos, Michelle Belanger. USA: English/Color/45m. Whitewolf Entertainment Inc./Bosch Media.

🦇🦇🦇

A modern look at the historical cases of vampirism throughout New England, as well as the legends behind Bram Stoker's fictional Count Dracula. Includes medical tests performed on a sanguinist and a psychic vampire, as a means to scientifically explain the nature of each person's affliction. Narrated by Stan Bernard.

This documentary suspiciously revisits many of the same ideas first presented in the "Vampires" episode from the NGC series *Is It Real?* (2006). However, it delves further into the historical case of "J.B.," a Connecticut man whose unmarked grave was disturbed shortly after his death; his remains were mutilated in a way befitting one suspected of vampirism. The program also explores the fictional Dracula, but breaks no new ground and rehashes nonsense about Bram Stoker and the inspiration behind his immortal Count. A sanguinist undergoes hematological testing, and in several unintentionally humorous segments, a paranormal investigator examines psychic vampire Michelle Belanger. It's more overwrought than the NGC program, but still worth watching.

Monster Mania

AMC. Oct 31, 1997. Culture/History. D: Kevin Burns. W: Kevin Burns, Raphael Simon. C: Jack Palance, Cassandra Peterson. USA: English/Color/60m. Van Ness Films/Foxstar Productions/AMC/20th Century Fox Film Corporation.

Count Dracula (Jack Palance) plans to turn Lucy Westenra into his undead bride in *Dracula* (Dan Curtis Productions Inc.)

From the first films of the silent era to the modern resurgence of the 1990s, stories that feature Dracula, Jekyll and Hyde, the Wolf Man, and Frankenstein's Monster have been retold over many generations. When their popularity diminished, other horrors took their place; the likes of aliens, robots, and even natural disasters kept us in fear until the classic monsters returned. Illustrated with film clips, commercials, and other media, host Jack Palance traces the pop culture evolution of the iconic horrors, from *Frankenstein* (1910) to *Mary Reilly* (1996).

This excellent documentary highlights the classic movie monster incarnations since 1910, and frames examples from each decade within a historical context, which illustrates how the genre evolved as it spread throughout North American popular culture. It's a wonderful introduction to the horror movie genre, and who better to have for your tour guide than actor Jack Palance? This production kicked off a horror film festival on AMC, which featured movies including *The Omega Man* (1971) and *Blacula* (1972).

 Released on DVD with an introduction by Elvira, Mistress of the Dark.

Monsters, Madness & Mayhem – "Creatures"

SyFy. 2003 (S01E03). Folklore/History. D: Garry Gibson, Michael Gibson. W: Peter Evans, Michael Gibson. C: Steve Van Dyke, Phillip Blackman, Bobby Hamilton, Dean Harrison. USA: English/Color/43m. Highland Entertainment/Starcast Incorporated.

Did we create monsters to explain what science and religion could not? Or are they a way for us to cope with the darkness that exists in human nature, perhaps as a reflection of the beast that lurks within us all? This episode explores the creatures of fantasy and folklore, and the real monsters that live in our world. Hosted by James Romanovich (as James Reeves).

Vampires are just a small part of this pastiche of a documentary, which presents a supernatural menagerie that ranges from dragons and trolls, to Bigfoot and werewolves—as well as the Kraken and even the Gorgon. But it doesn't stop there; the program also covers the duck-billed platypus and the coelacanth, as well as notorious killers including Tracey Wigginton. The host fails to tie everything together with jumbled segues, and there are so many topics covered that none are explored in any detail. The focus jumps around so much that the program is difficult to follow, and many of the sequences are compiled from a number of sources, so at any given time, the audience is presented with a mix of Australian, British and American-accented narration. What a mess.

This was part of a five-episode miniseries that also broadly covered the subjects of Witches, the Devil, Halloween, and Superstitions.

Monumental Mysteries – "Teen Vampire" / "King of Cons" / "First Escape From Alcatraz"

Travel Channel. May 9, 2013 (S01E01). History/Reality. D: Sterling Milan, Remy Weber. W: Don Wildman. C: Sarah L. Thomson, Sarah Henry, John Cantwell, John Borowski, Robert Horton, Nathaniel Orlowek. USA: English/Color/43m. Optomen Productions.

In this series, host Don Wildman travels nationwide to uncover the unusual histories of national monuments and other historically-significant landmarks. In the segment "Teen Vampire," he visits Exeter, Rhode Island, to examine the tombstone of Mercy Brown—and explore the macabre mystery surrounding her death which happened during New England's vampire panic in the 19th century. The series was rebranded *Mysteries at the Monument* for its third season.

The Most Evil Men and Women in History – "Vlad the Impaler 1431-1476"

Channel 5. Apr 8, 2002 (S01E01). Biography/History. D/W: Natalie Goldberg. C: Colin Imber, Raymond McNally, Brianna Caradja. UK: English/Color/25m. Uden Associates/Channel 5 Broadcasting.

The Wallachian prince Vlad Țepeș, also known as Dracula or "son of the dragon," is well known for his infamous and bloody reign. Yet to this day he's considered a national hero in Romania, where he's remembered for his crusades against the invading Turks. Scholars examine Vlad's life, his time on the throne, and the brutality he inflicted both on and off the battlefield. Narrated by Ben Taylor.

A thorough documentary that sticks to the facts and focuses on the life and times of the real Dracula, and leaves out any debate about his influence on Bram Stoker's fictional vampire. Features an interview with Princess Brianna Caradja, a descendent of Vlad Țepeș.

This ten-part documentary series is a sequel to the six-part series *The Most Evil Men in History* (2001). A book tie-in, *The Most Evil Men and Women in History* (2002), includes essays that cover the sixteen individuals profiled.

The Most Evil Men and Women in History – "Countess Dracula"

Channel 5. May 27, 2002 (S01E07). Biography/History. D/W: Mike Bluett. C: Tony Thorne, Raymond McNally, Terri Apter. UK: English/Color/24m. Uden Associates/Channel 5 Broadcasting.

At the high point of her life, Countess Elizabeth Báthory held more wealth and power than the King of Hungary. Yet today she is considered one of history's most prolific female serial killers, implicated in the torture and death of hundreds of young women. Narrated by Ben Taylor.

An interesting episode that examines the life of Báthory and her supposed crimes against Slovak peasants, which she carried out in collaboration with four of her senior servants (most of whom ended up as scapegoats for the atrocities). Báthory was neither tried nor convicted for these crimes, but was placed under house arrest, and imprisoned within a room inside her castle until she died. She was a sadist that had a compulsion for torture, but the exact nature and scope of her crimes is still under debate. Yet here these stories are presented as facts, including tales of eating the flesh of her young victims, and bathing in their blood.

Most Haunted: LIVE – "Dracula/Transylvania"

LivingTV. Feb 23-25, 2007 (S09E17-19). Folklore/Reality. D: Gary Brooks. W: Anon. C: Ciarán O'Keeffe, David Wells, Karl Beattie, Stuart Torevell, Catherine Howe, Lesley Smith, Paul Ross, Julian Clegg. UK: English/Color/180m. Antix Productions.

In search of the ghost of Vlad Țepeș, the Most Haunted team travels to Transylvania to explore Castle Hunyad, purported to be the location where the fifteenth century warlord was imprisoned in his youth—and where he lived for several years after he was deposed in 1462. Over the course of three nights, the team investigates several sections of the building, but nothing conclusive is drawn from their activities. Presented by Yvette Fielding.

My Strange Addiction – "Blood Drinker"

TLC. Mar 20, 2013 (S04E08). Biography/Reality. D: Anon. W: Kelly McClurkin, Andy Schwarcz. C: Michelle, Chad, Johnny, Boris Bagdasarian. USA: English/Color/21m. 20 West Productions/Violet Media.

This documentary series explores the often bizarre compulsive behaviors of people across the globe, and this episode is devoted to covering one of the more peculiar examples. Michelle, a 29 year-old tattoo artist, admits to drinking up to a liter of pig's blood a day; if she has to go without, it has a serious effect on her disposition. While she usually imbibes the red stuff directly, she will also sometimes cook with it—and is beginning to drink human blood, as well. This series, which seems to celebrate odd (and often life-threatening) behavior rather than focus on treating it, is narrated by Demetri Goritsas.

Mysterious Journeys – "The Hunt for Dracula"

Travel. Oct 24, 2007 (S02E05). Folklore/History. D/W: Megan Peterson. C: Andras Balogh, Andrei Nicolau, Ana Maria Ignat, Father Nicolae, Bishop Calinic, Adriana Antihi, Cristina Irina, Alex Briscu, Gabriel Moisescu, Evan Jonigkeit ♀. USA: English/Color/44m. Authentic Entertainment Inc./Travel Channel.

Most civilizations have a vampire tale in their native folklore, so why did Bram Stoker choose Romania as his source for inspiration? This documentary explores the country's bloody history, where fact is often stranger than fiction, and discovers that there was more than one potential role model that could have inspired Stoker's bloodthirsty creation. Narrated by Erik Todd Dellums.

Takes a questioning look at the reign of Vlad the Impaler as a source of inspiration behind Dracula; also discusses Romania's "Dark Prince" (Radu Negru a.k.a. Negru Vodă), as well as the local legend of the *strigoi*. In a nice change from the norm, the program avoids the standard group of North American scholars; instead, native Romanians discuss their history. It's an interesting exploration of local folklore, and how Bram Stoker's Dracula has been integrated into Romania's mainstream culture—which has led to such curiosities as Transylvania Live – Vampire Tours, Casa Dracul Restaurant, and the Dracula Castle Hotel.

📺 Radu Negru is believed to be the legendary founder of Wallachia (c. 1290); he supposedly had a pregnant woman buried alive within the foundation of the magnificent Curtea de Argeș Cathedral, to guarantee the stability of the structure.

Mysterious Worlds – "Vampires Among Us"

TLC. Oct 31, 2002 (S01E--). Culture/Media. D: Anon. W: Michele Gardner-Smith. C: Adam Carolla, Norinne Dresser, Aphrodite Jones, Elizabeth Miller, Drew Pinsky, Deita Klaus ♀. USA: English/Color/60m. GRB Entertainment.

From Bram Stoker's immortal tale of *Dracula* to the slate of modern-day horror films, bloodsucking fiends are part of our daily (and nightly) lives. This documentary discusses the vampire's continuing hold on our imagination; it features conversations with modern-day practitioners, and explores the Romanian roots behind these undead legends.

Nightmare: The Birth of Horror – "Dracula"

BBC One. Dec 18, 1996 (S01E02). Culture/History. D: Derek Towers. W: Christopher Frayling. C: Trevor St. John Hacker, Eileen Daly ♀, Vida Garman ♀, Vicky Lee ♀, Anthony Jackson. UK/USA: English/Color/47m. Wall to Wall Television/BBC.

This series examines the origins of four Victorian-era Gothic novels, and how each has become integrated into Western mythology. In this episode, writer, teacher and pop culture aficionado Christopher Frayling explores Bram Stoker's classic tale, *Dracula*. From the Villa Diodati at Lake

Geneva to the shores of Whitby, and inside the walls of the British Museum and Rosenbach Library, Frayling discusses vampire folklore, Stoker's life and research, and the enduring legend that the author's creation has had on our popular culture.

In this globetrotting adventure, Christopher Frayling follows in the footsteps of Jonathan Harker—often from within a caleche—to visit several real locations from the novel, as well as other key spots associated with Stoker during his life and times. It's a smartly-written and witty take on the man, the myth and the novel, and still holds up as one of the top documentaries on the subject. Rebroadcast in North America as part of "Tricks and Treats" week on A&E.

Noted scholar, writer, and teacher Christopher Frayling is often the go-to guest for documentaries exploring Bram Stoker's *Dracula* and its enduring legacy on popular culture.

Night Bites: Women and Their Vampires

WeTV. May 28, 2003. Culture/Media. D: Inbal B. Lessner. W: Maitland McDonaugh. C: Marti Noxon, John Landis, Elvis Mitchell, Stephanic Romanov, Ann Manguson, Nancy Collins, David S. Goyer, Maitland McDonaugh, Anne Rice, Michelle Belanger. USA: English/Color/60m. WeTV.

Showcases the evolution of the vampire, from its early roles in film and television, to the modern romantic incarnations. Why do women so easily succumb to the irresistible charms of these creatures of the night?

Night Visitors

TLC. Oct 29, 2000. Folklore/History. D/W: George C. Steitz. C: Troy Taylor, Gene Davidson, Raymond J. McNally, Faye Ringel, Christopher Rondina, Nick Bellantoni, Beth Trapani, Gwyneth Shahen, Joseph A. Citro. USA: English/Color/45m. Impact Television/Discovery Communications.

🦇 🦇 🦇

Released into the home video market as *Night Visitors: Strange Tales of Witches, Vampires & Ghosts,* this documentary features supernatural tales from the United States. It includes the story of Mercy Brown, the infamous Rhode Island vampire, who was thought to be responsible for a number of deaths in the late 1800s. Narrated by James P. Kisicki.

A very interesting production that highlights a number of American folk tales, the most recognizable of which is that of Mercy Brown. In 1883, her mother was infected by a mysterious illness and died; the death was attributed to a supernatural cause, although we now know it was consumption that killed her (and many others). One by one, Mercy and her siblings succumbed to the same illness, and locals were convinced that a dead member of her family was rising from the grave to prey on others. When Mercy's body was exhumed, it had not yet decayed; they assumed that she was the vampire, and her remains were destroyed via the superstitious methods of the day. Revealed here is a fact that is not often presented in tales about Mercy Brown: she was believed to be an energy vampire, who would draw forth the breath of her victim, which in turn drained their life force.

Paranormal Paparazzi – "Nicolas Cage Vampire"

Travel Channel. Nov 8, 2012 (S01E08). Culture/Media. D: Scott Preston. W: Kristen Pietropoli, Jenna Levine, Robin Keats. C: Aaron Sagers, Julie Alexandria, Rachel Fine, Scott Gruenwald, Sona Oganesyan, Joshua P. Warren, Branden Wellington. USA: English/Color/22m. My Tupelo Entertainment.

At the beginning of each episode in this short-lived series—which should technically be filed under variety programming—host Aaron Sagers tasks his band of peppy "reporters" with investigating various paranormal happenings across the United States. In this episode, Joshua P. Warren explores the infamous LaLaurie mansion in New Orleans, considered to be one of the most haunted locations in the French Quarter. Actor Nicolas Cage reportedly once owned the macabre manor, which leads to a discussion of the recent discovery of a Civil War-era photograph that seems to show the actor, looking much like he does today. Could Nicolas Cage be a real vampire? If so, could this be connected to the paranormal goings-on at LaLaurie mansion? Narrated by Dave Mitchell.

Paranormal State – "Lady Vampire"

A&E. Aug 11, 2008 (S02E05). Reality/Fantasy. D: Benjamin Wolf. W: Anon. C: Ryan Buell, Sergey Poberezhny, Eilfie Music, Katrina Weidman, Heather Taddy, CJ Sellers. USA: English/Color/30m. Four Seasons Productions/Go Go Luckey Productions.

Series follows the adventures of the Pennsylvania State Paranormal Research Society, a student-run club that studies supernatural occurrences. In this episode, the team heads to Texas to investigate the sighting of a hag nicknamed "Lady Vampire."

The Pier – "Long in the Tooth: A Century of Dracula"

ITV. Mar 21, 1997. Culture/Literature. D: Anon. W: Anon. C: Christopher Fraying, David Morse, Andrew Davies, Sue Birtwistle. UK: English/Color/25m. Antelope South Productions/Meridian TV.

UK magazine-style arts and entertainment series, which often broadcasts documentaries. In this episode, it's been a century since Bram Stoker penned his immortal tale, *Dracula*. Experts and fans weigh in on the legacy of the novel, and how it contributed to the current vampire craze.

A Place Among the Undead

(In Development). 2017 (6 Episodes). Culture/Horror. D: Juliet Landau. W: Juliet Landau, Deverill Weekes. C: Joss Whedon, Tim Burton, Gary Oldman, Willem Dafoe, Anne Rice, Ron Perlman, Nathan Fillion, Juliet Landau, Robert Patrick, Charlaine Harris, Kristin Bauer van Straten, Caroline Munro, Kevin Grevioux. USA: English/Color/360m. Miss Juliet Productions.

Juliet Landau, best known for portraying the vampire Drusilla in the TV series *Buffy the Vampire Slayer* and *Angel,* initially crowd-funded a "definitive vampire doc" to be produced along with her husband, cinematographer Deverill Weekes. The stand-alone feature planned to showcase interviews with a who's who in the world of undead popular culture. But after the financial campaign was an overwhelming success, the concept was expanded into a multi-part television documentary series, which allowed for them to dig deeper into the world of film, literature, comics, video games, music, and art. The series is expected to be sold to a broadcaster.

Places of Mystery – "Dracula's Castle"

Travel Channel. Aug 15, 2000. Folklore/History. D: Anon. W: Anon. C: Elizabeth Miller. USA: English/Color/30m. Team Entertainment/Travel Channel.

An exploration of "Dracula's Castle" in the Romanian countryside, the former stronghold of Vlad Țepeș. Narrated by Peter Cullen.

Primary Focus – "The Vampire Mystique"

PAX. Oct 29, 1999 (S01E10). Culture/Faith. D: Anon. W: Anon. C: Steve Weick, Lou Drabek, Russell Ulas, Mike Stackpole, Lydia Tross. USA: English/Color/30m.

This religious magazine series reports on cultural trends and current events. In this episode, with the popularity of role-playing games and the surge of the Gothic subculture, teenagers have become fascinated with the concepts of power, immortality and fantasy. But what lurks behind this dark, vampire mystique? This program unearths reaction to the role-playing game *Vampire: The Masquerade,* which most see as a means to temporarily escape the banality of their daily lives—but not everyone believes that the game is just harmless fun.

Project Runway: Under the Gunn - "Unconventional Vampire"

Lifetime. Feb 6, 2014 (S01E04). Drama/Reality. D: Matthew Bartley. W: Anon. C: Sarah Hyland, Jen Rade, Trina Turk, Zoey Deutch, Zanna Roberts Rassi, Mondo Guerra, Anya Ayoung-Chee, Nick Verreos, Michelle Überreste, Brady Lange. USA: English/Color/42m. Murray Productions/The Weinstein Company Television.

As a tie-in with the feature film *Vampire Academy* (2014), the aspiring designers are tasked with creating unconventional looks inspired by the bloodthirsty undead. Stumbling their way through the dark, the contestants have only minutes to grab fabric and accessories strewn about a spooky, fog-drenched landscape—not truly aware of what they have to work with until seeing it in the light of day! Presented by Tim Gunn.

The Real Vampire Chronicles

Channel 4. Oct 25, 2005 (S01E--). Crime/Culture. D: Helen Littleboy. W: Francine Shaw. C: Anon. UK: English/Color/60m. Blast! Films/Channel 4.

This production, one of four documentaries that covered real events associated with horror movies, explored how an obsession with a vampire film led to the death of two friends. In 2002, Allan Menzies killed his best friend, Thomas McKendrick, then mutilated his body and drank his blood. At his trial, Menzies stated that he was so obsessed by the film *Queen of the Damned* that he believed the lead character, Akasha, spoke to him; he claimed that she told him he would become an immortal vampire if he killed people. Menzies pleaded insanity, but the jury wasn't convinced; he was sentenced to life in prison, where he hanged himself in 2004.

The Real Vampire Files

History. Sep 7, 2010. Culture/History. D: David Mortin. W: Robert Colapinto. C: Norinne Dresser, Michelle Belanger, Joseph Laycock, Steve Biodrowski, Del Howison, Radu Florescu, Leslie Klinger, Elizabeth Miller, J. Gordon Melton, David J. Skal. CAN: English/Color/60m. MDF Productions Inc.

Is there any truth behind the spine-chilling undead legends of the silver screen? These creatures may just be a product of an active imagination, but what of those who call themselves modern-day vampires? In this documentary, real life practitioners discuss their dark secrets, the realities of their chosen lifestyle, and the truth behind the fiction. Narrated by Robert Latimer Cornell.

Real Vampires... Exposed!

UPN. Jan 20, 1998. Culture/Literature. D: Mack Anderson. W: Michael Kriz. C: Anon. USA: English/Color/60m. Bob Bain Productions.

This tabloid-like investigation takes a voyeuristic look at underground vampire roleplaying clubs. It includes interviews with the people who frequent them, and explores the history and lore that has led to this surge in vampire popularity. Hosted by Emmett Miller.

Real Vampires

Discovery. Oct 31, 2007. Culture/History. D/W: Daniel Richler. C: Elizabeth Miller, Nicolae Paduraru, Constantin Rezachevici, Robert Wood, Roderick Scott, Mark Benecke, Michael Watts, Tony Thorne, Seán Manchester. CAN/UK: English/Color/93m. Cream Productions Inc./IWC Media.

Using modern science to deconstruct the legends of historical vampires, this production crisscrosses the globe to explore the classic traits of vampirism—and touches on modern sanguinists, fetishism, and bloodsuckers in the natural world. Is there a rational, scientific explanation behind the vampire myth? Presented by archaeologist Timothy Taylor and anthropologist Kathryn Denning.

This documentary draws on hematology, pathology, and other scientific disciplines, to search for the truth behind the vampires of folklore—and manages to dispute, rather humorously, the horrors attributed to the likes of Vlad the Impaler and Elizabeth Báthory. Features a discussion of some modern killers, including Wayne Boden ("The Vampire Rapist"), Allan Menzies, Manuela and Daniel Ruda, and Marcelo Costa de Andrade ("The Vampire of Niterói"). The hosts' running commentary is presented as video travelogues from inside nondescript hotel rooms, and one of them is given the additional task of narrating the entire production; two odd choices that don't quite work. Many of the topics presented have been covered in countless other productions, but it's still a refreshing exploration of vampirism through the lens of science.

📺 According to a hematologist, over the course of a century, a vampire would gain close to four hundred pounds of excess weight from the iron in the blood that they imbibe.

Rear Window – "Dracula: The Undiscovered Country"

Channel 4. Aug 17, 1993. Culture/History. D: Sue Clayton. W: Anon. C: Ronan Vibert. UK: English/Color/40m. Bandung Productions.

Examines historical accounts of the origin of the vampire, and why it has become such an enduring icon in Western popular culture. How did it all come to be, and what influence, if any, did the Catholic Church have? Follow the path of the undead, from the depths of Transylvanian folklore, to its reinvention through Western eyes. Highlights include clips from Hammer horror movies, and excerpts from classic vampire tales.

Revealed – "Mysteries of the Vampire Skeletons"

Channel 5. Sep 13, 2011 (S08E09). History/Mystery. D/W: Mark Fielder. C: Chris Read, Mark Horton, Clare Downham, John Blair, Catriona McKenzie, Lisa Smith, Juliette Wood, Vintila Mihailescu, Mihai Fifor, John Burke. UK: English/Color/45m. Quickfire Media Ltd.

🦇 🦇 🦇 🦇

In 2007, archeologists in Ireland unearthed a mass grave of almost three thousand skeletons, and discovered three unique sets of remains deemed "deviant burials," due to the bizarre nature of how they were arranged. One skeleton in this Medieval cemetery had the legs twisted

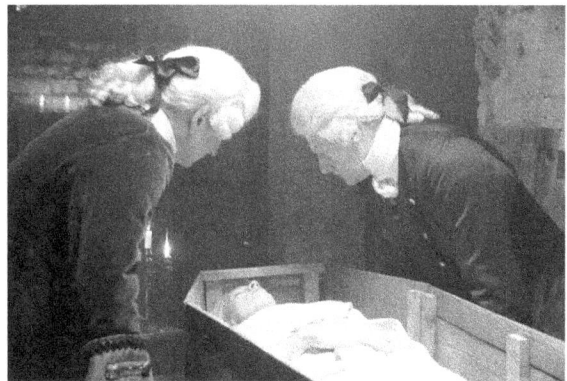

Doctors investigate a disturbing series of deaths in this re-enactment from *Revealed* - "Mysteries of the Vampire Skeletons" (Quickfire Media)

around a large boulder, while two others had a hefty stone jammed into the mouth; each was a superstitious act meant to prevent the dead from rising from the grave. Experts discuss the find and the history of these strange rituals, which are still practiced in some countries to this day. Narrated by Russell Boulter.

Today, vampires are a form of entertainment, but in the twelfth century, these revenants were considered by many to be a very real threat to their existence. This excellent documentary takes a detailed look at the investigation into these three strange skeletons, and includes an interesting overview of related folklore over the centuries. Highly recommended.

Riddles of the Dead - "Dracula Unearthed"

NGC. Oct 27, 2002. History/Science. D: Paulette Moore. W: Anon. C: Mark Benecke, Leanna Chamish, Elizabeth Miller. USA: English/Color/60m. Hoggard Films/National Geographic Television.

A superstitious burial from the twelfth century is unearthed in *Revealed* - "Mysteries of the Vampire Skeletons" (Quickfire Media)

Forensic entomologist Mark Benecke, affectionately known as "Dr. Maggot," journeys to Transylvania to explore the science behind the common vampire myths. The bug expert separates fact from fiction with the help of historians, scientists, skeptics and fans—and untangles the myths surrounding the literary Dracula and the historical Vlad Țepeș.

Ripley's Believe It or Not! - Ep. #1.01

TBS. Jan 1, 2000 (S01E01). Culture/History. D: Paul Nichols. W: Erik Nelson, Dan Jbara. C: Dean Ortner, Terri Ortner, Dennis Hite, Stephen Thomas, Thomas Hancock, Sue Johnson, Rose Siggins, David Siggins, George Vlosich. USA: English/Color/46m. Ripley Entertainment Inc./Angry Dragon Entertainment.

🦇 🦇 🦇

The Ripley archives hold over 22,000 objects, and there's a story behind each and every one of them. This includes a simple wooden box that is actually an authentic eighteenth century "vampire protection kit." It contains, in part, a small vial of holy water, a necklace of garlic, a wooden stake, and a crucifix—which encases a gun that fires silver bullets. Hosted by Dean Cain.

This stomach-churning, premiere episode begins with a story about the Aghori tribe, modern-day cannibals in India who believe that eating the flesh of the recently deceased will give them extraordinary spiritual powers—and a direct line to immortality. Another segment features members of the "Suspension Club," who form a nine-person "human mobile" anchored by stainless steel hooks passed through the skin on their backs. Next is a story about a medical treatment known as "maggot therapy," where fly larvae are intentionally utilized to eat away at gangrenous flesh. This episode contains minimal vampire content, but the additional stories are so extreme that it's still recommended viewing.

Scare Tactics – "Security Breach" / "Taste for Blood" / "Zombie Grandma" / "Killer Car"

Syfy. Sep 12, 2003 (S01E18). Culture/Reality. D: Mike Harney. W: Anon. C: Anon. USA: English/Color/30m. Hallock Healey Entertainment/The Sci-Fi Channel.

This spin on *Candid Camera* is aimed at a generation raised on the Internet and bad horror movies; the most gullible of the human stock are put into preposterous situations, which they actually believe are real. In the segment "Taste for Blood," a woman attends an interview for an assistant position, and discovers she is in the presence of a vampire. Hosted by Shannen Doherty.

Scare Tactics – "Motor Psychos" / "Attack of the Rat Monster" / "I Me Minefield" / "There Are Men Coming Here to Kill Me"

Syfy. Oct 6, 2004 (S02E09). Culture/Reality. D: Anon. W: Anon. C: Anon. USA: English/Color/30m. Hallock Healey Entertainment/The Sci-Fi Channel.

In "Motor Psychos," Ashley takes her best friend Karrina to an exclusive, invitation-only party—but along the way they cross paths with a gang of vampire bikers. Hosted by Shannen Doherty.

Scare Tactics – "Genie in a Beer Bottle" / "Vampire Spa" / "Escaped Mental Patient" / "Alien Eggs"

Syfy. Jul 16, 2008 (S03E03). Culture/Reality. D: Anon. W: Anon. C: Anon. USA: English/Color/30m. Hallock Healey Entertainment/The Sci-Fi Channel.

In the segment "Vampire Spa," a new employee discovers the secret ingredient to the facility's most popular treatment: human blood. This segment was repeated as "Blood Bath" in episode #12. Hosted by Tracy Morgan.

Scare Tactics – "Channeling the Dead" / "Black Project 2" / "Zombie Testing" / "A Quick Bite"

SyFy. Sep 30, 2008 (S03E16). Culture/Reality. D: Anon. W: Anon. C: Anon. USA: English/Color/30m. Hallock Healey Entertainment/The Sci-Fi Channel.

In "A Quick Bite," an interview with a vampire takes a turn for the worse once he starts to get a little hungry. Hosted by Tracy Morgan.

Scare Tactics – "Vampire Stakeout" / "Mind Killer" / "Wine to Die For" / "Grandpa Has Returned"

SyFy. Oct 25, 2010 (S04E04). Culture/Reality. D: Adam Brodie. W: Adam Brodie, Joey Case, Andy King. C: Lauren Ash, Adam Wilson ☥. USA: English/Color/22m. Hallock Healey Entertainment/The Sci-Fi Channel.

In the segment "Vampire Stakeout," Emma plays a joke on her best friend Rebecca. She convinces her to participate in an overnight ride-along with a private investigator; they monitor an empty shipping facility that is actually a vampire hangout. In "Wine to Die For," mom Pauline wants to give her daughter Latricia a good scare, so she persuades her to attend a wine tasting event at the home of a peculiar winemaker; his best vintage is infused with human blood. Hosted by Tracy Morgan.

The Scariest Places on Earth – "A Night in Dracula's Castle: The Transylvania Dare"

FOX Family. Oct 26, 2001 (S02E26). Reality/Suspense. D: Jeff Lengyel. W: Stephen Kroopnick. C: Nicolae Ceriser, Iochim Lazar, Raymond T. McNally, Tristan Codrescu, Florin Iepan, Maria Belus, Aurelia Moholea, Liviu Avram. USA: English/Color/87m. Triage Entertainment.

In this two-hour Halloween special, the Menegaux family from New York spends a night exploring Hunyad Castle in Hunedoara, Romania—once a home to Vlad the Impaler. Presented by Linda Blair with paranormal expert Alan Robson, and narrated by Zelda Rubinstein.

Considering the program comes with a disclaimer—that some scenes are re-creations or dramatizations, and may include created or enhanced effects—it's clear from the get-go that the line will be erased between reality and fantasy. There's no doubt that the family had some real scares, but what else would you expect? A group of urbanites has to trudge through a creepy, dimly-lit, centuries-old castle, and their imaginations run wild. With questionable, macabre mythology, and interviews with "locals" that appear to be staged, this program is of little interest to anyone over the age of thirteen. The episode initially presents an accurate account of Vlad the

Impaler, but then goes completely off the rails into fantasy land when it relates additional "facts" about him, which are completely fabricated for storytelling purposes.

📺 Includes possibly the last recorded interview with Dracula historian Raymond T. McNally, who died in 2002; these clips were also used in the episode "Return to Transylvania."

The Scariest Places on Earth – "Return to Romania Dare"

FOX Family. Apr 21, 2002 (S03E01). Reality/Suspense. D: Jeff Lengyel. W: Stephen Kroopnick. C: Linda Blair, Alan Robson, Zelda Rubinstein. USA: English/Color/60m. Mobile Video Productions Inc./Triage Entertainment/Fox Family Channel.

An American family spends a night in Hunyad Castle, a Romanian fortress once inhabited by Vlad the Impaler. This is most likely a rebroadcast/re-edit of the two-hour, 2001 Halloween special that featured the Menegaux family. Presented by Linda Blair with paranormal expert Alan Robson, and narrated by Zelda Rubinstein.

The Scariest Places on Earth – "Return to Transylvania"

FOX Family. Oct 21, 2002 (S03E03). Reality/Suspense. D: Jeff Lengyel. W: Stephen Kroopnick. C: Ana Roscas, Doru Cirstoi, Maria Belus, Florin Iepan, Aurelia Moholea, Tristan Codrescu, Raymond T. McNally, Maria Belus. USA: English/Color/44m. Triage Entertainment.

The Broders family from California travels to Romania, to spend a night at Vlad the Impaler's castle in Hunedoara. Presented by Linda Blair with paranormal expert Alan Robson, and narrated by Zelda Rubinstein.

Shares the same location, setup and outcome as the episode "A Night in Dracula's Castle: The Transylvania Dare"—except with a different family. It begins with the same cast of Romanians from the earlier episode, who try to sell the creepy nature of the castle. Next, the family gets suitably freaked out over bats, rats and other creepy crawlies, but nothing concrete is seen or heard by the audience. Rest assured, the family makes it through till morning—but there's still time to give them a closing speech filled with more utter nonsense.

📺 This same concept and location was used for *Most Haunted: LIVE* – "Dracula/Transylvania" (2007).

The Scariest Places on Earth – "Castle Transylvania"

ABC Family. Oct 22, 2005 (S04E02). Reality/Suspense. D: Jeff Lengyel. W: Stephen Kroopnick. C: Linda Blair, Alan Robson, Zelda Rubinstein, Monahan Family. USA: English/Color/60m. Mobile Video Productions Inc./Triage Entertainment/Fox Family Channel.

The Monahan family from California is the third unlucky group that travels abroad to check out the scares in Romania. But this time around, the location isn't Hunyad Castle; they'll be testing their mettle overnight within the famous Citadel of Făgăraș. Presented by Linda Blair with paranormal expert Alan Robson, and narrated by Zelda Rubinstein.

The Scariest Places on Earth – "Castle of the Blood Countess"

ABC Family. Oct 29, 2005 (S04E05). Reality/Suspense. D: Anon. W: Stephen Kroopnick. C: Linda Blair, Alan Robson, Zelda Rubinstein, Chris Fleming. USA: English/Color/60m. Mobile Video Productions Inc./Triage Entertainment/Fox Family Channel.

An unsuspecting family spends a night at Čachtice Castle in Slovakia, once home to the infamous Countess Elizabeth Báthory. She was accused of killing hundreds of girls, and although she was never tried or convicted of any crime, Báthory was imprisoned in her home, where she died in 1614. Presented by Linda Blair with paranormal expert Alan Robson, and narrated by Zelda Rubinstein.

The Search For Dracula

Discovery Channel. Feb 1996. Culture/Folklore. D: Joe Wiecha. W: Eleanor Grant, Mike Sinclair, Steven Zorn. C: Michael Bell. USA: English/Color/50m. A&E Television Networks.

Examines the origins of the Dracula legend, and discusses the possibility that vampires may have actually existed. Hosted by Eli Wallach.

The Secret Lives of Vampires

A&E. Oct 28, 2005. Culture/Folklore. D/W: Anon. C: Michelle Belanger, Don Henrie, Father Sebastiaan, David Skal, Rosemary Ellen Guiley, Elizabeth Miller, Michael Barsanti, Rob Eighteen-Bisang, Aphrodite Jones, Katherine Ramsland, Radu Florescu. USA: English/Color/91m. A&E Television Networks.

The modern vampire was born from the pages of *Dracula* (1897) and *Interview with the Vampire* (1976), and is barely recognizable from the revenants of folklore. Many who adopt the vampire's look and lifestyle do so just for fun, but some claim they are *true* vampires that feed on human vital energy—either through blood or life-force.

These modern vampires are all around us, from large urban centers to small towns, and they come from all walks of life. This in-depth exploration of contemporary vampires is a who's who of sorts; it includes interviews with experts, scholars, and the practitioners who are considered to be the modern face of vampirism. There is a breadth and depth to this once-secretive community, and for the first time, we get a well-balanced look at those who fall under the umbrella of "modern vampire." Unfortunately, too much time is spent exploring the vampires of folklore and the origins of *Dracula,* neither of which is a "secret" to anyone who has even a passing interest in the subjects. It is worthwhile to compare the folkloric vampire to its modern equivalent; however, if you're only interested in learning about the secret lives of modern vampires, then this extraneous information won't be of much use.

Secret Lives of Women – "Dirty Little Suburban Secrets"

WeTV. Jun 24, 2008 (S04E13). Culture/Lifestyle. D: Anon. W: Anon. C: Dominae Drakonis. USA: English/Color/60m. Burrud Productions/Reelistic Pictures/Women's Entertainment Channel.

A series that profiles real women who often lead secret lives, from fetishes to fantasies and other dirty little secrets. In this episode, four suburbanites reveal what happens behind closed doors, including a woman who's a vampire and professional Dominatrix.

Secret Lives of Women – "The Occult"

WeTV. Sep 16, 2008 (S04E25). Culture/Lifestyle. D/W: Abbey LeVine. C: Yvonne, Ronald Conway, Heather Saenz, Brian, Vampyra, Laura Holst, Lady Deberah, Ava Park. USA: English/Color/41m. Burrud Productions/Reelistic Pictures/Women's Entertainment Channel.

This episode profiles three very different women—a Vampire, a Satanist and a Wiccan—who discuss their uncommon spiritual beliefs and practices. Narrated by Sheila Head.

Any program that sheds light into the often secretive world of different belief systems is a positive way to enlighten the general public about these groups. However, careful attention must be given in choosing the interviewees, because they will greatly influence the audience's perception of these beliefs. Unfortunately, the three main women profiled here each come off as kooky role players, despite the fact that they are certainly very serious about their chosen ideologies.

Sexy Beasts: Vamps, Wolves, and Mutants

TV Guide Network. Oct 24, 2010. Culture/Media. D/W: Heather Konkoli. C: Chris Serico. USA: English/Color/60m. TV Guide Network.

A countdown of the top twenty-five "hottest" otherworldly creatures in popular culture, including werewolves, mutants and vampires.

Sightings – "Vampires" / "Gainesville Murders" / "Flight 19"

FOX. Jun 26, 1992 (S01E15). Culture/Folklore. D: Anon. W: Anon. C: Paul Sledzik, Norine Dresser, Catrina Coffin. USA: English/Color/30m. Fair Dinkum Productions/Ann Daniel Productions/Triage Entertainment.

Paranormal news magazine series that investigates strange happenings from across the globe. This episode features a segment that discusses the purported existence of an eighteenth century vampire cult, and includes an interview with a modern-day practitioner. Other topics include Visions of Death, and the Bermuda Triangle. Hosted by Tim White with correspondent Carla Wohl.

Sightings – "The Marfa Lights"

FOX. Sep 25, 1992 (S02E02). Culture/Folklore. D: Anon. W: Anon. C: Anon. USA: English/Color/30m. Fair Dinkum Productions/Ann Daniel Productions/Triage Entertainment.

Explores reports of a UFO dogfight, strange "vampire" rituals, and some paranormal experiences as submitted by viewers. Hosted by Tim White with correspondent Carla Wohl.

Sightings – "Halloween"

FOX. Oct 30, 1992 (S02E06). Culture/Folklore. D: Anon. W: Anon. C: Vincent Hillyer, Stephen Martin, Rosemary Ellen Guiley, Martin V. Riccardo, Vlad. USA: English/Color/30m. Fair Dinkum Productions/Ann Daniel Productions/Triage Entertainment.

Halloween special that discusses the ghosts of Scotland's "House of Horror," a self-proclaimed vampire named Vlad, and practitioners of modern witchcraft. Hosted by Tim White with correspondent Carla Wohl.

Sightings – Ep. #4.07

Syndicated. Oct 22, 1995 (S04E07). Culture/Folklore. D: Scott Firestone. W: Susan Michaels. C: Michael Bell, Lewis E. Peck, Paul Sledzik. USA: English/Color/60m. Fair Dinkum Productions/Ann Daniel Productions/Triage Entertainment.

Topics include: a ghost that haunts the Spirit of Oregon train; Tesla's death ray that destroyed part of Siberia in 1908; aliens and Roswell; and a report on the famous 1930s photograph of the Loch Ness Monster. The segment "Consumed by Vampires" explores the subject of Mercy Brown, and a purported New England vampire cult from the late 1800s. Hosted by Tim White with correspondent Carla Wohl.

The South Bank Show – "Birth of Frankenstein and Dracula"

ITV1. Feb 8, 1987 (S10E15). Arts/Culture. D: Chris Hunt. W: Chris Hunt, Frances Dickenson. C: Tim McInnerny, Miranda Richardson, Amanda Root, Tim Roth, Benedict Taylor. UK: English/Color/60m. London Weekend Television.

Traces the origins of the Gothic horror tradition from a circle of friends—Lord Byron, Mary and Percy Shelley, Claire Clairmont and John Polidori—who spent the summer of 1816 together at the Villa Diodati in Geneva. Includes clips from the Ken Russell film Gothic (1986). Presented by Melvyn Bragg.

The South Bank Show – "The Dracula File"

ITV1. Jan 24, 1993 (S16E11). Arts/Culture. D: Daniel Wiles. W: Melvyn Bragg. C: Leonard Wolf, Christopher Frayling, Tina Rath, Daniel Farson, Elaine Showalter, Stephen Jones, Christopher Lee, Stephen Kaplan, Seán Manchester. UK: English/Color/52m. London Weekend Television.

🦇 🦇 🦇 🦇

Examines the evolution of the Dracula character, from the evil monster in Bram Stoker's original tale to the romantic hero in his latest film incarnation. Includes interviews with the cast and crew of Bram Stoker's Dracula (1992), and showcases clips from other film versions that featured the infamous vampire. Presented by Melvyn Bragg.

This enjoyable episode gives insight into Stoker and the impact of his work, and is illustrated with numerous film clips from various adaptations. This version is superior to the re-edited production that was rebroadcast in the United States; it includes additional film clips, and an informative (and extended) conversation with Christopher Frayling—and should be sought out over the other.

📺 An edited version was rebroadcast in the United States as the "Dracula" episode of *Biography* on Oct 26, 1995; the original version was rebroadcast on TVO in Canada on Oct 31, 1995.

Studio 2 – Ep. #504

TVOntario. Oct 31, 1996 (S03E--). Culture/History. D: Blair Harley. W: Anon. C: Steve Paikin, Lynda Ciaschini, Randy Warren, Robert Kozinets, Elizabeth Miller, Carol Sloane. CAN: English/Color/60m. TVOntario.

🦇 🦇 🦇

The segment "Dracula" explores the most feared and revered vampire of all time, an iconic bloodsucker that has seen numerous changes over the course of a century. An unlikely scholar on the subject—university professor Elizabeth Miller—shares her keen interest in Bram Stoker's tale; she discusses how it's been transformed through popular culture, and its connection to the fifteenth century Wallachian prince Vlad Țepeș.

A news magazine report that features a lengthy interview with *Dracula* scholar Elizabeth Miller, who chats about the man, the myth, and the legend. She also discusses the 1995 World Dracula Congress in Bucharest, and the Dracula '97 centennial celebration in Los Angeles. When viewed today, it's an interesting look back at the resurgence of vampire pop culture of the mid-1990s—which was soon fueled by the debut of the iconic TV series *Buffy the Vampire Slayer*.

True Bloodlines – "Vampire Legends"

HBO. Sep 6, 2008. Culture/Folklore. D: Souzan Alavi. W: Anon. C: Thomas J. Garza, David J. Skal, Meagan Schenkelberg, J. Gordon Melton, Michelle Belanger, Tony Timpone, Elizabeth E. Fuller, Paul Bibeau, Nina Auerbach, Wil Gafney. USA: English/Color/27m. Home Box Office.

🦇 🦇 🦇

Explores the evolution of the vampire in Western popular culture, beginning with its origin in folklore and the exploits of Vlad Ţepeş and Elizabeth Báthory. Experts discuss the genesis of Bram Stoker's novel, and its various feature film incarnations. Concludes with a look at contemporary authors including L.A. Banks and Charlaine Harris, who discuss their own take on the vampire legend.

This fast-paced overview is a good starting point for anyone who is unfamiliar with the genre; wide in scope but short on detail, it definitely leaves one thirsting for more. It's the first of two short documentaries promoting the HBO series *True Blood,* which premiered the following evening. Features interviews with cast and crew from the show, including Alexander Skarsgård, Stephen Moyer, Alan Ball, Chris Offutt, Ryan Kwanten, Anna Paquin, Chris Bauer, Lois Smith and Sam Trammell.

True Bloodlines - "A New Type"

HBO. Sep 6, 2008. Culture/Film. D: Souzan Alavi. W: Anon. C: Tony Timpone, Patrick Rodgers, David J. Skal, Meagan Schenkelberg, Nina Auerbach, Michelle Belanger, J. Gordon Melton, Thomas J. Garza, Wil Gafney, Paul Bibeau, Lady Valfreyja. USA: English/Color/24m. Home Box Office.

Explores the romantic vampire, a creature that has evolved from a folkloric boogeyman to become a dark, sensual and often conflicted being. Experts survey the slate of modern vampire films, and reflect on the ever-changing myths and traits associated with contemporary bloodsuckers. Also features a brief look at the vampire subculture.

The first half of the documentary explores modern cinema classics (including *The Lost Boys, Near Dark* and *The Hunger),* yet it becomes an exercise in self-promotion as filmmakers gush over the (not so classic) movies created by some of the other interviewees. The second part covers the fluid mythology associated with modern vampires; this is simply a barrage of clips from authors and filmmakers who reveal what "their" vampires can do. This is the second of two short documentaries promoting the HBO series *True Blood,* which premiered the following evening. Features interviews with cast and crew from the show, including Alan Ball, Daniel Minahan, Alexander Woo, Chris Bauer, Sam Trammell, Nelsan Ellis, Anna Paquin, Chris Offutt and Kristin Bauer.

True Horror with Anthony Head - "Vampires"

Discovery Europe. Nov 17, 2004 (S01E01). Culture/Folklore. D: Rupert Miles. W: Eliza James. C: Tina Rath, Nicolae Paduraru, Mark Benecke, Mihai Fifor, Seán Manchester, Keith McLean, Richard Weisman, Marina Andronache. UK: English/Color/48m. October Films.

Who better to explore the truth behind our most nightmarish legends than the actor who's best known for portraying Rupert Giles on *Buffy the Vampire Slayer?* In this premiere episode, historians, scientists and other experts explore the real facts behind the vampire legend. Hosted by Anthony Head.

Giles may know everything about the undead, but the actor portraying him does not, which is why Anthony Head takes this personal journey across Europe to better understand the origins of the vampire myth. Intrigued by the 2003 vampire scare in Marotinu de Sus, the host begins and ends his journey in this small Romanian village—and along the way he unearths the truth behind Dracula, Vlad Țepeș, and vampire superstitions. If you are unfamiliar with these topics, and are looking for a documentary that'll quickly get you up to speed, then this is the one for you. Entertaining and factually accurate, the only misstep is a couple of cheesy reenactments, but the host is so engaging that you'll probably never notice.

📺 This five-part series also covered the topics of demons, werewolves, witches and zombies.

True Story of the Vampire

History Channel. Oct 31, 1997. Folklore/History. D: Anon. W: Anon. C: Anon. USA: English/Color/60m. Hearst Entertainment/A&E Television Networks.

A documentary that searches the world over for tales of the undead, exploring the folklore of Transylvania, Medieval Europe, eighteenth century Greece and nineteenth century New England. Little else is known about this production, which apparently was only broadcast on a single occasion. It was referenced in an Associated Press article published on October 26, 1997, as well as within a newsletter published by the International Documentary Association that same year.

Truth or Scare – "Dracula"

Discovery Kids. 2001 (S01E02). Culture/Literature. D: Trish Mitchell, Rasha Drachkovitch. W: Trish Mitchell. C: Leonard Wolf, David J. Skal, James V. Hart, Elizabeth Miller, Nina Auerbach. USA: English/Color/23m. 44 Blue Productions/The Cronkite Ward Company/Discovery Communications.

🦇 🦇 🦇

This true account of Count Dracula uncovers the facts behind the fiction; it explores the life and times of author Bram Stoker, and the real events that influenced his most famous novel. Hosted by Michelle Trachtenberg.

This is a repackaging of the excellent 1999 TLC documentary "Dracula" from the series *Great Books,* edited down and presented in a manner more suited towards young adults. The original production is superior, yet this trimmed version is still an excellent overview for the younger generation.

Truth or Scare – "Night Visitors"

Discovery Kids. 2002 (S01E11). Culture/Folklore. D: George C. Steitz, Rasha Drachkovitch. W: George C. Steitz. C: Gene Davidson, Gwyneth Shahen, Richard C. Gordon. USA: English/Color/22m. 44 Blue Productions/Impact Television/Discovery Communications.

American tales of ghosts, witches and vampires haunt this episode, including the story of Mercy Brown, the purported vampire from Exeter, Rhode Island, who in the late 1800s was thought to be responsible for a number of deaths in the area. Also included are tales of The Bell Witch of Tennessee; Emily's ghost at the Gold Brook Bridge in Vermont; and the haunted Hammond Castle in Cape Ann, Massachusetts. Hosted by Michelle Trachtenberg.

This is a repackaging of the TLC documentary *Night Visitors* (2000), pared down and presented in a manner more suited towards young adults. It doesn't cover as much ground as the original production, with fewer interviews and more narration. Those interested in these phenomena are better off seeking out the original documentary.

Tuesday's Documentary – "That Dracula Business"

BBC One. Aug 6, 1974. Culture/Literature. D: Anthony de Lotbinière. W: Daniel Farson. C: Michael Carreras. UK: English/Color/50m. BBC.

Writer and broadcaster Daniel Farson visits Romania to explore the places and myths behind the novel *Dracula,* written by his great-uncle Bram Stoker, and investigates the current vampire fascination within British society. Includes a look at how the Romanian government is attempting to cash in on the Dracula craze.

Twisted History: Vampires

Discovery. Oct 30, 2005. Culture/History. D: Justin Albert. W: Lucilla D'Agostino. C: Katherine Ramsland, Theresa Bane, Camden Toy, Konstantinos, Mike Mignola. USA: English/Color/60m. West Beach Entertainment.

Scientists, historians and filmmakers explore the enduring legends behind the vampire myths. From Vlad the Impaler to Blade the Vampire Hunter, this documentary takes an often irreverent look at our enduring fascination with the undead.

Ultimate Super Heroes, Vixens & Villains

Bravo. May 26-28, 2005 (3 Episodes). Culture/Media. D: Anon. W: Anon. C: George Lucas, Vivica A. Fox, Linda Hamilton, Robert Englund, Mark Hamill, Stan Lee, Bill Mumy, Lou Ferrigno, James Earl Jones, Hal Sparks, Todd McFarlane. USA: English/Color/180m. Van Ness Films/Prometheus Entertainment.

In this three-part special, the top twenty super-heroes, super-vixens and super-villains are counted down from film, television and comics. In their respective categories, both Blade and Dracula barely make the cut at #19, while Buffy fares much better at a respectable #5. Narrated by Adam West.

The Unexplained – "The Vampire Myth"

A&E. May 7, 1998 (S03E03). Culture/History. D/W: Terry Spencer. C: Nicolas Strathloch, J. Gordon Melton, Raymond McNally, Alexander Obolsky, Nicolae Paduraru, Don Jakoby, Dale McKinley, Catrina Coffin, Sabina Ispas, Michael Bell. USA: English/Color/46m. Towers Productions Inc.

From role players to real life sanguinists, this program takes a look at several modern vampires including those who frequent the Fang Club in Beverly Hills. They've based their lifestyle on the seductive vampire of literature, not the horrific revenant of folklore, and the inspiration behind their subculture is examined by scholars and esoteric experts. Narrated by Norm Woodel.

Early documentaries that featured vampiric practitioners tended to include guests that were a little more on the fringe, and such is the case in this production. Subjects include: a man who believes he was inhabited by a vampire god at age five; a woman who owns a hearse and sleeps in a coffin; and a couple who believes they have a psychic connection with Vlad Țepeș—who surprisingly has become a loving and positive force in their relationship (and his spirit can be channeled by either partner). This episode seems to have been made specifically to shock and amuse, rather than truthfully examine a thriving subculture. Definitely not a production that should be taken too seriously, but still worthwhile viewing for its entertainment value. For a more balanced look at modern vampire culture, check out the 2005 documentary *The Secret Life of Vampires*.

The Unexplained: Witches, Werewolves & Vampires

NBC. Oct 23, 1994. Culture/History. D: Terry Landau. W: Gregory Ross. C: Leonard George, Paul Barber, Harvey Rosenstock, Selena Fox, Alison D'Amario, Laurie Cabot, Raymond McNally, Catrina Coffin. USA: English/Color/47m. Landau Entertainment Inc.

In the realm of monsters, all roads lead to the graveyard. Tales of folklore were created by those who needed to put a face to their fears, in an attempt to explain the unknown. Today we no longer need these mythological monsters,

Creatures of the night abound in *The Unexplained: Witches, Werewolves & Vampires*, which explores real events that may have lead to the creation of these enduring myths (Landau Entertainment Inc/James Sorensen)

so why does the fascination live on? This program examines real events that possibly led to the fictional images of the witch, the werewolf, and the vampire. Hosted by Peter Graves.

Illustrated with clips from horror films, this documentary examines the three greatest monsters with the most significant and enduring mythology. It begins with an exploration of folklore versus mythology with respect to werewolves, and then delves into the Hollywood image of a witch versus real life Wiccans. The vampire is featured in the longest segment of the program, where experts weigh in on how its image was greatly influenced by Bram Stoker, and speculate on how much the author himself was influenced by the Medieval warlord Vlad Țepeș. It also takes a look at film adaptations and real vampires of history, including modern-day Romanian beliefs and the condition known as "Renfield's Syndrome." It's an entertaining program with some cheesy yet charming host segments, which were shot in a graveyard and a funeral home.

The Universal Story

Starz. 1995. History/Film. D: David Heeley. W: Joan Kramer, David Heeley. C: Lew Ayres, Alfred Hitchcock, Boris Karloff, Susan Kohner, Gregory Peck, Mary Pickford, Steven Spielberg, James Stewart, Lupita Tovar, Meryl Streep, Sigourney Weaver, Orson Welles. USA: English/B&W, Color/120m. Top Hat Productions/Universal Television.

In 1915, Carl Laemmle had a vision to create a studio that would "make the people laugh, or cry, or sit on the edge of their chairs the world over." In celebration of the 80th anniversary of Laemmle's Universal Studios, host Richard Dreyfuss narrates a tour that begins with the formation of Universal Film Manufacturing Company, with its silent screen stars like John Ford and Lon Chaney. The story continues into the era of the studio's signature horrors of the silver screen, followed by the evolution of its star system that included Rock Hudson, James Stewart, and Tony Curtis. Exploring over 100 films and filmmakers, this documentary includes clips from *Dracula* and *Frankenstein*, both of which were released in 1931 and led to successful horror franchises.

Universal Horror

TCM. Oct 9, 1998. History/Film. D: Kevin Brownlow. W: Patrick Stanbury. C: Ray Bradbury, Nina Foch, James Karen, Carla Laemmle, Sara Karloff, Forrest J Ackerman, David J. Skal, Gloria Stuart, Fay Wray. UK: English/B&W, Color/95m. Photoplay Productions/Universal TV.

🦇 🦇 🦇

This program explores the horror legacy of Universal Studios, featuring a detailed look at the early classics produced from the 1920s through the late 1940s. Includes both new and archival interviews with the actors, writers and directors who played a part in bringing these films to life. Narrated by Kenneth Branagh.

Some screen time is given to the frights produced by competing studios, but ultimately this is a love letter to Universal, so the majority of the films presented are produced by them alone. The documentary casts a wide net, covering many films from this era; there's so much information packed into ninety minutes that it's easier to digest if taken in over more than one sitting.

📺 This kicked off a horror-themed weekend on TCM that featured several of the films discussed in the program, including Tod Browning's *Dracula* (1931).

Unnatural History – "Vampires & Witches"

TLC. 1997 (S01E02). Folklore/History. D: Michael Tetrick. W: Michael Tetrick, Anne McGrail. C: J. Gordon Melton, Paul Barber, Norine Dresser, Catrina Coffin, Jeffrey B. Russell, Michael Shermer. USA: English/Color/53m. Dove Four Point Productions.

🦇🦇🦇

There was a time when our innate fears of the unknown led to the demonization of those who were different from the norm. These poor souls were usually blamed for strange maladies befalling a community, and often were named as a vampire or a witch. The situation rarely ended without tragedy. The first half of this episode traces the evolution of the vampire, from the Hebrew tale of Lilith to the revenants of folklore, and the ever-changing creatures depicted in film and literature. Killers with a penchant for blood are also profiled, from Vlad Țepeș to the infamous "vampire clan" in Kentucky, as well as modern sanguinists who only get their blood supply from willing donors. The program continues with a look at witchcraft over the ages and the persecution of its practitioners, primarily the result of plans executed by the Catholic Church in an attempt to quell any religion outside of their own. Narrated by Mark Hamill.

A thorough documentary that explores how a formerly-feared undead creature became the sexually-charged vampire that we know today, whose presence once had people running for the hills but is now actively welcomed into their lives. As the vampire was being staked in the forests of old, it was Gothic literature that saved it from certain extinction, and once Bram Stoker added veiled sexuality into the mix, the vampire was here to stay. Stoker's immortal creation has died a thousand deaths, yet Dracula still comes back for more—and we'd not have it any other way.

Unsolved Mysteries – Ep. #9.12

NBC. Jan 31, 1997 (S09E12). Crime/Mystery. D: Anon. W: Anon. C: Melissa Hines, James Ridgeway, Jill Morley, John M. Rhein, Floyd Merchant. USA: English/Color/60m. Cosgrove-Meurer Productions.

Features a segment on former *Village Voice* reporter Susan Walsh, who at one time investigated vampire nightclubs, yet lost her journalistic objectivity after being drawn into the subculture; she even started dating one of the "undead." She quit the newspaper after the publisher refused to print her article, and returned to her former life as an exotic dancer. She was last seen on July 16, 1996; her disappearance from Nutley, New Jersey remains an unsolved mystery.

Susan may have intentionally disappeared to make a clean break and leave her sordid life behind.

Some believe she was murdered, a result of her past investigation into both the vampire clubs of Greenwich Village and the Russian Mob, which she alleged was forcing young immigrant women to work as strippers (she received death threats upon publication of her findings).

Untitled Ian Holt Project

(Unproduced.) 2009.

Around the time of the publication of *Dracula the Un-dead* (2009), which he co-wrote with Dacre Stoker, Holt announced he was looking for a few vampires—real practitioners—who would be interested in being part of a new reality show. Holt's intention was to make it less game show and more documentary, and take an unbiased look at their lifestyle choice. His target for broadcast was the summer of 2011, but there's been no word since on the status of this project.

Vampire Secrets

History Channel. Oct 29, 2006. Culture/Folklore. D: Diana Zaslaw. W: Josh Rosen. C: Thomas Garza, Katherine Ramsland, J. Gordon Melton, Michelle Belanger, Loyd Auerbach, Mark Benecke, Father Sebastiaan, Jeffery Davis ⚥, Justin Rodgers Hall ⚥. USA: English/Color/91m. Indigo Films/Jeff Margolis Productions.

This documentary traces the history of vampire legends worldwide; it features interviews with historians and other experts, and explores related tales both past and present. Includes reenactments featuring "real" vampires throughout history. Narrated by Corey Burton.

Average presentation that takes a look into the truths lurking behind the vampire legends, beginning with the earliest folklore from the Far East, to historical and modern-day "vampire" serial killers. There's nothing here that hasn't been seen or explored before, and a few of the so-called facts—especially relating to Elizabeth Báthory—need to be taken with a grain of salt. It's also best just to ignore the reenactment of Rod Ferrell's crimes, because they've taken way too much artistic liberty.

📺 Rebroadcast on January 19, 2007 as part of History Channel's *Decoding the Past* series.

Vampires: Thirst For the Truth

TLC. Oct 27, 1996. Folklore/History. D/W: Ruben Norte. C: J. Gordon Melton, David J. Skal, Donald F. Glut, Leslie Shepard, Raymond McNally, Radu Florescu, Norine Dresser, Lupita Tovar Kohner, Maila Nurmi, Forrest J Ackerman, Mark Rein-Hagen. USA: English/Color/95m. Weller-Grossman Productions Inc.

Presents a detailed look at the world of the vampire, from its literary incarnations to the wide-ranging interpretations on film and television. Also traces the various undead legends throughout different cultures. Narrated by William Marshall.

An exhaustive program with some very interesting moments that unfortunately don't add up to an overall compelling documentary. Beginning with the genesis of Bram Stoker's *Dracula,* the program explores the many historical accounts of vampire myths the world over, and how they could have influenced the author; this segment seems a little haphazard at times, and features some corny imagery. This is followed by the common topics of Vlad Ţepeş and Elizabeth Báthory, but there's no counterpoint to the standard claims that are always made when these two historical figures are mentioned. There is an interesting section that covers how the tourism industry of contemporary Romania has been influenced by the novel, as well as a revealing look at the modern misconceptions surrounding standard vampire folklore. The documentary jumps around too much and isn't very coherent, and regretfully, the interview segments are overly theatrical and presented in a cheesy manner. Too bad, because the program contains some rare interview clips with actors from some of the popular films and TV shows of the 1970s and 1980s.

Vampires: Why They Bite

BBC Three. Feb 10, 2010. Culture/History. D: Ray Easmon. W: Ray Easmon, Jacqui Wilson. C: Charlaine Harris, Edi Gathegi, Xan Brooks, Toby Whithouse, Tina Rath, Christopher Frayling, Cecilia d'Felice, Dan Jones, Richard Shepherd, Kim Newman. UK: English/Color/60m. BBC.

Explores how writers and filmmakers have taken an undead revenant and turned him into a Hollywood heartthrob. Deeply rooted in our psyche, vampires permeate today's popular culture—but are they simply the stuff of nightmares, or is the truth behind their origins much more terrifying? Searching for answers is historian Lisa Hilton, who begins her journey in Whitby to explore the origins of Bram Stoker's *Dracula.* She spans the globe to trace the evolution of the vampire from the German silent film *Nosferatu, Eine Symphonie des Garuens* (1922) to the UK television series *Being Human* (2009).

Once only a two-dimensional character with no voice of his own, the vampire has evolved from a feared creature of the night to a romantic, sexual being—now often depicted as the hero of the story. Over the course of an hour, this stylish and informative documentary somehow manages to outline the history of the vampire in popular culture, without feeling rushed or missing any of the important milestones. Despite its focus on bloodsuckers in visual media, the program still gives mention to some tales of folklore and the more ground-breaking novels. Peppered with dry British wit, this excellent documentary is a fine introduction to the subject. The only aspect I take issue with is the assertion that the characterization of Count Orlok by Max Schreck is anti-Semitic. Sorry, but that absurd notion is complete rubbish!

Vampires in New England

CPTV. Feb 1996. Folklore/History. D: Anon. W: Anon. C: Michael Bell, Christopher Rondina. USA: English/Color/30m. Connecticut Public Television.

A discussion of local vampire legends, including the tale of Mercy Brown, the infamous Rhode Island vampire thought to be responsible for a number of deaths in the late 1800s.

Vlad the Impaler: The True Story of Dracula

Book TV. 2002. Folklore/History. D/W: George Angelescu. C: Garth Collins. CAN: English/Color/51m. C21ETV Inc.

Explores the life and times of the infamous Wallachian warlord Vlad Țepeș, charting his life from the ruins of Târgoviște to his rule from Hunyad Castle in Hunedoara, Romania. May be alternately titled *The Impaler: A Biographical/Historical Look at the Life of Vlad the Impaler, Widely Known as Dracula*.

Van Helsing: The Man and the Monsters – A Sci-Fi Lowdown

SyFy. May 2, 2004. Culture/Film. D: Anon. W: Joy Lissandrello. C: Kate Beckinsale, Hugh Jackman, Silvia Colloca, Shuler Hensley, Will Kemp, Richard Roxburgh, Josie Maran, Stephen Sommers, David Wenham. USA: English/Color/60m. New Wave Entertainment Television.

Promotional documentary that features clips from the cast and crew of *Van Helsing* (2004), and explores the myths behind the folklore of vampires and werewolves.

Why Horror?

Super Channel. Oct 28, 2014. Culture/Horror. D: Nicolas Kleiman, Rob Lindsay. W: Rob Lindsay. C: Chris Alexander, Simon Barrett, John Carpenter, Don Coscarelli, Rodrigo Gudiño, Liisa Ladouceur, Karen Lam, Brad Middleton, Steve Niles, Gary Pullin, Xavier Aldana Reyes, George A. Romero, Eli Roth, Jen Soska, Sylvia Soska, Andrea Subissati. CAN: English/Color/82m. Don Ferguson Productions.

Why Horror? co-director Nicolas Kleiman, along with star Tal Zimerman and sociologist Andrea Subissati, joined forces to discuss the documentary at a fan convention (Author Photo)

Writer, lecturer, and horror blogger Tal Zimerman wants to know why we like to be scared. While travelling worldwide to explore this fear-inducing genre in different cultures, Zimerman speaks with leading writers, actors, and filmmakers, in an attempt to uncover why it is so popular. From books, to movies, and other avenues of popular culture, intentionally being scared has become a worldwide phenomenon—so what does this say about horror fans themselves? The documentary premiered on Canada's Super Channel as part of their "12 Nights of Horror Movies" marathon event, although it first garnered attention at Toronto's *After Dark Film Festival,* where it was named one of the best films of the program.

Why We ♥ Vampires

NBC. Nov 1, 2013. Culture/Reality. D: Anon. W: Anon. C: Victoria Smurfit, Anne Rice, Kristin Bauer, Carrie Preston, Cassandra Peterson, James Marsters, Nicholas Brendon, Edward Herrmann, Chris Sarandon. USA: English/B&W, Color/60m. Peacock Productions.

MSNBC anchor Tamron Hall hosts this one-hour special that asks the question, why do we love vampires? Features numerous interview clips with actors, writers, and other personalities who wax poetic about their love affair with these bloodsucking creatures of the night.

The World of Hammer – "Peter Cushing"

Channel 4. Aug 12, 1994 (S01E01). History/Film. D: Robert Sidaway. W: Ashley Sidaway, Robert Sidaway. C: Oliver Reed. UK: English/Color/30m. Best of British Films & Television Production/Hammer Film Productions.

This episode focuses on actor Peter Cushing and his roles in various Hammer productions, including his notable performances as Baron Frankenstein, Van Helsing and Sherlock Holmes. Features clips from the vampire films *Brides of Dracula* (1960) and *Twins of Evil* (1971). Narrated by Oliver Reed.

The World of Hammer – "Dracula and the Undead"

Channel 4. Aug 19, 1994 (S01E02). History/Film. D: Robert Sidaway. W: Ashley Sidaway, Robert Sidaway. C: Oliver Reed. UK: English/Color/30m. Best of British Films & Television Production/Hammer Film Productions.

With a focus on the Peter Cushing/Christopher Lee *Dracula* films, this episode highlights the vampire movies of Hammer Film Productions. Features clips from *Horror of Dracula* (1958), *The Brides of Dracula* (1960), *Kiss of the Vampire* (1963), *Dracula: Prince of Darkness* (1966), *Scars of Dracula* (1970), *Twins of Evil* (1971), *Vampire Circus* (1972), *Captain Kronos: Vampire Hunter* (1974) and *The Legend of the Seven Golden Vampires* (1974). Narrated by Oliver Reed.

The World of Hammer – "Vamp"

Channel 4. Sep 1, 1994 (S01E04). History/Film. D: Robert Sidaway. W: Ashley Sidaway, Robert Sidaway. C: Oliver Reed. UK: English/Color/30m. Best of British Films & Television Production/Hammer Film Productions.

Although Hammer Film Productions is best known for their numerous Dracula films, the Count wasn't the only bloodsucker on the roster. This episode celebrates Carmilla and other female vampires, and features clips from *The Brides of Dracula* (1960), *The Vampire Lovers* (1970), *Twins of Evil* (1971) and *Lust for a Vampire* (1971). Narrated by Oliver Reed.

The World of Hammer – "Wicked Women"

Channel 4. Sep 9, 1994 (S01E05). History/Film. D: Robert Sidaway. W: Ashley Sidaway, Robert Sidaway. C: Oliver Reed. UK: English/Color/30m. Best of British Films & Television Production/Hammer Film Productions.

In the films of Hammer Film Productions, female characters were often more wicked and malicious than the men. This entry highlights the work of such screen icons as Ingrid Pitt, Martine Beswick, Joan Fontaine, and Bette Davis. Includes scenes from the vampire film *Countess Dracula* (1971), as well as several other classics like *The Nanny* (1965) and *Dr. Jekyll & Sister Hyde* (1971). Narrated by Oliver Reed.

The World of Hammer – "Mummies, Werewolves and the Living Dead"

Channel 4. Sep 30, 1994 (S01E08). History/Film. D: Robert Sidaway. W: Ashley Sidaway, Robert Sidaway. C: Oliver Reed. UK: English/Color/26m. Best of British Films & Television Production/Hammer Film Productions.

This episode features a gallery of the living dead, offering up examples of vampires, mummies and werewolves from the Hammer vault of horror. Includes a segment covering *The Legend of the 7 Golden Vampires* (1974). Narrated by Oliver Reed.

The World of Hammer – "Christopher Lee"

Channel 4. Oct 21, 1994 (S01E11). History/Film. D: Robert Sidaway. W: Ashley Sidaway, Robert Sidaway. C: Oliver Reed. UK: English/Color/30m. Best of British Films & Television Production/Hammer Film Productions.

This episode focuses on actor Christopher Lee and his starring roles in various Hammer productions, including his notable performances as Dracula, The Mummy, and Rasputin. Features clips from his vampire movies. Narrated by Oliver Reed.

The World of Hammer – "Hammer"

Channel 4. Oct 28, 1994 (S01E12). History/Film. D: Robert Sidaway. W: Ashley Sidaway, Robert Sidaway. C: Oliver Reed. UK: English/Color/30m. Best of British Films & Television Production/Hammer Film Productions.

This episode celebrates the forty-year history of Hammer Film Productions, with highlights that include a selection of clips from their Dracula movies. Narrated by Oliver Reed.

The World of Van Helsing

Channel 5. May 8, 2004. Culture/Film. D: Anon. W: David Hughes, Gordon Dale. C: Hugh Jackman, Kate Beckinsale, Stephen Sommers, Silvia Colloca, Will Kemp, Shuler Hensley, Richard Roxburgh. UK: English/Color/24m. Picture Production Company/Five.

Promotional documentary for the film *Van Helsing* (2004), featuring interviews with the cast and crew, as well as highlights of the special effects and stunts performed in the movie.

Promotional advertisement for the NBC series *Cliffhangers!* (Universal TV/TV Guide)

Promotional advertisement for the ABC TV movie *Vampire* (MTM Enterprises/TV Guide)

Original promotional advertisement for the ABC TV movie *The Halloween That Almost Wasn't* (New Horizons/TV Guide)

Promotional advertisement for the 1980 rebroadcast of *Salem's Lot* (Warner Bros. Television/TV Guide)

Artistic Endeavors
Variety Programming and TV Specials

Lucy (Tara Birtwhistle) surrenders to Count Dracula (Zhang Wei-Qiang) in Guy Maddin's
Dracula: Pages from a Virgin's Diary (Vonnie Von Helmolt Film/Bruce Monk)

3-2-1 – "The Magic of Merlin"

ITV. Nov 16, 1985 (S08E12). Culture/History. D: Ian Bolt, David Millard, Philip Casson, Paddy Russell. W: Anon. C: Kenneth Connor, Aimi MacDonald, Jon Pertwee ☥, Jeremy Connor, Chris Emmett. UK: English/Color/60m. Yorkshire Television.

It's a quiz! It's a game! It's fortune and fame! In this long-running game show, contestants vied for hidden prizes, and had to solve cryptic clues before they discovered what they won. If they disliked the prize, they could reject it in favor of winning a better one. But there was always a chance they'd end up with the booby prize (a garbage can), which was represented by the character "Dusty Bin"—the show's mascot. Hosted by Ted Rogers and Caroline Munro.

Part variety show, this series often had themed episodes, and featured up-and-coming musical acts and comedians (who performed for the audience, and then provided clues to the contestants). In this episode—most likely a Hollywood theme—actors portrayed Merlin, Marilyn Monroe, and Dracula.

📺 Co-host Caroline Munro appeared in the films *Dracula A.D. 1972* and *Captain Kronos - Vampire Hunter*. Jon Pertwee (Dracula) played a horror film star who is given a real vampire's cape in the segment "The Cloak" from the anthology film *The House That Dripped Blood*.

90 Minutes Live – Flora MacDonald / The Men of the Deeps

CBC. Dec 17, 1976 (S01E--). Culture/Music. D: Jack Sampson. W: Bob Ennis, Marrin Canell. C: Jonathan Edwards, Lynnie Edwards, Radu Florescu, David Brown ☥, Bonnie Bramlett, Flora McDonald, Men of the Deeps, Jan Todd, Terry Todd. CAN: English/Color/79m. CBC.

Host Peter Gzowski welcomes Radu Florescu, the forty-fifth descendent of Vlad the Impaler, who discusses his ancestry, author Bram Stoker and the novel *Dracula*, as well as the modern-day vampire beliefs of Romanian peasants. Also includes a monologue from *Dracula* performed by actor David Brown, fully costumed as the infamous vampire.

Radu Florescu, the 45th descendent of Vlad the Impaler, uncovered his family's connection to the infamous Romanian warlord while researching *In Search of Dracula* with Raymond McNally (Arthur Grace/HYT Pictures)

This episode features an engaging interview with Radu Florescu, who a few years earlier had co-written *In Search of Dracula* with Raymond McNally. Despite some trite questions, Florescu furnishes a good deal of information about the Vlad and his homeland, without letting the conversation become too sensational. The interview is followed by a *Dracula* monologue from

David Brown, who relates a charming story about his trip from Toronto to the TV Studios in Halifax. Because of delays due to inclement weather, he had to apply his makeup mid-flight so he could be ready for his appearance on the show—much to the shock of his fellow passengers. The actor also discusses his choice of makeup for the role, which appears to have been inspired by *La Cage aux Folles*—complete with pancake makeup, ruby-red lipstick and accentuated eyebrows.

90 Minutes Live – Salome Bey / Joyce Maynard / Offenbach

CBC. Mar 7, 1977 (S01E--). Culture/Music. D: Henry Pasilla. W: Anon. C: Salome Bey, Joyce Maynard, Offenbach, Jean Baillargeon, Stephen Kaplan, Don Chevrier. CAN: English/Color/77m. CBC.

This episode features a chat with Dr. Stephen Kaplan of the Vampire Research Centre of America, who discusses the increasing prevalence of real vampires in today's society (which include sanguinists and energy drainers). Hosted by Peter Gzowski.

The interview segment with Kaplan is quite odd, yet it is the best part of this episode. He comes off as a bit of a pseudo-intellectual, and is quite condescending to both the host and the audience. Although he tries his best to discuss his organization—and takes a serious approach to the topic of modern vampirism—the constant cackles from the audience are too much of a distraction for him. After his interview concludes and the show returns from a commercial break, he's nowhere to be found—even though all the other guests are still on set. It's a very bizarre bit of television, and in a show where the conversations tended to drag on for too long, it actually would have been nice to hear more from Dr. Kaplan.

The ABC Comedy Hour – Tony Curtis

ABC. Mar 29, 1972 (S01E12). Comedy/Music. D: Dwight Hemion. W: John Aylesworth. C: Rich Little, Frank Gorshin, George Kirby, Marilyn Michaels, Fred Travalena, Joe Baker. USA: English/Color/60m. Associated Television.

This short-lived variety series primarily featured a different guest host each week, plus a regular cast of impressionists who were collectively known as "The Kopycats." In this episode, guest host Tony Curtis appears as Count Dracula alongside the Frankenstein Monster (Frank Gorshin), with whom he sings a duet.

All That

Nickelodeon. 1994-2005. Comedy/Family. D: Anon. W: Anon. C: Chelsea Brummet, Jack DeSena ☥, Lisa Foiles, Giovonnie Samuels, Shane Lyons, Jamie Lynn Spears, Kyle Sullivan, Christina Kirkman. USA: English/Color/5520m. Tollin-Robbins Productions/Nickelodeon.

Seasons 7 through 10 of this youth-oriented sketch comedy show featured *The Unreal World*, a spoof of MTV's *The Real World*. Characters included a cool and wealthy vampire; a smart-mouthed mummy; the ghost of a cheerleader; an accountant who's a werewolf; a decaying zombie; and an idiotic Frankenstein Monster.

The Aunty Jack Show - "The Aunty Jack Horror Show"

ABC (AUS). Dec 27, 1972 (S01E07). Comedy/Music. D: Maurice B. Murphy. W: Grahame Bond, Geoff Atherden, John Brendan, Ronald Evans. C: Grahame Bond ☥, John Derum ☥, Rory O'Donoghue, Sandra MacGregor. AUS: English/B&W/30m. ABC-TV.

A Pythonesque sketch comedy series headlined by Aunty Jack (a mustachioed motorcycle-riding transvestite) and her band of misfits—which included Thin Arthur, Narrator Neville, and Flange Desire. In this horror-themed episode, Aunty Jack is turned into an undead bloodsucker, thus beginning a series of skits featuring vampires, witches, and ghosts. Oh my!

Barris & Company – Ep. #1.08

CBC. Nov 9, 1968 (S01E08). Comedy/Music. D: Pat King. W: Ken Gunton, Alfie Scopp, Alex Barris. C: Judy LaMarsh, Sandra O'Neill, Janet Baird, Guido Basso ☥, Les Rubie. CAN: English/B&W/33m. CBC.

This Saturday evening variety show aired live directly after the CBC's broadcast of *Hockey Night in Canada*. This episode includes interviews with Canadian politician Judy LaMarsh and singer Sandra O'Neill, and opens with a skit featuring orchestra leader Guido Basso dressed as Dracula. Hosted by Alex Barris.

The opening sketch sees Dracula creeping up to a buxom blonde lying in bed; she notices the vampire baring fangs and flatly says, "Don't be silly." She then delivers the punch line, "Besides, I gave at the office!" The joke hasn't aged well, but the rest of the episode is quite charming, and host Alex Barris is a good fit to his regular cast of performers. One skit in particular—a *Laugh-In* inspired "Alex's Restaurant"—garners a number of laughs.

The Bay City Rollers Meet the Saturday Superstars

NBC. Sep 8, 1978. Comedy/Music. D: Jack Regas. W: Mark Evanier, Lorne Frohman, Rowby Goren. C: The Bay City Rollers, Billie Hayes, Jay Robinson ☥, Billy Barty, Joe Namath, Erik Estrada, Scott Baio, Sharon Baird, Kaptain Kool and the Kongs. USA: English/Color/48m. Krofft Entertainment Inc.

A fall preview special that showcased the new *Krofft Superstar Hour* that premiered the next day. It was ostensibly a revamp of *The Krofft Supershow* (ABC, September 11, 1976 - September 2, 1978) and starred the Scottish pop group The Bay City Rollers, who performed several songs and acted in original comedy sketches. Included is a "Horror Hotel" segment that featured Wilhelmina

W. Witchiepoo (of *H.R. Pufnstuf* fame) as the proprietor of a run-down hotel, along with her assistant Horatio J. HooDoo (from *Lidsville*) and several other *H.R. Pufnstuf* characters. In this skit, Witchiepoo is all set to marry Count Dracula, that is, until football great Joe Namath stops into the hotel.

When athletes and musicians take a stab at acting—or even worse, comedy—things rarely turn out well. Thankfully in this case, they're surrounded by seasoned performers, who pick up the slack and help deliver a surprisingly entertaining program. Character actor Jay Robinson is in great form as a menacing Count Dracula; he's played for laughs, so the only real horror in this production is the 1950s-style love song performed by Erik Estrada.

The Benny Hill Show – "Leprechaun TV: Opening Night"

ITV1. Mar 14, 1979 (S10E02). Comedy/Variety. D: Dennis Kirkland. W: Benny Hill. C: Benny Hill ♀, Henry McGee, Jack Wright, Jenny Lee Wright, Geraldine, Sue Upton, Roger Finch, Nola Haynes, Jenny Westbrook, Johnny Vyvyan. UK: English/Color/30m. Thames Television.

In the segment "Wondergran Meets Dracula," the geriatric superwoman tries her best to stop the Count from biting the necks of young, bodacious women (as well as a couple of men). Features typical humor from Benny Hill, so if you appreciate his comedic antics, you'll enjoy his take on Dracula.

The Best of the Munsters

TBS. Oct 9, 1988. Comedy/Family. D: Anon. W: Anon. C: Al Lewis ♀, Pat Priest, Butch Patrick. USA: English/B&W, Color/60m. Kayro-Vue Productions/Universal Pictures/TBS.

This was a retrospective of the classic series, and was broadcast prior to the premiere episode of the new series *The Munsters Today*. With Lily and Herman away on vacation, Eddie and Marilyn visit Grandpa to reminisce about old times. Clips from *The Munsters* are introduced through one of Grandpa's new inventions—a TV set that allows them to view their memories.

Count Dracula (Benny Hill) considers having a quick bite in a sketch from *The Benny Hill Show* (Thames Television)

Beyond Reason – Ep. #2.37

CBC. Sep 19, 1978 (S02E37). Culture/Reality. D: Ernie Zuk. W: Richard Lubbock, Allen Spraggett. C: Geof Gray-Cobb, Marilyn Rossner, Irene Hughes, Sybil Leek, Stirling Moss. CAN: English/Color/25m. CBC.

A psychic game show where a panel of paranormal experts attempt to figure out the identities of two hidden guests. The panel features an Astrologer, who's given the guest's birth date and location; a Psychic Graphologist, who gets a handwriting sample; and a Clairvoyant, who gets a personal object. This week's "Psychic Clopedia" segment covers the topic of vampirism, and includes an interview with vampirologist Dr. Stephen Kaplan of the Vampire Research Center. Hosted by Allen Spraggett along with adjudicator Bill Guest.

The first guest, Sybil Leek, was a very influential figure in the advancement of the Wiccan religion during this period, and her segment is interesting in and of itself. But genre fans will of course be more interested in the interview with Kaplan, who discusses his organization as well as his research into three types of modern vampirism: sanguinists, energy drainers, and "vampire-like" individuals. Although another panelist gets the most points and essentially "wins" this time around, it's Geof Gray-Cobb who hits a home run—he correctly identifies race car driver Stirling Moss.

Beyond Reason – Ep. #3.34

CBC. Mar 28, 1979 (S03E34). Culture/Reality. D: Ernie Zuk. W: Richard Lubbock, Allen Spraggett. C: Geof Gray-Cobb, Marilyn Rossner, Irene Hughes, Helena de Silaghi-Sirag, Henry Morgan. CAN: English/Color/25m. CBC.

This episode features Countess Helena de Silaghi-Sirag, a distinguished painter and blood relative of Vlad Țepeș, who facetiously calls herself "Dracula's niece." The Psychic Clopedia segment covers the topic of Dracula; the host dresses up as the Count, and relates tales of Vlad Țepeș and the Hollywood vampire. Hosted by Allen Spraggett along with adjudicator Bill Guest.

Three paranormal experts guess the identities of hidden contestants on *Beyond Reason* (CBC Still Photo Collection)

Another great episode from this very unique game show, and although the panelists are unable to discern the identities of Helena de Silaghi-Sirag or Henry Morgan, it's a lot of fun watching them work their mojo.

Bizarre – Ep. #1.02

CTV. Oct 24, 1980 (S01E02). Comedy/Satire. D: Maurice Abraham. W: Allan Blye, Bob Einstein, Martin Tenney. C: John Byner ♀, Tom Harvey, Bob Einstein, Ziggy Lorenc, Beau Starr, Billy Van. CAN: English/Color/30m. Shiral Productions/CTV.

A risqué sketch comedy show where no topic is sacred. This episode features a skit where Dracula pays an unusual daytime visit to his doctor. The vampire relates a story about a Hollywood party, where he met a lot of famous people (and bit some of them on the neck).

Dressed as a typical Count Dracula, Byner recalls the events of the party, and breaks into several impersonations of the guests. These include Ted Kennedy, Johnny Mathis, Don Rickles, Paul Lynde (who bites Dracula!), and Rodney Dangerfield.

The Book Tower – "Vampire Master"

ITV. Jan 7, 1988 (S07E04). Drama/Literature. D: Richard Callanan. W: Anon. C: Anthony Benson, Gerry Cowan, Lawrence Cieslik, Dean Manning, Helen Stockdale. UK: English/Color/25m. Yorkshire Television.

Children's magazine show focusing on literature and reading, which includes dramatizations of extracts from featured books. This episode highlights *Vampire Master of Burlap Hall*, the 1987 book by Virginia Ironside, which is about a group of students who discover that their new biology teacher, Mr. A Culard, is really Dracula. Hosted by Mark Miwurdz.

Burr Tillstrom's Kukla and Ollie – "Buelah's Debut"

NBC. 1961 (S01E--). Family/Music. D: Anon. W: Anon. C: Burr Tillstrom. USA: English/B&W/5m. Kuklapolitan Productions/NBC.

This incarnation of puppeteer Burr Tillstrom's Kuklapolitan Troupe featured Kukla (a human), Ollie (a dragon), Mrs. Bufforfington (a chicken) and Buelah (a witch). In this episode, Buelah debuts a new song at the "Vampire Room" in the Hotel Kuklapolitan.

Canada After Dark – Ep. #1.32

CBC. Oct 31, 1978 (S01E32). Comedy/Culture. D: Henry Pasila. W: Alex Frame, Bob Ennis. C: Ricky Jay, Marilyn Brooks, Walter Stewart, Larry Palef, Jack Lens. CAN: English/Color/51m. CBC.

After the cancellation of *90 Minutes Live* in the mid-1970s, the CBC revisited the genre with this entertainment-oriented talk show, hosted by veteran actor Paul Soles. This special Halloween-themed episode opens with Soles dressed as Dracula, wearing a red-lined opera cape and adopting a Hungarian accent.

Clips from horror movies are run just before each commercial break, one of which is from an unknown vampire film. The second interview segment features fashion designer Marilyn Brooks, who illustrates four costumes for Halloween that can be made on the cheap from "anything in your closet." This includes a "Bride of Dracula" getup complete with horns, a pink mask, and a dime store set of fangs. Thanks in part to the engaging first interview with magician/actor Ricky Jay, this is one of the better episodes of the series, and includes a goofy mix of humor, sexual innuendo and vague drug references.

Québécois actor Jean LeClerc replaced Frank Langella for the Broadway touring production of *Dracula*, portraying the vampire across the United States and Canada in the early 1970s (Kenn Duncan)

Canada After Dark – Ep. #1.89

CBC. Jan 18, 1979 (S01E89). Comedy/Culture. D: Henry Pasila. W: Alex Frame, Bob Ennis. C: Ian Tyson, Liz Torres, Elwy Yost, Jean LeClerc, Brenda Lee. CAN: English/Color/51m. CBC.

Host Paul Soles interviews French Canadian actor Jean LeClerc, who discusses his role as the title character in the Broadway production of *Dracula*; he replaced Frank Langella when the play went on tour.

LeClerc tries his best to seriously discuss his role as the infamous vampire, but the host hams it up way too much and takes the whole conversation a little too frivolously. For a much more engaging interview about the subject, seek out Brian Linehan's chat with the actor from the Canadian arts series *Evening Out*.

The Carol Burnett Show – Ep. #6.11

CBS. Nov 22, 1972 (S06E11). Comedy/Music. D: Dave Powers. W: Stan Hart, Larry Siegel. C: Carol Burnett, Harvey Korman, Vicki Lawrence, Lyle Waggoner ⚲, Vincent Price, Ray Charles. USA: English/Color/60m. Bob Banner Associates/Burngood/Punkin Productions Inc./CBS.

In a salute to horror movies, Count Dracula introduces a spoof of *King Tut's Tomb* (1950) and *Bride of Frankenstein* (1935), which features guest star Vincent Price. Rebroadcast as part of S01E11 of the syndicated series *Carol Burnett and Friends*.

Carry on Christmas

ITV. Dec 24, 1969. Comedy/Satire. D: Ronnie Baxster. W: Talbot Rothwell. C: Sid James, Terry Scott, Charles Hawtrey, Hattie Jacques, Barbara Windsor, Bernard Bresslaw, Peter Butterworth ⚥, Frankie Howerd. UK: English/Color/50m. Thames Television.

This irreverent take on Charles Dickens' *A Christmas Carol* has Ebenezer Scrooge visited by three atypical spirits; they attempt to show him the error of his penny-pinching ways, through a glimpse into his past, present and future. First in a series of four stand-alone Christmas specials.

An average TV special with a handful of funny moments, the best of which is when scene-stealer Charles Hawtrey appears as the Ghost of Christmas Past. He relates the tale of a scientist, Dr. Frank N. Stein, who had asked Scrooge for a loan; his assistant, Count Dracula, had just procured the final appendage needed to finish off his latest creation. Even though the monster has a bride waiting for him, when he awakes, he's more attracted to the Doctor.

Cincinnati Pops Holiday: Erich Kunzel's Halloween Spooktacular

PBS. Oct 30, 1996. Dance/Music. D: Phillip Byrd. W: Phillip Byrd, John Meek. C: Robert Guillaume, Tom Wopat, Jonathan & Charlotte Pendragon, Aaron Douglas Smith, Marquis. USA: English/Color/57m. Brandenburg Productions/WCET-TV.

Pared down from a two-hour variety show that was recorded live over three nights at the Cincinnati Music Hall, this visual spectacle features horror-themed music, song and dance. Highlights include a Broadway medley performed by Tom Wopat, and a reading of *The Legend of Sleepy Hollow* by Robert Guillaume. Orchestra conducted by Erich Kunzel.

The costumed musicians represent all the well-known horrors, including a vampire piano player and the Frankenstein Monster on the marimba; there are also set pieces that feature a coven of witches, and a zombie that rises from inside a coffin. The barbershop quartet "Marquis"—all sporting red-lined opera capes—perform *The Cockroach That Ate Cincinnati,* while Robert Guillaume enthusiastically narrates a poetic adaptation of Washington Irving's classic tale. A children's choir caps off the evening with a Halloween medley, which features such songs as "Monster Mash" (sung by a vampire) and the theme to *The Addams Family.* It's a wonderful, seasonal program that's perfectly suited for the entire family.

Club Oasis - Ep. #2.05

NBC. Aug 2, 1958 (S02E05). Comedy/Music. D: Anon. W: Stanley Shapiro, Hugh Wedlock, Howard Snyder, Fred Fox. C: Joyce Jameson ⚥, Doodles Weaver, Billy Barty, Len Carrie, Kendall Kapps, The King Sisters, Spike Jones ⚥ and his City Slickers. USA: English/Color/30m. NBC.

A mix of comedy and music, this early NBC series attempted to evoke a chic nightclub atmosphere, and eventually became a showcase for the crazy antics of bandleader Spike Jones. In this episode, the story of Cinderella is reimagined as a "spooktacular scarytale" as if directed by Alfred Hitchcock. The skit featured Jones as Dracula, Joyce Jameson in the dual role of Cinderella/Vampira, and Len Carrie as the Frankenstein Monster. Hosted by Spike Jones.

📺 This episode likely led to the 1959 recording Spike Jones - In Stereo: A Spooktacular in Screaming Sound. During a publicity junket for the album, horror host Zacherley appeared alongside a Vampira lookalike.

Creature Feature

WDCA-TV. 1973 – 1987 (-- Episodes). Comedy/Horror. D: Anon. W: Dick Dyszel. C: Dick Dyszel ☥. USA: English/B&W, Color/--m. WDCA-TV.

Horror host Count Gore DeVol, a vampire, introduces classic monster movies to the masses. He often had special guests, including Forrest J Ackerman, and was the featured player in a number of skits and commercial parodies. Broadcast locally in Washington D.C. on the independent station WDCA-TV.

Daily Show - "Misty May-Treanor"

Comedy Central. Aug 14, 2012 (S17E140). Comedy/Politics. D: Chuck O'Neil. W: Tim Carvell, Jon Stewart, John Oliver. C: Jon Stewart ☥, John Hodgman, Misty May-Treanor. USA: English/Color/60m. Comedy Partners/Hello Doggie.

Due to the ratings bump after Robert Pattinson's appearance on the previous evening (to promote *Cosmopolis*), host Jon Stewart rebranded this episode as the "Democalypse 2012 - Wait! Don't Leave! Here is a Picture of Taylor Lautner" edition. Opening coverage refers to the race for the White House as an ongoing struggle between "a young and diverse feral group" of werewolves (Democrats), and "a very old pale clan" of vampires (Republicans)—with Stewart briefly donning false fangs, and sparkling in sunlight. Correspondent John Hodgman explores *Twilight's* vampires in his "Horrorotica" segment, which leads to Stewart tailoring his political analysis to make it more teen-friendly, and inexplicably tied to Stephenie Meyer's popular novel series.

The Danny Kaye Show – Ep. #3.11

CBS. Dec 1, 1965 (S03E11). Comedy/Music. D: Anon. W: Gary Belkin, Billy Barnes, Ron Friedman. C: John Astin, Gwen Verdon, D'Aldo Romano, Harvey Korman, Joyce Van Patten. USA: English/Color/60m. Dena Productions/CBS.

Danny Kaye welcomes John Astin from *The Addams Family*, as well as comedienne Gwen Verdon and singer D'Aldo Romano. A group of "dancing vampires"—four females dressed as a cross between Morticia Addams and Vampira—join Kaye and Astin in one sketch.

The Danny Kaye Show – Ep. #3.30

CBS. Apr 13, 1966 (S03E30). Comedy/Music. D: Robert Scheerer. W: Herbert Baker, Billy Barnes, Larry Gelbart. C: Edie Adams, Fred Gwynne, Glenn Yarbrough, Harvey Korman. USA: English/B&W/60m. Dena Productions/CBS.

🦇 🦇 🦇

Danny Kaye introduces Fred Gwynne in character as Herman Munster, who reveals that he wants to be more than just a television performer—his goal is to be a newscaster. This segues into a spoof of a newscast hosted by "Chet" Munster, who co-anchors the *Munster-Dracula Report* alongside Kaye as "David" Dracula. Edie Adams joins in the fun as "Tempera Tura," the weather ghoul, channeling Zsa Zsa Gabor while wearing a guise inspired by Vampira.

This charming skit of fake news features Gwynne in top form as Herman Munster, while Kaye is equally as engaging with his Lugosi-inspired take on Dracula—who's quite entertained by all the death and destruction in the day's headlines. An episode definitely worth watching if you can find it.

The David Frost Show – Ep. #4.118

CBS. Mar 2, 1972 (S04E118). Culture/Music. D: Anon. W: Anon. C: David Frost, Kris Kristofferson, Greg Morris, Jan de Hartog, Raymond McNally, Radu Florescu. USA: English/Color/60m. Group W Productions.

Host David Frost welcomes authors Raymond McNally and Radu Florescu, who discuss the legend of Dracula and their new book, *In Search of Dracula : A True History of Dracula and Vampire Legends*.

The Dick Cavett Show – Ep. #7.36

ABC. Nov 14, 1972 (S07E36). Culture/Music. D: Anon. W: Anon. C: Radu Florescu, Raymond McNally, Melba Moore, Bobby Rosengarden, Fred Foy. USA: English/Color/90m. Daphne Productions Inc./ABC.

Host Dick Cavett welcomes authors Raymond McNally and Radu Florescu, who discuss the origins of the vampire Dracula and their new book, I*n Search of Dracula : A True History of Dracula and Vampire Legends.*

Dinah Shore Chevy Show – Ep. #1.09

NBC. May 17, 1957 (S01E09). Comedy/Music. D: Bob Banner. W: John Bradford. C: Dinah Shore ☥, The Skylarks, Art Carney, Boris Karloff, Betty Hutton ☥. USA: English/Color/60m. Bob Banner Associates/NBC.

🦇 🦇 🦇 🦇

Boris Karloff performs his own take on the show's theme song (presented by "Shiverolet" instead of "Chevrolet"), which opens with a graphic of the NBC logo superimposed with a bat. This leads into a performance of "Mama Look at Bubu" from Borey Karloff and his All-Ghoul Orchestra.

The band features Art Carney wearing coke-bottle glasses and a set of malformed teeth, with both Betty Hutton and Dinah Shore dressed up as Vampira lookalikes. The group then sings a hilarious rendition of "Little Darlin'." Hosted by Dinah Shore.

Dr. Bundolo – Ep. #1.02

CBC. Oct 19, 1980 (S01E02). Comedy/Music. D: Don S. Williams. W: Dan Thatchuk, David King. C: Bill Buck, Norm Grohmann, Marla Gropper, Bill Reiter, Don Clark Band, Phil Reimer, Don Granbery, Al Foreman. CAN: English/Color/51m. CBC.

Evolving from the half-hour radio program *Dr. Bundolo's Pandemonium Medicine Show,* this Vancouver-based sketch comedy series was taped before a live studio audience, and featured a regular cast with special guests and musicians each week. This episode included a short sketch called "Vampire Coconuts," which was a mock promo for a new CBC movie of the week that shows a woman being attacked by bloodsucking coconuts. By no means the best skit of the bunch, it's far outshined by the highlight of the episode, "Prefab Holmes of Lumber Yard," where Grohmann and Reiter effectively take on the roles of Sherlock Holmes and Dr. Watson in a very funny skit.

Dracula: A Chamber Musical

CBC. Mar 16, 2000. Drama/Music. D/W: Richard Ouzounian. C: Juan Chioran ☥, June Crowley, Roger Honeywell, Michael Fletcher, Amy Walsh ☥, Benedict Campbell. CAN: English/Color/110m. Ontario Educational Communications Authority/TV Ontario.

A musical adaptation of Bram Stoker's immortal tale. This was recorded live at the Avon Theatre in Stratford, Ontario on November 16, 1999 during the Stratford Shakespeare Festival.

Dracula, Live From Transylvania

FOX. Oct 25, 1989. Culture/History. D: Roger Cardinal. W: John Joslyn, S.S. Schweitzer, Karl LaFong. C: George Hamilton, Radu Florescu, Norine Dresser, Bernard Davies, Raymond McNally, Françoise Robertson ☥. CAN: English/Color/92m. Joslyn Entertainment/Misha Televisual Productions/Omni Capital.

George Hamilton hosts this live event (with pre-taped portions) from Solomon's Tower in Visegrad, Hungary, a citadel that once held Vlad Țepeș under duress. As Hamilton wanders throughout the castle, he meets up with scholars and researchers, and learns about Bram Stoker, the genesis of his novel *Dracula,* and vampires—both real and historical. Narrated by Vlasta Vrana.

This is one of those television specials that needs to be seen to be believed; it's an odd mix of live interviews and dramatized segments, with a self-deprecating George Hamilton tying it all together in a light-hearted manner (using some off-color jokes at times). Some of Hamilton's segues were definitely taped, however it does appear that most if not all the interviews were live, as they are at times spotted with flubbed lines, uncomfortable silences, and noise from the television crew. The best interview segment is with McNally and Florescu, who come off as a bickering Odd Couple as they argue over who discovered what, regarding their research into Vlad Țepeș. Author Norine Dresser *(American Vampires)* also interviews "Brad" and "Monique," two modern sanguinists who discuss their lifestyle while blanketed in shadow. The special concludes in full fiction mode as Hamilton flees from the castle, after a couple of bodies are found with bite marks on the neck and completely drained of blood.

This was the last of a number of live, high-concept and overly-hyped television specials that ran in the 1980s, which also included *The Mystery of Al Capone's Vault* (1986) with Geraldo Rivera and *Return to the Titanic - Live!* (1987) with Telly Savalas.

George Hamilton hosts *Dracula, Live From Transylvania* from inside Solomon's Tower in Visegrad, Hungary (Joslyn Entertainment/Robert Szabo)

The Ed Sullivan Show – Ep. #20.38

CBS. May 28, 1967 (S20E38). Culture/Music. D: Anon. W: Anon. C: The Pickle Brothers, The Temptations, Robert Goulet, The Roselles, The Jovers, Tessie O'Shea, Peter Lawford. USA: English/Color/60m. Sullivan Productions/CBS.

Host Ed Sullivan welcomes several guests including the comedy trio The Pickle Brothers, who perform a vaudeville-style sketch featuring Dracula.

The Electric Company

PBS. Oct 25, 1971 – Apr 15, 1977 (780 Episodes). Educational/Family. D: Henry Behar. W: Jeremy Stevens. C: Morgan Freeman ⚥, Rita Moreno, Skip Hinnant, Judy Graubart, Mel Brooks, Jim Boyd, Joan Rivers, Gene Wilder. USA: English/Color/23400m. Children's Television Workshop.

A children's educational series where *Saturday Night Live* met *Sesame Street,* which taught basic grammar and language through a variety of songs, skits and cartoons. Morgan Freeman played several bloodsuckers on the show; one of his first appearances was during a performance by series regulars *Short Circus,* who sang about the menacing nature of the vampire. He also appeared as

Dracula in such regular skits as "Spidey Super Stories" and "Norman Neat, Man on the Street," and extoled the virtues of eating healthy in the guise of Vincent, the Vegetable Vampire. One noteworthy undead performance was a musical number where Freeman took a bubble bath inside a casket.

The Entertainers – Ep. #1.17

CBS. Jan 16, 1965 (S01E17). Comedy/Music. D: Dave Geisel. W: Vincent Bogert, Sydney Zelinka. C: Carol Burnett ⚲, Caterina Valente ⚲, Chita Rivera ⚲, Boris Karloff, Hendra & Ullett, Dom DeLuise, Ruth Buzzi, John Davidson. USA: English/B&W/60m. Bob Banner Associates/CBS.

Co-hosts Carol Burnett and Caterina Valente welcome Chita Rivera and Boris Karloff for an eerily good time. One performance features Burnett, Valente and Rivera as a trio of ghoulish women, who sing a tongue-in-cheek version of "I Enjoy Being a Girl" from the Rodgers and Hammerstein musical *Flower Drum Song* (1958). This performance takes place within a fog-laden graveyard, and the three are dressed as a cross between Vampira and Morticia Addams. They also wear the same guise when they introduce a musical number by Karloff, who performs "Chim Chim Cher-ee" from *Mary Poppins* (1964).

Evening Out – Ep. #1.16

CBC. Jan 11, 1979 (S01E16). Arts/Music. D: Anon. W: Anon. C: Frank Moore, Jean LeClerc, Tom Kneebone, Toby Tarnow, Neil Vipond. CAN: English/Color/24m. CBC.

Hosted by renowned Canadian celebrity interviewer Brian Linehan, this weekly series focused on the arts scene in Toronto, Canada. This episode featured an interview with actor Jean LeClerc, who at the time was starring in the Broadway touring production of *Dracula*, having taken over the role from Frank Langella.

A very engaging interview that takes place in a makeup room, where LeClerc discusses his take on the Dracula character, including the absence of the Bela Lugosi stylings. He rightly states that next to the role of God or the Devil, Dracula is one of the most fascinating characters that an actor can play.

The Ernie Kovacs Show

ABC. 1961-1962 (10 Episodes). Comedy/Variety. D: Ernie Kovacs, Maury Orr. W: Ernie Kovacs. C: Ernie Kovacs, Alice Novice, Spyros Tyro, Lester Newcomer, Jolene Brand ⚲, Bobby Lauher ⚲, Joe Mikalos, Maggi Brown ⚲. USA: English/B&W/300m. DuMont Entertainment Group.

Greetings over your orthocon tube! This largely forgotten but ground-breaking television entertainer got his start in Philadelphia, and had several variety series on CBS, NBC and ABC,

Television pioneer Ernie Kovacs unearthed some vampires for his variety series *The Ernie Kovacs Show* (DuMont Entertainment Group)

during a broadcasting career that spanned the years from 1950 to 1962. This incarnation of Ernie Kovacs' variety show featured several sketches with vampires and other monsters, first and foremost of which was the character of Auntie Gruesome, a storyteller with crazy white hair, long fingernails and pronounced fangs. It may be debatable that she (or he) was a true vampire, but such is not the case for at least three other skits that featured more traditional bloodsuckers.

One surreal vampire sketch is best described as a Western as if written by Rod Serling, and features a cowboy wandering through a strange forest, where the trees are covered in hanging moss and adorned with cattle skulls—and he's being stalked by two vampire cowgirls. In another vignette, set to music, Dracula enters the residence of a buxom beauty, and discovers that he should really take better care of his fangs—one of them breaks off when he attempts to bite her on the neck. In a third skit, the Frankenstein Monster invites Mr. and Mrs. Dracula over to his home, which is a simple cave with few creature comforts—most notably a pool table. Dracula teaches his host how to play the game, but he's shocked when the monster turns out to be a pool shark. A fourth segment spoofs soap opera storytelling, and features a woman who seems completely unfazed after her companion morphs into a creature that resembles some sort of vampire/witch.

📺 From April to June 1977, PBS aired a series of ten, thirty-minute programs under the banner "The Best of Ernie Kovacs." These were sourced mainly from his ABC specials, and included an introduction by Jack Lemmon.

The Fast Show – "Monster"

BBC Two. Dec 5, 1997 (S03E04). Comedy/Satire. D: Mark Mylod. W: Charlie Higson, Paul Whitehouse. C: Paul Whitehouse ☥, Charlie Higson, Simon Day, Caroline Aherne, Arabella Weir, Mark Williams, John Thomson, Ben Evans. UK: English/B&W, Color/30m. BBC.

A popular rapid-fire sketch comedy show, where each episode features a number of short skits. This outing includes a take on the German classic *Nosferatu, eine Symphonie des Grauens* (1922), and mimicks the scene where Graf Orlok is about to prey upon Ellen Hutter. But rather than attack his victim, in this case, the vampire gives her advice on which team to bet on in an upcoming soccer match—much to Ellen's confusion. The vampire resembles Orlok, yet his persona is based on the British publicist and sports agent Eric Hall, whose catchphrase was "Monster."

Finders Keepers

Nickelodeon/Syndicated. Nov 2, 1987 – Mar 10, 1989 (195 Episodes). Culture/Family. D: Kevin Gill. W: Geoffrey Darby, Michael Klinghoffer, Bonni Grossberg. C: John Harvey, Joe Conklin, Bob Lorman, Harry Stevens. USA: English/Color/5850m. Games Productions/Nickelodeon.

Children's game show that challenged two teams to find hidden objects within a large, eight-bedroom house. This scavenger hunt often found the kids searching through a room called "Dracula's Den," constructed to resemble the interior of a castle, and filled with bats, cobwebs and even a coffin—from which the Count himself would occasionally emerge. Presented by Wesley Eure (Nickelodeon) followed by Larry Toffler (syndication).

Frank & Drac

CBS. Oct 1987 – Jun 1988 (-- Episodes). Comedy/Horror. D: Anon. W: Robert Kokai. C: Allen Christopher, Robert Kokai ☥. USA: English/B&W, Color/--m. WOIO.

Horror hosts Frankenstein and Count Dracula teamed up on Saturday nights to present classic monster films, and often showed their comedic side in a series of skits. The show also featured Boom-Boom, Bambi and Thumper—Dracula's brides—who were collectively known as The Vampettes. Broadcast locally in Cleveland, Ohio on the CBS affiliate WOIO.

Front Page Challenge – Ep. #18.--

CBC. Mar 13, 1973 (S18E--). Culture/Media. D: Anon. W: John Aylesworth. C: Christopher Plummer, Devendra P. Varma, Pierre Berton, Betty Kennedy, Gordon Sinclair, Don Harron. CAN: English/Color/60m. CBC.

Quiz show where notable journalists are faced with a mystery guest, who supplies them with clues as they try to reason out which news story the challenger is associated with. In the segment "Dracula Legend Re-Vamped," the hidden participant is Devendra P. Varma, a leading authority on the Gothic novel, who discusses the recent surge in popularity of the Dracula character. Moderated by Fred Davis.

Full Moon Fright Night – "Vampire Journals"

SyFy. Aug 3, 2002 (S01E01). Comedy/Horror. D: Charles Band, Ted Nicolaou. W: Courtney Joyner, Chris Kreski, Ted Nicolaou. C: Jonathon Morris ☥, Kirsten Cerre ☥, David Gunn ☥, Ilinka Goya ☥, William Shatner ☥. USA: English/Color/91m. Full Moon MPC Inc./SyFy.

This low budget, short-lived anthology series attempted to bring back the weekly late night hosted horror program. This episode features *Vampire Journals,* the 1997 direct-to-video movie about a vampire who traverses Eastern Europe, exacting revenge on a lineage of fellow undead who are also the progeny of his master. Hosted by William Shatner.

The feature film often rises above B-movie standards, but the host segments are horrible. The film deserves better; forget this production and just rent the actual movie instead. Actor David Gunn seems to have since retired from the craft, which is too bad, as he turns in a strong performance as the tortured vampire Zachary, and gives Brad Pitt (Louis in *Interview with the Vampire*) a run for his money. At least one can appreciate that by the end of the film (and this episode), pretty much everyone is turned into a vampire—including Shatner.

The Garry Moore Show – Ep. #5.12

CBS. Dec 18, 1962 (S05E12). Comedy/Music. D: Anon. W: Anon. C: Carol Channing, Barbara McNair, Alan King, Durward Kirby ☥. USA: English/B&W/60m. Bob Banner Associates.

Host Garry Moore plays husband to Carol Channing in a skit where a horror movie addict comes face to face with Dracula (series regular Durward Kirby). This episode also features Channing and Barbara McNair singing several popular tunes, and Alan King performing a comedy routine that skewers lawyers.

The Garry Moore Show – Ep. #6.26

CBS. Mar 31, 1964 (S06E26). Comedy/Music. D: Anon. W: Anon. C: Chita Rivera ☥, Roy Castle, Alan King, Durward Kirby. USA: English/B&W/60m. Bob Banner Associates.

Features a sketch with Garry Moore satirizing Walter Cronkite as he visits the castle of an infamous bloodsucker, where he interviews the vampire's wife, Countess Dracula (guest star Chita Rivera).

The Generation Gap – Ep. #1.08

ABC. Mar 28, 1969 (S01E08). Culture/Family. D: Mike Gargiulo. W: Anon. C: Jonathan Frid ☥, Katherine Raht, Del Reeves, The Classics IV, Orson Bean, Barbara Cowsill, Janice Morgan, Cathy Willner, Tony Seaton. USA: English/Color/30m. Talent Associates/Norton Simon Inc./ABC.

Primetime game show where two teams, divided by age (over and under 30), were quizzed about each other's generation. In this episode, Jonathan Frid appeared as Barnabas Collins from *Dark Shadows* as a "mystery guest"—much to the delight of the enthusiastic audience. Hosted by Dennis Wholey.

📺 Actor David Henesy (David Collins from *Dark Shadows*) appeared along with his mother in the first episode of this series, while Jonathan Frid returned as a contestant in episode #9.

The Hilarious House of Frightenstein

The Count (Billy Van) has yet another bright idea on *The Hilarious House of Frightenstein* (CHCH-TV/David Cremasco)

CHCH. 1970-1971 (130 Episodes). Comedy/Family. D/W: Riff Markowitz. C: Billy Van ⚥, Fishka Rais, Vincent Price, Mitch Markowitz, Julius Sumner Miller, Guy Big, Joe Torbay. CAN: English/Color/7800m. CHCH-TV.

🦇 🦇 🦇

The thirteenth son of Count Dracula, Count Frightenstein, is exiled to Canada for failing to reanimate his creation, Brucie J. Monster. He now lives in Castle Frightenstein along with his big, green hapless assistant Igor, and a cast of other strange characters.

History Bites – "Dracula's Evil Twin"

History. Jan 11, 2001 (S03E09). Comedy/History. D: Rick Green. W: Rick Green, Amy McKenzie. C: Duncan McKenzie, Bob Bainborough, Danny DiTata, Amy McKenzie, Jeremy Winkels, Janet Van De Graff. CAN: English/Color/26m. History Bites Productions/S and S Productions.

Comedy series that explores world history as if seen through the lens of contemporary television programming. This episode features Vlad the Impaler, former Medieval prince of Wallachia, who wants reclaim his position as one of the most ruthless warlords of history. Hosted by Rick Green.

Hollywood Special

ABC. 1962-1968 (-- Episodes). Comedy/Horror. D: Anon. W: Mike Price. C: Mike Price ⚥, Dennis Calkins, Bill Eadie. USA: English/B&W/--m. WNYS-TV.

One of the earliest regional late-night vampire hosts of the Shock Theater era was Baron Daemon, portrayed by television announcer Mike Price (channelling Bela Lugosi). *Hollywood Special*, which aired Saturday nights on the ABC affiliate WNYS-TV in Syracuse, New York, offered selections from the Universal monster movie library. Baron Daemon became so popular that he spawned a second edition for kids that aired earlier in the afternoon, called the *Saturday Hollywood Special*, which was soon followed by another late-night edition (on either Friday or Sunday). A weekday afternoon show, *The Baron and His Buddies,* was then added to the list, and much like the Saturday afternoon broadcast, it also featured cartoons. His increasing popularity led to guest appearances at charity events, sock hops, and even on other WNYS programs. Price also recorded "The Transylvania Twist," a novelty song adapted from the Burl Ives tune "Fooba Wooba John." For marketing purposes, his band—Sam and the Twisters, along with backup singers The Bigtree Sisters—were collectively known as "The Vampires." Baron Daemon was resurrected in 1984 as part of a local FM radio station's Halloween broadcast, and once again on television in 2008 for *Baron Daemon's Halloween Fright Fest,* in celebration of the 40th anniversary of the *Hollywood Special.*

Homemade TV – "Fashion Day"

CBC. Oct 19, 1977 (S03E11). Culture/Family. D: Don Elder, Peter McLean. W: Larry Mollin, Phil Savath, Barry Flatman, Jed MacKay. C: Barry Flatman ⚢, Fred Mollin, Larry Mollin, Phil Savath ⚢, Susan Hart, Tessa Watt. CAN: English/Color/29m. CBC.

A variety series for teens that evolved into a magazine-style format, where audience members and viewers at home became active participants in driving the content for the show. This episode featured a Dracula makeup contest, where two teams competed to create the most monstrous monster in sixty seconds—and the winners received copies of the LP *Elvis in Hollywood*.

Although the intent of the series was honorable, it wasn't executed very well. However, the comedy skits were well written, and the topics—including skateboarding and a debate over uniforms in school—would have been of interest to the target audience.

The Horror Hall of Fame (1974)

ABC. Oct 31, 1974. Culture/Film. D: Charles Braverman. W: Bernard Rothman, Jack Wohl. C: Vincent Price, Billy Van ⚢, Frank Gorshin, John Carradine, John Astin, William Tuttle, Raymond T. McNally. USA: English/Color/67m. Braverman Productions Inc./Rothman-Wohl Productions Inc.

This program salutes the most famous names in the world of horror—Lon Chaney, Boris Karloff and Bela Lugosi—along with several other notable genre actors, including Lon Chaney Jr., Peter Lorre, Peter Cushing and Christopher Lee. Features clips from several classic horror films, such as *Mark of the Vampire* (1935), *Blacula* (1972) and *Dracula Has Risen from the Grave* (1968); interviews with Frank Gorshin, John Carradine and John Astin; and a transformation of actress Candy Clark by legendary makeup artist William Tuttle. Includes several scenes that take place in the "laboratory" of the Horror

Horror Hall-of-Famer John Carradine as Mr. Hawkins has a surprise in store for three curious kids in the *Night Gallery* vignette "Big Surprise" (Universal Studios Television)

Hall of Fame, where Murray Frankenstein, the great-great-grandson of the famous doctor, is close to completing a monster of his own. Hosted by Vincent Price.

This is a benchmark for how horror tribute shows should be done; it's a classy, stylish and witty program that never takes itself too seriously, but still shows respect for the genre and its influence on pop culture. Consummate professional Vincent Price is in top form, whether he's reminiscing about Hollywood while interviewing his notable guests, or while acting in several skits throughout the program. His co-host of sorts, Zuckman (the "curator" of the Horror Hall of Fame), is a vampire hunchback portrayed by Billy Van, in an inspired and hilarious performance. Price begins one of the more notable segments from within a coffin, where he discusses vampire folklore and then interviews Raymond T. McNally (co-author of *In Search of Dracula*)—who's sporting an opera cape.

The Horror Hall of Fame (1990)

Syndicated. Sep 30, 1990. Culture/Film. D: Ron de Moraes. W: Marc Juris, Michael J. Haigney. C: Forrest J Ackerman, Roger Corman, Joe Dante, Catherine Hicks, Rick Baker, John Landis, Janet Leigh, Anthony Perkins. USA: English/Color/94m. John Anthony Productions/Select Media Communications.

🦇 🦇 🦇

This first annual all-star tribute to terror, taped live in front of an audience at Universal Studios in Hollywood, pays tribute to several exceptional horror films of the past, as well as legendary actors of the genre. Honorees include Forrest J Ackerman, Boris Karloff and Vincent Price; and films such as *Psycho* (1960), *The Exorcist* (1973) and *Alien* (1979). Features cast and crew interviews, as well as a behind-the-scenes look at creating horror movie makeup for Halloween. Also included is an overview of the top fan-nominated films of the year, with best honors going to *Arachnophobia*. Hosted by Robert Englund and announcer Shadoe Stevens, with appearances by Chucky, Jason and The Cryptkeeper.

This ceremony—the *Academy Awards* for horror films (its statuette is the Grim Reaper!)—celebrates genre movies past and present. Fans will enjoy this, but parts of the telecast are painful to watch, most notably, the out of place comedy segments from the likes of Phyllis Diller and Sam Kinison. These faults are overshadowed by the best bits, including the induction of Vincent Price into the Horror Hall of Fame by Roddy McDowall. The special also includes a clip from *Dracula* (1931), as well as the remake of *Dark Shadows* (1991).

The Horror Hall of Fame II

Syndicated. Oct 5, 1991. Culture/Film. D: Ron de Moraes. W: Marc Juris, Michael J. Haigney. C: Adrienne Barbeau, Veronica Cartwright, Roger Corman, Elvira, Tippi Hedren, Vincent Price, Don Rickles, William Shatner, Dee Wallace Stone. USA: English/Color/92m. John Anthony Productions/Select Media Communications.

🦇 🦇 🦇

This second annual tribute to the masters of the macabre, past and present, was taped live in front of an audience at Universal Studios in Hollywood. Honorees include Bela Lugosi and Roger Corman; such films as *The Birds* (1963) and *The Texas Chainsaw Massacre* (1974); and horror publisher EC Comics. This year, the best horror film honor went to *The Silence of the Lambs*, which beat out *Jacob's Ladder* and *Misery*. Hosted by Robert Englund and announcer Shadoe Stevens, with an appearance by The Cryptkeeper.

Equally as enjoyable as the previous outing, this program will be of special interest to vampire fans because it features a fitting tribute to the life and career of Bela Lugosi. It also includes what is likely the last public appearance by Vincent Price, who hands out the award for best horror film. The excellent overview of *The Birds* will be of great interest to Hitchcock fans, and segments like this make up for the less-than-stellar aspects of the production. The most underwhelming of these are the "Scare Tactics" clips, where SFX wiz Steve Johnson illustrates some behind-the-scenes techniques for making your home videos more horrific. The tricks he shows are interesting enough, but the jokes are painfully unfunny.

The Horror Hall of Fame III

Syndicated. Oct 1992. Culture/Film. D: Norman J. Grossfeld. W: Marc Juris, Michael J. Haigney. C: James Curtis, Leonard Maltin, The Amazing Johnathan, Bobby "Boris" Pickett, Carel Struycken. USA: English/Color/90m. John Anthony Productions/Select Media Communications.

This third celebration of monsters, maniacs and madmen was taped live in front of an audience at Universal Studios in Hollywood. It featured a tribute to the film *Bride of Frankenstein* (1935), which was the sole honoree to be inducted that year, with the best horror film nod going to *The Addams Family*. Hosted by Robert Englund and announcer Shadoe Stevens, with an appearance by The Cryptkeeper.

Presented in a scaled-down venue with no notable guest stars, this third and final HHOF telecast primarily consists of repeat segments from the previous two outings (aside from the tribute to *Bride of Frankenstein*), and a countdown of the top films of the year. Additional new content includes a performance of "Monster Mash" by Bobby "Boris" Pickett, and the bloody comedy stylings of The Amazing Johnathan. There's a sneak peek into the slate of upcoming films, yet the movies are all forgettable, and represent just a few of the garbage horror films from the early 1990s. The best film of the year, *The Addams Family*, barely faced any competition, and easily beat out the likes of *Alien3* and a slew of other horror sequels. With the quality of horror films on the decline, and the reliance on previous content for this telecast, it's easy to see why a fourth incarnation never came to be—despite being promised by the host. Also features clips from *Dracula* (1931) and *To Sleep with a Vampire* (1993).

A large set piece showcased the faces of several well-known horrors: The Bride of Frankenstein (Elsa Lanchester), The Wolf Man (Lon Chaney Jr.), The Phantom of the Opera (Lon Chaney), The Frankenstein Monster (Boris Karloff), and Dracula (Bela Lugosi).

Tarantula Ghoul (Suzanne Waldron) presented horror films on Wednesday nights on the short-lived program *House of Horror,* which aired in Portland, Oregon from 1957-58 (KPTV)

House of Horror

NBC. Oct 9, 1957 - Nov 26, 1958 (-- Episodes). Comedy/Horror. D: Anon. W: Suzanne Waldron. C: Suzanne Waldron, John Burgess Hillsbury. USA: English/B&W/--m. KPTV.

This Wednesday late-night hosted horror movie program featured Tarantula Ghoul (Suzanne Waldron), a black-haired, pale-skinned "ghoul-friend" with an acerbic wit who in some respects was in homage to Vampira—as if played by Tallulah Bankhead. *House of Horror* was broadcast in Portland, Oregon, and included a series of horror films—most likely from Universal's *Shock Theater* package—interspersed with segments featuring 'Taranch' and her sidekick Milton, a retired grave-robber turned gardener; she also had a monstrous menagerie, including a boa constrictor named "Baby," a rattlesnake named "Heathcliff," and a shy tarantula named "Sir Galahad." Movies were introduced from within her haunted home, which overlooked a cemetery and was weirdly adorned with skulls, a few decapitated heads, and a macabre painting hanging over the fireplace. Sometimes, she and Milton were found outside on the patio, err, *planting things.* Some segments were themed to match the evening's feature film. For example, when making her grand entrance, she appeared from within a sarcophagus (for *Mummy* movies), and from a laboratory operating table (for *Frankenstein* films)—and when taking part in community events, she would often emerge from within a simple pine coffin, carried by pallbearers. Although no footage of her show is extant, Waldron recorded two novelty songs, as *Tarantula Ghoul & Her Gravediggers,* called "King Kong" and "Graveyard Rock." The show originally aired on the local NBC affiliate KPTV (which is now owned by FOX).

In Good Company – Ep. #1.--

CBC. Oct 31, 1975 (S01E--). News/Satire. D: Anon. W: Robert Gibbons. C: Rod Coneybeare, Ruthy Lunenfeld, Gail Dahms, Roger Abbott, Don Ferguson, Gene Di Novi Trio. CAN: English/Color/30m. CBC.

This Halloween special features the regular gang appearing in costumes of their own choosing, and includes a performance of "One More for the Road" by Rod Coneybeare, who's dressed as Dracula. Hosted by Hana Gartner.

In Living Color – "Lil' Magic: Working Girl" / "Your Face is Your Passport" / "Ugly Woman: Bram Stoker's Wanda"

FOX. Dec 13, 1992 (S04E11). Comedy/Music. D: Terri McCoy. W: Greg Fields, Les Firestein, James Carrey, Nancy Neufeld. C: James Carrey ⚥, David Alan Grier, Jamie Foxx, Kim Wayans, T'Keyah "Crystal" Keymah, Kelly Coffield, Tommy Davidson. USA: English/Color/30m.

In the sketch "Ugly Woman: Bram Stoker's Wanda," Count Dracula slips into Wanda's darkened bedchamber, where she's more than happy to fulfill the vampire's needs—but once the lights come on, Dracula quickly changes his mind. Hosted by Keenen Ivory Wayans.

Hilarious skit featuring Jim Carrey in a spot-on impression of Gary Oldman as Dracula, with Jamie Foxx reprising his Wanda Wayne character. Rather than face an eternity with Wanda as his undead bride, the Count ultimately chooses to end his existence by exposing himself to the sun.

Junior Roundup – "Sing Ring Around"

CBC. Jun 6, 1961 (S01E164). Family/Music. D: Anon. W: Michael Spivak, John Keogh. C: Donna Miller, Murray Westgate, Barbara Hamilton, Jack Mather, Claude Rae, Charles Telling, Linda Keogh, John Keogh, Paul Robin, Gustav Harsfai. CAN: English/B&W/58m. CBC.

Early children's series aimed at the pre-teen set, which was preceded by fifteen minutes of content for even younger viewers—in this case, "Sing Ring Around" with Donna Miller (and a monkey doll named Cheeky). The theme of this special episode of *Junior Roundup* was vaudeville, and each skit—performed entirely with marionettes—is introduced by host Murray Westgate in puppet form. One segment takes viewers to Spook Mountain and into the haunted nursery at Dracula's Castle, home to Auntie Vampira and her monster son Frankie.

This macabre segment is the best part of the "Junior Roundup Spring Vaudeville Show," and features a menagerie of monsters based on some very familiar creatures. These include: Auntie Vampira (inspired by Maila Nurmi's campy creation); her creepy son Frankie (who has a pet bat named Bartholomew); their butler named Bazzle (an invisible man); a pet werewolf named Walter; and two skeletons—Harem and Scarem—who dance the Cha-cha-cha! The other segments are often equally as strange, but mainly because the marionettes are all very creepy looking. Had I been a kid watching this back in the day I would have run from the television screaming—despite the good nature of the other skits, which include dancing poodles (doing the Can-can!) and a comedy troupe featuring two clowns named Fiddle and Faddle.

📺 The entire vaudeville show was rebroadcast on September 18, 1961.

The Kids in the Hall – Ep. #1.17

CBC. Jan 18, 1990 (S01E17). Comedy/Satire. D: John Blanchard. W: David Foley, Bruce McCulloch, Kevin McDonald, Mark McKinney, Scott Thompson. C: David Foley, Bruce McCulloch, Kevin McDonald, Mark McKinney ⚥, Scott Thompson. CAN: English/Color/24m. Broadway Video/CBC.

One skit takes place after a hockey game, when Leslie invites his new pal Brad back to his apartment for a beer. Brad is initially oblivious to what is in store for the evening, but the burly man realizes that something is amiss after Leslie emerges from the bedroom wearing a Dracula cape. It's a sidesplitting sketch featuring McKinney as a flamboyant gay man who *really* likes to dress up as Dracula, and does his best to seduce Brad even though the man is a confirmed heterosexual (McKinney's rant about Dracula and Vlad the Impaler is comedic gold).

The Kids in the Hall – Ep. #2.11

CBC. Dec 13, 1990 (S02E11). Comedy/Satire. D: John Blanchard. W: David Foley, Bruce McCulloch, Kevin McDonald, Mark McKinney, Scott Thompson. C: David Foley, Bruce McCulloch, Kevin McDonald, Mark McKinney ⚥, Scott Thompson. CAN: English/Color/24m. Broadway Video/CBC.

In one sketch, after a group of gay bashers chase a young man into a dank part of the subway system, their pursuit is interrupted by a flamboyant stranger who catches them all by surprise—and not just because he's dressed as a vampire. Mark McKinney reprises his character of Leslie, a gay man who has a fondness for wearing a Dracula cape and vamping it up.

Lamb Chop in the Haunted Studio

PBS. Oct 21, 1994. Family/Music. D: Bill Davis. W: Bernard Rothman, Mallory Tarcher. C: Shari Lewis, Alan Thicke ⚥, John Byner, Doug Cameron, Jan Rubeš. CAN/USA: English/Color/60m. Paragon Entertainment Corporation/CBC.

This Halloween special finds Shari, Lamb Chop and friends about to tape a scary-themed show in an old studio where the great monster movies were once filmed. But Lamb Chop is scared because the building is apparently haunted by a spooky phantom—and she was right. The Phantom of the Studio wreaks havoc on the production, and imprisons the guest stars so he can impersonate them for the Special—because, as a failed actor, he never had a chance to show anyone his versatility in scary roles.

A charming program for kids that has a good message about not judging a book by its cover, and adults will enjoy the humorous elements geared directly towards them. The guest stars really shine; Alan Thicke works his self-absorbed shtick to great aplomb (and makes for a pretty good Dracula), while John Byner shows off his skill for impressions as he channels Boris Karloff in his role as Doctor Frankenstein. But it's the celebrated Czech-Canadian opera singer and actor Jan Rubeš who is the standout, and his role as The Phantom is the most memorable of the monsters here.

📺 Nominated for a 1995 Emmy Award for Outstanding Children's Program.

The Late Late Show with Craig Ferguson – Ep. #6.65

CBS. Dec 15, 2009 (S06E65). Comedy/Music. D: Brian McAloon. W: Lynn Ferguson, David Harte, Philip McGrade, Craig Ferguson. C: Jason Schwartzman, Jason Segel, Maria Bello, Kristen Bell. USA: English/Color/60m. Worldwide Pants.

Jason Segel performs his song "Dracula's Lament" from the film *Forgetting Sarah Marshall* (2008), which features a Dracula puppet. Hosted by Craig Ferguson.

Late Night Horror – "No Such Thing as a Vampire"

BBC Two. Apr 19, 1968 (S01E01). Drama/Horror. D: Paddy Russell. W: Richard Matheson, Hugh Leonard. C: Andrew Keir, Meg Wynn Owen, Thomas Gallagher, Cynthia Etherington, Peter Blythe ☥. UK: English/Color/27m. BBC.

This was the first drama production at the BBC to be recorded in color, but unfortunately no archive material of this episode is known to exist. Dr. Petre Gheria is mystified after his wife is attacked while asleep, and although she has two small lacerations on her neck, she recalls nothing of the assault. Vowing to protect his wife, Gheria locks himself in her room the following evening, yet she is attacked once again—and he remembers nothing. Their servants suspect a vampire is behind the assaults; they convince the couple to protect themselves accordingly, while they seek out the monster's resting place.

📺 Matheson's short story was also adapted as part of the anthology telefilm *Dead of Night* (1977).

The Late Night Horror Show

ABC. Apr 21, 1989 – 1990 (-- Episodes). Comedy/Horror. D: Anon. W: Anon. C: Jim Kellett ☥. USA: English/B&W, Color/--m. KSPR-TV.

From his humble (yet creepy) chateau in the hills, host Count Norlock—a green-skinned Nosferatu-type vampire—presents a bevy of creature features. Broadcast locally in Springfield, Missouri on the ABC affiliate KSPR-TV.

Late Night With Jimmy Fallon – Ep. #2.168

NBC. Nov 8, 2010 (S02E168). Comedy/Music. D: Anon. W: A.D. Miles, David Angelo, Morgan Murphy. C: Scarlett Johansson, Chris Morris, Morgan Murphy, A.D. Miles, Bashir Salahuddin, Toots & The Maytals. USA: English/Color/60m. Universal Media Studios/Broadway Video.

Features a behind-the-scenes short film called "Suckers," where a new writer named Angelique joins the staff, and discovers that her co-workers—including host Jimmy Fallon—are bloodsucking vampires. The segment parodies the *Twilight* films, *True Blood* and *The Vampire Diaries*. In other episodes, Fallon performs in a series of hilarious skits called "Bothered with Robert Pattinson," where he impersonates the actor looking as he did in the *Twilight* movies. In these segments, Fallon hangs out in a tree and rants about things that bother him, occasionally hissing at the object in question, or expressing a sultry, pouting look towards the camera. Many things annoy him, including Christmas, the iPad, Snickers ads…and the title of the film *New Moon*.

The League of Gentlemen Christmas Special

BBC Two. Dec 27, 2000. Comedy/Horror. D: Steve Bendelack. W: Jeremy Dyson, Mark Gatiss. C: Jeremy Dyson, Mark Gatiss ♀, Steve Pemberton, Reece Shearsmith, Freddie Jones, Liza Tarbuck, Andrew Melville, Frances Cox, Bay White, Rusty Goffe. UK: English/Color/57m. BBC.

Reverend Bernice Woodall, the acerbic vicar of Royston Vasey, listens to three disturbing tales recounted by locals on Christmas Eve. In one story, a man named Matthew Parker reveals that in 1975, he was put in the care of Herr Lipp—the director of a boys choir—whom he believed was a vampire.

This Christmas special is definitely not standard fare for the holidays; it features adult situations, double entendre, and scenes more suited to a horror film. Yet these elements are often found in the dark comedy of The League of Gentlemen, a group of British performers. "The Vampire of Duisberg" is the best segment of the three, and reveals that Herr Lipp is a completely different kind of predator altogether. His wife is the real bloodsucker; she's already turned the entire choir into vampires, and has been actively biting Parker on the neck while he sleeps. There are several references to vampire films, most notably *Nosferatu*. In one scene, Lipp utters the words, "The absence of love is the most abject pain," which is a direct quote from the Werner Herzog adaptation from 1979. When he climbs a stairway, his shadow casts a reflection on the wall, much like the iconic scene from the original 1922 film. It should also be noted that the head vampire seems to be based on Kurt Barlow from the 1979 TV miniseries *Salem's Lot*.

MADtv – Ep. #3.08

FOX. Nov 15, 1997 (S03E08). Comedy/Satire. D: Paul Miller. W: Fax Bahr. C: Alex Borstein, Nicole Sullivan, Will Sasso ⚥, Lisa Kushell, Pat Kilbane, Chris Hogan, Debra Wilson, Aries Spears, Mary Scheer. USA: English/Color/60m. Bahr-Small Productions/David Salzman Entertainment.

🦇🦇🦇

In the segment "Buffy the Umpire Slayer," the hit TV series is reimagined…sort of. In this spoof, Buffy battles bloodsucking *umpires,* instead of your run-of-the-mill vampires (she uses pointy baseball bats to stake them). They've been the scourge of humanity for centuries, pre-dating Christianity; it's believed that the entire population of Atlantis was undead umpires! They only fear three things: wild pitches, Buffy, and Roberto Alomar (who once got into a heated argument with an umpire, and spit in his face).

MADtv – Ep. #7.07

FOX. Nov 24, 2001 (S07E07). Comedy/Satire. D: Amanda Bearse. W: Garry Campbell. C: Alex Borstein, Stephanie Weir, Will Sasso, Frank Caliendo, Andrew Daly ⚥, Michael McDonald, Debra Wilson, Mo Collins, Aries Spears. USA: English/Color/60m. Bahr-Small Productions/David Salzman Entertainment.

🦇🦇

In the sketch "Bunny the Vampire Slayer," Ms. Swan takes over slaying duties after Buffy leaves Sunnydale to go visit Angel. Her sister Dawn isn't impressed, until Swan reveals that she's actually their aunt.

MADtv – Ep. #9.07

FOX. Nov 15, 2003 (S09E07). Comedy/Satire. D: Bruce Leddy. W: Lauren Dombrowski. C: Ike Barinholtz, Bobby Lee, Frank Caliendo, Mo Collins ⚥, Josh Meyers, Michael McDonald, Paul Vogt, Stephanie Weir, Aries Spears, Nicole Parker. USA: English/Color/60m. Bahr-Small Productions/David Salzman Entertainment.

🦇🦇🦇

In the music video "Me Against Madonna" (a parody of Britney Spears and Madonna's "Me Against the Music"), Britney attempts to escape the clutches of Madonna, a desperate vampire who wants to steal her youth so she can be fashionable once again.

Macabre Theatre

Syndicated. 2002-2006 (-- Episodes). Comedy/Horror. D: Anon. W: Todd Livingston, Gary Lycan, Natalie Popovich. C: Natalie Popovich, Butch Patrick. USA: English/Color/--m. Just N Entertainment/KDOC-TV.

Macabre Theatre aired over small regional and satellite affiliates that were part of the *America One* television network. Raven-haired seductress Ivonna Cadaver—a quick-witted, sardonic version of Elvira, Mistress of the Dark—presented mostly Z-grade movies along with her sidekick Butch

Patrick (of *The Munsters* fame), including such classics as *King of the Zombies* (1941), *Lady Frankenstein* (1971), *The Brain That Wouldn't Die* (1962), and *Satan's School For Girls* (1973). There were also a couple of Halloween specials, but the show was cancelled around 2006, although it continued sporadically in reruns for several years after that. In 2012, *Macabre Theatre* was resurrected (without Eddie Munster) as part of *Youtoo America*, an interactive, social television network with several regional affiliates across the United States.

Marineland Carnival

CBS. April 18, 1965. Comedy/Family. D: Anon. W: Anon. C: Fred Gwynne, Yvonne De Carlo ☥, Al Lewis ☥, Pat Priest, Butch Patrick. USA: English/Color/60m. CBS.

The Munster family visits the famous Marineland of the Pacific, where they take part in the Marineland Carnival along with The New Christy Minstrels. This was the fourth in a series of annual Easter specials that featured popular television characters visiting the tourist attraction. Other guests over the years included Jim Backus (Thurston Howell III from *Gilligan's Island*), and Irene Ryan, Donna Douglas and Max Baer (Granny, Elly May and Jethro from *The Beverly Hillbillies*).

Shock Theater was a package of 52 Universal Studios horror films that were released into television syndication in 1957, which led to a number of regional late-night horror programs hosted by ghouls, vampires, and other creatures of the night (Universal Pictures)

Matinee Theatre – "Dracula"

NBC. Jan 6, 1956 (S01E49). Drama/Romance. D: Lamont Johnson. W: Robert Esson, Bram Stoker. C: John Carradine ☥, Lisa Daniels, John Conte. USA: English/Color/60m. NBC.

This anthology series aired daily in the afternoon, often live. This first television adaptation of Bram Stoker's *Dracula* has John Carradine starring as the famous Count, who falls for a local girl after losing his bride. Hosted by John Conte.

The Mike Douglas Show – Ep. #14.26-14.30

CBS. Oct 6 – 10, 1975 (S14E26-30). Comedy/Music. D: Anon. W: Anon. C: Frank Gorshin, Darren McGavin, William Marshall, Harry Blackstone, Leonard Wolf, Zacherley, Adrienne Barbeau, Dick Cavett, Arte Johnson, Forrest J Ackerman. USA: English/Color/300m. Group W/Westinghouse Broadcasting Company.

Mike welcomes co-host Frank Gorshin in a special, week-long salute to the famous monsters of

Hollywood. Features an interview with Leonard Wolf, author of *The Annotated Dracula,* and a demonstration of special effects, including a casket, cobweb machine and vampire bat.

Mr. Dressup – "Casey in the Moon"

CBC. Feb 19, 1990 (S23E--). Family/Music. D: Don Brown. W: Lilly Barnes. C: Ernie Coombs, Judith Lawrence, Alyson Court. CAN: English/Color/29m. CBC.

Mr. Dressup shows his crafty side and makes a dragon costume for Finnegan using sparkles and felt. He then reveals two paper-bag hand puppets sent in by viewers—one is a beaver while the other is Dracula. He chats with the two puppets; the beaver says he likes to build dams and chew on trees, while Dracula says he likes to scare people on Halloween. He then joins Casey for a game of "moon" while Finnegan takes a nap.

Mr. Dressup – "Scary Dress-up Party"

CBC. Nov 22, 1993 (S26E--). Family/Music. D: Lorraine Barton. W: Robin White. C: Ernie Coombs ⚥, Nina Keogh, Cheryl Wagner, Marc Marut. CAN: English/Color/29m. CBC.

Marc arrives dressed as a monster, so Truffles suggests they have a scary dress-up party. Mr. Dressup chooses to go as the vampire "Count Down"—because he likes to count backwards. He scours the Tickle Trunk and finds a red-lined cape, white gloves, and a wig of jet-black hair—and since every vampire needs a pet bat, he creates one out of black construction paper (and names it "Betty"). Mr. Dressup makes for a very amicable vampire, and Betty the bat is a fun little addition—which he uses to teach his viewers about echolocation.

Monty Python's Flying Circus – "You're No Fun Anymore"

BBC One. Nov 30, 1969 (S01E07). Comedy/Satire. D: Ian MacNaughton. W: Graham Chapman, John Cleese, Eric Idle, Terry Jones, Michael Palin, Terry Gilliam. C: Graham Chapman ⚥, John Cleese, Eric Idle, Terry Jones, Michael Palin, Terry Gilliam. UK: English/Color/30m. Python (Monty) Pictures Limited.

In one of the vignettes, Dracula approaches a buxom blonde in her bedroom, but his fangs fall out of his mouth just as he's about to bite her on the neck. Disappointed, the woman laments, "You're no fun anymore…" (this expression is repeated in other skits throughout the episode). Short and to the point, the vampire skit is funny for what it is, but the best sketches are based around the main premise of the episode, where a UFO invasion turns the British into Scotsmen.

Movie Macabre

Syndicated. 1981–1993. Comedy/Horror. D: Larry Thomas. W: Larry Thomas. C: Cassandra Peterson, John Paragon, Joan Leizman. USA: English/B&W, Color/16800m. Panacea Entertainment.

Hosted by Elvira, Mistress of the Dark, who made light of the often low-budget films she presented. She's actually a witch, even though she shares some of the common physical traits that are often associated with vampires. This long-running series showcased several vampire films, including *Grave of the Vampire, Blacula, Count Yorga: Vampire, Count Dracula's Great Love, The Fearless Vampire Killers, The Return of Count Yorga, Curse of the Vampires* and *House of Dark Shadows*.

The Muppet Show – Ep. #1.19

Syndicated. Oct 19, 1976 (S01E19). Comedy/Family. D: Peter Harris. W: Jack Burns, Marc London. C: Vincent Price ♱, Frank Oz, Jim Henson ♱, Jerry Nelson ♱, Richard Hunt, Dave Goelz, Eren Ozker. UK/USA: English/Color/24m. The Jim Henson Company/Associated Television.

Vincent Price guest stars in this Halloween-themed episode that features vampires, ghosts, ghouls and other creatures of the night. Price appears as a vampire in the closing sketch, as does Kermit the Frog! Dracula also makes an appearance; he attends a monster ball and takes a bite out of his dancing partner. One of the most charming segments is the musical number "I'm Looking Through You," where three ghosts cover the Beatles tune—with voices that sound like Boris Karloff.

Mystery and Imagination – "The Flying Dragon"

ITV1. Nov 5, 1966 (S02E03). Mystery/Suspense. D: Bill Bain. W: John Bowen, J. Sheridan Le Fanu. C: Ann Bell, Derek Smith, John Moffatt, John Phillips, David Buck, John Bryans, Mark Burns. UK: English/B&W/60m. ABC Television.

In this episode, now thought to be lost, an Englishman traveling through Europe encounters vampires. Based on J. Sheridan Le Fanu's short story "The Room in the Dragon Volant" (1872).

Mystery and Imagination – "Carmilla"

ITV1. Nov 12, 1966 (S02E04). Mystery/Suspense. D: Bill Bain. W: Stanley Miller, J. Sheridan Le Fanu. C: Jane Merrow ♱, Joseph O'Conor, Natasha Pyne ♱, Roy Marsen, Laurel Mather, Sonia Dresdel, Vernon Dobtcheff, Terence Bayler. UK: English/B&W/60m. ABC Television.

In this production, no longer extant, a female vampire wreaks havoc on members of the Karnstein family. Based on J. Sheridan Le Fanu's novella "Carmilla" (1872).

Mystery and Imagination – "Feet Foremost"

ITV1. Jun 27, 1968 (S03E06). Mystery/Suspense. D: Toby Robertson. W: Charles Graham, L.P. Hartley. C: Clive Morton, Fanny Rowe, Fiona Hartford, Neil Stacy, Timothy West, Trevor Baxter, Fiona Walker. UK: English/B&W/60m. ABC Television.

In this episode, now thought to be lost, a couple moves into an old house believed to be cursed. According to local legend, an evil ghost attacks anyone living at the home; it enters their body, and then kills them from the inside out. Based on L.P. Hartley's short story "Feet Foremost" (1938).

📺 Remade in 1983 for the UK series *Shades of Darkness*.

Mystery and Imagination – "Dracula"

ITV1. Nov 18, 1968 (S04E03). Mystery/Suspense. D: Patrick Dromgoole. W: Charles Graham. C: Denholm Elliott ♀, James Maxwell, Corin Redgrave, Suzanne Neve, Bernard Archard, Joan Hickson, Susan George ♀, Hedley Goodall. UK: English/B&W/81m. Thames Television.

Doctor John Seward is not impressed by Count Dracula, a suave man from Transylvania who has relocated to Whitby and appears to be smitten by his fiancée, Lucy Weston. Yet the doctor is preoccupied by the strange case of Patient #34—a John Doe—whose erratic behavior, especially at night, has prompted Seward to seek out the assistance of his colleague, Professor Van Helsing. As Patient #34 unlocks his past, Lucy is stricken with a grave illness, and both misfortunes seem to be tied to the arrival of the mysterious foreigner from the East.

This slimmed down adaptation of Bram Stoker's novel primarily takes place in Whitby, with one flashback to Transylvania that involves Harker, Dracula and his three brides. Aside from a few missteps that are overly theatrical and lean towards camp, each actor is quite effective in their role. Corin Redgrave as Patient #34, the manic-depressive minion to Dracula—an amalgam of Jonathan Harker and Renfield—is a pleasure to watch, and Denholm Elliott as the infamous Count gives a performance that oozes pure menace and raw sexuality. This adaptation explores the concept of the vampire's bite as a sexual act, and even hints at a bisexual longing between Mina and the vampire Lucy, as well as Jonathan and Dracula. Much like in *Nosferatu, eine Symphonie des Grauens* (1922), Dracula has rat-like fangs, and is destroyed by sunlight—two elements that aren't in the original novel. Fueled by the faith of Seward and Van Helsing, the vampire's death scene is befitting to a Hammer horror film, complete with rotting flesh and a corpse that crumbles to dust.

Mystery Science Theater 3000 – "The Wild Wild World of Batwoman"

Comedy Central. Nov 13, 1993 (S05E15). Comedy/Crime. D: Jim Mallon. W: Michael J. Nelson, Trace Beaulieu. C: Trace Beaulieu, Michael J. Nelson, Jim Mallon, Kevin Murphy, Frank Conniff, Katherine Victor ♀, Lucki Winn ♀. USA: English/B&W, Color/92m. Best Brains, Inc./Medallion TV Enterprises Inc.

Trapped on a space station, a man and his robot friends provide running commentary as they watch terrible, low-budget movies. In this episode, they view what may be the worst "vampire" film in history, the 1966 disaster *The Wild Wild World of Batwoman*. In the movie, a busty crime fighting vampire, along with her crack team of bodacious Bat Girls (who are also fabulous dancers), face off against a mysterious masked man named Rat Fink. The plot, such as it is, involves the theft of a hearing aid that's been converted into an atomic bomb.

It's amazing how such a terrible film, barely viewable on its own, becomes must-see television thanks to the crew of MST3K. This one's a doozy; the point of the movie isn't really to tell a coherent story, so much as it is to showcase a group of curvy, scantily-clad babes who spend most of their time dancing variations of "The Jerk" and "The Monkey" (not that there's anything wrong with that). None of the women are classic undead; in the words of their leader, "We're vampires all right, but only in a synthetic sense. Drinking the real stuff went out with Count Dracula!" She's referring to blood; their initiation involves drinking a red elixir that is a mixture of strawberries, honey, cherries and yogurt. They're basically a cult of role players who don't really do any role playing. It's one of those movies that's so bad it's good, but be warned: it is a frustrating experience at times, and this presentation is really the only way in which the film should be viewed.

Mystery Science Theater 3000 – "Samson vs. the Vampire Women"

Comedy Central. Mar 25, 1995 (S06E24). Comedy/Sci-Fi. D: Jim Mallon. W: Michael J. Nelson, Frank Conniff. C: Trace Beaulieu, Michael J. Nelson, Frank Conniff, Santo, Lorena Velázquez ♀. MEX/USA: English/B&W, Color/92m. Best Brains, Inc./American International Television.

Mike and his robot friends watch the 1963 Mexican film *Samson vs. the Vampire Women (Santo vs. las mujeres vampiro)*. In the movie, a professor seeks the help of a great wrestler to protect his daughter. She's being stalked by a group of the undead, who believe she's destined to become their new vampire queen.

The host segments are sub-par for this episode, but the running commentary during the film more than makes up for it. The movie itself is pretty horrid, and today's audiences will see it as more comedy than horror; however it does retain a certain B-movie charm.

National Lampoon Presents Disco Beaver from Outer Space

HBO. Feb 23, 1979. Adult/Comedy. D: Joshua White. W: Peter Elbling, Jeff Greenfield. C: Rodger Bumpass, Peter Elbling , Alice Playten, James Widdoes, Lee Wilkof, Michael Simmons, Sarah Durkee, Lynn Redgrave. USA: English/Color/52m. National Lampoon Players Inc.

As a couple channel surfs through various cable stations, they're presented with a series of comedy sketches in the guise of television programs; the stories eventually bleed into one another as characters cross over into each other's segments. The first of two main stories involves a human-sized Canadian beaver from beyond the stars, which has several misadventures while exploring New York City. The second showcases the exploits of Dragula, Queen of Darkness, a gay vampire whose bite instantly turns any man into a homosexual.

This is a risqué, non-PC comedy special with some very funny segments—especially the story arc that features Dragula. As his "evil" spreads throughout the city, macho men fall under his spell. These include a construction worker, NHL hockey players, a sports broadcaster, and a Country and Western singer. His final victim, Mr. Murray, is an allusion to the character Mina Murray from Bram Stoker's novel. The story features Lynn Redgrave in a hilarious performance as Vanessa Van Helsing, a sexology columnist and vampire hunter who wards off the "haemosexualist" until he is destroyed after facing his biggest weakness: the giant spacefaring beaver. Dragula is repelled by several objects that definitely fall outside of the standard lore: a cheap charm bracelet from Woolworth's; family-style meatloaf; pictures of Lloyd Bridges; TV dinners; breakfast nooks; café curtains; and of course, any image of a beaver.

The sketches were based on the horror comic parody "Dragula" by Tony Hendra & Neal Adams, from *National Lampoon Magazine* #20 (November 1971).

Nightmare Classics – "Carmilla"

Showtime. Sep 10, 1989 (S01E01). Drama/Suspense. D: Gabrielle Beaumont. W: Jonathan Furst. C: Ione Skye , Meg Tilly , Roy Dotrice, Roddy McDowall, John Doolittle, Armelia McQueen. USA: English/Color/54m. Think Entertainment/Showtime Networks.

Marie is an only child living on a plantation in the post-Civil War United States, under the watchful

Carmilla (Meg Tilly) befriends a young girl and her family in *Nightmare Classics* - "Carmilla" (Think Entertainment/Showtime Networks)

eye of her overly-protective father. After a carriage overturns nearby, she finds solace in a pale young woman named Carmilla, the sole survivor of the accident. Her arrival coincides with the onset of a deadly illness that has gripped the South—and a police inspector believes that a vampire is responsible.

This is a faithful adaptation of J. Sheridan Le Fanu's novella, albeit transplanted to the United States circa 1865. It's not your typical Carmilla adaptation; there are no fangs, little blood, and the erotic overtones, while still present, are very subdued.

Roy Dotrice (Marie's father) played the vampire Count Draco in "My Ghostwriter – The Vampire" from the series *Tales from the Darkside* (1987).

Nightmare Theatre

CBS. Sep 26, 1964 - Oct 31, 1978 (-- Episodes). Comedy/Horror. D: Anon. W: Joe Towey. C: Joe Towey ☥, Chris Wedes. USA: English/B&W, Color/--m. KIRO-TV.

The *Nightmare Theatre* television program was brought to life by *Emmy* award-winning director and actor Joe Towey, which aired locally in Seattle, Washington on CBS affiliate KIRO-TV. Initially a Friday late-night horror program that just aired movies, Towey's creation, The Count, was introduced four years into its run, first appearing on Halloween night in 1968. Movies, often shown as double-features, included *Horrors of the Black Museum* (1959), *A Bucket of Blood* (1959), *Black Sunday [La maschera del demonio]* (1960), and *The Bloody Vampire [El vampiro sangriento]* (1962). Based on the Lugosian archetype, with a very sinister laugh, this "dime-store Dracula whose shtick was worse than his bite" hosted the program until 1975, after which time *Nightmare Theatre* returned to airing movies on their own. The character had become so popular locally that Towey continued to appear as The Count at special events throughout Washington State, and at least once he was resurrected on KIRO-TV during Halloween.

Oddville, MTV

MTV. 1997 (S01E--). Comedy/Variety. D: Kit Carson. W: Steve Korn. C: Father Sebastiaan, Melissa Gabriel, Kendall Gill, John Walsh. USA: English/Color/30m. MTV Networks.

Recorded in New York City, this series showcased the hidden talents of a wide range of Americans (no matter how strange or obscure), and gave them their "fifteen minutes of fame." It was also part traditional talk show, and featured guest entertainers and musicians. One episode included an interview with Father Sebastiaan, a central figure in the New York vampire scene of the 1990s, who was often tapped for documentaries during that decade. Hosted by Rich Brown (as Frank Hope) and David Greene.

Opening Night – "Dracula: Pages from a Virgin's Diary"

CBC. Feb 28, 2002 (S01E17). Dance/Film. D: Guy Maddin, Alan Burke. W: Mark Godden. C: Zhang Wei-Qiang ⚥, Tara Birtwhistle ⚥, David Moroni, CindyMarie Small, Johnny Wright, Stephane Leonard, Guy Maddin, Elizabeth Miller. CAN: English/B&W, Color/115m. CBC.

🦇🦇🦇🦇

Guy Maddin, Don McKellar and Elizabeth Miller discuss *Dracula* on *Opening Night* (CBC Still Photo Collection)

This episode features the world television premiere of Guy Maddin's art film (commissioned especially for *Opening Night*), which is based on the Royal Winnipeg Ballet's production of *Dracula*. This is followed by a panel discussion covering the movie, Bram Stoker's book, and the underlying themes found in both. Presented by Don McKellar.

This is one of the best adaptations of the novel; a ballet at its core, it never really feels like a "ballet film," and is completely accessible, enjoyable, and stunning in its execution. Evoking the style of early German expressionist film, this production is chiefly presented in black and white, with a subtle but effective use of the color red (a handful of scenes are also fully tinted in different colors to evoke mood). Using the original dancers from the critically-acclaimed 1998 ballet production—itself a very faithful adaptation—Maddin also revisited the novel to ensure the most faithful version possible. He shifts the focus of the story onto the lead women—Lucy and Mina—and much like in Bram Stoker's book, Dracula is not ever-present. Fans of the novel will be thrilled to see elements of the story that have never made it to film until now, and Maddin deftly explores the underlying themes of xenophobia, misogyny and sexual awakening. The panel discussion that follows is essentially a dialogue between Maddin and Elizabeth Miller (a *Dracula* scholar), and their conversation about the film and the novel is quite interesting.

📺 Fittingly, the CBC rebroadcast this episode on October 31, 2002.

The Passion of Dracula

Showtime. Jan 17, 1980. D: J. Edward Shaw. W: Bob Hall, David Richmond. C: Christopher Bernau ⚥, Gordon Chater, Brian Bell, Alice White ⚥, K.C. Wilson, Elliott Vileen, Julia Mackenzie. USA: English/Color/105m. The Dracula Theatrical Company/Leslie Kleiman International Inc.

🦇🦇🦇

Very loosely based on the classic novel, this televised stage play was recorded at the Ed Sullivan Theatre in New York City. Dr. Seward is concerned about the weakening health of his niece,

Christopher Bernau portrays Count Dracula in the televised stage play *The Passion of Dracula*, recorded at the Ed Sullivan Theatre in New York City (The Dracula Theatrical Company/Leslie Kleiman International Inc)

Wilhemena "Willie" Murray, who has been displaying odd behavior of late. She's quite lethargic during the day, but has renewed vigor at night, and often wanders around as if in a trance—unaware of her nocturnal activities. Considering the recent events in Whitby—where three young women were killed, their throats torn out and bodies drained of blood—Seward seeks the help of Professor Abraham Van Helsing. Coincidentally, a suave aristocrat, Count Dracula, recently purchased the nearby Abbey—and many locals believe that he's responsible for the terrible events plaguing their village.

This adaptation is an irreverent take on *Dracula*, with some very dry humor that doesn't always work. Separated into three acts, the story takes place entirely in England (with no reference to any events in Transylvania)—which makes sense, considering Jonathan Harker is now a reporter working for the London *Globe*. He's known for his salacious headlines, and often speculates about the goings-on behind the closed doors of the Seward Sanatorium. Other characters from the novel have been dropped in favor of two new ones. Dr. Helga Van Zandt is a visiting Freudian psychiatrist studying Renfield, and she's having a secret, passionate affair with Lord Godalming. There's also Mr. Jameson, the caretaker of the facility, who's occasionally used for comic relief. Dracula—who's introduced as a Transylvanian nobleman studying English folklore—is a descendent of the infamous warlord Vlad Țepeș. But it's revealed that he's the *real* Vlad Țepeș; according to legend, Vlad was a vampire who drank the blood of his captives, and through this act gained immortality. Christopher Bernau is quite engaging as the Count, as is Malachi Throne as Van Helsing; I equally enjoyed the Van Zandt character (but only after she was turned into a vampire).

Christopher Bernau was a cast member of the original *Dark Shadows* from 1969-70, where he played the character "Philip Todd." Barnabas Collins turned Philip's wife into a vampire, who bit him in one scene.

Prisoners of Gravity - "Vampires"

TVO. Jan 30, 1992 (S03E17). Literature/Sci-Fi. D: Gregg Thurlbeck. W: Rick Green. C: Gene Colan, Forrest J Ackerman, Julian Grant, Robert Hadji, Garfield Reeves-Stevens, Ellen Datlow, Nancy Collins, Brian Lumley, Tanya Huff, Jewelle Gomez. CAN: English/B&W, Color/30m. TV Ontario/OECA.

🦇🦇🦇

Commander Rick built a homemade rocket in order to leave the Earth and all its strife behind, but he inadvertently crashed into an orbiting telecommunications satellite. He now spends his days examining the themes and issues explored through fantasy and sci-fi literature, and broadcasts a pirate television show to the populace below. This episode starts with the trailer for *The Vampire's Coffin (El ataúd del Vampiro,* 1958), and discusses the evolution of the Western vampire through literature, folklore, and early *Dracula* film adaptations. Contemporary authors reflect on their own interpretations of the vampire mythos, and how these creatures can be used to explore issues such as death, sex, greed and isolation.

This outing is a shining example of why this low-budget Canadian series attained such a cult following. The host takes a serious look—with a healthy dose of humor—at vampires and their evolution in film, comics and literature. With very little flash, Commander Rick interacts with pre-taped interviews from several renowned authors, resulting in a half hour of fascinating conversation; it's a talk show of sorts that takes place in a very non-traditional setting.

📺 Features a cooking show skit where the host prepares "Bram Stoker's recipe for Vampire Alfresco:" take two pounds of Vlad (skin off), add one tablespoon of ground Nosferatu, and then season with sexual subtext; most importantly, avoid garlic! This meal "will feed on four to six people" and make "a nice change from blood pudding."

Prisoners of Gravity – "Vampires"

TVO. Mar 16, 1994 (S05E19). Literature/Sci-Fi. D: Gregg Thurlbeck. W: Rick Green, Mark Askwith. C: Poppy Z. Brite, Nancy A. Collins, Nancy Baker, Chelsea Quinn Yarbro, Suzy McKee Charnas, Jewelle Gomez, Tanya Huff, Anne Rice. CAN: English/Color/30m. TV Ontario/OECA.

🦇 🦇 🦇 🦇

The focus of this episode is on the new wave of female authors of vampire literature, and how they represent women (and vampires) in their stories. Includes discussions of which trappings from the vampire mythos they've kept, and what they have discarded.

Another great POG episode featuring a topic that rarely gets such attention, with interview clips from several popular contemporary authors who chat about their characters and their craft. The host's only gaffe is the insinuation that Bram Stoker's immortal vampire was heavily influenced by Vlad Țepeș, but this can be forgiven considering it was the popular theory at the time. Several notable books are mentioned in this episode, each of which are required reading for all vampire fans: *Lost Souls* (Poppy Z. Brite); *Sunglasses After Dark* and *In the Blood* (Nancy A. Collins); *Darker Passions Dracula, Love Bite* and *Night Inside* (Nancy Baker); Atta Olivia Clemens series (Chelsea Quinn Yarbro); *The Vampire Tapestry* (Suzy McKee Charnas); *The Gilda Stories* (Jewelle Gomez); *Blood Price* and *Blood Lines* (Tanya Huff); *The Vampire Lestat, Queen of the Damned* and *Tale of the Body Thief* (Anne Rice).

Play for Today - "Vampires"

BBC One. Jan 9, 1979 (S09E11). Drama/Horror. D: John Goldschmidt. W: Dixie Williams. C: Peter Moran ☥, Paul Moran, Tommy White, Linda Beckett ☥, Jimmy Coleman, Bert Edgar, Vera Kelly, Paul Shane, Terri Griffin, John G. Heller ☥. UK: English/Color/50m. BBC.

Stu Perry is a young lad with a bleak future, who often skips school to spend his day drifting around his poor, working-class neighborhood. He loves all things horror, especially vampires, and even buys some fake plastic fangs so he can pretend to be one. After his younger brother Davey claims to have actually seen a bloodsucker in the local cemetery, a skeptical Stu checks it out for himself—and discovers a pale, gaunt man wandering the crypt underneath a derelict chapel.

This story has some allusions to the famous "Gorbals Vampire" incident of 1954, when a group of children in Scotland, armed with knives and other sharp objects, gathered in a local cemetery to hunt down the vampire that they believed was preying on local boys. This incident led to the introduction of strict censorship laws in the UK, which effectively banned the sale of American horror comics and magazines; concerned parents believed that these publications were responsible for inducing fear and anxiety in their children. There is a vampire in this story, but is it just a figment of an overactive imagination, or something very real? Perhaps the creature is being used as a metaphor for the evil inside us all, and in the case of one character, an evil that could no longer be contained. The reality (or fantasy) is never fully explained, and this ambiguity leads to a frustratingly unsatisfactory conclusion.

📺 The movie that the kids watch on TV is the classic Hammer production *Dracula: Prince of Darkness* (1966).

Purple Playhouse - "Dracula"

CBC. Mar 25, 1973 (S01E05). Drama/Romance. D: Jack Nixon-Browne. W: Rod Coneybeare. C: Norman Welsh ☥, Nehemiah Persoff, Dan MacDonald, Blair Brown, Steven Sutherland, Charlotte Blunt ☥, Marie Romain Aloma ☥, Marcella Saint Amant ☥. CAN: English/Color/50m. CBC.

Purple Playhouse was an eight-episode Canadian dramatic series that adapted both novels and stage plays. This story opens with Jonathan Harker already at Dracula's castle in Transylvania, but he's soon trapped within the walls of the fortress. Dracula heads to England and quickly sets his sights on Lucy Murray. Includes an introduction from author Robertson Davies.

This is one of the more faithful adaptations of Bram Stoker's novel, even though corners are cut and the story is streamlined to tell the tale within one hour. The characters of Renfield and Quincey Morris are dropped, as is any mention of the Demeter, and Lucy and Mina are now sisters. Surprisingly, the story concludes in England, with Mina delivering the final blow; she stakes Dracula before a reluctant Jonathan can do the deed himself. Some key scenes typically absent from most adaptations are included here, such as Dracula's head-first climb down the castle wall, and Van Helsing's use of the communion host to sanctify (and thereby desecrate) one of

Dracula's coffins. Like many productions of this era, this one feels like a filmed stage play, yet it does utilize technology of the day to show the vampires transforming back and forth into dogs. The Count himself is closer to Stoker's original vision; he has very pronounced fangs, long fingernails, flowing white hair, and bloodshot eyes topped by unkempt eyebrows.

Reach for the Crypt

BookTelevision. Oct 2001. D: Anon. W: Daniel Richler. C: Daniel Richler, Elizabeth Miller, Liisa Ladoucer, Baron Marcus, Renee, Singuala, Peter Mansfield, Stephanie Quinlan. CAN: English/Color/47m. CHUM Television Ltd.

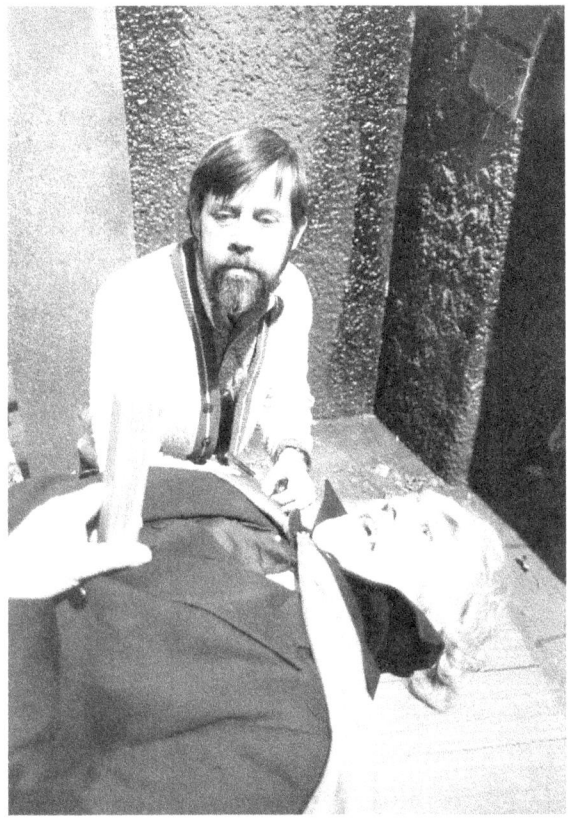

Writer Rod Coneybeare looks on as Norman Welsh prepares for a scene in *Purple Playhouse* - "Dracula" (CBC Still Photo Collection)

This TV special examines classic literature under the guise of a Gothic game show. Host Daniel Richler directs questions to competing teams from "Shapeshifter University" and "Bloodsucker College," with answers verified by Dracula scholar Elizabeth Miller. Topics fall within several categories, all relating to some aspect of Bram Stoker's novel—sourced from Miller's book, *Dracula: Sense and Nonsense*.

The concept is great, and wordsmith Daniel Richler keeps it entertaining and light-hearted, which makes up for the obvious low-budget nature of the production. Unfortunately the group of "contestants" appear at times to be just vaguely interested in the topic, while the studio audience seems to tune out altogether. The program gets bonus points for clearing up the most common misconceptions about the novel, and is one of the more unique ways of exploring *Dracula* and its influence on contemporary pop culture.

Real People - "Family Reunion Special"

NBC. Nov 21, 1979 (S01E--). Culture/Family. D: David N. Caldwell. W: Anon. C: Fred Willard, John Barbour, Sarah Purcell, Jimmy Breslin, Mark Russell, Skip Stephenson, Byron Allen, Bill Rafferty. USA: English/Color/90m. NBC.

This was a landmark weekly primetime show that profiled real people from across the United States, in stories that ran the gamut from the humorous to the heartwarming, and from the peculiar to the bizarre. In this special extended episode, current and former hosts gather to pay tribute to their favorite segments from past programs, including a story about a modern-day vampire hunter. Other segments feature a bicyclist who rides backwards; the "world's fastest oil painter"; a private eye who specializes in finding lost pets; a six-year-old pool shark; the official witch of Salem, Massachusetts; a ten-year-old disc jockey; and a man who runs a school for beggars.

Promotional advertisement for NBC's *Real People* 90-minute special (NBC/TV Guide)

Promotional advertisement for a Halloween-themed episode of NBC's *Real People* (NBC/TV Guide)

Real People – "Where the Ghouls Are" / "Dracula's Wedding" / "One More Time" / "Maskmaker"

NBC. Oct 29, 1980 (S02E--). Culture/Family. D: David N. Caldwell. W: Anon. C: Sarah Purcell, John Barbour, Skip Stephenson, Byron Allen, Bill Rafferty. USA: English/Color/60m. NBC.

In this special Halloween episode, the segment "Dracula's Wedding" features Sarah Purcell in attendance at a wedding where the bride, groom and guests all dress up like monsters. Other segments include John Barbour visiting a haunted house; a young boy who thinks he's a reincarnation of his uncle; a Medium who attempts to contact the spirit of Elvis Presley; and a behind-the-scenes look at a company that produces rubber masks for Halloween.

The Red Skelton Show – Ep. #3.40

NBC. Jun 15, 1954 (S03E40). Comedy/Music. D: Seymour Berns. W: Red Skelton. C: Red Skelton, Peter Lorre, Lon Chaney Jr., Bela Lugosi, Maila Nurmi, David Rose and His Orchestra. USA: English/B&W/30m. Van Bernard Productions.

Lugosi appeared in a mad scientist skit alongside Nurmi as Vampira, and although this episode is no longer extant, surviving publicity stills show the two hamming it up together. There is a dispute over the actual broadcast date of their appearance; some sources claim that it was actually part of a Halloween special from 1953—although Nurmi's creation didn't appear on television until the debut of *The Vampira Show* in April of 1954. However, much as with his appearance on the *Texaco Star Theater* in 1949, Lugosi didn't fare well in this live situation once Skelton started ad-libbing his lines.

The Red Skelton Show – Ep. #4.18

NBC. Jan 18, 1955 (S04E18). Comedy/Music. D: Anon. W: Red Skelton. C: Red Skelton, Peter Lorre, Muriel Landers, Mary Beth Hughes, Maila Nurmi, The Redettes, Art Gilmore, David Rose and His Orchestra. USA: English/B&W/30m. Van Bernard Productions.

Features a macabre parody of *The Honeymooners,* with Lorre as Ralph Kramden, Maila Nurmi (in the guise of Vampira) as "Malice Kramden," and Skelton as Ed Norton. There is some debate as to whether or not this was actually Nurmi performing, and upon close examination of surviving video, indeed it does not appear to be her. Some sources suggest that it was actually actress Mary Beth Hughes who was made up to look like the Vampira character.

The Riddlers – "Legend of the Vampire Hedgehog"

CITV. 1993 (S05E06). Educational/Family. D: Chris Ryder. W: Rick Vanes. C: Victoria Williams, Peter Llewellyn Jones, Richard Robinson, Mike Gallant. UK: English/Color/30m. Yorkshire Television Ltd.

As the gang plans a trip to Whitby in search of Glossup, Postie warns that they should avoid the area altogether—for it is the home of legendary monster Snackula the Vampire Hedgehog. Marjorie and Mr. Grimley believe he's just getting confused by the legend of Dracula, while Mossop dismisses the tale entirely. Only young Tiddlup believes the story is true, and during a sleepless night, she insists that Mossop investigate a strange noise coming from the garden—where he discovers a terrible sight hiding in the bushes.

The Ron James Show – Ep. #1.09

CBC. Nov 20, 2009 (S01E09). Comedy/Satire. D: Dale Heslip. W: Ron James, Garry Campbell. C: Ron James ⚥, Matt Baram, Naomi Snieckus, Colin Mochrie, Nicole Stamp, Debra McGrath. CAN: English/Color/23m. Ron James Entertainment Inc./Enter the Picture Productions Inc./CBC.

In the segment "Newfie Vampire," a tourist stops at Buddy's bar looking for directions, unaware that the proprietor is a vampire. This is the first in a limited series of skits featuring Buddy McNabb, an amicable vampire, which all have the underlying theme of the kindness of Newfoundlanders—who freely offer their blood for Buddy to drink.

The Ron James Show - Ep. #2.06

CBC. Oct 29, 2010 (S02E06). Comedy/Satire. D: Dale Heslip. W: Ron James, Garry Campbell. C: Ron James ♀, Eric Peterson, Mark Day, Jennifer Gibson ♀, Torquil Colbo. CAN: English/Color/23m. Ron James Entertainment Inc./Enter the Picture Productions Inc./CBC.

In the segment "Newfie Vampire: Origins," it's the year 1908, and a bartender named Buddy McNabb has a fateful run-in with a beautiful, mysterious woman. A few days later, Buddy realizes that he's been turned into a vampire; distraught over what he's become, Buddy convinces his friends that he's a "Draclear"—and must be staked through the heart. But the caring locals refuse; instead, they offer themselves up as donors—because Newfoundlanders stick together.

A charming and very funny skit about the renowned kindness of Newfoundlanders, even towards one of their own who has been turned into a vampire. Some of the best moments occur as Buddy adjusts to his new undead life; he has difficulty with the transition, and inadvertently breaks off one of his fangs in an attempt pry the cap off of a bottle of beer. The running joke of calling himself a "Draclear" ("drah-klee-air") is one of the highlights, and used throughout the related skits.

The Ron James Show - "New Year's Eve Edition 2010"

CBC. Dec 31, 2010 (S02E12). Comedy/Satire. D: Dale Heslip. W: Ron James, Garry Campbell. C: Ron James ♀, Jennifer Gibson ♀, Salvatore Antonio ♀, Torquil Colbo, Scott Thompson, Aurora Browne. CAN: English/Color/46m. Ron James Entertainment Inc./Enter the Picture Productions Inc./CBC.

In the segment "Newfie Vampire Soul," two strangers walk into Buddy's bar; one of them is Valentina, the temptress who turned him one hundred and eighteen years ago. She's confused by Buddy's demeanor; her companion, Eduardo, is dark and moody, yet Buddy has maintained a cheery disposition—despite the "lonely crush of immortality" that they all face.

This is likely the last "Newfie Vampire" sketch, and is the best segment from this TV special. Buddy maintains his positive attitude thanks to the giving compassion of Newfoundlanders (and his vampire dog); he loses his remaining fang after a fight with Eduardo—but gains the hand of the lovely Valentina.

Royal Canadian Air Farce - Ep. #2.08

CBC. Nov 25, 1994 (S02E08). Comedy/Politics. D: Perry Rosemond. W: Gord Holtam, John Morgan, Rick Olsen. C: Roger Abbott, Don Ferguson, Luba Goy, John Morgan ♀. CAN: English/Color/22m. Air Farce Productions Inc./CBC.

Includes the sketch "Interview with a Canadian Vampire," where a woman is attacked in her boudoir by a polite, overly apologetic vampire (who asks for permission before biting her). It's an obvious reference to *Interview with the Vampire* (1994), which hit theaters a couple weeks earlier, and pales in comparison to the best skit of the bunch: Richard Simmons "Sweatin' to the News Headlines."

Royal Canadian Air Farce – Ep. #10.11

CBC. Jan 17, 2003 (S10E11). Comedy/Politics. D: Perry Rosemond. W: Gord Holtam, Rick Olsen, Rob Lindsay, Wayne Testori. C: Roger Abbott, Don Ferguson, Luba Goy, Craig Lauzon ☥. CAN: English/Color/22m. Air Farce Productions Inc./CBC.

🦇🦇

In one skit, the "Pfaisal Pfarmaceutical Pcompany" is hard at work developing an exciting new way to fight strokes, using an enzyme extracted from the saliva of vampire bats. Unfortunately for one lab assistant, these creatures aren't as harmless as he had first thought. This segment garners some laughs thanks to the physical comedy of Craig Lauzon; he's attacked and then bitten by the bat, and transforms into a Dracula-type vampire.

Royal Canadian Air Farce – Ep. #13.01

CBC. Oct 28, 2005 (S13E01). Comedy/Politics. D: Perry Rosemond, Rob Lindsay. W: Don Ferguson, Alan Park, Craig Lauzon. C: Roger Abbott, Don Ferguson, Luba Goy, Jessica Holmes, Craig Lauzon, Alan Park ☥. CAN: English/Color/22m. Air Farce Productions Inc./CBC.

🦇

This episode features a Monty Python-esque animated sketch where a vampire discovers the hidden dangers of Hepatitis C. It's a fake PSA that ends with the statement "Hepatitis C. No one's immune to it."

SCTV

Global/CBC/NBC. 1976–1984 (135 Episodes). Comedy/Satire. D: Milad Bessada, John Bell. W: Var. C: Joe Flaherty ☥, Eugene Levy, Andrea Martin, Dave Thomas, John Candy, Catherine O'Hara, Rick Moranis, Dave Thomas, Martin Short, Harold Ramis. CAN: English/Color/6660m. Old Firehall Productions/Second City Entertainment.

🦇🦇🦇🦇

A small-town television station fills its broadcast day with a wide range of original programming, including "Monster Chiller Horror Theatre." The host, Count Floyd, is a vampire who howls like a

Vampire horror host Count Floyd gets stuck with airing Z-grade films on "Monster Chiller Horror Theatre," a recurring segment on *SCTV* (Old Firehall Productions/Second City Entertainment)

wolf (and he's actually news anchor Floyd Robertson in costume). Due to budget constraints, he's limited to showcasing non-horrific Z-grade movies, such as Tip O'Neil's 3D House of Representatives, Dr. Tongue's House of Cats, and Dr. Tongue's 3D House of Stewardesses. This groundbreaking sketch-comedy series first aired in Canada, but was rebranded over the years as it switched networks and production locales.

SM:TV Live – Ep. #129

ITV. Feb 10, 2001 (S03E24). Comedy/Family. D: Anon. W: Anon. C: Anthony McPartlin, Declan Donnelly, Cat Deeley, Helen Soraya, Ant McPartlin, Dane Bowers ⚥, Mel B. UK: English/Color/125m. Blaze Television/Gallowgate.

This British Saturday morning sketch comedy series for kids often skewered contemporary popular culture, such as with the recurring segment "Chums," which was a parody of the sitcom *Friends*. In this edition—"The One with the Vampire"—the gang meets Handy Andy, a contractor who'll be working on their flat. What's really odd is that he asks to stay there overnight, then drags in a coffin! It seems he also casts no reflection, never works during the day, and is allergic to garlic. Could he be a vampire? The Chums offer up a tasty buffet, and after devouring a sausage roll doused in holy water, Andy dies—killed by "Buffet, the Vampire Slayer"! This segues to a mock *Buffy: The Vampire Slayer* opening, which stars a sausage roll, scotch egg, and a slice of quiche. However, it turns out that Andy isn't a vampire after all—although Dane Bowers certainly appears to be.

Saturday Night Live – Desi Arnaz / Desi Arnaz, Jr.

NBC. Feb 21, 1976 (S01E14). Comedy/Music. D: Dave Wilson, Gary Weis. W: Chevy Chase, Herb Sargent, Al Franken. C: Desi Arnaz, Desi Arnaz, Jr., Dan Aykroyd, John Belushi, Jane Curtin, Laraine Newman ⚥, Gilda Radner. USA: English/Color/90m. Broadway Video/NBC.

In the skit "Luciana Vermicelli's Beauty Regimen," a woman pops out of a coffin and reveals the secret to her everlasting youth, which includes eating the faces of young virgins and drinking the blood of Girl Scouts. Hosted by Desi Arnaz with musical guests Desi Arnaz and Desi Arnaz, Jr.

Saturday Night Live – Christopher Lee / Meat Loaf

NBC. March 25, 1978 (S03E15). Comedy/Music. D: Dave Wilson. W: Dan Aykroyd, Herb Sargent, Al Franken. C: Christopher Lee, Dan Aykroyd, John Belushi, Jane Curtin, Laraine Newman, Gilda Radner, Bill Murray. USA: English/Color/90m. Broadway Video/NBC.

Christopher Lee chose not to appear on SNL as Dracula, but in one sketch, he plays the role of a Van Helsing-inspired vampire hunter. He's hired to stake the memoirs of the disgraced former President Richard Nixon, before the book can be published.

Saturday Night Live – Buck Henry / Sun Ra

NBC. May 20, 1978 (S03E20). Comedy/Music. D: Dave Wilson. W: Dan Aykroyd, Herb Sargent, Al Franken. C: Buck Henry, Dan Aykroyd, John Belushi, Jane Curtin, Laraine Newman ☥, Gilda Radner, Bill Murray. USA: English/Color/90m. Broadway Video/NBC.

The segment "Mr. Mike's Least Loved Music" features the song "Baby Ghouls" by Michael O'Donoghue, which includes backing vocals by a vampire (who ends up biting his neck). Hosted by Buck Henry with musical guest Sun Ra.

Christopher Lee plays a vampire hunter in a sketch from *Saturday Night Live* (Broadway Video/NBC)

Saturday Night Live – James Woods / Don Henley

NBC. Oct 28, 1989 (S15E04). Comedy/Music. D: Dave Wilson, Tom Schiller. W: James Downey, Herb Sargent. C: Dana Carvey, Nora Dunn, Phil Hartman, Jan Hooks, Victoria Jackson, Jon Lovitz, Mike Myers, Kevin Nealon, Dennis Miller. USA: English/Color/90m. Broadway Video/NBC.

In the sketch "AIDS-Aware Dracula," it's apparent that the Count is well aware of the deadly blood-borne disease that's raging across the country—since he chooses his victims solely based on how chaste they are. Hosted by James Woods with musical guest Don Henley.

Saturday Night Live – John Travolta / Seal

NBC. Oct 15, 1994 (S20E03). Comedy/Music. D: Dave Wilson. W: James Downey, Al Franken. C: Ellen Cleghorne, Chris Elliott, Janeane Garofalo, Chris Farley, Norm MacDonald, Tim Meadows, Michael McKean, Mike Myers, Jay Mohr. USA: English/Color/90m. Broadway Video/NBC.

In the skit "Dracula's Not Gay," the Count is offended by his unexpected guests, who mistake him for a man with homosexual tendencies (it turns out Renfield is gay, as is their werewolf neighbor). Hosted by John Travolta with musical guest Seal.

Saturday Night Live – Sarah Michelle Gellar / Portishead

NBC. Jan 17, 1998 (S23E11). Comedy/Music. D: Beth McCarthy-Miller. W: Adam McKay, Tina Fey. C: Jim Breuer ☥, Will Ferrell ☥, Ana Gasteyer, Chris Kattan, Norm MacDonald, Tim Meadows, Darrell Hammond ☥, Cheri Oteri. USA: English/Color/90m. Broadway Video/NBC.

In one sketch, the WB reimagines *Buffy the Vampire Slayer* to attract fans of the sitcom *Seinfeld*, which just ended its series run. This mash-up has Buffy now living in New York City, where she essentially takes on the role of Elaine from *Seinfeld*—but her friends (Jerry, George and Kramer) are all vampires. Hosted by Sarah Michelle Gellar with musical guest Portishead.

Saturday Night Live – Sarah Michelle Gellar / Faith Hill

NBC. Oct 12, 2002 (S28E02). Comedy/Music. D: Beth McCarthy-Miller. W: Tina Fey, Dennis McNicholas. C: Fred Armisen, Rachel Dratch ☥, Jimmy Fallon, Tina Fey, Will Forte, Darrell Hammond, Chris Kattan ☥, Seth Meyers, Amy Poehler ☥. USA: English/Color/90m. Broadway Video/NBC.

The opening monologue is interrupted by a family of the undead; they're offended, because the actress who plays a vampire hunter on TV is hosting this week. Hosted by Sarah Michelle Gellar with musical guest Faith Hill.

Saturday Night Live – Hugh Laurie / Beck

NBC. Oct 28, 2006 (S32E04). Comedy/Music. D: Don Roy King. W: Seth Meyers. C: Fred Armisen, Will Forte, Bill Hader, Darrell Hammond, Seth Meyers, Amy Poehler, Maya Rudolph, Andy Samberg, Jason Sudeikis ☥, Kristen Wiig. USA: English/Color/90m. Broadway Video/NBC.

In the sketch "The Curse of Frankenstein," a mob of angry villagers hunts down the Frankenstein Monster. He tries to convince them that he's not the one they're looking for; instead, they should be attacking the castle across the moor—which turns out to be the home of Dracula. Also, in the animated segment "TV Funhouse," President George W. Bush introduces two new political attack ads targeting Democrats. The first features Ted Kennedy wearing a Dracula costume, while the second shows Barack Obama in the guise of Count von Count (who crunches some numbers: "one gay marriage, two gay marriage…"). Hosted by Hugh Laurie with musical guest Beck.

Saturday Night Live – Ellen Page / Wilco

NBC. Mar 1, 2008 (S33E06). Comedy/Music. D: Don Roy King. W: Seth Meyers, Paula Pell. C: Fred Armisen, Will Forte, Bill Hader, Darrell Hammond, Amy Poehler, Seth Meyers, Andy Samberg, Jason Sudeikis ☥, Kenan Thompson, Kristen Wiig. USA: English/Color/90m. Broadway Video/NBC.

Features the SNL Digital Short "The Mirror," where a young woman sees a crazed psycho reflected behind her in the bathroom mirror, over and over again. But it's just a bad dream—for the both of them. Hosted by Ellen Page with musical guest Wilco.

Saturday Night Live – Taylor Swift

NBC. Nov 7, 2009 (S35E05). Comedy/Music. D: Don Roy King. W: Seth Meyers, Alex Baze. C: Fred Armisen, Will Forte, Bill Hader, Darrell Hammond, Amy Poehler, Seth Meyers, Andy Samberg ☥, Jason Sudeikis, Kenan Thompson, Kristen Wiig. USA: English/Color/90m. Broadway Video/NBC.

In the SNL Digital Short "Firelight" (a trailer for a film parody of *Twilight*), a high school girl falls for Philip Frank, a student who comes from a family of Frankenstein Monsters. But her friend—a mummy named Lomax—isn't impressed with the budding relationship. Instead of the typical vampire/werewolf struggle, this story features the lesser-known Frankenstein Monster/mummy conflict (who knew?)—and includes a glimpse of the Edward Cullen vampire character. Hosted by Taylor Swift, who also performs two songs.

Secrets of the Cryptkeeper's Haunted House

CBS. Sep 14, 1996 – Aug 23, 1997 (-- Episodes). Education/Reality. D: Eytan Keller. W: Jack Wohl, Sally J. Maisel, Michelle Johnson. C: John Kassir, Danny Mann, Van Snowden. USA: English/Color/--m. Goldwyn Entertainment Company/Keller Productions/The Wohl Company.

A macabre, Saturday morning game show for kids taped at Universal Studios Florida, which featured two teams competing in five different challenges in and around a haunted house. One set piece was called "The Vampire's Lair," which was a darkened room with a bloodsucker hidden inside. Presented by Steve Saunders.

Sesame Street

PBS. Nov 10, 1969 – 2016 (4384 Episodes). Education/Music. D: Var. W: Var. C: Caroll Spinney, Frank Oz, Jim Henson, Jerry Nelson ☥, Sonia Manzano, Bob McGrath, Loretta Long, Kevin Clash, Emilio Delgado, Fran Brill ☥. USA: English/Color/263040m. Children's Television Workshop/Jim Henson Productions.

🦇 🦇 🦇

One of the most endearing characters from the long-running children's show *Sesame Street* is Count von Count, pictured here with Jerry Nelson, the man who brought life to the vampire (Children's Television Workshop/Jim Henson Productions)

On a quaint inner-city street, residents teach children about preschool subjects through games, songs, cartoons and comedy. Features the recurring character Count von Count, a vampire obsessed with numbers (whose look is based on the Dracula archetype).

The Count also had several vampire "lady friends" on the series, beginning with The Countess Natasha in 1977. In 1980, he romanced Countess Dahling von Dahling, and a decade later, Countess von Backwards entered his life (his vampire mother also made a brief appearance). An episode from 1987 included the soap opera spoof *All My Letters,* which starred a vegetable vampire named Walter.

Sesame Street All-Star 25th Birthday: Stars and Street Forever!

ABC. May 18, 1994. Family/Music. D: Anon. W: Anon. C: Joe Pesci, Corbin Bernsen, Danny DeVito, Rhea Perlman, John Goodman, Julia Louis-Dreyfus, Rosie O'Donnell, Susan Sarandon, Barbara Walters, Regis Philbin, Kathie Lee Gifford. USA: English/Color/45m. Children's Television Workshop.

Celebrating the twenty-fifth anniversary of the long-running series for children, this TV special features clips from past episodes (some of which include Count von Count). Intermixed is a framing story about a rich Tycoon, Ronald Grump, who wants to give Sesame Street a major makeover—by demolishing buildings and erecting a skyscraper (to be called Grump Tower).

Sesame Street Jam: A Musical Celebration

PBS. 1994. Family/Music. D: Mustapha Khan, Jon Stone. W: Sara Compton, Judy Freudberg. C: Caroll Spinney, Martin P. Robinson, Fran Brill, Jerry Nelson ⚥, Kevin Clash, David Rudman, Joey Mazzarino, Pam Arciero, Frank Oz, Jim Henson. USA: English/Color/45m. Children's Television Workshop.

Count von Count and the other muppet regulars appear alongside celebrity guests, in scenes primarily taken from segments originally broadcast during the twenty-fifth season. Guest stars include En Vogue, Little Richard, Aaron Neville, Queen Latifah, Los Lobos and Maya Angelou. Originally produced for the twenty-fifth anniversary of the series, it wasn't broadcast on PBS until the 1994 pledge drive season (it was released six months earlier on home video, as *Sesame Street: 25 Wonderful Years).*

Sesame Street, Special

PBS. 1988. Family/Music. D: Jon Stone. W: Christopher Cerf, Cathi Rosenberg-Turow. C: Jim Henson, Kevin Clash, Richard Hunt, Jerry Nelson ⚥, Frank Oz, Caroll Spinney, Northern Calloway, Bob McGrath, Linda Bove. USA: English/Color/45m. Children's Television Workshop.

Mixing new material with older segments from the series, this TV special opens with Gladys Night and the Pips singing a jazzed-up version of the opening theme. All the regular muppets are here, including Count von Count, as well as a number of guest stars such as Phil Donahue, Martina Navratilova, Barbara Walters and Ralph Nader. Several comedians and musicians take part, including Paul Simon, Patti LaBelle, James Taylor, John Candy, Andrea Martin and Paul Reubens. Released into the home video market as *Put Down the Duckie: An All-Star Musical Special.*

Sesame Street Stays Up Late! A Monster New Year's Eve Party

PBS. Dec 29, 1993. Family/Music. D: Chuck Vinson. W: Lou Berger. C: Alison Bartlett, Linda Bove, Ruth Buzzi, Lily Tomlin, Annette Calud, Emilio Delgado, Savion Glover, Angel Jemmott, Jerry Nelson ☥. USA: English/Color/60m. Children's Television Workshop/The Jim Henson Company.

As everyone prepares to welcome in the new year, Elmo hosts the Monster News Network, which includes segments that show how New Year's Eve is celebrated around the world. Features clips of international *Sesame Street* co-productions, from such countries as Japan, Israel, Germany, Mexico, Portugal and Norway. Although meant as a New Year's Eve special, it was actually first broadcast in some markets on December 29, and then repeated on the 31st (and still ends with a countdown to midnight, despite being broadcast at 8:00 p.m.). It was released into the home video market as *Sesame Street Celebrates Around the World*.

Shock Theatre

ABC. 1968-1976 (-- Episodes). Comedy/Horror. D: Anon. W: Tommy Reynolds. C: Tommy Reynolds ☥, Patricia Abney, Baxter Eaves, Dan East. USA: English/B&W, Color/--m. Ruckerstein Enterprises/WTVC-TV.

Dracula, under the moniker of Doctor Shock, hosted this Saturday late-night horror movie program with help from his assistant, Nurse Badbody (likely in parody of Nurse Goodbody, from *Hee Haw*). This was essentially a stand-up act by Tommy Reynolds (as Dr. Shock), the Program Director of the station who dressed in typical Dracula garb, with pale makeup and large, black circles under his eyes; he also carried a cane adorned with a human skull. His sidekick—an irreverent vampire bat named Ding Bat (created and voiced by puppeteer Dan East)—would often introduce humorous

Shock Theatre was a late-night cult horror program hosted by Dr. Shock, a Lugosi-inspired Dracula, on Saturday nights in Chattanooga, Tennessee (Ruckerstein Enterprises/WTVC-TV)

breaking news by crying, "FLASH, FLASH, FLASH!" The cast of kooky characters, who entertained viewers around commercial breaks, also included corrupt Congressman Wilbur Ripsnort, Walter Crankcase, Batgorilla, and many others. Broadcast locally in Chattanooga, Tennessee on the ABC affiliate WTVC-TV, *Shock Theatre* developed a cult following. After cancellation, it briefly resurfaced on CBS affiliate WDEF-TV.

📺 In 2011, a new cast resurrected the program for a two-hour Christmas special featuring Reynolds doppelgänger Jack Gray as Doctor Shock, April Sinclair as Nurse Goodbody ("or Badbody, depending on her mood"), and Teddy Whittenbarger as Dingbat (as well as a playing new character, named Dirge). They have since taken the show online.

Show of the Week – "Wayne & Shuster Take an Affectionate Look at Abbott and Costello"

CBC. Jan 25, 1965 (S01E04). Comedy/Film. D: Norman Campbell. W: Arthur Knight, Johnny Wayne, Frank Shuster. C: Johnny Wayne, Frank Shuster. CAN: English/B&W/60m. CBC.

Wayne and Shuster chat about the career of madcap duo Abbot and Costello, from their early work in burlesque and vaudeville, to their extensive career in radio and film. Clips include their run-ins with the famous monsters of the silver screen, including Dracula, the Wolf Man, and the Frankenstein Monster.

Show of the Week – "Wayne & Shuster Take an Affectionate Look at the Monsters"

CBC. Jan 10, 1966 (S02E02). Comedy/Film. D: Norman Campbell. W: Arthur Knight, Johnny Wayne, Frank Shuster. C: Johnny Wayne, Frank Shuster. CAN: English/B&W/60m. MCA/CBC.

Johnny Wayne and Frank Shuster highlight some great moments in the history of horror film and television. Features clips from *The Cabinet of Dr. Caligari* (1920), *Nosferatu, eine Symphonie des Grauens* (1922) and *Dracula* (1931).

Silents Please – "Dracula"

ABC. 1960/61 (S01E31). History/Film. D: Anon. W: Ernie Kovacs. C: Ernie Kovacs. USA: English/B&W/30m. Gregstan Enterprises.

Series explored the history of silent-era motion pictures, and covered "the great stars, the excitement, the thrills, the laughter and heartbreak of Hollywood's golden era." This episode featured a condensed version of F. W. Murnau's 1922 classic film *Nosferatu, eine Symphonie des Grauens*. Presented by Ernie Kovacs.

The Sonny and Cher Comedy Hour – Ep. #4.02

CBS. Sep 19, 1973 (S04E02). Comedy/Music. D: Art Fisher. W: Paul Wayne, Bob Arnott, Bob Einstein. C: Sonny Bono, Cher, Danny Thomas, Telly Savalas, Billy Van ♀, Ted Zeigler, Teri Garr, Freeman King, Peter Cullen. USA: English/Color/60m. Yosh Productions.

Guest star Danny Thomas sings his rendition of "If I Didn't Care," and is joined onstage by the Frankenstein Monster and Count Dracula—played by Billy Van. The comedian also portrayed "Count Frightenstein" (the thirteenth son of Count Dracula) on the Canadian series *The Hilarious House of Frightenstein* (1970).

The Sonny and Cher Comedy Hour – Ep. #4.08

CBS. Oct 31, 1973 (S04E08). Comedy/Music. D: Art Fisher. W: Paul Wayne, Bob Arnott, Bob Einstein. C: Sonny Bono, Cher, Jerry Lewis, Billy Van ☥, Ted Zeigler, Teri Garr, Freeman King, Peter Cullen, Murray Langston. USA: English/Color/60m. Yosh Productions.

This Halloween special has Sonny and Cher welcoming special guest Jerry Lewis, and features a skit involving Dracula (Billy Van reprises his role as the Count).

The Sonny & Cher Show - Ep. #1.02

CBS. Feb 8, 1976 (S01E02). Comedy/Music. D: Tim Kiley. W: Frank Peppiatt, John Aylesworth. C: Sonny Bono ☥, Cher ☥, Raymond Burr ☥, Billy Van, Ted Zeigler, Linda Hoxit, Susan Buckner, Gailard Sartain, Jack L. Harrell. USA: English/Color/60m. Yosh Productions.

Barely live, from television city, comes the *Sonny & Cher Monstrel Show!* This segment, from the revamped incarnation of the couple's first variety series (which was canceled two years earlier), featured both Sonny and Cher, as well as guest-star Raymond Burr, as vampires. They were surrounded by a cast of monsters, including Frankenstein's creation, The Wolf Man, the Bride of Frankenstein, and various mummies, witches, skeletons, and other ghouls. Sketches within the segment included "Stab-it and Costello," "The Great Ghoulo," and a Halloween-themed song performed by Cher—who is introduced as "Ms. Vampira."

Sonny with a Chance – "A So Random! Halloween Special"

Disney. Oct 17, 2010 (S02E17). Comedy/Music. D: Eric Dean Seaton. W: Adam Schwartz. C: Tiffany Thornton, Brandon Smith, Doug Brochu, Allisyn Ashley Arm, Demi Lovato, Shaquille O'Neal ☥, AllStar Weekend. USA: English/Color/22m. It's a Laugh Productions/Varsity Pictures.

🦇 🦇

Follows the adventures of Sonny Munroe, who joins the cast of the teen sketch comedy series *So Random!*. In this episode, the show-within-a-show presents a Halloween special with musical guest AllStar Weekend (Munroe also performs a song), and features guest host Shaquille O'Neal as Dracula in several sketches. It's an average episode, with forgettable pop music manufactured for the masses, but it's not all bad. The skits featuring the obnoxious "check it out girls," and the music video for the song "Making Babies Cry," are both quite funny.

The Steve Allen Show

NBC/ABC. 1956-1964. Comedy/Music. D: Anon. W: Stan Burns, Herb Sargent, Mike Marmer, Don Hinkley. C: Steve Allen, Don Adams, Edia Adams, Dayton Allen, Gabe Dell ☥, Herbert Hartig, Skitch Henderson. USA: English/B&W, Color/10020m. NBC.

This groundbreaking American variety show occasionally featured regular cast member Gabriel

Dell showcasing his famous Dracula impersonation. In 1963, Wonderland Records released a double LP that featured a story written by Cherney Berg with voices by Gabriel Dell. Titled *Famous Monsters Speak,* the album told the story of a reporter who meets Dracula and the Frankenstein Monster. The individual stories were titled "Frankenstein's Monster Talks" and "Dracula's Return."

Super Scary Saturday

TBS. Oct 1987 – 1989 (-- Episodes). Comedy/Horror. D: Anon. W: Anon. C: Al Lewis ⚰. USA: English/B&W, Color/--m. Turner Broadcasting System.

From deep within a dungeon, horror movie host "Grampa"—ostensibly Grandpa Dracula from *The Munsters*—presents B-grade horror and sci-fi films. He's joined by Igor the bat and Slim the skeleton. Around this same time, Al Lewis (in his vampire guise) was featured in a commercial that promoted the "Junior Vampires of America Club," a pay-per-minute 900-number service for kids, which they could call in order to hear scary monster stories. As an incentive, they were offered a free "vampire patch" and a list of "vampire tricks and secrets."

Superspecial – "Boo!"

CBC. Oct 26, 1980 (S07E--). Comedy/Music. D: Danny Mann. W: Riff Markowitz. C: Peter Cullen, Jack Duffy, Ben Gordon ⚰, Barbara Law ⚰, Ted Zeigler, Dionne Warwick, Rip Taylor. CAN: English/Color/45m. BOO! Productions Inc./CBC.

🦇 🦇 🦇 🦇

Count Dracula and his wife the Countess headline this variety special from a haunted castle in Transylvania, along with Dr. Frankenstein, his creation Frankie, and their feral friend Wolfie the werewolf. Special guests Dionne Warwick and Rip Taylor add their talents to this frenzied mix of comedy and music—with a few bloodcurdling screams to boot.

The program opens with Count Dracula, who appears from inside a coffin and exclaims, "Dead! From television central in Transylvania, it's BOO!" This leads into a catchy, disco-infused theme song performed by the five main characters, supported by three backup singers (all mummies) and a large group of dancers (a mix of zombies and vampires). So begins this very entertaining variety special that features cheesy jokes, rapid-fire skits, two songs performed by Dionne Warwick ("Déjà Vu" and "Just the Way You Are") and the prop comedy of Rip Taylor. Dracula and his wife explain to the live audience that they're tired of frightening people, so they decided to sing and dance their way into the hearts of the country. This is one of the most entertaining variety specials produced during this decade, especially for fans of the horror genre; it's a shame that it's been forgotten and will likely never see a DVD release.

Superspecial – "Wayne and Shuster #4"

CBC. Sep 23, 1979 (S06E04). Comedy/Music. D: Trevor Evans. W: Johnny Wayne, Frank Shuster, Kate Lonsdale, Ted Lonsdale. C: Johnny Wayne ⚲, Frank Shuster ⚲, Paul Kligman, Don Cullen, Tom Harvey, John Davies, Carol Robinson. CAN: English/Color/50m. CBC.

🦇🦇🦇

Variety show hosted by Canadian comedy duo Johnny Wayne and Frank Shuster, featuring song, dance and extended comedic sketches. One segment, "Newsnose," has a number of short skits, including a story about an all-vampire band making their musical debut. The group performs "Transylvania 6-5000," which is based on the Glenn Miller hit "Pennsylvania 6-5000."

A very funny segment featuring an entire big band dressed up as Dracula, with pale faces, slick-backed hair and red-lined capes. The bandleader points out that they do not take requests, especially when asked to play such classics as "Peg O' My Heart." The best skit of the bunch, however, is the Shakespearean tragedy *Hamlet* reimagined as a Western, where the Dane is "The Fastest Soliloquy in the West." It's an overall enjoyable production with some very smart writing.

📺 The "Transylvania 6-5000" skit was rebroadcast on Aug 20, 1988 as part of *Wayne and Shuster International*, a best-of series consisting of repackaged sketches from previous Wayne and Shuster broadcasts.

Tales from the Darkside Special

Syndicated. Sep 27, 1986. Horror/Thriller. D: Bob Balaban, Ted Gershuny. W: Edithe Swensen. C: Barnard Hughes, Harsh Nayyar ⚲, Marcia Cross ⚲, Patrick Kilpatrick ⚲, Seth Green. USA: English/Color/120m. Laurel Entertainment Inc./Jaygee Productions/Tribune Entertainment.

Renowned impressionist Rich Little hosts this two-hour special that features his favorite episodes from *Tales from the Darkside*: "Inside the Closet," "Strange Love," "Monsters in My Room," and "Trick or Treat." The episode "Strange Love" is the tale of a doctor who makes a fateful house call late one night, and is held captive in the home of a vampire couple. "Monsters in My Room" doesn't have any bloodsuckers, but features a young Seth Green well before he attained fame as the werewolf Oz in *Buffy the Vampire Slayer*.

Texaco Star Theater – Ep. #2.02

NBC. Sep 27, 1949 (S02E02). Comedy/Music. D: Edmund Cashman. W: Milton Berle, Mike Marmer. C: Bela Lugosi ⚲, Billie Burke, Bill Robinson, Jackie Robinson, Ole Olsen, Chic Johnson, Fatso Marco, Alan Roth. USA: English/B&W/60m. Texaco Gasoline Company/NBC.

A variety show that started on radio in 1938; when it transitioned to television in the late 1940s, it featured a rotating slate of guest hosts before settling on comedian Milton Berle. In this episode, although not called Dracula by name, Lugosi appeared in one skit dressed as the iconic vampire, and tried to hypnotize Berle in a very Dracula-like fashion. Lugosi fared well in unfamiliar comedic territory, but after he flubbed a punch line, Berle ad-libbed "You kill people on the screen and you also kill jokes!" A favorable review in *The Billboard* magazine stated that "Berle should make it a must to get one wild sketch into each show, the sort of slapstick, cornball idiocy built around Bela Lugosi."

📺 Considered the first appearance of a vampire on television!

That's So Weird – "That's So Scary"

YTV. Oct 2010. Comedy/Family. D: Dennis Saunders. W: Gary Pearson, Duncan McKenzie. C: James Hartnett ☥, Hannah Hogan, Alana Johnston ☥, Kayla Lorette, Joey Lucius ☥, Alex Spencer, AJ Vaage ☥. CAN: English/Color/19m. Halifax Film Company/YTV.

🦇🦇

Sketch comedy show featuring a group of teenagers who work at "So Weird TV," a fictional television station where employees create commercials and PSAs, often resulting in oddball spots. This creature-filled Halloween special features the sketch "dusk 3," a parody of the *Twilight* movies.

In "dusk 3," a vampire—the new bloodsucker in school—fails to impress a hip gang of fangless, vegetarian vampires. Other sketches feature the disenfranchised Dracula reflecting on the negative aspects of his condition (he often receives a baseball bat as a joke gift). The vampire sketches are the best of the bunch, with most of the other monster-related skits missing the mark.

📺 A version of this episode, with a few different sketches, was first presented on YTV's website in October 2009.

That's So Weird – "Space Thunder"

YTV. Oct 6, 2010 (S02E01). Comedy/Family. D: Anon. W: Anon. C: James Hartnett, Hannah Hogan, Alana Johnston, Kayla Lorette, Joey Lucius, Alex Spencer, AJ Vaage. CAN: English/Color/30m. Halifax Film Company/YTV.

The staff creates a show called "Space Thunder," which is just a spoof of past sci-fi movies. Includes sketches that parody the *Twilight* franchise and its rabid fan base.

The Tommy Ambrose Show – Ep. #2.--

CBC. Jan 11, 1963 (S02E--). Comedy/Music. D: Bill Davis. W: Bernard Rothman, Stan Jacobson. C: Frank Gorshin, Denny Miller. CAN: English/B&W/26m. CBC.

🦇🦇🦇🦇

Musical variety show hosted by Canadian singer-songwriter Tommy Ambrose, who welcomes American impressionist Frank Gorshin. As they chat about their predictions for the coming year, Gorshin states that the recent success of the novelty song "Monster Mash" will mean that the hit parade will soon be dominated by the Hollywood Gangland. The two then perform a version of "I've Grown Accustomed to Her Face," while trading off impressions of Bela Lugosi, Alfred

Hitchcock, Edward G. Robinson, Boris Karloff, and James Cagney.

The vampire element is minimal; Tommy Ambrose channels Bela Lugosi as he sings one verse of the duet as Dracula. The episode is still quite entertaining, and features a great routine from Gorshin, where he mimics several deceased stars—who now reside in Heaven at "Holy Wood." His impressions include: Ward Bond, Clark Gable, James Dean, Al Jolson, and Jeff Chandler. The two men joke that they should team up as a nightclub act, which leads into an extended routine where they do impressions of popular duos of the day, including: Martin and Lewis, The Everly Brothers, and Allen & Rossi.

The Tonight Show with Conan O'Brien

NBC. Sep 24, 2009 – Jan 11, 2010. Comedy/Music. D: Allan Kartun. W: Mike Sweeney, Conan O'Brien. C: Eric Callero ☥, Andy Richter, Max Weinberg. USA: English/Color/600m. Conaco/Universal Media Studios.

Host Conan O'Brien satirically jumped on the *Twilight* bandwagon with the introduction of a new personal assistant, Cody Devereaux. Born in 1589, the Edward Cullen-inspired character was a brooding, misunderstood vampire "full of heartache and longing." In each of his ten appearances, Cody ended up so blinded by grief that he ran outside into the daylight—and burst into flames. Each segment ended with the title card "Cody Devereaux: 1589 – Today."

📺 Eric Callero (Devereaux) also appeared as the male vampire who was staked during the opening moments of the *Scream Awards* (2010) on Spike TV.

The Tracey Ullman Show – Ep. #2.11

FOX. Dec 20, 1987 (S02E11). Comedy/Satire. D: Ted Bessell. W: Matt Groening. C: Tracey Ullman, Julie Kavner, Dan Castellaneta, Nancy Cartwright, Yeardley Smith, Liz Georges, Sam McMurray, Joseph Malone. USA: English/Color/30m. Gracie Films/20th Century Fox Television.

Hosted by British comedienne Tracey Ullman, this sketch comedy series featured the debut of The Simpson family, who appeared in forty-eight one-minute animated shorts over the course of three years. In the segment "Scary Stories," Bart terrifies his siblings with several macabre tales—one of which features a vampire. The shorts were crudely animated, but they hinted at the quirky humor that would be the cornerstone of early years of *The Simpsons* series.

The Tyra Banks Show – "Vampires!"

Syndicated. Oct 31, 2008 (S04E40). Culture/Reality. D: Scot Titelbaum. W: Anon. C: Don Henrie, Sarah Lester, Lucien, Vampyra. USA: English/Color/60m. Handprint Entertainment/Telepictures Productions/Bankable Productions.

Tyra delves into the mysterious world of the undead as she welcomes a group that lives the vampire lifestyle. But these aren't role players, or people who dress up as a vampire on Halloween—they're real blood drinkers, and take their subculture very seriously. Hosted by Tyra Banks.

V Graham Norton – Ep. #1.43

Channel 4. Jul 3, 2002 (S01E43). Adult/Comedy. D: David Coyle, Steve Smith. W: Jon Magnusson, Graham Norton. C: Graham Norton, Anthony Head, Betty Hoskins ☥. UK: English/Color/30m. So Television.

🦇 🦇 🦇

In the sketch "Poofy the Vampire Slayer," Anthony Head reprises his role as Rupert Giles in a spoof that features a geriatric vampire (and a lot of sexual innuendo). It also makes reference to his pre-*Buffy* series of television commercials for Taster's Choice instant coffee.

The Vampira Show

ABC. Apr 30, 1954 – Apr 2, 1955 (-- Episodes). Comedy/Horror. D: Hap Weyman. W: Hunt Stromberg, Jr. C: Maila Nurmi ☥. USA: English/B&W/--m. KABC-TV.

Vampira (Maila Nurmi) scares up a selection of creature features on *The Vampira Show* (KABC-TV)

As Vampira, television's first horror movie hostess, Maila Nurmi created an image (and format) that would be copied across the nation. There are no extant episodes; the show aired live, and the kinescope process was not utilized to create any recordings (although some promotional clips exist). Broadcast locally in Los Angeles on the ABC affiliate KABC-TV.

The Vampyr: A Soap Opera

BBC Two. Dec 29, 1992 – Jan 2, 1993 (5 Episodes). Drama/Music. D: Nigel Finch, Robert Chevara. W: Charles Hart, Janet Street-Porter. C: Omar Ebrahim ☥, Fiona O'Neill, Philip Salmon, Richard van Allan, Willemijn van Gent. UK: English/Color/150m. A&E Network/Virgin Classics/BBC.

🦇 🦇 🦇

Buried for two hundred years, Ripley—a vampire—is accidentally unearthed from the catacombs underneath old London. His predatory instinct and deceptive nature quickly takes him to the top of the business world—and Satan comes calling. Lest he be forever damned, Ripley must take the lives of three women in as many days, after which time his soul will be renewed for another year. Marriage, too, is on the horizon for the vampire; but his betrothed—society heiress Miranda Davenant—is being forced into the nuptials by her father. Bankrupt, the man believes that Ripley is actually the Earl of Marsden, and sees his fortune as a means to get out of debt. To complicate matters, Miranda's secret lover, Alex, is also Ripley's personal assistant. After both men discover the truth about each other's nocturnal activities, Ripley offers Alex a choice: leave Miranda, or be killed along with her. Will Alex sacrifice the woman he loves in order to save his own soul from the clutches of the vampire? Narrated by Robert Stephens.

If the story seems complicated, well, it *is* a soap opera after all. Based on a Victorian-era opera, the setting and libretto have been updated to modern times. The production is quite unique and engaging, and includes narration to help drive the story; this is necessary, because sometimes the vocals are difficult to understand. The vampire lore is a mishmash of sorts: Ripley walks in the sun, uses moonlight to heal, transforms into a wolf and fears the cross—yet he has no problem with being in a church. Definitely for genre fans only.

The story is based on the 1898 opera *Der Vampyr* by Heinrich Marschner and Wilhelm August Wohlbrück, which itself was an adaptation of John Polidori's "The Vampyre" (1819). This production was broadcast in other markets as a single, two-hour telefilm.

The Vegas Vampire Show

KVVU-TV. 1965 – 1975 (-- Episodes). Comedy/Horror. D: Anon. W: Jim Parker. C: Jim Parker ☥. USA: English/B&W, Color/--m. KVVU-TV.

The Vegas Vampire spent his Friday nights presenting a series of B-grade horror and science fiction films produced by Universal Pictures. During its nine-year run, the show developed a fan base among entertainers, including Frank Sinatra, Red Buttons, and Sammy Davis Jr. Initially a version of *Shock Theater*, the show was broadcast locally in Las Vegas, Nevada on the independent station KVVU-TV.

W.O.W. – "Just Us"

CBC. Mar 2, 1979 (S01E--). Education/Family. D: Stan Swan. W: Pat Patterson. C: Don Harron ☥, Catherine McKinnon, Leon Bibb, Kelley Harron ☥, Nancy Ferguson, Chuck Flanders, Judith Ann Miller, David Wood. CAN: English/Color/27m. CBC.

This musical variety show for kids stars a young girl named Kelley, her TV parents Don and Catherine, and their friend Leon; they each perform songs and discuss problems that children often face. This episode focuses on how tough it is for kids to discuss their feelings with adults, and includes a segment where Dracula sings a song about why it's okay to sometimes feel a little grumpy.

Also known as *Wonderful One-of-a-Kind Weekend,* this series was definitely a product of its time; it had a psychedelic look, and used minimal sets with solid black or colored backdrops. But content is key: the topics are successfully presented in a straight-forward manner, and feature some very catchy songs that seem right out of a Broadway musical. Dracula's "grumpy song" is quite charming: sometimes he feels unfriendly, impolite, and just wants to bite! (Kelley transforms into a kid vampire after hearing the song).

Wake, Rattle & Roll

Syndicated/Disney. Sep 19, 1990 – 1992 (50 Episodes). Education/Family. D: Doug Rogers. W: Don Dougherty. C: R. J. Williams, Rob Paulsen, Avery Schreiber, Terri Ivens, Frank Welker, Pat Musick, Charlie Adler ♀, Jonathan Winters. USA: English/Color/1500m. Four Point Entertainment/Hanna-Barbera Productions Inc.

A live-action kid's morning show with several animated segments, including "Monster Tails"—which featured a group of pets whose owners are famous monsters. Each animal took on the personality of its master, including Dracula's cat—aptly named Catula—who had a penchant for magic. After the first season, the series was broadcast exclusively on The Disney Channel and was retitled *Jump, Rattle & Roll.*

Wayne & Shuster – Ep. #1.02

CBC. Aug 1, 1986 (S01E02). Comedy/Music. D: Trevor Evans. W: Johnny Wayne, Frank Shuster, Robert Cormier. C: Johnny Wayne ♀, Frank Shuster, Carol Robinson, Don Cullen, John Davies, Roy Wordsworth, Tom Harvey, Renee Cherrier, Les Ruby. CAN: English/Color/50m. CBC.

In the segment "The Wayne and Shuster Festival of Your Favorite Commercials," the comedy duo lampoon television advertising with several skits, one of which is for a product called "Dracu-Grip," a denture cream endorsed by Count Dracula.

From within a cellar in Transylvania, Dracula emerges to promote the benefits of the product—because loose-fitting dentures can lead to inappropriate bites elsewhere on the body. The skit also features a cute kid playing the role of Dracula's vampire son, Wolfgang.

📺 Dracu-Grip is made from an old Romanian recipe that mixes Crazy Glue, Mămăligă and chicken fat; Mămăligă is a traditional Romanian porridge made from yellow maize flour.

Whatever Turns You On – "Fright" / "Repeats"

CTV. Oct 23, 1979 (S01E07). Comedy/Music. D: Geoffrey Darby. W: Roger Price, Geoffrey Darby. C: Ruth Buzzi, Les Lye ☥, Marc Baillon, Jonathan Gebert, Rodney Helal, Christine McGlade, Kevin Somers ☥. CAN: English/Color/30m. Carleton Productions Ltd./CTV.

A sketch comedy show geared towards teens, which stars a young cast alongside two veteran performers who play all the adult roles. This short-lived series also features performances by notable Canadian musical acts of the day, including Max Webster and Trooper. Although this episode focuses on the nature of re-runs in television (and other repetitious situations), a couple of sketches feature Dracula and his teenage vampire son. Unfortunately, the majority of the program is not quite as funny as the laugh track would suggest.

Where in the World is Carmen Sandiego? – "The Return of Dracula's Castle"

PBS. Dec 13, 1991 (S01E55). Education/Family. D: Dana Calderwood. W: Jamie Greenberg, McPaul Smith, J.M. Stifle. C: Penn & Teller, Rockapella, Gahiji Barrow, Jennifer Levy, Dhaval Shah. USA: English/Color/29m. WGBH Educational Foundation/QED Communications Inc.

Youth-oriented game show where three amateur sleuths use their knowledge of geography to track down one of Carmen Sandiego's cronies. The successful contestant is then given the chance to capture the infamous international thief herself. In this episode, Robocrook has committed a felonious foreclosure in Romania: he's stolen Bran Castle, once home to Vlad the Impaler. Presented by Greg Lee, with Lynne Thigpen as The Chief.

An enjoyable episode that's a little off the mark with its facts about Vlad Țepeș, however, it's refreshing to see vampires used in such an educational context. Even Count Dracula takes part; he offers up two clues: once as himself, and the second time in the form of a bat.

Whose Line Is It Anyway? – Ep. #7.04

ABC. Jan 24, 2005 (S07E04). Comedy/Music. D: Arthur Forrest. W: Wayne Brady, Colin Mochrie, Ryan Stiles, Chip Esten. C: Wayne Brady, Colin Mochrie, Ryan Stiles ☥, Chip Esten, Laura Hall. USA: English/Color/30m. Hat Trick Productions/Warner Bros. Television.

A wholly improvised, audience-driven game show, where "everything's made up and the points don't matter." In the segment "Whose Line," moments before sunrise, Buffy the Vampire Slayer (Colin Mochrie) confronts Dracula (Ryan Stiles), who has just drained the last drop of blood from his latest victim. Presented by Drew Carey.

The X Factor – "Live Show #4"

ITV1. Oct 30, 2010 (S07E17). Music/Reality. D: Jonathan Bullen. W: Ivor Baddiel. C: Mary Byrne, Aiden Grimshaw, Belle Amie, Rebecca Ferguson, Treyc Cohen, Matt Cardle, Wagner Fiuza-Carrilho, Paije Richardson, Cher Lloyd, Katie Waissel, One Direction. UK: English/Color/83m. Fremantle Media/Talkback Thames.

This Halloween-themed live broadcast features songs from the eleven remaining contestants, including the boy band One Direction with their rendition of "Total Eclipse of the Heart." The group's look for this performance was inspired by the *Twilight* films, complete with bloody bite marks on their necks. Also getting into the spirit of things is judge Simon Cowell, who wears fake fangs during the broadcast. Presented by Dermot O'Leary.

Although a few of the performances were worthy of some praise, one might believe they were all destined for stardom based on the constant accolades from judge Louis Walsh. This series illustrates everything that's wrong with the music industry today—it's all style and no substance. Excluding One Direction's undead façade (and the fact that watching the boy band drains a bit of one's soul), there are no real vampire elements here. If you are at all prone to motion sickness or epileptic seizures, then you should avoid this altogether; the hyperkinetic camera shots, fast editing, and strobe effects may trigger an adverse reaction.

The X Factor – Season 8

ITV. Aug 20 – Dec 11, 2011 (31 Episodes). Music/Reality. D: Adam Chapman. W: Anon. C: Gary Barlow, Louis Walsh, Kelly Rowland, Tulisa Contostavlos, Alexandra Burke, Peter Dickson, Jade Richards ☥. UK: English/Color/1860m. Syco Television/Fremantle Media/Talkback Thames.

The eighth season featured contestant Jade Richards, a young Scottish singer who liked to perform under the guise of a vampire (using the alter-ego Jade von Horror). Presented by Dermot O'Leary.

The Xtra Factor

ITV2/IVT3. Aug 20 – Dec 11, 2011 (31 Episodes). Music/Reality. D: James Howard. W: Anon. C: Gary Barlow, Louis Walsh, Kelly Rowland, Tulisa Contostavlos, Peter Dickson, Jade Richards ☥. UK: English/Color/1860m. Syco Television/Fremantle Media/Talkback Thames.

A companion show to *The X Factor,* featuring a behind-the-scenes glimpse of contestants and judges, and extra footage from the parent show. One of the contestants from this season is twenty-one-year-old Goth girl Jade Richards, who often donned the guise of a vampire. Presented by Caroline Flack and Olly Murs.

You Asked For It – "Bela Lugosi"

ABC. Jul 27, 1953 (S03E--). Culture/Family. D: Anon. W: Robert Lees. C: Bela Lugosi, Shirley Patterson. USA: English/B&W/30m. DuMont Television Network.

An audience-driven show where viewers were asked to mail in postcards describing something or someone they wanted to see on television. In this episode, Bela Lugosi performs a "weird vampire bat illusion," where he rises from a coffin and then "hypnotizes" a girl. After he places her inside a "magic cabinet," she transforms into a bat. Afterwards, Lugosi promotes the upcoming 3-D film *Phantom Ghoul,* as well as a television series called *Dr. Acula*—neither of which ended up being produced. Hosted by Art Baker.

Your Hit Parade – Ep. #6.--

NBC. Jun 9, 1956 (S06E--). Comedy/Music. D: Bill Colleran. W: Dan Lounsbery. C: Dorothy Collins, Snooky Lanson, Gisèle MacKenzie ⚥, Russell Arms, Tom Hanson, Raymond Scott, André Baruch. USA: English/B&W/30m. The American Tobacco Co./NBC.

🦇🦇🦇

Featured a regular cast of performers singing the seven top-rated songs of the week, presented in elaborate production numbers (modified from week-to-week if the song remained on the charts). In this special "vacation edition," the segment "Guide to a Wretched Vacation" features the song "Heartbreak Hotel" sung by Gisèle MacKenzie, who's the proprietor of a creepy inn and is made up to look like Vampira.

Zingrr's Projections

KTVW. 1971-1976 (-- Episodes). Comedy/Horror. D: Anon. W: Robert O. Smith. C: Robert O. Smith. USA: English/B&W, Color/--m. KTVW-TV.

KIRO-TV's *Nightmare Theatre* (featuring The Count) had already established itself by the time Dr. ZinGRR appeared on the independent broadcaster KTVW-TV—however, this hipster horror host soon grabbed the attention of Seattle's counter-culture crowd. Played by local deejay Robert O. Smith, Dr. ZinGRR, a German scientist, sported long white hair and a goatee—but he was just one character in Smith's repertoire that also included The DreamMaker, The Masked Doily, Film Lorre, and Count Lickula, among others. His sidekick—named "Raw Surrealism"—was a puppet made in the image of Rod Serling, which was later replaced by someone on set, who wore gory makeup and lip-synced to dialogue that Smith pre-recorded. (He would change characters about every fifteen minutes, often transforming just in time for the next commercial break.) Count Lickula, the "world's oldest whampire," was based on Lugosi's Dracula, and would "gum" his victims on the neck since he no longer had fangs. Undeniably, the draw was Smith's cavalcade of kooks, since his show aired sub-Z-grade films that most horror hosts wouldn't even touch… and when the movie was *really* bad, he spliced himself into scenes to liven it up! Very little archival material exists for this show, which is also fondly remembered as *Dr. ZinGRR's Astro-Projections* and *Dr. ZinGRR's Astral Projections,* among other variations.

In *Count Dracula*, a charming yet arrogant vampire (Louis Jourdan) travels to England in search of fresh blood. This promotional photo was used for the 1978 rebroadcast on the PBS series *Great Performances* (British Broadcasting Corporation)

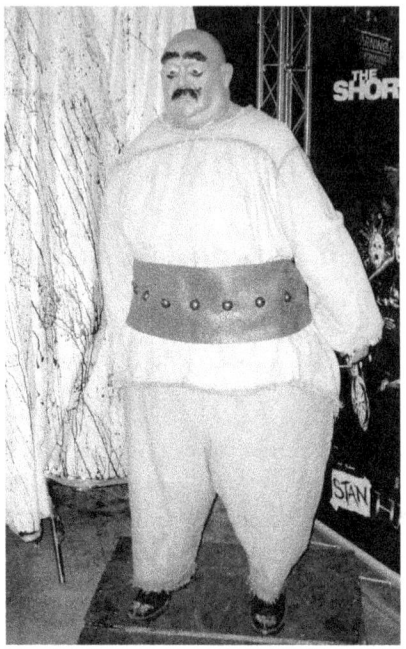

Spied at a comic convention was this life-size statue of Igor (Fishka Rais), who was Dracula's hapless assistant in *The Hilarious House of Frightenstein* (Author Photo)

The Count (Billy Van) and Igor (Fishka Rais) pledge allegiance to Transylvania on *The Hilarious House of Frightenstein* (CHCH-TV/David Cremasco)

What's in a Name?
Non-Traditional Vampires

A Vorvon takes a great interest in Col. Wilma Deering in
Buck Rogers in the 25th Century — "Space Vampire"
(Glen A. Larson Productions/Universal TV)

The Adventures of Sinbad – "Heart and Soul"

Syndicated. Oct 19, 1997 (S02E03). Action/Adventure. D: Alan Simmonds. W: Ed Naha. C: Zen Gesner, Paryse Allen, George Buza, Gérard Rudolf ⚥, Michele Burgers ⚥. CAN: English/Color/42m. All American Television/Atlantis Films Limited.

Sinbad and his crew are captured by the Baroness Kalilah Orlock. She and her husband are life-force-draining vampires, yet Kalilah is tired of being a monster. She longs for death, but can only be killed if Sinbad retrieves her heart—which was literally stolen by her husband centuries ago.

I doubt this series was known for its fine acting or plausible storylines, and this episode is no exception. Why would a vampire choose for his resting place a room with exceptionally large windows, with only meager curtains to keep out the daylight? Seems like an obvious health risk to me. This is a prime example of lazy vampire storytelling.

Adventures of the Quest – "Visiting the Vampire"

Discovery Channel. Feb 1, 2000 (S01E05). Adventure/Nature. D: Geoff Fitzpatrick, Claire Masters. W: Andrew Wight, Liz Wight. C: Andrew Wight. AUS: English/Color/60m. Quest Australia Productions/Beyond Properties/Great Wight Productions.

The Quest team heads to the jungles of Belize, home to a wide and diverse population of bats, including a species that thrives on the blood of other animals. Presented by Andrew Wight.

Animal X – "Chupacabras" / "Magic Cows" / "Black Dogs"

Discover Channel. Apr 30, 1999 (S01E01). Culture/Mystery. D: Carolyn Bertram, Mike Searle. W: Rob McGlynn, Carolyn Bertram, Mike Searle. C: Bill Kerr, Natalie Schmitt, Daniel Searle, Ted Loman, Jim Griffith. AUS: English/Color/24m. Storyteller Media Group/ScreenWest.

Australian series that investigates the paranormal and creatures of legend. In this episode, the Animal X team explores the mystery of the *chupacabra,* which has become one of the most intriguing paranormal puzzles since first being sighted in Puerto Rico during the mid-1990s.

Animal X – "Chupacabra" / "Essex Panther" / "Pet Detectives"

Animal Planet. Apr 2, 2001 (S02E15). Culture/Mystery. D: Carolyn Bertram, Mike Searle. W: Rob McGlynn, Carolyn Bertram, Mike Searle. C: Bill Kerr, Natalie Schmitt, Daniel Searle. AUS: English/Color/23m. Storyteller Media Group/ScreenWest/Discovery Channel.

In the segment "Chupacabra," the Animal X team delves deeper into the mystery of this elusive creature from Puerto Rico.

Animal X: Natural Mystery Unit – "El Chupacabras"

Animal Planet. Aug 11, 2006 (S01E08). Culture/Mystery. D: Carolyn Bertram, Mike Searle. W: Rob McGlynn, Carolyn Bertram, Mike Searle. C: Bill Kerr, Natalie Schmitt, Daniel Searle. AUS: English/Color/48m. Storyteller Media Group/ScreenWest.

This spin-off series followed two investigators specifically looking for creatures whose existence has yet to be scientifically proven. This episode is devoted entirely to the strange paranormal creature known as *el chupacabra,* which was first sighted in Puerto Rico in the mid-1990s.

Batman: The Animated Series – "On Leather Wings"

FOX. Sep 6, 1992 (S01E02). Crime/Drama. D: Kevin Altieri. W: Mitch Brian. C: Kevin Conroy, Bob Hastings, Richard Moll, Lloyd Bochner, Robert Costanzo, Clive Revill, Marc Singer ♀, Rene Auberjonois, Pat Musick. USA: English/Color/23m. Warner Bros Television.

A strange bat-like creature is terrorizing Gotham City, and the police believe that the Dark Knight is to blame. Batman locates a team of researchers specializing in the study of bats; the lead scientist, Dr. Kirk Langstrom, seems to be hiding a dark secret.

A very stylish episode with not much substance, but the story is funny at times. Langstrom and his team discovered a formula to create a totally new species—neither man nor bat, but the best of both—and the doctor used himself as a test subject. But the bat inside of him takes over, and forces Langstrom to hunt down the chemicals necessary to make the transformation into beast-form a permanent one. Ultimately, the Man-Bat doesn't cause too much trouble, and Langstrom is cured of his affliction.

Batman: The Animated Series – "Tyger, Tyger"

FOX. Oct 30, 1992 (S01E30). Crime/Drama. D: Frank Paur. W: Randy Rogel, Michael Reaves, Cherie Wilkerson. C: Kevin Conroy, Efrem Zimbalist Jr., Adrienne Barbeau, Marc Singer ♀, Joseph Maher, Jim Cummings. USA: English/Color/30m. Warner Bros Television.

Selina Kyle is abducted by an evil scientist, who transforms her into a real cat woman to provide a mate for Tygrus, a monster of his creation. Batman seeks out the help of Dr. Kirk Langstrom, in order to find a way to revert Selina back to her normal self.

Batman: The Animated Series – "Terror in the Sky"

FOX. Nov 12, 1992 (S01E37). Crime/Drama. D: Boyd Kirkland. W: Mark Saraceni, Steve Perry. C: Kevin Conroy, Loren Lester, Efrem Zimbalist Jr., Bob Hastings, Marc Singer ♀, Rene Auberjonois, Meredith MacRae, Pat Musick. USA: English/Color/30m. Warner Bros Television.

Dr. Kirk Langstrom has a nightmare where he's the Man-Bat, committing crimes and terrorizing

Gotham City—but is it only a dream? For Batman once again battles the creature, but he's not entirely convinced that this time around Langstrom is the man behind the beast.

Batman Beyond – "Splicers"

WB. Sep 18, 1999 (S02E01). Crime/Drama. D: Curt Geda. W: Evan Dorkin, Sara Dyer. C: Will Friedle ⚲, Kevin Conroy, Ian Buchanan, Cree Summer, Ice-T, Tim Dang, Stockard Channing, Paul Winfield, Yvette Lowenthal, Teri Garr. USA: English/Color/21m. DC Comics/Warner Bros. Television.

Fifty years in the future, teenager Terry McGinnis dons the cape and cowl to fight corruption in Gotham City. In this episode, Batman is suspicious of the latest trend: teens are getting animal DNA spliced in with their own, which leads to a change in their physical appearance as they take on certain aspects of the beast. While Batman investigates the procedure, he's captured and injected with a massive overdose of vampire bat serum—which transforms him into a strange humanoid creature.

Interesting premise in an episode where Batman becomes a large, vampire bat/man hybrid, similar to the DC Comics character "Man-Bat." The transformation is quickly reversed before he can do too much damage. This concept would have been best suited to a multi-episode story arc, since it's resolved too quickly—but it is still one of the better episodes from this series.

📺 In "The Curse of Krypton" from *World's Finest Comics* (DC, Vol. 1 No. 258, September 1979), Batman contracts a virus and literally mutates into a "bat man."

Batman: The Brave and the Bold – "Last Bat on Earth!"

Cartoon Network. Jun 19, 2009 (S01E22). Action/Adventure. D: Ben Jones. W: Steven Melching. C: Diedrich Bader, Richard McGonagle, Greg Ellis, Dee Bradley Baker, Mikey Kelley, John Di Maggio, Diane Delano, Yuri Lowenthal. USA: English/Color/24m. Warner Bros. Television.

In this incarnation of the Batman franchise, the Caped Crusader teams up with other heroes in the DC Universe to battle super villains. In this episode, Batman follows Gorilla Grodd into a future ruled by intelligent animals. He teams up with Kamandi, the Last Boy on Earth, who's attempting to free a human populace enslaved by the beasts. Looking for an advantage to use against Grodd, Batman heads to the bat cave in search of some old technology—and finds dilapidated ruins inhabited by a race of intelligent, humanoid man/bat creatures.

Even though the group of Man Bats initially warns Batman that they'll "feast on his blood and suck the marrow from his bones," the humanoids eventually team up with him to battle Grodd and his minions. It's not a bad story, but I just couldn't be sold on Diedrich Bader as the voice of Batman.

The Batman – "The Man Who Would Be Bat"

Kids' WB/TeleToon. Oct 30, 2004 (S01E05). Action/Adventure. D: Seung Eun Kim. W: Tom Pugsley, Greg Klein. C: Rino Romano, Steve Harris, Ming-Na, Peter MacNicol ⚲. USA: English/Color/22m. DC Comics/Warner Bros. Animation.

Dr. Kirk Langstrom, an employee of Wayne Industries, is researching sonar in bats—and hopes to someday use it as a basis to cure deafness in humans. When Bruce Wayne discovers the research is just a front for more nefarious plans, Langstrom imbibes a formula that transforms him into a large bat-like creature. As he terrorizes Gotham City, several animals are found completely drained of blood. Batman must find a way to stop Langstrom before the transformation becomes permanent.

It's a nice take on a more evil Langstrom, with excellent animation and great voice work by Peter MacNicol. In this version, Langstrom uses vampire bats in his research, and ostensibly becomes a vampiric Man-Bat (only hinted at but never mentioned directly).

📺 MacNicol played "Thomas Renfield" in the Mel Brooks spoof *Dracula: Dead and Loving It* (1995).

The Batman – "Pets"

The CW. Jun 18, 2005 (S02E06). Action/Adventure. D: Sam Liu. W: Christopher Yost. C: Rino Romano, Alastair Duncan, Peter MacNicol ⚲, Tom Kenny. USA: English/Color/30m. DC Comics/Warner Bros. Animation.

The Penguin discovers a sonic transmitter that allows him to take control over Man-Bat.

The Batman – "Rumors"

The CW. Mar 3, 2007 (S04E11). Action/Adventure. D: Matt Youngberg. W: Joseph Kuhr. C: Rino Romano, Evan Sabara, Kevin Michael Richardson, Tom Kenny, Ron Perlman. USA: English/Color/22m. DC Comics/Warner Bros. Animation.

Rumor, a new vigilante in town, is about to cross a line that Batman never could—he plans to permanently rid Gotham City of all its villains. There are no real vampires here, just a cameo by Dr. Langstrom/Man-Bat as one of the villains captured by Rumor. It's an average story elevated by the presence of a rogue's gallery of Batman's arch-enemies, all together in one room.

The Batman – "Attack of the Terrible Trio"

The CW. Feb 2, 2008 (S05E09). Action/Adventure. D: John Fang. W: Stan Berkowitz. C: Rino Romano, Danielle Judovits, Grey DeLisle, Peter MacNicol ⚲, Rob Paulsen, David Faustino, Chris Pratt, Googy Gress. USA: English/Color/30m. DC Comics/Warner Bros. Animation.

Batman deals with three deviant college students, who use the Man-Bat formula—stolen from Dr. Langstrom—to transform themselves into monstrous beasts.

Ben 10 - "Last Laugh"

Cartoon Network. Feb 25, 2006 (S01E09). Action/Adventure. D: Scooter Tidwell. W: Joe Casey, Duncan Rouleau. C: Tara Strong, Meagan Smith, Paul Eiding, Dee Bradley Baker, Steve Blum, Jeff Doucette, Cree Summer, John Kassir ☥. USA: English/Color/23m. Cartoon Network Studios.

While visiting the circus, Ben must overcome his fear of clowns after realizing that the star attraction, Zombozo, is up to no good. The evil entertainer is draining the positive energy from those around him, becoming more powerful as he feeds on their happiness—which leaves his victims sad, lethargic, and completely drained of vitality.

A "psi-vampire" story in the guise of a "psi-clown," who Ben calls "a goofball emotional vampire." It's a pretty dark tale featuring an exceptionally creepy clown, and is definitely a unique take on this type of vampirism.

Beyond Reality - "Keepsake"

USA Network. Feb 27, 1993 (S02E21). Horror/Sci-Fi. D: William Fruet. W: Marc Scott Zicree. C: Shari Belafonte, Carl Marotte, Nicole de Boer, Linda Griffiths, Joel Bissonnette ☥. CAN/USA: English/Color/24m. Paragon Entertainment Corporation.

In 1968, John Woodbridge died suddenly of a cerebral hemorrhage; he reappears in the present day, unaware of who he is. Through hypnosis, Laura gleans his name and address. They travel to his home and meet Cassie, a woman who claims to be John's mother—but she's hiding a dark secret.

After Laura begins to feel weak, Cassie confesses that she's actually John's wife. She brought him back from the dead using a magical spell—but unfortunately he's now draining the life-force of others. The story starts out well but becomes far too melodramatic by the end.

📺 Joel Bissonnette (John) played a disturbed man who thought he was a real vampire in the *CSI: Crime Scene Investigation* episode "Suckers" (2004).

Big Life - "Smoking" / "Vampires"

Newsworld. May 23, 1996 (S01E07). Culture/Media. D: Anon. W: Daniel Richler. C: Jonathan Franzen, Fran Lebowitz, Jan Wong, Tim Ward, Michelle Cheung, Scott McEwan, Tee. CAN: English/Color/45m. CBC.

In the segment "Who's Drinking All the Blood?" host Daniel Richler chats with Michelle Cheung in Mexico, where she reports on the recent sightings of *el chupacabra*—a creature that locals claim is attacking livestock and sucking their blood. Presented by Daniel Richler.

Is a creature really attacking animals, or is it just a hoax? Opposition parties claim that the government created this beast in order to draw the public's attention away from the poor state of the economy. Real or not, the Mexican people are captivated by the *chupacabra,* and many are finding ways to ward off the creature—including painting the front of their homes white, and placing large wooden crosses in the front yard. This entire episode is exceptional, and features interesting conversations about the pervasiveness of advertising, Big Tobacco and the sex appeal of smoking, body piercing and tattoos—and even tantric sex.

Blakes 7

BBC One. Jan 2, 1978 – Dec 21, 1981 (52 Episodes). Adventure/Sci-Fi. D: Var. W: Var. C: Gareth Thomas, Sally Knyvette, Paul Darrow, Jan Chappell, Michael Keating, David Jackson, Stephen Greif, Brian Croucher. UK: English/Color/3120m. BBC.

In the post-apocalyptic future, a group of political exiles, led by Roj Blake, are on the run. They're chased through space by a Federation ship helmed by the evil Commander Travis, whose crew is manned by Mutoids—modified humans that subsist on a greenish blood-serum. In a pinch, this can be substituted by actual human blood, which the Mutoids ingest via a needle-like proboscis that extends from the wrist.

Exceptional British sci-fi series created by prolific TV writer Terry Nation. These pseudo-vampires—who really dislike being called "vampire"—made eight appearances throughout the series, first in "Duel" (February 20, 1978 / S01E08) and last in "Games" (November 16, 1981 / S04E08).

Buck Rogers in the 25th Century – "Space Vampire"

NBC. Jan 3, 1980 (S01E14). Adventure/Sci-Fi. D: Larry Stewart. W: Kathleen Barnes, David Wise. C: Gil Gerard, Erin Gray, Patty Maloney, Nicholas Hormann ☿, Lincoln Kilpatrick. USA: English/Color/42m. Bruce Lansbury Productions/Glen A. Larson Productions/Universal TV.

Buck and Wilma are on a stopover at Theta Station when the I.S. Demeter, a derelict spaceship, crashes into the vessel. All her crew are found dead, possibly victims of the EL-7 virus; it's later discovered that they're in a state of cellular suspension, as if their souls have been drained from their bodies. The creature behind the attacks—a Vorvon—wreaks havoc aboard the space station, and he wants Wilma as his new partner-in-crime.

The story is interesting enough, and the Vorvon creature—which at times sounds like Tim Curry from *The Rocky Horror Picture Show*—makes for a decent villain. He looks like a cross between

Max Schreck (Count Orlok from *Nosferatu*, 1922) and a Talosian (from the *Star Trek* episode "The Cage," 1966)—with a major unibrow. He has pronounced fangs, but has no use for them; his *modus operandi* is to use the elongated nails on his pinky and forefinger to straddle the neck of his victim, through which he drains their soul. The best scene is when Wilma falls under the spell of the Vorvon; her morals loosen, and she begins to sound a little like Kathleen Turner. She morphs into what I consider my ideal vampire bride: long feathered hair, an overabundance of lip gloss, and a voice deeper than my own. Good campy fun.

Buzz Lightyear of Star Command

Syndicated. Oct 2, 2000 – Jan 13, 2001 (62 Episodes). Family/Sci-Fi. D: Var. W: Var. C: Patrick Warburton, Nicole Sullivan, Larry Miller ☥, Craig Ferguson ☥, Diedrich Bader, Dan Castellaneta. USA: English/Color/1364m. Buena Vista Television.

The continuing adventures of Space Ranger Buzz Lightyear and his friends at Star Command, based on the character from the *Toy Story* movies. In the first season of this series, one of their enemies is a robotic energy vampire called NOS-4-A2, created by the evil mastermind Emperor Zurg and voiced by Craig Ferguson.

An overall charming series by Pixar, given high marks for this well-defined and entertaining vampire character—which feeds on the energy of other robots, then takes control of them with a bite on the neck. NOS-4-A2 (based, of course, on "Nosferatu") made five appearances; first in "NOS-4-A2" (October 8, 2000 / S01E06) and last in "Revenge of the Monsters" (November 14, 2000 / S01E38).

Charmed – "Death Takes a Halliwell"

WB. Mar 15, 2001 (S03E16). Comedy/Drama. D: Jon Paré. W: Krista Vernoff. C: Shannen Doherty, Holly Marie Combs, Alyssa Milano, Julian McMahon, Christopher Shea ☥, Wade Williams ☥. USA: English/Color/42m. Spelling Television/Northshore Productions Inc.

Cole is hunted by two vampire-like demons called Seekers, who drain knowledge from their victims by biting into their brain stems.

I can't speak to the overall quality of the series, but in this episode, the monsters of the week are quite menacing. For some reason they were given the ability to levitate, which seems to be more of a gimmick rather than of any practical use; perhaps the writer was inspired by the "Gentlemen" characters from the Buffy episode "Hush" (1999). I must admit, the draining of knowledge directly via the brain stem is a novel idea.

CSI: Crime Scene Investigation – "Justice is Served"

CBS. Apr 26, 2001 (S01E21). Crime/Drama. D: Thomas J. Wright. W: Jerry Stahl. C: William Petersen, Marg Helgenberger, Gary Dourdan, George Eads, Jorja Fox, Paul Guilfoyle, Eric Szmanda, Alicia Coppola ☥. USA: English/Color/42m. Jerry Bruckheimer Television/Alliance-Atlantis/CBS.

Grissom, Warrick and Nick investigate the death of a jogger who appears to have been killed by an animal, and had his organs removed after death with surgical precision. The case leads to an eccentric nutrition guru, Dr. Susan Hillridge, who has a taste for protein shakes with peculiar ingredients.

Hillridge tells Grissom, "One man's corpse is another man's candy." She suffers from porphyria—in this case, cutaneous—and ingests the dried remains of blood-rich organs in order to halt the progression of the disease. The underlying symptoms and reasoning behind her actions are relatively factual, although she's a psychotic killer who goes to extremes in order to deal with her affliction.

📺 This case is mentioned in the Season 11 episode "Blood Moon" (2010).

Danny Phantom

Nickelodeon. Apr 3, 2004 – May 25, 2007 (53 Episodes). Adventure/Family. D: Butch Hartman. W: Steve Marmel. C: David Kaufman, Colleen O'Shaughnessey, Rickey D'Shon Collins, Martin Mull ☥, Grey DeLisle, Kath Soucie, Rob Paulsen. CAN/USA: English/Color/1590m. Billionfold/Nickelodeon Animation Studios.

Follows the adventures of fourteen-year-old Danny Fenton, the son of ghost-hunting parents, who becomes infused with ectoplasm. This transforms him into half human/half ghost; he calls himself "Danny Phantom" when in full-on ghost form. The main antagonist of the series is Vladimir Masters, whose evil alter-ego, Vlad Plasmius, is patterned after the Dracula archetype (he has green skin, noticeable fangs, and wears a long, flowing cape). He first appeared in the seventh episode, "Bitter Reunions."

📺 Vlad Plasmius was originally going to be a vampire, but the series creator wanted to avoid any association with the occult. The character was changed to a ghost, yet still retained the guise of a vampire.

Dark Angel – "Love in Vein"

FOX. Mar 8, 2002 (S02E14). Action/Sci-Fi. D: David Grossman. W: Michael Angeli. C: Jessica Alba, Michael Weatherly, Jensen Ackles, Martin Cummins, Kevin Durand, Richard Gunn, Sam Witwer ☥. USA: English/Color/45m. Cameron-Eglee Productions/20th Century Fox Television.

After Max confronts a gang that appears to have super-human abilities, she believes they too are *transgenics*. But they're only mimicking their leader, Marrow, who is the only transgenic in the group. He's been feeding them his blood, in order to build up an army of humans with enhanced abilities.

Sam Witwer chews the scenery as Marrow, a transgenic who jokingly calls himself "the bank of sangria," a "holy vampire" whose followers get the benefits of increased strength, endorphins, coagulants, and "feel good" enzymes. The vampire connotations are rampant throughout, and Marrow dies after being impaled through the heart. Surely there are other ways to kill a wayward transgenic, however this method fits the story quite well.

📺 Sam Witwer played the reluctant vampire Aidan on the SyFy series *Being Human* (2011).

Da Vinci's Demons – "The Devil"

Starz . May 17, 2013 (S01E06). History/Fantasy. D: Paul Wilmshurst. W: Brian Nelson, Marco Ramirez. C: Tom Riley, Laura Haddock, Blake Ritson, Elliot Cowan, Lara Pulver, Paul Ryhs, Shaun Parkes, Alexander Siddig, Garnon Davies, Simon Gregor, Gilbert Wynne, Ian Pirie, Jason Langley, Andrew Brooke, Asha Cecil. UK/USA: English/Color/55m. Tonto Films and Television Ltd./Phantom Four Films.

With great aplomb (and perhaps reckless abandon), this series fictionalized the early life of Leonardo da Vinci, an artist, inventor, and restless adventurer living in Renaissance Florence. In this episode, Da Vinci is on the hunt for a missing cartographer who is being held captive by the notorious Romanian warlord, Vlad the Impaler—who regained his throne by selling his soul to Lucifer. Although not a blood-drinking vampire, Vlad shares many undead traits, such as immense strength, and an ethereal visage—and he is very hard to kill. After being burned and impaled, and apparently falling to his death, Vlad's body disappears without a trace.

Deepwater Black – "Refugee"

SyFy. Sep 8, 1997 (S01E07). Drama/Sci-Fi. D: George Mendeluk. W: Jeff Copeland, Barry Pearson. C: Gordon Michael Woolvett, Nicole de Boer, Kelli Taylor, Tara Sloan ☥. CAN/USA: English/Color/30m. Empire Entertainment/Orbit 1 Productions Inc./Sunbow Entertainment/YTV.

This series aired as *Mission Genesis* in the USA, and tells the story of cloned humans on a return voyage to Earth, which was devastated after a virus decimated the population. In this episode, an unconscious female is found inside a drifting life pod, and the crew discovers she's a fugitive who has escaped from several ships over the past decade. Upon awakening, she elicits extreme emotions from the crew, who begin to turn on one another. Teeming with wooden acting, this tepid tale of an emotional vampire was almost watchable up until the ending—when the woman is saved by love.

Destination Truth – "Ropen" / "Chupacabra"

SyFy. Jun 20, 2007 (S01E03). History/Mystery. D: Anon. W: Chip Brown, Shanon Hayes, Ian Shorr. C: Alberto Urquiza, Ignacio Idalsoaga, Naomi Grossman, Elizabeth Wictum, Eric Wing. USA: English/Color/44m. Realand Productions LLC./Mandt Bros. Productions.

In the segment "Chupacabra," the team travels to Chile in pursuit of the legendary goatsucker, which locals claim is killing their livestock. Hosted by Josh Gates.

As with all of these investigative shows, nothing supernatural is ever found, but there's always an unexplained element that makes up for the lack of proof. Although the eyewitness accounts of the *chupacabra* are compelling, its existence is not supported by any scientific evidence. None of that matters, however, because the charm lies in host Josh Gates, whose sarcastic running commentary is the best part of this episode.

Dexter's Laboratory – "Techno Turtle" / "Surprise!" / "Got Your Goat"

Cartoon Network. Oct 29, 1997 (S02E16). Adventure/Sci-Fi. D: Genndy Tartakovsky. W: Jason Butler Rote, Seth MacFarlane. C: Christine Cavanaugh, Kath Soucie, Rob Paulsen, Kat Cressida, Frank Welker. USA: English/Color/30m. Rough Draft Studios/Hanna-Barbera Productions Inc.

Follows the adventures of Dexter, a boy who has an extensive secret laboratory that houses his inventions. In the segment "Got Your Goat," Dexter and Dee Dee head to South America in search of the *chupacabra*—which turns out to be one of his wayward experiments.

📺 Director Genndy Tartakovsky would go on to helm *Hotel Transylvania* (2012), *Hotel Transylvania 2* (2012), and *Hotel Transylvania 3* (2018). This trilogy of animated films follows the antics of Dracula, who runs an upscale resort in Transylvania far from the prying eyes of humans, where monsters can safely bring their families on holiday.

Discover Magazine – "Bloodsuckers"

Science Channel. Sep 30, 1998 (S04E02). Nature/Science. D/W: Chris Gidez. C: Michael Bell. USA: English/Color/30m. Big Rock Productions/Pinball Productions.

A look at nature's bloodsuckers: fleas, leeches and vampire bats—furry fliers that may hold the key to treating heart disease.

Doctor Who – "The Claws of Axos"

BBC One. Mar 13 – Apr 3, 1971 (S08E11–14). Adventure/Sci-Fi. D: Michael Ferguson. W: Bob Baker, Dave Martin. C: Jon Pertwee, Nicholas Courtney, Roger Delgado, Katy Manning, Richard Franklin, John Levene, Peter Bathurst, Paul Grist, Donald Hewlett. UK: English/Color/98m. BBC.

In this four-part story, an alien spaceship lands carrying the bug-eyed, golden-skinned Axons, who are in desperate need of fuel. In exchange, they'll provide "Axonite," a miracle molecule that can replicate any substance. The Axonite is actually part of a single parasitic entity—which feeds on a planet's energy—and its real goal is to learn the Doctor's secret of time travel, so it can broaden its feeding base.

Axonite is simply bait for human greed, something that's too good to be true: a growth technology that can build any form of energy or duplicate any substance, even a human being. It ultimately drains the life-force from the body, leaving behind a corpse that's as white as a ghost and disintegrates on touch. The story is interesting enough, although the creatures are dated and look rather silly by today's standards.

The working title for this story was "The Vampire from Space," and the Axons were referred to as a kind of "space vampire." It was novelized by Terrance Dicks in 1977.

Doctor Who – "The Stones of Blood"

BBC One. Oct 28 – Nov 18, 1978 (S16E09–12). Adventure/Sci-Fi. D: Darrol Blake. W: David Fisher. C: Tom Baker, Mary Tamm, Nicholas McArdle, Beatrix Lehmann. UK: English/Color/100m. BBC.

In this four-part story, the Doctor and Romana discover the Nine Travelers, a group of standing stones worshipped by a local Druidic sect. The stones are actually alive and require blood to survive, and are being controlled by the Druids—who are actually aliens.

Doctor Who – "Vampires of Venice"

Syndicated. May 8, 2010 (2nd Series / S05E06). Adventure/Sci-Fi. D: Jonny Campbell. W: Toby Whithouse. C: Matt Smith, Karen Gillan, Arthur Darvill, Helen McCrory ♀, Alex Price ♀, Lucian Msamati, Alisha Bailey ♀. UK: English/Color/49m. BBC.

The Doctor takes Amy and her fiancée to sixteenth century Venice, but it's sealed off for protection from the Plague by command of the powerful Rosanna Calvierri. She isn't quite human, and has trapped residents inside as part of her nefarious plan for the city.

Calvierri is an alien refugee; of all of those who were once with her, only the males survived. To save her race, she actively recruits local women and converts them to her species—and plans to sink Venice to make it more conducive to the aquatic living conditions that they require. She uses a "perception filter" that makes her appear human; however, the façade has a self-preservation feature built in, so her large, vampire-like teeth are exposed when she feels threatened or feeds on her victim. Very vampiric in the sense that she feeds in order to gain liquid nutrients; she also converts humans into her species by draining them completely of blood, which she replaces with her own.

Episode writer Toby Whithouse created the UK series *Being Human* (2008).

Equinox Special – "Do Vampire Bats Have Friends?"

Channel 4. Dec 20, 1995. D/W: Chris Sykes. C: Celia Hayes. UK: English/Color/60m. Christopher Sykes Productions/Channel 4.

This series of one-off specials explores the question of animal consciousness—do they think at all, or are they just programmed to simply survive and reproduce? This episode takes a deeper look into the world of vampire bats.

 Rebroadcast in 1997 under the banner *Animal Nights*, which was an evening of programming focused on the animal kingdom.

Fangface – "Space Monster Mishap"

ABC. Oct 28, 1978 (S01E08). Adventure/Family. D: Rudy Larriva. W: Elana Lesser, Mark Jones, Norman Maurer, Cliff Ruby. C: Frank Welker, Susan Blu, Bart Braverman, Jerry Dexter, John Stephenson, Ted Cassidy. USA: English/Color/30m. Ruby-Spears Productions.

🦇

The gang ends up on the Space Station after inadvertently starting up the Space Shuttle during a tour of the rocket ship on Earth. Things go awry after a cosmic creature is taken aboard the facility; it escapes and attacks the scientists, draining their minds and turning them ghostly white in the process.

The fanged, green monster uses a device to store the brilliant minds he's stolen, so he can keep them sustained until he returns to his home planet. This is a stretch to be considered as vampirism, but the creature "feeds" on the scientists and steals a life essence (their minds)—and the characters are noticeably affected after being attacked.

The Flintstone Kids – "Camper Scamper" / "Bone Voyage" / "The Cream-Pier Strikes Back"

ABC. Jan 25, 1988 (S02E05). Comedy/Family. D: Ray Patterson. W: Lane Raichert, Bill Matheny. C: Mel Blanc ♀, Charles Adler ♀, Ronnie Schell ♀, Bever-Leigh Banfield ♀, Scott Menville, Elizabeth Lyn Fraser, Hamilton Camp. USA: English/Color/30m. Hanna-Barbera Productions Inc.

In the segment "The Cream-Pier Strikes Back," the kids are making a batch of rock cakes when they're interrupted by the broadcast of their favorite prehistoric crime fighter cartoon, *Captain Caveman and Son*. In this show-within-a-show, one by one the population of Bedrock is turned into a comedian, after being hit with one of the Yuckster's "cuckoo-nut" cream pies. After Captain Caveman is victimized by the diabolical punster, it's left up to Cavey Jr. to prevent Bedrock from becoming the silliest city in the world.

A vampire tale in its most watered-down, kid friendly sense, where each of the Yuckster's victims takes on the guise of the one who bites…er, slams them with a cream pie. Rather than attain fangs and facial deformities, the victims take on the features of Groucho Marx; these include a crazy hairdo, glasses, a thick moustache, and large eyebrows. They inflict pain and suffering on those around them—by telling bad puns.

FreakyLinks – "Subject: Live Fast, Die Young"

FOX. Jun 1, 2001 (S01E10). Horror/Fantasy. D: David Barrett. W: Michael R. Perry. C: Ethan Embry ☥, Lisa Sheridan, Karim Prince, Ryan Bollman, Eric Balfour ☥, Paige Moss ☥. USA: English/Color/44m. Haxan Films/ Regency Television/20th Century Fox Television.

Barnes uncovers footage of a man who is unharmed after jumping off of a bridge, and he's captured by the couple seen on the tape. He discovers that they can't be killed; their secret lies in "joy juice," an adrenaline-based serum that they inject directly into their hearts—which temporarily renders them invincible.

No traditional vampires here, and even categorizing them as non-traditional may be a stretch. But the couple's sustenance, called "necromorphine," is a chemical secreted by humans during periods of extreme distress—and once it is harvested from a victim, they die. After injection, these "vampires" become invincible, and if they continue to use necromorphine, they'll effectively be immortal. It's a great story that is well-acted, and definitely feels like a vampire tale in the way it is presented.

Eric Balfour had a more traditional undead role, albeit a small one, in the first two episodes of *Buffy the Vampire Slayer* (1997-2003). He played Jesse McNally, a student at Sunnydale High who was sired by a vampire, and then accidentally staked by his best friend, Xander Harris.

Friday the 13th: The Series – "Master of Disguise"

Syndicated. Nov 11, 1988 (S02E06). Horror/Suspense. D: Tom McLoughlin. W: Bruce Martin. C: John D. LeMay, Louise Robey, Chris Wiggins, John Bolger, Hrant Alianak, Chapelle Jaffe, Jason Blicker, Joyce Gordon. CAN: English/Color/47m. Lexicon Productions/Hometown Films.

William Pratt has it all; he's a great actor, and his good looks propelled him to leading man status in record time. But like any entertainer, Pratt has certain quirks; he does his own makeup, which he stores within a special old case marked with the initials "J.W.B." Unfortunately for Pratt, every time he makes a film, someone dies accidentally; on the set of his latest movie, it's happening a little too often. After Curious Goods is hired to provide props for the film, the gang discovers that Pratt's makeup case is special indeed: it's a cursed object that once belonged to John Wilkes Booth, the actor who assassinated President Abraham Lincoln in 1865.

Despite needing to suspend disbelief a little too often (even for a supernatural series), this is an inspired and exceptionally bloody episode where Micki learns that beauty is only skin deep—and definitely in the eye of the beholder. She falls in love with Pratt, but he's a serial killer who requires fresh blood to supercharge the makeup in the kit; when applied, it hides his numerous facial deformities for a short period of time. It's an interesting take on *Beauty and the Beast,* except here the monster first appears as the prince, but eventually reveals his true self.

"William Pratt" is the birth name of actor Boris Karloff, who made a career out of playing monsters on the silver screen.

Friday the 13th: The Series – "Night Hunger"

Syndicated. Jan 9, 1989 (S02E10). Horror/Suspense. D: Martin Lavut. W: Jim Henshaw. C: John D. LeMay, Louise Robey, Chris Wiggins, Richard Panebianco, Réal Andrews, Elliot Smith, Nick Nichols, Gaston Poon. CAN: English/Color/47m. Lexicon Productions/Hometown Films.

Michael Fiorno is a troubled young man; he's taking part in a series of illegal drag races that will culminate in a final challenge against Deacon, a gang leader under whose shadow he's lived since they were both children. Despite owning a less than race-worthy vehicle, Michael wins each challenge, and coincidentally, there's been a surge of hit-and-runs in the area. As Michael races towards his final goal, the increasing body count alerts the proprietors of Curious Goods, who discover that he's in possession of a cursed object.

Talk about holding a grudge! Coming from an abusive family, Michael has been forced to compare himself to Deacon for years, but he's found a way to finally best his rival, and prove to his father that he isn't worthless—which he is, considering he's developed a fondness for vehicular homicide. His car is supercharged by a blank key on a silver chain—but only after it has been coated in the blood of a victim whom he's killed while driving. This silly tale of revenge doesn't work, especially since the audience has no compassion for Michael. It may be a stretch to label the car as a vampire, but when the bloodied key is inserted into the ignition, the automobile attains increased energy through this "taste" of its victim's blood—in all honesty, this knockoff of *Christine* (1983) has nothing else going for it.

Friday the 13th: The Series – "The Sweetest Sting"

Syndicated. Jan 16, 1989 (S02E11). Horror/Suspense. D: David Winning. W: Rick Butler. C: John D. LeMay, Louise Robey, Chris Wiggins, Art Hindle, David Palffy, Tim Webber. CAN: English/Color/60m. Lexicon Productions/Hometown Films.

A cursed antique hive gives a swarm of bees the ability to drain a person's life-force, and when it is injected into another, the recipient is transformed into the one who was victimized. But the only way this new identity can be maintained is through a special blood-honey mixture—and it's only available (at a price) through a crazed beekeeper.

Friday the 13th: The Series – "The Spirit of Television"

Syndicated. Apr 30, 1990 (S03E18). Horror/Suspense. D: Jorge Montesi. W: Robert Holbrook. C: Louise Robey, Steven Monarque, Chris Wiggins, Marj Dusay ☥, Paul Humphrey, Belinda Metz, Paul Bettis, Nancy Cser. CAN: English/Color/46m. Lexicon Productions/Hometown Films.

Ilsa Van Zandt is a psychic to the stars; she has the uncanny ability to put her clients in contact with their dearly departed loved ones, who speak to them through an old television set in Van Zandt's parlor. Her abilities draw the attention of the proprietors of Curious Goods, after several of her clients die under mysterious circumstances—and each death occurred in the vicinity of a television set.

A very engaging episode where the dead first present themselves as kindly, forgiving spirits, who have a change of heart once they reappear in the client's own television. In each case, the spirit has been wronged by the one who sought them out, so it exacts revenge, killing the person and feeding their soul back to the cursed object—Van Zandt's old television set. This in turn gives the psychic a new lease on life, because she suffers from a degenerative illness; for every soul delivered, she maintains her health for an additional two weeks.

Futurama – "Fry Am the Egg Man"

Comedy Central. Aug 11, 2011 (S06E22). Comedy/Sci-Fi. D: Dwayne Carey-Hill. W: Michael Rowe. C: Billy West, Katey Sagal, John Di Maggio, Tress MacNeille, Lauren Tom, Phil LaMarr, Maurice LaMarche. USA: English/Color/22m. The Curiosity Company/20th Century Fox Television.

After a bad experience with awful take-out food, Leela forces the gang to eat an organic, home-cooked meal. Fry discovers that the eggs she purchased are still fertile, with little infant creatures growing inside; horrified, he rescues one and nurtures it until it hatches. The cute, rat-like creature grows up into a monstrous beast; it's a *"bonus vampirus"*—a bone-sucking vampire—and it's the last of its kind. They reintroduce the creature into the wild; even though it was raised a vegetarian, it soon targets its natural prey—and starts sucking the skeletons from livestock.

An average episode with typical *Futurama* humor, although it's apparent that the series is beginning to lose steam. One of the most inspired moments occurs at the end, in a scene that's in homage to *Scooby-Doo*.

Ghost Story – "Alter-Ego"

NBC. Oct 27, 1972 (S01E06). Suspense/Thriller. D: David Lowell Rich. W: D.C. Fontana, Stanley Ellin. C: Helen Hayes, Michael-James Wixted ☥, Charles Aidman, Collin Wilcox-Horne, Janet Mac Lachland, Gene Andrusco. USA: English/Color/47m. William Castle Productions/Screen Gems Television.

Robert Cameron is at home recovering from an accident; unable to go outside, he's stuck in his bedroom, with no one to talk to or to play with. One afternoon, as he starts yet another solo game of chess, an opponent suddenly materializes—a boy who looks exactly like him. Initially Robert is overjoyed with his new friend, but the boy is somehow different, as if they were opposite sides of a coin. Robert discovers the *doppelgänger* has taken his place outside the home; as his twin becomes stronger and more malevolent, Robert gets weaker. The two play a final game of chess to determine which one of them survives, and gets to live the life of Robert Cameron. Hosted by Sebastian Cabot (as Winston Essex).

Exceptionally creepy tale about an imaginary friend that wants to replace the boy who created him; the *doppelgänger* gains strength by draining the life of insects, then animals, and then finally Robert. What the twin does to Miss Gilden, Robert's favorite teacher, is the greatest of his atrocities; it's completely believable thanks to the exceptional work of Oscar-winning actress Helen Hayes, who shines in the fateful role of the school teacher. But the highlight is child actor Michael-James Wixted, who manages to pull off two distinct roles; his performance makes this episode truly memorable.

The Godzilla Power Hour – "The Energy Beast" / "The Animal Snatchers"

NBC/TV Tokyo. Oct 14, 1978 (S01E07). Adventure/Family. D: Ray Patterson. W: Don Heckman, Duane Poole. C: Ted Cassidy, Jeff David, Al Eisenman, Hilly Hicks, Don Messick, Brenda Thomson, B.J. Ward. USA: English/Color/60m. Hanna-Barbera Productions Inc./Toho Company.

In the segment "The Energy Beast," a meteorite crashes near the Sundance Mesa Dam, releasing an alien creature. It targets the structure, growing in size as it drains the electrical energy produced by the turbines. Godzilla confronts the alien, but the lizard is hit with a powerful energy blast that sends it reeling back into the sea. Godzilla later attacks a power plant in search of energy, and then sets his sights on a nuclear reactor.

A silly cartoon that can only be enjoyed by kids, with a friendly Godzilla and his annoyingly cute nephew Godzooky (a character loosely based on Minira from the 1967 film *Son of Godzilla*). Appearances are deceiving; the alien is actually a chameleon of sorts, and mimics Godzilla as it continues its path of destruction. But in the way the story is presented, it appears that Godzilla is turned into an energy drainer as well, after being hit by the alien's energy blast.

Godzilla: The Series – "Underground Movement"

FOX. Apr 1, 2000 (S02E15). Adventure/Sci-Fi. D: Sam Liu. W: Marsha F. Griffin. C: Ian Ziering, Malcolm Danare, Rino Romano, Charity James, Brigitte Bako, Max Brooks, Kevin Dunn. USA: English/Color/21m. Adelaide Productions/Centropolis Television/Toho Company.

While most of the team goes to Court—fallout from a recent mission that saw the destruction of a giant vampire bat (and parts of Miami)—Randy and Craven investigate complaints of a "giant beanstalk" that's destroying farmland. The creature responsible is a parasitic fungus; due to pesticides, it has mutated to the point where plant life can no longer sustain it—so it's now targeting any living thing, including humans.

This giant fungus uses its extensive underground network of tapeworm-like tentacles to drain the amino acids from any living creature, including team member Monique—who gets bitten on the neck and turns ashen white. The story is a little flat, although it gets high marks for including some real science...and the opening tale of a giant vampire bat.

The Grim Adventures of Billy & Mandy – "Little Rock of Horrors"

Cartoon Network. Oct 18, 2002 (S01E13). Comedy/Family. D: Robert Alvarez. W: Gord Zajac. C: Grey DeLisle, Greg Eagles, Richard Horvitz, Jennifer Hale, Vanessa Marshall, Phil LaMarr ♀, Dorian Harewood. USA: English/Color/8m. Castle Creek Productions/Cartoon Network.

Billy hopes to find a new friend, and wishes upon a shooting star; that instant, a meteorite crashes into the neighborhood. Inside is an alien that subsists on human brains, and it convinces Billy to bring everyone in town to the crash site so it can feed its never-ending hunger—but Mandy's grey matter is too much for it to handle. This episode features an extended, infectious sing-along performed by the alien, a creature that could be considered vampiric.

The Grim Adventures of Billy & Mandy – "Duck!" / "Aren't You Chupacabra To See Me"

Cartoon Network. Jun 24, 2005 (S05E04). Comedy/Family. D: Shaun Cashman. W: Jeremy Bargiel, Ian Wasseluk. C: Grey DeLisle, Greg Eagles, Richard Horvitz, Jennifer Hale, Vanessa Marshall. USA: English/Color/23m. Castle Creek Productions/Cartoon Network.

In "Duck!," Grim dreams that he stars in a sitcom called *The Reapers* (an allusion to *The Munsters*). In the second segment, Grim takes the kids to Underworld Video to rent a movie, and Billy chooses *The Legend of the Chupacabra*. Upon watching the film, Billy is attacked by one of the creatures, after it escapes from the television set and into reality. Even though the *chupacabra* drain's Billy's life-force, he's happy to have a new friend—so he names it "Daisy."

Billy's new pet is a corporeal manifestation of the video images, a cursed, bloodsucking creature that sucks the life-force from its victims. This take-off on *The Ring* has a couple of laughs, and there's even a green-skinned vampire in the video store.

Grimm - "Tarantella"

NBC. Feb 10, 2012 (S01E11). Drama/Horror. D: Peter Werner. W: Alan DiFiore, Dan E. Fesman. C: David Giuntoli, Russell Hornsby, Bitsie Tulloch, Silas Weir Mitchell, Sasha Roiz, Reggie Lee, Amy Acker ⚥, Nicholas Gonzalez, Sharon Sachs, Robert Blanche, Mike Massa, Kyle Vahan, Danny Bruno, Nicole McCullough. USA: English/Color/45m. GK Productions/Universal Television.

Series follows Detective Nick Burkhardt of the Portland police force, who discovers he's a "Grimm" and comes from a long line of monster hunters tasked with killing *Wesen,* fabled supernatural creatures that are able to hide their true nature behind a human façade. In this episode, after two men are found dead with their internal organs completely dissolved—and missing!—Nick discovers that the killer is a *Spinnetod,* a Black Widow-like *Wesen* that, in order to maintain her youth and immortality, must take three victims every five years by seducing them and then dissolving their innards—which she then consumes.

Grimm - "Mommy Dearest"

NBC. Mar 7, 2014 (S03E14). Drama/Horror. D: Norberto Barba. W: Brenna Kouf. C: David Giuntoli, Russell Hornsby, Bitsie Tulloch, Silas Weir Mitchell, Sasha Roiz, Reggie Lee, Bree Turner, Claire Coffee, Freda Foh Shen ⚥, Alain Uy, Tess Paras, Robert Blanche, Damien Puckler, Bethany Jacobs, Susannah Mars, Sumilang Angeles. USA: English/Color/45m. GK Productions/Universal Television.

Nick is at odds with his partner Hank (who knows his dark secret) over how to handle Sgt. Wu, who somehow recently witnessed a malevolent creature called an *Aswang*—and has since been convinced that he's losing his mind. Resembling a *Manananggal,* this creature of nightmares is on the hunt for an unborn child—and the potential victim is very close to home.

Grimm - "Chupacabra"

NBC. Dec 12, 2014 (S04E08). Drama/Horror. D: Aaron Lipstadt. W: Brenna Kouf. C: David Giuntoli, Russell Hornsby, Bitsie Tulloch, Silas Weir Mitchell, Sasha Roiz, Reggie Lee, Bree Turner, Claire Coffee, Alexis Denisof, Max Arciniega ⚥, Alyssa Diaz, Will Rothhaar, Bernhard Forcher, Philip Anthony-Rodriguez, Robert Blanche. USA: English/Color/45m. GK Productions/Universal Television.

A blood-borne disease that only affects canid *Wesen* turns them feral, resulting in a disfiguring condition that leads to hemorrhaging around the eyes, nose and ears, with patches of bloody skin and fur. The resulting creature is completely visible to humans, which has led to the legend of *el chupacabra.* Unless Nick can find a cure for a young *Wesen* who is fighting the disease, he'll be permanently transformed into a bloodthirsty creature that thirsts for both humans and animals alike.

H.R. Pufnstuf

NBC. Sep 6, 1969 – Sep 4, 1971 (17 Episodes). Comedy/Family. D: Hollingsworth Morse. W: Lennie Weinrib. C: Jack Wild, Billie Hayes, Joan Gerber, Lennie Weinrib, Walker Edmiston, Joy Campbell, Roberto Gamonet. USA: English/Color/425m. Sid & Marty Krofft Television Productions.

A shipwrecked boy named Jimmy is befriended by a group of kooky characters who reside on Living Island. They're constantly threatened by a wicked witch named Wilhelmina W. Witchiepoo, whose henchmen include a large, purple vampire bat she "affectionately" calls "Stupid Bat."

Hi Hi Puffy AmiYumi – "Talent Suckers" / "Talent Suckers Return" / "A Grave Mistake"

Cartoon Network. Nov 19, 2004/Nov 25, 2005/Apr 21, 2006 (S01E02/S02E13/S03E06). Comedy/Family. D: Darrell Van Citters, Scott Gray. W: Adam Beechen, Joelle Sellner. C: Yumi Yoshimura, Keone Young, Nathan Carlson, Grey DeLisle, Ami Onuki, Janice Kawaye. USA: English/Color/30m. Cartoon Network Studios.

Animated series based on vocalists Ami Onuki and Yumi Yoshimura, who perform as PUFFY, a Japanese pop/rock duo (known as Puffy AmiYumi in the United States). In "Talent Suckers," a gang of Goth groupies—who are actually vampires—attack the girls and suck the talent out of them, because they want to start their own rock band. In "Talent Suckers Return," the vampires are now penniless, and they owe an arena manager a tidy sum; he offers to let them work it off—with disastrous results. In "A Grave Mistake," the vampires recruit zombies in an attempt to be more popular, but the plan backfires after the walking dead take a dislike to their music.

Honey, I Shrunk the Kids: The TV Show – "Honey, You Drained My Brain"

Syndicated. Feb 14, 1998 (S01E14). Comedy/Family. D: Scott McGinnis. W: Dan Studney, Kevin Murphy, Kat Likkel. C: Peter Scolari, Barbara Alyn Woods ♀, Thomas Dekker ♀, James Dugan, Lorena Gale. USA: English/Color/60m. Buena Vista Television/Disney.

Wayne creates a "thinky ring"—an electrochemical Q-wave enhancer—to help Diane focus her thoughts for an upcoming case. But it has a side effect: she becomes an evil, brain-sucking cerebral vampire, who absorbs Q-waves and dumbs down her victim in the process.

A quirky episode that was more enjoyable than expected. After Wayne and Diane's son Nick steals the ring, he absorbs so many Q-waves that he ends up looking like a cross between a Vorvon *(Buck Rogers)* and a Talosian *(Star Trek)*. This turns him into an evil genius with a large, bald head, bent on world domination.

The Hunger – "Necros"

Showtime/TMN. Jul 20, 1997 (S01E03). Drama/Horror. D: Russell Mulcahy. W: Steven Salzburg, Audrey Thaler Salzburg, Brian Lumley. C: Philip Casnoff, Céline Bonnier ⚧, Leonardo Cimino, Tony De Santis, Richard Jutras. CAN/UK/USA: English/Color/28m. Telescene Film Group Productions/Scott Free Productions.

🦇🦇

William Cobb, recently single and looking for love, falls for a beautiful woman named Helma—even though he's warned that her elderly companion is a vampire. As he becomes romantically involved with her, Cobb discovers the couple has a strange relationship; the elderly man doesn't care about the affair, and is more concerned that Cobb learns how to play Bridge. Presented by Terence Stamp.

Definitely a strange tale, and it's not clear what sort of monster Helma is—although she's likely a succubus. She drains the life-force from her victims, which quickly ages them in the process; considering the strong sexual overtones of the story, she definitely fits the mold. Her elderly companion isn't a vampire, he's just her protector. Why worry about teaching Cobb how to play Bridge? Because after Helma preys on the man, he joins her other victims—who spend their remaining days playing the game.

📺 Released into the home video market as part of the DVD set *Hunger: Vampires,* along with the episodes "Fly By Night," "A Matter of Style," and "Footsteps."

The Hunger – "Clarimonde"

Showtime/TMN. Mar 20, 1998 (S01E21). Drama/Suspense. D: Tom Dey. W: Gerald Wexler. C: David La Haye, Audrey Benoît ⚧, James Bradford, Sheena Larkin, Pierre LeBlanc, Guy Héroux, Frank Fontaine. CAN/UK/USA: English/Color/27m. Telescene Film Group Productions/Scott Free Productions.

🦇🦇🦇

Clarimonde dies moments before Romuald, a newly-ordained priest, arrives to perform the last rites. He's drawn towards the young woman, and inexplicably gives her a kiss—which brings her back to life. As he begins a torrid affair with her, Romuald questions his faith in God and his devotion to the Church—and loses his grip on reality. Is he a priest who dreams that he is Clarimonde's lover, or her lover who dreams that he is a priest? Presented by Terence Stamp.

Set in 1856 in Québec, this is an engaging tale of temptation with otherworldly undertones. Clarimonde chose the young priest because of his strong devotion to God—for only the stolen love of the most devout can sustain her. The story is based on "La Morte Amoureuse" by Théophile Gautier, first published in *La Chronique de Paris* in 1836. This adaptation follows the same basic premise, but here Clarimonde is more of a succubus-type creature, and not the true vampire from the source material (where it was actually Romuald's blood that sustained her and not his faith). Features strong performances all around, and is one of the better vampire-themed episodes in this series.

The Hunger – "Footsteps"

Showtime/TMN. Mar 27, 1998 (S01E22). Drama/Horror. D: Jimmy Kaufman. W: Gerald Wexler, Cordwainer Bird. C: Paul-Anthony Stewart ♀, Sofia Shinas ♀, Cédric Noël, Jean-Guy Bouchard, Doris Milmore. CAN/UK/USA: English/Color/26m. Telescene Film Group Productions/Scott Free Productions.

Claire is driven each night to seduce and kill, and targets men who enjoy the finer things in life—for the better they eat, the tastier her meal. But her nocturnal activities have not gone unnoticed, and she meets a man who claims to be just like her—who has curbed his affliction through a change in diet. Presented by Terence Stamp.

Based on Harlan Ellison's short story of the same title, where Claire is a werewolf who's driven by nature to seduce and kill—a sympathetic succubus who meets a very different kind of man. But in this mess of an adaptation, it's not very clear what she is. Claire transforms into something that snacks on men, but it's too ambiguous to tell if she's a lycanthrope, succubus, or some other creature that feeds on meat and/or blood. We don't feel the same empathy for her that worked so well in the original story, and here the vegetarian character is just downright cheesy.

📺 "Cordwainer Bird" is the pseudonym Harlan Ellison often uses in credits when the adaptation doesn't live up to his standards.

The Hunger – "Replacements"

Showtime/TMN. Nov 28, 1999 (S02E12). Drama/Horror. D/W: Bruce M. Smith. C: Andreas Apergis, Stellina Rusich, Howard Rosenstein, Pascale Devigne, Jacklin Webb, David Rigby, Penny Mancuso. CAN/UK/USA: English/Color/27m. Telescene Film Group Productions/Scott Free Productions.

Dr. Lang notices odd behavior in some of his female co-workers—they've developed cold, indifferent attitudes towards men. As the insolence spreads throughout the town, Lang's wife is also affected—and he discovers a small, hairless creature suckling at her breast. Presented by David Bowie.

Based on Lisa Tuttle's 1992 short story of the same title, which is the tale of a man's growing insecurity over his wife's flourishing independence, after she takes in an odd pet that becomes the focus of her attention. In this adaptation, these odd little creatures drink the blood of their female hosts, who lose their self-control once the blood exchange begins. With elements from *Invasion of the Body Snatchers* and *The Stepford Wives*, this predictable story isn't very memorable—despite the creepy little *chupacabra*-like creatures.

Huntik: Secrets & Seekers – "The Bookshop Hunter" / "The Vampire Loses its Fangs"

Jetix. Jan 19/20, 2009 (S01E16/17). Action/Adventure. D/W: Iginio Straffi. C: Marc Thompson, Yuri Lowenthal, Rebecca Soler, Karen Strassman, Mike Pollock, Maddie Blaustein, Kirk Thornton, Richard Epcar. ITA: English/Color/60m. Big Bocca Productions/Rainbow/Rai Fiction.

A group of "Seekers" search the globe for ancient amulets that contain Titans—powerful deities they invoke while fighting an evil organization. In this two-part story, the heroes find the Spear of Vlad the Impaler, which once held the Titan called "Antedeluvian." They travel to Wallachia in search of Vlad's other objects, which are hidden within his castle and protected by powerful magic.

Vlad the Impaler was an evil Seeker who possessed several powerful Titans, including the Antedeluvian—a vampire-like humanoid that drains energy from its foes. With fangs, pale blue skin, and large bat-like wings, this Titan became the basis for the Dracula legend. Vlad wasn't a vampire; he's long dead, but the Titan is still around to cause the heroes some grief.

📺 Antedeluvian also battled the Seekers in the episode "Lok's Leadership" (S02E17 / May 15, 2012).

Is It Real? – "Chupacabras"

NGC. Nov 14, 2005 (S02E01). History/Mystery. D: Paulette Moore. W: Paulette Moore, Eleanor Grant. C: Benjamin Radford, Luiseppi Quinones, Edmundo Torres, Ricky Lummus, Rick O'Kelley, David Arshawsky. USA: English/Color/46m. National Geographic Television and Film.

What's behind the increase in mutilated, dead animals found throughout Latin American and the southern United States? Is it a bloodthirsty hybrid—part reptile, kangaroo, and vampire bat—with glowing red eyes and pronounced fangs? Is it an alien creature, or perhaps a genetic experiment gone horribly awry? Eyewitnesses, skeptics, and experts weigh in on the cause of these unexplained deaths.

This over-the-top episode leaps directly from the pages of a tabloid newspaper, yet surprisingly provides a balanced look at these mysterious events. Eyewitness accounts range from the believable to the absurd, and unlike most documentaries on the subject, this program takes a highly skeptical approach. A combination of natural predation and decay, hoaxes, and possibly intentional mutilation has led to these animal deaths; nothing points to a weird, bloodsucking cryptid. The *chupacabra* joins the ranks of Bigfoot and the Loch Ness Monster as another highly-contested creature whose existence has yet to be proven—but they still provide fodder for television, the tourist trade, and tales around the campfire.

📺 The program reveals that the term "chupacabra" ("goat sucker") was actually coined by the media in 1995.

Jackie Chan Adventures – "The Curse of El Chupacabra"

WB. Oct 15, 2001 (S02E08). Adventure/Family. D: Phil Weinstein. W: Mark Seidenberg. C: Jackie Chan, James Sie, Stacie Chan, Sab Shimono, Candi Milo, Franco Velez, Miguel Sandoval ☥. USA: English/Color/30m. The JC Group/Blue Train Entertainment/Columbia TriStar Television.

Jackie and the gang head to Mexico at the behest of El Toro; an evil spirit known as the *chupacabra* is killing his livestock. They defeat the beast, but it scratches El Toro during battle—which curses him to become the next *chupacabra*.

Jackie Chan Adventures – "Chi of the Vampire"

WB. May 4, 2002 (S02E35). Adventure/Family. D: Chap Yaep. W: Rob Hoegee, Adam Beechen. C: Jackie Chan, James Sie, Stacie Chan, Sab Shimono ☥, Dee Bradley Baker ☥, George Kee Cheung. USA: English/Color/23m. The JC Group/Blue Train Entertainment/Columbia TriStar Television.

The gang heads to a dilapidated castle to pick up some antiques. While exploring the old estate, Jade inadvertently awakens an ancient vampire—who gains strength by draining the *chi* from his victims.

An interesting adventure that features vampire folklore from China. Traditionally, *chi* is considered one's life-force or vital energy; in this story, once it's drained, the victim becomes an undead minion of the vampire—and can only revert to normal if their *chi* is restored. The vampire, Kiang Chi, is based on the Chinese creature *chiang-shih,* which shares some traits with the undead in Slavic folklore; he's also influenced by the "hopping" vampire of Chinese mythology.

Kolchak: The Night Stalker – "Demon in Lace"

ABC. Feb 7, 1975 (S01E16). Horror/Thriller. D: Don Weis. W: Stephen Lord, Michael Kozoll, David Chase. C: Darren McGavin, Simon Oakland, Keenan Wynn, Jackie Vernon, Kristina Holland, Carolyn Jones. USA: English/Color/51m. Francy Productions Inc./Universal TV.

Kolchak investigates the deaths of several young college students; each man died of a heart attack despite being in perfect health. Coincidentally, the body of a young woman is found near each male victim, yet the two deaths don't appear to be related. The men were students of a professor who just returned from the Middle East, and brought back an ancient stone tablet with a cursed past.

The ten-thousand-year-old tablet holds a recipe for creating precious metals by divine means, a secret that is protected by a succubus. Now that it has been unearthed, the demon attacks the unsuspecting students, because they're trying to decipher the symbols on the tablet. The succubus seeks out a woman who dies accidentally, and then takes over her body. She uses it as a vessel to seduce one of the men, then reveals her true face—which is so shocking that it bursts his heart (this scenario repeats as she targets each student). Aside from the high body count, it's an enjoyable episode; the succubus scenes are quite thrilling, and balance out the funny situations that Kolchak encounters during his investigation.

📺 Carolyn Jones, who played The Registrar, starred as the macabre matriarch Mortia Addams in *The Addams Family* (1964-66).

The Krofft Superstar Hour

NBC. Sep 9, 1978 – Jan 27, 1979 (13 Episodes). Comedy/Music. D: Jack Regas. W: Mark Evanier, Lorne Frohman. C: The Bay City Rollers, Billie Hayes, Billy Barty, Patty Maloney, Van Snowden, Jay Robinson, Sharon Baird. USA: English/Color/630m. Krofft Entertainment Inc.

This short-lived children's variety show starred the Scottish pop band The Bay City Rollers, who performed songs and acted in skits. One regular segment, "Horror Hotel," featured Wilhelmina W. Witchiepoo (of *H.R. Pufnstuf* fame) as the proprietor of a run-down hotel. One of her minions was a large, purple vampire bat she "affectionately" called "Stupid Bat."

Lidsville

ABC. Sep 11, 1971 – Sep 2, 1973 (17 Episodes). Adventure/Family. D: Tony Charmoli. W: Larry Alexander. C: Charles Nelson Reilly, Billie Hayes, Butch Patrick, Lennie Weinrib, Joy Campbell, Hommy Stewart, Jerry Maren, Buddy Douglas, Van Snowden. USA: English/Color/510m. Krofft Entertainment Inc.

At a magic show, curiosity gets the best of Mark, who sneaks backstage to get a closer look at the props. Suddenly a magical hat expands in size, and Mark falls into it—landing in the strange dimension of Lidsville, a garish world populated by talking hats. The land is ruled by an evil magician, Horatio J. HooDoo, who enlists four corrupt hats to do his bidding—including Bela, the Vampire's Cowl.

📺 Butch Patrick, who starred as Mark, played the role of the young, feral boy Eddie in *The Munsters* (1964-66) television series. He later co-hosted the low-budget horror movie program *Macabre Theatre* (2002-2006).

Lost Girl

Showcase. Sep 12, 2010 – Oct 25, 2015 (77 Episodes). Drama/Fantasy. D: John Fawcett. W: M.A. Lovretta, Peter Mohan. C: Anna Silk ⚢, Kris Holden-Ried, Ksenia Solo, Richard Howland, Zoie Palmer, K.C. Collins, Clé Bennett, Emmanuelle Vaugier. CAN: English/Color/4620m. Prodigy Pictures/CanWest Broadcasting.

A young woman learns that she is a succubus who must choose between warring factions of Fae in *Lost Girl* (Prodigy Pictures/CanWest Broadcasting)

Bo, a confused young woman, learns that she's

a "Fae"—a group of folkloric creatures that look human, but possess otherworldly abilities. She's a succubus that feeds on the sexual energy of others, but she can only safely mate with another Fae—any human partner could inadvertently be killed. As she investigates what she is and where she came from, Bo discovers there are two opposing factions of Fae—one good, one evil—and both want her to join their ranks.

Lost Tapes - "Chupacabra"

Animal Planet. Oct 30, 2008 (S01E01). Culture/Drama. D: Anon. W: Anon. C: Anon. USA: English/Color/30m. Go Go Luckey Entertainment/Discovery Communications.

A family from Mexico tries to enter the United States illegally, but they're abandoned in a remote part of the Sonora Desert by the man who was supposed to smuggle them across the border. As they desperately try to finish the journey on foot, a creature with a taste for blood stalks them in the night.

Martin Mystery - "The Vampire Returns"

YTV. Sep 8, 2004 (S02E02). Action/Adventure. D: Stéphane Berry. W: Rob Hoegee. C: Samuel Vincent ♀, Dale Wilson, Kelly Sheridan ♀, Teryl Rothery. CAN/FRA: English/Color/22m. Marathon Animation/Image Entertainment Corporation Inc.

The team travels to Paris to investigate the disappearance of two teens at an amusement park. An ancient vampire is responsible; she wants to rebuild her species and enslave mankind, but her brethren can only return if she opens a passage to the banished realm—and Martin holds the key.

This vampire doesn't have a taste for blood; she steals the souls of her victims, which turns them into her undead minions. She can morph into a large, bat-like humanoid, but is still susceptible to sunlight—which ultimately leads to her demise. It's a good story with a nasty vampire (and some very creepy minions), and is more entertaining than many vampire films of recent memory.

Moby Dick and the Mighty Mightor - "Vampire Island" / "The Saucer Shells" / "Cult Of Cavebearers"

CBS. Nov 4, 1967 (S01E09). Adventure/Family. D: William Hanna, Joseph Barbera, Charles A. Nichols. W: David Scott, Ed Brandt. C: Paul Stewart, Bobby Diamond, Patsy Garret, Norma McMillian, John Stephenson. USA: English/Color/30m. Hanna-Barbera Productions Inc.

Tor, a teenage caveman, protects his village from danger by transforming into Mightor, a mighty warrior who brandishes a mystical club. In the segment "Vampire Island," Sheera and Lil Rok get stranded on an island populated by vampire men. Can Mightor save his friends before they succumb to the strange creatures and their gigantic vampire bats?

The vampires resemble feral humanoids with fangs, and can fly utilizing a set of wings strapped to their backs. Their cohorts are your basic gigantic bat, with big yellow eyes and large white fangs. It's a charming early genre tale where the monsters of the week aren't classic undead; they have fangs, but don't drink blood, and are probably just called vampires to make them seem more menacing.

📺 Adapted as "The Mighty Mightor Battles the Vampire King" in the comic book *Hanna-Barbera Super TV Heroes* #1 (Gold Key, April 1968).

MonsterQuest – "Vampire Beast"

History Channel. Jun 4, 2008 (S02E03). History/Mystery. D: Mike Wafer. W: Mike Wafer, Meredith Fowke. C: Berry Lewis, Doris Avant, Tom Padgett, William Robinson, George Feldhamer, Leon Williams. USA: English/Color/45m. Whitewolf Entertainment Inc./Bosch Media, LLC.

🦇🦇🦇

The MonsterQuest team travels to North Carolina to investigate the legendary "Beast of Bladenboro," a fifty-year-old mystery that has remained unsolved. In 1954, residents of Bolivia faced an unknown predator that attacked pets and livestock at night—and these horrible events are happening again. Witnesses describe the culprit as a dark brown creature about four feet long, with the face of a cat, the claws of a dog, and the teeth of a vampire. Their peaceful lives shattered, residents are looking for answers—can modern science identify this nocturnal hunter? Narrated by Stan Bernard.

This enthralling episode feels like an *X File*—but it's a genuine story about a group of North Carolinians dealing with a mysterious creature that has a thirst for blood, and their concerns are justified. In 2007, dozens of incidents were reported; the animals weren't killed for food, and were undisturbed except for deep wounds on the neck. Experts use science to search for clues, while residents conduct their own investigation in the remote woodlands. Neither group comes up with any solid evidence; a single, blurry photograph supports the theory that cougars have returned to the region. Yet some residents still believe the "Beast of Bladenboro" is a cryptic creature that has resurfaced and expanded its hunting ground.

MonsterQuest – "Chupacabra"

History. Jul 23, 2008 (S02E08). History/Mystery. D: Joseph Schneier. W: Joseph Schneier. C: Phylis Canion, Gustavo Rodriguez, Hommy Vasquez, Devin McAnally, Ken Gerhard, Benjamin Radford, Joe Palermo, Irving Kornfield. USA: English/Color/45m. Whitewolf Entertainment Inc./Bosch Media, LLC.

Since 1995, from Puerto Rico to Texas, reports have surfaced of *el chupacabras*. The description of the dreaded beast varies from place to place, but the evidence remains consistent: livestock is found dead, with bite marks on the neck, and bodies drained of blood. Through eyewitness accounts, interviews with experts, and scientific testing, this program tries to determine what is killing these animals. Narrated by Stan Bernard.

Is the *chupacabra* an animal unknown to science, perhaps a type of feral canine? Or is it actually a gargoyle-like beast with glowing red eyes and spines on its back? After watching this episode, you'll still have no idea; it reveals nothing about this nocturnal predator. As with many of these programs, traps are set and cameras are placed in an attempt to capture one of these creatures alive—which of course never happens. (You'd think such an elusive beast would be easily caught within the time constraints of a weekly documentary series.) This overly-dramatic production includes an account of a bipedal, gargoyle-like creature, but there's no evidence to back up this claim. So the investigation starts and ends with the ramblings of a single eyewitness.

The "goat sucker" is likely just an urban myth, the go-to creature that's blamed for unexplained animal deaths (and possibly even a few hoaxes).

Monsters - "The Offering"

Syndicated. Feb 18, 1990 (S02E18). Horror/Suspense. D: Ernest Farino. W: Dan Simmons. C: Orson Bean, Robert Krantz, Bob Larkin, Karen Hittelman. USA: English/Color/22m. Laurel EFX Inc./Tribune Broadcasting Company/Worldvision Enterprises Inc.

After a car accident, a young man begins to see visions of a horrible, giant insect—which he describes as a "cancer vampire"—injecting his mother with small slug-like bugs. He believes that these monsters have been using humans as incubators, invisibly planting their larvae into them which leads to the growth of what the medical community believes are cancerous tumors—but in reality it's just these creatures growing inside. Dan Simmons's original teleplay was published in *Prayers to Broken Stones* (1990), which also included "Shave and a Haircut, Two Bites," a story adapted for season three of *Monsters*.

¡Mucha Lucha!: Gigante – "I Was a Pre-Teenage Chupacabra" / "Carnival of Masked Terror"

WB. Nov 27, 2004 (S03E09). Comedy/Family. D: Ken Kessel. W: Mitch Watson. C: Carlos Alazraqui, Kimberly Brooks, Tasia Valenza, Candi Milo, Scott McNeil, Michael Donovan. USA: English/Color/21m. Warner Bros. Animation.

In the segment "I Was a Pre-Teenage Chupacabra," the gang tries out the latest hairstyles, but Flea doesn't have enough on his head to work with. A huckster sells him a vial of "Honest Miguel's Super Cure-All Syrup," which he claims will assist in hair growth. After applying the concoction, Flea grows so much hair that he's mistaken for the *chupacabra*—and the real beast isn't impressed once it learns there's an imposter running around town. It's a forgettable cartoon with only one really funny scene: when Flea is first mistaken for the *chupacabra,* frightened locals immediately hide their goats.

Mutant X – "Lazarus Syndrome"

Syndicated. Feb 18, 2002 (S01E15). Action/Sci-Fi. D: John Bell. W: Mark Amato. C: John Shea, Victoria Pratt, Lauren Lee Smith, Victor Webster, Andrew Kenneth Martin ☥, Larissa Laskin. USA: English/Color/42m. Fireworks Entertainment/Mutant X Productions Ltd.

Four genetically engineered mutants seek out others like themselves, while on the run from the scientist who created them. In this episode, empath Emma DeLauro is captured by Caleb Mathias, a modern-day psychic vampire who feeds on the life-force of other mutants.

Many psychic vampire stories are poorly written, and this one is no exception. The premise goes nowhere: if the vampire dies, he can come back to life, but can only stay regenerated if he quickly drains the life-force of another mutant. The process can only be initiated by kissing his victim, which seems to be his Achilles' heel (it's obvious, then, how this one ends). Since his victims all come back to life after he permanently dies, by the end of the story we're right back at the beginning.

The Natural World – "Vampires, Devilbirds and Spirits Tales of the Calypso Isles"

BBC Two. Apr 3, 1994 (S12E07). Nature/Science. D/W: Nick Upton. C: Paul Keens-Douglas. UK: English/Color/50m. National Geographic Society/Green Umbrella.

Focuses on the wildlife of Trinidad and Tobago, which plays an important role in local folklore. From the forest canopy to the mangrove swamps, the program highlights the menagerie of unique beasts found on the islands, including two species of vampire bat. Presented by Paul Keens-Douglas.

The Natural World – "Islands of the Vampire Birds"

BBC Two. Mar 14, 1999 (S17E16). Nature/Science. D: David Parer. W: David Parer, Elizabeth Parer-Cook. C: David Attenborough. UK: English/Color/55m. National Geographic Society/BBC/Australian Broadcasting Corporation.

Explores how the finch made its way to the barren Galapagos Islands and evolved into one of the most intriguing avian species on the planet. The two northernmost islands of the archipelago are home to the oddest bird of all: the "vampire finch." It pecks at the base of a seabird's wing feathers until the skin breaks, and then sips the blood as it begins to flow. Presented by David Attenborough.

📺 Broadcast in Australia on ABC-TV as a stand-alone program on October 13, 1999.

Nature – "Bloody Suckers"

PBS. Nov 17, 2002 (S21E04). Nature/Science. D: Mark Ferns. W: Nigel Zega. C: Mark Ferns. USA: English/Color/30m. Thirteen-WNET/Natural History New Zealand Limited.

Wildlife filmmaker Mark Ferns explores the broad spectrum of creatures in nature that thrive on the blood of other beings.

The New Adventures of Captain Planet – "The Energy Vampire"

TBS. Nov 20, 1993 (S01E12). Adventure/Education. D: Don Lusk. W: Nick Boxer, Sean Catherine Derek. C: David Coburn, LeVar Burton, Joey Dedio, Janice Kawaye, Scott Menville, Kath Soucie, Margot Kidder, Maurice LaMare ☥, Tim Curry. USA: English/Color/24m. Hanna-Barbera Cartoons Inc./TBS Productions Inc.

Doctor Blight's latest experiment gives Duke Nukem the ability to recharge from any energy source, which turns him into a glutton for power—an energy vampire. To satiate Nukem's growing needs, Dr. Blight plans to build a huge dam on a major river system—and the eco-conscious Planeteers look for a way to stop the nefarious plan.

Although the vampire allusions are minimal, it's actually a well-written story with a great message about the power addict in all of us (and even includes a homage to the classic film *King Kong*). This episode is ostensibly from the fourth season of the long-running *Captain Planet and the Planeteers* series, which was retitled when the production company changed from DiC Entertainment to Hanna-Barbera Cartoons.

Neverwhere

BBC Two. Sep 12 – Oct 17, 1996 (6 Episode Miniseries). Drama/Fantasy. D: Dewi Humphreys. W: Lenny Henry, Neil Gaiman. C: Gary Bakewell, Laura Fraser, Paterson Joseph, Clive Russell, Hywel Bennett, Peter Capaldi, Tamsin Greig ☥. UK: English/Color/180m. Crucial Films/BBC.

Richard Mayhew's life turns upside down after he meets a mysterious woman named Door, who's battered, bruised and bloodied. Chased by two assassins, Richard follows her into "London Below," a parallel world that exists underneath the streets of London. In this supernatural realm, he helps Door investigate the murder of her family.

Three episodes ("Knightsbridge," "Down Street," and "As Above, So Below") feature the seductive

Lamia and The Velvets, a group of vampire-like sirens who drain warmth from the bodies of their victims.

📺 In 1998, Neil Gaiman published a novel based on the TV series, which expanded the story and included scenes that did not make it into this production.

Nick's Quest - "Vampire Bats"

Channel 5. Mar 3, 1999 (S01E03). Nature/Science. D/W: Wendy McLean. C: Nick Baker. UK: English/Color/30m. Available Light Productions.

An eight-part series where a Naturalist travels the world in search of endangered and often dangerous species. In this episode, the host journeys to Costa Rica in a quest to find the rare vampire bat, and tries to dispel the common fears about this intriguing hematophage. Presented by Nick Baker.

Night Gallery - "The Girl with the Hungry Eyes"

NBC. Oct 1, 1972 (S03E02). Suspense/Thriller. D: John Badham. W: Robert Malcolm Young, Fritz Leiber. C: Rod Serling, James Farentino, John Astin, Joanna Pettet ☥, Kip Niven. USA: English/Color/26m. Universal TV.

🦇 🦇 🦇

Photographer David Faulkner has a gold mine in his mysterious new model, whose face graces billboards and advertisements city wide. She represents life, death, and everything in between—the culmination of every man's wants and desires. The woman has an alluring effect on several men she meets—healthy men who end up dead, apparently the victims of a heart attack.

This is essentially a succubus story: the woman feeds on the wants and desires of her victims, after drawing them in with a seductive glance (and glowing eyes). It's never fully explained, but she's likely a manifestation made whole by the photographer; when he burns the photographic negatives of her, she's destroyed. This varies from the ending in the original 1949 short story by Fritz Leiber, but the premise is the same. It's an allegory about the power of advertising and the constant search for the next "it" girl, whose smile can trick you into throwing away your money (and in this case, your life).

The Night Strangler

ABC. Jan 16, 1973. Horror/Thriller. D: Dan Curtis. W: Richard Matheson, Jeff Rice. C: Darren McGavin, Jo Ann Pflug, Simon Oakland, Scott Brady, Wally Cox, Margaret Hamilton, John Carradine, Al Lewis, Nina Wayne, Virginia Peters, Richard Anderson ☥. USA: English/Color/90m. ABC Telefilms.

🦇 🦇 🦇 🦇

After losing his job in Las Vegas, newspaper reporter Carl Kolchak relocates to Seattle, where he lands in the middle of yet another bizarre killing spree that hints of the supernatural. Young women are found strangled to death, with a small amount of blood extracted from their body through a puncture wound just below the scalp. Residue found on the victims' skin appears to be rotted human flesh—as if the women were strangled by a dead man.

In this satisfying sequel to *The Night Stalker* (1972), Kolchak discovers that since 1889, five identical sets of murders have occurred every twenty-one years. They were committed by the same man: a one-hundred-and-forty-four-year-old alchemist who discovered the secret ingredients to the "elixir of life," which gives the imbiber immortality. The most precious component is human blood, which must be extracted from the brain of a young woman within seven seconds of her death. Since first taking the potion over a century ago, the alchemist has been looking for a way to make the effects permanent; until then, he must resurface every couple of decades to siphon blood for a new batch of the elixir. The telefilm features charming cameos from Al Lewis (Grandpa from *The Munsters*), Margaret Hamilton (The Wicked Witch of the West from *The Wizard of Oz*), and John Carradine (Dracula from *House of Frankenstein* and *House of Dracula*). There's even a delightful nod to Carradine's past vampire roles; one character jokes that "he may be old, but his fangs are potent!"

Legendary producer Dan Curtis was a champion of Gothic television, bringing vampires and a horde of otherworldly creatures to life in such productions as *Dark Shadows, Dead of Night, The Night Stalker,* and *Dracula* (Dan Curtis Productions Inc)

📺 A third telefilm, *The Night Killers*, was co-written by Richard Matheson and William F. Nolan, but the production was dropped when the characters and premise were sold as a weekly series. In this story, set in Hawaii, Kolchak investigates an alien plot to replace political figures with androids.

The Paranormal Borderline – Ep. #1.01

UPN. Mar 12, 1996 (S01E01). Drama/Mystery. D: Mark Cole. W: Carl Buehl. C: Anon. USA: English/Color/60m. First Television/UPN.

Series explores unexplained phenomena, including reports of UFOs and paranormal experiences. This episode features a segment that investigates a "vampire killer" in Puerto Rico—the "goat sucker," locally known as *el chupacabras*. Presented by Jonathan Frakes.

Paranormal Paparazzi – "San Diego Chupacabra"

Travel Channel. Nov 2, 2012 (S01E07). Culture/Media. D: Scott Preston. W: Kristen Pietropoli, Jenna Levine, Robin Keats. C: Aaron Sagers, Julie Alexandria, Rachel Fine, Scott Gruenwald, Sona Oganesyan, Joshua P. Warren, Branden Wellington. USA: English/Color/22m. My Tupelo Entertainment.

This episode of the paranormal documentary series (which should really begin with the disclaimer "for entertainment purposes only") finds Scott Gruenwald heading to San Diego to determine if a bizarre, hairless creature found on a beach proves the existence of the legendary *el chupacabra*. Features an interview with noted cryptozoologist Loren Coleman. Narrated by Dave Mitchell.

The Plastic Man Comedy/Adventure Show – "The Dangerous Dr. Dinosaur" / "The Spider Takes a Bride" / "Who Do the Voodoo" / "The Perils of Paulette" / "The Dangerous Dr. Gadgets" / "The Super-Duper Race Cage"

ABC. Nov 3, 1979 (S01E07). Adventure/Family. D: Rudy Larriva, Manny Perez, Charles A. Nichols, John Kimball. W: Var. C: Frank Welker, Susan Blu, Bart Braverman, Jerry Dexter, Joe Baker, Michael Bell, Melendy Britt. USA: English/Color/120m. Ruby-Spears Productions.

In the segment "Who Do the Voodoo," Count Drako—an evil magician—escapes from Carfax Prison by morphing into a mist monster and draining the spirits of the guards (which turns them into zombies). As the diabolical man continues to syphon spirits in order to restore his body, Fangface and Fangpuss must find a way to stop his criminal pursuits and return his victims back to normal. Features a scary-looking antagonist, despite being a cookie-cutter villain. Even though it alludes to *Dracula* and vampires in general, it's just a banal tale that has been told far too often.

The Plastic Man Comedy/Adventure Show – "Ghostfinger" / "Highbrow" / "Dog Gone Days" / "The Evil Evo-Ray" / "The Count Draculon Caper" / "The Film Fiasco of Director Disastro"

ABC. Dec 1, 1979 (S01E11). Adventure/Family. D: Rudy Larriva, Manny Perez, Charles A. Nichols. W: Var. C: John Anthony Bailey, Dee Timberlake, Bobby Ellerbee, Johnny Brown, Al Fann. USA: English/Color/120m. Ruby-Spears Productions.

In the *Rickety Rocket* segment "The Count Draculon Caper," the teen detectives investigate the wrongdoings of the vampiric madman Count Draculon, who used his hypo-beam to turn passengers aboard a rocket liner into zombies. Far out!

The Real Adventures of Jonny Quest – "Eclipse"

Cartoon Network. Dec 27, 1996 (S02E12). Adventure/Family. D: Larry Houston. W: Glenn Leopold. C: Quinton Flynn, Jennifer Hale, Rob Paulsen, Jennifer Lien ☥, Michael Carven, James Barbour, Troy Evans, Mary Gregory, John de Lancie. USA: English/Color/20m. Hanna-Barbera Studios Inc.

While in New Orleans to watch a lunar eclipse, Hadji rescues a beautiful woman from two assailants, and falls deeply in love with her. But Jonny discovers she's a demon that drains the life essence of others to sustain her youth—yet Hadji is so completely under her spell that he won't believe a word of it. After she captures Jessie, Jonny tries to save his friends before they become part of a nefarious plan that will rejuvenate the demon for another fifty years.

A better than average succubus story with a vicious antagonist in the guise of Elise Lenoire. She can transform into a large, bat-like flying demon, and mummifies her victims after draining them of their vitality.

📺 The succubus storyline was supposedly based on an unproduced episode from the animated series *SWAT Cats* (1993).

Reaper – "Cancun"

The CW. May 20, 2008 (S01E18). Comedy/Drama. D: Stephen Cragg. W: Michele Fazekas, Tom Spezialy. C: Bret Harrison, Tyler Labine, Rick Gonzalez, Missy Peregrym, Ray Wise, Cindy Sampson ⚲, Ken Marino. CAN/USA: English/Color/42m. The Mark Gordon Company/Fazekas & Butters.

Sam must capture the escaped soul of Madame Ozera, a Romanian fortune teller, unaware that a group of demons plan to trap him for an eternity in Solomon's Cage. Meanwhile, Sock meets up with Marlena, whom he describes as a "hot demon chick"—each time they kiss, she steals a year of his life. It's another entertaining *Reaper* episode with a good mix of comedy and drama. Sock's interaction with Marlena—who's a succubus—leads to some hilarious scenes. Highly recommended viewing.

📺 Tom Spezialy also co-wrote the vampire episode "Gary & Wyatt's Bloodsucking Adventure" from the series *Weird Science* (1996).

Sealab 2021 – "Isla de las Chupacabras"

Cartoon Network. Nov 14, 2004 (S04E07). Comedy/Satire. D: Adam Reed, Matt Thompson. W: Matt Thompson, Pat Piper. C: Michael Goz, Brett Butler, Bill Lobley, Chris Ward, Kate Miller, Ellis Henican, Angela Gibbs. USA: English/Color/11m. Seventy-Thirty Productions/Williams Street.

Captain Shanks takes the crew to "Happy Fun Time Island" for a team building seminar. The main event is a *chupacabra* hunt, but they inadvertently maim one another—which leaves them unable to fend off the *chupacabras*. Or the tree cobras. Or the nasty shore crabs and man-eating trees!

This painfully unfunny episode has only a single saving grace: one of the characters misunderstands the focus of the hunt, and believes the prey is actually Chewbacca, the wookie from *Star Wars*. The *chupacabras* resemble the Creature from the Black Lagoon, with bulging eyes, webbing under their arms, and large protruding fangs.

📺 This series features new animation mixed with reused footage and characters from the Hanna-Barbera kids cartoon *Sealab 2020* (1972). This revamped show has adult-themed stories and situations that apparently have not impressed the creators of the original series.

Sherlock Holmes in the 22nd Century – "The Adventure of the Sussex Vampire Lot"

FOX. Oct 30, 1999 (S01E07). Adventure/Sci-Fi. D: Robert Brousseau. W: Phil Harnage. C: Jason Gray-Stanford, John Payne, Akiko Morison, Jennifer Copping, Richard Newman, Ian James Corlett, Viv Leacock, William Samples. USA: English/Color/30m. DiC Entertainment/Scottish Television.

In this futuristic series, the discovery of cellular rejuvenation allows Sherlock Holmes to be brought back to life, in order to battle his arch-nemesis, James Moriarty—who has somehow returned from the dead. In this episode, a vampire is terrorizing New London and breaking into what were believed to be inaccessible locations. The culprit drains computer systems of every bit of data—but then restores it just days later. Why would the vampire steal the information only to give it back, and moreover, why is Moriarty so interested in finding him before Holmes does?

An average genre tale that takes place in the future but references several vampires of the past. Holmes reads *Dracula* as part of the investigation and finds it most engaging—for fiction. He's a practical man and doesn't believe that a real vampire is involved, even though this being appears to feed on electrical data. Turns out the "vampire" was just an avatar, created by a young hacker to draw attention to the flaws in various security systems. She discovered that Moriarty was also illegally hacking the systems in order to steal financial data.

📺 This tale was "inspired" by Sir Arthur Conan Doyle's short story "The Adventure of the Sussex Vampire" (1924), although the similarities are limited to the title.

South Park – "The Succubus"

Comedy Central. Apr 21, 1999 (S03E03). Adult/Satire. D: Trey Parker. W: Trey Parker. C: Trey Parker, Matt Stone, Isaac Hayes, Michelle Unger ♀. USA: English/Color/22m. Braniff/Comedy Partners.

Chef has quit his job and completely changed his image; he's now engaged to Veronica, his new girlfriend. In a desperate attempt to get their mentor back, the boys turn to Mr. Garrison, who facetiously explains that she's a typical woman—a succubus sent from hell to drain men dry.

Turns out he was right: Veronica is a blood-sucking demon in disguise.

A typically smart and funny episode that benefits from the introduction of Chef's parents and the secondary plot involving Cartman's dealings with an optometrist. The succubus is suitably evil, and Garrison's take on the entire situation is hilarious.

Space Precinct - "Predator and Prey"

Syndicated. Feb 20, 1995 (S01E14). Action/Sci-Fi. D: Sidney Hayers. W: Nicholas Sagan. C: Ted Shackelford, Rob Youngblood, Simone Bendix, Nancy Paul, Jerome Willis, Rolf Saxon, Natalie Roles, Joe Mydell, Nic Klein, Megan Olive, Mary Woodvine, Richard James ☥, Lou Hirsch, David Quilter. UK/USA: English/Color/44m. Grove Televentures/Mentorn.

This series, which takes place in the year 2040, follows the adventures of Lieutenant Patrick Brogan, a 20-year veteran of the NYPD who transfers to another precinct…in space! In this episode, a pale, bald humanoid—which resembles a Talosian from *Star Trek* (with a fondness for opera capes)—is on the hunt to recharge its fading vital energy. A parasite of sorts, the creature temporarily inhabits its victim while draining their life force.

Space Stars - "Rampage of the Zodiac Man" / "The Buccaneer" / "The Haunted Space Station" / "The Ultimate Battle" / "Magnus"

NBC. Oct 17, 1981 (S01E06). Adventure/Sci-Fi. D: Ray Patterson. W: Donald Glut, Kathleen Barnes. C: Gary Owens, Steve Spears, Alexandra Stewart, Frank Welker, Mike Road, Virginia Gregg, Don Messick, Keene Curtis. USA: English/Color/60m. Hanna-Barbera Productions Inc.

In "The Haunted Space Station," an automated S.O.S. call draws Space Ghost and company to Outworld Station. Her entire crew has been turned into zombies by a Vorvolaka, a soul vampire that feeds on the vital energies of others—and this interstellar Dracula wants to create a master race of vampires throughout the galaxy.

A supernatural space story that's peppered with bad puns, and features a short, portly and balding soul vampire that wears a one-piece blue jumpsuit and a black cape. One can't take him very seriously, because he's dressed as though he's on the way to party at an intergalactic Studio 54.

Special Unit 2 - "The Years"

UPN. Oct 17, 2001 (S02E03). Comedy/Sci-Fi. D: John T. Kretchmer. W: Evan Katz. C: Michael Landes, Alexondra Lee, Danny Woodburn, Richard Gant, Jonathan Togo, Lola Glaudini ☥, Antonio Cupo, Tania L. Pearson ☥. USA: English/Color/42m. Paramount Television/Rego Park.

Follows a group that investigates mysterious deaths attributed to "links"—monsters from folklore and mythology that are considered the missing link between humans and beasts. In this episode, a nineteen-year-old male is found dead; the cause of death was congestive heart failure due to old age. He was the victim of a centuries-old "year witch," who drained his life-force to maintain her youth. The prime suspect is the founder of an emerging cosmetics company, but conflict arises after the enigmatic businesswoman takes a liking to the lead detective in the case.

This predictable episode features the closest thing to a vampire that could be found in this series, because the premise implies that all myths are true—except for these creatures. Too bad, because the story really could have used a little more bite.

Star Trek – "The Man Trap"

NBC. Sep 8, 1966 (S01E01). Adventure/Sci-Fi. D: Marc Daniels. W: George Clayton Johnson. C: William Shatner, Leonard Nimoy, DeForest Kelley, George Takei, Nichelle Nichols, Jeanne Bal ♀, Alfred Ryder. USA: English/Color/60m. Desilu Productions/Norway Corporation.

The Enterprise makes a routine stop to check in on Professor Robert Crater and his wife Nancy, a couple studying the remains of an ancient civilization. An unknown predator stalks the crew, killing them at random and draining the salt from their bodies—and the only clues left behind are strange red marks dotting the faces of the victims.

Star Trek – "Obsession"

NBC. Dec 15, 1967 (S02E13). Adventure/Sci-Fi. D: Ralph Senensky. W: Art Wallace. C: William Shatner, Leonard Nimoy, DeForest Kelley, George Takei, Nichelle Nichols, James Doohan, Walter Koenig, Majel Barrett. USA: English/Color/60m. Desilu Productions/Norway Corporation.

The Enterprise encounters a strange, gaseous being that subsists on human red blood cells. Captain Kirk first encountered the creature over a decade ago, but he failed to destroy it—which resulted in the deaths of several crew members. Racked by guilt and fixated on revenge, Kirk becomes obsessed with hunting down the creature—and nothing is going to stop him from killing it once and for all.

Stargate: Atlantis

SyFy. Jul 16, 2004 - Jan 9, 2009 (100 Episodes). Adventure/Sci-Fi. D: Martin Wood. W: Robert C. Cooper. C: Joe Flanigan, David Hewlett, Rachel Luttrell, Jason Momoa, Torri Higginson, Paul McGillion, Christopher Heyerdahl ♀, James Lafazanos ♀, Andee Frizzell ♀. CAN/USA: English/Color/4500m. Pegasus Productions/Acme Shark.

An outpost is discovered in the Antarctic; it's a "stargate," part of a network of portals created by an ancient race of humans, which they used to quickly travel from one world to another. This particular gateway leads to the lost city of Atlantis, which lies in the Pegasus Galaxy. An international team of scientists and the military is sent to explore the region, but they get trapped and are unable to return to Earth. The group aligns with another humanoid race to battle a common enemy known as the Wraiths, vampire-like telepaths that feed on the life-force of human beings.

Strange – "Incubus"

BBC One. Jun 21, 2003 (S01E04). Horror/Mystery. D: Simon Massey. W: Andrew Marshall. C: Richard Coyle, Samantha Janus, Ian Richardson, Imelda Staunton, Paul Shearer, Martin Ball. UK: English/Color/60m. Big Bear Films/BBC.

🐎 🐎 🐎 🐎

Series follows ex-vicar John Strange in his quest to hunt down and destroy demons. In this episode, something is killing young woman, and they're being mauled—from the inside out! These incidents are eerily similar to the "Milan incubi attacks" of the late seventeenth century—when bloodthirsty demons wreaked havoc on the populace.

A very entertaining story that features an incubus, a demon disguised as a human male that sexually preys on women. In this case, it's less humanoid, and yearns for human blood rather than sexual contact. The method of its incubation—updated for our modern times—is brilliant.

Strange – "Dubik"

BBC One. Jun 28, 2003 (S01E05). Horror/Mystery. D: Joe Ahearne. W: Andrew Marshall. C: Richard Coyle, Samantha Janus, Ian Richardson, Ana Sofrenovic, Ralph Ineson ☥, Liz Daniels. UK: English/Color/60m. Big Bear Films/BBC.

🐎 🐎 🐎 🐎

A British surveyor working abroad in Herzegovina is murdered, and when Canon Black's elderly sister dies under similar circumstances—both victims were drained of blood—he reluctantly asks Strange for help. The ex-vicar uncovers a Baltic folk legend called a *dubik* ("blood eater"), and his investigation leads to Mina—a mysterious peasant girl who recently emigrated from the same region.

The *dubik* ensnares its victim by tricking them into believing it's a deceased loved one; this is reminiscent of the episode "Horror in the Heights" from *Kolchak: The Night Stalker* (1974), where a demon takes on the form of the person whom its victim trusts the most. The *dubik's* true form is revealed at the end, and it's a little silly—even though it's accurate according to folklore. But this episode still gets high marks for originality; it keeps you guessing, and is one of the more enjoyable productions in this section. Alternately titled "Dubuykk."

Superboy – "Succubus"

Syndicated. May 20, 1989 (S01E25). Adventure/Sci-Fi. D: David Nutter. W: Cary Bates. C: John Haymes Newton, Stacy Haiduk, Jim Calvert, Sybil Danning ⚲. USA: English/Color/22m. Alexander & Ilya Salkind/Cantharus Productions N.V./Viacom.

T.J. falls for romance novelist Pamela Dare, who's actually an ancient succubus that remains forever young by draining the youth of others. She plans to steal Superboy's extraordinary life-force, hoping that the supercharged energy will fulfill her needs so that she'll never have to feed again.

Another middle-of-the-road story that stands out only because it involves a succubus and stars Sybil Danning in the role. After Pamela absorbs Superman's life-force, she becomes too youthful. She reverts to a teenager, then a young girl, then a baby—and then regresses even further into something that looks like a pile of rock salt. This makes little sense, considering a succubus is a demon that takes on the form of a woman, so whatever she reverted to is completely inexplicable. But I suppose the idea serves the premise of the story, so just take it with a grain of salt (ha!).

📺 Sybil Danning starred in several B-movies as well as the vampire-themed TV series *The Lair* (2009).

Supernatural – "Something Wicked"

The CW. Apr 6, 2006 (S01E18). Horror/Thriller. D: Whitney Ransick. W: Daniel Knauf. C: Jared Padalecki, Jensen Ackles, Jeffrey Dean Morgan, Colby Paul, Ridge Canipe, Venus Terzo, Adrian Hough ⚲. USA: English/Color/42m. Kripke Enterprises/Wonderland Sound and Vision/Warner Bros. Television.

Sam and Dean investigate a mysterious illness effecting children in a quaint Wisconsin town. Unresponsive to antibiotics, the kids become comatose, as if their bodies simply wear out. A *shtriga* is responsible; it's a witch that feeds on their life-force—and the same creature attacked Sam when he was a boy. This is an atmospheric episode that deftly intertwines mythology with past and present events in the lives of the Winchester family.

📺 In Albanian folklore, the *shtriga* is a creature that disguises itself as an old woman during the day, while at night it sucks the blood of infants as they sleep.

Supernatural – "The Kids Are Alright"

The CW. Oct 11, 2007 (S03E02). Horror/Thriller. D: Phil Sgriccia. W: Sera Gamble. C: Jared Padalecki, Jensen Ackles, Kathleen Munroe, Cindy Sampson, Margot Berner ⚲, Nicholas Elia. USA: English/Color/43m. Kripke Enterprises/Wonderland Sound and Vision/Warner Bros. Television.

The brothers investigate a suspicious death in Indiana and discover that a changeling is taking over a gated community, one child at a time. It captures the kids and leaves mimics in their place, which feed on the synovial fluid of their surrogate mothers.

This average episode features hollow-eyed, multi-fanged creatures that bite into the back of a neck as they feed (and the kid monsters are quite chilling). Dean has another reason for being there—it's the home of a former lover, Lisa Braeden, and he believes that he's the father of her child. This story arc seems forced at times, yet Lisa and her son become a prominent fixture in Dean's life after the events of Season 5.

One character is reading Elizabeth Kostova's The Historian (2005), a contemporary Gothic adventure that interweaves real history, vampires, and Vlad Țepeș.

The Super Mario Bros. Super Show! – "Magician" / "Count Koopula"

Syndicated. Sep 27, 1989 (S01E18). Adventure/Family. D: Dan Riba. W: Phil Harnage. C: Lou Albano, Danny Wells, Harvey Atkin ♀, Jeannie Elias, John Stocker ♀, Robert Bockstael. USA: English/Color/22m. Binder Entertainment/DiC Entertainment/Nintendo of America Inc.

In the animated segment "Count Koopula," a bat steals Mario's spaghetti leftovers. The gang pursues the creature to a creepy castle, where they seek refuge from the inclement weather. It's the home of Count Koopula, a vampire that has a taste for the red stuff: tomato sauce.

Tales from the Darkside – "Hush"

Syndicated. Jul 10, 1988 (S04E18). Horror/Thriller. D: Allen Coulter. W: John Sutherland, Zenna Henderson. C: Nile Lanning, Eric Jason, Bonnie Gallup. USA: English/Color/22m. Laurel Entertainment Inc./Jaygee Productions/Tribune Entertainment.

Jennifer babysits Buddy, a sickly boy who invents small robots and other curiosities. He's most proud of the "noise eater," a vacuum-like device that can suck the sound out of any object—rendering it silent. But after the robot takes on a life of its own, the two discover that it actually drains the energy from anything it touches, destroying the object in the process—and it wants to silence them forever.

About as thrilling as you would expect from a story that features a 1950s-era vacuum cleaner that plays hide-and-seek with Jennifer and Buddy, who try to stay quiet so the life-draining vampire can't find them. It's a silly concept that's poorly executed, featuring ridiculous characters who have great difficulty outrunning decades-old technology.

Tales of Tomorrow – "Youth on Tap"

ABC. Sep 26, 1952 (S02E04). Horror/Thriller. D: Don Medford. W: Lona Kenney, Mann Rubin. C: Robert Alda, Harry Townes ♀, Mary Alice Moore, Bernard Burke, Ralph Porter. USA: English/B&W/30m. George F. Foley Productions/The Science Fiction League of America.

🦇 🦇 🦇

Jeff is down on his luck; he desperately needs a thousand dollars to buy a gas station, so he can begin a new life with his girlfriend. Dr. Platan offers him a dubious proposition: in exchange for the money, all he wants is a pint of Jeff's blood.

After extracting the blood through a "special process," Platan injects it into his own veins, gaining a new lease on life; as his youth is restored, Jeff rapidly ages. Even though the conclusion is a little too tidy, it's still an interesting tale about an energy vampire. At one hundred and sixty years old, Platan maintains his vigor by stealing the life essence from his young victims, through what he calls the "youth derivative" in their blood.

Tales of Tomorrow – "The Fury of the Cocoon"

ABC. Mar 6, 1953 (S02E29). Horror/Sci-Fi. D: Don Medford. W: Frank de Felitta. C: Nancy Coleman, Peter Capell, Cameron Prud'Homme. USA: English/B&W/25m. George F. Foley Productions/The Science Fiction League of America.

🦇 🦇 🦇

A relief team is sent to rendezvous with a crew investigating a meteor impact deep in the jungle. They discover two of them dead, their throats pierced and bodies completely drained of blood. The sole survivor claims that the meteorite was carrying life from beyond our universe: a group of invisible, dog-sized insects that subsist exclusively on human blood.

Having invisible monsters certainly adds suspense, and the story effectively works around the fact that they're not seen for most of the episode. The aliens are definitely vampire-like in nature—even though the word is never mentioned—and they look like "E.T. the Extra-Terrestrial" with two large, pronounced fangs.

To the Ends of the Earth – "The Fearless Vampire Hunters"

Channel 4. May 4, 1998 (S03E03). Folklore/Nature. D: Norman Hull. W: Jonathan Downes. C: Jonathan Downes. UK: English/Color/60m. AVP Productions.

This series of adventure documentaries explores the lesser-known parts of the planet. In this episode, a team travels from Puerto Rico to Miami in search of the mythical *chupacabra,* purported to be a nocturnal flying beast that sucks the blood from its victims.

Torchwood – "Day One"

BBC Three. Oct 22, 2006 (S01E02). Action/Sci-Fi. D: Brian Kelly. W: Chris Chibnall. C: John Barrowman, Eve Myles, Burn Gorman, Naoko Mori, Gareth David-Lloyd, Kai Owen, Sara Lloyd Gregory , Adrian Christopher, Ross O'Hennessy. CAN/UK: English/Color/48m. BBC Wales/CBC.

🦇🦇🦇

Gwen's first day on the job isn't going well. At the scene of a meteor crash, she inadvertently releases a gaseous alien life-form that takes over the body of a young woman. The alien is addicted to the sexual energy produced at the point of orgasm, and uses its host body to drain the life from her male victims—which turns them into piles of dust.

In a story reminiscent of the movie *Species* (1995), the Torchwood team chases a sex-addicted alien—a succubus of sorts—throughout the boroughs of Cardiff. This tale is definitely meant for adults, and is a nice mix of sexual humor and wanton behavior.

📺 The resident aliens in this series, *Weevils,* are hideous-looking humanoids with pronounced fangs. They're not vampires, but are definitely influenced by the *Nosferatu* archetype—and one is even seen biting a man's neck and apparently drinking his blood.

Julie Eldridge (Karen Black) is a wolf in sheep's clothing in "Julie," one of three supernatural stories collected in *Trilogy of Terror* (ABC Circle Films/Dan Curtis Productions)

Trilogy of Terror

ABC. Mar 4, 1975. Horror/Suspense. D: Dan Curtis. W: Richard Matheson, William F. Nolan. C: Karen Black, Robert Burton, John Karlin, George Gaynes, James Storm, Kathryn Reynolds, Orin Cannon, Gregory Harrison. USA: English/Color/72m. ABC Circle Films/Dan Curtis Productions.

🦇🦇

A collection of three short horror stories—"Julie," "Millicent and Therese," and "Amelia"—that feature Karen Black playing four different women, each seeking revenge over the forces tormenting them. In the first tale, Chad—a handsome college student—inexplicably falls for his mousy professor, Julie Eldridge.

Based on Richard Matheson's short story "The Likeness of Julie," this strange tale leaves too many unanswered questions. Chad drugs Julie, rapes her, and then blackmails her so that she'll do whatever he asks. But Julie was behind the entire scheme; she implanted irrational thoughts into Chad, controlling his actions and using him for sex. It's not clear how she accomplishes this feat, but just like her other victims over the years, she kills Chad once she gets bored with the game (he dies of a heart attack). Julie is probably a succubus; considering these demons take on the form of women, the "likeness" part of the original title may refer to this (and her last name may allude to "eldritch," which means "weird" or "eerie"). It should be noted that issue #3 of *Fangoria* magazine (December 1979) featured an article on the career of Richard Matheson—and a list of his credits indicated that Julie was a succubus.

This was the first of two pilots for a proposed anthology series called *Dead of Night*; the second attempt featured three different stories under that title, and was produced in 1977.

Unsolved Mysteries – Ep. #8.24

NBC. Apr 26, 1996 (S08E24). Drama/Mystery. D: Anon. W: Jan Kimbrough. C: Eliezer Rivera, Luis Guadalupe, Madelyne Tolentino, David Negron, Jorge Martin, Jose Soto, Carlos Soto, David Morales. USA: English/Color/60m. Cosgrove-Meurer Productions.

One segment reports on a mysterious animal blamed for numerous attacks on livestock in Puerto Rico—a creature that locals call *el chupacabras*. Witnesses describe the beast as having fangs, red luminous eyes, three-fingered claws, and a boney ridge along the top of its head. Hosted by Robert Stack.

This is one of the earliest investigations into the *chupacabra* phenomenon, and featured several eyewitness accounts. First reported in late 1995, the number of incidents grew exponentially; the municipality of Canóvanas saw the greatest concentration—an upwards of seventy attacks on livestock and domesticated animals.

URBO: The Adventures of Pax Afrika – "Monster Plague"

SABC3. Aug 29, 2008 (S02E26). Adventure/Sci-Fi. D: Charlie Alves. W: Sarah Lotz, Sam Wilson. C: Anelisa Phewa, Nicholas Pauling, Precious Kofi, Siphokazi Jan, Mike Westcott, Nicola Jackman, Jon Falkow. RSA: English/Color/30m. Octagon CSI (Clockwork Zoo).

In a post-apocalyptic South Africa, Maximilian Malice rules with a heavy hand over the residents of iKapa City; only a handful of teenagers, led by Pax Afrika, are willing to stand up to the evil industrialist. In this episode, a vicious swarm of vampiric locusts heads towards the city, and leaves a trail of destruction in its wake.

Vampire Bats

CBS. Oct 30, 2005. Sci-Fi/Thriller. D: Eric Bross. W: Doug Prochilo. C: Lucy Lawless, Dylan Neal, Craig Ferguson, Timothy Bottoms, Liam Waite, Jessica Stroup, Tony Plana, Brett Butler. USA: English/Color/120m. LIFT Productions/VZS Productions/Violet Blue Productions.

After a student is violently killed by a colony of vampire bats, professor Maddy Rierdon discovers that the furry fliers have mutated due to industrial pollution dumped into a river. As the attacks continue, Rierdon faces local corruption as she tries to halt the advancement of the aggressive, mutated bats. This is a sequel to the TV movie *Locusts* (2005), where Maddy Rierdon protects the populace from a deadly swarm of bio-engineered grasshoppers.

The Vampire Hunter With Nigel Marven

ITV. Aug 28, 2000. Reality/Science. D: Anon. W: Anon. C: Anon. UK: English/Color/60m. United Television Productions/HTV.

This stand-alone special features wildlife enthusiast Nigel Marven as he experiments with nature's blood drinkers: he allows fleas, leeches, and vampire bats to tap into his veins.

Van-pires

Syndicated. Sep 14 - Dec 7, 1997 (13 Episodes). Adventure/Family. D/W: Anthony Gentile, John Gentile. C: Garikayi Mutambirwa, Melissa Marsala, Marc Schwarz, Jason Hayes, Susan Varon, Ron Kaehler, Charles Wayne Loflin. USA: English/Color/390m. Abrams Gentile Entertainment Inc./MSH Entertainment.

Four teenagers seek shelter in derelict vehicles as a meteor crashes into a junk yard. The fallout radiation infuses them with the ability to transform into human/automobile hybrids, but it also creates an evil horde of sentient vehicles: the Van-Pires. Led by Tracula, their primary goal is to drink the gas from unsuspecting cars, and drain the planet of all its fuel. The teen heroes—led by their friend, Van He'llsing—form a group called the "Moto-Vators," to protect the night from the voracious, vampiric vehicles.

Released on DVD as *Van-Pires Transform,* this series was live-action combined with computer-animated segments—which look surprisingly good considering the available technology at the time. The evil Van-Pires are the best thing about the show, which is abysmal in all other aspects. The four teenage leads overact to the point of aggravation, and the groan-worthy dialogue is peppered with ridiculous car-speak. Too violent for children and too lame for teens, this series is about as much fun as bumper-to-bumper traffic.

Warehouse 13 - "Age Before Beauty"

SyFy. Jul 27, 2010 (S02E04). Comedy/Fantasy. D: Tawnia McKiernan. W: Andrew Kreisberg. C: Eddie McClintock, Joanne Kelly, Saul Rubinek, Genelle Williams, Allison Scagliotti, Tawny Cypress, Phillip Rhys ☥, Nolan Gerard Funk. USA: English/Color/44m. Universal Media Studios.

Series follows two Secret Service Agents tasked with retrieving supernatural objects stolen from a secret government storage facility. In this episode, Pete and Myka investigate the case of a woman who died of old age—yet she was actually a nineteen-year-old supermodel. Someone is stealing the youth from runway models—and each case is linked to an old camera once owned by photographer Man Ray.

In a story that takes a few jabs at the fashion industry, an energy vampire of sorts uses an old camera to steal the youth from someone to transfer it into another—through a simple double exposure of both the donor and recipient. The photographer was the first to experience the exchange of life energy in the 1930s; once the good guys find the camera and reverse the process, he rapidly ages and dies.

Weird Science – "Grampira"

USA Network. Apr 22, 1995 (S03E03). Comedy/Sci-Fi. D: Max Tash. W: Kari Lizer. C: Michael Manasseri, John Mallory Asher, Vanessa Angel, Gloria Le Roy ⚧. USA: English/Color/22m. St. Clare Entertainment/Universal Television.

Wyatt asks Lisa to restore his Grandmother's vitality so she can feel young again. But this turns the elderly woman into an energy vampire; she drains the life-force from her victims, which ages them in the process. It's a fun story of a geriatric woman's day on the town; as she begins to feel more like a teenager, the young folk around her take on the aspects of the elderly.

Wheelie and the Chopper Bunch – "Dragster Net" / "Dragula" / "Boot Camp"

NBC. Nov 16, 1974 (S01E11). Adventure/Family. D: Charles A. Nichols. W: Anon. C: Don Messick, Franklin Welker, Lennie Weinrib, Paul Winchell ⚧, Judy Strangis, Rolinda Wolk. USA: English/Color/30m. Hanna-Barbera Productions Inc.

This animated series features Wheelie, a red Volkswagen Beetle, which communicates through a sequence of honks and images displayed on its windshield; his nemeses are a gang of anthropomorphic motorcycles. In the segment "Dragula," the Chopper Bunch is targeted by a vampire dragster that awakens with a thirst for a quart of "Type O"—oil that is!

A very charming story with one of the most peculiar takes on the Dracula archetype, featuring a benign vampire in the guise of a white racing car. "Dragula" has two pronounced fangs on the front grill, a large cape that drapes over the back wheels, and a voice that sounds like Bela Lugosi—with an unrelenting thirst for the *dark* stuff. He can also transform into a bat, which is just a smaller version of him that sports a set of wings. Although Dragula constantly tries to drain the oil from other cars, he's never successful—but receives a fresh new barrel of sustenance from Wheelie, as a thank-you present for scaring away the Chopper Bunch.

📺 "DRAG-U-LA" was the name of Grandpa Munster's racing car in *The Munsters* (1964-66).

Wolverine and the X-Men – "Shades of Grey" / "Foresight"

YTV. Mar 9-12, 2009 (S01E23-26). Action/Adventure. D: Doug Murphy. W: Greg Johnson, Craig Kyle. C: Steven Blum, Susan Dalian, Danielle Judovits, Jennifer Hale, Yuri Lowenthal, Nolan North, April Stewart ☥. USA: English/Color/88m. Toonz Entertainment/Liberation Entertainment/EVA.

Jean Grey suffers from memory loss; in a fit of rage, she unintentionally releases a wave of psychic energy that alerts Emma of her whereabouts. She's captured by the Inner Circle, a group dedicated to controlling the Phoenix force living inside of her—and they intend to release the beast from within. As the X-Men fight to keep the Phoenix from rising, Magneto amasses his sentinels and plans to destroy the human race.

This engaging, four-episode story ends with a cliffhanger—but unfortunately the series lasted only a single season. Psychic vampire Selene makes an appearance in these final episodes, as a secret member of the Inner Circle.

The World's Strangest UFO Stories – "Alien Vampire Chronicles"

Discovery. Mar 23, 2006 (S01E07). Nature/Sci-Fi. D/W: Robin Bicknell. C: Virgilio Sanchez, Ron McGill, Ismael Aguayo, Madelyne Tolentino, Norka Albandoz, Seth Shostak, Scott Corrales, Marco Reynoso, Orlando Pla, Dennis Murray. CAN: English/Color/44m. Proper Television Inc.

This episode investigates *el chupacabra,* the blood-sucking creature that supposedly feasts on animals from the jungles of Latin America to the sunny shores of Miami. Could it be some sort of mutated monster, the result of a sinister CIA experiment gone wrong? Or perhaps an interdimensional alien that has traveled to Earth in order to feed on our indigenous species? Narrated by Mark Williams.

A cheeky yet engaging look at the history of this elusive beast, an infamous "goat sucker" that was first implicated in the deaths of livestock in the 1990s. It's a surprisingly thorough examination of what has become a cultural phenomenon, and covers the history of the attacks while exploring several common theories about the creature. Yet the program takes a further leap into the depths of space, and offers an interdimensional alien as yet another possible origin for this bloodthirsty being. It's all in good fun, of course; despite featuring several interviews from those who firmly believe in the more otherworldly theories, the narrator never lets the tone get too serious.

The X Files – "2Shy"

FOX. Nov 3, 1995 (S03E06). Mystery/Sci-Fi. D: David Nutter. W: Jeff Vlaming. C: David Duchovny, Gillian Anderson, Timothy Carhart ☥, James Handy, Suzy Joachim, Catherine Paolone, Glynis Davies. USA: English/Color/60m. Ten Thirteen Productions/20th Century Fox Television.

The team investigates a strange murder in Cleveland, where a corpse was found in an advanced state of decay—even though the victim had only been missing for a short time. Mulder connects the homicide to a number of earlier cases in a different city, where each victim had responded to a personal ad in the newspaper. The women had the lipids drained completely from their bodies—as if by a fat-sucking vampire—and the killer is now using Internet chat rooms to seek out his prey.

The X Files – "Avatar"

FOX. Apr 26, 1996 (S03E21). Mystery/Sci-Fi. D: Jim Charleston. W: Howard Gordon, David Duchovny. C: David Duchovny, Gillian Anderson, Mitch Pileggi, William B. Davis, Jennifer Hetrick, Tom Mason. USA: English/Color/60m. Ten Thirteen Productions/20th Century Fox Television.

Assistant Director Skinner is the prime suspect in the murder of a woman with whom he had a one-night stand. She was found in his bed, dead with a broken neck, yet he can't remember anything of the incident. Mulder believes a succubus is to blame, after Skinner reveals that he's had a series of nightmares where he's visited by an old woman.

The X Files – "El Mundo Gira"

FOX. Jan 12, 1997 (S04E11). Mystery/Sci-Fi. D: Tucker Gates. W: John Shiban. C: David Duchovny, Gillian Anderson, Mitch Pileggi, Rubén Blades, José Yenque, Raymond Cruz, Simi Mehta, Susan Bain. USA: English/Color/60m. Ten Thirteen Productions/20th Century Fox Television.

After a bizarre storm teeming with yellow rain, a young migrant worker is found dead—and locals believe *el chupacabra* is to blame. Mulder is quick to jump on the supernatural bandwagon, yet Scully determines that the victim died from a substantial fungal infection. The investigation leads to another migrant worker who's feared by others in the community; he carries a contagious fungus that can potentially kill anyone with whom he comes in contact.

The X Files – "Patience"

FOX. Nov 19, 2000 (S08E03). Mystery/Sci-Fi. D/W: Chris Carter. C: Gillian Anderson, Robert Patrick, Bradford English, Gene Dynarski, Dan Leegant, Jay Caputo ♀, Eve Brenner, Annie O'Donnell. USA: English/Color/45m. Ten Thirteen Productions/20th Century Fox Television.

With Mulder missing, Scully reluctantly teams up with her new partner, John Doggett, to investigate a strange double murder in Idaho. An undertaker and his wife died from massive blood loss through deep wounds on their bodies; the bite marks appear to be human, but footprints at the crime scene suggest that an animal was responsible. These murders mimic similar deaths from forty-four years earlier, when a "human bat" was killed by a group of hunters.

Another one of these creatures—neither man nor animal—has returned to seek revenge against the sole survivor of the original hunting party. The creature chooses its victims by scent, so anyone who has come in contact with the man—including the FBI Agents—is a potential target. This is one of the better monster-of-the-week episodes from the later seasons, and sets up the new team dynamic where Scully takes on the role of the believer—now that Mulder is out of the picture.

Yin Yang Yo! – "The Howl of the Weenie"

Jetix. Oct 13, 2008 (S02E27). Adventure/Comedy. D: Ted Collver. W: Eric Trueheart. C: Scott McCord, Stephanie Morgenstern, Martin Roach, Jonathan Wilson, Linda Ballantyne, Tony Daniels, Gerard Butler, Ron Rubin ☥. CAN/USA: English/Color/22m. Walt Disney Television Animation.

In this animated series, siblings Yin and Yang use their special martial arts skills to battle Eradicus, the original Night Master. This episode takes place during Weenie Howl; it was once a night of terror, when peasants hid themselves from roaming packs of were-weenies. But these days it's all about candy and costumes, a concept that does not sit well with Eradicus. So he creates the "terror weenie," a tube-steak horror that subsists on fear, and summons his minions to frighten the locals—which feeds his creation, making it powerful enough to destroy the city.

Loosely based on the energy vampire concept (and Halloween), the terror weenie devours fear, becoming increasingly powerful in the process. There are several costumed monsters on the night of Weenie Howl; one is dressed as Dracula from *Bram Stoker's Dracula* (1992). Most of the laughs come from Yin, who repeatedly dresses up in lame costumes—but her too-cute nature ultimately saves the day.

Take a Breather
No Vampires Here!

Early promotional photograph for the ABC series *The Addams Family*, about an eccentric clan with a taste for the macabre (Filmways Pictures)

30 Rock – "Plan B"

NBC. Mar 24, 2011 (S05E18). Comedy/Satire. D: Jeff Richmond. W: Josh Siegal, Dylan Morgan. C: Tina Fey, Tracy Morgan, Jane Krakowski, Jack McBrayer, Scott Adsit, Judah Friedlander, Alec Baldwin. USA: English/Color/22m. Broadway Video/Little Stranger Inc./Universal Media Studios.

TGS goes on a "forced hiatus," and the cast and crew believe that the show will soon be canceled. With no Plan B, Liz implores her agent to find her another gig, but she's told to just write something about vampires (since they're so popular). She pitches a new show to her boss, explaining that it's about "a girl television writer trying to have it all in the city"—but when he shows little interest, Liz adds "…also, she's a vampire…I guess" (he only likes the last part). It's a really fun episode even though the vampires are limited to Liz's story pitch. The underlying theme is about the importance of good writing in the age of Facebook, and includes nods to both *Star Wars* and *The West Wing*.

The Addams Family (1964)

ABC. Sep 18, 1964 – Sep 2, 1966 (64 Episodes). Comedy/Family. D: Sidney Lanfield. W: Harry Winkler, Hannibal Coons. C: John Astin, Carolyn Jones, Jackie Coogan, Ted Cassidy, Ken Weatherwax, Lisa Loring, Marie Blake. USA: English/B&W/1920m. Filmways Pictures.

Based on the cartoons of Charles Addams from *The New Yorker* magazine, this series features a wealthy and eccentric family that loves the macabre. This good-natured clan is oblivious to the fact that what they deem as "normal" behavior is actually quite shocking to the rest of society. The matriarch is Morticia, a woman with pale skin and long black hair, who is more of a vamp (in the *femme fatale* sense of the word) as opposed to a traditional vampire.

Shortly after the series was canceled, Lurch (Ted Cassidy) appeared in the *Batman* episode "The Penguin's Nest," in a scene accompanied by *The Addams Family* theme. Carolyn Jones appeared as Morticia Addams in the first episode of the short-lived children's game show *Storybook Squares* (1969).

The Addams Family (1973)

NBC. Sep 8, 1973 – Aug 30, 1975 (16 Episodes). Comedy/Family. D: Charles A. Nichols. W: Bill Raynor, Bud Atkinson. C: John Stephenson, Leonard Weinrib, Jackie Coogan, Janet Waldo, Don Messick, Pat Harrington, Jr., Jodie Foster, Ted Cassidy. USA: English/Color/480m. Hanna-Barbera Productions Inc.

This animated series, featuring character designs based on the original cartoons of Charles Addams, follows the macabre family in their trek across the United States. They explore the country in their custom RV along with a menagerie of pets, including Ocho the octopus, Ally the alligator, Abigail the bat, and Sparky the eel.

This cheaply-made series put an effort into animating the Addams Family to some degree of satisfaction, yet all the other characters are poorly drawn with cookie-cutter designs. The incessant laugh track only brings attention to the sub-par writing; none of Gomez's puns register any real chuckles. The majority of the episodes follow the exact same premise: the family arrives in a new city, where they immediately flaunt their inordinate wealth. This brings them the unwanted attention of two crooks, who are already preying on the locals. The criminals grift the Addams for as much cash as possible; the family never catches on, yet they always manage to foil the bad guys and save the day.

📺 There are some minor undead references; in episodes #3 and #11, the family calls a famous New York landmark "The Vampire State Building." In episode #10, Gomez and Morticia dress up as vampires, and even Grandmama gets in on the act; her costume resembles Edward C. Burke (in his vampire guise) from the movie *London After Midnight* (1927).

The Addams Family (1992)

ABC. Sep 12, 1992 – Nov 6, 1993 (21 Episodes). Comedy/Family. D: Robert Alvarez. W: Bill Matheny, Lane Raichert. C: John Astin, Nanci Linari, Rip Taylor, Debi Derryberry, Jeannie Elias, Carol Channing, Jim Cummings, Rob Paulsen. USA: English/Color/630m. Hanna-Barbera Productions, Inc.

🦇🦇

Even though they're genuinely friendly, the creepy and kooky Addams Family don't quite fit in with the other suburbanites of Happydale Heights. One meddlesome neighbor, Norman Normanmeyer, wants to get rid of them altogether. Faced with his nefarious schemes—as well as several villains who try to abscond with their fortune—the Addams clan is subjected to a number of miserable situations, yet they'd have it no other way.

Aimed at kids, this animated series watered down the macabre nature of the famous family, and put more emphasis on their "kooky" aspect. This increase in the silliness quotient works fine for the target audience, but fans of the original series will be disappointed by the changes. The character designs are based on the original drawings of Charles Addams, but not as closely as the previous incarnation from 1973. Their new arch-nemesis, Norman Normanmeyer, seems to be a less-snarky take on the persona of Paul Lynde.

📺 The creative consultant for this series was Barbara Estella Barb (credited as "The Lady Colyton"); she was briefly married to Charles Addams from 1954 to 1956, and wound up controlling the television and movie rights.

The Addams Family Fun-House

ABC. Aug 19, 1973. Comedy/Music. D: Anon. W: Jack Riley, Liz Torres. C: Jack Riley, Liz Torres, Stubby Kaye, Pat McCormack, Butch Patrick, Jim Nabors. USA: English/Color/30m. Viacom Enterprises.

Produced in late 1972 (but broadcast in August of 1973), this pilot for a musical variety show featured an all-new cast of the Addams Family as they "welcome great guests for comedy, song and dance." The public disliked seeing Charles Addams' famous family in such a different light; the series would have featured a new guest star each week, but the concept never made it past the pilot stage. Just as well, because a similar idea led to one season of *The Brady Bunch Variety Hour* (1976), and most associated with that train wreck—including the unfortunate audience—would just as soon forget it ever happened.

Alias – "Nocturne"

ABC. Feb 9, 2005 (S04E06). Action/Adventure. D: Lawrence Trilling. W: Jeff Pinkner. C: Jennifer Garner, Ron Rifkin, Michael Vartan, Victor Garber, Michael A. Goorjian, Kevin Weisman. USA: English/Color/60m. Bad Robot/Touchstone Television/Buena Vista International Television.

Follows the adventures of a graduate student who moonlights as a secret agent. In this episode, Sydney loses touch with reality after being infected with a hallucinogen during a fight with a rogue CIA agent.

Undead red herrings abound: Sydney gets bitten on the neck by a crazed agent, whose ramblings on paper show Nosferatu-like creatures and the word "vampire." The hallucinogenic drug is called "nocturne," and the sleazy dealer is nicknamed "The Count." Heck, the story even takes place in Romania. But alas, no vampires here—just an unstable man who bites Sydney, passing on a chemical originally designed to suppress a soldier's need for sleep.

Alvin and the Chipmunks – "Trick or Treason"

USA Network. Oct 28, 1994. Comedy/Family. D: Walt Kubiak. W: Janice Karman, Ross Bagdasarian. C: Ross Bagdasarian, Janice Karman, Vanessa Bagdasarian, Michael Bagdasarian. USA: English/Color/22m. Bagdasarian Productions Inc.

Alvin desperately wants to be a part of "The Monster Club," a group of kids with cruel intentions; they think it's cool to make jokes at the expense of others. Their current target is Michael, a kid with a facial deformity whom they nicknamed "pumpkinhead." Alvin must decide if it's more important to be a member of this exclusive group, or be true to his friends.

The story is a good life lesson for kids, however adults may find the shrill voices of the Chipmunks too much to bear, especially in their rendition of Bobby "Boris" Pickett's novelty song "Monster Mash." On the cover of the 2006 DVD release, Alvin appears dressed as a vampire, although this never actually happens in the story.

Animaniacs – "Scare Happy Slappy" / "Witch One" / "Macbeth"

FOX. May 3, 1994 (S01E62). Comedy/Family. D: Michael Gerard, Jeff Siergey, Jon McClenahan. W: John P. McCann. C: Rob Paulsen, Jess Harnell, Tress MacNeille, Colin Wells. USA: English/Color/30m. Amblin Entertainment/Warner Bros. Television Animation.

This episode includes the short "Randy Beaman's Pal #6," where Colin relates a story about his friend Randy—who encounters Dracula (we never see the vampire, only hear of him). Seventeen of these shorts were produced, which feature the thirty-second ramblings of a young boy who tells tall tales.

Banned From the Bible II

History Channel. Apr 8, 2007. History/Religion. D: Geoffrey Madeja. W: Marcy Marzuki. C: Kenneth Hanson, David Copeland, Linda Moulton Howe, Duane L. Dobbert, Jacque Vallee. CAN: English/Color/100m. A&E Networks Inc.

Explores several books that were excluded from the Biblical canon, including the legend of Lilith, Adam's first wife. Narrated by Edward Herrmann.

The Ben Stiller Show – Pilot

FOX. Sep 27, 1992 (S01E01). Comedy/Satire. D: Paul Miller. W: Ben Stiller, Judd Apatow. C: Ben Stiller, Janeane Garofalo, Andy Dick, Bob Odenkirk, Roseanne Arnold, Garry Shandling, Tom Arnold, Dave Madden. USA: English/Color/22m. HBO Independent Productions.

In the sketch "Cape Munster" (a parody of 1992 film *Cape Fear*), former child delinquent Eddie Munster is released from prison. He exacts revenge on a television producer whom he believes was responsible for canceling *The Munsters*. Eddie is covered in tattoos, including the words "Fester is mine" and "Grampa sucks."

Canadian Reflections – "Carpathian Tales" / "Wild Voices"

CBC. Apr 6, 1980. Folklore/History. D: J. Fijalkowski. W: Mihail Corvinus. C: Anon. CAN: English/Color/15m. CBC.

The segment "Carpathian Tales" takes a look at the highly superstitious Romanian peasants who populate the small villages on the slopes of the Carpathian Mountains. Narrated by William Whitehead.

City Guys – "Video Killed the Radio Star"

NBC. Dec 1, 2001 (S05E22). Comedy/Family. D: Frank Bonner. W: Bernie Ancheta. C: Wesley Jonathan, Scott Whyte, Caitlin Mowrey, Dion Basco, Marissa Dyan, Steven Daniel, Marcella Lowery, Nadiyah Jones, Amanda Ware. USA: English/Color/20m. Peter Engel Productions.

The school receives funding to start up a TV department, so Dawn, Cassidy, El-Train and Al create a show called *Muffy the Werewolf Slapper*. Their production is sabotaged right around the same time that radio hosts Chris and Jamal discover that the TV show is stealing their audience.

Average fanged fare where this spoof of *Buffy the Vampire Slayer*—which features cheerleader Muffy, her pal Sunset, and two werewolves named Howl and L-Fang—is the best part of the episode. Truthfully, *Muffy* is more entertaining than the original *Buffy* feature film.

Community – "Origins of Vampire Mythology"

NBC. Apr 12, 2012 (S03E15). Comedy/Culture. D: Steven Tsuchida. W: Dan Harmon. C: Joel McHale, Gillian Jacobs, Danny Pudi, Yvette Nicole Brown, Alison Brie, Donald Glover, Jim Rash. USA: English/Color/22m. Harmonius Claptrap/Krasnoff Foster Productions.

The Bar Association suspends lawyer Jeff Winger after discovering he falsified his education; he enrolls at a Community College, and creates a study group so he can be closer to a fellow student. In this episode, Britta's ex-boyfriend is in town with a traveling carnival. He's bad news, but Britta can't resist him—so she asks Annie to stop her from going anywhere near him.

Her ex-boyfriend's name is Blade; this leads to several scenes where his namesake (the half human/half vampire from the movies and comic books) is mentioned. Aside from numerous references to the feature film *Blade* (1998), there are no real vampires here.

The Cosby Show – "Adventures in Babysitting"

NBC. Feb 7, 1991 (S07E17). Comedy/Family. D: Oz Scott. W: Steve Kline. C: Bill Cosby, Phylicia Rashad, Keshia Knight Pulliam, Raven-Symoné. USA: English/Color/30m. Bill Cosby/Carsey-Werner Company/NBC.

Rudy babysits Olivia while the Huxtables are away at a pinochle tournament. The girls watch *Vampire-Werewolves of London* on TV, then barricade themselves in the bedroom—because they believe the creatures are lurking outside. They leave several traps throughout the house, hoping the devices will keep the beasts at bay.

No real vampires here, but the kids' reaction to the horror movie—and the scenes involving the imagined vampire-werewolves—are pretty funny. Cliff and Clair return home to find the two asleep, surrounded by cloves of garlic. Rudy holds a cross made out of a wooden fork and spoon, while Olivia clutches a piece of meat—a "steak" to drive through the vampire's heart. The premise of *Vampire-Werewolves of London* is intriguing: a man is a vampire on most nights, unless it's a full moon—when he turns into a vampire-werewolf. Finally, a mixed breed destined to put a stop all those regrettable vampire/werewolf conflicts.

📺 This episode may have been inspired by Bill Cosby's famous "Chicken Heart" comedy routine, in which he confesses that as a child he believed that stories from the old-time radio shows (like *Lights Out*) were actually real. To prevent the monsters from getting him, he'd smear Jell-O all over the floor—so they'd slip and fall.

Counterstrike – "In the Blood"

USA Network/CTV. Dec 7, 1991 (S02E12). Action/Adventure. D: René Bonnière. W: Michael Leo Donovan. C: Simon MacCorkindale, Christopher Plummer, Nigel Bennett, James Purcell, Ariana Cervenka. CAN/FRA: English/Color/60m. Alliance Communications/Gaumont Télévision/Grosso Jacobson.

Alexander sends his team to protect a rising tennis sensation, Carmilla Jannovic, who received a death threat after her coach was murdered—but his replacement has a sinister plan in store for her. This story appears to be about a blood doping scheme, and probably has no vampiric element (even though characters are named Carmilla and Vlad). This series has yet to be released into the home video market, so no confirmation can be made about specific elements of the story.

Dark Prince: The True Story of Dracula

USA Network. Oct 31, 2000. Drama/History. D: Joe Chappelle. W: Tom Baum. C: Rudolph Martin, Jane March, Roger Daltrey, Michael Sutton, Christopher Brand, Peter Weller. USA: English/Color/88m. The Kushner-Locke Company.

As Vlad Țepeș wages war against the Ottoman Empire, the Orthodox Church questions his methods and allegiances: he's accused of horrific acts against his own people, abandoning his religion, and conspiring with the Papacy in Rome. To avoid excommunication—which may put his very soul at risk—Vlad recounts tales of his past to refute the misconceptions about him.

Don't let the cheesy DVD cover art fool you; there are no vampires here, which is actually refreshing for a tale about Vlad Țepeș—who's still considered a national hero in Romania. Most stories about the Wallachian prince turn him into a vampire at some point, but this one avoids that trap—although it is far from being the "true" story of Dracula. The creators have taken liberties with dates, places, events, and characters—and have made Vlad much more of a romantic hero.

📺 Probably the most accurate (yet one-sided) biopic about Vlad is the Romanian film *Vlad Țepeș* (1979). Worthwhile viewing if you can hunt it down.

Days of Our Lives – Ep. #10710

ABC. Sep 21, 2011 (S42E181). Drama/Romance. D: Michael V. Pomarico. W: Lorraine Broderick, Addie Walsh. C: Eva La Rue, Bobbie Eakes, Vincent Irizarry, Ricky Paull Goldin, Cady McClain, Debbi Morgan. USA: English/Color/60m. Creative Horizons/ABC.

Sarah Michelle Gellar has a cameo role as a patient who claims that vampires are everywhere—and they're out to get her! She also believes that she's the daughter of Erica Kane, and that the people and places of Pine Valley seem eerily familiar. In this character mash-up, Gellar is ostensibly playing the role of Buffy Summers from *Buffy the Vampire Slayer,* and the person she claims to be—Kendall Hart Lang—is a character she portrayed on *Days of Our Lives* from 1993 to 1995.

Deadliest Warrior – "Vlad the Impaler vs. Sun Tzu"

Spike. Jun 29, 2010 (S02E10). History/War. D: Michael S. Ojeda. W: Anon. C: Geoffrey Desmoulin, Armand Dorian, Max Geiger, Vaclav Havlik, Brahm Gallagher, Johnny Yang, Tommy Leng, Rusty Locke. USA: English/Color/42m. 44 Blue Productions/Morningstar Entertainment.

This series tests history's deadliest weapons, using twenty-first century technology to pit two legendary warriors against one another. In this episode, the infamous Wallachian prince Vlad Țepeș, known as The Impaler, faces off against the Chinese master strategist Sun Tzu, author of *The Art of War*. It's brute strength versus precision fighting—who will claim victory? Narrated by Drew Skye.

This testosterone-infused farce of a program actually provides a relatively accurate history of Vlad and his methods, despite one expert commenting that he liked to dip bread into the blood of his enemies—a fable that has never been proven. For those interested in seeing dead pigs repeatedly hacked into pieces by ancient weaponry, or perhaps a graphic reconstruction of an impalement using a lifelike human body: this episode is for you. But for the majority who would never touch this with a ten-foot pole, I'll let you in on a little secret: Vlad wins the competition!

The Flintstone Kids – "Frankenstone" / "Yard Wars" / "Freezy Does It"

ABC. Sep 13, 1986. Comedy/Family. D: Anon. W: Mel Gilden, John K. Ludin. C: Lennie Weinrib, Hamilton Camp, Julie Dees, B.J. Ward, Marilyn Schreffler, Susan Blu, Mel Blanc. USA: English/B&W, Color/30m. Hanna-Barbera Productions Inc.

This series reimagines the Bedrock gang as children, with an assorted cast of new characters who take part in their adventures. In the segment "Frankenstone," Freddy and Barney fix broken toys to earn some money. The kids let their imaginations run wild, and create the ultimate Pebble Patch doll: it walks, talks, and ties its own shoes. But the creation—"Frankenpebble"—runs amok, taking Wilma hostage.

With the title of "Frankenstone," one is reminded of *The Flintstones Meet Rockula and Frankenstone* (1980). But unlike that classic, there are no vampires here—and the story is geared towards a much younger audience.

Foster's Home for Imaginary Friends – "Squeakerboxxx"

Cartoon Network. May 13, 2005 (S02E08). Comedy/Family. D: Craig McCracken. W: Craig Lewis. C: Grey DeLisle, Keith Ferguson, Tom Kane, Tom Kenny, Phil LaMarr, Sean Marquette, Candi Milo. USA: English/Color/23m. Cartoon Network.

The gang wins lots of tickets at the arcade, except for Bloo; when it comes time to turn them in for prizes, he comes up short. He wants a set of glow-in-the-dark Dracula teeth, and convinces his friends to pool their tickets to claim a shared prize—but instead of the teeth, they choose a pink elephant that squeaks.

A charming episode, especially if you ever obsessed over owning a pair of fake vampire teeth. Seriously, who wants a pink elephant when you can have poorly-fitting plastic teeth, which make you drool uncontrollably and render you completely inarticulate?

Frankenstein Jr. and The Impossibles – "Smogula" / "The Alien Brain From Outer Space, Part 1" / "The Sinister Speck"

CBS. Oct 1, 1966 (S01E04). Adventure/Family. D: William Hanna, Joseph Barbera. W: Michael Maltese. C: Ted Cassidy, Dick Beals, Don Messick, Hal Smith, Paul Frees, John Stephenson. USA: English/Color/30m. Hanna-Barbera Productions Inc.

In the segment "Smogula," a villain threatens to conquer Empire City—and if he faces any resistance from The Impossibles, he'll just obliterate it instead. There's not a bloody fang to be found in this story, but it's listed because writers often come up with vampire character names that are a take on "Dracula." In this case, "Smogula" is simply a generic villain with weather-based weapons, who rides around in a large, gray cloud.

Frankenstein Jr. and The Impossibles – "The Anxious Angler" / "The Mad Monster Maker" / "The Rascally Ringmaster"

CBS. Dec 17, 1966 (S01E15). Adventure/Family. D: William Hanna, Joseph Barbera. W: Eddie Brandt. C: Ted Cassidy, Dick Beals, Don Messick, Hal Smith, Paul Frees, John Stephenson. USA: English/Color/30m. Hanna-Barbera Productions Inc.

In the segment "The Mad Monster Maker," Baron von Ghoul—a former movie director—hides out in an abandoned studio, where he assembles three colossal creatures from his old horror films. After the Baron sets them loose on the city, it's up to Buzz and his thirty-foot crime-fighting robot Frankie to stop the rampaging cine-monsters.

The crime fighting duo includes a Frankenstein Monster; they battle Baron von Ghoul, a madman who creates three creatures: a werewolf, a mummy, and…a giant firefly? Really? This story needs a vampire, but Baron von Ghoul obviously never made any *Dracula* pictures.

Freddie – "Halloween"

ABC. Oct 26, 2005 (S01E03). Comedy/Family. D: John Pasquin. W: Conrad Jackson. C: Freddie Prinze Jr., Jacqueline Obradors, Brian Austin Green, Jenny Gago, Chloe Suazo, Mädchen Amick, Benjamin King. USA: English & Spanish/Color/21m. Hunga Rican/Excitable Boy!.

Freddie Moreno's life gets complicated after his grandmother, sister, niece, and sister-in-law move in with him. In this episode, young Zoe is stuck without a costume for school, because her mom accidentally ruined her vampire outfit in the wash. The replacement getup that Freddie makes for Zoe is an absolute disaster; to make amends, he sneaks her into a theater to watch *The Rocky Horror Picture Show*. It's an average episode that tries too hard to get laughs, however, seeing Brian Austin Green dressed as Frank-N-Furter almost makes up for it.

Ghost in the Water

BBC One. Dec 31, 1982. Family/Fantasy. D: Renny Rye. W: Geoffrey Case. C: Judith Allchurch, Ian Stevens, Jane Freeman, Joanne James, Dave Mitty, Lynda Higginson, Hilary Mason, Paul Marks, Paul Copley, Daniel D'Arcy ☥. UK: English/Color/50m. BBC.

In this story, adapted from the book of the same name by Edward Chitman, a young girl is drawn into past events after she investigates the death of a blood relative who died in 1860. The woman drowned, and her family believed she committed suicide after her lover was killed in a mining accident—but the girl discovers the real truth behind the unfortunate event. Daniel D'Arcy is credited as playing Dracula in the production, which is true. However, he has nothing to do with the actual story; he briefly appears in a film that the young girl, Teresa, watches on television.

The Ghost Writer

FOX. Aug 15, 1990. Comedy/Family. D: Alan Rafkin. W: Alan Spencer. C: Anthony Perkins, Leigh Taylor-Young, Joshua Miller, Juliet Sorcey, Pam Matteson ☥, Cindy Sorenson, Lisabeth Aubrey, Kurt Paul. USA: English/Color/27m. Alan Spencer Productions/The Indieprod Company.

Acclaimed horror author Anthony Strack suffers from writer's block, and he's distracted by recent family issues. His new wife and daughter have moved in; they're having difficulty adjusting to life with his teenage son and their eccentric housekeeper. Ten years ago, Strack's first wife died after an accident in the home—and now that there's a new woman in his life, her ghost has returned to protest the union.

This failed pilot, written by the creator of the excellent *Sledge Hammer!* TV series, is a cross between *Soap* and *The Brady Bunch,* with a touch of *The Addams Family.* The star attraction is Anthony Perkins, who shows off his comedic side; he's having as much fun as the live audience. Equally entertaining is Joshua Miller; he plays Perkins' son, a macabre teen who fancies himself the anti-Christ. Pam Matteson channels Madeline Kahn in her humorous turn as Miss Blasko, the housekeeper; she's probably not a vampire, but certainly comes off as one.

"Miss Blasko" alludes to Béla Blaskó, better known as Bela Lugosi, the actor most famous for his iconic turn as Dracula.

Halloween Monster Bash

NBC. Oct 1991. Culture/Film. D/W: Larry Thomas. C: John Astin, Bobby Kelton, Rhonda Shear, S.D. "Doc" Nemeth, Bobby "Boris" Pickett. USA: English/Color/46m. MOSO Productions/Larry Thomas Productions/Goodman Entertainment Group Inc.

John Astin hosts this Halloween special that showcases various B-movie classics, with additional running commentary from co-hosts Bobby Kelton, Rhonda Shear, and S.D. Nemeth. Also features a performance of "Monster Mash" by Bobby "Boris" Pickett.

This TV special has largely been forgotten, with good reason; it has a cringe-worthy script and extremely low production values. Dressed as Gomez Addams, John Astin navigates through a series of lesser-known B movies—the most recognizable is *Night of the Living Dead* (1968)—while his questionable co-hosts utter bad puns and even worse scripted commentary. The program also features clips from: *The Evil Mind* (1934), The Human Monster (1939), *Invisible Ghost* (1941), *The Corpse Vanishes* (1942), *The Ape Man* (1943), *Creature from the Haunted Sea* (1961), *Dementia 13* (1963), *The Terror* (1963), *The Devil's Nightmare* (1971), *Horror Express* (1972), *The Loch Ness Horror* (1981), and *Blood Song* (1982).

Halloween with the New Addams Family

NBC. Oct 30, 1977. Comedy/Family. D: Dennis Steinmetz. W: George Tibbles. C: John Astin, Carolyn Jones, Jackie Coogan, Ted Cassidy, Vito Scotti, Henry Darrow, Jane Rose. USA: English/Color/74m. Charles Fries Productions Inc./Wilshire Productions Inc./Worldvision Enterprises Inc.

As Gomez and Morticia Addams prepare their home for a Halloween party, a band of criminals are planning a heist. They want to crash the festivity in disguise, and steal whatever valuables they can find.

The cast from the original television series has returned, including the grown-up actors who played Wednesday and Pugsley; two new children, Wednesday Jr. and Pugsley Jr., are played by young actors. It's definitely strange seeing the famous macabre family in full color, but the main problem lies with the horrible script—it's a major disappointment. This was intended as a pilot for a new series, but wasn't picked up by any network.

Hammer House of Horror – "Carpathian Eagle"

ITV. Nov 8, 1980 (S01E09). Horror/Suspense. D: Francis Megahy. W: Bernie Cooper, Francis Megahy. C: Anthony Valentine, Suzanne Danielle, Siân Phillips, Barry Stanton, Jonathan Kent, Matthew Long, Ellis Dale, Pierce Brosnan. UK: English/Color/53m. Chips Productions Ltd./Hammer Films.

Unwanted guests crash Morticia and Gomez's festive fall party in the TV movie *Halloween with the New Addams Family* (Charles Fries Productions Inc/Wilshire Productions Inc)

Author Natalie Bell's latest true crime novel is based on a three-hundred-year-old Carpathian legend, in which a Countess murdered over one hundred of her young lovers by ripping out their hearts. After two men are murdered in the same manner as detailed in the book, Det. Inspector Clifford believes that there's a copycat killer on the loose—and he has a short list of suspects, considering the novel hasn't yet been published.

This Hammer production has no vampires, although the inspector jokes that the killer is actually the Countess herself—a "Lady Dracula" who has survived the ages by devouring the hearts of young men (the myth alludes to the legend of Countess Elizabeth Báthory). It's a very suspenseful and well-acted episode that keeps you hooked right up until the macabre twist ending, even though the killer's identity is revealed halfway through the story.

The Highwayman – "Billionaire Body Club"

NBC. Apr 15, 1988 (S01E06). Action/Sci-Fi. D: Ivan Nagy. W: Glen A. Larson. C: Sam J. Jones, Mark Jackson, Jane Badler, Tim Russ, Christopher McDonald, Cindy Morgan, Kim Ulrich, Ken Swofford, Mark Lonow, Ed Hooks. USA: English/Color/48m. New West Entertainment.

A cross between *Knight Rider* and *Mad Max,* this series takes place in a world "just beyond now," where a group of lawmen—aided by a futuristic, high-tech transport truck—patrols the outer fringes of society while investigating bizarre crimes. In this episode, bodies are found in shallow graves, completely drained of blood, and some are missing organs. The Highwayman believes that a renowned transplant surgeon, Joshua Towler, is having healthy people killed—so he can use their organs to restore the failing health of his rich clients.

Towler is facetiously referred to as a vampire; the story plays with this theme, and he even tries on a red-lined opera cape for a masquerade ball (and Dracula is mentioned in passing). Despite a promising opening that almost screams "vampire!" there are no undead creatures here. The first body is unearthed in a cemetery by a film crew, while shooting an exercise video titled *So You Wanna Beat the Grave?* Too bad the rest of the episode doesn't live up to this inspired scene.

Home to Roost – "Open House"

ITV. Sep 12, 1986 (S02E02). Comedy/Family. D: David Reynolds. W: Eric Chappell. C: John Thaw, Reece Dinsdale, Elizabeth Bennett, John Rowe, Jean Rimmer, Julia Gilbert. UK: English/Color/25m. Yorkshire Television.

Series follows the relationship between a divorced man, Henry Willows, and his eighteen-year-old son Matthew—both of whom have a hard time adjusting to living under the same roof. In this episode, after his father returns home early from a business trip, Matthew attempts to hide the fact that he's having a party. One of his friends is a statuesque woman nicknamed Dracula; she's a *femme fatale* who works at a mortuary, and takes a liking to Henry.

Hungarian Dracula

MTV. 1983. Adventure/Drama. D: Géza Böszörményi. W: Péter Müller. C: Dzsokó Rossich, Gábor Reviczky, Ildikó Bánsági, András Bálint. HUN: Hungarian/Color/70m. Magyar Televízió Művelödési Föszerkesztöség.

This production is listed in a couple of vampire books because it has "Dracula" in the title—but it's not a *Dracula* adaptation. The story has nothing to do with the undead; it's about a professional boxer who's nicknamed "Hungarian Dracula."

It's What's Happening, Baby!

CBS. Jun 28, 1965. Comedy/Music. D: Barry Shear. W: Anon. C: Fred Gwynne, Ray Charles, Marvin Gaye, Bill Cosby, Martha Reeves and the Vandellas, The Supremes, The Ronettes, Jan and Dean, The Dave Clark Five, The Temptations. USA: English/B&W/90m. CBS Productions.

Hosted by influential disc jockey Murray the "K," this variety special promoted government services from the U.S. Office of Economic Opportunity, and included performances from popular musical acts of the day. An extended built-in commercial for the "New Chance" program featured Fred Gwynne as Herman Munster, who wanders through a beach party and terrifies all the dancing teenagers (they faint at the sight of him). He chats with Murray the "K" about the program, gives the mailing address, then continues on his journey.

Kung Fu: The Legend Continues – "Sunday at the Museum with George"

Syndicated. Oct 31, 1994 (S02E18). Action/Fantasy. D: Jon Cassar. W: Michael Sloan. C: David Carradine, Chris Potter, Robert Lansing, Geordie Johnson, Michele Scarabelli, Patrick Monckton, Scott Wentworth. CAN/USA: English/Color/44m. Warner Bros. Television.

Caine worries about the patrons attending an upcoming museum gala. There's a new exhibit of priceless objects connected to an ancient, bloodthirsty Chinese warrior—including his sarcophagus. He believes that thieves are going to steal from the collection, and their actions will awaken the soul of the ruthless warlord—and release a deadly curse upon everyone in attendance.

The man behind the robbery is George Vladpallin, a master thief played by actor Geordie Johnson; this performance is a sly nod to his role as Alexander Lucard from *Dracula: The Series* (1990). Often it's as if Vladpallin is Lucard himself; he has a mesmerizing effect on women, and in one scene, he runs into a Bat Cave exhibit—and disappears. Johnson's performance is the highlight of this episode, which is otherwise horribly acted and silly beyond belief. There's a brief mention of Vlad the Impaler, and although the Chinese warrior drank the blood of his victims, he wasn't a vampire.

MADtv – Ep. #3.23

FOX. May 2, 1998 (S03E23). Comedy/Satire. D: Paul Miller. W: Fax Bahr. C: Alex Borstein, Nicole Sullivan, Will Sasso, Lisa Kushell, Pat Kilbane, Chris Hogan, Debra Wilson, Aries Spears, Mary Scheer. USA: English/Color/60m. Bahr-Small Productions/David Salzman Entertainment.

In the "Celebrity Funeral" sketch, David Boreanaz shows up for a friend's wake, much to the delight of those in attendance. Rather than mourn the loss of the deceased, the group inundates the actor with questions about his character Angel from *Buffy the Vampire Slayer*. Boreanaz also appears as himself in the first "This 'N' That with Rusty" sketch (S06E14), when nerdy host Rusty Miller visits the set of *Angel*.

The Making of "The Addams Family"

UPN. Dec 7, 1991. Culture/Media. D: Anon. W: Anon. C: Anjelica Huston, Raul Julia, Christopher Lloyd, Christina Ricci, Dan Hedaya, Jimmy Workman, Christopher Hart, Carel Struycken, M.C. Hammer. USA: English/Color/30m. Backstage Productions.

An inside look at the making of the 1991 film *The Addams Family,* featuring interviews with cast and crew, and the debut of the new M. C. Hammer music video "Addams Groove."

The Man from U.N.C.L.E. – "The Bat Cave Affair"

NBC. Apr 1, 1966 (S02E28). Action/Spy. D: Alf Kjellin. W: Jerry McNeely. C: Robert Vaughn, David McCallum, Leo G. Carroll, Joan Freeman, Martin Landau. USA: English/Color/50m. Arena Productions/MGM Television.

Kuryakin travels to Transylvania in search of Count Zark, who plans to use bats with altered sonar to interfere with defense systems worldwide. After Kuryakin gets caught, Zark gives him a first-hand look at his colony of vampire bats; he chose this species because they're perfect for such an evil scheme—and they're the most bloodthirsty.

No real bloodsuckers here, although the vampire bats attack Kuryakin. Martin Landau, who shines as Count Zark, both looks and sounds like a stereotypical Count Dracula (although he's never called a vampire by name). This shows how deeply Bela Lugosi's iconic portrayal is embedded in our popular culture; even without mentioning "vampire" or "Dracula," the audience can still easily identify the character.

Three decades later, Martin Landau won an Academy Award for his portrayal of Bela Lugosi in *Ed Wood* (1994).

Monsters – "Half as Old as Time"

Syndicated. Dec 17, 1989 (S02E11). Horror/Suspense. D: Christopher Todd. W: Thomas Babe, Taenha Goodrich, Jake West. C: Leif Garrett, Valerie Wildman, Nick Ramus. USA: English/Color/22m. Laurel EFX Inc./Tribune Broadcasting Company/Worldvision Enterprises Inc.

A man with terminal cancer gets help from his estranged daughter, an archaeologist who knows the location of a secret Native American temple. It contains a pool of water believed to cure all ills; after the man imbibes the liquid, both his youth and health are restored—but immortality comes at a very high price.

This dialogue-heavy story features a human monster, who sacrifices the life of his daughter so he can remain healthy forever. He should have read the fine print; he's granted "eternal youth," which really means that time will just pass slowly for him. One second will last a month and one minute will last a decade, for all of eternity—essentially turning him to stone. This could have been an interesting study of mankind's strive for immortality, but the poor acting and unimaginative execution just make for a really dull episode.

The New Addams Family

FOX Family/YTV. Oct 19, 1998 – May 29, 1999 (65 Episodes). Comedy/Family. D: Ed Anders. W: Arnold Rudnick, Rich Hosek. C: Glenn Taranto, Ellie Harvie, Brody Smith, Nicole Fugère, Betty Phillips, Michael Roberds, John DeSantis. CAN: English/Color/1950m. Shavick Entertainment/Saban Entertainment.

A contemporary version of the 1960s sitcom featuring a different cast of actors except for John

Astin, who plays Gomez's grandfather. The iconic theme from the original series was not used, but several of its storylines were reworked and updated to reflect the world of the 1990s.

The New Scooby-Doo Movies – "Wednesday Is Missing"

CBS. Sep 23, 1972 (S01E03). Adventure/Comedy. D: William Hanna, Joseph Barbera. W: Jameson Brewer. C: Casey Kasem, Don Messick, Frank Welker, Heather North, Nicole Jaffe, John Astin, Carolyn Jones, Jackie Coogan, Jodie Foster. USA: English/Color/42m. Hanna-Barbera Productions Inc./CBS.

🦇🦇🦇

The Mystery Machine breaks down on a foggy night, so the amateur sleuths seek refuge in a nearby mansion. It's the home of the Addams Family; mistaken for housekeepers, the gang babysits the kids while Gomez and Morticia spend the weekend away. Wary of their surroundings, they have to explore the creepy estate after Wednesday Addams is kidnapped by a mysterious stranger.

The eccentric, macabre clan from the classic 1960s sitcom lives on in *The New Addams Family* (Shavick Entertainment/Saban Entertainment)

It's a treat seeing the Scooby gang alongside this first animated incarnation of the Addams Family, even though the jokes are lame and the canned laughter gets on your nerves. The story is standard fare, but there's a neat twist: the Scooby gang has prior knowledge of the Addams clan, because they've seen them on TV. Voiced by four of the main cast members from the original live-action series, this appearance led to their own spin-off cartoon in 1973 (although John Astin and Carolyn Jones didn't participate in that series).

The Norliss Tapes

NBC. Feb 21, 1973. Drama/Horror. D: Dan Curtis. W: William F. Nolan, Fred Mustard Stewart. C: Roy Thinnes, Angie Dickinson, Claude Akins, Don Porter, Nick Dimitri. USA: English/Color/72m. Metromedia Producers Corporation/Dan Curtis Productions Inc.

🦇🦇🦇

David Norliss had planned to write a book about the commercialization of spiritualism and the occult, to expose the phonies who make millions of dollars off of their gullible victims. But after a year of research, he's too terrified to put pen to paper; after a frantic call to his publisher, Norliss disappears. He leaves behind a series of audio cassettes on which he recorded his research, beginning with a fateful meeting with Ellen Cort—a widow who claims that she was attacked by her recently-deceased husband.

Blood and immortality play important roles, but this story is about a zombie—not a vampire. The husband, James Cort, was a sculptor who got involved in the occult just before he died from a terminal illness. He possessed an Egyptian ring that brought him back to life, yet he's not much more than a mindless zombie with a single task. Using blood-laced clay, he's creating a sculpture of a demon; once completed, the statue will come to life—and the demon will grant Cort immortality. More serious in tone than *The Night Stalker* (1972), this is another fine production from Dan Curtis, with solid acting, an interesting story, and a few genuine scares. Meant as a pilot for a weekly series, the story is left open-ended—so the supernatural adventures of David Norliss end here.

William F. Nolan penned a sequel, *The Return,* where Norliss goes back in time and encounters his boyhood self. According to the writer, the script was bought by NBC but never produced, because the 1973 Writers Guild of America strike "killed the Norliss series."

The Ray Bradbury Theater – "The Emissary"

USA Network. Feb 13, 1988 (S03E03). Mystery/Sci-Fi. D: Sturla Gunnarsson. W: Ray Bradbury. C: Helen Shaver, Keram Malicki-Sanchez, Linda Goranson, Neil Munro, Stuart Kenny, Eric Hebert. CAN: English/Color/26m. Atlantis Films Limited/Wilcox Productions Inc.

Due to an illness, teenager Martin Bailey is confined to bed. He relies on his loyal dog to keep him connected to the outside world, and lives vicariously through his pet's outdoor adventures. After Martin attaches a note to the dog explaining his lonely situation, it returns with a schoolteacher, and the two become fast friends. She continues to stop by daily to visit the teen, but one day she doesn't show up—because she's been killed in a car accident. Saddened by the news, Martin laments that he'll never see her again—but his faithful dog digs her up in the cemetery. Under the light of a full moon, Martin's teacher comes back from the dead—but all we see is her pallid, decaying hand. It's not quite clear what sort of creature has returned, but in folklore, newly-undead vampires often visit friends and loved ones.

Rambo: The Force of Freedom – "Deadly Keep"

Syndicated. Sep 19, 1986 (S01E10). Adventure/Family. D: John Kimball, Charles A. Nichols. W: Matt Uitz. C: Neil Ross, Mona Marshall, Alan Oppenheimer, Peter Cullen, Michael Ansara, James Avery, Robert Ito. USA: English/Color/22m. Ruby-Spears Productions/Carolco International N.V.

John Rambo—based on the character from the 1982 film *First Blood*—is part of an elite military team that battles terrorists and other evildoers. In this episode, a Nobel Prize-winning physicist is kidnapped, because he discovered the secret to neutron fusion. The abductor is a Romanian named Count Vladimir, the great-grandson of Vlad the Impaler—and he's holding the physicist hostage in his ancestral home high atop the Moldavian mountains. Rambo and crew must find a way to breach the impenetrable fortress, before the Count can use the secret energy source for his own wicked purposes.

The majority of the action takes place at Vladimir's home, which vaguely resembles Poenari Castle—given a facelift. The Count claims that no one has been able to invade the fortress in the past four hundred years, yet Rambo manages to do so with a simple air balloon. This makes sense, because in this universe, Rambo can defy gravity, dodge bullets, and pretty much do anything that Superman can—except fly (although he can jump really high). One would think that turning an excessively violent Soldier of Fortune character into a children's cartoon hero would never work—and it doesn't.

Rambo: The Force of Freedom – "Return of the Count"

Syndicated. Oct 21, 1986 (S01E27). Adventure/Family. D: John Kimball, Charles A. Nichols. W: Matt Uitz. C: Neil Ross, Mona Marshall, Alan Oppenheimer, Peter Cullen, Michael Ansara, James Avery, Robert Ito. USA: English/Color/22m. Ruby-Spears Productions/Carolco International N.V.

On Halloween night, Colonel Trautman's nephew is abducted by a strange man who has pale skin and wears a cape—just like Dracula. Rambo discovers that an old foe has returned, and is once again in league with the terrorist organization known as S.A.V.A.G.E.

Another tepid story that features the return of Count Vladimir, descendent of Vlad the Impaler, who in this episode dons the guise of a vampire (I guess because it's Halloween?). It's not a stretch really, considering he already looks and sounds like Dracula—so all he had to do was slap on some white greasepaint. It's too bad the actor voicing the character has so much difficulty maintaining the accent; it often changes from scene to scene, and even line by line.

Rats, Bats and Bugs

History Channel. Oct 27, 2003. Culture/Nature. D/W: Karen Thorsen, Chris Gidez. C: Bruce A. Colvin, Elizabeth Miller, Doug Moench, Debbie Ducommun, Donald R. Griffin, Greg Auger. USA: English/Color/180m. HTV Productions/A&E Television Networks.

This three-part documentary—where science meets culture—explores the world of rats, bats and bugs, three creepy creatures that have troubled mankind throughout the ages. Includes a discussion of how bats are tied to vampire mythology. Presented by Alice Cooper and narrated by Harry Prichett.

Robot Chicken – "A Day at the Circus"

Cartoon Network. Oct 29, 2006 (S02E17). Adult/Comedy. D: Tom Root. W: Jordan Allen-Dutton, Mike Fasolo. C: Seth Green, Eugene Byrd, Leah Cevoli, Jamie Kaler, William Mapother, Lisa Rohr. USA: English/Color/12m. Shadowmachine Films/Stoopid Monkey/Williams Street.

This mediocre episode includes a segment where Thing (the disembodied hand from *The Addams Family*) goes through various life situations. Gomez and Morticia Addams believe that it's time for Thing to make a life of his own, so they send him off into the big bad world. He does remarkably well; he lands a good job, has an office romance, and even finds his true soul mate.

Saturday Night Live – Dolly Parton

NBC. Apr 15th, 1989 (S14E17). Comedy/Music. D: Paul Miller, Tom Schiller. W: James Downey, Conan O'Brien. C: Dana Carvey, Nora Dunn, Phil Hartman, Jan Hooks, Mike Myers, Al Franken, Jon Lovitz, Kevin Nealon, Dennis Miller, Ben Stiller. USA: English/Color/90m. Broadway Video/NBC.

Includes a "Sprockets" sketch, where Dieter welcomes Butch Patrick, the former child actor who played the werewolf Eddie on *The Munsters* (1964). The series has just become a hit in Germany, so the actor is capitalizing on his new-found popularity in the country—and he's dressed exactly like he was when he played Eddie twenty-five years earlier. Patrick claims that he still doesn't know what sort of creature Eddie is; Dieter believes that he was an energy vampire, since the interview becomes "tiresome." Hosted by Dolly Parton, who is also the musical guest.

Ben Stiller also portrayed an adult Eddie Munster in the pilot episode of his own sketch comedy series, *The Ben Stiller Show* (1992).

Ship's Reporter – Ep. #--

ABC. Dec 1951 (S--E--). Culture/News. D: Chick Vincent. W: Anon. C: Bela Lugosi. USA: English/B&W/15m. National Television Guild.

In this series, host Jack Mangan interviewed celebrities as they arrived or disembarked at New York Harbor. One of the interviews in this episode was with Bela Lugosi, who just returned from England after filming *Mother Riley Meets the Vampire* (which he calls "Vampire Over London"); he was also in a British touring production of *Dracula*. Of his career, and about being typecast as a horror star, Lugosi said that "Dracula never ends. I don't know whether I should call it a fortune or a curse, but it never ends." Aired in New York City on the local ABC affiliate WJZ-TV.

The Simpsons – "Lisa's Wedding"

FOX. Mar 19, 1995 (S06E19). Comedy/Satire. D: Jim Reardon. W: Greg Daniels. C: Dan Castellaneta, Julie Kavner, Nancy Cartwright, Yeardley Smith, Hank Azaria, Harry Shearer, Phil Hartman, Pamela Hayden, Maggie Roswell. USA: English/Color/22m. Gracie Films/20th Century Fox Television.

While attending the Springfield Renaissance Fair, Lisa visits a fortune teller who gives her a glimpse into the future—including events leading up to her wedding in 2010. There's minimal vampire content here: in the future, Kent Brockman—who now works for CNNBCBS (a division of ABC)—announces a list of celebrities who have recently been arrested; the names include "Senator and Mrs. Dracula."

The Simpsons – "A Fish Called Selma"

FOX. Mar 24, 1996 (S07E19). Comedy/Satire. D: Mark Kirkland. W: Jack Barth. C: Dan Castellaneta, Julie Kavner, Nancy Cartwright, Yeardley Smith, Hank Azaria, Harry Shearer, Jeff Goldblum, Phil Hartman, Pamela Hayden. USA: English/Color/22m. Gracie Films/20th Century Fox Television.

After being spotted by a reporter while on a date with Selma, has-been actor Troy McClure realizes that having a woman on his arm generates the positive press that he needs to restore his failing career. It's a fun episode with a minor vampire reference: after Homer suggests that Troy should make movies about World War II, the actor dismisses the idea because there's already been too many of them—so Homer proposes "Dracula" as an alternative (the gag being that there are probably even more movies about Dracula than World War II).

The Simpsons – "Treehouse of Horror VIII"

FOX. Oct 26, 1997 (S09E04). Comedy/Satire. D: Mark Kirkland. W: Mike Scully, David S. Cohen. C: Dan Castellaneta, Julie Kavner, Nancy Cartwright, Yeardley Smith, Hank Azaria, Harry Shearer, Marcia Wallace, Tress MacNeille, Maggie Roswell. USA: English/Color/22m. Gracie Films/20th Century Fox Television.

In the segment "The HΩmega Man," tensions mount between Springfield and France over an off-color joke by Mayor Quimby—and they want an apology. Quimby refuses, so the French annihilate the town with a neutron bomb. Homer—who escaped the blast—is now the last man on earth in a world populated by mutant freaks with a taste for human skin.

In this spoof of *The Omega Man* (1971), Homer plays the role made famous by Charlton Heston. This story has no vampires, but was based on the novel *I Am Legend* (1954) by Richard Matheson, an apocalyptic story about the sole survivor of a pandemic that has turned the rest of humanity into vampires.

Other adaptations of Matheson's novel include: *The Last Man on Earth* (1964) starring Vincent Price, *I Am Legend* (2007) starring Will Smith, and *I Am Ωmega* (2007) starring Mark Dacascos.

The Simpsons – "Simpson Tide"

FOX. Mar 29, 1998 (S09E19). Comedy/Satire. D: Milton Gray. W: Joshua Sternin, Jeffrey Ventimilia. C: Dan Castellaneta, Julie Kavner, Nancy Cartwright, Yeardley Smith, Hank Azaria, Harry Shearer, Rod Steiger, Bob Denver, Pamela Hayden. USA: English/Color/22m. Gracie Films/20th Century Fox Television.

Homer joins the Naval Reserve, and is assigned to a nuclear submarine because of his past work experience. His captain becomes incapacitated during a war games exercise, which puts Homer in charge—with disastrous results. As for vampires, while Homer is channel surfing, he comes across a promo for three exploitation films: *Blacula, Blackenstein,* and *The Blunchblack of Blotre Blame* (the first two are real movies).

The Simpsons – "Treehouse of Horror X"

FOX. Oct 31, 1999 (S11E04). Comedy/Satire. D: Pete Michels. W: Donick Cary, Tim Long. C: Dan Castellaneta, Julie Kavner, Nancy Cartwright, Yeardley Smith, Hank Azaria, Harry Shearer, Marcia Wallace, Pamela Hayden. USA: English/Color/22m. Gracie Films/20th Century Fox Television.

In the segment "I Know What You Diddily-Iddly-Did," the Simpsons are fleeing from a nest of vampires (unseen) when they inadvertently run over and kill Ned Flanders. After they try to cover up the accident by claiming he had a heart attack, Flanders returns from the dead to teach them all a lesson.

The Simpsons – "Tales from the Public Domain"

FOX. Mar 17, 2002 (S13E14). Comedy/Satire. D: Mike B. Anderson. W: Andrew Kreisberg, Josh Lieb. C: Dan Castellaneta, Julie Kavner, Nancy Cartwright, Yeardley Smith, Hank Azaria, Harry Shearer, Pamela Hayden, Tress MacNeille, Karl Wiedergott. USA: English/Color/22m. Gracie Films/20th Century Fox Television.

Homer receives an overdue notice from the library, for a children's book that he checked out just after Bart was born. He still hasn't read it, so he gathers his family and narrates the three tales within: "Homer's Odyssey," "Joan of Arc" and "Hamlet." No bloodsuckers here, but during the show opening, Bart writes on the blackboard *Vampire is Not a Career Choice*.

The Simpsons – "The Greatest Story Ever D'ohed"

FOX. Mar 28, 2010 (S21E16). Comedy/Satire. D: Michael Polcino. W: Michael Price. C: Dan Castellaneta, Julie Kavner, Nancy Cartwright, Yeardley Smith, Hank Azaria, Harry Shearer, Sacha Baron Cohen, Yael Naim, Pamela Hayden, Tress MacNeille. USA: English/Color/22m. Gracie Films/20th Century Fox Television.

In an attempt to make Homer a better man, Flanders offers to take the Simpsons on a pilgrimage to Israel. After getting lost in the desert, Homer becomes delusional; he believes he's the Messiah, given the divine task of uniting all faiths of the Holy Land. Prior to this earth-shattering event, while touring King David's tomb, Flanders begs Homer to turn off his video camera; he replies, "If you say it like Dracula I will." It's a slim vampire reference in an episode that has few laughs and is largely forgettable.

Starsky & Hutch – "Texas Longhorn"

ABC. Sep 17, 1975 (S01E02). Crime/Drama. D: Jack Starrett. W: Michael Mann. C: David Soul, Paul Michael Glaser, Antonio Fargas, Bernie Hamilton, Med Flory, Charles Napier, George Loros, Stefanie Auerbach. USA: English/Color/50m. Spelling-Goldberg Productions.

Starsky and Hutch investigate the case of two men who raped and murdered the wife of a Good Samaritan; he's hunting the killers, and plans to take the law into his own hands once he finds them. There are no vampires here, but during the investigation, the officers visit a blood bank. Starsky makes a disparaging remark about the attending nurse, saying "She is a vampire. Now that's the first lady vampire I ever met!" (In Season 2, Starsky and Hutch investigate a bloodthirsty killer who appears to be the real deal.)

The Steve Allen Show – Ep. #5.14

NBC. Jan 11, 1960 (S05E14). Comedy/Music. D: Dwight A. Hemion. W: Stan Burns, Herb Sargent. C: Steve Allen, Tony Bennett, Caroline Richter, Monica Zetterlund, Jayne Meadows, Louis Nye, Gabe Dell, Bill Dana. USA: English/Color/60m. Bell-Meadows Enterprises/NBC.

🦇 🦇 🦇

This episode features crooner Tony Bennett, Swedish singing sensation Monica Zetterlund, and comedienne Caroline Richter—in a humorous original monologue about a "friendly" divorce. In the "Wife of Frankenstein" sketch, Doctor Frankenstein makes a bride for his monster, which is on the loose and terrorizing locals. The doctor hopes that if the creature gets married and settles down, the added responsibility will set him straight.

This mock musical features familiar fiends, but Dracula is not one of them—despite being indicated as such in several print and online sources. Gabe Dell, who often plays Dracula in this variety series, takes on the role of the Bürgermeister. Steve Allen plays the madcap doctor, Jayne Meadows is the bride, while Louis Nye is the standout in his hilarious turn as the Frankenstein Monster.

Superspecial – "Nadia: From Romania with Love"

CBC. Nov 21, 1976 (S03E--). Culture/Sports. D: Anon. W: Tom Egan. C: Nadia Comăneci, Theodora Ungureanu. USA: English/Color/60m. Clerow Productions Inc./Radioteleviziunea/CBS.

Follows teenager Nadia Comăneci, the winner of three Olympic gold medals for gymnastics, as she returns home to showcase the sights and sounds of Romania. Includes performances by the

Bucharest Circus and popular Romanian entertainers—and a trip to Count Dracula's castle. Hosted by comedian Flip Wilson, this American/Romanian co-production was primarily recorded in Nadia's hometown of Oneşti (at the time, called Gheorghiu-Dej) in the Carpathian Mountains. In the United States, the program was broadcast on CBS two days later.

Tales of the Wizard of Oz – "The Reunion"

Syndicated. 1961 (S01E101). Adventure/Family. D: Harry Kerwin. W: Arthur Rankin Jr. C: Carl Banas, Corinne Conley, James Doohan, Peggi Loder, Larry D. Mann, Bernard Cowan, Alfie Scopp. USA: English/Color/5m. Rankin-Bass Productions/Crawley Films/Videocraft International.

The Wicked Witch returns to the Oz School for Sorcerers for a class reunion, where she reconnects with Frankie Dracula—her former high school crush—and her kooky friend, Velma Villain. Despite his last name, Frankie isn't a vampire—he's a Frankenstein Monster-type who sounds like Boris Karloff.

To the Ends of the Earth – "The Transylvanian Job"

Channel 4. Mar 30, 1997 (S01E02). Folklore/Nature. D: Neil Rawles. W: Mike Chamberlain. C: Anon. UK: English/Color/60m. Channel 4/Stampede.

This series of adventure documentaries explores the lesser-known parts of the planet. In this episode, two amateur archaeologists from Britain team up with a group of elderly Americans to search for lost treasure in Dracula country. Guided by an expert in the field, the group travels throughout Romania, where they're hampered by bureaucracy and personality conflicts.

True Horror – "Dracula"

History Channel. Nov 23, 2009 (S01E02). History/Literature. D/W: Ben Chanan. C: Mei Trow, Kim Newman, Tessa Dunlop, Mark Benecke, Laura Richards, David Holmes, Francis Magee, Barry Aird, Stuart Bowman, Dominykas Vaitiekunas. UK: English/Color/43m. Hardy Pictures.

This three-part docudrama series explores the truth behind real historical horror stories, and features dramatizations of actual events interspersed with interview clips from academics. In this episode, Vlad Ţepeş—the fifteenth century Voivod of Wallachia—imprisons three monks. As they await their fate, the two older men relate tales of Vlad's atrocities to Jacob, the youngest of their ranks.

This production is a unique, informative and entertaining way to tell the story of Vlad Ţepeş, and the dramatic segments are based on the famous tale of three monks who were unfortunate enough to meet him in person. Several versions of this anecdotal story exist, but they each have one thing in common: one monk lives to tell the tale. His name was Brother Jacob; after he left Vlad's castle, Jacob traveled to Austria, where he was interviewed by the German minstrel Michael Beheim. In 1463, his misadventure was turned into the poem "Story of a Bloodthirsty Madman Called Dracula of Wallachia"—and this singular account is most likely why the story of Vlad Țepeș was not lost to history.

Unnatural History – "Mythical Beasts and Monsters"

TLC. 1997 (S01E03). Folklore/History. D/W: Michael Tetrick. C: Roy Mackal, Scott Harriet, Michael Shermer. USA: English/Color/55m. Dove Four Point Entertainment.

Throughout history, different cultures have created similar stories—from brave warriors battling horrific monsters, to fiendish creatures stalking us in the night. This episode explores monsters of legend and folklore, including present-day creatures that still defy explanation. Narrated by Mark Hamill.

From Biblical monsters to the folklore of Greece and Japan, this program casts a wide net as it explores the creatures that have captivated humanity over the centuries—including modern-day enigmas such as Bigfoot and the Loch Ness Monster. It's a thorough look that still manages to inform, despite the vast number of topics covered. Shape shifters and werewolves are explored in detail, but there is only a passing reference to vampires. This allows for the inclusion of some of the lesser-known legends, which is acceptable, because the undead are the focus of another episode in this series: "Vampires & Witches."

Werewolf – "The Black Ship"

FOX. Aug 1, 1987 (S01E04). Horror/Suspense. D: James Darren. W: Allan Cole, Chris Bunch. C: John J. York, Lance LeGault, Stefan Gierasch, Claude Earl Jones, Chuck Connors, Lillian Garrett. USA: English/Color/23m. TriStar Television.

Eric Cord suffers from lycanthropy, and searches for the one responsible for his cursed bloodline—a malicious werewolf named Janos Skorzeny, whom he has to kill in order to be cured. In this episode, Eric meets Otto Renfield, a cantankerous old seaman who offers to help him find Skorzeny—but the man has a hidden agenda.

Eric travels from town to town in search of Skorzeny; along the way he helps locals with their problems, just like David Banner in *The Incredible Hulk* (1978). These werewolves are immortal; the actual originator of the bloodline is Nicholas Remy, a two-thousand-year-old character based on the real-life Inquisitor and witch hunter of the same name. There are no vampires in the series, but this episode alludes to the novel *Dracula*. Otto Renfield, who was once the thrall of Skorzeny, lives on a derelict ship that is "on its last run...a last voyage"—a veiled reference to the *Demeter,* the Russian vessel that brought Dracula to England. The evil werewolf, Janos Skorzeny, is named after the vampire antagonist in *The Night Stalker* (1972).

📺 In 1988, Blackthorne Publishing produced a five-issue comic adaptation; around this same time, the ninety-minute first episode—the series pilot—was released into the European home video market.

Wildlife On One – "Vampire"

BBC One. Feb 7, 1980 (S--E--). Nature/Science. D/W: Adrian Warren. C: Uwe Schmidt. UK: English/Color/25m. BBC Wales.

Explores the vampire bats of Trinidad, including research into the creature's physiology being conducted at the University of Bonn in West Germany. Narrated by David Attenborough.

Wild Carpathia

Travel Channel. Oct 30, 2011. History/Nature. D: Alasdair Grant. W: Charlie Ottley. C: Mihai & Mihaela Constantinescu, Nicoleta Carpineanu, Erika Stanciu, Caroline Fenerland, Nat Page, Radu Mot, Christoph Promberger, Tibor Kalnoky, HRH The Prince of Wales. UK: English/Color/47m. Almond Films.

🦇 🦇 🦇

Because of Bram Stoker's novel *Dracula,* many believe that the Carpathian Mountains are a forbidding location. The region is actually more reminiscent of the landscape in a Tolkien novel, yet it remains a place of myth and legend. Host Charlie Ottley travels the countryside to explore the history, culture, and wildlife of the region—and brings attention to its greatest threat: illegal logging.

This lavish documentary—which will surely bring an increase in tourism to the area—showcases the natural beauty of the region historically known as Transylvania. Some pockets of civilization still live a Medieval existence, while more modern settlements are restoring old traditions that were lost under Communist rule. One of the greatest champions of this unspoiled landscape is Prince Charles, who jokes that he has a "stake" in the country because he's a descendent of Vlad the Impaler. He believes that the centuries-old farming traditions should be preserved, and that modern society can learn from such ancient rural practices. Unlike most documentaries about the region, this one focuses on deforestation and the environment. There's no discussion of folklore, and the only vampire content is a brief mention of Bram Stoker and Vlad Țepeș (and a glimpse of Hunyad Castle in Hunedoara).

Wild Explorer – "Vampire Bats and Spectacled Bears"

Channel 5. Aug 30, 1999 (S01E04). Nature/Science. D: Michael Bodnarchuk. W: Anon. C: Anon. UK: English/Color/30m. Channel 5/Catspaw Pictures.

Alternately titled "Vampire Bats and River Dolphins," this episode features the wildlife of South America, including river dolphins, spectacled bears, and vampire bats. Narrated by John Telfer.

Will & Grace – "Love Plus One"

NBC. Nov 9, 2000 (S03E06). Comedy/Drama. D: James Burrows. W: Richard Rosenstock. C: Eric McCormack, Debra Messing, Megan Mullally, Sean Hayes, Patrick Dempsey, Jeremy Piven, Maria Pitillo, Eric Roth. USA: English/Color/21m. KoMut Entertainment/Three Sisters Entertainment/NBC.

🦇 🦇 🦇

Grace decides whether to join an ex-boyfriend and his new partner for an intimate encounter. Meanwhile, Jack employs Will as a modern-day Cyrano de Bergerac; he wants to date a brainy customer, but has difficulty talking to him. This very funny episode doesn't have any vampires, but Jack makes a passing reference to them. While chatting with the customer, he mentions how important the *Buffy the Vampire Slayer* TV series is to him, and how happy he is that Willow is a lesbian.

Word Travels – "Romania: On the Run"

OLN. Feb 22, 2009 (S02E06). Folklore/Travel. D: Michael Bodnarchuk. W: Deb Wainwright. C: Robin Esrock, Julia Dimon. CAN: English/Color/30m. Omni Film Productions.

Series follows two globetrotting journalists as they try to write the best travel articles possible—considering they constantly face jet lag, looming deadlines, and culture shock. In this episode, Robin and Julia take part in a cultural tour of the Transylvanian countryside, where they explore rural life in a village that has changed little over the centuries. They discover that there's much more to Romania than Gothic buildings and vampire folklore—yet they still uncover a few local legends that have a paranormal twist.

Non-English Programming

Promotional advertisement for the Argentinian miniseries *The Amazing Siege: Once Again, Dracula* (Canal 9)

SINGLE EPISODES

Birdman Task Force Jetman – "A Kiss That Calls for Death" / "Maria...Her Love and Death"
[*Chojin sentai Jettoman* – "Shi o yobu kuchizuke" / "Maria...Sono ai to shi"]

TV Asahi. Jan 24/31, 1992 (S01E48/49). Action/Fantasy. D: Keita Amemiya. W: Toshiki Inoue, Naruhisa Arakawa. C: Kotaro Tanaka ♀, Toshihide Wakamatsu, Tomihisa Naruse, Rika Kishida, Sayuri Uchida, Maho Maruyama ♀. JPN: Japanese/Color/60m. Toei Company/Bandai.

In this two-part story, after offering to share his power with Maria, Radiguet creates a parasitic creature out of his blood, and attaches it to her neck. This turns her into a vampire, and she kills a number of people in order to drink their blood—and then uses the parasite to infect Ryu, the leader of the Jetman. As Ryu suppresses his newfound bloodlust, he works at getting Maria to remember the good person she once was—because he'll need her by his side in the final showdown with Radiguet. Narrated by Tsutomu Tareki.

Dandelion – "Peter and the Dance of the Vampires"
[*Löwenzahn* – "Peter und der Tanz der Vampire"]

ZDF. Mar 21, 2001 (S21E02). Education/Family. D: Hannes Spring. W: Kai Rönnau. C: Peter Lustig, Helmut Krauss, Marc Bischoff. GER: German/Color/30m. Studio-TV-Film GmbH/Zweites Deutsches Fernsehen.

Children's television series where each episode is dedicated to one specific topic, which is explored through several related segments (both live-action and animation). In this episode, one of Peter's neighbors comes across a bat in their yard, so he alleviates their fears by clearing up the misconceptions about these furry fliers.

Films to Keep You Awake: A Real Friend
[*Películas para no dormir: Adivina quién soy*]

Telecinco. 2006. Horror/Suspense. D: Enrique Urbizu. W: Enrique Urbizu, Jorge Arenillas. C: Goya Toledo, José María Pou, Eduardo Farelo ♀, Aitor Mazo, Andrés Marí, Sandra Aguilera, Mark Ullod, Roelkis Bueno. ESP: Spanish/Color/73m. Filmax.

A young girl uses her imagination to create monsters that befriend and protect her. After she starts hanging out with her latest creation—a vampire—she discovers that this creature may not be the product of her imagination. This was part of a series of six films commissioned in July 2004, which were shelved until 2006 when they finally went to air.

Forbidden Love – Ep. #1.3702
[Verbotene Liebe]

Das Erste. Oct 5, 2010 (S16E--). Drama/Romance. D: Anon. W: Anon. C: Wolfram Grandezka, Jens Hartwig, Antonius Hermlin, Stephan Käfer, Milan Marcus, Krystian Martinek, Thomas Ohrner, Sebastian Schlemmer. GER: German/Color/60m. Grundy UFA TV/Produktions GmbH.

A German soap opera that was originally based on the Australian series *Sons and Daughters*. In this episode, Nathalia and Constantin fight their mutual attraction, despite having strange dreams of vampire-like adultery.

Journey to the Unexpected – "You Have to Kill Dracula"
[Viaje a lo inesperado – "Hay que matar a Drácula"]

Canal 13. Dec 15, 1979 (S01E07). Drama/Horror. D: Alberto Rinaldi. W: Máximo Soto. C: Narciso Ibáñez Menta, Gianni Lunadei ⚰, Elizabeth Killian, María Ibarreta, Luisa Kuliok, Pepe Novoa, Patricio Contreras, Graciela Dufau. ARG: Spanish/B&W/120m. Proartel S.A.

Jonathan Harker travels to Transylvania at the behest of Van Helsing, and is given the task of killing Dracula. But the Count has already left for England, where he intends to spread his evil across the land. Hosted by Narciso Ibáñez Menta.

This was a televised version of a stage play originally performed from January through March 1979 at the Lola Membrives theater in Buenos Aires—but only Gianni Lunadei (Dracula) reprised his role. Narciso Ibáñez Menta also starred as Van Helsing the previous year in a Spanish theatrical adaptation of the Balderston/Deane play, and he portrayed Dracula in the 1970 miniseries *Otra vez Drácula*. It should also be noted that several online sources incorrectly list this as a ninety-minute production from 1968.

Journey to the Unexpected – "Dracula"
[Viaje a lo inesperado – "Drácula"]

Canal 13. Mar 29, 1980 (S01E22). Drama/Horror. D: Terence Fisher. W: Jimmy Sangster, Bram Stoker. C: Christopher Lee ⚰, Peter Cushing, Michael Gough, John Van Eyssen, Melissa Stribling, Janine Faye, Valerie Gaunt ⚰. UK: English/Color/90m. Hammer Film Productions.

Initially this series rebroadcast episodes of *Quinn Martin's Tales of the Unexpected* (1977), but then featured a number of television movies and feature films. This episode is a special broadcast of the Hammer film *Horror of Dracula* (1958). Hosted by Narciso Ibáñez Menta.

Letters from Felix : A Rabbit on a World Tour – "Caution, Vampires!" / "Gondola Regatta in Venice"
[*Briefe von Felix: Ein Hase auf Weltreise* – "Vorsicht, Vampire!" / "Gondelregatta in Venedig"]

ZDF/KI.KA. 2003 (S02E19). Adventure/Family. D: Hanan Kaminski, Alan Simpson. W: John Patterson, Annette Langen. C: Patrick Flecken, Gilbert Nash, Stéphanye Dussud. GER: German/Color/30m. Caligari Film GmbH/ TV-Loonland AG/Neue Deutsche Filmgesellschaft.

Animated series about a rabbit with a poor sense of direction, who has wild adventures as he roams across the globe; he relates the tales back to his owner through a series of letters. In the segment "Caution, Vampires!" Felix makes an emergency landing at Dracula's Castle, where he's greeted by the Count's butler, a vampire bat.

Macaroni tout garni – Episode #--.--

Télé-Québec. 2003 (S--E--). Family/Fantasy. D: Pierre Lord. W: Denis Thériault. C: Nathalie D'Anjou, Louis-Martin Despa, Julie Le Breton, Jean Harvey, Chantal Collin, Anne Casabonne, Pierre Gendron ♀. CAN: French/Color/30m. Productions Jeunesses Bouchard Morin Inc.

Best friends Snoro and Macaroni are boisterous young dogs brought to life from the drawings of magician Louise-Martin. Through their numerous adventures they meet a cast of interesting historical and fictional characters, including Count Dracula.

Midnight DJ – "Vampires"

TV5. 2008 (S01E05/06). Horror/Suspense. D: Lore Reyes. W: Aloy Adlawan, Jessel Duque. C: Paolo Contis, Desiree del Valle, Joaqui Tupas, Ryan Eigenmann ♀, Dimples Romana ♀, Chubi del Rosario ♀. PHI: Filipino/Color/60m. BIGTOP Media Productions/Double Vision.

This series follows an overnight radio station disc jockey named Patrick, a Medium who sidelines as a paranormal investigator to solve the supernatural problems of his listeners. Each episode features Filipino myths and legends, several of which include vampire-like creatures. In this two-part story, Patrick investigates an underground club called Rojo, rumored to be a vampire hangout. After getting bitten by a bloodsucker, the only way he can halt his transformation is to destroy a mysterious gem known as the "bloodstone."

Midnight DJ – "Ghost"
["Aswang"]

TV5. Dec 13, 2008 (S02E04). Horror/Suspense. D: Lore Reyes. W: Anon. C: Oyo Boy Sotto, Desiree del Valle, Joaqui Tupas. PHI: Filipino/Color/30m. BIGTOP Media Productions/Double Vision.

After the death of the previous host, LXFM hires a man named Samboy as their new Midnight DJ, who in this episode confronts an evil vampire/witch known as an *aswang*.

Midnight DJ – "Vampire on Campus" / "Vengeance of Death"
["Manananggal sa Campus" / "Higanti ng Kamatayan"]

TV5. Aug 8/29, 2009 (S04E10/13). Horror/Suspense. D: Lore Reyes. W: Anon. C: Oyo Boy Sotto, Desiree del Valle, Joaqui Tupas. PHI: Filipino/Color/60m. BIGTOP Media Productions/Double Vision.

In this two-part story, the Midnight DJ crew investigate a series of attacks at a local university, and discover that there's a *manananggal* on the loose—an evil vampire-like creature that dines on humans.

Midnight DJ – "Vampire Family"
["Pamilyang Aswang"]

TV5. Nov 14, 2009 (S05E09). Horror/Suspense. D: Lore Reyes. W: Anon. C: Oyo Boy Sotto, Desiree del Valle, Joaqui Tupas. PHI: Filipino/Color/30m. BIGTOP Media Productions/Double Vision.

After their car breaks down, the crew from LXFM unknowingly takes shelter in a house populated by a family of *aswangs* (vampire/witches).

Midnight DJ – "Campus Vampire"
["Campus Bampira"]

TV5. Dec 5, 2009 (S05E12). Horror/Suspense. D: Lore Reyes. W: Anon. C: Oyo Boy Sotto, Desiree del Valle, Joaqui Tupas. PHI: Filipino/Color/30m. BIGTOP Media Productions/Double Vision.

The gang heads back to school as they investigate a series of vampire attacks at a university.

Midnight DJ – "Ghost Village"
["Barangay Aswang"]

TV5. Nov 13, 2010 (S09E08). Horror/Suspense. D: Lore Reyes. W: Anon. C: Oyo Boy Sotto, Desiree del Valle, Joaqui Tupas, Meg Imperial, Gilbert Telis. PHI: Filipino/Color/30m. BIGTOP Media Productions/Double Vision.

A dying reporter leads the crew to Sitio La Magra, a small village not marked on any map, and for good reason: every resident is an *aswang* (vampire/witch).

Midnight DJ – "Vampire!"
["Baklitang Manananggal!"]

TV5. Dec 4, 2010 (S09E11). Horror/Suspense. D: Lore Reyes. W: Anon. C: Oyo Boy Sotto, Desiree del Valle, Joaqui Tupas, Meg Imperial, Gilbert Telis, Epi Quizon ☥, Kitkat, Jade Lopez. PHI: Filipino/Color/30m. BIGTOP Media Productions/Double Vision.

The crew joins forces with a battle-scarred hunter named Isay, to assist a hairdresser who believes he's being stalked by a *manananggal*. After the man takes on the aspects of the vampire, the group must find a way to cure him before the transformation is complete.

Stone-Faces – "Bat Castle"
[Kivikasvot – "Lepakko-linna"]

MTV3. Mar 29, 1980. Comedy/Music. D: Vesa Nuotio, Ismo Sajakorpi. W: Ismo Sajakorpi. C: Maija Lokka, Ismo Sajakorpi, Petra Frey, Matti Siitonen, Ilkka Hemming, Georg Dolivo ♀, Martti Liimo, Sirkka Sandrén, Risto Mäkelä. FIN: Finnish/Color/50m. MTV Viihdetoimitus.

In a story that takes place in the nineteenth century, an eclectic group of travelers—including an opera singer, her pianist, and a vampire hunter—end up at Dracula's castle. They face the Count and his butler, and try their best to save themselves from becoming creatures of the night. This is a made for TV movie created by the same musical comedy troupe that had a popular television series in Finland.

Yellow Thrill – "A Night in the Cemetery"
[*Brivido giallo* – "Una notte nel cimitero"]

Canale 5. Aug 1988 (S01E01). Horror/Thriller. D: Lamberto Bava. W: Dardano Sacchetti, Lamberto Bava. C: Gregory Lech Thaddeus, Lea Martino, Beatrice Ring, Gianmarco Tognazzi, Karl Zinny, Lino Salemme. ITA: Italian/Color/97m. Reteitalia/Dania Film/Devon Film.

Brivido giallo was an Italian television series of four unrelated feature-length horror films, all of which were directed by Lamberto Bava. In this film, five delinquent teenagers end up in a remote wooded area after their van breaks down. They find a tavern nearby, and inside is a large cache of valuables—including jewelry, money, gilded objects, and even credit cards. The bartender speaks of an old legend dating back centuries, when a thief once boasted that he could steal the thirty pieces of silver from the tomb of Judas. But like so many since that time, the bandit failed in his quest, so he had to surrender all of his possessions that held value. If the teens can survive one night in the cursed crypt below the church, then the tavern treasure is theirs for the taking.

This was released into the English-language market as *Graveyard Disturbance;* in such stories, the body count of unsuspecting teenagers tends to be quite high. Here all five survive, but by the end of the movie you'll wish they hadn't. It starts out quite good, with a fitting Gothic atmosphere, but once the teens head to the crypt, the "horrors" they meet are unintentionally funny (such as the zombie-vampires). The main problem is that nothing horrific or thrilling ever happens; each time the teens are confronted by a creature, they simply run in another direction. The group makes it out alive, but the bartender is really the Grim Reaper—and he's going to kill them. Then one of the teens just stabs him, and he dies. The moral of the story? Don't rent it!

Yellow Thrill – "Dinner with a Vampire"
[Brivido giallo – "A cena col vampire"]

Canale 5. Aug 1988 (S01E04). Comedy/Horror. D: Lamberto Bava. W: Dardano Sacchetti, Luciano Martino. C: George Hilton ☥, Patrizia Pellegrino, Riccardo Rossi, Valeria Milillo, Yvonne Sciò, Isabel Russinova ☥. ITA: Italian/Color/87m. Dania Film/Devon Film/Reteitalia.

After an open audition, four aspiring artists are selected to join a famous horror film director at his remote castle for the weekend. They believe their host, Jurik, will offer them a contract to work on his next movie. But the man is an ancient vampire who longs to end his boring existence, and his death can only be met at the hands of an innocent. The group has until sunrise to kill him, otherwise he'll drink their blood and turn them into creatures of the night—just like all the other failed hopefuls who haunt the basement of his castle.

This tale is an improvement over the previous entry, but it doesn't really work as a comedy or a horror film. The vampire isn't affected by the usual trappings such as garlic, crosses, or even stakes, which makes finding a way to kill him all the more difficult. The trouble is, the group spends more time talking about their predicament than they do figuring out way to destroy Jurik. Much like in *A Night in the Cemetery,* everyone survives, although you'd just as well prefer it if they had not. The makeup for the aged vampire is fantastic, but the same can't be said for the special effects, which range from bad to laughable.

SERIES

The Amazing Siege: Once Again, Dracula
[El cerco alucinante: Otra vez Drácula]

Canal 9. Jul 30 – Aug 27, 1970 (5 Episode Miniseries). Drama/Horror. D: Narciso Ibáñez Menta, Alberto Rinaldi. W: Horacio S. Meyrialle. C: Narciso Ibáñez Menta ☥, Marta González, Carlos Muñoz, Graciela Pal, Luisina Brando, Rodolfo Morandi. ARG: Spanish/B&W/450m. Canal 9.

In modern-day Buenos Aires, a troupe of theatre actors stage a play satirizing Count Dracula, unaware that the vampire is alive and well—and living in the catacombs underneath the building. Unimpressed with being made a fool of, Dracula seeks vengeance against the actors—with the help of his undead brides. Narciso Ibáñez Menta plays both Dracula and the actor portraying him on stage.

Drácula

América 2. Mar 5 – May 14, 1999 (11 Episode Miniseries). Drama/Horror. D: Diego Kaplan. W: Horacio del Prado, Ana Franco. C: Carlos Calvo ♀, Lorenzo Quinteros ♀, Magalí Moro, Juan Ignacio Machado, Alejandro Awada, Carolina Fal. ARG: Spanish/Color/550m. América TV.

In 1476, the warrior prince Vlad Țepeș turned his back on God, and participated in a satanic ritual that transformed him into an immortal vampire. To stop the evil man, God summoned a challenger named Zordan, and armed him with a special stake to drive through Vlad's heart—but he failed in his quest. Five centuries later, in 1978, a coffin drifted onto the banks of the Río de la Plata in Argentina. Vlad Țepeș was inside, and Zordan reappeared to confront the vampire—but he was captured by police and locked up in a mental institution. Now twenty years later, Vlad is known as Professor Dreshko, and lives in Buenos Aires where he teaches hematology at the School of Medicine. He falls in love with a beautiful student named Lourdes, but his activities have once again attracted the attention of his nemesis. The series was initially planned to span thirteen episodes, but after lead actor Carlos Calvo became ill, this number was reduced to eleven. Calvo experienced a series of unfortunate events in his personal life, which led him to believe that he had been cursed by playing Dracula. For the final two episodes, the role was taken over by actor Lorenzo Quinteros.

Dracula, a Love Story
[Drácula, uma História de Amor]

TV Tupi. Feb 1980 (4 Episodes). Drama/Romance. D: Atílio Riccó. W: Rubens Ewald Filho. C: Rubens de Falco ♀, Carlos Alberto Riccelli, Cleyde Yáconis, Paulo Goulart, Bruna Lombardi, Isabel Ribeiro, Flávio Galvão, Cláudia Alencar. BRA: Portuguese/Color/240m. TV Tupi.

Count Dracula travels to Brazil in search of his long-lost son, who as an infant was taken by his wife. The two are reunited, but Dracula falls in love with his son's spouse—and believes she is the reincarnation of a past love. This short-lived *telenovela* was cursed from the start; the director was fired before it was broadcast, and only four episodes aired before production was halted. Days after broadcaster TV Tupi was shut down, a rewritten version aired on Rede Bandeirantes under the title *Um Homem Muito Especial (A Very Special Man)*. It was spearheaded by the same writer and director, and included much of the same cast.

Dracula's Ring

Danmarks Radio. Oct 15-21, 1978 (7 Episode Miniseries). Drama/Horror. D/W: Flemming la Cour, Edmondt Jensen. C: Bent Børgesen ♀, Brita Fogsgaard, Søren Steen, Ejnar Hans Jensen, Gitte Herman, Mary C. Collieri, Lene Axelsen, Jørgen de Mylius. DEN: Danish/Color/105m. DR TV-uha.

Three young Danes are on vacation in Malta, where they explore the ruins of an old, decrepit castle. Inside they steal an ornate ring, and inadvertently loosen a series of chains that are entwined around a stone sarcophagus. Their actions come back to haunt them upon returning home, for Dracula has escaped from his grave and has followed them to Denmark—and he wants his stolen property back. This "bedtime story for adults" was serialized into seven fifteen-minute episodes, and aired just once on Denmark's national broadcaster.

Frankenstein's Aunt
[Teta / Teta Frankenstein]

Syndicated. 1987 (7 Episodes). Comedy/Fantasy. D: Juraj Jakubisko. W: Juraj Jakubisko, Jaroslav Dietl, Joachim Hammann. C: Viveca Lindfors, Ferdy Mayne ♀, Gerhard Karzel, Flavio Bucci, Mercedes Sampietro, Martin Hreben, Jacques Herlin. AUT/ESP/FRA/GER/ITA/SWE/TCH: Slovak/Color/420m. Ceskoslovenská Televize Bratislava/Films du Sabre.

Baron Frankenstein flees his castle in Transylvania, and leaves behind the monster he created and several other inhabitants. Hannah, Frankenstein's aunt, travels to the castle to take care of those left behind—including Count Dracula, Larry Talbot (a werewolf), Elizabeth Báthory (the White Lady), and several other mystical creatures. Endeavoring to make the lives of her new friends as normal as possible, Hannah keeps their existence hidden from the local villagers. This seven country co-production is based on the Swedish novel *Frankenstein's Aunt* (1978) by Allan Rune Pettersson. It was also edited down into the ninety-six-minute film *Pehavý Max a strasidlá (Freckled Max and the Spooks)*. Actor Ferdy Mayne, who played Count Dracula, also portrayed the vampire Count von Krolock in the feature film *The Fearless Vampire Killers* (1967).

Freeze

Home CGV. Oct 27-31, 2006 (5 Episode Miniseries). Drama/Romance. D: Jeong Jae-hoon. W: Lee Jin-u, Han Seon-jae. C: Lee Seo Jin ♀, Son Tae Young ♀, Park Han Byul, Lee Han Wie, Lee Joon, Ji Dae Han. KOR: Korean/Color/300m. Yellow Film/YA Entertainment Holdings Ltd.

Joong-Won is a three-hundred-and-fifty-year-old vampire, turned by the beautiful E-Hwa when he was near death, after he rescued her from the clutches of crazed villagers. The two vampires are now business partners in present-day Seoul, yet Joong-Won tires of immortality and secretly longs for death. He has a change of heart after he chances upon a young woman, who reminds him of a long-lost love back when he was human.

Hello Franceska
[Annyeong! Peurancheseuka]

MBC. Jan 24, 2005 – Feb 27, 2006 (52 Episodes). Comedy/Family. D: Do-Cheol No. W: Jeong-ku Shin, Hyun-hee Kim. C: Hye-jin Shim, Ryeo-won Jeong, Du-il Lee, Seul-ki Park, Soo-mi Kim, Seul-gi Park, Kyeon Lee, Daniel Henney. KOR: Korean/Color/3120m. MBC-TV Korea.

One of the few remaining vampire clans in Romania splits up to hide safely amongst the human population, where they'll bide their time until their glorious empire can be restored. As they spread across the Earth, one group stows away on the wrong ship and ends up in Korea. Disguised as human and living a new life in Seoul, the vampires await the return of their leader—despite the fact that he probably has no idea where they have ended up.

Immortal
[Imortal]

ABS-CBN. Oct 4, 2010 – Apr 29, 2011 (148 Episodes). Drama/Horror. D: Chito S. Roño. W: Var. C: John Lloyd Cruz ☥, Angel Locsin, Maricar Reyes ☥, Rico Blanco, Niña Dolino, Jomari Yllana ☥, Jake Roxas ☥. PHI: English, Filipino/Color/8880m. Star Television.

Unaware that they belong to warring supernatural clans—and are destined to become mortal enemies—a vampire and a werewolf fall hopelessly in love. During the series run, the official website hosted a related sequence of short webisodes under the banner *Anino't Panaginip,* which revealed hidden chapters of the series.

Kiss of the Vampire
[O Beijo do Vampiro]

Rede Globo. Aug 26, 2002 – May 3, 2003 (215 Episodes). Drama/Fantasy. D: Marcos Paulo. W: Antônio Calmon, Álvaro Ramos. C: Tarcísio Meira ☥, Cláudia Raia ☥, Kayky Brito ☥, Flávia Alessandra, Tato Gabus, Deborah Secco ☥. BRA: Portuguese/Color/10750m. Rede Globo de Televisão.

In this Brazilian *telenovela,* Count Bóris Vladescu—an eight-hundred-year-old evil vampire—protects his newborn son from his wife by placing him in the care of another couple. Thirteen years later, Zeca, now a teenager, becomes aware of his vampiric nature, which coincides with his father's attempt to locate him. When they finally reunite, the elder vampire has the surprise of his life: his heir is innately good, and won't harm humans or drink their blood. Although they don't see eye to eye, father and son eventually respect their differences, and join forces to face an ultimate evil—an ancient vampire named Nosferatu.

Koishite Akuma: Vampire Boy
[Vanpaia bôi]

Fuji TV. Jul 7 - Sep 8, 2009 (10 Episodes). Drama/Romance. D: Junichi Tsuzuki. W: Ogawa Satoko, Okubo Tomomi. C: Nakayama Yuma ☥, Shiro Ito, Keiko Horiuchi, Morimoto Shintaro, Masahiko Kondo ☥. JPN: Japanese/Color/600m. Kansai Telecasting Corporation.

Ruka Kuromiya is a fledgling vampire, secretly hiding among the human population. His transformation won't be complete until he tastes the blood of one who loves him—which seems next to impossible, considering his frigid attitude towards humans. After he enrolls in high school, he meets a young teacher named Makoto Natsukawa, and falls for the beautiful mortal.

Little Kaibutsu
[Kaibutsu-kun]

NTV. Apr 17 - Jun 12, 2010 (9 Episodes). Adventure/Family. D: Nakajima Satoru. W: Nishida Masafumi. C: Ohno Satoshi, Kaga Takeshi, Yashima Norito ⚥, Ueshima Ryuhei, Choi Hong Man, Kawashima Umika, Hamada Tatsuomi. JPN: Japanese/Color/270m. Nippon Television.

Before he can assume his rightful throne, a young prince from monster land travels to the human realm with three companions—Wolfman, Dracula and Franken—where they battle a group of demons attempting to take over the world. This is a live-action remake of two previous animated incarnations (a feature film adaptation, directed by Yoshihiro Nakamura, was released in November 2011).

The Little Vampire: New Adventures
[Der kleine Vampir: Neue Abenteuer]

ARD/BBC Two. Dec 5, 1993 – 1994 (13 Episodes). Adventure/Family. D: Christian Görlitz. W: Sabine Thiesler. C: Jan Steilen ⚥, Matthias Ruschke, Nadja Engelbrecht, Lena Beyer ⚥, Andreas Nickl ⚥, Peter Lohmeyer. GER: German/Color/390m. Polyphon Film-und Fernsehgesellschaft.

This German production followed the continuing adventures of vampire siblings Rüdiger and Anna, and their best friend Anton Bohnsack. Based on the books *The Little Vampire Takes a Trip* (1984) and *The Little Vampire on the Farm* (1988) by Angela Sommer-Bodenburg.

Man, Next Natural Girl: 100 Nights in Yokohama / N-Girls vs. Vampire
[Tennen shôjo Man next: Yokohama hyaku-ya hen]

WOWOW. Nov 25/26, 1999 (2 Episode Miniseries). Action/Horror. D: Takashi Miike. W: Itaru Era, Yûji Ishida. C: Ayana Sakai, Chiaki Ichiba, Takashi Nagayama, Chikako Ôba, Erika Yamakawa, Eri Nomura. JPN: Japanese/Color/202m. Dentsu Inc./Pony Canyon Inc.

Several teenagers recently hired by a modeling agency are turned into vampires. High school student Man Kôda discovers that the organization is a front for a gang of the undead, who are using the agency to lure in young virgins.

The Mutants: Pathways of the Heart
[Os Mutantes: Caminhos do Coração]

Rede Record. Jun 3, 2008 – Mar 23, 2009 (243 Episodes). Drama/Fantasy. D: Alexandre Avancini. W: Tiago Santiago. C: Bianca Rinaldi, Leonardo Vieira, Marcos Pitombo, Maytê Piragibe, Carolina Holanda, Fernanda Nobre, Julianne Trevisol. BRA: Portuguese/Color/7290m. Rede Record.

A mutation spreads among the population of São Paulo, changing humans into a bevy of creatures including cats, snakes, spiders, werewolves, and vampires. As the epidemic continues to claim victims, the terrified residents fight back.

My Date with a Vampire
[Ngo wo geun see yau gor yue wui]

ATV. Nov 30, 1998 – Jan 15, 1999 (35 Episodes). Drama/Romance. D: Sin Chi Wai. W: Chan Sap Sam. C: Eric Wan Tin Chiu ☥, Joey Meng Yee Man, Kenneth Chan Kai Tai ☥, Lui Yau Wai, Kristy Yang, Chapman To Man Chat. HKG: Chinese/Color/2100m. Asia Television Limited.

When the Japanese invaded China in 1938, guerilla freedom fighter Fong Kwok-Wai battled one-on-one with Lieutenant Katsuo Yamamoto, in order to protect his neighbor's son. Mortally wounded, the three men were turned by the vampire king Cheung Sun. Upon the arrival of powerful ghost hunter Ma Da-Na, Cheung Sun escaped, as did his three new vampire progeny. Sixty years later, Fong now lives and works as a police detective, and he adopted the young vampire as his own son. Ma Siu Ling, the descendent of ghost hunter Ma Da-Na, knows that Fong is a vampire—but that hasn't stopped her from falling in love with him. If she continues along this path, there's a chance she will lose her supernatural abilities—but she needs them now more than ever. The vampire Yamamoto has returned to settle his score with Fong, to finish the battle they started sixty years earlier. The plot for this series was loosely based on what would have been the third installment of *Vampire Expert,* which was canceled in 1997 after its star, Lam Ching Ying, was diagnosed with a terminal illness.

My Date with a Vampire II
[Ngo wo geun see yau gor yue wui II]

ATV. Mar 6 – Apr 30, 2000 (42 Episodes). Drama/Romance. D: Sin Chi Wai. W: Chan Sap Sam. C: Eric Wan Tin Chiu ☥, Joey Meng Yee Man, Kenneth Chan Kai Tai ☥, Simon Yam ☥, Ruby Wong, Kristy Yang, Chapman To Man Chat, Pinky Cheung Man Chi ☥. HKG: Chinese/Color/2520m. Asia Television Limited.

It's the turn of the millennium, and the vampire king Cheung Sun has risen from the grave. He anxiously awaits the return of the woman he loves, the all-powerful goddess Nüwa. Cheung Sun worries that even though Nüwa created the Earth, she'll want to destroy it after witnessing what the self-serving human race has done to it. So he plans to turn the world's population into vampires, as a means to please her and keep the Earth intact. Meanwhile, during an investigation in England, vampire detective Fong Kwok-Wai is killed; his doppelgänger and grandfather, Fong Tin-Yau, assumes his identity. He returns to Hong Kong, and Fong's lover—ghost hunter Ma Siu Ling—is completely unaware of the switch. With the fate of the world held in balance, the couple faces off against Nüwa and Cheung Sun, in an ultimate battle of good versus evil.

My Date with a Vampire III
[Ngo wo geun see yau gor yue wui III]

ATV. Oct 25 – Dec 11, 2004 (36 Episodes). Drama/Romance. D: Tam Yau Yip. W: Chan Sap Sam. C: Eric Wan Tin Chiu ☥, Joey Meng Yee Man, Kenneth Chan Kai Tai ☥, Cheung Kwok Kuen, Pinky Cheung Man Chi ☥, Bert Ting Yip Ng ☥. HKG: Chinese/Color/2160m. Asia Television Limited.

The last remaining holy goddess, Yiu Chi Sing Mo, has returned to Earth in search of her long lost holy god, Yun Wong. Yet he no longer loves her, and only wishes to live a normal life with a human woman—so in order to get his attention, Yiu Chi Sing Mo plans to destroy the Earth. These events lead to the return of legendary warriors Fong Tin-Yau and Ma Siu Ling, who reunite to stop the two gods before the Earth can be destroyed.

RH Plus

Tokyo MX. Jan 2 – Mar 26, 2008 (13 Episodes). Action/Horror. D: Ichino Ryuuichi. W: Sasano Megumu, Ueno Kimiko. C: Hassei Takano ☥, Yū Miura ☥, Naoya Ojima ☥, Rakuto Tochihara ☥, Haruka Tomatsu. JPN: Japanese/Color/780m. RH Plus Production Committee.

Kiyoi is an elder vampire who takes care of three others living under his charge. As they adjust to life disguised as humans, they investigate crimes that the police won't touch. Based on Ayako Suwa's manga series of the same name.

Schuster's Ghosts
[Schusters Gespenster]

ARD. Sep 10 – Oct 8, 1978 (5 Episode Miniseries). Adventure/Family. D: Bruno Voges. W: Klaus-Dieter Lang. C: Balduin Baas, Paul Dahlke, Ingrid Froehlich, Sandra Michaelis, Kurt Schmidtchen ☥, Karl-Heinz von Hassel, Clara Walbröhl. GER: German/Color/125m. Pidax Film Media Ltd.

The Shuster family inherits an old mansion, and to their shock, three friendly ghosts live in the attic. Their neighbor, an equally amicable Eugene Dracula, often stops by for a nighttime visit.

Spectreman - "Hunt for Kyudora" / "Battle the Evil"
[Supekutoruman - "Uchu no Tohri-ma Kyudorah-seijin" / "Pal-yuusei-jin yo Eien nare"]

FujiTV. Oct 30/Nov 6, 1971 (S01E44/45). Action/Sci-Fi. D: Keinosuke Tsuchiya. W: Daiji Kazumine, Tomio Sagisu. C: Tetsuo Narikawa, Takanobu Toya, Kazuo Arai, Kiyoshi Kobayashi, Machiko Konishi, Koji Ozaki, Tôru Ôhira. JPN: Japanese/Color/44m. P Productions.

This live-action series followed the cyborg Spectreman, a monster-fighting, Ultraman-like hero disguised as Jôji (George) Gamou, a human being who can transform into his alter-ego by calling on the power of the Nebula 71 Star. The main protagonist was an evil, mutant scientist named

Dr. Gori, who with his henchman Karras aimed to take over the Earth by creating monsters that fed off of the pollution that plagued the planet. In this 2-part "Cosmic Vampire" story, after over twenty women have been killed, with their blood completely drained, a mysterious alien enlists Spectreman to battle the notorious space vampire Kyudora. (These episodes were also collectively known as "The Vampire from Outer Space.")

📺 The sixty-three episode series was divided into three segments, each of which had a different title. However, the show was rebroadcast, in English, under a single title when it was syndicated across the United States in 1978 (airing on broadcasters such as TBS Superstation).

Split
[Hatsuya]

HOT. 2009 – 2010 (135 Episodes). Drama/Romance. D: Shai Kapon. W: Ilan Rozanfeld, Shira Alon. C: Amit Farkash ♀, Yon Tumarkin ♀, Yedidia Vital, Maya Sho'ef, Avi Kornick, Anna Zaikin, Idan Ashkenazi, Yussuf Abu Warda ♀. ISR: Hebrew/Color/4050m. Dori Media Darset.

Israeli supernatural series that follows an introverted teenager, Ella Rosen, who learns of her true destiny through a chance meeting with a new classmate: a centuries-old bloodsucker. Ella is a "split"—half human, half vampire—and is drawn into an ancient battle between humans and the undead, a conflict that she's been preordained to resolve. Unknown to her, the school Principal is the head of the "Order of Blood," a shadow organization whose purpose is to forever rid the world of vampires. Ella also has to deal with personal conflict; she falls in love with both her vampire mentor and her human best friend. The series was originally produced for video on demand, but proved to be so popular that it became part of the regular broadcasting schedule on the family-oriented Children's Channel. It has since been sold into 35 foreign markets.

Vamp

Rede Globo. Jul 15, 1991 – Feb 8, 1992 (179 Episodes). Comedy/Romance. D: Jorge Fernando. W: Antonio Calmon, Vinícius Vianna. C: Ney Latorraca ♀, Cláudia Ohana ♀, Reginaldo Faria, Joana Fomm, Patrícia Travassos ♀, Fábio Assunção. BRA: Portuguese/Color/10740m. Rede Globo de Televisão.

Newlyweds Jonas Rocha and Carmen Maura are beginning a new life with their twelve children in a small town off the coast of Rio de Janeiro. Their peaceful existence is disrupted upon the arrival of a rock superstar named Natasha, who rose to fame after making a pact with the ancient vampire Vlad Polanski. Natasha wants to be rid of him, and is looking for the Cross of St. Sebastian, a relic that she believes can be used to kill him.

Vampire Expert

ATV. Oct 16, 1995 – 1996 (30 Episodes). Comedy/Horror. D: Anon. W: Anon. C: Lam Ching Ying, Annie Man, Kingdom Yuen, Wong Shu Kei, Philip Keung, Sin Ho Ying, Norman Tsui. HKG: Chinese/Color/900m. Asia Television Limited.

World War II has just ended, and a monk named Mon Siu Fong arrives in Hong Kong along with his disciple Ma Fan, in pursuit of a centuries-old vampire. They meet a master fighter named Wan Fei Yeung, who is actually a vicious man trying to become the most powerful vampire ever known. Fong and Fan must stop the madman before he can become the King Vampire, a transformation that will give him the power to destroy the city.

Vampire Expert II

ATV. Oct 7, 1996 – 1997 (50 Episodes). Comedy/Horror. D: Benny Chan. W: Anon. C: Lam Ching Ying, Annie Man, Kiki Sheung, Philip Keung, Sin Ho Ying, Mung Hoi, Eric Wan, Frankie Lam, Berg Ng, Kristy Yang. HKG: Chinese/Color/1500m. Asia Television Limited.

After looting an old crypt, a thief inadvertently resurrects a clutch of vampires, and the vicious horde attacks a small village. Mo Siu Fong, a Taoist monk, fends off the marauding evil with the help of his two disciples. That's just the first of many foes that the trio will face; a number of malevolent forces are about to surface, including a powerful fighter whom the monk once considered a friend. In 1997, production began on a third installment of this series, however it was halted after star Lam Ching Ying was diagnosed with liver cancer; he passed away later that year. The story was reworked to become the basis for the ATV series *Ngo wo geun see yau gor yue wui* (*My Date with a Vampire*).

Vampire Idol
[Baempaieo Aidol]

MBN. Dec 5, 2011 – 2012 (120 Episodes). Comedy/Music. D: Lee Geun-Wook. W: Lee Seong-Eun, Ha Cheul-Seung. C: Lee Jung ☥, Kim Soo Mi, Kang Min Kyung, Lee Soo Hyuk ☥, Shin Dong Yup ☥, Oh Kwang Rok. KOR: Korean/Color/3600m. Sidus HQ Productions.

A vampire prince from an alien world travels to Earth with one goal in mind: to become the next global pop idol.

Vampire Prosecutor
[Baempaieo Geumsa]

OCN. Oct 2 – Dec 18, 2011 (12 Episodes). Drama/Fantasy. D: Kim Byeong-Soo. W: Han Jung-Hoon. C: Yun Jung Hoon ☥, Lee Won Jong, Kim Joo Young, Lee Young Ah, Jang Hyun Sung, Kim Ye Jin. KOR: Korean/Color/720m. CMG Chorok Stars.

Lawyer Min Tae Yeon has become a vampire, but he refuses to lead an evil existence. He only drinks the blood of the dead, and uses his enhanced abilities to prosecute powerful criminals who were once considered untouchable.

Vampire Syndrome: Hatu

KBS Kyoto/TV Kanagawa. 2002 (13 Episodes). Horror/Thriller. D: Naoyuki Tomomatsu. W: Chisato Okawara. C: Atsushi Harada, Kazumi Murata, Aimi Nakamura, Hitomi Miwa, Ryuuji Yamamoto, Tarou Suwa, Hoshimi Asai. JPN: Japanese/Color/390m. Happinet Pictures.

This live-action series apparently features an excessive amount of blood and gore—for television, anyway—however no further information is available about the show.

A Very Special Man
[Um Homem Muito Especial]

Rede Bandeirantes. Jul 1980 – Feb 1981 (10 Episodes). Drama/Romance. D: Antônio Abujamra. W: Rubens Ewald Filho, Jaime Camargo. C: Rubens de Falco ♀, Bruna Lombardi, Carlos Alberto Riccelli, Isabel Ribeiro, Sandra Barsotti, Cláudia de Alencar, Cleyde Yáconis. BRA: Portuguese/Color/600m. Rede Bandeirantes.

Count Dracula leaves Transylvania for Brazil in search of his long-lost son Raphael, who was taken away by his mother when he was an infant. The vampire falls in love with his son's wife Mariana, whom he believes is the reincarnation of a past love. This is a remake of sorts by the same creative team behind *Drácula, una História de Amor (Dracula, a Love Story)*, a short-lived *telenovela* that was canceled just months before this production went to air. A decade later, in 1991, actress Cleyde Yáconis appeared in the vampire-themed soap opera *Vamp*.

TELEFILMS AND PILOTS

Carmilla

TVP. Nov 13, 1980. Horror/Romance. D: Janusz Kondratiuk. W: Janusz Kondratiuk, Maciej Kozłowski. C: Izabela Trojanowska ♀, Monika Stefanowicz ♀, Leon Niemczyk, Anna Milewska, Barbara Rachwalska, Tomasz Grochoczyński, Zofia Rysiówna, Jerzy Łapiński. POL: Polish/B&W, Color/68m. Telewizja Polska.

The secluded lives of Laura and her widower father are shattered upon the arrival of a mysterious woman named Carmilla, whom they take in after she claims to be ill while traveling with her mother. A plague affects the local populace, and as the body count rises, the family realizes that the source of the outbreak is a little too close to home. It's a faithful adaptation of J. Sheridan Le Fanu's novella, and was broadcast primarily in black and white with a few scenes tinted in amber.

Carmilla: The Petrified Heart
[Carmilla: Le coeur petrifié]

FR3. Mar 10, 1988. Horror/Romance. D: Paul Planchon. W: Antoine Robert, Paul Planchon. C: Emmanuelle Meyssignac ♀, Aurelle Doazan, Marc Michel, Roland Kieffer, Paulette Schlegel, Yvette Stahl, Dinah Faust, André Pommarat. FRA: French/Color/60m. France 3 Alsace.

Laura and her father live in a remote castle in the Alsace region of France, and on one fateful evening, a stagecoach crashes just outside their home. The sole occupant of the vehicle, a woman named Carmilla, is taken in by the family and befriended by Laura—with disastrous results.

Count Dracula
[Hrabě Drakula]

Ceskoslovenská Televize. 1970. Drama/Horror. D: Anna Procházková. W: Anna Procházková, Oldrich Zelezný. C: Ilja Racek ♀, Jan Schánilec, Klára Jerneková, Jiří Zahajský, Hana Maciuchová ♀, Ota Sklencka, Václav Mares. CZE: Czech/B&W/75m. Ceskoslovenská Televize.

🦇 🦇 🦇

Jonathan Harker travels to Transylvania in order to meet Count Dracula, a peculiar man who's interested in purchasing a home near London. He becomes trapped in the Count's castle, and discovers his host and three females sleeping in coffins. He escapes and returns to London, but the terror from Transylvania follows him home. This is a condensed yet faithful Czechoslovakian adaptation of Bram Stoker's novel that includes several key scenes, and has a suitable Gothic atmosphere despite the generic sets. The raven-haired Count, who sports a full beard, is genuinely menacing despite being somewhat short in stature. He has fangs, despises mirrors, and has no trouble with sunlight; he commands packs of wild dogs, transforms into a bat, and climbs head-first down the castle wall. The ending is true to the novel; Harker, Holmwood, Morris, Seward, and Van Helsing—along with Mina—chase Dracula back to Transylvania, where he is killed by a knife through the heart.

Little Kaibutsu: All New Special
[Mou Kaette Kita Yo!! Kaibutsu-kun Subete Shinsaku SP]

NTV. Jun 26, 2010. Adventure/Family. D: Matsuoka Masahiro. W: Nishida Masafumi. C: Ohno Satoshi, Kaga Takeshi, Yashima Norito ♀, Ueshima Ryuhei, Choi Hong Man, Kawashima Umika, Hamada Tatsuomi, Matsuoka Masahiro. JPN: Japanese/Color/90m. Nippon Television Network.

At the end of the live-action series *Kaibutsu-kun* (2010), the young prince returned to the land of the monsters after completing his training among the humans—but he's back. This ninety-minute special features three separate episodes: "Kaiko," "Detective" and "Wolfman's Lie." Includes additional content recorded before a live studio audience.

The Moth
[Leptirica]

RTB. Apr 15, 1973. Horror/Suspense. D: Đorđe Kadijević. W: Đorđe Kadijević, Milovana Glišića. C: Mirjana Nikolić ♀, Petar Božović, Slobodan Perović, Vasja Stanković, Aca Stojković, Tanasije Uzunović, Ivan Đurđević. SRB: Serbo-Croatian/Color/63m. Radio-televizija Beograd.

Strahinja is a young man in love with the beautiful Radojka, but their relationship is forbidden because her father doesn't want his daughter to marry a pauper. Strahinja's fortunes will improve if he relocates to a larger town, so he offers to work at the local mill to earn some money for the trip. Unfortunately for him, there has been a series of deadly attacks on workers at the mill, and the village elders believe that a centuries-old vampire named Sava Savanovic is responsible. Based on the short story "After Ninety Years" by Milovana Glišića.

The Phantom
[Upiór]

TVP. Feb 11, 1968. Horror/Suspense. D: Stanisław Lenartowicz. W: Ziemowit Fedecki. C: Jadwiga Chojnacka ♀, Aleksandra Zawieruszanka, Jan Machulski, Ryszard Ronczewski, Zdzislaw Karczewski ♀, Witold Pyrkosz, Edward Lubaszenko. POL: Polish/B&W/28m. Film Polski/Telewizja Polska.

A story about a young woman whose family is cursed with vampirism. Loosely based on the 1841 short story "Upyr" by Alexey Tolstoy, which was the first vampire story written by a Russian author.

The Vampire Family
[Semya vurdalakov]

YST. 1990. Horror/Suspense. D/W: Gennadiy Klimov, Igor Shavlak. C: Igor Shavlak, Nikolai Kochegarov, Nikita Simanovsky, Yelena Karadzhova, Ivan Shchyogolev, Yelena Zemlyanikina, Yuri Katin-Yartsev, Nikolai Voloshin. SOV: Russian/Color/78m.

A newspaper reporter travels to the Russian countryside to investigate rumors of strange activities in the area. He meets a family of peasants who claim that their deceased grandfather, on this very night, will return from the grave as a vampire—and they were right. Based on the 1884 novella "The Family of the Vourdalak" by Alexey Tolstoy, this story was also adapted as "The Wurdalak" segment in Mario Bava's 1963 film *I Tre volti della paura (Black Sabbath)*.

Documentaries and Reality TV

The 30 Most Mysterious Stories
[*Les 30 histoires les plus mystérieuses*]

TF1. May 26, 2006 – Aug 5, 2011 (6 Episodes). Mystery/Fantasy. D: Franck Broqua. W: Carole Rousseau, Jacques Legros. C: Anon. FRA: French/Color/720m. Case Productions.

Presented in a ranked format, hosts Carole Rousseau and Jacques Legros count down the top thirty mysterious stories from a wide range of topics. These include the paranormal, folklore, and other incredible subjects—as well as modern vampires, the *chupacabra,* and the Vampire of Highgate.

AVRO Close-Up – "Bela Lugosi: Dracula's Doppelgänger"
[*AVRO Close-Up* – "Bela Lugosi: Dracula's Dubbelganger"]

Nederland 2/AVRO. Dec 9, 2007. Biography/History. D: Florin Iepan. W: Florin Iepan, Ramona Iepan. C: Otilia Hedesan, Bela Lugosi Jr., Péter Müller, Gary D. Rhodes, Helen Richman, Boris Karloff. BEL/GER/NED: Dutch/B&W, Color/52m. Belgische Radio en Televisie/Zweites Deutsches Fernsehen.

Examines the roller-coaster life of Lugosi, from his early days on stage to his iconic film role in *Dracula* (1931)—which shot him to stardom yet ultimately killed his career in Hollywood. The program explores his fall from grace, his drug use and recovery, and his questionable roles in a series of B-movies towards the end of his life. Also known as *Le vampire déchu (The Fallen Vampire).*

Galileo Mystery – "Vampire: The True Story of the Leech"
[*Galileo Mystery* – "Vampire: Die wahre Geschichte der Blutsauger"]

Pro7. Feb 15, 2008 (S03E18). Education/History. D: Anon. W: Anon. C: Mario Ludwig. GER: German/Color/60m. Story House Productions/ProSieben.

This pseudo-documentary series, an offshoot of *Galileo* magazine, explores folklore and mythology; this particular episode delves into the legends of the vampire. Presented by Aiman Abdallah.

Mysteries – "The Highgate Vampire"
[*Mystères* – "Hypnose" / "Jeanne Fretel" / "Au clair de la Lune" / "Contre-expertise Moto en aveugle" / "Le vampire de Highgate" / "Le mystère de la maison hantée de Normandie: Les pommes volantes" / "Les Prophéties de Nostradamus"]

TF1. Mar 4, 1994 (S02E07). Mystery/Fantasy. D: Anon. W: Anon. C: Anon. FRA: French/Color/60m. Plaisance Films.

In one of the first French series to explore the supernatural in depth, host Alexandre Baloud covered several different topics in each episode. These were supported by reports, reenactments, interviews and personal accounts, and concluded with a group discussion. The segment "The Highgate Vampire" examined the mystery of a vampire that was said to have haunted London's Highgate Cemetery in the 1970s.

Myth and Truth – "Dracula Lives: The Legacy of the Count"
[Mythos und Wahrheit – "Dracula lebt: Das Vermächtnis des Grafen"]

ZDF. Jan 7, 2012 (S--E--). Literature/Folklore. D: Marvin Entholt. W: Marvin Entholt. C: Elizabeth Miller, Mark Benecke, Nicola Bardola, Charlie Bewley, Lydia Benecke, Dacre Stoker, Otilia Hedeşan, Mihai Fifor, Hagen Schaub. GER: German/Color/43m. Februar Film/ZDF.

This documentary explores the evolution of the Western vampire, from the hideous revenant in *Nosferatu* to the stylish Cullen clan from the *Twilight* films. Scholars discuss the genesis of Bram Stoker's novel, and the ancient, superstitious rituals that Romanians still practice to this day.

Sphinx: Secrets of History – "The Vampire Princess"
[Sphinx: Geheimnisse der Geschichte – "Die Vampirprinzessin"]

ZDF. Oct 27, 2007 (S14E--). Folklore/History. D: Klaus Steindl. W: Andreas Sulzer, Klaus Feichtenberger. C: Michal Ernée, Christa Kletter, Christian Reiter, Rainer Köppl, Pater Albin Scheuch, Silvia Hladky, Ulrich Scherzer. AUT/FRA/GER/USA: German/Color/60m. Pro Omnia Film/Zweites Deutsches Fernsehen.

In the Czech Republic, excavations near the castle of Princess Eleonore von Schwarzenberg revealed three bodies buried in the style of *magia posthuma,* a ritual once used on those suspected of being a vampire—thought to prevent the undead from rising again. The princess led an unorthodox lifestyle and believed in the occult; she died from cervical cancer in 1741. Could tales of von Schwarzenberg and these strange burial customs be the real inspiration behind Bram Stoker's immortal *Dracula?* A dubbed version with English narration by Brad Abelle was broadcast on the Smithsonian Channel on Oct 19, 2008 (and on the History Channel in the UK).

The Truth About Dracula
[Die Wahrheit über Dracula]

Arte. Oct 27, 2011. Education/History. D/W: Stanislaw Mucha. C: Vittorio Ballerotti, Walther G Seidner, Winfred Hutter, Dieter Schlesak, Gheorghe Gigel, Valentina Savu, Eginald Schlattner, Ileana Scurtu, Anna Zeck. GER: German/Color/82m. U5 Filmproduktion GmbH.

A journey through Transylvania that explores the boom in tourism, thanks to the popularity of Bram Stoker's novel *Dracula*.

U-KISS' Vampire

MBC. Jan 22 – Mar 26, 2010 (10 Episodes). Comedy/Music. D: Anon. W: Anon. C: Alexander Lee Eusebio, Shin Soo Hyun, Kim Ki Bum, Lee Kiseop, Eli Kim, Kevin Woo, Shin Dong Ho. KOR: Korean/Color/300m. NH Media.

Reality show that follows a seven-member boy band from South Korea—*Ubiquitous Korean International [Idol] Super Star*—who live together in a dorm during the course of the series. As a means to illustrate the "psychological differences" inherent to one's blood type, band members are separated into teams based on this criterion; in the opening credits, each member is dressed as a vampire. This was part of a series of film and television projects used to promote the band, which was manufactured by NH Media in 2008. Presented by Sun Shin Ae.

Animation

Adventures of Puss-in-Boots – "Pierre Turned into a Vampire!"
[Nagagutsu o haita neko no bôken – "Kyûketsuki ni sareta pieeru!"]

TV Tokyo. Sep 9, 1992 (S01E24). Adventure/Family. D: Susumu Ishizaki. W: Takashi Yamada, Shun'ichi Yukimuro. C: Chieko Honda, Banjô Ginga, Chika Sakamoto, Ryô Horikawa, Takehito Koyasu, Hirotaka Suzuoki, Kazuhiko Inoue. JPN: Japanese/Color/30m. Toei Company.

A loveable cat helps a poor boy in his quest to win the heart of a princess. No specifics are known about this episode, aside from a probable vampire theme based on the title.

Astro Boy – "Vampire Vale"
[Tetsuwan Atomu – "Vampire Vale"]

Fuji TV/NBC. Jan 18, 1964 (S01E55). Adventure/Sci-Fi. D/W: Fred Ladd. C: Billie Lou Watt, Cliff Owen, Gilbert Mack. JPN: Japanese/B&W/30m. Mushi Productions/Video Promotions Inc./NBC Enterprises.

While traveling through the mountains of Transmelvania, adventurers Tick and Tock discover a small remote village; each home has garlic flowers and crosses covering the windows. They camp inside an abandoned castle on the outskirts of town, and are attacked by a vampire—but Tock escapes. Dr. Elefun discovers that the bloodsucker is his former colleague, Ray Sergum, a scholar well-versed in the legend of Atlantis—and he has a mysterious connection to this civilization that was lost twelve thousand years ago.

A decent episode that begins strong, yet becomes a little convoluted once the hidden society of

Poseidon (once part of Atlantis) is introduced—which leads to a good laugh after one character deadpans, "are you making this up?" Even though Sergum has an aversion to sunlight and is immortal, he's not a true vampire. He's using the guise as a front for something even more sinister: he's kidnapping the village youth and taking them to Poseidon, because the inhabitants cannot produce offspring themselves. This children's cartoon also includes a creepy scene where Astro Boy has his feet shot off.

📺 This series was produced in Japan, although half of the episodes were adapted for the North American market.

Bandar Book: One Million Year Trip
[Ai wa Chikyû wo Sukuu – Hyakumannen chikyû no tabi: Bandâ bukku]

NTV. Aug 27, 1978. Adventure/Fantasy. D: Osamu Tezuka, Hisashi Sakaguchi. W: Osamu Tezuka. C: Yuu Mizushima, Toru Ohira, Fumi Koyama, Masato Ibu, Chiba Koichi ⚥, Katsuta Hisashi, Kosei Tomita, Iemasa Ieyumi. JPN: Japanese/Color/93m. Tezuka Productions Co. Ltd.

Bandar Book was Japan's first feature-length animated movie made for television, and was broadcast as part of a twenty-four hour programming special that celebrated Nippon Television's twenty-fifth anniversary. Bandar is a human teenager who grew up on a distant planet populated by peaceful shape-shifters. Their tranquil lives are shattered upon the arrival of an invading army, which forces Bandar to return home to Earth—where he confronts evil on a world that he never knew existed.

In one segment, Bandar visits a creepy castle with an interior layout inspired by M. C. Escher's *Relativity* drawing. Inside the cave-like dwelling, Bandar confronts Don Dracula, and breaks off the vampire's fangs before he's attacked by a large mummy. The pursuit takes to the skies, where Dracula eventually succumbs to the rays of the sun. Don Dracula (and his daughter Chocola) resurfaced in their own short-lived television series in 1982.

Bibi Blocksberg – "B.B. and the Vampires"
[Bibi Blocksberg – "B.B. und die Vampire"]

Premiere. Dec 28, 1997 (S01E08). Adventure/Family. D: Royce Ramos. W: Christian Matzerath, Ulli Herzog. C: Susanna Bonasewicz, Hallgerd Bruckhaus, Barbara Ratthey, Guido Weber, Katrin Neusser ⚥, Konrad Bösherz ⚥, Joachim Pukaß. GER: German/Color/30m. Kiddinx Films/Hahn Film AG.

The series follows a teenage witch who's still learning her craft, and lives at home with her mother Barbara (a witch) and her father Bernhard (a normal man). In this episode, Bibi's dad is quite unnerved after the family wins a surprise trip to Transylvania—even though he loves vampire movies.

Black Blood Brothers

Tokyo MX. Sep 8 – Nov 24, 2006 (12 Episodes). Fantasy/Horror. D: Hiroaki Yoshikawa. W: Yuu Sugitani. C: Miyuki Sawashiro, Ryoko Nagata, Omi Minami, Takahiro Sakurai, Hiroki Yasumoto, Ayumi Tsuji, Jun Fukuyama, Hisao Egawa. JPN: Japanese/Color/360m. Studio Live/BBB Partners.

Ten years ago, the Black Bloods (old vampires) and Red Bloods (humans) combined forces to defeat a new group of vampires—the Kowloon Children. But the surviving members haven't given up; they're attempting to once again raise an evil army to take up arms against their enemies.

Black Lagoon: The Second Barrage – "The Vampire Twins Comen"

Tokyo MX. Oct 3, 2006 (S01E01). Crime/Suspense. D/W: Sunao Katabuchi. C: Daisuke Namikawa, Megumi Toyoguchi, Jun Karasawa, Mami Koyama, Hiroaki Hirata, Tsutomu Isobe, Banjou Ginga. JPN: Japanese/Color/30m. Black Lagoon Committee/Geneon Entertainment.

Bounty hunters from across the globe descend on Roanapur. A sizeable sum has been placed on the head of whoever was responsible for killing gang members at Hotel Moscow.

Bleach - "Another Side Story! This Time's Enemy is a Monster!?"
[Bleach - "Gaiden futatabi! Kondo no teki ha monsutā!?"]

TV Tokyo. Jan 11, 2011 (S14E39). Action/Fantasy. D: Noriyuki Abe. W: Masashi Sogo. C: Masakazu Morita, Yuki Matsuoka, Fumiko Orikasa, Kentaro Ito, Noriaki Sugiyama ♀, Hiroki Yasumoto, Toru Okawa, Takako Honda. JPN: Japanese/Color/24m. TV Tokyo/Studio Pierrot.

This long-running animated series centres around teenager Ichigo Kurosaki, who has the ability to see spirits and eventually becomes a Soul Reaper. In this episode, two hunters arrive at a dilapidated castle in search of a legendary jewel, the Snow Crystal, which can force monsters to turn back to human form. Inhabiting the castle is Kurosaki, who has been trapped and turned into a Frankenstein Monster, along with his enemy Uryū, who appears in the guise of a lethargic, somewhat anemic vampire who prefers to drink milk. Based on the manga of the same name by Tite Kubo.

Blood+

MBS/TBS. Oct 8, 2005 – Sep 23, 2006 (50 Episodes). Action/Horror. D: Var. W: Var. C: Eri Kitamura ♀, Akiko Yajima, Hiroyuki Yoshino, Hôchû Ôtsuka, Jûrôta Kosugi, Katsuyuki Konishi, Takashi Nagasako. JPN: Japanese/Color/1500m. Production I.G./Aniplex/Mainichi Broadcasting System.

With no memory of her past, Saya Otonashi discovers that she's a warrior destined to battle a race of immortal bat-like creatures called Chiropterans—and that she can only survive by living off the blood of humans. This is an alternate retelling of the *anime* film *Blood: The Last Vampire* (2000). Dubbed into English and broadcast in North America on the Cartoon Network from March 11, 2007 to March 23, 2008.

Blood-C

MBS/TBS. Jul 8 – Sep 22, 2011 (12 Episodes). Action/Horror. D: Tsutomu Mizushima. W: Jun'ichi Fujisaku, Nanase Ohkawa. C: Nana Mizuki ♀, Keiji Fujiwara, Kenji Nojima, Masumi Asano, Misato Fukuen, Atsushi Abe, Tatsuhisa Suzuki. JPN: Japanese/Color/360m. CLAMP/Production I.G.

Saya Kisaragi is a seemingly normal girl living an average life, except at night—when she protects her village from hordes of supernatural creatures. This is the third interpretation of stories and characters first presented in the film *Blood: The Last Vampire* (2000).

Carland Cross – "The Highgate Vampire"
[Carland Cross – "Le Vampire de Highgate"]

TF1. 1996 (S01E21). Crime/Mystery. D: Michel Oleffe, Olivier Grenson. W: Michel Oleffe. C: Robert Guilmard, Daniel Dury, Véronique Biefnot, Philippe Allard, Peppino Capotondi, Léon Dony, Nicole Shirer. BEL/CAN/FRA: French/Color/30m. ODEC-Kid Cartoons/TF1/Canal+.

Series follows a British private investigator in the 1930s, who takes on unexplained and mysterious cases. In this episode, the working-class neighborhood of Highgate is being robbed, and the prime suspect is an acrobat named Krolock—whose stage persona is a vampire. This story may be inspired by the infamous "Highgate Vampire" sensation from the early 1970s, and "Krolock" may allude to the vampire Count von Krolock from the 1967 film *Dance of the Vampires* (a.k.a. *The Fearless Vampire Killers*).

A Certain Magical Index – "Vampire Killer (Deep Blood)"
[Toaru Majutsu no Index – "Kyuuketsu koroshi (diipuburaddo)"]

Animax SK. Nov 29, 2008 (S01E09). Action/Drama. D: Hiroshi Nishikiori. W: Masanao Akahoshi. C: Yuka Iguchi, Rina Satou, Akeno Watanabe, Atsushi Abe, Kimiko Koyama, Kana Asumi, Kishô Taniyama. JPN: Japanese/Color/30m. Geneon Entertainment/J.C. Staff.

Series follows a young nun named Index, a sorceress whose brain has been implanted with thousands of magical writings from the *Index Librorum Prohibitorum;* due to the toll this takes on her mind, she is only expected to live for one year. In one story arc, a new student arrives at the Kirigaoka Academy for Girls. She's given the nickname "Deep Blood," because vampires are inexplicably drawn to her. In this episode, alchemist Aureolus Izzard uses the girl to snare a vampire; he plans to extract the creature's blood and use it to extend Index's life—although there's a chance she may turn into a vampire herself. The *Index Librorum Prohibitorum*—first published in the mid-sixteenth century by the Catholic Church—compiled a list of heretical authors and prohibited books, which included the writings of some early philosophers and astronomers whose work promoted pantheism and heliocentrism. The last edition was published in 1948, and the Index was officially abolished in 1966. Thirty years later, the Vatican allowed scholars to view all archives associated with the Index, and researchers have been surveying the material ever since.

D.Gray-man –"The Vampire of the Ancient Castle" / "Do Your Best, Mr. Exorcist" / "Krory, Attack" / "Eliade's Truth" / "The Vampire I Loved"
[*D.Gray-man* – "Kojô no Kyūketsuki" / "Ganbare Exorcist-sama" / "Kurôrī, Shūgeki" / "Eriāde no Shinjitsu" / "Watashi ga Aishita Kyūketsuki"]

TV Tokyo. Feb 13 – Mar 13, 2007 (S01E19-23). Horror/Fantasy. D: Osamu Nabeshima. W: Reiko Yoshida. C: Sanae Kobayashi, Hiroki Touchi, Hiroshi Yanaka, Ai Shimizu, Hozumi Gôda, Kenichi Suzumura, Junpei Takiguchi. JPN: Japanese/Color/150m. TMS Entertainment/TV Tokyo.

In this five-part story, Allen heads to Romania in search of his mentor, General Cross Marian, and discovers the locals are living in fear of a bloodthirsty vampire.

Dance in the Vampire Bund
[Dansu in za vanpaia bando]

AT-X. Jan 7 – Apr 1, 2010 (12 Episodes). Action/Horror. D: Akiyuki Shinbo, Masahiro Sonoda. W: Hiroyuki Yoshino. C: Aoi Yuki ♀, Yuuichi Nakamura, Asuka Tanii, Eri Kitamura, Akeno Watanabe, Chiwa Saito, Ken Narita. JPN: Japanese/Color/360m. Vampire Bund Gyouseifu.

Mina Tepes, the princess and ruler of all vampires, believes the undead should no longer be hidden from the human population. In a deal with the Japanese government, she pays off the entire national debt, in exchange for the right to build an exclusive district for her kind—which she calls "The Bund." After the existence of vampires is revealed to the world, tensions run high as extremist factions—from both races—undermine the fragile state of peace.

A Dark Rabbit Has Seven Lives
[Itsuka Tenma no Kurousagi]

Syndicated. Jul 8 – Sep 23, 2011 (12 Episodes). Adventure/Fantasy. D: Takashi Yamamoto. W: Shigeru Morita. C: Megumi Takamoto ♀, Shinnosuke Tachibana, Chika Horikawa, Iori Nomizu, Aya Goda, Kenichi Suzumura, Jun Fukuyama. JPN: Japanese/Color/360m. ZEXCS.

When he was a boy, Taito Kurogane met a girl named Himea Saito, a vampire who gave him the gift of eternal life. They were separated, and Taito lost all memory of his time with her. Nine years later, after he survives yet another accident that should have killed him, Taito reunites with Himea—and his memories of the past come flooding back.

Demon Corpse
[Shiki]

Fuji TV. Jul 8 – Dec 30, 2010 (22 Episodes). Drama/Mystery. D: Tetsuro Amino. W: Kenji Sugihara. C: Kouki Uchiyama, Toru Ohkawa, Aoi Yuki ♀, Kazuyuki Okitsu, Haruka Tomatsu ♀, Nobuhiko Okamoto, Ai Orikasa. JPN: Japanese/Color/660m. DENTSU Music and Entertainment/Darks Production.

Sotoba is a remote village where time passes slowly and nothing much happens—but the quiet lives of its residents are shattered upon the discovery of three dead bodies. The village doctor believes it's an isolated incident, yet the killings continue; he concludes that vampires are to blame.

Descendants of Darkness – "The Nagasaki File"
[Yami no matsuei – "The Nagasaki File"]

WOWOW. Oct 2-16, 2000 (S01E01-03). Comedy/Fantasy. D: Hiroko Tokita. W: Masaharu Amiya. C: Shinichiro Miki, Mayumi Asano, Shô Hayami, Toshihiko Seki, Yuka Imai ♀, Yumiko Nakanishi. JPN: Japanese/Color/75m. J.C. Staff/Central Park Media.

🦇 🦇 🦇

Series follows Tsuzuki—a guardian of death—who works for the Ministry of Hades to help guide lost souls that are stuck in the mortal world. In this three-part story, Tsuzuki reluctantly teams up with a new partner, Kurosaki, to investigate a bizarre murder in Nagasaki. The prime suspect is Maria Wong, a singer who committed suicide several months earlier.

Wong is reanimated by her mother, a malevolent woman who wants to continue to profit from her daughter's fame. When not performing, the reluctant vampire wanders the streets of Nagasaki, seeking out victims to satiate her uncontrollable bloodlust. It's a richly-animated and quirky story, with many funny moments; those unfamiliar with its *bishounen* and *yaoi* themes may be surprised by the suggestively homoerotic scenes between the cast of androgynous male characters. An English-dubbed version aired in 2008 on SyFy in the USA, and the Super Channel in Canada.

Detective Conan - "Vampire Villa"
[Meitantei Conan – "Dorakyura sou satsujin jiken"]

NTV. Jan 26/Feb 2, 1998 (S04E06/07). Comedy/Drama. D: Kenji Kodama. W: Fumiharu Kamanaka. C: Minami Takayama, Akira Kamiya, Wakana Yamazaki, Ami Koshimizu, Ai Orikasa, Ikue Ohtani, Koji Yusa. JPN: Japanese/Color/60m. FUNimation Entertainment/Tokyo Movie Shinsha.

In this two-part story, a famous horror novelist is murdered at his estate. His body is found in a room locked from within, and there are no footprints in the snow outside of the windows. The author often wrote about vampires, and Conan believes that one of these creatures may be behind the attack. The series was retitled *Case Closed* for the North American release.

Dr. Slump & Arale-chan – "Fearful Monsters Night" / "Scary! Monster Prince"
[Dr. Slump & Arale-chan – "Kyoufu no Monsters Night" / "Kowaai! Monsutā purinsu"]

Fuji TV. Aug 5, 1981/Jun 30, 1982 (S01E17/62). Adventure/Family. D: Minoru Okazaki. W: Masaki Tsuji, Shun'ichi Yukimuro, Michiru Shimada. C: Kenji Utsumi, Mami Koyama, Isamu Tanonaka, Hiroshi Ohtake, Nachi Nozawa, Kazuko Sugiyama, Masaharu Satou. JPN: Japanese/Color/60m. Tôei Company Ltd.

Follows the adventures of Professor Senbei Norimaki, a.k.a. Dr. Slump, an inventor who lives in

Penguin Village with his wife and their unruly android daughter Arale. In this two-part story arc, a female vampire preys on the family: she attempts to steal money from Senbei, and get a taste of Arale's blood (but fails on both counts). She later returns to claim Senbei's soul, but Arale interferes and saves the day.

Dr. Zitbag's Transylvania Pet Shop
[Docteur Globule]

TF1. Jun 16, 1994 - Jul 27, 1998 (65 Episodes). Adventure/Family. D: Xavier Picard. W: Tony Barnes. C: Jean-Claude Donda, Marc Moro, Max André, Danièle Hazan. FRA/UK: French/Color/1625m. Shanghai Morning Sun Animation.

A mad scientist in Transylvania spends his days inventing all sorts of crazy devices, few of which turn out as planned. He hopes to someday get rich from selling the items, so he can marry the women of his dreams: Sinistra and Bimbella, twin sisters who are vegetarian vampires.

Don Dracula

TV Tokyo. Apr 5 – 26, 1982 (8 Episodes). Adventure/Family. D: Masamune Ochiai. W: Osamu Tezuka, Takao Koyama. C: Kenji Utsumi ♀, Saeko Shimazu ♀, Junpei Takiguchi, Takao Ohyama, Kaneta Kimotsuki, Masaru Ikeda. JPN: Japanese/Color/240m. Tezuka Productions Co. Ltd.

An old house is transported from Romania to Japan with the occupants still inside—Don Dracula, his daughter Chocola, their henchman Igor, and their animal companion Bat Yasubei. A group of vampire hunters, led by Professor Lip Van Helsing, don't exactly give them a warm welcome. Out of a planned twenty-six episodes, only eight were produced; only four of these were broadcast before the sponsor went out of business, which led to the cancelation of the series.

Dracula: Sovereign of the Damned
[Yami no teiô kyûketsuki Dorakyura]

TV Asahi. Aug 19, 1980. Drama/Romance. D: Minoru Okazaki. W: Tadaaki Yamazaki. C: Ryo Ishihara, Nachi Nozawa ♀, Keiko Mari, Hidekatsu Shibata, Hiroko Suzuki, Junpei Takiguchi. JPN: Japanese/Color/94m. Tôei Animation Company/Harmony Gold Ltd./Northstar Entertainment.

Dracula relocates to Boston and falls in love with the beautiful Dolores, whom he saves from becoming the bride of Satan. They have a child together, which doesn't sit well with the Devil and his worshipers—but they're not Dracula's only enemies. A rag-tag group of hunters, which include the descendants of Abraham Van Helsing and Jonathan Harker, also want to destroy the vampire.

Loosely based on Marvel's seventy-issue *Tomb of Dracula* comic book series, this adaptation is a bloody mess. Dialogue-heavy with far too much exposition, the production tries to cram several years of storyline into ninety minutes. Despite all its faults, it's still worthwhile viewing, because a feature-length animated vampire story from this period is pretty rare. It was dubbed into English in 1983 (crediting "Robert Barron"—a fabricated person—as writer and director), and then broadcast on cable channels in the USA.

Dragonball – "The Five Fighters"

Fuji TV. Jul 15, 1987 (S02E42). Adventure/Fantasy. D: Anon. W: Anon. C: Tôru Furuya, Masako Nozawa, Mami Koyama, Naoko Watanabe, Mitsuko Horie, Junpei Takiguchi, Kôji Totani ♀. JPN: Japanese/Color/20m. Tôei Company Ltd.

Goku and friends accept a challenge to fight five warriors one on one; if they win, Baba will reveal the location of the final dragonball. These are no ordinary opponents; in the first match, Krillin faces a crazed beast: Fangs the vampire. This bizarre children's cartoon is unexpectedly violent and a little creepy. The vampire sinks his fangs into Krillin's skull to feed, and the head wounds constantly squirt and drip blood. The name of the character is officially "Dracula Man" (or "Draculaman"), and is defeated by garlic breath. The series was dubbed into English as *Dragon Ball*, and broadcast on the Cartoon Network (this episode was retitled "We Are the Five Warriors").

Ernest the Vampire
[*Ernest le Vampire*]

FR3. 1988 – 1991 (117 Episodes). Adventure/Family. D: Bruno Desraisses, José Xavier. W: François Bruel. C: Pascal Woyciechowski. FRA: French/Color/293m. Quartier Latin/SEK Studio/Col.Ima.Son/France 3/WDR.

Ernest is a lonely vampire who lives in a large castle along with some bats and mice. He looks like a cross between a bat and an elephant, with upper canines that resemble those of a walrus. Each episode begins with a surreal dream sequence, in which Ernest has an adventure that usually ends poorly, and he wakes up with a start from inside his coffin.

Ghost Sweeper Mikami

TV Asahi. Apr 11, 1993 – Mar 6, 1994 (45 Episodes). Comedy/Horror. D: Akinori Yabe. W: Masaharu Amiya. C: Hiromi Tsuru, Ryou Horikawa, Mariko Koda, Toshiyuki Morikawa ♀, Kazuyuki Sogabe, Shigeru Chiba, Maria Kawamura. JPN: Japanese/Color/1350m. Tôei Company Ltd.

In Japan, overpopulation has reached the point to where it's affecting the spirit world, and the ethereal beings no longer have any space of their own—so they have no choice but to encroach on the land of the living. Reiko Mikami is trained in the art of exorcism, and she works tirelessly to rid the city of its ghostly pests—for a modest fee. This series features Pietro de Bloodeau, a seven-hundred-year-old half-vampire who's related to Dracula through marriage. He's the current disciple of the same Catholic priest who trained Reiko, up until she became dissatisfied with living a life of poverty—and chose to use her skills for profit.

Heartbeat Tonight
[Tokimeki Tonight]

NTV. Oct 7, 1982 – Sep 22, 1983 (34 Episodes). Comedy/Romance. D: Hiroshi Sasagawa. W: Toshio Okabe, Akiyoshi Sakai. C: Eriko Hara, Yuu Mizushima, Yoshito Yasuhara ⚲, Miina Tominaga, Hideyuki Tanaka, Junpei Takiguchi. JPN: Japanese/Color/1020m. Group TAC.

Ranze Etō comes from an extraordinary family; her mother is a werewolf and her father is a vampire. She appears to be an ordinary teenager, but she hides a special ability: through a simple bite, Ranze can turn into a carbon-copy of anything—yet she can only revert back to normal by sneezing. She falls in love with a star athlete, Shun Makabe, but her parents won't allow her to date a human—but Shun is hiding a magical secret of his own.

Hellsing
[Herushingu]

Fuji TV. Oct 10, 2001 – Jan 16, 2002 (13 Episodes). Action/Horror. D: Umanosuke Iida. W: Chiaki J. Konaka, Yuuji Hosono. C: Jôji Nakata ⚲, Yoshiko Sakakibara, Fumiko Orikasa ⚲, Nachi Nozawa, Takumi Yamazaki ⚲, Motomu Kiyokawa, Hideyuki Tanaka. JPN: Japanese/Color/390m. Gonzo.

The last descendent of Van Helsing teams up with an ancient vampire to battle a host of supernatural creatures bent on destroying the world. Dubbed into English and rebroadcast in the United States from October 4 to December 27, 2003 on *Starz! Encore Action.* Nine additional OVA episodes have since been produced under the banner *Hellsing Ultimate,* and follow the storyline of the original manga more closely than the *anime* series.

Hipira: The Little Vampire
[Hipira-kun]

NHK. Dec 21 – 25, 2009 (10 Episodes). Adventure/Family. D: Shinji Kimura. W: Katsuhiro Otomo. C: Yumiko Kobayashi ⚲, Bin Shimada, Chihiro Suzuki, Sayaka Ohara, Ayumi Fujimura, Fumiko Orikasa, Genki Yoshimoto. JPN: Japanese/Color/50m. Sunrise.

Follows the adventures of Hipira, a young boy who's part of a community of vampires living in the city of Salta—where the sun never shines.

I'm Gonna Be an Angel
[Tenshi ni Narumon]

TV Tokyo. Apr 7 – Sep 29, 1999 (26 Episodes). Comedy/Romance. D: Hiroshi Nishikiori. W: Mamiko Ikeda. C: Issei Miyazaki, Tomoko Kawakami, Yukana Nogami, Nobutoshi Hayashi ☥, Juurouta Kosugi, Noriko Hidaka, Tomoko Naka. JPN: Japanese/Color/780m. Kyoto Animation/Studio Pierrot.

Yuusuke lives alone until one fateful day when he meets Noelle, an angel in training. She moves into his house with her extended family in tow; they're a group of supernatural creatures that include her older brother Gabriel, who's a vampire.

Illusion at Midnight / Midnight Fantasy – "8653 yen no onna"
[Genso Midnight – "8653 yen no onna"]

TV Asahi. 1997 (S01E09). Drama/Fantasy. D: Toshio Oi. W: Mitsuru Tanabe. C: Kanako Enomoto ☥, Shigeru Saiki, Ken Izawa, Jun'ichirou Asano, Hiroshi Ishii, Etsuko Kishimoto, Hiroshi Harada, Yoshitaka Yanagida. JPN: Japanese/Color/30m. Tôei Company Ltd.

An eleven-part fantasy series that was not released outside of Japan; each episode features a supernatural subject such as ghosts, vampires, psychics, and other entities from local folklore. This episode was based on the short story of the same title by Baku Yumemakura.

Karin

WOWOW. Nov 3, 2005 – May 11, 2006 (24 Episodes). Comedy/Horror. D: Shinichiro Kimura. W: Masaharu Amiya. C: Sayuri Yahagi ☥, Katsuyuki Konishi, Hiroshi Matsumoto ☥, Emi Shinohara ☥, Aya Hisakawa, Junichi Suwabe ☥. JPN: Japanese/Color/720m. Karin Seisaku Iinkai.

Based on the *Chibi Vampire* manga series by Yuna Kagesaki, the story follows pureblood vampire Karin Maaka, who hides a terrible secret: she produces too much blood, so instead of drinking it, she injects her own into her victims. Despite her unusual vampiric tendencies, Karin passes for human and keeps her true self hidden—until the arrival of Kenta Usui, a new transfer student. Narrated by Junpei Takiguchi.

The Ketchup Vampires
[Die Ketchup Vampire]

ZDF. 1991 - 1994 (26 Episodes). Adventure/Family. D: Alexander Zapletal. W: Bettina Matthaei. C: Marek Erhardt ☥, Simone Seidenberg ☥, Sabine Hahn, Christian Stark ☥, Hildegard Krekel, Rolf Jülich, Marianne Kehlau ☥. CZE/GER: German/Color/780m. Zweites Deutsches Fernsehen.

Members of a reformed vampire clan are vegetarian, and subsist only on ketchup. Their patriarch, Maurice, stole a sacred tome that details how to become evil; since then, all vampires have changed their ways. But some clans want to regain their wicked nature, so the hunt is on to find the book. It's hidden somewhere inside the castle of Edgar von Ravenstein, who's unaware that Maurice and his other new tenants are vampires. Some episodes were dubbed into English and compiled into two ninety-minute programs released on VHS (with narration by Cassandra Peterson as Elvira, Mistress of the Dark).

Kitou the Six-Eyed Monster – "Coffin' Up a Vampire"
[Kitou Scrogneugneu – "Le vampire de ces monstres"]

TF1/Radio-Canada. Nov 27, 2003 (S01E17). Adventure/Family. D: Frédéric Dybowski. W: Tony Scott. C: Jan Sebastian Panesak, Max Felder, Simone Brahmann, Katharina Berthold, Beate Pfeiffer, A.J. Henderson ⚲. CAN/FRA: French/Color/15m. Belvision/RTBF/Dargaud Marina.

Kitou is a curious and good-natured six-eyed monster who leaves home to begin a new life in the human realm of Lilacville, where he's befriended by a young girl named Lucy. In this episode, the evil Count Brakula comes to town, hoping to make everyone miserable—but Kitou has other plans for the vampire.

Legend of Duo
[Rejendo obu duo]

AT-X. Oct 27, 2004 – 2005 (12 Episodes). Drama/Fantasy. D: Koichi Kikuchi. W: Toshiki Inoue, Daisuke Ishibashi. C: Hisashi Nakamoto ⚲, Tomokazu Sugita ⚲, Haruhisa Okumura, Yuu Amano. JPN: Japanese/Color/60m. mobanimation/Duo Project.

A mysterious disease drives humanity towards extinction. Duo, a vampire, reveals a secret cure that saves mankind; in doing so, he discloses the existence of his once-hidden race, which turns humans against the vampires. Now considered a traitor to his own people, Duo is hunted by Zieg, a man he once considered a good friend—but who's now his immortal enemy.

Little Drac
[Draculito mon saigneur]

M6. Sep 1991 – 1993 (26 Episodes). Family/Fantasy. D: Bruno-René Huchez. W: France-Hélène Joubaud. C: Françoise Blanchard ⚲, Pascale Jacquemont, Bernard Bollet ⚲, Patrice Baudrier. FRA/GER: French/Color/780m. Renaissance-Atlantic Films/Société Française de Production.

In this series, based on the books by Martin Waddell and Joseph Wright, Little Dracula tries to be a normal ten-year-old kid—even though he's the only son of the legendary vampire. This French-language version of the English series *Little Dracula* (1991) is distinct from the original, because a full twenty-six episodes were commissioned whereas only thirteen were produced for the English market.

Little Kaibutsu
[Kaibutsu-kun]

TBS. Apr 21, 1968 – Mar 23, 1969 (50 Episodes). Adventure/Family. D: Masaaki Osumi. W: Masaya Yamazaki, Shima Namie. C: Fuyumi Shiraishi, Minori Matsushima, Mariko Mukai, Hiroshi Ohtake ♀, Shingo Kanemoto, Masao Imanishi. JPN: Japanese/B&W/1500m. Tokyo Movie Shinsha/Zero Studio.

As he prepares to become King, a boisterous young prince from the land of Kaibutsu goes to the human realm for training. He takes along three attendants: Wolfman, Franken, and Dracula—who prefers to dine on tomato juice rather than blood. Narrated by Nagaharu Yodogawa.

Little Kaibutsu 2
[Kaibutsu-kun 2]

TV Asahi. Sep 2, 1980 – Sep 28, 1982 (188 Episodes). Adventure/Family. D: Hiroshi Fukutomi. W: Masaya Yamazaki. C: Masako Nozawa, Katsue Miwa, Chiyoko Kawashima, Kaneta Kimotsuki ♀, Takuzou Kamiyama, Taro Sagami. JPN: Japanese/Color/5640m. Shin-Ei Animation.

In this remake of the original series, a young prince from the land of Kaibutsu travels to the human realm. With the help of his three companions—Wolfman, Franken and Dracula—Kaibutsu battles a horde of supernatural creatures.

Little Vampire
[Petit Vampire]

FR 3. Oct 24, 2004 – 2005 (52 Episodes). Adventure/Family. D: Christian Choquet. W: Sandrina Jardel, Riad Sattouf. C: Kevin Sommier, Riad Sattouf, Emmanuel Fouquet, Isabelle Laporte, Vincent Azé, Michel Vignaud. FRA/IRL: French/Color/780m. Tele Media Group/France Animation S.A.

Based on a series of comic books by Joann Sfar, this story features a boy named Michel Douffon and his vampire friend Fernand. During their secret nighttime adventures, they often meet other friendly monsters. In August 2011, Sfar announced that he'll write and direct an animated film adaptation.

Lunar Legend Tsukihime
[Shingetsutan Tsukihime]

TBS/BS-TBS. Oct 9 – Dec 25, 2003 (12 Episodes). Drama/Mystery. D: Katsushi Sakurabi. W: Hiroko Tokita. C: Kenichi Suzumura, Hitomi Nabatame ♀, Hiroyuki Yoshino ♀, Kana Ueda, Fumiko Orikasa ♀, Akiko Kimura. JPN: Japanese/Color/360m. J.C. Staff/Geneon Entertainment Inc.

After surviving a life-threatening injury, Shiki Tohno gained the ability to see the invisible threads that bind everything together, which wear down and snap as a person ages and dies (or as an object is destroyed). He meets a stranger named Arcueid Brunestud; consumed by inexplicable rage, he kills her—or so he thinks. Arcueid is alive and well, but instead of being angry, she offers him a job as her bodyguard.

Lupin the 3rd – "Lupin Becomes a Vampire"
[Rupan Sansei: Part II – "Vampire ni natta Lupin"]

Animax/NTV. May 29, 1978 (S02E08). Comedy/Thriller. D: Kyosuke Mikuriya. W: Kiyoshi Miyata. C: Yasuo Yamada ♀, Kiyoshi Kobayashi, Eiko Masuyama, Goro Naya, Makio Inoue, Michiko Oyano ♀. JPN: Japanese/Color/30m. Tokyo Movie Shinsha (TMS) Entertainment.

Series follows the adventures of the infamous thief Arsène Lupin III and his partners in crime, who travel the world in search of ill-gotten gains. In this episode, a two-thousand-year-old casket is excavated, and the woman found inside still has vital signs. Born a vampire, her name is Camilla—and she claims to be the twin sister of Jesus Christ. Lupin attempts to steal the treasure that was buried along with her: a golden statuette of the Virgin Mary. When he fails, Camilla turns him into her vampire henchman. For the English DVD release, this episode was retitled "But Your Brother was Such a Nice Guy."

Magipoka
[Renkin 3-kyu Magical? Pokaan]

Syndicated. Apr 4 – Jun 20, 2006 (12 Episodes). Adult/Comedy. D: Kenichi Yatagai. W: Yasunori Ide. C: Hitomi Nabatame, Aya Hirano ♀, Satomi Akesaka, Momoko Saito, Shoko Tsuda. JPN: Japanese/Color/360m. GENCO/Media Factory/Magipoka Group.

Four princesses from the Netherworld—a werewolf, an android, a witch, and a vampire—travel to Earth. Unfamiliar with their new surroundings, the group is constantly hounded by the wicked scientist Doctor K-Ko, who wants to use them to prove the existence of the supernatural. The series was followed by three OVA episodes that continued the story.

Master of Mosquiton '99

TV Tokyo. Sep 30, 1997 – Mar 31, 1998 (26 Episodes). Adventure/Comedy. D: Hiroshi Negishi. W: Sumio Uetake, Kenichi Araki. C: Yuka Imai, Takehito Koyasu ♀, Banjou Ginga, Atsuko Tanaka, Yuji Ueda, Michiko Neya. JPN: Japanese/Color/780m. Zero-G Room/Sotsu Agency.

Teenager Inaho Hitomebore defeats a powerful vampire, Alucard von Mosquiton, then revives him with a drop of her blood. Now bound to serve her, Mosquiton takes a job as a teacher at Inaho's school, and follows her on a series of adventures. This is a reimagining of the OVA series *Master of Mosquiton* (1996), a six-volume story adapted from the manga of the same name (which was set in the 1920s).

Mon Colle Knights - "The Vampire Strikes Back"
[Rokumon Tengai Monkore Naito - "Dokkiri kan no vampire"]

TV Tokyo. Jan 31, 2000 (S01E04). Action/Adventure. D: Yasunaga Aoki. W: Satoru Akahori. C: Yui Horie, Tomo Saeki, Kyoko Hikami, Shigeru Chiba, Kazuhiko Inoue, Takehito Koyasu, Shinichiro Miki, Yuko Mizutani, Maria Yamamoto. JPN: Japanese/Color/30m. Studio DEEN.

Adventurers Mondo and Rokuna travel through the Six Gate World—a land of magical creatures—looking for six special items. When combined, the objects will form a connection between their universe and the Earth (no episode synopsis is available). Narrated by Kyoko Hikami.

MoonPhase
[Tsukuyomi Moon Phase]

TV Tokyo. Oct 4, 2004 – Mar 28, 2005 (25 Episodes). Comedy/Romance. D: Akiyuki Shinbo. W: Mayori Sekijima. C: Hiroshi Kamiya, Chiwa Saito ☥, Mai Kadowaki, Michiko Neya, Fumihiko Tachiki, Sawa Ishige, Yumi Kakazu ☥. JPN: Japanese/Color/750m. SHAFT.

Photographer Kohei Morioka is on assignment in Germany, to capture paranormal phenomena for an occult magazine. A teenage vampire, Hazuki, feeds on Kohei and claims him as her servant; much to her surprise, Kohei resists her charms and retains his free will. She follows him back to Tokyo, where their friendship develops over a series of adventures. The 2006 DVD release included a bonus episode.

Mythical Detective Loki Ragnarok - "The Traps of Castle Dracula"
[Matantei Loki Ragnarok - "Dorakyura Jyou no Wana"]

TV Tokyo. Jun 21, 2003 (S01E12). Action/Adventure. D: Hiroshi Watanabe. W: Kenichi Kanemaki. C: Yuriko Fuchizaki, Takahiro Sakurai, Yui Horie, Kouichi Toochika, Hirofumi Nojima, Mai Nakahara, Hiroaki Ishikawa ☥. JPN: Japanese/Color/30m. Studio DEEN.

The mischievous god Loki is exiled to Earth, and now runs a detective agency. His mission is to hunt down the evil auras that plague humanity, a task that must be fulfilled before he can return to the realm of the gods. In this episode, his partner Mayura is trapped within the video game *Dracula's Castle,* and Loki must complete each level before he can rescue her.

Negima!

TV Tokyo. Jan 5 – Jun 29, 2005 (26 Episodes). Adventure/Comedy. D: Nagisa Miyazaki, Nobuyoshi Habara. W: Ichiro Okouchi. C: Rina Satou, Akemi Kanda, Akeno Watanabe, Ai Nonaka, Hazuki Tanaka, Yu Kobayashi, Yuki Matsuoka ☥. JPN: Japanese/Color/780m. Xebec.

A young wizard in training, Negi Springfield, faces one final challenge before he can become a master of his craft: he must teach English at an all-girl boarding school. These are not ordinary students; each one is a supernatural being, including Evangeline—who's a pure-blood vampire (she was turned at age ten during the Hundred Years' War).

Negima!?

TV Tokyo. Oct 4, 2006 – Mar 28, 2007 (26 Episodes). Action/Comedy. D: Akiyuki Shinbo. W: Kenichi Kanemaki. C: Rina Satou, Akemi Kanda, Akeno Watanabe, Ai Nonaka, Ai Bandou, Akane Omae, Yuki Matsuoka ☥. JPN: Japanese/Color/780m. Deep Side/SHAFT.

This is an alternate retelling of *Negima!,* featuring the same characters redesigned, and using many of the original voice actors—but with a focus on action.

Netherworld Battle Chronicle: Disgaea
[Makai Senki Disgaea]

Chiba TV. Apr 4 – Jun 20, 2006 (12 Episodes). Action/Adventure. D: Kiyotaka Isako. W: Chinatsu Houjou. C: Kaori Mizuhashi, Yuko Sasamoto, Tomoe Hanba, Chiwa Saito, Nobuo Tobita, Chihiro Suzuki ☥. JPN: Japanese/Color/360m. PCB Productions/Ankoku Gikai.

Prince Laharl Krichevskoy fights to claim the Netherworld for his own, after the death of his father throws the realm into chaos. His chief rival, Count Vyers, is a demon known as the "Dark Adonis;" he has several vampire-like traits but doesn't drink blood. The series is based on the Nippon Ichi video game *Makai Senki Disugaia (Disgaea: Hour of Darkness).*

Nightwalker: Midnight Detective
[Mayonaka no tantei: Nightwalker]

TV Tokyo. Jul 9 – Sep 24, 1998 (12 Episodes). Comedy/Horror. D: Kiyotoshi Sasano. W: Ryota Yamaguchi. C: Takumi Yamazaki ☥, Emi Shinohara, Maaya Sakamoto, Akira Ishida, Hidetaka Takeda, Hideyuki Tanaka ☥. JPN: Japanese/Color/360m. Bandai Visual Company/AIC.

Shido Tatsuhiko came to Japan after fleeing Transylvania, where he ruled alongside Cain, the cruel and powerful vampire who turned him. To atone for his past sins, Tatsuhiko now hunts *Nightbreed*—humans who have succumbed to supernatural influence—with the help of his partner, government agent Yayoi Matsunaga.

Nyanpire: The Animation

Kids Station. Jul 6 – Sep 21, 2011 (12 Episodes). Adventure/Family. D: Takahiro Yoshimatsu. W: Natsuko Takahashi. C: Ami Koshimizu ☥, Noriaki Sugiyama, Jun Fukuyama, Yuko Goto, Shinnosuke Tachibana ☥, Nozomi Maeda, Shion Hirota. JPN: Japanese/Color/360m. Gonzo.

Nyanpire is a kitten that was abandoned and near death; she was saved by a dose of vampire blood, and adopted by a young girl named Misaki-chan. Nyanpire enjoys blood (or any other red foods), and has a series of adventures with the other neighborhood cats.

Phantom Stories
[Bakemonogatari]

Tokyo MX. Jul 3, 2009 – Jun 25, 2010 (15 Episodes). Action/Romance. D: Akiyuki Shinbo. W: Fuyashi Tô. C: Hiroshi Kamiya ⚲, Chiwa Saito, Emiri Kato, Miyuki Sawashiro, Kana Hanazawa, Aya Hirano ⚲. JPN: Japanese/Color/450m. Aniplex/Kodansha/SHAFT.

Teenager Koyomi Araragi was once a vampire, but his affliction has been cured—yet he still retains traces of his former self (he has exceptional night vision and can heal very quickly). He helps those who are dealing with supernatural problems, guided by Meme Oshino—the homeless man who cured him of vampirism.

Princess Resurrection
[Kaibutsu oujo]

TBS. Apr 12 – Sep 27, 2007 (26 Episodes). Comedy/Horror. D: Masayuki Sakoi. W: Yasunori Mitsunaga. C: Ayako Kawasumi, Fuyuka Oura, Rika Morinaga, Ai Shimizu, Mamiko Noto, Hôchû Ôtsuka ⚲, Yûko Kaida, Shiho Kawaragi. JPN: Japanese/Color/780m. Madhouse.

Hiro dies while saving the life of a beautiful woman; she's a princess of the demon royal family, and she resurrects him for a second chance at life—as long as he serves her. The undead appear in several episodes of this series, including an ancient pureblood vampire named Duke Dracul.

Red Riding Hood Chacha – "Date with Que-chan" / "Que-chan Strikes Back!" / "Go! Legendary Soldiers"
[Akazukin Cha Cha – "Kyu-chan to Deto" / "Kyu-chan no Gyakushu!" / "Yuke! Densetsu no Senshi-tachi"]

TV Tokyo. Feb 4/Mar 11/Dec 9, 1994 (S01E05/10/49). Adventure/Fantasy. D: Hatsuki Tsuji. W: Hiroshi Toda, Shigeru Yanagawa. C: Masami Suzuki, Shingo Katori, Noriko Hidaka, Mayumi Akado, Tohru Senrui, Junko Ohtsubo, Noriko Namiki. JPN: Japanese/Color/90m. Studio Gallop.

Chacha, a young magician-in-training, has a number of adventures with her schoolmates Riiya and Shiine. The vampire Que-chan makes three appearances over the course of the series.

Rosario + Vampire

Tokyo MX/Chiba TV. Jan 3 – Mar 27, 2008 (13 Episodes). Action/Adventure. D: Takayuki Inagaki. W: Hiroshi Yamaguchi. C: Nana Mizuki ⚲, Daisuke Kishio ⚲, Kimiko Koyama, Rie Kugimiya, Kikuko Inoue, Misato Fukuen, Shuuichi Ikeda. JPN: Japanese/Color/390m. Gonzo.

Tsukune Aono discovers that his classmates at Yokai Academy are monsters disguised as human beings. Although he fears for his own safety, he remains at the school, because his less-than-stellar grades don't give him a lot options. He's smitten by fellow student Moka Akashiya, a caring vampire whose true nature is only revealed if the rosary around her neck is removed. Later in the series, Tsukune adopts some aspects of the vampire, after Moka saves him from death by injecting him with her blood.

Rosario + Vampire Capu.02

Tokyo MX/Chiba TV. Oct 1 – Dec 24, 2008 (13 Episodes). Action/Adventure. D: Takayuki Inagaki. W: Hiroshi Yamaguchi. C: Nana Mizuki ♀, Daisuke Kishio ♀, Chiwa Saito ♀, Kimiko Koyama, Rie Kugimiya, Kikuko Inoue, Misato Fukuen. JPN: Japanese/Color/390m. Gonzo.

Chronicles a group of students attending the second semester at Yokai Academy, a private school for monsters, where pupils take on the guise of human beings to keep their true nature hidden. Tsukune Aono—the only real human student at the school—also keeps his true self hidden, because only monsters are allowed. His friend Moka Akashiya knows the real truth; after her unruly half-sister Kokoa enrolls at the academy, he discovers there's a lot of bad blood between the vampire siblings.

Samba of Ghosts
[Obake no Samba, Mon Mom Monster]

TV Tokyo. May 1, 1980 – Mar 26, 1981 (46 Episodes). Comedy/Music. D: Yukito Aizawa. W: Shun-ichi Yukimuro. C: Hitoshi Omeae, Minorv Sado ♀, Takeshi Sasano, Midori Fukuhara, Jiro Sakagami. JPN: Japanese/Color/1380m. Watanabe Kikaku/Tokyo Hoso 12.

Little is known about this series; it seems to be a musical sitcom that features the gruesome threesome—Dracula, the Wolf Man, and the Frankenstein Monster.

The School for Vampires
[Die Schule der kleinen Vampire]

RBB. Aug 26, 2006 – Nov 3, 2010 (104 Episodes). Adventure/Family. D: Robert Arkwright, Greg Manwaring. W: William R. Pace. C: Till Völger ♀, Marianne Graffam ♀, Hannes Maurer ♀, Santiago Ziesmer ♀, Sebastian Schulz ♀. GER: German/Color/3120m. Hahn Film AG.

In this special school, students are taught skills that will make them better vampires—from how to avoid crosses, garlic and the sun, to flying lessons and transformation techniques. One student, Oskar, faints at the sight of blood, but he tries his best at school. His thoughts often turn to a human girl named Sunshine, whose grandfather Paulus Polidori is a vampire hunter. Adapted from the popular series of books by Jackie Niebisch.

Those Obnoxious Aliens - "What a Dracula!"
[*Urusei Yatsura* – "Tonda Dorakyura"]

Fuji TV. May 12, 1982 (S02E06). Comedy/Sci-Fi. D: Mamoru Oshii. W: Hiro Iwasaki. C: Toshio Furukawa, Fumi Hirano, Ichirô Nagai, Akira Murayama, Kazuko Sugiyama, Issei Futamata, Machiko Washio, Kaneta Kimotsuki ☥. JPN: Japanese/Color/30m. Studio Pierrot/Studio DEEN.

The Oni, an alien race, intends to invade Earth. Instead of taking it by force, they challenge mankind to a competition similar to the game of "tag." Representing humanity is Ataru Moroboshi, an unlucky high school student; his challenger is Lum, an alien girl whose father commands the invading force. In this episode, Count Dracula rises from the grave thirsting for blood—and he sets his sights on Lum.

Titeuf – "Father Dracula"
[*Titeuf* – "Pépé Dracula"]

FR3. May 2, 2002 (S01E57). Adventure/Family. D: Daniel Duda. W: Jérôme Richebon, Claire Paoletti. C: Donald Reigneaux, Sabrina Lorquin, Vincent Ropion, Caroline Pascal, Thierry Raguenot, Daniele Hazan. FRA: French/Color/8m. France Animation/Canal J./Editions Glénat/SMEC.

Titeuf and his best friend Manu visit his grandfather's house, where they find a set of dentures soaking in a drinking glass. This leads them to believe that the man is actually the notorious vampire Count Dracula.

Topo Gigio: In the Castle of Count Dracula
[*Topo Gigio:* "No Castelo do Conde Drácula"]

TV Bandeirantes. 1987. Adventure/Family. D: Pedro Siaretta. W: Anon. C: Marthus Mathias, Samanta Monteiro. BRA: Portuguese/Color/60m. Rede Bandeirantes.

Topo Gigio, a mouse puppet, debuted on Italian television in 1959, and was a regular on the *Ed Sullivan Show* in 1963 (making over ninety appearances). Over the years, the character has appeared in different television productions from several countries, including Brazil, Italy, Japan, and Spain. In this spin-off animated special, the friendly little mouse is transported to Dracula's castle, after his friend Samantha inadvertently switches on a time machine.

Topo Gigio – "Drachula the 102"
[*Toppo Jijo* – "Drachura 102-sei"]

TV Asahi. Aug 31, 1988 (S01E18). Adventure/Family. D: Noboru Ishiguro. W: Takashi Hayashi, Taku Sugiyama. C: Ryusei Nakao, Toshiko Fujita, Daisuke Gouri, Youko Kawanami, Naoko Kyooda, Yuko Mizutani, Kenichi Ogata. JPN: Japanese/Color/30m. Nippon Animation.

Topo Gigio—a spacefaring mouse from the future—gets stranded on present-day Earth, where he's befriended by a young girl. In this episode, the gang watches an old *Dracula* movie on TV.

They tell Topo Gigio that vampires really exist, and one has been spotted in the ruins of an old castle—so he investigates their claim.

Trinity Blood

WOWOW. Apr 28 – Oct 27, 2005 (24 Episodes). Horror/Sci-Fi. D: Tomohiro Hirata. W: Yuuji Hosono. C: Mamiko Noto, Hiroki Touchi ♀, Junko Minagawa, Shinya Kitade, Junichi Suwabe, Michiko Neya ♀, Kenichi Suzumura, Kazuya Nakai. JPN: Japanese/Color/720m. Gonzo.

In the distant future, Armageddon throws the world into chaos, and there's a bitter war between humans and vampires. Humanity's last hope is an international group run by the Vatican, which includes a covert team of elite holy warriors led by a Catholic priest named Abel Nightroad—an ancient vampire who protects the human race from his own kind.

Ultraviolet: Code 044
[Urutoravaioretto: Kôdo 044]

Animax. Jul 1 – Sep 16, 2008 (12 Episodes). Action/Sci-Fi. D: Osamu Dezaki. W: Anon. C: Romi Park, Tomokazu Seki ♀, Rikiya Koyama, Kenyuu Horiuchi, Michio Hazama ♀, Kaori Yamagata, Akio Ohtsuka. JPN: Japanese/Color/360m. Madhouse Studios/Sony Pictures Entertainment.

Loosely based on the feature film *Ultraviolet* (2006), this series follows 044, a female clone who has been genetically manipulated to excel in combat. Her mission is to destroy a group of vampire-like humans known as the Phage, but after an intense battle with one of their soldiers, she can't bring herself to kill him. Considered a traitor, 044 flees with the injured soldier in tow, and becomes the target of her both own government and the Phage population.

Vampire Host
[Vanpaia hosuto]

TV Tokyo. Apr 4 – Jun 27, 2004 (12 Episodes). Drama/Romance. D: Hitoshe One. W: Takuro Fukuda. C: Satoshi Matsuda ♀, Minako Komukai, Seijun Nobukawa, Shiro Sano, Ryoji Suzuki, Isao Yamamoto, Masahiro Kuranuki. JPN: Japanese/Color/360m. Toho Co Ltd.

While investigating the disappearance of her best friend, Kanou Rion uncovers a woman's club hosted by a group of men who dress up as vampires, to serve as escorts for the clientele. She takes a part-time job there, and discovers that one of the men is the real thing. Loosely based on the one-shot manga *Blood Hound*—which was serialized in the magazine *Hana to Yume*—this series was retitled *Bloodhound: Vampire Gigolo* in North America.

Vampire Knight
[Vanpaia naito]

TV Tokyo. Apr 7 – Jun 30, 2008 (13 Episodes). Drama/Romance. D: Kiyoko Sayama. W: Mari Okada. C: Yui Horie, Daisuke Kishio ♀, Mamoru Miyano ♀, Fumiko Orikasa, Hiroki Yasumoto, Daisuke Kishio, Jun Fukuyama. JPN: Japanese/Color/390m. Studio DEEN.

Ten years ago, an undead creature attacked Yuki Cross, but she was saved by the vampire Kaname Kuran. Unable to remember anything prior to the incident, Yuki was adopted by the Headmaster of Cross Academy—home to both human and vampire students. She now works alongside her best friend Zero to maintain peace between the two groups.

Vampire Knight Guilty
[Vanpaia naito II]

TV Tokyo. Oct 6 – Dec 29, 2008 (13 Episodes). Drama/Romance. D: Kiyoko Sayama. W: Mari Okada. C: Yui Horie, Daisuke Kishio ♀, Mamoru Miyano ♀, Fumiko Orikasa, Hiroki Yasumoto, Daisuke Kishio, Jun Fukuyama. JPN: Japanese/Color/390m. Studio DEEN.

In this sequel to *Vampire Knight,* Yuki Cross uncovers clues to her forgotten past. A series of events forces Yuki into making a choice between her best friend Zero and the vampire Kaname Kuran.

Vampire Princess Miyu
[Kyûketsuki Miyu]

TV Tokyo. Oct 6, 1997 – Mar 30, 1998 (26 Episodes). Horror/Fantasy. D: Toshiki Hirano. W: Yuji Hayami, Yasutomo Yamada. C: Miki Nagasawa ♀, Chiharu Tezuka, Megumi Ogata, Kokoro Shindou, Asako Shirakura, Akio Ohtsuka. JPN: Japanese/Color/780m. Miyu Production Committee/AIC.

Although Miyu is a vampire, she poses as a teenager while secretly battling wayward demons known as *shinma*. Tasked with sending them back into the dark depths of hell, she cannot return herself until all *shinma* are banished from the face of the Earth.

Vampiyan Kids
[Banpaiyan Kizzu]

FujiTV. Oct 13, 2001 – Mar 30, 2002 (26 Episodes). Comedy/Family. D: Masatsugu Arakawa. W: Masaaki Yuasa. C: Hiroki Takahashi, Eiji Takemoto, Hiromi Tsuru ♀, Kenichi Ogata, Junko Takeuchi, Kinya Aikawa ♀, Mami Koyama ♀. JPN: Japanese/Color/780m. Production I.G.

A family of vampires—who subsist on orange juice instead of blood—is kicked out of the monster realm because their patriarch is no longer deemed scary. Trapped on Earth, they can only return if he frightens a thousand people—but his daughter falls in love with a human boy, and decides that she never wants to go back. The last three episodes were not broadcast on television, but instead were released on DVD.

NON-TRADITIONAL VAMPIRES

Kamen Rider Kiva

TV Asahi. Jan 27, 2008 – Jan 18, 2009 (48 Episodes). Horror/Fantasy. D: Ryuta Tasaki. W: Shoji Yonemura. C: Koji Seto, Kouhei Takeda, Keisuke Kato, Yu Takahashi, Nana Yanagisawa, Kouhei Kumai, Katsumi Shiono ☥. JPN: Japanese/Color/1440m. Ishimori Productions/Toei Company.

This series takes place in two different timelines: 1986 and 2008. The first story follows Kurenai Wataru, a young man destined to become Kamen Rider Kiva; the second involves his father Kurenai Otoya, a warrior who disappeared twenty-two years earlier. In both time periods, each man battles a common enemy known as the Fangires, a race of life-draining vampires who can disguise themselves as human. The story continued as "Kamen Rider Kiva: King of the Vampires" in the January 2010 issue of Hobby Japan magazine.

Vampire

Fuji TV. Oct 3, 1968 – Apr 5, 1969 (26 Episodes). Adventure/Family. D: Yamada Ken. W: Shun-ichi Yukimuro, Yoshiyuki Fukuda. C: Yutaka Mizutani ☥, Osamu Tezuka, Fumio Watanbe, Hiroshi Satô ☥, Hiroshi Iwashita, Kiyomi Kadena. JPN: Japanese/Color/780m. Tezuka Productions/Mushi Productions.

Toppei is a young boy from a small village of vampires, each of whom can shape shift into animals. His dream of becoming an animator takes him to Tokyo, where he lands a job working for the famous illustrator Osamu Tezuka. An evil vampire discovers Toppei's secret, and plans use the boy as part of his scheme to overthrow the human population. This was primarily a live-action series, but animation was used for the animals that the vampires transform into. These vampires don't drink blood nor are they immortal; akin to lycanthropes, they can morph into different animals including wolves, snakes, and bats—and the stimulus that triggers the transformation is different for each of them.

Wild Arms: Twilight Venom

WOWOW. Oct 18, 1999 – Mar 27, 2000 (22 Episodes). Action/Adventure. D: Itsuro Kawasaki. W: Aya Matsui. C: Mayumi Asano, Fumiko Osaka, Nariko Fujieda ☥, Junpei Morita, Mitsuo Iwata, Kaori Asou. JPN: Japanese/Color/660m. Bee Train/SPE Visual Works.

A group of escaped prisoners encounter a young boy who's actually the renowned gunslinger Cheyenne Rainstorm; he's trapped in the child's body and is searching for his own. One member of the group is Mirabelle Graceland, a thief from the vampire-like race known as the Crimson Nobles.

Dracula (Judd Hirsch) is just one of several fiends featured in the 1979 ABC TV special *The Halloween That Almost Wasn't* (Concepts Unlimited/New Horizons)

A Trivial Pursuit

After viewing over thirteen hundred hours of vampire television, common themes and practices become evident. Many plot devices are rehashed time and time again, while certain subjects (and running jokes) are often revisited.

Poor dental hygiene.
Of all the creatures in monsterdom, one would expect vampires to be the most diligent about oral hygiene—especially considering their halitosis problem! Yet bloodsuckers have been shown to lose a fang every now and again. *(The Ernie Kovacs Show, Benny Hill, The Ron James Show, Monty Python's Flying Circus, T-Bag and the Rings of Olympus, Bandar Book)*

An apple a day keeps Van Helsing away.
After a few centuries of unrelenting bloodlust, being chased by rabid humans with pointy wooden accoutrements must surely get on a vampire's nerves. Perhaps this is why a few of them have changed their diet to become vegetarian. *(Sesame Street, The Electric Company, Count Duckula, Growing Up Creepie, DuckTales, I'm Gonna Be an Angel, The Ketchup Vampires, Mr. Majeika, Dr. Zitbag's Transylvania Pet Shop, The Super Mario Bros. Super Show!)*

Romania is not one of the fifty states.
For some reason, modern vampires are cursed with a desire to return to high school (you'd never catch Dracula going back to Sighișoara High!). Yet a continuing education may be useful to those who confuse Pennsylvania with Transylvania. *(Supernatural, Animaniacs, The Beatles, Roger Ramjet, The Simpsons, The Bugs Bunny/Road Runner Hour, Superspecial)*

Bloodsucking waterfowl.
Next time you think of feeding a harmless brace of ducks, be careful, because one or two of them may have a bite worse than their quack! *(Danger Mouse, Count Duckula, Galaxy Goof-Ups, Quacula, Family Guy, Daffy Duck and Porky Pig Meet the Groovie Goolies, DuckTales, Tiny Toon Adventures)*

Dare to dream.
Although it's a cool notion, the famous one-hundred-and-two-story skyscraper in New York City is not called the "Vampire State Building." *(The Addams Family (1973), The Richie Rich/Scooby-Doo Show, The Horror Hall of Fame II, Groovie Goolies)*

Open the pod bay doors, DRAC.
Vampires are traditionally considered to be creatures of horror, but they often bleed into the realm of science fiction. Spacefaring undead? It could happen. *(Buck Rogers in the 25th Century, Duck Dodgers, Galaxy Goof-Ups, Blakes 7, Buzz Lightyear of Star Command, Doctor Who, Bloodsuckers, Fangface, Space Stars, The World's Strangest UFO Stories)*

The Impaler: a triple threat.
Vlad Țepeș is a national hero to Romanians, and is an integral part of their undead tourism

industry. He's also very useful in storytelling: he can play himself, a vampire, or be used as a convenient plot device. *(B.J. and the Bear, Da Vinci's Demons, Dark Prince: The True Story of Dracula, Dracula (1973), Drácula (1999), Dracula (2002), Dracula: Sovereign of the Damned, Dracula: The Series, Hellsing, Hercules: The Legendary Journeys, Huntik: Secrets & Seekers, The Librarian: The Curse of the Judas Chalice, Mentors, The Middleman, Mr. and Mrs. Dracula, Murdoch Mysteries, Nash Bridges, The Passion of Dracula, Rambo: The Force of Freedom, Relic Hunter, Road to Avonlea, So Weird, Where in the World is Carmen Sandiego?, The Young Indiana Jones Chronicles)*

The "vampire disease."
Porphyria was once believed to be an explanation for the origin of vampire legends, mainly because of the burning effect that sunlight has on the undead. But the vampires of folklore were never harmed by the sun; this was invented by the German director F.W. Murnau in 1922. The disorder remains closely tied to vampires, and is sometimes used in storytelling. *(Castle, CSI: Crime Scene Investigation, Trapper John M.D., Dracula: The True Story)*

Play it again, Vlad.
It's a rare occasion when Dracula shows off his musical side; it's no surprise that he's a great pianist! But you'd think after a few centuries he'd learn to play something other than Beethoven's "Moonlight Sonata." *(Mystery and Imagination, Cliffhangers)*

Surely you jest.
Living for an eternity would be dreadful without a good laugh every now and again, which is why vampires are usually pretty good at taking a joke. But they may be offended if you playfully ask if their favorite show tune is "Peg o' My Heart." *(Superspecial, Cliffhangers).*

That's no excuse.
When being attacked by a vampire, never joke that you "gave at the office," because they'll just roll their eyes—and then rip your throat out! *(Barris & Company, Night Gallery)*

Déjà vu.
This entry lists overused story ideas; now that they've been brought to light, let's hope that new writers will avoid revisiting them:
- Monster cage fighting *(Angel, Sanctuary, Blood Ties, Lost Girl, Being Human)*
- Vampires with cool convertibles *(Forever Knight, Angel, Moonlight)*
- Undead crime fighters *(Forever Knight, Angel, Moonlight, Blood Ties)*
- Monster dream sequences *(The Lucy Show, Happy Days, Gilligan's Island, Forever Knight)*
- Exploring Hunyad Castle *(Ghost Hunters International, Most Haunted: LIVE, The Scariest Places on Earth)*
- People become their Halloween costumes *(Buffy the Vampire Slayer, The Simpsons, Ned's Declassified School Survival Guide, The Adventures of Jimmy Neutron: Boy Genius)*
- Vampire abducts a woman to be his undead bride *(Dracula (1973), Mom's Got a Date with a Vampire, The Amazing Spider-Man and The Incredible Hulk, The Flintstones Meet Rockula and

Frankenstone, In Living Color, Dracula: Sovereign of the Damned)
- ◊ *Zoltan is a popular name (The Super Mario Bros. Super Show, Young Dracula, Attack of the Killer Tomatoes)*

Seventy-one bits of silliness.

One common element is seen time and time again: fake film titles. Writers seem to enjoy sneaking these non-existent movies into their stories; often it's just a movie poster, but sometimes there are a few scenes from the actual fake film. Some are so quirky that I'd pay good money to see the real thing!

- ◊ *Assisted Living Dracula* - Aqua Teen Hunger Force ("Bus of the Undead")
- ◊ *Attack of the Vampire with Fangs and Tentacles* - Darkwing Duck ("Night of the Living Spud")
- ◊ *Big D at Sunnybrook Farm* - Drak Pack ("Dred Goes To Hollywood")
- ◊ *Big D Bites Again* - Drak Pack ("Dred Goes To Hollywood")
- ◊ *Black Shroud* - Yellow Thrill ("Dinner with a Vampire")
- ◊ *Blacula Meets Black Dracula* - The Simpsons ("All's Fair in Oven War")
- ◊ *Blood Curse of the Vampire* - Shadow Zone ("The Undead Express")
- ◊ *Blood Horror 2* - Yellow Thrill ("Dinner with a Vampire")
- ◊ *The Blood of Mindy Hadlemen* - Sabrina, the Teenage Witch ("Really Big Season Opener")
- ◊ *Bloodsucker Diaries* - My Babysitter's a Vampire
- ◊ *Bloodsucking on the 23rd Floor* - Sabrina, the Teenage Witch ("Really Big Season Opener")
- ◊ *The Boo-Hoo* - Clifford the Big Red Dog ("Boo!")
- ◊ *Buff-Bot: The Human Slayer* - Futurama ("Fear of a Bot Planet")
- ◊ *Buffay the Vampire Layer* - Friends ("The One Where Chandler Can't Cry")
- ◊ *Charlie's Angels III: The Legend of Charlie's Gold* – Futurama ("I Dated a Robot")
- ◊ *Colonel Dracula Joins the Navy* - The Simpsons ("The Old Man and the Lisa")
- ◊ *Demons at Dusk* - Dear Dracula
- ◊ *Don't Drink the O-Positive* - Sabrina, the Teenage Witch ("Really Big Season Opener")
- ◊ *Dracula and the Sherriff's Daughter* - Disneyland ("The Mystery in Dracula's Castle")
- ◊ *Dracula's Horror Show* - Yellow Thrill ("Dinner with a Vampire")
- ◊ *Dream of the Vampires* - Supernatural ("Live Free or Twihard")
- ◊ *Dusk III: Unbitten* - My Babysitter's a Vampire
- ◊ *dusk 3* - That's So Weird ("That's So Scary")
- ◊ *Early Evening* - Phineas and Ferb ("The Curse of Candace")
- ◊ *The Eggplant That Ate Philadelphia* - The Lucy Show ("Lucy and the Monsters")
- ◊ *The Electroflying Firefly* - Frankenstein Jr. and The Impossibles ("The Mad Monster Maker")
- ◊ *Fangs* - B.J. and the Bear ("A Coffin with a View")

- *Fangs* - Tales from the Cryptkeeper ("Fare Tonight")
- *Fangs for the Memories* - The New Scooby-Doo Mysteries ("Scooby's Peep-Hole Pandemonium")
- *The Fearless Vampire Hunters* - Tales from the Cryptkeeper ("Fare Tonight")
- *The Fifty Foot Midget* - The Phil Silvers Show ("Bilko's Vampire")
- *Frankenstein's Doctor* - Happy Days ("Welcome to My Nightmare")
- *Frankenstone and Poltergravel* - The Flintstone Kids ("Frankenstone")
- *The Gallows Hang High* - The Snoop Sisters ("A Black Day for Bluebeard")
- *Grave of Frankenstein* - The Phil Silvers Show ("Bilko's Vampire")
- *Gravely Yours* - The Snoop Sisters ("A Black Day for Bluebeard")
- *Graveyard Confidential* - The Phil Silvers Show ("Bilko's Vampire")
- *High Noon for Big D* - Drak Pack ("Dred Goes To Hollywood")
- *How Dracula Got His Groove Back* - The Simpsons ("Treehouse of Horror IX")
- *Hyena Men From Outer Space* - Alfred Hitchcock Presents ("The Greatest Monster of Them All")
- *The Legend of the Chupacabra* - The Grim Adventures of Billy & Mandy ("Aren't You Chupacabra To See Me")
- *The Menacing Mummy* - Frankenstein Jr. and The Impossibles ("The Mad Monster Maker")
- *Mr. Big D Goes To Washington* - Drak Pack ("Dred Goes To Hollywood")
- *Mongo, Space Vampire* - The Jetsons ("Haunted Halloween")
- *Monster and the Beast* - Alfred Hitchcock Presents ("The Greatest Monster of Them All")
- *The Monsters Below* - Alfred Hitchcock Presents ("The Greatest Monster of Them All")
- *Muffy the Werewolf Slapper* - City Guys ("Video Killed the Radio Star")
- *The Mummy's Hand* - The Phil Silvers Show ("Bilko's Vampire")
- *My Summer of Blood* - Supernatural ("Live Free or Twihard")
- *Nosferatu: The Demon Vampire* - Are You Afraid of the Dark? ("The Tale of the Midnight Madness")
- *Nosferatu the Vampire* - One Foot in the Grave ("Tales of Terror")
- *Octopus Man* - The Adventures of Jimmy Neutron: Boy Genius ("Nightmare in Retroville")
- *Please Do Not Bite on the Neck* - Yellow Thrill ("Dinner with a Vampire")
- *The Return of Big D* - Drak Pack ("Dred Goes To Hollywood")
- *The Revenge of Count Krelski* - Mom's Got a Date with a Vampire
- *Revenge of the 48-Foot Eggplant* - Attack of the Killer Tomatoes ("Spatula, Prinze of Dorkness")
- *Revenge of the Killer Bat Zombies* - The New Adventures of Captain Planet ("Going Bats, Man")

- *The Rock and Roll Monster* - The Phil Silvers Show ("Bilko's Vampire")
- *Same Neck Next Year* - Sabrina, the Teenage Witch ("Really Big Season Opener")
- *Song of the Blood Suckers* – Love, American Style ("Love and the Monsters")
- *Sorority Vampire Beach Party* - Big Wolf on Campus ("Blaim It on the Haim")
- *Surfing Werewolf* - The Lucy Show ("Lucy and the Monsters")
- *A Thirst for Blood* - Midsomer Murders ("Death and the Divas")
- *Trapped Door of the Vampires* - The Evil Touch ("The Fans")
- *Vampire's Revenge* - The Littlest Hobo ("Day for Fright")
- *The Vampire's Tomb* - Dracula: The Series ("What a Pleasant Surprise")
- *Vampires Everywhere* - Hey Arnold! ("Sid the Vampire Slayer")
- *Vampire-Werewolves of London* - The Cosby Show ("Adventures in Babysitting")
- *The Werewolf of Paris* - The Phil Silvers Show ("Bilko's Vampire")
- *The Wicked Weird Wolf* - Frankenstein Jr. and The Impossibles ("The Mad Monster Maker")
- *Witch's Brew* - Yellow Thrill ("Dinner with a Vampire")

Beyond Buffy.

The cultural impact of *Buffy the Vampire Slayer* is visible in many other productions—in homage and in parody:

- *Archie's Weird Mysteries* – "Scarlet Night/I Was a Teenage Vampire/Halloween of Horror"
- *Being Erica* – "Erica the Vampire Slayer"
- *City Guys* – "Video Killed the Radio Star"
- *Friends* – "The One Where Chandler Can't Cry"
- *Futurama* – "Fear of a Bot Planet"
- *Grosse Pointe* – "Halloween"
- *House of Mouse* – "Gone Goofy"
- *MADtv* – Ep. #3.08
- *MADtv* – Ep. #3.23
- *MADtv* – Ep. #7.07
- *Reaper* – "I Want My Baby Back "
- *Robot Chicken* – "Plastic Buffet"
- *Saturday Night Live* – "Sarah Michelle Gellar/Portishead"
- *SM:TV Live* – Ep. #129
- *Unhappily Ever After* – "Ryan, Vampire Slayer"
- *V Graham Norton* – Ep. #1.43
- *Whose Line Is It Anyway?* – Ep. #7.04
- *Will & Grace* – "Love Plus One"
- *Xena: Warrior Princess* – "The Play's the Thing"

Appendix 1
Sources Consulted

Production information has been primarily obtained from viewing the actual programming. A number of publications proved useful in cross-checking facts and details, with special thanks going to the authors and editors of the books listed below.

Broadcasting Complaints Commission. *Annual Report*. Dublin, Ireland: Minister for Communications, Marine and Natural Resources, December 31, 2005. http://www.bcc.ie/BCC%20Report%202005.pdf.

Brooks, Tim, and Earle Marsh. *The Complete Directory to Primetime Network and Cable TV Shows, 1946-Present*. New York, N.Y.: Ballantine Books, 2007.

Browning, John Edgar, and Caroline Joan Picart. Dracula in Visual Media. Jefferson City, N.C.: McFarland, 2011.

Castleman, Harry, and Walter J. Podrazik. *Watching T.V., Four Decades of American Television*. New York, Toronto: McGraw-Hill, 1982.

Cheung, Theresa. *The Element Encyclopedia of Vampires: An A-Z of the Undead*. London: HarperElement, 2009.

Erickson, Hal. *Television Cartoon Shows: An Illustrated Encyclopedia, 1949 Through 1993*. Jefferson City, N.C.: McFarland, 1995.

Flynn, John L. *Cinematic Vampires: The Living Dead on Film and Television, From The Devil's Castle (1896) to Bram Stoker's Dracula (1992)*. Jefferson, N.C.: McFarland & Co., 1992.

Fulton, Roger. *The Encyclopedia of TV Science Fiction*. London: Boxtree, 2000.

Grossman, Gary H. *Saturday Morning TV*. New York, N.Y.: Arlington House, 1987.

Haining, Peter, ed. *The Television Late Night Horror Omnibus: Great Tales from TV Anthology Series*. London: Orion, 1993.

Hartman, Butch. Interview by Zcat6 of the Danny Phantom Online Forums. March 30, 2006. http://mysite.verizon.net/zcat6/IntBH2006p1.html.

Johnson, Catherine. *Telefantasy*. London: BFI, 2005.

Jones, Stephen. *The Illustrated Vampire Movie Guide*. London: Titan, 1993.

Jones, Stephen, and Forrest J Ackerman. *The Essential Monster Movie Guide: A Century of Creature Features on Film, TV and Video* (1st ed.). London: Titan Books, 1999.

Joshi, S. T. *Encyclopedia of the Vampire: The Living Dead in Myth, Legend, and Popular Culture*. Westport, CT: Greenwood Press, 2010.

Lackmann, Ronald W. *The Encyclopedia of American Television: Broadcast Programming Post World

War II to 2000. New York, N.Y.: Facts on File, 2003.

Ladd, Fred. *Astro Boy and Anime Come to the Americas: An Insider's View of the Birth of a Pop Culture Phenomenon.* Jefferson, N.C.: McFarland & Co., 2009.

Lentz, Harris M. *Science Fiction, Horror & Fantasy Film and Television Credits: Over 10,000 Actors, Actresses, Directors, Producers, Screenwriters, et al.* Jefferson, N.C.: McFarland, 1983.

---. *Science Fiction, Horror & Fantasy Film and Television Credits* (Supplement 1: Through 1987). Jefferson, N.C.: McFarland, 1989.

---. *Science Fiction, Horror & Fantasy Film and Television Credits* (Supplement 2: Through 1993). Jefferson, N.C.: McFarland, 1994.

McNeil, Alex. *Total Television: The Comprehensive Guide to Programming from 1948 to the Present* (4th ed.). New York, N.Y.: Penguin Books, 1996.

Melton, J. Gordon. *The Vampire Book: The Encyclopedia of the Undead* (3rd ed.). Canton, MI: Visible Ink Press, 2010.

Morton, Alan. *The Complete Directory to Science Fiction, Fantasy and Horror Television Series: A Comprehensive Guide to the First 50 Years, 1946 to 1996.* Peoria, IL: Alan Morton, 1997.

Muir, John Kenneth. *Terror Television: American Series, 1970-1999.* Jefferson, N.C.: McFarland, 2001.

Newcomb, Horace, ed. *Museum of Broadcast Communications Encyclopedia of Television.* Chicago, IL: Fitzroy Dearborn Publishers, 1997.

Riccardo, Martin V. *Vampires Unearthed: The Complete Multi-Media Vampire and Dracula Bibliography.* New York, N.Y.: Garland Pub., 1983.

Stanley, John. *Creature Features: The Science Fiction, Fantasy, and Horror Movie Guide* (Updated ed.). New York, N.Y.: Berkley Boulevard Books, 2000.

Terrace, Vincent. *Encyclopedia of Television: Series, Pilots and Specials.* New York, N.Y.: New York Zoetrope, 1985.

---. *Television Character and Story Facts: Over 110,000 Details from 1,008 Shows, 1945-1992.* Jefferson, N.C.: McFarland & Co., 1993.

Thompson, Jeff. *The Television Horrors of Dan Curtis: Dark Shadows, The Night Stalker and Other Productions, 1966-2006.* Jefferson, N.C.: McFarland & Co., 2009.

Thousand Oaks Library, and American Radio Archives. *Television Series and Specials Scripts, 1946-1992: A Catalog of the American Radio Archives Collection.* Jefferson, N.C.: McFarland & Co., 2009.

Watson, Elena M. *Television Horror Movie Hosts: 68 Vampires, Mad Scientists, and Other Denizens of the Late-Night Airwaves Examined and Interviewed.* Jefferson, N.C.: McFarland, 1991.

Wright, Gene. *Horror Shows: The A-to-Z of Horror in Film, TV, Radio and Theater.* New York, N.Y.: Facts on File, 1986.

Numerous online sources were consulted, and the following websites were particularly useful during the research phase.

Anime News Network. http://animenewsnetwork.com.

British Film Institute Film & TV Database. http://www.bfi.org.uk.

The Big Cartoon DataBase. http://www.bcdb.com.

The Classic TV Archive. http://ctva.biz.

Dresdencity.org. http://dresdencity.org.

E-gor's Chamber of TV Horror Hosts. http://myweb.wvnet.edu/e-gor/tvhorrorhosts

The Encyclopedia of Fantastic Film and Television. http://www.eofftv.com.

Internet FAQ Archives. http://faqs.org.

The Internet Movie Database. http://www.imdb.com.

Japanese Horror Movies Database. http://jhmd.jp.

Saturday Night Live Transcripts. http://snltranscripts.jt.org.

Tezukaosamu.net. http://tezukaosamu.net.

TVArchive.ca. http://www.tvarchive.ca.

TV.com. http://www.tv.com.

TV Guide. http://tvguide.com.

QuestFan. http://questfan.com.

Vampyres Only. http://vampyres.ca.

Appendix 2
Country Acronym Legend

ARG	Argentina	ITA	Italy
AUS	Australia	JPN	Japan
AUT	Austria	KOR	South Korea
BEL	Belgium	LUX	Luxembourg
CAN	Canada	MEX	Mexico
CZE	Czech Republic	NED	Netherlands
DEN	Denmark	NZL	New Zealand
ESP	Spain	PHI	Philippines
FIN	Finland	POL	Poland
FRA	France	PUR	Puerto Rico
GER	Germany	RSA	South Africa
HKG	Hong Kong	SOV	Soviet Union
HUN	Hungary	TCH	Czechoslovakia
IRL	Ireland	UK	United Kingdom
ISR	Israel	USA	United States

Appendix 3
Adaptations of Classic Literature and Popular Fiction

Bram Stoker's novel *Dracula* has been adapted in several countries. While most productions were faithful to the source, some were very loose with the translation.

Matinee Theatre – "Dracula" (USA 1956)
Mystery and Imagination – "Dracula" (UK 1968)
Count Dracula (TCH 1970)
Purple Playhouse – "Dracula" (CAN 1973)
Dracula (USA 1973)
Count Dracula (UK 1977)
Journey to the Unexpected – "You Have to Kill Dracula" (ARG 1979)
The Passion of Dracula (USA 1980)
Defenders of the Earth – "Dracula's Potion" (USA 1986)
Hello Kitty's Furry Tale Theater – "Catula" (USA 1987)
Drácula (ARG 1999)
Bad Blood (UK 1999)
Dracula: A Chamber Musical (CAN 2000)
Lexx – "Walpurgis Night/Vlad" (CAN 2001)
Dracula (ITA 2002)
Opening Night – "Dracula: Pages from a Virgin's Diary" (CAN 2002)
Duck Dodgers – "I'm Gonna Get You, Fat Sucka" (USA 2003)
Dracula (UK 2006)
Penny Dreadful (CAN/UK/USA 2014)

Adaptations of J. Sheridan Le Fanu's haunting novella, "Carmilla."

Mystery and Imagination – "Carmilla" (UK 1966)
Carmilla (POL 1980)
Carmilla: Le coeur petrifié (FRA 1988)
Nightmare Classics – "Carmilla" (USA 1989)

John William Polidori's short story "The Vampyre."

The Vampyr: A Soap Opera (UK 1992)

E.F. Benson's short story "Mrs. Amworth."

Classics Dark and Dangerous – "Mrs. Amworth" (CAN/UK 1975)

Manly Wade Wellman's short story "The Devil Is Not Mocked."

Night Gallery – "The Devil Is Not Mocked" (USA 1971)

The classic vampire/ghost story "Feet Foremost" by LP Hartley.
Mystery and Imagination – "Feet Foremost" (UK 1968)
Shades of Darkness – "Feet Foremost" (UK 1983)

'Salem's Lot, the horror fiction novel by Stephen King.
Salem's Lot (USA 1979)
'Salem's Lot (USA 2004)

Bryce Walton's short story "The Greatest Monster of Them All."
Alfred Hitchcock Presents – "The Greatest Monster of Them All" (USA 1961)

Harlan Ellison's short story "Footsteps."
The Hunger – "Footsteps" (USA 1998)

Lisa Tuttle's short story "Replacements."
The Hunger – "Replacements" (USA 1999)

Del Howison's short story "The Lost Herd."
Fear Itself – "The Sacrifice"(USA 2008)

John Ajvide Lindqvist's vampire novel *Låt den rätte komma in*.
Let the Right One In (TNT, 2017)

Cassandra Clare's popular series *The Mortal Instruments*.
Shadowhunters: The Mortal Instruments (Freeform, 2016)

Charlaine Harris's book trilogy *Midnight, Texas*.
Midnight, Texas (NBC, 2016)

The Southern Vampire Mysteries series by Charlaine Harris.
True Blood (HBO, 2008)

Dan Simmons's short story "Shave and a Haircut, Two Bites."
Monsters – "Shave and a Haircut, Two Bites" (Syndicated, 1990)

Tanya Huff's Blood Books.
Blood Ties (Lifetime, 2007)

Sarah Beth Durst's YA novel *Drink, Slay, Love*.
Drink, Slay, Love (Lifetime, 2017)

Appendix 4
Top Rated Productions

Animation:
ABC Weekend Specials – "Bunnicula, The Vampire Rabbit"
The Adventures of Jimmy Neutron: Boy Genius – "Nightmare in Retroville"
The Amazing Screw-On Head – "Pilot"
Attack of the Killer Tomatoes – "Spatula, Prinze of Dorkness"
Challenge of the Superfriends – "Attack of the Vampire"
Drak Pack
Duck Dodgers – "I'm Going to Get You, Fat Sucka"
Grim Adventures of Billy & Mandy – "Dracula de Bergerac"
Johnny Bravo – "Going Batty"
Octonauts – "Vampire Squid"
Oh Yeah! Cartoons – "Mina & The Count: The Vampire Who Came to Dinner"
Robot Chicken – "Tubba-Bubba's Now Hubba-Hubba"
Roswell Conspiracies: Aliens, Myths and Legends
Scary Godmother Halloween Spooktakular
The Simpsons – "Treehouse of Horror IV" and "Treehouse of Horror XXI"
Tales of the Wizard of Oz – "The Count"

Single Episodes:
Adventure Inc. – "Legacy of a Pirate"
Alfred Hitchcock Presents – "The Greatest Monster of Them All"
Are You Afraid Of The Dark? – "The Tale Of the Midnight Madness"
B.J. and The Bear – "A Coffin with a View"
Big Wolf on Campus – "Blaim It on the Haim" and "Everybody Fang Chung Tonight"
Burke's Law – "Who Killed Purity Mather?"
Castle – "Vampire Weekend"
CSI: Crime Scene Investigation – "Suckers"
The Dresden Files – "Bad Blood" and "Storm Front"
Freakylinks – "Live Fast Die Young"
Friday the 13th: The Series – "Night Prey"
Gilligan's Island – "Up at Bat"
Happy Days – "Welcome To My Nightmare"
The Hardy Boys/Nancy Drew Mysteries – "The Hardy Boys and Nancy Drew Meet Dracula"
Highlander – "The Vampire"
The Hitchhiker – "Nightshift"
The Hunger – "Nunc Dimittis"
Kolchak: The Night Stalker – "The Vampire"

Monsters – "The Waiting Game"
Quantum Leap – "Blood Moon"
Reaper – "I Want My Baby Back"
Sledge Hammer! – "The Last of the Red Hot Vampires"
The Supernatural (UK) – "Dorabella"
Supernatural – "Fresh Blood" and "Monster Movie"
Trapper John, M.D. – "Dark Side of the Loon"
The Twilight Zone – "Monsters!" and "Red Snow"
The X Files – "Bad Blood"
The Young Ones – "Nasty"

Series:
Angel
Being Human (UK)
Penny Dreadful
Young Dracula

Telefilms and Pilots:
The Dresden Files: Storm Front (pilot)
The Halloween That Almost Wasn't
The Midnight Hour
The NBC Wednesday Mystery Movie – "The Snoop Sisters: A Black Day for Bluebeard"
The Night Stalker

Non-Traditional Vampires:
Big Life with Daniel Richler – "Smoking/Vampires"
The Man From U.N.C.L.E. – "The Bat Cave Affair"
The Night Strangler
Reaper – "Cancun"
Strange – "Incubus"

Variety and TV Specials:
Beyond Reason – Ep. #2.37 and Ep. #3.34
Cincinnati Pops Holiday: Erich Kunzel's Halloween Spooktacular
Dinah Shore Chevy Show – Ep. #1.09
The Horror Hall of Fame (1974)
The Kids in the Hall – Ep. #1.17
Mystery Science Theater 3000 – "The Wild Wild World of Batwoman"
Opening Night – "Dracula: Pages from a Virgin's Diary"
Prisoners of Gravity – "Vampires"
SCTV
Superspecial – "Boo!"

The Tommy Ambrose Show – Ep. #2.--

Documentaries and Reality TV:

American Vampires
Biography – "Bela Lugosi: Hollywood's Dark Prince"
Bookmark – "The Vampire's Life"
Dracula: Fact and Fiction
Dracula: The True Story
Flesh and Blood: The Hammer Heritage of Horror
FRONTLINE/World – "Romania, My Old Haunts"
Great Books – "Dracula"
Hammer: The Studio That Dripped Blood!
A History of Horror with Mark Gatiss
Hollywood and The Stars - "Monsters We've Known and Loved"
The Horror of It All
In Search of... - "Dracula"
Lost Worlds – "The Real Dracula"
Monster Mania
MSNBC Investigates – "Dark Heart, Iron Hand: The Vampire Killers"
　　　　　"Interview with a Vampire"
Nightmare: The Birth of Horror – "Dracula"
Revealed – "Mysteries of the Vampire Skeletons"
The South Bank Show – "The Dracula File"
True Horror – "Dracula"
True Horror with Anthony Head – "Vampires"
The Unexplained: Witches, Werewolves & Vampires
Vampires: Why They Bite

Appendix 5
Lowest Rated Productions

Animation:
The Addams Family (1973)
The All-New Scooby and Scrappy-Doo Show – "Who's Minding the Monster?"
Alvin and the Chipmunks – "Trick or Treason"
Billy & Mandy's Big Boogey Adventure
The Cleveland Show – "Beer Walk!" and "A Nightmare on Grace Street"
Ed, Edd n' Eddy – "Ed, Edd n' Eddy's Boo Haw Haw"
Family Guy – "Lottery Fever"
The Flintstone Kids – "Frankenstone"
The Fonz and the Happy Days Gang – "The Vampire Strikes Back"
The Godzilla Power Hour – "The Energy Beast"
Grim Adventures of Billy & Mandy – "Aren't You Chupacabra To See Me"
Hanna-Barbera Superstars 10 – "Scooby-Doo and The Ghoul School"
James Bond Jr. – "The Inhuman Race"
Mad Jack The Pirate – "The Horror Of Draclia"
The Pink Panther Show – "Transylvania Mania"
Robot Chicken – "Nutcracker Sweet"
The Scooby and Scrappy-Doo Puppy Hour – "Vild Vest Vampire"
Scooby's All-Stars – "South America and Transylvania"
Sealab 2021 – "Isla De Las Chupacabras"
The Simpsons – "The Greatest Story Ever D'ohed"
Spider-Man – "Secret Wars: The Gauntlet of the Red Skull"
Tales from the Cryptkeeper – "Transylvania Express"
Yogi's Treasure Hunt – "Countdown Drac"

Single Episodes:
Baywatch – "Search & Rescue"
Baywatch Nights – "Night Whispers"
Bette – "Halloween"
Beyond Belief – "Night Walker"
chromiumblue.com – "The Eternal/The Eternal II"
The Collector – "The Vampire"
CSI: Crime Scene Investigation – "Blood Moon"
CSI: NY – "Sanguine Love"
Deepwater Black – "Refugee"
Frasier – "Halloween"
Freddy's Nightmares – "Prime Cut"

Friday the 13th: The Series – "Bottle Of Dreams"
Harry & Cosh – "Vampire"
The Highwayman – "Billionaire Body Club"
The Hunger – "Fly-By-Night"
Kids Unlimited – "Kids Undead"
Las Vegas – "Hide and Sneak"
Lost Tapes – "Vampire" and "Strigoi Vampire"
Monsters – "Half as Old as Time"
Mutant X – "Lazarus Syndrome"
Nash Bridges – "Superstition"
Nightman – "Constant Craving" and "Book of the Dead"
Night Gallery – "A Midnight Visit To The Neighborhood Blood Bank," "Smile, Please"
"How To Cure the Common Vampire"
PSI Factor: Chronicles of the Paranormal – "Valentine"
Sliders – "Stoker"
Smallville – "Thirst"
Superboy – "Young Dracula"
Supernatural – "Bloodlines"
Swamp Thing – "Powers Of Darkness"
Thrills – "Club Plasma"

Series:
Demons
The Munsters Today
Van-pires

Telefilms and Pilots:
Asylum Night
Emmanuelle the Private Collection – "Emmanuelle vs. Dracula"
Halloween with the New Addams Family
Munster, Go Home!
The Munsters' Scary Little Christmas
The Munsters Today
Slayer
Ultraviolet (pilot)
Wolvesbane

Non-Traditional Vampires:
Fangface – "Space Monster Mishap"
Friday the 13th: The Series – "Night Hunger"
The Hunger – "Footsteps"

Lost Tapes – "Chupacabra"
¡Mucha Lucha!: Gigante – "I Was a Pre-Teenage Chupacabra"
Tales from the Darkside – "Hush"

Variety and TV Specials:
Canada After Dark – Ep. #1.89
Halloween Monster Bash
Homemade TV – "Fashion Day"
The Horror Hall of Fame III
Royal Canadian Air Farce – Ep. #13.01
The X Factor – "Live Show #4"
Wayne & Shuster – Ep. #1.02

Documentaries and Reality TV:
The 700 Club – "Haiti/Michele Bachmann/Anne Rice"
America's Next Top Model – "America's Next Top Vampire"
Beyond - "Vampires"
Books Into Film – "Anne Rice"
Cake Boss – "Coffins, Costumes and a Cake on a Gurney"
Deadliest Warrior – "Vlad the Impaler vs. Sun Tzu"
Explorer – "Vampire Forensics"
Ghost Hunters International – "Dracula's Castle"
Mad Mad House
Monsters, Madness & Mayhem – "Creatures"
Secret Lives of Women – "The Occult"
Scare Tactics – "Vampire Stake Out"
The Scariest Places on Earth – "A Night in Dracula's Castle: The Transylvania Dare"
 "Return to Transylvania"
The World of Hammer – "Mummies, Werewolves and the Living Dead"
True Bloodlines – "A New Type"

Appendix 6
Yearly Breakdown

This graph illustrates the amount of vampire-themed television year by year, based on the entries listed in this book.

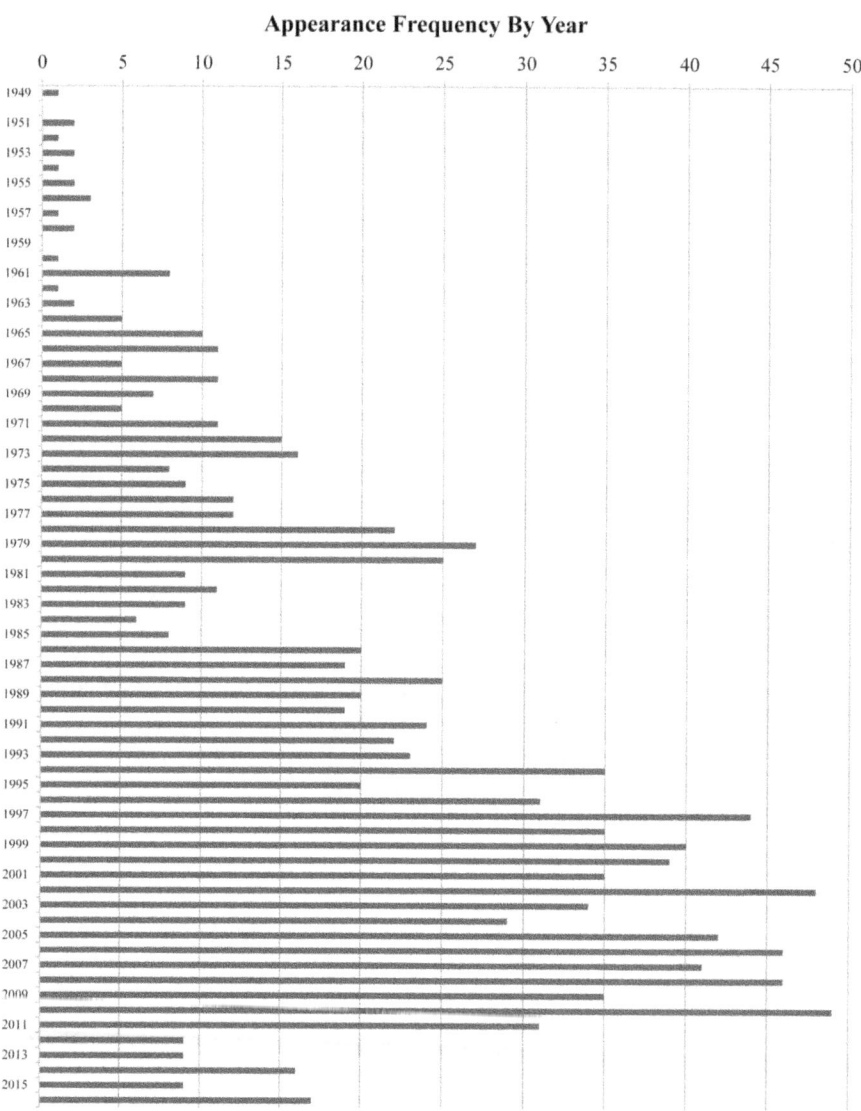

APPENDIX 7
WEB SERIES

Television and the Internet are converging; this is merely a sample of the vampire web series and webisodes that have exploded onto the Interwebs.

Becoming Human
Beyond the Rave
Bleed
Bleeder
Blood and Bone China
Chad Vader: Day Shift Manager – "Vampire Market"
Cherub: The Vampire with Bunny Slippers
Count Jeff
Deathless
Diary of a Teenage Vampire
Elevator: Harold the Vampire
End Transmission
Fangoria: Here There Be Monsters
The Ghouligans! Super Show!
Goodbye Light
The Hunted
I Kissed a Vampire
I <3 Vampires
Intercourse with a Vampire
The League of S.T.E.A.M. – "New Moon Vampire Hunt"
Monster High
The Naked Underground – "Was there a Female Dracula?"
Sanctuary
Suck & Moan
Super Scary Horror Theater
SuperNews! – "Vampires: Hollywood Bloodsuckers"
30 Days of Night – "Blood Trails" and "Dust to Dust"
Too Shy to Be a Vampire
Transitions: The Series
Transylvania Television
True Blood – "A Drop of True Blood"
Twilight: 5 Years Later
Valemont
The Vamps Next Door
Vamped Out
The Vampire Diaries – "A Darker Truth"
The Vampire Mistress
Vampire Killers
Vampire Trucker
Vampire Mob
The Vampire Secrets
Vampire Zombie Werewolf
Vampirism Bites
Venin Abyss

Index of Main Program Titles

A

Aaahh!!! Real Monsters 190
Abbott & Costello 190
The ABC Comedy Hour 339
ABC News Nightline 276
The ABC Saturday Superstar Movie 190, 191, 192
ABC Weekend Specials 192
The Addams Family (1964) 448
The Addams Family (1973) 448
The Addams Family (1992) 449
The Addams Family Fun-House 449
Adderly 16
Adventure Inc. 16
The Adventures of Jimmy Neutron: Boy Genius 193
Adventures of Puss-in-Boots 493
The Adventures of Sinbad 400
Adventures of the Quest 400
Adventure Time with Finn & Jake 193
AFI's 100 Years: 100 Heroes & Villains 276
Ai wa Chikyû wo Sukuu - Hyakumannen chikyû no tabi: Bandâ bukku. *See* Bakemonogatari: One Million Year Trip
Akazukin Cha Cha. *See* Red Riding Hood Chacha
Alfred Hitchcock Presents 17
Alias 450
The All-New Popeye Hour 193
The All-New Scooby and Scrappy-Doo Show 194
All Saints 18
All That 339
All Together Now 18
Alvin and the Chipmunks 450
The Amazing Adrenalini Brothers! 194
The Amazing Screw-On Head 194
The Amazing Siege: Once Again, Dracula 479
The Amazing Spider-Man and The Incredible Hulk 195
America Undercover 276
American Dragon: Jake Long 195
American Vampires 278
America's Next Top Model 277
The Anatomy of Horror 278
Ancient Aliens 276
Ancient Mysteries 277
Angel 18, 122, 154
Angel / Spike / Willow / Faith 154
Animal X 400
Animal X: Natural Mystery Unit 401

Animaniacs 196, 451
Anna in Wonderland 278
Annyeong! Peurancheseuka. *See* Hello Franceska
A.N.T. Farm 19
Aqua Teen Hunger Force 196, 197
Archie's Weird Mysteries 196
Are You Afraid of the Dark? 19, 20
Arrest & Trial 279
Astro Boy 493
Asylum Night 155
Attack of the Killer Tomatoes 197
Auction Kings 279
The Aunty Jack Show 340
AVRO Close-Up 491

B

B.J. and the Bear 20
Baby Looney Tunes 198
Backstory 279
Bad Blood 123
Bakemonogatari. *See* Phantom Stories
Bandar Book: One Million Year Trip 494
Banned From the Bible II 451
Banpaiyan Kizzu. *See* Vampiyan Kids
Barris & Company 340
The Basil Brush Show 21
The Baskervilles 198
The Batman 403
The Batman 403
Batman Beyond 402
Batman: The Brave and the Bold 198
Batman: The Animated Series 401
Batman: The Brave and the Bold 402
Baxter 21
The Bay City Rollers Meet the Saturday Superstars 340
Baywatch 21
Baywatch Nights 22
The Beatles 199
Beavis and Butt-Head 199
Behind the Fame 279
Being Erica 22
Being Human (CAN) 124
Being Human (pilot) 155
Being Human (UK) 123
Being Human Unearthed 280
The Ben Stiller Show 451
Ben 10 404
The Benny Hill Show 341

The Best of the Munsters 341
Bette 23
Beyond 280
Beyond Belief: Fact or Fiction 23, 24
Beyond Reality 24, 404
Beyond Reason 342
Bibi Blocksberg 494
Big Bad Beetleborgs/Beetleborgs Metallix 123
The Big Easy 25
Big Life 404
Big Wolf on Campus 25, 26, 27
Bigfoot and Wildboy 27
Biography 280, 281, 282, 283, 308, 309, 323
Birdman Task Force Jetman 474
Bizarre 343
Black Blood Brothers 495
Black Lagoon: The Second Barrage 495
Blade: The Series 124
Blakes 7 405
Blood+ 495
Blood-C 496
Bloodlines 283
Bloodsuckers 155
Bloodsucking Cinema 284
Blood Ties (FOX) 156
Blood Ties (Lifetime) 125
Blue Murder 28
The Book Tower 343
Bookmark 284
Books into Film 285
Boo to You Too! Winnie the Pooh 199
Brand Spanking New! Doug 200
Brandy & Mr. Whiskers 200
Briefe von Felix: Ein Hase auf Weltreise. *See* Les 30 histoires les plus mystérieuses: A Rabbit on a World Tour
Brivido giallo. *See* Yellow Thrill
Buck Rogers in the 25th Century 405
Buffy the Vampire Slayer (pilot) 157
Buffy the Vampire Slayer: The Animated Series (pilot) 200
Buffy the Vampire Slayer 125
The Bugs Bunny/Road Runner Hour 201
Bugs Bunny's Howl-Oween Special 201
Burke's Law 28
Burr Tillstrom's Kukla and Ollie 343
Buzz Lightyear of Star Command 406

C

Cake Boss 285
Canada After Dark 343, 344

Canadian Reflections 451
Captain N: The Game Master 202
Carland Cross 496
Carmilla 488
Carmilla: Le coeur petrifié. *See* Carmilla: The Petrified Heart
Carmilla: The Petrified Heart 489
The Carol Burnett Show 344
Carry on Christmas 345
The Casebook of Sherlock Holmes 28
Casper and the Angels 202
Cast a Deadly Spell 158
Castle 29
CatDog 203
Centurions 203
A Certain Magical Index 496
Challenge of the Super Friends 203
Charmed 30, 406
Chojin sentai Jettoman. *See* Birdman Task Force Jetman
chromiumblue.com 30
The Chronicle 31
ChuckleVision 30
Cincinnati Pops Holiday: Erich Kunzel's Halloween Spooktacular 345
Cities of the Underworld 286
City Guys 452
Class of the Titans 204
Classics Dark and Dangerous 32
The Cleveland Show 204, 205
Cliffhangers! 126
Clifford the Big Red Dog 205
Club Oasis 345
Codename: Kids Next Door 206
The Collector 32
The Comic Strip 206
Coming Up Rosie 33
Community 452
The Completely Mental Misadventures of Ed Grimley 206
The Conspiracy Show 286
Coronation Street 33, 34
The Cosby Show 452
Count Dracula 158, 489
Count Duckula 207
Counterstrike 453
Cow and Chicken 207
Creature Feature 346
Creepy Canada 286
Criminal Minds 34
Crossing Jordan 34
Crown Court 35

CSI: Crime Scene Investigation 35, 36, 404, 407
CSI: Miami 36
CSI: NY 37
The Curse of Dracula 159
Cyberchase 207

D

Daily Show 346
Dance in the Vampire Bund 497
Dandelion 474
Danger Mouse 208
The Danny Kaye Show 346, 347
Danny Phantom 407
Dansu in za vanpaia bando. *See* Dance in the Vampire Bund
Daring & Grace: Teen Detectives 37
Dark Angel 407
Dark Prince: The True Story of Dracula 453
A Dark Rabbit Has Seven Lives 497
Dark Realm 38
Dark Shadows (1966) 127
Dark Shadows (1991) 128
Dark Shadows (2004) 159
Darkroom 38
DarkStalkers 209
Darkwing Duck 209
Daughter of Darkness 160
The David Frost Show 347
Da Vinci's Demons 408
Days of Our Lives 38, 454
Dead of Night (pilot) 146
Dead of Night (telefilm) 161
Deadliest Warrior 287, 454
Deadly Love 160
Deadly Women 287
Dead of Night 161
Dear Dracula 210
Death Valley 129
Deepwater Black 408
Defenders of the Earth 210
Demon Corpse 497
Demons 129
Dennis the Menace 211
Der kleine Vampir: Neue Abenteuer. *See* That's So Weird: New Adventures
Descendants of Darkness 498
Destination Truth 409
Detective Conan 498
Dexter's Laboratory 409
D.Gray-man 497

Diagnosis Murder 38
The Dick Cavett Show 347
Die Ketchup Vampire. *See* The Ketchup Vampires
Die Schule der kleinen Vampire. *See* The School for Vampires
Die Wahrheit über Dracula. *See* The Truth About Dracula
Dinah Shore Chevy Show 347
Disappeared 288
Discover Magazine 409
Docteur Globule. *See* Dr. Zitbag's Transylvania Pet Shop
Dr. Terrible's House of Horrible 39
Doctor Who 39, 40, 41, 409, 410, 515
Don Dracula 499
Dracula (1973) 162
Dracula (2006) 163
Dracula (2012) 146
Dracula 130
Dracula: A Chamber Musical 348
Dracula, a Love Story 480
Drácula (ARG) 480
Dracula: Fact and Fiction 288
Dracula, Live From Transylvania 348
Dracula's Bram Stoker 289
Dracula
 [Il bacio di Dracula / Dracula's Curse] 130
Dracula: Sovereign of the Damned 499
Dracula's Ring 480
Dracula: The Series 131
Dracula: The True Story 289
Drácula, uma História de Amor. *See* Dracula, a Love Story
Draculito mon saigneur. *See* Little Drac
Dragonball 500
Drak Pack 211
Dr. Bundolo 348
The Dresden Files (pilot) 164
The Dresden Files 41
The Drew Carey Show 42
Drink, Slay, Love 164
Dr. Slump & Arale-chan 498
Dr. Zitbag's Transylvania Pet Shop 499
D-TV 208
Duck Dodgers 212
Duck Dodgers 212
DuckTales 212

E

Ed, Edd n' Eddy 213
The Ed Sullivan Show 349
El cerco alucinante: Otra vez Drácula. *See* That's So Weird: Once Again, Dracula

The Electric Company 349
Emmanuelle, the Private Collection: Emmanuelle vs. Dracula 165
Encounters: The Hidden Truth 289
ennen shôjo Man next: Yokohama hyaku-ya hen. *See* The Man from U.N.C.L.E.: 100 Nights in Yokohama
The Entertainers 350
Equinox Special 411
Ernest le Vampire. *See* Ernest the Vampire
Ernest the Vampire 500
The Ernie Kovacs Show 350
Evening Out 350
Everybody Loves Raymond 42
The Evil Touch 43
Explorer 289

F

F Troop 43
Faces of Evil 290
Faith the Vampire Slayer 146
Family Guy 213, 214
Family Matters 43
Fanboy and Chum Chum 214
Fang vs. Fiction: The Real Underworld of Vampires and Werewolves 290
Fangface 411
Fantasy Island 44
The Fast Show 351
Fear Itself 44
Films to Keep You Awake: A Real Friend 474
Finders Keepers 352
The Fixer 165
Flesh and Blood: The Hammer Heritage of Horror 291
The Flintstone Kids 411, 454
The Flintstones Meet Rockula and Frankenstone 215
The Fonz and the Happy Days Gang 215
Forbidden Love 475
Forever Knight 132
Foster's Home for Imaginary Friends 455
Frank & Drac 352
Frankenstein Jr. and The Impossibles 455
Frankenstein's Aunt 481
Frasier 45
Freaks and Geeks 46
FreakyLinks 412
Freaky Stories 215
Fred 2: Night of the Living Fred 166
Freddie 456
Freddy's Nightmares 46
Freeze 481
Friday the 13th: The Series 46, 47, 412, 413, 414

Friends 47
Fries With That? 48
From Dusk Till Dawn 132
FRONTLINE/World 292
Front Page Challenge 352
Full Moon Fright Night 352
Futurama 216, 414

G

Galaxy Goof-Ups 216
Galileo Mystery 491
Garfield and Friends 217
Garfield in Disguise 217
The Garry Moore Show 353
The Gates 134
General Hospital 48
The Generation Gap 353
Genso Midnight. See Illusion at Midnight / Midnight Fantasy
Get Smart 48, 49
Ghost & Vampire Legends of Rhode Island 292
The Ghost Busters 49
Ghost Hunters International 292
Ghost in the Water 456
Ghost Story 50, 414
Ghost Sweeper Mikami 500
Ghost Whisperer 51
The Ghost Writer 456
Ghostbusters 218
Gidget Gets Married 166
Gilligan's Island 51
Glee 51
Glory Days 52
The Godzilla Power Hour 415
Godzilla: The Series 415
Goosebumps 52
Gothica 167
Gravedale High 219
The Great Bear Scare 219
Great Books 293
The Gregory Hines Show 52
Greg the Bunny (1st Series) 134
Greg the Bunny (2nd Series) 135
The Grim Adventures of Billy & Mandy 219, 220, 221, 222, 266, 416
The Grim and Courage Hour 222
Grimm 417
Groovie Goolies 222
Grosse Pointe 53
Growing Up Creepie 223

H

H.R. Pufnstuf 418
The Halloween That Almost Wasn't 167
Halloween Monster Bash 457
Halloween Wars 294
Halloween with the New Addams Family 457
Hammer House of Horror 458
Hammer: The Studio That Dripped Blood! 294
Hanna-Barbera Superstars 10 223, 224
Happy Days 53
The Hard Times of RJ Berger 54
The Hardy Boys/Nancy Drew Mysteries 54
Harry & Cosh 54, 55
Hatsuya. *See* Split
HBO First Look 295
Heartbeat Tonight 501
Heartstoppers: Horror at the Movies 295
Heathcliff and Dingbat 224
Hellboy Animated 225
Hello Franceska 481
Hello Kitty's Furry Tale Theater 225
Hellsing 501
Hemlock Grove 135
Hercules: The Legendary Journeys 55
Here Come the Munsters 168
Herushingu. *See* Hellsing
Hey Arnold! 226
Hidden 296
Hideous Crime 296
Highlander 56
The Highwayman 458
Hi Hi Puffy AmiYumi 418
Hi Honey, I'm Home! 55
The Hilarious House of Frightenstein 354
Hill Street Blues 56
Hipira-kun. *See* Hill Street Blues: The Little Vampire
Hipira: The Little Vampire 501
History Bites 354
A History of Horror with Mark Gatiss 296
The Hitchhiker 57
Hollywood and The Stars 297
Hollywood Chronicles 297
Hollywood Special 354
Homemade TV 355
Home to Roost 459
Honey, I Shrunk the Kids: The TV Show 418
The Horror Hall of Fame 355, 356
The Horror Hall of Fame II 356

The Horror Hall of Fame III 357
The Horror of It All 298
Hotel Transylvania 226
Hotel Trubble 58
Hot in Cleveland 58
Hot Type 298, 299
House of Frankenstein 135
House of Horror 358
House of Mouse 226
How'd They Do That? 299
Hrabě Drakula. *See* Count Dracula
Hungarian Dracula 459
The Hunger 58, 59, 85, 132, 302, 324, 419, 420
Huntik: Secrets & Seekers 421

I

I, Desire 169
Il bacio di Dracula / Dracula's Curse 130
Illusion at Midnight / Midnight Fantasy 502
I Love Mummy 60
I'm Gonna Be an Angel 502
Immortal 482
Imortal. *See* Immortal
In Good Company 358
In Living Color 359
In Search of… 300
In Search of History 300
Incredible Stories 301
The Independent Lens 301
Insomniac with Dave Attell 301
Inspector Gadget 227
Invader ZIM 227
Is It Real? 301, 421
Itsuka Tenma no Kurousagi. *See* A Dark Rabbit Has Seven Lives
It's What's Happening, Baby! 459

J

Jackie Chan Adventures 422
James Bond Jr. 227
The Jerry Springer Show 302
The Jetsons 228
Jibber Jabber 228
Johnny Bravo 229
The Journal 302
Journey to the Unexpected 475
Junior Roundup 359

K

Kaibutsu-kun. *See* Little Kaibutsu
Kaibutsu-kun 2. *See* Little Kaibutsu 2
Kaibutsu oujo. *See* Princess Resurrection
Kamen Rider Kiva 513
Karin 502
Kentucky Teenage Vampires 302
The Ketchup Vampires 502
The Kids in the Hall 360
Kids Unlimited 60
Killer Trials: Judgment Day 302
Kim Possible 229
Kindred: The Embraced 136
Kiss of the Vampire 482
Kitou Scrogneugneu. *See* Kitou the Six-Eyed Monster
Kitou the Six-Eyed Monster 503
Kivikasvot. *See* Stone-Faces
Koishite Akuma: Vampire Boy 482
Kolchak: The Night Stalker 61, 422
The Krofft Superstar Hour 423
Kung Fu: The Legend Continues 460

L

L.A. Heat 62
The L Word 61
The Lair 137
Lamb Chop in the Haunted Studio 360
Land of the Giants 62
Las Vegas 63
The Last Precinct 63
The Late Late Show with Craig Ferguson 361
Late Night Horror 361
The Late Night Horror Show 361
Late Night With Jimmy Fallon 362
Laurell K. Hamilton's Anita Blake: Vampire Hunter 169
Law & Order: Criminal Intent 64
The League of Extraordinary Gentlemen 169
The League of Gentlemen Christmas Special 362
The Legend of Dick and Dom 64
Legend of Duo 503
Leptirica. *See* The Moth
Les 30 histoires les plus mystérieuses. *See* The 30 Most Mysterious Stories
Letters from Felix : A Rabbit on a World Tour 476
Let the Right One In 170
Lexx 65
The Librarian: The Curse of the Judas Chalice 170
Lidsville 423

Lights Out 66
The Little Vampire 137
The Little Vampire: New Adventures 483
Little Drac 503
Little Dracula 229
Little Kaibutsu 483, 504
Little Kaibutsu 2 504
Little Kaibutsu: All New Special 489
Little Vampire 504
The Littlest Hobo 66
London After Midnight 170
The Lost Boys 138
Lost Girl 423
Lost Tapes 67
Lost Tapes 66, 424
The Lost World 67
Lost Worlds: The Real Dracula 303
Love, American Style 68
The Love Boat 69
The Love Boat: The Next Wave 69
The Loves of Dracula 171
Löwenzahn. *See* Dandelion
The Lucy Show 69
Lucy, the Daughter of the Devil 230
Lugosi: The Forgotten King 303
Lunar Legend Tsukihime 504
Lupin the 3rd 505

M

Macabre Theatre 363
Macaroni tout garni 476
Madame's Place 70
Mad Jack the Pirate 230
Mad Mad House 305
MADtv 363, 460
Magic School Bus 231
Magipoka 505
Magnificent Obsessions 305
Makai Senki Disgaea. *See* Negima!?: Disgaea
The Making of "The Addams Family" 460
The Man from U.N.C.L.E. 461
Man, Next Natural Girl: 100 Nights in Yokohama 483
Marineland Carnival 364
Martina Cole's Lady Killers 306
Martin Mystery 231, 424
Mary Shelley's Frankenhole 232
Master of Mosquiton '99 505
Masters of Horror 71

Matantei Loki Ragnarok. *See* Mythical Detective Loki Ragnarok
Matinee Theatre 364
Mayonaka no tantei: Nightwalker. *See* Night Visitors: Midnight Detective
McCloud 70
McHale's Navy 71
Meitantei Conan. *See* Detective Conan
Mentors 72
The Middleman 72
Midnight DJ 476, 477
The Midnight Hour 171
Midnight, Texas 138
Midsomer Murders 73
Mighty Max 232
Mighty Mighty Monsters in Halloween Havoc 232
Mighty Mighty Monsters in New Fears Eve 233
Mighty Mighty Monsters in Pranks for the Memories 233
The Mike Douglas Show 364
Milton the Monster Show 233
Moby Dick and the Mighty Mightor 424
Mockingbird Lane 172
The Modifyers 146, 234
Mom's Got a Date with a Vampire 173
Mona the Vampire 234
Mon Colle Knights 506
The Monkees 73
Monster Auditions 234
MonsterFest 2000: The Classics Come Alive 306
Monster Force 234
Monster High 235
Monster Mania 307
Monster Mash 235
MonsterQuest 306, 425
Monsters 74, 75, 76, 426, 461
Monsters, Madness & Mayhem 307
Monster Squad 138
Monty Python's Flying Circus 365
Monumental Mysteries 308
Moonlight 138
Moonlight Desire 139
MoonPhase 506
The Most Evil Men and Women in History 308, 309
Most Haunted: LIVE 309
The Moth 490
Mother, May I Sleep with Danger? 173
Mou Kaette Kita Yo!! Kaibutsu-kun Subete Shinsaku SP. *See* Little Kaibutsu: All New Special
Movie Macabre 366
Mr. and Mrs. Dracula 174
Mr. Dressup 365
Mr. Majeika 73

Mr. Meaty 76
MSNBC Investigates 304
¡Mucha Lucha!: Gigante 236, 426
Munster, Go Home! 174
The Munsters 139
The Munsters' Revenge 175
The Munsters' Scary Little Christmas 176
The Munsters Today 140
The Munsters Today 176
The Muppet Show 366
Murder, She Wrote 77
Murdoch Mysteries 77
Must Be Santa 177
Mutant X 427
The Mutants: Pathways of the Heart 483
My Babysitter's a Vampire (telefilm) 177
My Babysitter's a Vampire: The Series 140
My Date with a Vampire 484
My Date with a Vampire II 484
My Date with a Vampire III 485
My Fair Munster 178
My Parents are Aliens 78
Mystères. *See* Mysteries
Mysteries 491
Mysterious Journeys 310
Mysterious Worlds 310
Mystery and Imagination 366, 367
Mystery Science Theater 3000 368
My Strange Addiction 309
Myth and Truth 492
Mythical Detective Loki Ragnarok 506
Mythos und Wahrheit. *See* Myth and Truth

N

Nagagutsu o haita neko no bôken. *See* Adventures of Puss-in-Boots
Nash Bridges 78
National Lampoon Presents Disco Beaver from Outer Space 369
The Natural World 427
Nature 428
The NBC Wednesday Mystery Movie: The Snoop Sisters: A Black Day for Bluebeard 178
NCIS: New Orleans 79
Ned's Declassified School Survival Guide 79
Negima! 506
Negima!? 507
Netherworld Battle Chronicle: Disgaea 507
Neverwhere 428
The New Addams Family 461
The New Adventures of Captain Planet 236, 428

The New Adventures of Mighty Mouse and Heckle and Jeckle 236
The New Scooby-Doo Movies 462
The New Scooby-Doo Mysteries 237
The New Shmoo 238
Ngo wo geun see yau gor yue wui. *See* My Date with a Vampire
Ngo wo geun see yau gor yue wui II. *See* My Date with a Vampire II
Ngo wo geun see yau gor yue wui III. *See* My Date with a Vampire III
Nick Knight 179
Nick's Quest 429
Night Bites: Women and Their Vampires 311
Night Court 80
Night Gallery 43, 81, 82, 83, 84, 253, 265, 355, 429
Nightmare Theatre 370
The Night Stalker 181
The Night Strangler 429
Night Visitors 311
Nightlife 180
NightMan 79, 80
Nightmare Classics 369
Nightmare: The Birth of Horror 310
Nightwalker: Midnight Detective 507
Ninja Turtles: The Next Mutation 84
Nip/Tuck 84
The Norliss Tapes 462
Nyanpire: The Animation 507

O

Obake no Samba, Mon Mom Monster. *See* Samba of Ghosts
O Beijo do Vampiro. *See* Kiss of the Vampire
Octonauts 238
Oddville, MTV 370
The Odyssey 85
Oh Yeah! Cartoons 239, 240, 267
Olliver's Adventures 241
One Foot in the Grave 85
Opening Night 371
The Originals 140
Os Mutantes: Caminhos do Coração. *See* That's So Weird: Pathways of the Heart

P

Pac-Man 241
Pac-Man and the Ghostly Adventures 241, 242
The Paranormal Borderline 430
Paranormal Paparazzi 312, 430
Paranormal State 312
Parks and Recreation 86
The Passion of Dracula 371

Películas para no dormer: Adivina quién soy. *See* Fear Itself: A Real Friend
Penny Dreadful 141
Petit Vampire. *See* Little Vampire
The Phantom 490
Phantom Stories 508
The Phil Silvers Show 86
Phineas and Ferb 242
The Pier 312
The Pink Panther and Friends 242
The Pink Panther Show 243
A Place Among the Undead 313
Places of Mystery 313
The Plastic Man Comedy/Adventure Show 243, 431
Play for Today 374
Podge & Rodge: A Scare at Bedtime 87
Police Academy: The Series 87
Poltergeist: The Legacy 87, 88
Port Charles 142
Power Rangers Mystic Force 142
Preacher 142
Primary Focus 313
Princess Resurrection 508
Prisoners of Gravity 372, 373
Private Practice 88
Project Runway: Under the Gunn 313
Providence 88
PSI Factor: Chronicles of the Paranormal 88
Psych 89
Purple Playhouse 374

Q

Quantum Leap 89

R

Rambo: The Force of Freedom 463, 464
Rats, Bats and Bugs 464
The Ray Bradbury Theater 90, 463
Reach for the Crypt 375
Read All About It! 91
The Real Adventures of Jonny Quest 431
The Real Ghostbusters 244
Real People 375, 376
The Real Vampire Chronicles 314
The Real Vampire Files 314
Real Vampire Housewives 143
Real Vampires 314
Real Vampires... Exposed! 314

Reaper 91, 432
Rear Window 315
Red Riding Hood Chacha 508
The Red Skelton Show 376, 377
Rejendo obu duo. *See* Legend of Duo
Relic Hunter 91, 92
Renegade 92
Renkin 3-kyu Magical? Pokaan. *See* Magipoka
Revealed 315
RH Plus 485
The Richie Rich/Scooby-Doo Show 244, 245
The Riddlers 377
Riddles of the Dead 316
Ripley's Believe It or Not! 245, 316
Ripper 181
R.L. Stine's The Haunting Hour 90
Road to Avonlea 92
Robot Chicken 232, 246, 247, 248, 465
Roger Corman's The Phantom Eye 182
Roger Ramjet 248
Rokumon Tengai Monkore Naito. *See* Mon Colle Knights
The Ron James Show 377, 378
Rosario + Vampire 508
Rosario + Vampire Capu.02 509
Roswell Conspiracies: Aliens, Myths and Legends 248
Round the Twist 93
Roxy Hunter and the Horrific Halloween 182
Royal Canadian Air Farce 378, 379
Rugrats 249
Rupan Sansei: Part II. *See* Lunar Legend Tsukihime

S

Sabrina, the Teenage Witch 93
Sabrina the Teenage Witch (anim) 249
'Salem's Lot (2004) 145
Salem's Lot 145
Salem's Lot 146
Salem's Lot (1979) 144
Samba of Ghosts 509
Sanctuary 143
Saturday Night Live 349, 380, 381, 382, 383, 465
Scare Tactics 317, 318, 357
The Scariest Places on Earth 318, 319, 320
Scary Godmother Halloween Spooktakular 250
The School for Vampires 509
Schusters Gespenster. *See* Schuster's Ghosts
Schuster's Ghosts 485
The Scooby and Scrappy-Doo Puppy Hour 250

The Scooby-Doo/Dynomutt Hour 250
Scooby-Doo and Scrappy-Doo 252
Scooby Doo, Where Are You! 252
Scooby's All-Star Laff-A-Lympics 251
Scooby's All-Stars 251
Scrubs 94
SCTV 379
Scully 146
Sealab 2021 432
The Search For Dracula 320
The Secret Adventures of Jules Verne 94
The Secret Lives of Vampires 320
Secret Lives of Women 321
Secret Diary of a Call Girl 94
Secrets of the Cryptkeeper's Haunted House 383
Sesame Street 383
Sesame Street All-Star 25th Birthday: Stars and Street Forever! 384
Sesame Street Jam: A Musical Celebration 384
Sesame Street, Special 384
Sesame Street Stays Up Late! A Monster New Year's Eve Party 385
Sexy Beasts: Vamps, Wolves, and Mutants 321
Shades of Darkness 95
Shadow Chasers 146
Shadowhunters: The Mortal Instruments 146
Shadow Zone 183
Sherlock Holmes in the 22nd Century 433
Sherlock Holmes: The Case of the Whitechapel Vampire 183
She-Wolf of London 95
Shiki, *See* Demon Corpse
Shingetsutan Tsukihime, *See* Lunar Legend Tsukihime
Ship's Reporter 465
Shock Theatre 385
Show of the Week 386
Sightings 321, 322
Silents Please 386
The Simpsons 196, 253, 254, 255, 256, 257, 391, 466, 467
Slayer 184
Slayer School 147
Sledge Hammer! 95
Sliders 96
SM:TV Live 380
Smallville 96
Smoke and Shadows 147
Snorks 257
The Sonny and Cher Comedy Hour 386, 387
The Sonny & Cher Show 387
Sonny with a Chance 387
The South Bank Show 322, 323

South Park 258, 433
So Weird 97
Space Ghost and Dino Boy 258
Space Precinct 434
Space Stars 434
Spawn 258
Special Unit 2 434
Spectreman 485, 486
Sphinx: Geheimnisse der Geschichte. *See* Special Unit 2: Secrets of History
Sphinx: Secrets of History 492
Spider-Man 259, 260
Spider-Woman 260
Split 486
SpongeBob SquarePants 261
St. Elsewhere 93
Star Trek 435
Stargate: Atlantis 435
Starsky & Hutch 97, 468
The Steve Allen Show 387, 468
Stone-Faces 478
The Strain 147
Strange 436
Struck by Lightning 98
Studio 2 323
Summer in Transylvania 148
The Super Hero Squad Show 262
Superboy 98, 437
SuperFriends 261
The Super Mario Bros. Super Show! 105, 438
Super Scary Saturday 388
Supernatural 17, 33, 99, 100, 101, 102, 103, 104, 262, 437
Supernatural (UK) 99
Superspecial 388, 389, 468
Swamp Thing 105
SWAT Kats: The Radical Squadron 262
The Sylvester & Tweety Mysteries 262

T

Tales from the Crypt 106, 107, 108
Tales from the Cryptkeeper 263
Tales from the Darkside 108, 109, 438
Tales from the Darkside Special 389
Tales of the Unexpected 109
Tales of the Wizard of Oz 264, 469
Tales of Tomorrow 439
T-Bag and the Rings of Olympus 106
T-Bag and the Wonders in Letterland 106
Tenshi ni Narumon. *See* I'm Gonna Be an Angel

Teta / Teta Frankenstein. *See* Frankenstein's Aunt
Tetsuwan Atomu. *See* Astro Boy
Texaco Star Theater 389
That's So Weird 390
The Unexplained: Witches, Werewolves & Vampires 327
Third Watch 110
Those Obnoxious Aliens 510
Thriller 110, 111
Thrills 111
Thundarr the Barbarian 264
Tiny Toon Adventures 265
Titeuf 510
Toaru Majutsu no Index. *See* A Certain Magical Index
Tokimeki Tonight. *See* Heartbeat Tonight
The Tommy Ambrose Show 390
The Tonight Show with Conan O'Brien 391
Topo Gigio 510
Topo Gigio: In the Castle of Count Dracula 510
Toppo Jijo. *See* Topo Gigio
Torchwood 440
To the Ends of the Earth 439, 469
The Tracey Ullman Show 391
Transylvania (2004) 184
Transylvania (2016) 184
Trapper John, M.D. 112
Trilogy of Terror 440
Trinity Blood 511
True Bloodlines 323, 324
True Blood 148
True Horror 469
True Horror with Anthony Head 324
True Story of the Vampire 325
The Truth About Dracula 492
Truth or Scare 325, 326
Tsukuyomi Moon Phase. *See* MoonPhase
Tuesday's Documentary 326
Twilight 185
The Twilight Zone 112
Twisted History: Vampires 326
The Tyra Banks Show 391

U

Ugly Americans 265
U-KISS' Vampire 493
Ultimate Super Heroes, Vixens & Villains 326
Ultraviolet (UK) 149
Ultraviolet (US) 185
Ultraviolet: Code 044 511

Um Homem Muito Especial. *See* A Very Special Man
Underfist 266
The Unexplained 327
Unhappily Ever After 113
Universal Horror 328
The Universal Story 328
Unnatural History 329, 470
Unsolved Mysteries 329, 441
Untitled Ian Holt Project 330
Untitled Kevin Williamson Project 186
Upiór. *See* The Phantom
Urban Gothic 113
URBO: The Adventures of Pax Afrika 441
Urusei Yatsura. *See* Those Obnoxious Aliens
Urutoravaioretto: Kôdo 044. *See* Ultraviolet: Code 044

V

V Graham Norton 392
Vamp 486
The Vampira Show 392
Vampire 186
Vampire (JPN) 513
Vampire Bats 441
The Vampire Diaries 149
Vampire Expert 486
Vampire Expert II 487
The Vampire Family 490
Vampire High 150
Vampire Host 511
The Vampire Hunter With Nigel Marven 442
Vampire Idol 487
Vampire Knight 512
Vampire Knight Guilty 512
Vampire Princess Miyu 512
Vampire Prosecutor 487
Vampire Secrets 330
Vampire Syndrome: Hatu 488
Vampires: Brighter in Darkness 150
Vampires in New England 332
Vampires: Thirst For the Truth 330
Vampires; Why They Bite 331
Vampiyan Kids 512
The Vampyr: A Soap Opera 392
Van Helsing 150
The Van Helsing Chronicles 187
Van Helsing: The Man and the Monsters – A Sci-Fi Lowdown 332
Vanpaia bôi. *See* Kivikasvot: Vampire Boy
Van-pires 442

The Vegas Vampire Show 393
The Venture Bros. 266
Verbotene Liebe. *See* Forbidden Love
A Very Special Man 488
Viaje a lo inesperado. *See* Journey to the Unexpected
Virtual Murder 114
Vlad Dracula 151
Vlad the Impaler: The True Story of Dracula 332

W

Wacky Races Forever 267
Wacky Races 266
Wacky Races Forever 473
Wake, Rattle & Roll 394
Warehouse 13 442
The Watcher 114
Wayne & Shuster 394
Weird Science 114, 443
Werewolf 470
What a Cartoon Show 267
What I Like About You 115
What's New, Scooby-Doo? 268
Whatever Turns You On 395
Wheelie and the Chopper Bunch 443
Where in the World is Carmen Sandiego? 395
Whose Line Is It Anyway? 395
Why Horror? 332
Why We ♥ Vampires 333
Wild Arms: Twilight Venom 513
Wild Carpathia 471
Wild Explorer 472
Wild Kat 115
The Wild Thornberrys 268
Wildlife On One 471
Will & Grace 472
Wings 115
Witch's Night Out 268
Wizards of Waverly Place 151
Wolverine and the X-Men 444
Wolvesbayne 187
Women: Stories of Passion 116
The Wonderful World of Disney 116
Word Travels 472
The World of Dracula 187
The World of Hammer 333, 334, 335
The World of Van Helsing 335
The World's Strangest UFO Stories 444
W.O.W. 393

X

The X Factor 396
Xena: Warrior Princess 118
The X Files 17, 22, 35, 98, 101, 116, 117, 159, 169, 249, 444, 445
The Xtra Factor 396

Y

Yami no matsuei. *See* Descendants of Darkness
Yami no teiô kyûketsuki Dorakyura. *See* Dracula: Sovereign of the Damned
Yellow Thrill 478, 479
Yin Yang Yo! 446
Yogi's Treasure Hunt 269
You Asked For It 396
You Wish 118
Young Dracula 151
Young Hercules 118
The Young Indiana Jones Chronicles 119
The Young Ones 119
Your Hit Parade 397

Z

Zingrr's Projections 397
Zombie Hotel 270
Zombies vs. Vampires 152

Numbers

3-2-1 338
5th Quadrant 45
10 Vampires We Love 272
13 Thirteenth Avenue 154
20/20 272, 273
The 30 Most Mysterious Stories 491
30 Rock 448
90 Minutes Live 338, 339
100 Greatest 273
100 Years of Horror 273, 274, 275
The 700 Club 275

www.ingramcontent.com/pod-product-compliance
Lightning Source LLC
Chambersburg PA
CBHW081331080526
44588CB00017B/2586